RAJ

— ◆ —

THE MAKING AND
UNMAKING OF
BRITISH INDIA

— ◆ —

Lawrence James

First published in Great Britain in 1997
by Little, Brown and Company
This edition published by The Softback Preview, 1998

A CIP catalogue record for this book
is available from the British Library.

ISBN: 0 316 64072 7

Maps by Neil Hyslop

Typeset in Bembo by M Rules
Printed and bound in Great Britain
by Clays Ltd, St Ives plc

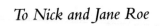

To Nick and Jane Roe

Contents

· Contents ·

· Contents ·

List of Maps

Acknowledgements

I would first like to thank my wife, Mary, for her forbearance, patience and good humour during the preparation and writing of this book. Thanks are also due to my sons, Edward and Henry, who have provided many valuable services. Help, suggestions, advice and information were also provided by Vice-Admiral Manohar Awati, Dr Richard Boyden, Dr Ian Bradley, Geordie Burnett-Stuart, Mrs Elsie Butler, William Dalrymple, Richard Demarco, Dr and Mrs Martin Edmonds, Sir Gerald Elliot, Professor Ray Furness, Dr Nile Gardiner, Andrew Gordon, Ian Gordon, Ruth Guilding, John Hailwood, Robert Harvey, Mr and Mrs Guli Juneja, Professor Bruce Lenman, Andrew Lownie, Philip Mason, Lieutenant-Colonel David Murray, Professor Alan Pat, Liz Pert-Davies, Professor Jeffrey Richards, the late General Sir Ouvry Roberts, Professor and Mrs Nick Roe, Trevor Royle, Alan Samson, Dr Bill Shields, Linda Silverman, W. A. Simms, Captain James Squire, Emma Strouts of Christie's Images, Deepak Vaidya, Andrew and Cherry Williams and Andrew Wilson.

I am greatly indebted to the staff of St Andrews University Library and the India Office Library for their courtesy and efficiency in handling all manner of enquiries. I would also like to thank the staff of the British Library, the National Library of Scotland, the Bodleian Library, Strathclyde Record Office, the Scottish Record Office, the National Army Museum, the Imperial War Museum, the Public Record Office and the Ministry of Defence. All have been generous with their time and knowledge.

Quotations from Crown Copyright collections appear by permission of the Controller of Her Majesty's Stationery Office, and those from the papers of General Sir Richard Savory by kind permission of his Literary Trustees.

Picture Credits

SECTION ONE
1, 4, 7, 8, 9, 10: The Hulton Getty Picture Collection; 2: Popperfoto; 3: Christie's Images; 5: Trustees of the Blair Athol Estate: 6: Victoria & Albert Museum; 11, 12, 17, 18: India Office Library; 15, 16: Courtesy of Deepak Vaidya

SECTION TWO
1, 12: Popperfoto; 6: Christie's Images; 8: Trustees of the Blair Athol Estate; 11: The Hulton Getty Picture Collection; 16, 17, 18, 19, 20: Courtesy of Geordie Burnett-Stuart; 21, 22: Imperial War Museum

SECTION THREE
1, 2, 3: Courtesy of Geordie Burnett-Stuart; 5, 6, 10, 11, 12, 15, 17: The Hulton Getty Picture Collection; 9: Camera Press; 13, 14: National Army Museum; 16, 18: Popperfoto

PART ONE

THE COMPANY ASCENDANT: 1740–84

1

— ◆ —

Prologue: Mughal Twilight

I

India is a land of vanished supremacies. Each proclaimed its power and permanence by architecture on the grand scale, designed to inspire admiration, awe and even fear. Always the observer is compelled to look upwards. One cranes one's neck to see the strongholds of Rajput warlords, perched precariously on the hilltops of Rajputana (Rajasthan), and one stands back to view the great mosques and mausoleums of their overlords, the Mughal emperors. Approach requires a degree of supplication; one trudges up the hillside to reach the Jaipur maharajas' palace at Amber and vast flights of steps skirt the government offices of the British Raj in New Delhi. The overall impression is of a country where power has been concentrated in a few hands and always flowed downwards.

There is much truth in this. The public buildings of the Mughals, the Indian princes and the Raj were expressions of their authority, reminding the onlooker of his place in the scale of things. Wealth went hand in hand with political power; the elaborate and intricate marblework, jewelled inlays and painted panels which decorated mosques and palaces announced their patrons and owners as men of infinite richness. The British were more cautious about this sort of ostentation. Sir Edwin Lutyens, the mastermind behind that complex of official buildings which was to form the heart of 'imperial' Delhi, considered traditional Indian architecture too florid and therefore unsuitable for a regime whose chief characteristics were integrity and firmness. Like other, earlier architects of the Raj, he preferred to assert its supremacy with solid stonework and severe classical motifs, which was understandable given that they and their patrons saw Britain as the new Rome. The fashion had been set in the early 1800s by the Marquess Wellesley, who believed that the dignity of a Governor-General of Bengal required a colonnaded mansion in the contemporary Georgian neo-classical style. Opposite his austere but imposing Government House was a triumphal arch surmounted by a vigilant imperial lion, which soon became a popular roost for Calcutta's cranes, vultures and kites.

India's official architecture was a backdrop for the traditional public rituals of state. The formal processions in which a ruler presented himself to his subjects and undertook his devotions, and the *durbars* (assemblies) where great men met, exchanged gifts and compliments and discussed high policy, required settings appropriate to what was, in effect, the theatre of power. At the heart of the Emperor Shahjahan's great palace in Delhi, now called the Red Fort, are the great audience halls, one a vast open courtyard, the other enclosed and reserved for foreign ambassadors and other elevated visitors. Both are now stripped of their awnings and wall-hangings and the private chamber lacks the Peacock Throne, a stunning construction of gold and jewels surmounted by a golden arch and topped by two gilded peacocks, birds of allegedly incorruptible flesh which may have symbolised not only the splendour of the Mughals but also their durability.

When Shahjahan held durbars for his subjects, dispensing justice and settling quarrels, he overlooked them from a high, canopied dias with a delicately painted ceiling. If he glanced upwards, he saw a panel which portrays Orpheus playing his lute before wild beasts who, bewitched by his music, are calmly seated around him. The scene was a reminder to the emperor and his successors that they were Solomonic kings. Like the Thracian musician, they were bringers of harmony, spreading peace among subjects who, if left to their own devices, would live according to the laws of the jungle. It was a nice and revealing conceit, a key to the nature of Mughal kingship and, for that matter, its successor, the British Raj.

Shahjahan's Delhi palace (he renamed the city Shahjahanabad) was completed in the middle years of the seventeenth century. He was a Timurid, a dynasty of interlopers who had founded their Indian empire in the mid-sixteenth century, and whose pedigree stretched back to the fourteenth-century conqueror, Timur the Great (Marlowe's Tamburlaine). By Shahjahan's time, Timurid domination extended from the Himalayan foothills to the borders of the Deccan. Even in the period of their ascendancy, the Mughals were never absolute masters of the whole of India; there were many remote, inaccessible regions where their will never penetrated. There were also areas, particularly in central India, where their authority rested on the submission and co-operation of local princes.

For outsiders, the physical boundaries of Mughal power were immaterial. Contemporary Europeans, fed on travellers' tales of the magnificence of his courts at Agra and Delhi, rated India's emperor as one of the great princes of earth, equal in stature to the Sultan of Turkey or the Emperor of China. The Mughal emperor was a figure of immense dignity and grandeur, a potentate who was imagined to hold absolute sway over millions. For European intellectuals seeking to understand the nature of political power, the Great Mughal was the embodiment of that despotism which was thought to be natural to the Orient. And yet, the Mughals complied with the Renaissance ideals of kingship, for they were renowned as connoisseurs and patrons of the arts. On an embassy to the imperial court in 1615, Sir Thomas Roe judged the palace at Agra as 'one of the great works and wonders of the world' and admitted to the Emperor Jahangir, who later had the Taj Mahal built, that his portrait painters surpassed those of James I.[1] It was, of course, easy for Western visitors to be bowled over by the splendour of Mughal architecture and the magnificence of their state pageantry, and to imagine that together they were the façade of a power which was total and limitless.

Appearances were misleading. Whatever its architecture announced to the contrary, the Mughal empire was never monolithic, nor did the emperor's will run freely throughout India. He was *shah-an-shah*, a king of kings, a monarch whose dominions were a political mosaic, whose tessera included provinces administered by imperial governors and semi-independent petty states. In the Deccan alone there were over a thousand fortified towns and villages, each under the thumb of its own *zamindar* (landowner), who was both a subject of the emperor and his partner in government.[2] The machinery of Mughal government needed the goodwill and co-operation of such men, as well as the services of its salaried administrators who enforced the law and gathered imperial revenues.

Timurid power rested ultimately on the cash raised from the land tax. Its burden was heaviest on the *ryots* (peasants) and it was theoretically yielding an annual 232 million rupees (£31.3 million) at the close of the seventeenth century.[3] Taken from an official revenue manual, this estimate ignored the often considerable sums siphoned off by venal officials. Nonetheless, the Mughals possessed, at least on paper, the wherewithal to play a political masterhand in their dominions: cash procured soldiers, allies and a loyal civil service. It could also seduce the discontented and purchase the allegiance of enemies. In the early 1690s, when the Emperor Aurangzeb's armies were fighting in Karnataka, he lured back a renegade raja, Yacham Nair, with an offer of a *jagir* (a lifetime annuity from land revenue) worth 900,000 rupees (£121,500) a year. Not long after, Aurangzeb ordered Yacham's arrest and murder.[4]

This was a typical exercise in Mughal statecraft. Dynastic survival and India's tranquillity depended upon an emperor's mastery of the arcane arts of political fixing; he gave or withheld patronage, he bargained with lesser princes, and played ambitious courtiers, nobles and officials against each other. Shahjahan's choice of Orpheus, the mollifier and enchanter, as a source of political inspiration was therefore very apt. It was also a very daring gesture, for the presence of a figure from pagan mythology above the imperial seat of power would certainly have made many of the emperor's fellow Muslims uneasy.

Like the Turkish and Persian empires, Mughal India was an Islamic state. It had, in 1700, an estimated population of about 180 million, of whom at least two-thirds were unbelievers, mostly Hindus. Although the emperors enjoyed the title *khalifa* (Caliph), and with it a claim to be regarded by Muslims as successors to Muhammad, they could only govern with the co-operation of the Hindus. A policy of pragmatic toleration was adopted, but unevenly and in ways which never wholly satisfied the Sikhs of the Punjab or the Hindu warrior castes, the Jats of Rajasthan and the Marathas of the Deccan. Integrated within the Mughal system, these groups submitted grudgingly and were always ready to spring to arms if their faith appeared to be in danger. Aurangzeb's policy of destroying Hindu temples during the suppression of insurrections in Karnataka and Rajasthan stiffened rather than reduced resistance.

Ever since the genesis of the Timurid empire under Akbar the Great (1556–1605), dynastic survival had depended on genetic good fortune in the form of emperors who were forceful, energetic and skilled manipulators. This luck ran out with the death of Aurangzeb in 1707, and the empire passed into nerveless and fumbling hands. Even so, it would have required rulers with superhuman talents to have preserved an inheritance which was already beset by difficulties, let alone overcome the problems which raised themselves during the next sixty years.

The Mughal empire fell apart swiftly. In what turned out to be the final surge of Mughal expansion, Aurangzeb overstepped himself by undertaking a series of campaigns designed to extend and consolidate his rule in the Deccan and Hyderabad. They became a war of attrition which stretched imperial resources beyond their breaking point, and by 1707, after nearly twenty years of intermittent fighting, the empire was exhausted. There was no breathing space; an eighteen-month war for the succession followed Aurangzeb's death. Moreover, the repercussions of the stalemate in central and southern India and the civil war were felt across the country. From the early 1680s onwards the Jats of Rajasthan launched a sequence of insurrections against oppressive taxation, seizing whole districts, occupying towns and, growing more audacious, were raiding the suburbs of Delhi by 1717.

Strong men flourished as anarchy spread. It was a period of making and breaking as determined and ambitious men snatched at opportunities to enrich themselves and usurp authority. Imperial officials, increasingly isolated and starved of funds, found their loyalty withering and looked for ways to preserve and advance themselves in a suddenly mutable world. There were fortunes to be made among the wreckage of an empire which was cracking up, and success went to the cunning and ruthless.

The adventures of Riza Khan, an Afghan professional soldier in the imperial service, may serve as a template for the stories of many others. In about 1700 he was appointed governor of Ramgir in the Deccan, but found his entry barred by his predecessor. Riza, a determined and resourceful figure, gathered extra men and entered the town by force, and turned it into a private power base. Turning his back on an emperor who was no longer able to reward his servants, Riza decided to make his own destiny; he turned bandit and enriched himself by diverting imperial taxes into his own pocket and looting caravans. He prospered and attracted followers, men like himself who had been cast adrift in a violent and disorderly world and whose only assets were their wits and their swords. His horde grew, swollen by deserters, unpaid soldiers from other armies, and those whose livelihoods had been destroyed by war and brigandage. Within six years Riza Khan was the leader of 10,000 freelances and an important piece on the chessboard of local power politics. His services were sought and obtained by Mughal officials in Hyderabad, once to help run down another bandit. He might have ended his life as a landowner, perhaps the founder of a dynasty, but his luck ran out in 1712 when he was tricked, taken prisoner and executed by a new governor.[5]

Others were more fortunate. Daud Khan Ruhela, another Afghan and the alleged son of a slave, made himself the master of a cluster of villages in the region north-east of the old imperial capital, Agra. It was an area where Akbar the Great had encouraged Afghan settlement in the sixteenth century, no doubt with an eye to swelling the numbers of his Muslim subjects. Daud Khan proceeded in what was becoming the classic manner for ambitious freebooters: he first hired himself and his brigands to another man on the make, a local zamindar, and then picked up property and helped himself to imperial revenues. Playing a double game with the Raja of Kumaun, he came unstuck, was captured and tortured to death in 1720. It was onwards and upwards for his adopted heir, Ali Muhammad Khan, who showed a remarkable virtuosity in switching alliances and, as his estates and prestige grew, meddling in the intrigues of the imperial court. When he died in 1748 he was the dominant figure in the constellation of petty Ruhela states which had emerged over the past thirty years and now stretched from the foothills of the Himalayas southwards across the Ganges valley to a line between Delhi and Agra. Princes deferred to him; the Raja of Garwhal paid him 160,000 rupees (£21,600) a year in protection money, and he was deeply engaged in the factional strife at court.[6]

One of Ali Muhammad Khan's greatest opportunities had come in 1739–40, when a Persian army under Nadir Shah invaded India, defeated the Emperor Muhammad at the battle of Kamal and then occupied Delhi. The city was thoroughly plundered, its inhabitants massacred and, in a gesture which combined cupidity with political symbolism, the Peacock Throne was carried off to Persia. While Delhi was in chaos, Ali Muhammad Khan engrossed a handful of *parganas* (imperial tax districts). Like every other predator on the loose in India, his motive in acquiring imperial revenues was a mixture of greed and political acumen. By encroaching on imperial rights, India's new masters transformed themselves into the heirs of the emperor.

By the mid-eighteenth century the self-made heirs of the Timurid emperors had changed the political map of India. New polities had appeared: the large states of Mysore, Hyderabad, Awadh (Oudh), Bengal and the Maratha principalities of Deccan. There was also a body of looser political units formed by the Ruhelas, the Sikhs of the Punjab and the Rajputs of Rajasthan. The masters of both the larger and smaller states behaved as independent rulers and presented themselves to their subjects as the legitimate successors of the Mughals. These 'lesser Mughals' upheld all the administrative codes and practices of traditional imperial government, particularly and for obvious reasons those concerned with the imposition of taxes.

And yet, curiously, India's *arriviste* princes continued to treat the emperor's person with customary respect and reverence long after his real power had evaporated. Even after 1784, when he became the virtual prisoner of the Maratha prince, Mahadji Scindia, his captor insisted that he was merely a 'servant' of the emperor. Although little more than ornaments, the Timurid emperors were still the sole source of legitimate political authority within India. They had none themselves, but they could be induced to bestow it on others, which was why nobody wished to get rid of them.

Mughal traditions and culture set the tone in all the new states. Ali Muhammad Khan was the patron of poets and musicians. Like the emperors, he generously endowed mosques and had a mausoleum built in his capital, Aonla (south-west of Bareilly), which is still an object of veneration.[7] Murshid Quli Khan, *Nawab* (governor) of Bengal, who delicately balanced his duties as a Mughal agent in the province with establishing himself as its effective ruler, followed imperial custom by renaming its capital, Murshidabad. It was embellished, at his expense, with a splendid, five-domed mosque. Hindu princes also imitated Mughal munificence by founding temples and building palaces in the Mughal style with audience halls, private apartments and elaborate gardens. Former Mughal artisans and artists were employed in all these enterprises; humble men, like great ones, had to follow where advantage led them.

III

One of the most ominous features of the power struggles which accompanied the collapse of Mughal power was the willingness of contestants to enlist external help. In the early 1740s the warring princes of Karnataka sought and gained military assistance from the British East India Company and the French Compagnie des Indes and paid for it by assignments of land and taxation. The four invasions of northern India by the Afghan ruler Ahmad Shah Abdali (1748, 1749, 1751 and 1757–61) revealed a variety of collaborators who were willing either to remain neutral or provide him with fighting men, whichever best suited their private interests. During the final incursion, Safdar Jang, the Nawab of Awadh, offered the Afghans lukewarm support,while Najib-ud Daula, an Afghan and former imperial commander, supplied them with Ruhela troops. He did so partly to further his own ambitions and partly because he knew the Ruhelas could only overcome their enemies, the Marathas, with Afghan backing. They did so at the decisive battle of Panipat in January 1761, which opened the way for Najib to secure the position of regent for the Afghan-nominated, puppet emperor Shah Alam II. It might be added that before the battle the Maratha *peshwa* (prince), Balaji Baji Rao, had attempted a deal with the East India Company, offering land in exchange for batteries of artillery and European-trained gunners.[8]

Although adding to India's chronic instability and the sum total of its people's suffering, the Afghan and Persian invasions were no more than smash-and-grab raids. Neither Nadir Shah nor Ahmad Shah Abdali had the inclination to supplant the Timurids, although the Afghans temporarily occupied the Punjab. Their interventions did, however, swell the numbers of professional cavalrymen who sold themselves to the highest bidder or, when unemployed, lived off the peasantry. In some cases, these parasites followed the example of those who hired them, and hoisted themselves up in the world to become zamindars. Armies were also a burden on those who could not survive without them, and participants in India's civil wars were often driven to borrow heavily from bankers to finance their campaigns. The peshwa, Balaji Baji Rao, faced mutinies by unpaid soldiers and once complained of his creditors, 'I am falling at their feet, till I have rubbed the skin from my forehead.' His successor borrowed fifteen million rupees (over £2 million) between 1740 and 1760, on which he was forced to pay interest of between 12 and 18 per cent.[9] The spiral of debt helped make war self-perpetuating, for it compelled princes to seek new sources of income through conquest and plundering raids. Maratha princes 'invited' into Rajasthan by local magnates in the 1730s, ostensibly to settle local disputes, used the opportunity to levy a form of protection money.

The Indian economy as a whole did not suffer unduly from the upheavals which accompanied the disintegration of Mughal power. Agricultural production proved resilient; warfare was localised and never continuous; and, mercifully, the first half of the eighteenth century witnessed no large-scale famines. There is evidence of growth, such as the colonisation of new lands, although the population was increasing slowly.

Nonetheless, chronic disruption occurred in the regions adjacent to Delhi, which suffered more than elsewhere because they were transformed into a cockpit in which, at different times, Persian, Mughal, Jat, Ruhela and Maratha forces did battle. The city's population fell, as did that of Agra, and elsewhere fragile economic structures were damaged by marauders. Maratha raiders burned mulberry bushes in the Birghum district, damaging the local silk industry.[10]

Localised anarchy hindered the exchange of goods. Throughout this period the British, French and Dutch trading companies grumbled about the losses they suffered from an upsurge in brigandage and coastal piracy. The East India Company's embassy to the Emperor Furrukhsiyar, with its cumbersome baggage train containing sumptuous bribes for him and his courtiers, needed a 450-strong escort in 1714. This would have been a reasonable precaution at any time, but it was insufficient to deter bandits between Patna and Benares (Varanasi), who had to be bought off with various gifts, including horse pistols and magnifying glasses.[11] There were complaints, too, about princes asserting their new independence, like the 'impertinent and troublesome rajahs' who imposed levies on goods passing down the Ganges.[12]

With valuable trade at stake, Europeans naturally attempted to keep track of India's power struggles. It was not easy; one East India Company agent in Madras admitted that it was impossible to follow exactly the serpentine manoeuvres of the princes of Karnataka in the 1730s. And yet from what he and others could discover, they were able to identify the key to success in the hurly-burly of Indian politics. It was a perpetually full purse, for experience showed that the individual Indian soldier would only follow a prince with well-primed coffers and when unpaid he would happily switch sides, even in the middle of a battle.[13] Once the British and French companies had taken the plunge and intervened actively in the local wars, their officers quickly realised how profitable it could be to play kingmaker. News of rich pickings travelled fast. Writing from the Cape and *en route* for Madras, Alexander Campbell told his parents in April 1748 that he had every chance of 'making a fortune . . . in a few years'. He dreamed of staying in India as an officer in the Company's new army, to 'try my luck'.[14]

This young Scot had expectations in common with those Indians of similar temper who had been trying their luck in various ways for the past forty years. One who came out well from the political free-for-all was the ruler of the small hilltop town of Mandawa, in the rolling countryside of

Rajasthan. He may well have been a superior sort of Rajput zamindar and he certainly possessed considerable self-esteem, for he built himself a fortified palace which, in design, if not scale, resembles those of greater princes.

Around the palace are clustered the houses of his officials – in all likelihood their master gave them Mughal titles such as *diwan* (treasurer). The exterior walls and courtyards of their houses are decorated with brightly coloured and lively murals which, one assumes, reflect something of the pretensions of their overlord. In them he rides on richly caparisoned camels and elephants to make war or hunt. His soldiers also appear: the cavalry armed with lances are probably Maratha or Afghan mercenaries; the infantrymen carry tulwars (curved swords) and matchlocks and wear red jackets. For this reason, the local guides mistakenly identify them as East India Company sepoys. The error is understandable: from the later years of the eighteenth century onwards some Indian rulers dressed their soldiers in red jackets in the belief that this colour possessed talismanic powers, which would make those who wore it fight as well as the Company's troops. This change in military fashion was more than a princely foible; it was a mark of a new and momentous shift in the balance of power within India.

2

A Glorious Prospect: Robert Clive's Wars, 1740–55

I

The life of Robert Clive might easily have been the plot for a picaresque novel by, say, Defoe or Smollett. The scapegrace youth leaves England to make his fortune in India and in the process gets into all sorts of scrapes. He extricates himself by displaying hitherto dormant energy, courage and an ability to turn every situation to his advantage. Clive's would not have been a moral tale, and eighteenth-century readers would have been hard pressed to discover any virtues within his character beyond patriotism, and this was offset by guile, ruthlessness and rapacity. In sum, he was temperamentally well suited to play a decisive role in Indian politics during the years of Mughal decline.

Clive was nineteen when he disembarked at Fort St George, Madras, in June 1744. He was a writer, a junior tally clerk, and, like many of his colleagues, came from a minor gentry background. He had been, not unusually for one of his birth, a harum-scarum schoolboy, but he had some preparation for his future career at a business school in Hemel Hempstead. As a younger son, he had to make his own way in the world, and clerking for the East India Company was an honourable occupation in which he could, if lucky, make himself a man of independent means. Whether he did or not, his family was relieved of the burden of supporting him, although it had to find two men willing to pledge £500 for his good behaviour and further sums for his voyage out and kit. The bill for a junior officer's clothing and household utensils came to just under £140 in 1781.[1]

Mettlesome, short-tempered and prone to depression, Clive was not happy pushing a pen, but his urge to help himself and his family was sufficiently strong to enable him to overcome his boredom and periodic fits of gloom. The boy who, allegedly, had clambered up the steeple of Market Drayton church and defied the world sitting astride a weathercock, resolved to steel himself to his humdrum duties and make the best of things. If he escaped the rigours of the climate and the local microbes, and large numbers of aspirants did not, Clive stood a good chance of returning home with enough capital to live as a gentleman. This was what Sir Archibald Forbes had in mind when he wrote a Polonius-like instruction to his son, who joined the Company at the same time as Clive. The youth was to show: 'Fortitude . . . courage and Resolution to encounter Danger, perform all duties to God and man and bear with pain and trouble.' If he conducted himself in this manner, a 'Glorious prospect' lay ahead of him.[2] The lure of India was therefore one of enrichment, but as matters stood in the early 1740s, this could only come as a result of making money from trade. First, the Company's employee undertook what was in effect a five-year apprenticeship as a writer, and then moved up the ladder to become successively a factor, a junior merchant, a senior merchant, a councillor and, finally, a governor. Salaries were not high, but men holding senior posts were free to trade on their own account.

The East India Company was one of those enterprises which floated on what Defoe had called the 'unbounded Ocean of Business', a sea which encompassed the whole globe. Britain lay at the hub of a thriving, expanding and highly complex system of international trade. 'Our ships are laden with the Harvest of every Climate,' wrote Joseph Addison in 1711. 'Our Tables are stored with Spices, and Oils, and wines: Our Rooms are filled with Pyramids of *China*, and adorned with the workmanship of *Japan*: Our morning's Draught comes to us from the remotest Corner of the Earth: We repair our Bodies by the Drugs of *America*, and repose ourselves under *Indian* canopies.'[3] The scope and benefits of British commerce were advertised, appropriately, on the tomb of Sir William Baker, a London merchant, who died in 1770 and was buried among the fashionable in Bath abbey. Above the confident inscription '*Orbis Terrarum Felicitas*' is a carved panel on which the symbolic figure of London, an elegant female classically draped and crowned with a battlemented tiara, receives the tribute of America and Asia. The first, a naked boy, offers a beaver, from whose skins hats and fortunes were made. Asia is represented by a tur-banned Indian who steps over an elephant's tusk and leads a camel laden with panniers.

The contents of the camel's pack may well have been Indian textiles, the bales of cottons, calicoes, muslins and chintzes which young Clive marked up in his ledger. His employers paid their shareholders with the profits from cargoes of these fabrics, pepper, indigo and spices, which were unloaded at the East India Company's Poplar dock, and, in many cases, re-exported to the Continent and North America. Since the late seventeenth century, when the Company had opened up direct trade with Canton, it had added fine chinaware, silks and tea to its imports. The British taste for the latter proved insatiable and, by 1744, annual sales of china tea were worth £348,000. Chinese and Indian products were bought for silver, which had been earned by Britain's trade with Europe and the New World.

The Company traded in a fiercely competitive world. 'Our trade,' Defoe had written in 1727, 'is the Envy of the World, and they are con-spiring to break in upon it, either to anticipate it, or block it out.' Not only was the prosperity of the nation at stake, but the stability of its ordered society. 'The poor would eat us up' if Britain's international trade col-lapsed.[4] Defoe was defending the current economic dogma, mercantilism, which laid down that the world's trade was finite and that, in consequence, the commercial powers would find themselves in perpetual conflict over raw materials and markets. Monopolies in both were the sole basis for national prosperity.

II

No one country had a monopoly on India's trade. The principal com-petitors for its business were the British and French companies, with the overstretched Dutch in third place and slipping. The Portuguese, who had opened up Indian commerce in the early 1500s, were out of the race, and two newcomers, the Danish and Ostend companies, were soon exhausted. By contrast, the East India Company had kept up a steady pace since its foundation at the very end of Elizabeth I's reign. It had acquired trading bases at Madras in 1639, Bombay in 1664 (as part of the dowry presented by Catherine of Braganza to Charles II) and Calcutta in 1696.

As its interests grew, the East India Company's profits spiralled. In 1701 an anonymous pamphleteer claimed that: 'The cheapest things are ever bought in *India*. . . . Manufacture may be had there for two Pence [1p], as in *England* for a shilling [6p].'[5] Even with transport costs and customs duties, there was a wide of margin for profit, especially on imported textiles. As a result, in 1718 English weavers complained that:

> *Every jilt of the town*
> *Gets a callicoe gown;*
> *Our own manufact[ur]es are out of fashion.*[6]

British and European demand for cheap calico, chintz bedspreads and hangings, silks, fine china and tea kept the price of East India stock high. During the first half of the century its annual dividends were between 6 and 8 per cent. In the two decades before Clive's arrival in Madras, the yearly value of imported Indian and Chinese goods averaged £1 million, and in 1744 the Company had even been able to loan the government £1 million.

The beneficiaries of this success were largely men of substance. There were just under 2,000 stockholders, the majority of whom lived in Britain, although there were some foreign, mostly Dutch, investors. The Company deliberately encouraged holdings of more than £500, which qualified the shareholder to a vote at the annual meeting at its headquarters in Leadenhall Street for the election of the directors. Policy-making, therefore, was in the hands of that elite which dominated the country's commercial and political life.[7] More than a third lived in London and the Home Counties, and so a typical investor of Clive's time was a Kentish or Surrey equivalent of Fielding's Squire Allworthy. His investment would have been worth between one and two thousand pounds, and in all likelihood he was a figure of eminence in his county, who voted in Parliamentary elections and perhaps sat for the shire or a local borough. The opinions and interests of such men counted for something in the world, for they were the natural partners of the nation's rulers, that small knot of great landed aristocrats who filled the ministries of the first two Georges. A Company which could lend money to the government and whose investors carried political clout was well placed to procure political favours. In 1730 its support in the House of Commons had been strong enough to see off a challenge from Bristol and Liverpool merchants who wanted to break into its monopoly of India's trade.

The Compagnie des Indes was less fortunate in its connections and never enjoyed the same financial security as its rival. It had been formed in 1719 by the merger of three other French Asian and Far-Eastern concerns, each of which had a history of under-funding and mismanagement. Like its forerunners, the Compagnie never secured the capital needed to match its pretensions, although it somehow produced an annual profit of about £1 million during the 1730s. Its assets, acquired between 1674 and 1740, were Pondicherry, its headquarters, and subsidiary trading stations at Chandanagar on the Hughli, Yanam at the mouth of the Godvari, and Mahé and Karaikal on India's south-west coast. Lines of communication with France were secured by the occupation of the islands of La Réunion and Mauritius, where work began in 1735 on a naval base at Port Louis to which French men-o'-war could retire to escape the autumnal monsoons.

Inside France, the Compagnie had few influential friends. Its capital was mainly concentrated in the hands of its directors, who were under official supervision. The prospects of Indian trade never captured the imaginations of French investors in the same way as it had their British counterparts. French investment flowed to the sugar islands of the Caribbean and North America, and it was in these regions that the government intended to enlarge and consolidate its colonies. Moreover, in some quarters there was hostility to trade with India: the peasantry feared an influx of Indian food, and textile manufacturers protested against imports of cheap Indian fabrics. On one occasion Indian cloth was publicly burned, an early example of what would become a traditional French reaction to foreign competition.[8]

For all that its agents had achieved in India, the Compagnie seemed destined to remain in second place to the East India Company. To escape this fate and avoid stagnation, the Compagnie needed to find a source of capital which did not depend upon the whims of French investors or the unpredictable fluctuations of trade. One was available: the rights of taxation which went with the ownership of territory. If the Compagnie could accumulate territory it would acquire a reliable source of revenues from the customary imposts levied on the Indian peasantry. It might also, and this was a tempting but still distant prospect, lay the foundations of a French empire in India. What today's businessmen would call diversification seemed the only way ahead, despite the objections of the directors in Paris who wanted the Compagnie to stick strictly to what it had always done. The men on the spot were more venturesome. They had their fortunes to make and they knew local conditions and how best to exploit them. Geography was their most valuable ally: a decision taken by the governor in Pondicherry in February 1747 was relayed by a letter which reached Paris by the end of the year and was approved in January 1748. The directors' sanction reached Pondicherry in August 1748.[9] This was an extreme example of the length of time messages took to reach their destination, but even in the most favourable conditions a letter sent from India to either Paris or London might take six to seven months to deliver.[10] Distance gave enormous power to local officials, enabling them to take decisions which could not be officially repudiated for at least nine months, probably longer.

What amounted to a free hand to the men on the spot was of vital importance as events unfolded during the 1740s. It allowed servants of both companies to act as they saw fit in the knowledge that their masters had no means of checking them until long after the event, by which time local circumstances might have changed radically. At the same time, and this too was highly important given that after 1744 Britain and France were engaged in a global war, the men in India were ignorant of developments on other fronts. They were, in effect, their own masters with a licence to devise strategies which best served the interests of their respective countries and employers. In exercising this liberty, the agents of both companies never forget that they had come to India to make their own fortunes and they shaped their policies accordingly.

III

In the summer of 1740 Rahugi Bhonsle's Maratha army swept across Karnataka. It defeated the forces of the nawab, Dost Ali, and roamed across the countryside, looting, raping and murdering. Refugees poured into Pondicherry, and its governor, Benoît Dumas, defied Rahugi, who withdrew rather than assault a city defended by fortifications built in brick and in the most up-to-date European style. Dumas's gesture raised French prestige in India. It was a straw in the wind, as were two minor engagements between Maratha cavalry and detachments using European weaponry and tactics. At Bahur a small party of musketeers routed twice their number of horsemen with volley fire, and rapid artillery and musket fire from the Dutch fort at Sadras scattered another, far larger body of Marathas.[11]

Dumas's tough line was part of a new and still evolving strategy, designed to elevate France's standing among the local princes and to cultivate their friendship and so acquire territory and revenues. This policy was already paying off; in 1739 Chandra Singh, the son-in-law of Dost Ali, had presented the French with the port of Karaikal as a reward for aid in his war against the Raja of Tanjore (Thanjavur). Dumas retired at the beginning of 1742 and was replaced by Joseph François Dupleix, a man of dynamic energy who combined ambition, cupidity, anglophobia and belligerence in roughly equal parts. He was forty-six, from bourgeois stock, and, like Clive, may have been driven by an urge to prove himself in the eyes of a distant and dismissive father.[12] Whether or not this was the mainspring behind his actions, Dupleix saw India as a treasure house from which he could help himself while simultaneously promoting the interests of France and his employer. His greed was contagious; his accomplices, Charles-Joseph Bussy, Jacques Mainville and Jean-Louis Gonpil, all helped themselves to the taxes which the governor was channelling into the Compagnie's coffers. For Dupleix these misdemeanours were '*petites affaires*', not worth bothering with.[13] Rumours of how much individual Frenchmen were making from Dupleix's enterprises filtered through to their British counterparts and naturally aroused envy and emulation.[14]

In defence of his actions, Dupleix once observed that his ultimate objective was '*la domination française dans l'Inde*', which may explain why his enemies considered him a megalomaniac. He understood, better than most of his contemporaries in India, how local dynastic rivalries and power struggles between states might be exploited. But before the Compagnie could barter military assistance for land, it had to demonstrate that its soldiers were unbeatable. Quite simply, French soldiers and sepoys trained and led by French officers had to defeat British as well as princely armies.

The chance to show the Compagnie's military muscle came in the autumn of 1744, when the news reached Pondicherry that Britain and France were at war. Intelligence was also received that a formidable British naval squadron was heading for the Indian Ocean. Dupleix had no choice but to propose a local truce, a suggestion which was welcomed by the governor of Madras, who was all too aware of the weakness of the city's defences and the smallness of its garrison. The new Nawab of Karnataka, Anwar-ud Din, fearful that his province might become a battlefield, insisted that both companies kept the peace. There were no constraints on the commanders of British men-o'-war, who attacked French shipping in the Indian Ocean; in September 1745 the Compagnie's China fleet was taken off the Malayan coast, yielding £92,000 in prize money.

The companies could no longer hope to stand aloof from the global war. During the winter of 1744–45, Bertrand Le Bourdonnais, the

Governor of Mauritius, had been building up and training a scratch squadron of French merchantmen, stiffened by a ship of the line. This force gave Dupleix the wherewithal to launch a land and sea attack on Madras, which fell after a half-hearted defence in September 1746. Soon afterwards, a monsoon storm sank two of Le Bourdonnais's ships and dismasted the rest. The crippled flotilla limped back to Mauritius for repairs and the balance of sea power swung back in Britain's favour. Backed by Royal Navy warships, the garrisons of Fort St David and Cuddalore were able to beat off French assaults in December 1746 and March 1747.

In the meantime, Anwar-ud Din had taken the field, ostensibly to forestall the attack on Madras and so demonstrate his authority in Karnataka. His army, 10,000-strong and commanded by his son, Mahfuz Khan, collided with a force of 230 Europeans and 700 sepoys led by a gallant and daring engineer officer, Captain Louis Paradis, near Saint Thomé at the beginning of November. Formed up in lines, the French troops fired a conventional musket volley and then charged their adversaries. Unnerved by this novel form of attack, the Indians crumbled and fled with their general, mounted on an elephant, making the pace. Paradis's men gave chase and added impetus to the rout by firing further volleys into the flying men. This spectacular victory, secured so quickly and against what seemed overwhelming odds, astounded everyone. Thinking of the Turks, a British officer remarked that hitherto Muslims had always enjoyed a reputation as formidable warriors, but the small French force had 'broke through the charm of this timorous opinion by defeating a whole army with a single battalion'.[15] It soon became axiomatic that European leadership, soldiers, weaponry and tactics were infinitely superior to Indian. A Royal Navy officer who witnessed engagements at Fort St David, Cuddalore and Pondicherry concluded that Indians 'are ill-calculated for war, and except when they are led on by *English* with other *Europeans,* seldom make any great figure in the field'.[16]

Another lesson emerged from the war: sea power held the key to success on the Indian battlefield. Lack of it had frustrated Dupleix's campaigns and made possible a British counter-attack on Pondicherry in the summer of 1748. The Royal Navy now enjoyed complete command of the seas, thanks to a squadron of thirteen battleships and twenty smaller vessels under the command of Rear-Admiral Edward Boscawen, which had hove to off the Coromandel coast in July. Dupleix had nothing with which to challenge this fleet. In May 1747 a sixteen-strong squadron, bound for Pondicherry, had been intercepted and largely destroyed by Admiral Lord

Anson off Cape Finisterre. So long as the British dominated the Atlantic, France's Indian, and for that matter West Indian and North American possessions, could expect only intermittent and fragmentary help from home. Nonetheless, Pondicherry withstood a seven-day bombardment and, on the approach of the monsoon, British land and sea forces pulled back. In January 1749 news reached India of the signing of the preliminaries of the treaty of Aix-la-Chapelle. Not long after, the representatives of the two companies heard that nothing was to be changed in India; bargaining for boundaries and strongholds in the Caribbean and North America had been the chief concern of the peacemakers.

IV

It had been a hard fight under the walls of Pondicherry. The besiegers had shown, in the words of a recently arrived young officer, 'all the conduct and courage that men could do'.[17] Among those who conspicuously distinguished himself was Robert Clive. In a war that had been undertaken by hastily improvised armies, command had been almost entirely in the hands of former clerks who, like Clive, learned the art of war on the march and on the battlefield. He was an adept pupil, who quickly revealed bravery and a knack of winning the obedience and devotion of Indian soldiers. Once, in the forward trenches, Clive found himself isolated with a none-too-steady platoon which was about to receive a French sally. He rallied his men by reminding them of the honour and glory they were about to win. The result of his harangue was reported by an eyewitness:

> All the company's troops had an affection for this young man,
> from observing the alacrity and presence of mind which always
> accompanied him in danger; his platoon animated by his
> exhortation, fired again with new courage and great vivacity
> upon the enemy.[18]

The volley brought down twenty of the French and sent the survivors scrambling back to their emplacements.

Incidents like this enhanced Clive's growing reputation as a cool-headed, self-confident commander who led by example from the front. A public emergency had released hidden talents in a young man, who had hitherto been regarded as 'a very quiet Person' with, as he frequently admitted, a distaste for his dull existence as a tally clerk. War gave him excitement and, since he was good at it, satisfied his craving for admiration. This was the age in which a man's honour and public standing were closely bound to his ability to display courage, that indispensable virtue of a gentleman. It also mattered to Clive that soldiering would bring him rewards far richer than those he could have expected from pen-pushing. As events turned out, he was soon in a position to fulfil deeply felt obligations to his family in England and, at the same time, make himself wealthy. So long as he grasped at the opportunities which were now emerging, Clive could only move upwards.

Dupleix and the Compagnie had come out of the war badly. The Royal Navy and British privateers had inflicted losses which totalled £750,000, and the value of the Compagnie's stock had fallen to a tenth of what it had been in 1741.[19] A financial crisis, possibly bankruptcy, could only be averted by making the Compagnie a territorial power rather than a commercial enterprise. Desperate to recoup recent losses, Dupleix redoubled his efforts and raised his sights; by mid-1749 he was preparing to make the Compagnie the kingmaker of southern India. The East India Company had been invigorated by the war which had reinforced its garrisons and placed a powerful fleet at its agents' disposal. The Company could afford to be truculent and in June 1748 the directors ordered that, if the Nawab of Bengal proved refractory in trade negotiations, he was to be reminded that George II

> having the Protection of the Company greatly at heart, as they [the directors] may perceive by the Strong Force he hath sent to the East Indies to chastise the French for their Insolence at Madras, His Majesty will support the Company in whatever they think fit to do for their further Security.[20]

The fleet was in fact used to assist Company forces invited into Tanjore by its deposed raja, Shahaji, who had appealed for help at the end of 1748. Once restored to his throne, he promised to hand over the port of Devikott together with an annual revenue of between ten and twelve thousand pagodas (£40–£48,000). The Madras council agreed, with strong support from Boscawen, and a short and far-from-easy campaign followed in which Clive's conduct was again praised. The port and the annuity (the raja could only manage £9,000 a year) were welcome, and by extending its influence over Tanjore, the Company strengthened its commercial position. The upheavals of the 1740s, particularly the Maratha incursions, had severely disrupted the production of the handloom weavers of the hinterland on whom the Company depended for cotton. Obviously any measure which encouraged them to remain in the same place was welcome, and once the Company gained physical control of an area it was free to eliminate Indian middlemen and deal directly with producers.[21]

Further north, Dupleix was engineering the overthrow of the Nawab of Karnataka, Anwar-ud Din, and his replacement by a French stooge, Chandra Singh. In August 1749 the nawab was killed and his army trounced at the battle of Ambur where, again, a larger Indian army was overcome by a smaller one using European weapons and tactics. The thankful Chandra gave the commander, Louis-Hubert D'Auteil, an annual grant of 4,000 rupees (£640) and doled out 75,000 rupees (over £10,000) to his soldiers, who had already taken their pick of the treasure abandoned in Anwar's camp, which was thought to be worth three and a half lakhs of rupees (£38,500).[22]

Dupleix now turned his attention to making his ally, Muzafar Jang, ruler of the Deccan. This was achieved by yet another victory against overwhelming odds, this time roughly ten to one, at Velimdonpet in December 1750. Even the French commanders were stunned by what they had witnessed. Bussy described it as: 'A victory which no one could believe possible in Europe.' Chandra's gratitude was boundless: gifts and grants of land were showered on French commanders, with Dupleix picking up £77,500 and a jagir (annuity) worth £20,000. Lesser men got lesser presents: 400,000 rupees (£64,000) was distributed among the 5,300 soldiers according to rank and, at the end of the pecking order, the Compagnie picked up two lakhs (£22,000).[23]

Mufazar was murdered by Pathan mercenaries on his way to his capital, Hyderabad, so Bussy had his uncle, Salabat Jang, installed as *nizam* (ruler). For this service he received another handsome subvention. In just over eighteen months, Dupleix had made himself the power broker of southern India, secured a substantial land revenue for the Compagnie and, according to Madras gossip, engrossed for himself £200,000. It was not entirely a one-way traffic; Dupleix distributed various gifts to his Indian allies, including telescopes, glasses and French tapestries. Salabat and Chandra had hoped to receive portraits of their new, distant patron, Louis XV, and his family, but Dupleix could not obtain them. He was now a high-ranking Mughal official, having been declared Salabat Jang's *subadar* (lieutenant) throughout the southern Deccan. And yet his achievements were illusory;

sudden and often temporary switches of fortune were commonplace in India during this period of political flux, and there was no way of knowing for how long Dupleix and his protégés would enjoy their power undisturbed. Moreover, his masters in Paris were horrified by what they regarded as reckless gambling. In September 1752, the Controller-General of Finances vainly reminded him that 'we want only some outposts to protect our commerce: no victories, no conquests, only parity of merchandise and some augmentation of dividends'.[24]

By now Dupleix was engaged in a proxy war with the East India Company. It had refused to tolerate a French puppet in charge of Karnataka, able to impede, perhaps throttle, vital trade with the hinterland. Pretenders were plentiful in mid-eighteenth-century India and one, Muhammad Ali, the son of Anwar-ud Din, was on hand and glad to take whatever the Company would offer him. He had fled to Trichinopoly after his father's death and in May 1751 Chandra Singh began a campaign to evict him. The siege of Trichinopoly opened a contest between himself with his French sponsors and the Company for the control of Karnataka.

The departure of Boscawen's squadron at the end of 1749 restricted the Company to land operations which, for the next four years, were undertaken to expel the French and their stooges from the hinterland of Madras. The immediate tactical objective in 1751 was the relief of Trichinopoly and the release of Muhammad Ali. Since the army encircling the city outnumbered the Company's forces, only one option was open: a diversionary coup against Arcot, the capital of Karnataka. Leading an army of 200 white troops and 600 sepoys, Clive surprised Arcot on 1 September. It was undefended, for the garrison had run off after its commander lost his nerve on hearing the reports of his spies, who had described a foreign army marching calmly and resolutely through a monsoon thunderstorm. Despite having gained a psychological advantage, Clive's situation was extremely tricky, for while he had been presented with Arcot's well-stocked arsenal, its inhabitants were malevolent neutrals. As the Company's soldiers marched into the city, a sergeant observed how they passed through 'a millaion Spectators whose looks betrayed their traytours notwithstanding their pretended friendship and dirty presents'. Humble Indians, like their princes, understood the arts of duplicity. Almost immediately, Arcot was encircled by a 10,000-strong Franco-Indian army and the same NCO calculated that there were at least 2,000 of Chandra Singh's secret sympathisers lurking in the city, all 'willing to cut our throats had not that their dastardly spirits hindered them'.[25]

Clive responded to the enemy within and without the city by keeping both on their toes and never losing the initiative. His adversaries, at first short of suitable artillery and poorly commanded by Chandra's son, Raja Sahib, were continually surprised and demoralised by sudden forays, sometimes at night. An attempt to batter down the main gate with elephants with spiked iron plates on their heads failed when they were peppered by musketry. Enraged by pain, the pachyderms turned round and trampled their escorts and the waiting assault troops. Elephants were the unfortunate accessories to Indian warfare then and for the next hundred or so years but, as Clive quickly realised, they were a double-edged weapon in a pitched battle. Wounded or frightened by the noise of gunfire, they naturally tried to escape, charging down those who had brought them to the battlefield.

The siege of Arcot lasted fifty days, during which Clive and his men resisted bribes, threats, bombardment and assaults. Losses were heavy, with the Company's strength down to 240 in the final phase of the siege. On 14 November a small relief force arrived, commanded by Major James Killpatrick. Without pausing, Clive went on to the offensive. Reinforced by 600 horse under Morari Rao, a Maratha chief with whom he had made a secret alliance, Clive harried Raja Sahib's army and turned its retreat into a rout.

The siege of Arcot was destined to become an imperial epic, one of those symbolic moments of empire when heavily outnumbered British forces refused to give up, first defying and then driving off their assailants in apparent contravention of all the laws of war. Heroic sieges punctuated the history of the British in India. Arcot, Jalalabad, Lucknow and Chitral entered imperial mythology as shining examples of the discipline, doggedness and steady courage of the British race. In the later examples those who manned the ramparts were presented as the defenders of order and civilisation and their strongholds were breakwaters around which surged the waters of chaos and barbarism. It was strangely appropriate that a siege marked the foundation of the Raj.

Arcot deserved its fame. It was a turning point in the fortunes of the British, for it had revealed that the French were not invincible. Clive's reputation as a natural leader soared to new heights, and rightly so; he had displayed almost superhuman stamina, an ability to think on his feet and that quality which Napoleon desired most in his generals, luck. This amateur soldier had established two principles which would be followed by the professionals who succeeded him as commanders of British armies in

India. The first was audacity at all times; whenever a tactical choice existed it was best to take the most daring alternative, for it was commonly believed that Indian fighting men were always discountenanced by the unexpected. When Indians were under British orders, it was essential that they learned to respect and admire their white officers. A magic touch was needed to transform the sepoy into a tiger, for the experience of the 1740s and 1750s seemed to indicate that the Indian soldier was instinctively timid. Clive saw more deeply into the sepoy's psychology and realised that he possessed both courage and a sense of duty, which could be aroused by showing him how to be brave. Time and time again, Clive deliberately took risks under enemy fire to encourage his men. They responded and called him '*sabit jang*' – steady in battle.[26]

After Arcot the tide of the war turned slowly in Britain's direction. Bussy's incursion into Maratha lands in 1751 had gone awry after his opponents had harassed his supply lines. Most importantly, an Anglo-Indian army was capable of beating a French one, and the lesson was punched home repeatedly during 1752 and 1753 by Clive and the Company's new commander-in-chief, Colonel Stringer ('The Old Cock') Lawrence. He was a veteran of wars of the Continent, Culloden, and the Indian campaigns of 1747–48. Versatile and without the professional's customary arrogance towards the amateur, Lawrence recognised Clive's value and helped instruct him in the finer points of soldiering. The pair proved irresistible, winning a sequence of small-scale actions during the first half of 1752 which finally broke the siege of Trichinopoly and sealed the fate of Chandra Singh, who was captured and beheaded at the orders of his old foe, the Raja of Tanjore.

French power in Karnataka was now falling apart, but neither side had gained a decisive advantage. A stalemate ensued in which Dupleix found himself unable to sustain his pretensions. The Compagnie was after his blood, for he had dragged it into a conflict which it had not wanted and which it now seemed unable to win. His resignation had been demanded in 1752, but he ignored the summons home in the hope that he might still snatch some irons from the fire. He found none and grudgingly accepted the inevitable, leaving Pondicherry in October 1753. He had no regrets for what he had done: '*Je trouve des contrariétés partout, mais mon courage et ma fermeté ne sont point alterés: ma confiance est toujours dans la Providence.*' Dupleix was able to face personal setbacks in comfort; it was estimated that he returned to France with £200,000. He had overreached himself as a politician, but had the consolation of knowing that he had raised French prestige in India. Three years after his departure, it was reported that the Bengalis 'look upon [the French] as an enterprizing people with more of the spirit of the soldier than the merchant in them'.

VI

Dupleix's replacement, Charles Godeheu, a Breton merchant and director of the Compagnie, arrived in Pondicherry with powers to bring the fighting to an end. He did so in January 1755, in an agreement which provided a breathing space during which the antagonists prepared for the next round. The scope of the conflict was widening, since both companies had appealed to their governments for assistance in what was becoming a struggle for political and economic supremacy in southern India. In the spring of 1755 the British Cabinet approved the despatch of a squadron of three men-o'-war under Rear-Admiral Charles Watson to the Indian Ocean. On board one ship were regular soldiers of the 39th Regiment and a detachment of artillery.

The ships and the men were a token of the British government's willingness to support its trade against France. Their appearance in India marked a new phase in an Anglo-French arms race which had begun four years before. The Compagnie had procured over 4,000 men in four years, recruiting French, Swiss, German, émigré Irish and Polish mercenaries as well as prisoners from the Paris gaols. The East India Company was trawling British slums and lock-ups for extra men; a band which disembarked at Madras in 1752 were described by an onlooker as 'the refuse of the vilest employment in London'. Whatever their origins, these men were transformed into units which were making a considerable impact on the Indian consciousness. A young Armenian recalled his reactions on first seeing European troops, probably Swiss, drilling in Calcutta in the early 1750s. 'There I saw the Fort of the Europeans and the Soldiers Exercise, and the shipping and that they were dexterous and perfect in all things.' Events to the south were proving that even small numbers of such fighting men could dominate campaigns in which, one officer noted, a platoon could have as much if not greater influence on a battle than a whole battalion in Europe.

Tactical deployment and greater firepower were not the only reasons why millions of men and women in Karnataka and the Deccan were gradually passing under British and French control. They did so because of the faults of their rulers. In their analyses of what was happening, the men-on-the-spot repeatedly stressed what they considered were the inadequacies of character shared by the Indian ruling class. 'Honour is never a principle which governs the actions of Orientals,' concluded Dupleix, although to judge by his actions he would have been hard pressed to define virtue. Bussy agreed, reminding his countrymen that to succeed they would have to surpass the Indians in dissembling. 'Among a people as doublefaced as are those with whom we have to deal, to show only straightforwardness and probity is, to my thinking, only to be their dupe, and we shall inevitably be that if we do not conform to the usages of the country.'

British observers concurred, adding further shortcomings to the moral character of the Indians. 'The governments of Indostan have no idea of national honour in the conduct of their affairs' wrote Robert Orme, who was both eyewitness to and historian of events in the 1740s and 1750s. The fault lay in the upbringing and moral outlook of the Indian aristocracy:

> The vain notions in which they have been educated inspire them with such love of outward show, and the enervating climate in which they are born render them so incapable of resisting impulses of fancy, that nothing is so common than to see them purchasing a jewel or ornament of great price, at the very time that they are in the greatest distress of money to answer the necessities of government.

Orme's explanation of why Indian princes were unfit to rule proved to be the first paragraph in a dismal compendium in which successive British commentators detailed the waywardness and follies of an élite that was almost universally regarded as incapable of ruling efficiently or fairly. He offered a diagnosis of India's malady which, seen from the perspective of Karnataka in the 1750s, was perfectly valid. No cure was recommended, nor was it required, since Orme's employers did not see themselves as India's future rulers with a mandate to unseat the fickle and self-indulgent. The Company was still solely concerned with securing conditions in which it could continue its business without interruption or coercion.

In doing this the East India Company and its French counterpart joined the ranks of the powerful predators at large in mid-eighteenth-century India. They were welcomed by their Indian allies who had quickly learned that small numbers of European and European-trained soldiers could tip the balance on the Indian battlefield. The pay-offs individual commanders were coming to expect were an enticement to the adoption of belligerent policies: what might be called the power-brokers' fees made Dupleix and his lieutenants rich men. The British seem to have done marginally less well, although Clive was said to have taken £40,000 with him when he sailed for England in October 1753, which was enough to propel him into the ranks of the politically active gentry. After paying off £6,000 of his parents' mortgage and buying a town house in Queen Square, Ormonde Street, he laid out £5,000 for a seat in Parliament. This sum purchased thirty of the fifty voters of the Cornish rotten borough of Mitchell, but Clive's election was overturned by a petition to the Commons. Not that Clive would have taken his seat in the chamber, for the Company had appointed him deputy-governor of Fort St David with the promise of the governorship of Madras, and George II had given him the local rank of lieutenant-colonel. He was back in India in October 1755, aware that a war between Britain and France was imminent.

Clive's ascent from rags to riches was a powerful incentive for other men on the spot to meddle in Indian affairs whenever the chance occurred, irrespective of whether or not their actions benefitted the Company. Of course, it could always be argued, and it was after the event, that the acquisition of land and political power meant higher returns in the long run. By establishing what amounted to protectorates over Tanjore and Karnataka, the Company was free to impose stringent conditions on internal trade which were designed to increase its profits. Within twenty years of Arcot, the Company was dictating how the weavers of southern India organised production and systematically squeezing out Indian investors and entrepreneurs. Having been delivered from the depredations of Maratha horsemen, the artisans of Karnataka found themselves at the mercy of the Company's agents.

The nawab could not help them, even had he wished to, for he owed his throne to the Company's army. In less than ten years, and encouraged by a knot of persuasive, self-seeking officials like Clive, the Company had discovered that a felicitous combination of war and trade was making it richer and more powerful. There was no way of knowing where this new course would lead and, equally, no way of guaranteeing that by following it the Company would continue to prosper. A few, siren voices in London predicted an eventual disaster of the kind which had overtaken the French. They were ignored in India, where the Company servants were now dreaming of the fortunes which were the rewards for audacity and shrewdness.

3

New Strength from
Conquest: Bengal,
1755–65

I

Bengal was the richest, most fertile and densely populated region of
India. No one was sure how many people lived there. Counting
Indians was an innovation of British rule, and to begin with it was undertaken in a rough and ready manner. Clive conjured up the figure of fifteen
million, which was far too low. An official and well-informed guess of
1801 estimated the total population of Bengal as about forty million, over
four times that of Great Britain.[1] The figure may have been higher in the
1750s, for it was calculated that a fifth of Bengalis had perished in the great
famine of 1769–70. Most Bengalis were ryots, peasant farmers with varying sizes of holdings and degrees of status, who lived in villages. They,
together with landless labourers and artisans, occupied the lower reaches of
a dynamic and thrusting society. At the top were the zamindars and a
growing class of Hindu bankers, merchants and entrepreneurs who were
celebrated for their enterprise and shrewdness. Newcomers to India were
warned to be wary of Calcutta's *banias*, money agents with a keen nose for
profit who could easily outwit inexperienced young Britons.[2]

There were three sources of power within Bengal which co-existed
more or less harmoniously during the first half of the century. The power
of the sword was exercised by Murshid Quli Khan and his successors. His
had been a typical success story of the years of Mughal decline; an

imperial governor, he transformed his province into a private domain while maintaining all the outward forms of deference to the emperor in Delhi. Creating a new state was an expensive business, and Murshid and his son, Alivardi Khan, needed the co-operation and loans of Bengal's second power, its bankers and proto-capitalists. The third power in Bengal was the East India Company which, under the generous terms of the *firman* (edict) granted in 1717 by the Emperor Furrukhsiyar, enjoyed extensive commercial privileges. Most prized were the *dastaks*, certificates which gave the Company and private merchants operating under its umbrella exemption from all levies on goods passing from district to district. These concessions, granted by a moribund empire to a private company, were an affront to the nawabs' sovereignty which deprived them of revenues and hurt native traders.

The Company was jealous of its rights and regarded the growing number of protests about their misuse as tiresome quibbles. In the end it did not matter how the rules were applied, for the governor and councillors in Calcutta, in common with their countrymen everywhere, were convinced that they had a God-given right to trade where and how they liked. For an eighteenth-century Briton any restriction on legitimate commerce was tyrannical, and the forcible removal of hindrances, even when they had the power of local law, was perfectly justifiable. This logic, which combined motives of profit with a conviction that the natural rights of Britons travelled with them to every quarter of the globe, had led to a war with Spain in 1742. A major clash with the Nawab of Bengal was therefore unavoidable.

By the mid-1740s relations between the Company and Alivardi Khan were taking a turn for the worse. More was at stake than legal interpretations of the firman. As the Company's economic penetration of Bengal gathered momentum, the nawab was forced to consider the political implications for a Muslim state whose roots were still shallow among a predominantly Hindu population. Alivardi died in April 1756, bequeathing his anxieties to his grandson and heir, Siraj-ud Daula. The 21-year-old nawab was determined to engineer a showdown with the intruders which would confirm his supremacy throughout Bengal. He was ill-equipped for the task: resolute by starts, he was easily disheartened and his fickle vindictiveness lost him friends among his courtiers and more powerful subjects. He did not, for instance, help himself by threatening forcibly to convert and circumcise leading members of the Hindu banking oligarchy.[3]

Siraj's geatest error was to misjudge the resources and determination of his adversary. This mistake was forgiveable given the remarkable ease with which his troops occupied the Company's bases at Kasimbazar and Calcutta during the summer of 1756. The one-sided war had been the consequence of the Company's refusal to stop strengthening the defences of Fort William, work then being undertaken in expectation of a war with France. This challenge was contemptuously dismissed by Roger Drake, the governor in Calcutta, who went so far as to remark that he could easily overthrow Siraj if he continued to make trouble.[4] This was empty bluster from a coward who lacked the muscle to carry out his threats. Kasimbazar was guarded by a polyglot rabble largely untrained in arms, and Calcutta had neglected to send replacements for its worm-eaten gun carriages. Fort William was also weakly defended; in 1753 its arsenal had contained only 200 serviceable muskets and its garrison of twice that size was largely made up of Swiss mercenaries of fragile loyalty.[5]

Kasimbazar surrendered and Calcutta was taken on 20 June in circumstances which combined farce with tragedy. On the approach of Siraj's army, Drake and a handful of officers took flight to the ships anchored off shore. In the meantime, the leaderless and disheartened garrison took to the bottle.[6] During the night of 20–21 June, an unknown number of Siraj's prisoners were herded into a small room where over half suffocated during a hot and airless night. For the British, 'the Black Hole of Calcutta' was an atrocity which demanded vengeance and, on one level, the events of the following year could be interpreted as the punishment of a brutal autocrat. In fact, no one was certain how many were crammed into the Black Hole and how many perished. Estimates vary between 100 and 200 incarcerated and between 40 and 140 dying. Siraj may not have been directly responsible, and one Indian writer has blamed the incident on Eastern 'negligence, indifference and inefficiency'.[7] This explains but does not excuse: by the same token the deaths of sixty-seven Mapillas (Malabari Muslims), stifled in railway cars in 1921, was the consequence of Western incompetence. It might well be added that neither Siraj nor the British authorities in Malabar were unduly disturbed by what had happened.

The loss of Calcutta was a signal blow to the Company's prestige and temporarily overturned the myth of European invincibility. It disappointed those Bengal Hindus who had secretly hoped that Siraj might get a bloody nose from the British.

News of the disaster reached Madras on 16 August. There was no question that a counter-offensive had to be launched to recapture Calcutta and bring Siraj to heel. Delivering it was an unwelcome distraction from the task then occupying the minds of the Madras authorities: a campaign in partnership with the Marathas to extinguish all French influence in the Deccan. The recovery of Calcutta took precedence and an expeditionary force was mustered of 600 white soldiers and 900 sepoys who were conveyed to the port by five warships. Command was placed in the hands of Clive and the local senior naval officer, Admiral Charles Watson, a straightforward sailor of impeccable character who found himself dominated by his more forceful and devious partner. Both men hoped to profit from the expedition, but Watson shrank from compromising his integrity by playing politics in the Indian fashion.

II

Clive had no such inhibitions and complete freedom of action. His mandate from the Madras council was to reoccupy Calcutta and restore all the Company's trading concessions. No one was yet clear just how this could be achieved, although Watson imagined that, once he had been 'well thrashed', Siraj would toe the line. Before he could be taught his lesson, it was imperative to expel his garrison from Calcutta, which was achieved with little bloodshed on New Year's Day, 1757. By then, if not before, Clive had convinced himself that the Company's trade in Bengal could only be truly safe when Siraj had been dethroned and replaced by a puppet nawab. The means to carry out this coup were at Clive's disposal; he had men-o'-war, including two ships of the line, and a well-trained army. This force would soon have to withdraw to engage the French, and so it was necessary to strike immediately. The alternative was to leave behind a wounded and therefore dangerous tiger; so long as he occupied the throne of Bengal, Siraj was free to take his vengeance on Calcutta, possibly with French assistance.

For the next six months Clive threw himself into organising what he and the council in Calcutta afterwards called a 'revolution'. It was a consummate exercise in chicanery in which Clive was abetted by two colleagues, Luke Scrafton and William Watts, men of quick wits and elastic conscience, who acted as emissaries to Siraj. The nawab had been taken aback by the speed of the Company's reactions and the strength of its forces, although the fighting which followed the recovery of Calcutta had been indecisive. Realising that he may have bitten off more than he could

chew, Siraj grudgingly agreed to make peace in February. He was probably no more sincere in his professions of goodwill than Clive, but for the
time being he had to tread carefully. Large Afghan forces were operating in
the Punjab and might strike south-east into Awadh and Bengal, and therefore he was glad to hear that George II and the Company were now his
friends and would come to his rescue if his lands were invaded. British soldiers and ships could not render this service without first capturing the
French base at Chandanagar, and so Siraj was persuaded to stand back and
permit it to be taken in March.

Siraj had been gulled; it now remained for him to be ensnared and
dethroned. Shedding whatever scruples they may have had, Clive and his
accomplices proceeded swifly and with serpentine cunning. During April
and May they cobbled together an alliance of influential Bengali dissidents,
all of whom had much to gain from Siraj's deposition. At the heart of
the conspiracy were Bengal's leading money men, the Sikh merchant
Omichand, and the two brothers who headed the Jagat Seth (merchants of
the world) banking house. Bengal's commerce relied heavily on the silver
with which the Company paid for its goods and, so long as the province
was ruled by a prince at loggerheads with the British, their company and
fortunes were in danger. There was also an alternative nawab, Mir Jafar, a
nobleman and one of Siraj's senior commanders. All the plotters were to
have their rewards: Mir Jafar would get a throne, the European community
in Calcutta would receive £550,000 for property looted by Siraj's army,
the Hindu community £222,000, the Armenian £77,000, the army and
navy £275,000 and members of the Company's council £275,000.
Omichand set a high price on his co-operation and got it according to a
bogus agreement on which Clive had faked Watson's signature. This piece
of legerdemain was a victory of guile over greed, although in the eyes of
Clive's enemies it was a disgraceful example of an Englishman dropping his
own moral code and embracing that of the Orient.

Clive knew that he, as a council member and commander-in-chief of
the Company's land forces, would rake in the lion's share of the compensation, not to mention whatever customary gifts that might have come his
way from the grateful Mir Jafar. He also knew that there was no intrinsic
dishonour in merging his own interests with those of his country and
employer. The age in which he lived allowed its public men the right to
grow rich through their service to the state, although there was, as Clive
would soon discover, much disagreement as to where the line between
public and private interest should be drawn. He sincerely believed that in

all his decisions he had achieved a proper balance and was therefore beyond reproach, and yet there can be no question that he was well aware that he would be the chief British beneficiary from the coup and, like everyone else involved, expected to leave Bengal a richer man.[8]

With the agreement signed, Clive was ready to pounce. The plot required a battle in which Siraj would be defeated by a combination of the Company's army and defectors from his own led by Mir Jafar. Clive had about 3,000 troops and sailors, two-thirds of them sepoys who marched from Kasimbazar. The white fighting men travelled by boat, the better to preserve them from fevers and the sultry midsummer heat. Against them Siraj had 50,000 men, many unpaid and disgruntled.

The two armies collided at Plassey on 23 June and a battle followed which, by European standards, was little more than a skirmish, and a messy one at that. Much of it was taken up by an exchange of cannon fire in which the Bengalis came off worst. They had massive twenty-four and thirty-two pounder pieces, each mounted on platforms dragged by forty or fifty yoke of bullocks and nudged into position by elephants. Their transport proved the gunners' undoing, for three elephants were killed and the rest became 'unruly'. The oxen, too, were terrified by the fire and stampeded, taking their drivers with them.[9] If this was not enough, one observer noticed that the Indian gunners seemed clumsy and once accidentally set alight their own powder barrels, which exploded and added to the pandemonium. All this was watched by Mir Jafar, who, judging the moment right, sent a message to Clive warning him of his imminent defection. The trouble was that Clive was unaware of where Mir Jafar's contingent was placed and had already accidentally bombarded his troops. The fire was so hot that the messenger refused to cross the lines. In the end, the bungling on both sides did not matter; Siraj's hesistant army disintegrated and took to its heels, with the nawab leading the way on a camel.

He was eventually taken and stabbed to death by the servants of his successor, Mir Jafar, who seems to have imagined that Clive would have asked for him to be spared. This exercise in king-making had cost few lives: British casualties were only seventy and 'those chiefly blacks', according to Clive's report to the directors.[10] No one counted the dead Bengalis, but a rough and probably exaggerated estimate put them at about 500.[11]

III

No one who had taken part in the battle of Plassey imagined for a moment that it had marked a turning point in British and Indian history. For them it was merely a solution to a local problem: the future security of the Company's operations in Bengal. It also offered a means of dealing with another problem, the French, as Clive pointed out in his despatch to the directors written in August. With Mir Jafar's cash in the Company's war chest, the balance of power in southern India would swing further against the French. In Bengal the Company was henceforward free to trade as it wished with the blessing of a grateful nawab. It was this aspect of Plassey which George II's poet laureate, William Whitehead, had in mind when he wrote in 1759:

> *If protected Commerce keep*
> *Her tenor o'er yon heaving deep,*
> *What have we from War to fear?*
> *Commerce steels the nerves of war:*
> *Heals the havoc Rapine makes,*
> *And new strength from conquest takes.*[12]

There were distant political gains as well, vaguely discerned by Clive, who told the directors that they now possessed the 'power to be as great as you please in the kingdom of Bengal'.[13]

Plassey's significance became apparent only with hindsight. In 1823 the compiler of the *East India Military Calendar*, following what was already a standard line of imperial mythology, detected the hand of Providence at work. Clive and his brother officers had behaved 'as if decreed by fate to erect the British standard in the East'.[14] As that flag advanced, the battle assumed a symbolic significance; in the words of one Victorian school-room text, Plassey laid 'the foundation of the British empire in India'.[15] Another historian was more emphatic: 'In 1757 the English had established their dominion of India by their conquest of Bengal.'[16] And yet, strangely given the Raj's obsession with public monuments, no attempt was ever made to distinguish the site of Plassey. By 1800 much of the battlefield had been washed away by the adjacent Bhagrithi river and all that remained of the village was 'a few miserable huts'. Eighty years later, when the Raj was enjoying its heyday, the whole area had reverted to jungle.[17]

Just as well, many Indians may have thought, for the battle marked the beginning of an era of alien government and the disturbance of ancient habits and customs. Plassey was also an uncomfortable reminder that there had been many Indians, especially from the country's élite, who willingly collaborated with the intruders and helped them win this and many subsequent victories. Their behaviour was evidence that at a crucial moment in their history there had been no 'national' sentiment among Indians, a fact which nineteenth- and twentieth-century nationalists frequently deplored.

And yet, Plassey assumed a supernatural significance for some Hindus as the starting point of a predestined historical cycle that would take a century to run its course. The Muslim, Mughal Raj had been supplanted by a British one, which would last exactly one hundred years according to predictions found in some obscure Hindu scriptures. Then, reassuringly, a Hindu Raj would emerge to rule India. Rumours of this upheaval were current during the early 1830s and their circulation increased in the years immediately before 1857.[18] The sepoy mutiny at Meerut on 10 May 1857 and the sudden collapse of the Raj in northern India was naturally taken as a fulfilment of the prophecy. Its new potency was exploited by the insurgent leader, Nana Sahib, who chose the precise anniversary of Plassey, 23 June, for a major assault on the residency of Cawnpore (Kanpur).

After the Indian Mutiny, even the most improbable seditious prophecies were taken seriously by the authorities. Official nerves were on edge during 1906–07, when a spate of nationalist agitation coincided with the fiftieth anniversary of the Meerut uprising.[19] The 150th anniversary of Plassey had not been forgotten and the ex-Viceroy Lord Curzon was soliciting contributions for Clive memorials in London and Calcutta. His successor, Lord Minto, was dismayed and asked, 'How would Bengal in these stormy days look upon a monument to Clive coupled with Plassey?'[20] As wormwood was the answer, Minto scotched a project which would have raised tension everywhere in India. Meanwhile, Curzon was badgering Indian princes for subventions, reminding the Maharaja of Bikaner that money offered in Clive's memory was an a token of loyalty to Britain.[21] In the space of 150 years, Plassey had become, in turn, a glorious victory which established the Raj; a source of hope for those who longed for its collapse; and finally an embarrassment to its rulers.

IV

On 23 June 1763, the sixth anniversary of Plassey, a handful of traders and army officers gathered at the Company's factory (business premises) at Patna for a commemorative dinner.[22] They had much to celebrate, for Plassey had been a key which had opened a treasure house whose contents they were now pillaging. The past six years had been quite literally a golden age, during which the Company's servants had scooped up the riches of Bengal. The bonanza began with delivery of the compensation promised by Mir Jafar and the gifts he made to those who had engineered his elevation. Then there were the land taxes extracted from the Bengali ryots, whose parganas (tax districts) had been ceded to the Company and which, in time, would provide it with the means to buy goods with cash raised in India, rather than imported silver. Lastly, and most importantly for the men on the spot, were the new and lucrative openings in the huge internal commerce of Bengal.

The inland trade of Bengal had always been minutely regulated by the nawabs, who allocated monopolies to individuals and consortiums. With Mir Jafar's accession, the system of state control fell apart under pressure from private traders seeking quick profits. The salt, betel-nut and opium concessions attracted the sharks who identified them as offering the best returns. Henry Vansittart, who followed Clive as Governor of Bengal in 1759, made the running and was later charged with abusing his authority to get the biggest possible share of the province's trade. Warren Hastings, resident at the court of Mir Jafar at Murshidabad, presided over a large-scale venture dealing in salt, opium, tobacco, timber and boat-building which had a capital of £30,000 and employed five Europeans. It was calculated that he and other predator entrepreneurs were making over £500,000 a year by 1760.

The methods of these men were brutal. They and the Hindu and Armenian merchants who were their factotums used coercion to dominate markets. The sword intruded into everyday business life, for the more ruthless commodity dealers encouraged their *gumastahs* (Indian clerks and business agents) to employ sepoys wherever pressure was needed to secure the best bargain. Competitors were scared off and unwilling suppliers or customers who objected to inflated prices were flogged.[23] Vansittart noted with wry amusement that gumastahs, 'who in Calcutta walk in rags', once inland would 'lord it over the country, imprisoning the ryots, and merchants, and writing and talking in the most insolent, domineering manner to the *fougedars* [rural policemen] and officers'.[24] Minatory business methods were copied in southern India; in the early 1770s the native factor employed by Anthony Sadleir to buy cloth in the Vizagapatam district was accompanied by sepoys who beat those weavers who set what was thought to be too a high a price on their goods.[25] In Bengal, dastaks (tax exemption certificates) were liberally doled out to Indian and Armenian as well as British traders, some of whom flaunted their privileges by flying the Company's flag on their boats.

The three years of unbridled and systematic economic exploitation that followed the battle at Plassey proved mortal for the Bengal state. Its economy was in the hands of the Company and its servants; the nawab's authority was circumscribed by a British resident; and Company sepoys garrisoned his cities. Mir Jafar's impotence was demonstrated early in 1759, when Bengal was threatened by what turned out to be a half-hearted incursion by a Mughal army commanded by the emperor's eldest son, the future Shah Alam II. Brushing aside Mir Jafar's suggestion of buying him off, Clive led a force to Patna where he discovered that the young prince's unpaid army had dispersed. Clive used this bloodless victory as the excuse to squeeze an annuity of £27,000 a year from the nawab. Disdainful of the profits from trade being made by his more unscrupulous colleagues, he had been angling for an award of this kind for six months.[26] The sum was to be paid from the revenues of parganas close to Calcutta, which Mir had previously allocated to the Company.

By rewarding Clive with a jagir rather than the usual cash gift, Mir Jafar revealed the parlous state of his treasury. It had been drained by the Plassey pay-off and customs revenues were dwindling. Solvency, and with it a semblance of sovereignty, could only be secured by stemming the haemorrhage of Bengal's wealth. In what turned out to be the first round in a struggle to regain independence, Mir Jafar demanded some curtailment of the commercial activities of the Company's servants in 1760. Governor Vansittart refused to tolerate any challenge to the sacred right of the Company and its employees to trade as they wished, even though he was well aware of the abuses they committed. Clive's puppet had, in the governor's words, revealed himself as unfit to govern, being 'of a Temper extremely tyrannical and avaricious at the same time very indolent and the People about him being either abject Slaves and flatterers, or else the basest Instruments of his Views'.[27] Siraj-ud Daula had been vilified in almost exactly the same terms, and like him, Mir Jafar was deposed by the Company, this time without a fight. His successor, his son-in-law Mir

Kasim, was described by one official as a 'very enterprizing man of great abilities', which may be interpreted as a tractable prince willing to do whatever he was told.[28] Like the old, the new nawab was obliged to pay the power-brokers' fees; Vansittart and a knot of councillors were believed to have pocketed at least £200,000.[29] The Company's reward for supporting Mir Kasim were the districts of Burdwan, Chittagong and Midnapur.

Mir Kasim fell short of his patrons' expectations. During the next three years, he prepared to reverse the verdict of Plassey and restore Bengali independence. He sorted out his finances and rebuilt his army, which he equipped with modern cannon and stiffened with 200 European mercenaries, mostly artillerymen. Mir Kasim also shifted his capital away from Murshidabad to Munger, where his activities were monitored by the *hircarras* (spies) supervised by Henry Lushington in Patna. During the first half of 1762 they reported, among other things, that the nawab was spending large sums on hiring Ruhela cavalry, had banned his subjects from dealing with British gumastahs and was waiting for news from Europe on the outcome of the war with France.[30] His open hostility and preparations for war did not create undue alarm; rather there was complacency in Calcutta, where one official observed that the Company would depose thirty nawabs if it needed to and could profit by it.[31]

The war opened in June 1763 with an underhand trick which went awry. While the Company was negotiating with Mir Kasim, officials in Patna undertook a pre-emptive *coup de main* against the city. What was easily gained was easily lost, thanks in large part to slackness and the unexpected difficulties of street fighting. The Patna garrison was evicted and its remnants were pursued across country with heavy losses. News of this reverse demoralised sepoys serving in the forces under Majors Thomas Adams and John Carnac, who were advancing on Murshidabad.[32]

What Carnac called 'this truly just and necessary war' had to be won quickly and decisively in order to repair the damage inflicted on the Company's prestige. He was an aggressive, confident officer with sufficient experience of Indian warfare to appreciate that silver counted as much as steel on the battlefield. As he approached Burdwan, he requested Vansittart's permission to confiscate its 'collections' (tax revenues) and use the cash to entice unpaid soldiers away from the local raja's army.[33] For their part, his adversaries identified lines of communications as a weakness in an army whose commanders insisted that their men did not live off the land. Raids were therefore made against Carnac's supply columns which, on occasions, had to fight their way through.

Carnac's and Adams's brigades also had to endure cross-country marches in the hot season, often through flooded paddy fields. The enemy made a better showing than at Plassey, and after the engagement at Sooti on 2 August an astonished Carnac reported the 'most obstinate resistance infinitely above whatever was made by a black army before'. At one stage, Afghan cavalry penetrated behind British lines and it was only the 'coolness and intrepidity' of Adams, who rallied the wavering 84th Regiment, that staved off disaster. Adams was a commander in the Clive mould, careless of his personal safety and indifferent to odds, whose nerve was vital in a crisis. 'Good God! How much depends on the life of one man,' Carnac wrote after one of Adams's displays of audacity and coolheadedness.[34] The strain proved too much and Adams died from the effects of his exhaustion on his way back to England to recuperate. Such men were desperately needed as the army pushed on towards Munger and Patna, and both officers and men became weary and disheartened.

Patna was retaken by a night attack and Mir Kasim, having lost the initiative, fell back threatening to kill the prisoners taken during the retreat from Patna if the Company's forces engaged him. He kept his word and the hostages were murdered in October, despite a warning from Adams that this act of savagery would assure his own destruction. In the new year, Mir Kasim's fortunes seemingly revived when he was reinforced by soldiers of his allies, Shuja-ud Daula, the Nawab of Awadh, and the Emperor Shah Alam II. Lukewarm partners, the two princes' troops enabled Mir Kasim to field an army of about 40,000, strong in Afghan cavalry and with modern cannon manned by European gunners; Carnac had been dismayed to find that captured guns had screw elevators of the most up-to-date kind which enabled them to be aimed more accurately than those deployed at Plassey.[35]

In spite of these hurried innovations, the army of Mir Kasim and his allies was heavily defeated by a much smaller one commanded by Major Hector Munro at Buxar on 23 October 1764. It was very much a classic engagement of a kind which would occur across India during the next hundred years. On each occasion the ingredients of the Company's victories were the same: iron discipline; the steadiness of its men, both Indian and European, in defence; and their ferocity when the moment came for a counter-attack with bayonet. Unflinching soldiers firing carefully timed volleys shattered cavalry charges at Buxar and broke the attackers' nerve. One described the line of sepoy infantry as a 'wall which vomited fire and flame'.[36]

V

The consequences of Buxar were as far-reaching as at Plassey. It marked the final disintegration of the Bengal state, brought Awadh firmly into the Company's orbit and was an additional blow to the standing of the Mughal dynasty, which was still reeling from the Afghan invasion of three years before. A power vacuum had been created which only the Company was rich and strong enough to fill. The political settlement was masterminded by Clive, who had returned to Calcutta as governor in May 1765 with instructions from the directors to stamp out corruption and devise an orderly system of government.

Buxar made possible the last, for it gave him the opportunity to forgo what had proved to be the highly unsatisfactory procedure of picking a suitable nawab and then hoping that he would do as he was told. Clive was now able to deal directly with the emperor and secure his formal approval for a legally impeccable settlement which gave the Company absolute authority throughout Bengal. There was no question of Shah Alam II refusing; the emperor was a fugitive with an empty purse and therefore pleased to accept Clive's offer of an annual tribute of £272,000 from the revenues of Bengal and also those of Allahabad and Korah, which lay inside Awadh. In return for solvency and security (Company soldiers were stationed close by his palace at Allahabad), Shah Alam II granted the Company the diwan of Bengal, Bihar and Orissa in perpetuity, giving it the sole right to collect taxation estimated to be worth approximately £33 million a year. Clive also secured the imperial imprimatur for his personal jagir (annuity) and concessions for the Company's ally, the Nawab of Karnataka.

There was still a nawab of Bengal, the sixteen-year-old Najm-ud Daula, whom the Company had installed as ruler with the by-now ritual distribution of bribes and presents to British officials. Henceforward, he and his successors would be ornamental ciphers whose trappings of state were paid for by Company pensions. Real power, that which came from free access to the taxes of Bengal and the day-to-day governance of the province, was in the hands of the Company.

Looking back on these events nearly twenty years later, a Company official reminded the government that 'we acquired our Influence and Possessions by force, it is by force we must maintain them'.[37] It was a phrase which would be repeated in various forms until the last days of the Raj, and it contained much truth. It became an article of faith for generations of British officers of all ranks, who believed unquestioningly that armed force alone had been the foundation of the Raj and remained the guarantee of its survival in the face of external and internal threats. This assumption was more than an interpretation of history; it was the basis of a powerful claim by military men for their views to have paramountcy whenever questions of security were under consideration.

It would be impossible to discount the value of the victories in Bengal. What might be called the stand-off at Plassey and the pitched battles of 1763–64 delivered the province into British hands and prepared the way for the political and economic penetration of Awadh. Quite simply, the Company's army was better-trained, more inspiringly commanded and technically better equipped than its adversaries. Elsewhere, its achievements were equally impressive; despite some early hitches it overcame the French and their allies in southern India. Pondicherry fell in 1761 and four years later the new French governor, Jean Law, wrote despairingly: 'The city was like another Jerusalem, razed to the ground, its walls overthrown, its houses destroyed and its inhabitants led to captivity.'[38]

Unlike the Jews, the French never recovered from their Babylonian captivity. In 1764 the Compagnie's debts totalled £12.2 million and were increasing by the year as its trading losses rose. It was now just a commercial concern, for, by the terms of the Treaty of Paris signed in February 1763, the Compagnie had been allowed to keep all its former trading stations. But it was forbidden to indulge in politics, and to make sure it did not, its bases were to be unfortified and their garrisons severely limited. In 1776 Pondicherry was guarded by just over 200 white soldiers and 32 sepoys, a detachment equal to that which might have been stationed in some Company outpost in up-country Awadh. Although Clive still feared a recrudescence of French influence in India, possibly backed by a fleet sent from France, the Compagnie had been all but destroyed both as a political power and an economic force.

What is perhaps most striking about the events in India between 1756 and 1765 was their pace and decisiveness. In less than a decade two formidable powers, the Compagnie des Indes and the state of Bengal, were knocked out of the political ring. Awadh had begun an irreversible slide into British control and a Mughal emperor had been driven to go begging to the Company for money and protection. The catalysts for these astonishing reversals of fortune had been a small band of what might be called private-enterprise imperialists, who had found themselves in a position to shape Company policy as they proceeded and were more or less free of any restraint from above.

They had followed no pre-conceived plan, nor did any one of them justify himself with a vision of imperial destiny or mission. They were pragmatic, flexible men who reacted to events as they happened. Most significantly, Clive and those who followed his example were quite willing to adopt that moral elasticity vital to political success in India. All regarded themselves as patriots and were so, save that their sense of duty to their country was always tempered by what they would have considered enlightened selfishness. Private and public advantage proceeded hand in hand. Vansittart proclaimed that the Company's interests were automatically those of Britain and it followed, at least by his logic, that by advancing them alongside his own, he was doing a favour for his countrymen.[39] Clive thought along similar lines, arguing that his and his colleagues' endeavours had created a new and extremely valuable national asset. In 1770 he reminded the Prime Minister, Lord North, of the considerable 'annual advantages' that now flowed into Britain from the rise in income from customs duties on Indian imports. The nation as a whole was benefitting from an injection of capital in the form of private fortunes, such as his own, and he warned that if these gains were somehow lost, there would be widespread 'Accusation and Resentment'.[40]

Britain's new possessions in India were indeed generating plenty of accusations and resentments, but not the kind Clive had in mind. His countrymen were becoming disturbed by the often distressing details of how exactly this empire had been obtained, and were growing uneasy about how its possessions might undermine or corrupt what was called 'the national character'.

4

An Empire Within an Empire: British Reactions to Indian Conquests

I

Samuel Foote had a jobbing playwright's knack of knowing what his audiences wanted. The *bon ton* of the early 1770s was obsessed by 'nabobs': the word was a corruption of nawab and was used to describe anyone who had come home from India with a fortune. Nabobs were *arrivistes* whose efforts to thrust themselves into fashionable society and politics were a source of amusement and indignation. Foote detected a market and responded to it with a comedy, *The Nabob*, which was first performed in Dublin's Theatre Royal in November 1773. It was topical, rollicking stuff and enjoyed considerable success.

The nabob of the title is Sir Matthew Mite, a brash vulgarian. Theatregoers would have immediately recognised features of Clive in his character and behaviour; he had been a scapegrace schoolboy whose misdeeds included throwing a barrow woman into the Fleet ditch and throwing a firework at a Methodist preacher, a prank for which he got someone else to take the blame.[1] The scoundrel flourishes in India and, at the start of the play, we hear:

Sir Matthew Mite, from the Indies, came thundering amongst

us; and, profusely scattering the spoils of ruined provinces, corrupted virtue and alienated the affections of all the old friends to the family.

Mite has two ambitions: first to win acceptance in elegant society, and secondly to purchase that ultimate token of social success, a seat in the Commons. His endeavours to assume the standing of a gentleman are ludicrous. A waiter teaches him to cast dice in the modish manner and instructs him in the 'oathes and phrases that are most in use at the club'. He also wishes to cut a figure with men of learning and has been gulled into buying bogus antiques, which he intends to deposit in a national collection. They include: Falstaff's corkscrew, Henry VIII's nutcrackers and the toecap of the slipper worn by Cardinal Pandulf when he kicked King John. This Gothic junk impresses the ignoramuses of the Society of Antiquaries, who elect him a fellow, and Mite returns the honour with a donation of more curios, including a green chamber pot, allegedly the sarcophagus of Mark Antony's coachman.

There is a sinister side to Mite. He once confesses, 'I have thoughts of founding in this town a seraglio,' and adds that his odalisques will be guarded by 'three blacks from Bengal'. He is warned against this scheme and pointedly reminded that imprisoning women was unthinkable and illegal 'in a country of freedom'.[2] Here is the central theme of the comedy: Mite has been seduced by the morals of India, a none-too-difficult process, given his character, and has returned determined to corrupt his fellow countrymen.

Mite's attempts to subvert common British decency provide the plot of the play. His plans to enter Parliament involve a challenge to Sir John Oldham, the impoverished but honourable head of an ancient family. At every turn, Mite behaves in an underhand manner. He has secretly taken over Oldham's debts, which he promises to repay in return for the borough which he controls. He adds, impudently, that he will settle a 'jaghire' on Oldham; pay for the shipping of his two daughters to Calcutta 'and there procure them suitable husbands'; and provide junior Company posts for their brothers. Faced with this bargain, Oldham's brother-in-law complains, 'No wonder that so much contrivance and cunning has been an overmatch for a plain English gentleman, or an innocent Indian one.' Lady Oldham concurs: 'With the wealth of the East, we have too imported the worst of its vices.'

In the end Mite is frustrated through the intervention of Oldham's brother, a merchant whose code of honour has not been contaminated by trade. He tells Mite that 'corrupt as you may concieve this country to be, there are superior spirits living, who would disdain an alliance with grandeur obtained at the expense of honour or virtue.' Lady Oldham warns that: 'The possessions arising from plunder very rarely are permanent; we every day see what has been treacherously and rapaciously gained, as profusely and full as rapidly squandered.' Mite is genuinely puzzled by the absence of any 'gratitude of the country to those who have given it dominion and wealth', a complaint which was echoed by Clive, among others.

In essence, *The Nabob* is a tale of a knave whose moral infirmities have been made worse by his life in India. Sympathy is shown towards those Indians he has deceived, and throughout the author claims that Indian riches are tainted because they have been fraudulently acquired. Corruption is contagious, and the play strongly suggests that Mite and his kind are debauching domestic society and politics with vices endemic to India, but hitherto absent from Britain. Moreover, as *The Nabob* makes clear, gentlemen with pedigrees and pretensions were revolted by the entry into their world of a pack of crass *nouveaux riches* who not only aped their manners but could outspend them. Warren Hastings, who represented old money fallen on hard times, was keen to restore his family's status, whatever the cost. When he purchased the manor of Daylesford in Gloucestershire, which his family had been forced to sell in 1715, he instructed his agent to 'give as much for it as it is worth and if you give something more for it I shall not be sorry'.[3]

There was little in *The Nabob* which would have shocked audiences. During 1772 and the first the half of 1773, Parliamentary investigations were uncovering the methods by which the nabobs had made their fortunes. The country heard details of chicanery, double-dealing and extortion, which gave an added edge to blue-blooded jealousy. These revelations contributed to a widespread apprehension that a novel and unwholesome source of political power was on the rampage.

Snobbery and fears about the moral and political pollution of the nation combined in Horace Walpole's frequent outbursts against nabobs. In July 1773 he wrote:

> What is England now? – A sink of Indian wealth, filled by nabobs and emptied by Maccaronis! A senate sold and despised! A country overrun by horse-races! A gaming, robbing,

wrangling, railing nation without principles, genius, character
or allies.

He damned all nabobs as the spawn of Macheath, the highwayman anti-
hero of *The Beggars' Opera*, and once asserted that the arch-nabob Clive
was the begetter of all Macaronis, Italianate fops who, it was whispered,
indulged the 'Italian vice', as sodomy was then called.[4] Walpole was the
son of an earl and a dilettante who preferred an idealised Gothic past to
what he considered to be a degenerate present, which partly explains the
ferocity of his outbursts.

There were two complementary issues at stake. The first was the possibly harmful impact of the nabobs on British political life, and the second
concerned how far the British people were prepared to tolerate a despotism being exercised in their name in India. There had never been any
objection in principle to nabobs buying Parliamentary seats in an age
which accepted that wealth and political influence were synonymous.
What upset contemporaries were the methods employed by nabobs seeking election. Like the fictional Sir Matthew Mite, they were men in a
hurry and unconcerned with common political courtesies. They never
bothered to cultivate constituencies and were indifferent to the feelings of
those they had swept aside. It appeared, particularly to their victims, that
the nabobs were behaving in Britain as they had in India. Furthermore,
they were able to offer more than the going rate, either in bribes to voters
or payments to the owners of rotten boroughs. The nabobs were making
politics more expensive and this, above all, made them enemies among a
political establishment whose wealth came from the ownership of land.

By 1767, Clive, his cousin George (who had made £20,000 during the
Plassey campaign), his friend John Walsh and two ex-governors of Madras
had secured seats in the Commons.[5] Thereafter, the numbers of nabob
MPs rose steadily; there were twenty-six between 1774 and 1780 and
forty-five between 1784 and 1790, an increase which reflected the fact that
during this period ultimate power over Indian affairs had passed from the
Company to Parliament.[6] Given that the total membership of the Commons was 558, nabobs were in a strong position to exert pressure on
ministries whenever Indian legislation was under discussion.

Parliamentary interest in India was focused on the conduct of the
Company's officials in India. Their behaviour was scandalous; according to
a hack pamphleteer of 1773:

Lacks and crowes [lakhs and crores] of rupees, sacks of diamonds, Indians tortured to disclose their treasure; cities, towns and villages ransacked and destroyed, jaghires and provinces purloined; Nabobs dethroned, and murdered, have found the delights and constituted the religions of the Directors and their servants.

The government ignored these outrages at its peril, for if the Company was not bridled in time it would become 'subversive of the Liberties of Englishmen, and creative of a set of tyrants'.[7]

II

The Company had become a sort of Frankenstein's monster, out of control and capable of wreaking havoc both in India and Britain. In the revealing words of one of its directors, it was 'an empire within an empire', possessing vast resources and answerable to no one but its own shareholders.[8] It was essentially an alien empire: it possessed no roots in Britain, unlike the American colonies whose people were of British stock and shared British liberties and traditions. Indeed, as Clive told the Commons in 1772, India was the antithesis of Britain in terms of its political system, its rulers' moral code, and its peoples' freedom:

Indostan was always an absolute despotic government. The inhabitants, especially in Bengal, in inferior stations are servile, mean, submissive and humble. In superior stations they are luxurious, effeminate, tyrannical, treacherous, venal, cruel.[9]

Clive was in a tight spot, forced to defend his honour to a House of Commons which had been stunned by the recent revelations about his activities in Bengal. The Company also had its back to the wall in 1772, having enjoyed a brief period of unprecedented prosperity which had been followed by an unlooked-for and potentially fatal slump. News that Clive had secured the entire revenues of Bengal sparked off what turned out to be an artificial boom based upon wild exaggerations of the province's wealth. The price of Company shares rocketed and there was a period of giddy speculation between 1767 and 1769. The bubble was pricked by reports of the invasion of Karnataka by Haidar Ali and of the

Bengal famine. After 1770, the Company was wobbling and fears began to grow that it might crash, particularly after it had been driven to seek short-term loans from the Bank of England. Anxious investors, fearing that another South Sea fiasco was imminent, turned to the government for a life-line.

The financial crisis which seemed likely to break the Company placed it and Lord North's ministry in a tricky position. On one hand, the government was confronted with demands for curbs on the Company's activities in India and shadowy fears that somehow it posed a threat to national freedoms. On the other, it was conscious that by imposing restraints on the Company the ministry might stand accused of trampling on the rights of private property. The Company was, in the words of one of its champions, 'a great corporate body' with rights and privileges which had been granted by Parliament and, therefore, had the protection of the law. Its chartered liberties and possessions were sacrosanct, like those of the colleges of Oxford and Cambridge, the Church of England, and the civic corporations. Any infringement of the Company's rights, even if undertaken for the best of reasons, was liable to be interpreted as a blow against the rights of property in general. Lord North had to tread carefully to prevent the issue of how the Company should be run from becoming a constitutional battle.

Fortunately for Lord North, the Company had already made a token submission to the government. In the summer of 1766 the then Prime Minister Lord Chatham (William Pitt the elder) had secured the Company's agreement to an annual subvention of £400,000, which, in theory, represented payment for the assistance rendered by the army and navy during the recent war. This sum was also a contribution to the costs of the Royal Navy, which was India's first line of defence, and the small garrison of British troops that supplemented the Company's army. The same principle was also being applied to the American colonies, where it provoked a storm of protest which led directly to the rebellion of 1775–76. The directors of the Company did not complain; they imagined that they had got off lightly, even though the annual payments turned out to be excessive. Chatham had also toyed with the idea of taking responsibility for the government of Bengal away from the Company and placing it in the hands of the government. This was too radical and the directors and their political allies denounced the plan as an attempt to engross the Company's patronage, which was growing in direct proportion to the enlargement of its lands.

The circumstances of 1772–73 made it easier for the Cabinet to intervene in the Company's affairs. Its credit was dwindling and the value of its stock plummeting. The main source of its difficulties was the dramatic fall in income which followed the great Bengal famine of 1769–70. The province's revenues had dropped to £174,300 in 1770–71 whilst overheads, such as the annual military budget of between £600,000 and £1 million, remained the same. Preoccupied with finding fresh sources of credit, the directors had to make the best bargain they could with a government which, in January 1773, obligingly sanctioned a Bank of England loan to the Company of £1 million.

A further blow to the Company was the tarnished reputation of its servants, who were widely regarded as a pack of brutal bloodsuckers, guilty of what the Whig leader, Lord Rockingham, called 'rapine and oppression' in Bengal. This had been the conclusion reached by the Commons select committee, chaired by the playwright soldier General John Burgoyne (later famous for the Saratoga débâcle of 1777), after it had disentangled the events in Bengal over the past sixteen years. When it reported to the House, the committee asked for the 'harmonising' of the Bengal administration with 'the principles and spirit' of the British constitution.

This demand was a landmark in Anglo-Indian history, in so far as it insisted that the Company's Indian subjects deserved fair treatment and that the Company's Indian territories were somehow within the pale of English law. This assertion was a reproof to those who had assumed that the Company was justified in perpetuating the cruel and despotic methods of the government it had inherited just because Indians had grown accustomed to them. No one would have gone so far as to argue that Indians were automatically entitled to the same consideration as Britons, but they did have a right to be governed honestly and benevolently. As a token of its concern for the legal rights of Indians, the government passed the Judicature Act of 1773, which established a Supreme Court in Calcutta whose judges were English jurists and from which appeals could be made to the Privy Council in London.

The future administrative structure of the Company's government was established by the 1773 Regulating Act. Like all compromises, it solved some problems and created others, but it did at least make absolutely clear the British government's right to oversee and regulate the affairs of India. Calcutta became the seat of the Company's administration and the Governor-General of Bengal henceforward enjoyed superiority over the presidencies of Madras and Bombay. He was to be advised by a Supreme

Council, with some members appointed by the Crown. There was some tinkering with the internal organisation of the Company, intended to prevent factional squabbles among its directors, and its accounts and correspondence were opened for Treasury inspection. Little was done to reform the day-to-day governance of India, although the act stipulated that in future Company officials and army officers 'shall not accept, receive or take directly or directly . . . from any of the *Indian* princes or Powers, or their Ministers or Agents (or any natives of *Asia*) any Present, Gift, Donation, Opportunity or Reward'. This clause turned out to be a piece of legislative wishful thinking, for it was ignored by the men-on-the-spot whose lodestar was still the career of Clive.

Clive had survived the Parliamentary campaign of vituperation with an intact fortune but a blemished reputation. It suffered further, in the eyes of posterity, by his suicide in November 1774, although it was more likely to have been prompted by a painful illness than remorse. In the next century, Clive became something of an embarrassment for historians such as James Mill and Thomas Macaulay, for whom the Raj was one of the highest attainments of Christian civilisation. Clive was indisputably the founder of British India, but his methods and character were those of an adventurer who turned public emergencies to his own advantage. He was never, and Victorian imperialists found this unforgiveable, an idealist; he cared little for and knew less of Indian culture and did not consider it the Company's duty to uplift and improve its new subjects. He died when the Romantic movement was gaining headway and with it a new humanitarianism; his legacy was a popular image of the Company as a tyranny which encouraged and exploited human suffering.

IV

Public disquiet at how Bengal was being governed was not dissipated by the 1773 Regulating Act. It broke surface again in May 1782, when the Commons demanded the dismissal of the Governor-General of Bengal, Warren Hastings, on the grounds that he had 'acted in a manner repugnant to the honour and policy of the British nation'. The rumpus which followed formed the background to a two-year Parliamentary wrangle over fresh regulations for the Company. Controversy over Hastings's objectives, methods and rewards led to his impeachment in the spring of 1786, a process which dragged on for a further nine years and ended with his acquittal.

The object of this contention had been born in 1732 into a family of decayed gentry whose last days of glory had been under the Tudors. Hastings was proud of his surname and ancestry, and among the luxuries he purchased on his first return from India in 1765 was a carriage 'of a pleasant pompadour' emblazoned with the ancient arms of his family. This dashing, crimson vehicle and sundry other luxuries were paid for by the £30,000 he had brought back from Calcutta, some of it made in private trade and the rest from gifts received for helping nawabs on and off their thrones. Some of the cash went on a portrait rendered by Sir Joshua Reynolds in which Hastings's face is a mask of aristocratic hauteur. One of his hands rests on a pile of business papers, the other hangs limply, which was a nice touch since the subject swung between extremes of energy and lassitude in his public life.

By 1769 Hastings was in debt, from which he was saved by an appointment to the Madras council, and three years after he was made Governor-General of Bengal. He spent lavishly on a sumptuous household, but during his twelve years in office he managed to accumulate a fortune of roughly £218,000, an amount almost equal to his salary for the period. Among his acquisitions was a huge diamond tinged with red which was valued at £10,000 and offered to the Czaritsa Catherine, but she was not tempted.[10] He was the nabob *par excellence*, although, like Clive, he was certain that he acted honourably, balancing private gain with public service. He explained his outlook to the Prime Minister, William Pitt the Younger, in a letter of December 1784:

> It has been my Lot to desire from long Possession and casual Influence Advantages which have overcome the worst Effects of my own Deficiencies, and it has been a Maxim of my Conduct . . . to do what I knew was requisite for public safety, though I should doom my own Life to legal Forfeitures, or my name to Infamy.[11]

Hastings's vision was imperial. Had it been fulfilled, he claimed in 1783, then, 'British Dominion might by this time have acquired the Means of its Extension, through a virtual Submission to its Authority, of every region in Indostan and Deccan'.[12] Creating a greater imperium in India was not what the government or the Company had wanted, especially as it involved them in a series of expensive and far from conclusive wars against Mysore and the Maratha polity.

Hastings had exceeded his brief, which had been to collect taxes, maintain civil order, administer justice and do all within his power to promote relations with the Indian states which would favour British trade.

Leaving aside Hastings's culpability, his record as it was appreciated in Britain raised a fresh hue and cry against the Company. Towards the end of 1781 there were Whig demands for a 'Magna Charta' for India which, as its name suggested, was intended to end the Company's despotism.[13] The prime movers were Charles James Fox and Edmund Burke, whose India bill presented at the end of 1783 was designed to place British possessions there under direct Crown administration. Not only would this bill extend the blessings of a benevolent government to George III's Indian subjects, it would, according to Burke, serve as a 'guard to preserve the British Constitution from its worst corruption' – in other words the influence of the East India Company. The Company responded with its old battlecry: 'Our property and charter are forcibly invaded'. Five counties and forty-five boroughs rallied to its defence and petitioned the Commons on its behalf.[14] George III was also alarmed by this assault on property and put pressure on the Lords, who threw out the bill. He intervened again in what had become a constitutional crisis by dissolving Parliament and calling a general election in the spring of 1784.

The nabobs and their bank balances were mobilised, and when he was returned to power the younger Pitt was able to count on over forty to swell his majority. Burke was bitter and prophesied that the government might soon be overwhelmed by these venal men, aided and abetted by Hastings when he finally returned from India. What he failed to realise was that his spiteful, obsessive campaign against Hastings had alienated many within the Commons, a body which has always shown misgivings about members who ride their hobby-horses relentlessly.

Having dished the Whigs, Pitt anticipated Disraeli by stealing their clothes, or at least some of them. Not wholly convinced by Burke's allegations against Hastings, Pitt was well aware that the affairs of India needed to be placed on a new footing. The upshot was the India Act of 1784 which placed the Company's territories under a form of dual government. The court of directors retained their old powers of patronage. Executive control of Indian affairs passed to a new body, the Board of Control, whose president was a member of the Cabinet and answerable to Parliament.

It was a cumbersome arrangement which still allowed local administrators considerable freedom of action. A despatch from Viscount Castlereagh, then president of the Board of Control, to the Governor-General,

Marquess Wellesley, written on 17 December 1802, arrived in Calcutta on 6 May 1803. Another, written on 14 February 1803, was opened at Government House on 6 July 1803. There were some improvements in communications, most importantly the establishment of an express route by way of the Mediterranean and the Suez isthmus. Even so, it took between 102 and 142 days for a letter from England to reach Bombay in 1815.[15]

V

An example of what officials in India might get up to if they were left to their own devices was the squalid Ruhela war of 1774. It had been waged by Company troops on behalf of the Nawab of Awadh, who had paid for their services, so helping Hastings to balance his budget. The affair naturally attracted the attention of the Commons during the Governor-General's impeachment and several officers involved were closely cross-examined. One, Major Marsack, revealed that the Hindu peasantry had been benevolently ruled by their Ruhela masters and as a consequence the country reached 'the greatest Height of Opulence'. After conquest and on the arrival of the nawab's tax collectors, the region's prosperity disappeared.[16]

The incident raised one significant question: by what moral right did the Company conquer lands in India? The evidence strongly suggested that the Ruhela state was orderly and flourishing and, therefore, in the eyes of eighteenth-century Englishmen, deserved to be considered as civilised. Moreover, its inhabitants were fulfilling, unknowingly of course, the will of God, who had ordained that the fruits and treasures of the earth belonged naturally to those who used them to the best advantage. Post-Reformation theology had provided a mandate for European expansion in America and Africa where, it was alleged, native populations had ignored or neglected what God had provided. Amerindians and Negroes could be evicted from their lands by interlopers who had the will and capacity to develop them. The law of man concurred with that of God: at the time of the Ruhela war Captain James Cook was cruising in the Pacific armed with a ruling of Justice Sir William Blackstone, who had declared that Australia was '*terra nullius*', a land owned (as yet) by no one.

By no stretch of the imagination could India, or any other Asian country, be considered an empty, uncultivated land, lacking what the philosopher John Locke had called 'industrious and rational people' to exploit it. Nor was it without a society whose hierarchy and government would have been recognisable as 'civilised' by men of reason. India lay firmly within the compass of that civilised world which had been known to Greek and Roman historians and geographers and, unlike America, it had always had cultural and economic relationships with Europe.

James Forbes, an amateur anthropologist of indefatigable curiosity, who served the Company in the Bombay presidency between 1765 and 1783, detected a closeness between Hindu morality and legends and those of the ancient Greeks. Hindu 'village nymphs' appeared to wear robes similar to those of Greek maidens as they appeared on statues. The natives of the Malabar coast had enjoyed exchanges with the civilisations of Egypt, Assyria, Persia, Greece and Rome, but Forbes regretted that the cumulative effect of these associations had been limited, for the Malabari inhabitants had remained 'for a thousand years in the same state of mediocrity'. Like many others, he blamed imaginary Indian stagnation on the heat. Nonetheless, he concluded that the Indians were on a far higher plane of civilisation than the Amerindians and Negroes, since India possessed 'eloquence, poetry, painting and architecture, in a considerable degree of perfection'.[17]

Forbes was also impressed by the skills of Indian eye surgeons, and William Gilchrist, a surgeon and proto-vet in the Company's service, was happy to use native remedies when treating sick elephants.[18] An officer in the Company's army noticed that Indian junior officers and NCOs displayed 'greater penetration and intelligence' than their European counterparts.[19] His judgement confirmed a view which was already well established. Thomas Bowrey, who visited India during the second half of the seventeenth century, encountered clever craftsmen, merchants and mathematicians and judged Indians as intelligent a race as any on earth.[20] Ample evidence of this was provided by Indian art, architecture and artefacts: an eighteenth-century man of discrimination would happily fill his house with Indian chintzes and miniatures, but would disdain the native handiwork of Africa or America as barbaric.

Visitors to Bombay regularly undertook sightseeing trips to the Elephanta Island cave temples to examine the erotic sculpture, which were taken by some as a basis for the 'supposition of high civilisation among the Hindus'.[21] The Marquess of Hastings, who became Governor-General in 1814, compared the statues of gods in Indian temples to the carved figures he had seen in mediaeval churches.[22] James Mill, relying on illustrations, disagreed and contemptuously dismissed both Gothic and Indian art as products of a 'very low stage of civilisation'.[23] Indian sculpture stood comparison with Greek and Roman, at least in the eyes of connoisseurs of pornography. An engraving of one carving showing, among other things, fellatio, found its way into *An Account of the Remains of the Worship of Priapus*, a series of engravings which appeared in 1786. The original drawing had been made by a naval officer.[24]

All travellers to India were alternately fascinated and repelled by the connection between religious practises and sexual enjoyment, something unknown in Europe since pre-Christian times. Alexander Hamilton, a Scot who toured India at the end of the seventeenth and beginning of the eighteenth centuries, came across one Hindu holy man, a giant with a massive penis to which was attached a gold ring. He was greatly revered by young married women who knelt before 'the living *Priapus*, and taking him devoutly in their Hands, kist him, whilst his bawdy Owner strokt their silly Heads, muttering some filthy prayers for their Purification'.[25] This was but one manifestation of what other visitors saw as the mindless submission of the Hindus to their clergy. Thomas Bowrey was shocked by the 'Seduceing and bewitchinge Brahmins' who misled the simple-minded with superstitious fancies.[26] A naval officer, visiting the Coromandel coast in the 1750s, was appalled by the sight of 'Pagans of many Sects, who have a great number of *Pagodas* or *Temples* in which they worship Images of different kinds of Animals &c., being grossly and ridiculously impos'd upon by their Priests and Brahmins'.[27]

Both observers held to that Protestant world-view which coloured the thinking of most Britons. It had found its most trenchant expression in John Milton's *Second Defence of the People of England* (1654), in which he contrasted the 'liberty' and civil life and worship of his countrymen with the abjectness of peoples who were 'stupified by the wicked arts of priests' and 'merely worship as gods those demons they are unable to put to flight'. The author had in mind Roman Catholics, but he could have easily been referring to Hindus as they were perceived by Britons then and during the next century. When not deriding the follies of India's Hindus, Hamilton was jeering, in typically Protestant vein, at its Catholics. In Portuguese Goa he heard the church bells ringing continuously and remarked: 'They have a specifick Power to drive away all Manner of evil Spirits, except Poverty in the Laity and pride in the clergy.'

If traveller-writers such as Hamilton were to believed, and they generally were, Hinduism and an enervating climate were together responsible for the Indian character. By the end of the century the stereotype of the sly, timid and servile Bengali was well established in the British consciousness, and in this unflattering form he took his place in a gallery of national caricatures, alongside the foppish Frenchman, the ridiculous Italian and the haughty Spaniard.[28] Imagined deficiencies in character did not, however, give the Company the right to conquer and govern Indians. Whatever their moral disabilities, they were clearly a hard-working, skilful people whose industry qualified them for a place in that Divine ordering of the world under which all races were judged according to their usefulness and productivity. Unlike the African Negroes, the Indians were never condemned wholesale to a life of plantation slavery. Indeed, by the early 1800s the Company was endeavouring to suppress domestic slavery within its territories and those of its princely allies and clients.

Clive and Hastings had created an empire in what was, in effect, a moral vacuum. Their only justification for their actions had been political expediency. To protect its commerce, the Company had been driven to take control of Karnataka and Bengal and the quest for security proved unending. From 1770 onwards the Company found itself engaged in one war after another, either against hostile neighbours or its rebellious subjects. What one warrior proconsul later called 'the Red Mark of the British Empire' was spreading crablike and inexorably across the map of India.[29]

Seen from an Indian perspective, the Company was a highly successful competitor in the power struggles which marked the disintegration of Mughal authority. It was acting according to that local political theory which was summed up by the Persian proverb: 'He who can wield the sword shall have money struck in his name.' This philosophy did not prevail in Britain where, for the past century and a half, traditions of government through consent and individual liberty had taken deep root. Moreover, as Parliamentary scrutiny of the Company's affairs revealed, an empire based upon military might was being governed without justice or humanity. Even those involved were repelled; an officer who had taken part in the infamous Ruhela campaign of 1774 felt that it had destroyed 'our Character for Justice and Clemency'. It was painful, therefore, to find that those virtues which underpinned the eighteenth-century Briton's sense of superiority had somehow been jettisoned in India.

The controversies about how the affairs of India ought to be managed occurred at a time when there was a far wider and more far-reaching public debate about the nature of Britain's overseas empire. To some extent, India was peripheral to the disputes which centred on relations with the American colonies and whether or not their inhabitants were entitled to the same political and legal rights enjoyed by their kinsfolk in Britain. The matter had been resolved by the end of 1782, with the end of the War of Independence and the emergence of the independent United States of America. Superficially, India presented a very different set of moral problems: the Company's provinces had been acquired by conquest; its peoples possessed their own culture and systems of government which were utterly unlike those of Britain; and its British population was transient. Were Indians, therefore, perpetually excluded from the enjoyment, even in the least degree, of the rights which their rulers considered as their special birthright? Put another way, would India remain an Oriental despotism overseen by British officials in the name of commerce?

The answer had been a qualified 'no'. Public opinion in the late eighteenth century had refused to tolerate a tyranny run in Britain's name and had insisted, in the teeth of the Company's opposition, on extending to India the framework of honest and fair government. While British politicians had been seeking some kind of ethical basis for the new empire, officials in India were groping towards a moral justification for the fledgling Raj. The result was a compound of pragmatism and idealism. Experience showed that for the time being Indians lacked that sense of public responsibility which was necessary if a people were to govern themselves. In the words of one official, their 'Disposition, Manners and Prejudices require that the legislative and executive Powers be lodged in one Hand', which, it went without saying, would be British. John Shore, a member of the Calcutta council who became Governor-General in 1793, justified what amounted to an alien autocracy on the grounds of the superiority of the British character. 'A Sense of Humour and Virtue' and a reputation for 'Bravery, Clemency and Good Faith' were the distinguishing marks of the Company's servants which ideally qualified them to rule over those without these virtues. Such paragons might bring about a limited regeneration of the Indians:

> The more we are aquainted with their [the Bengalis'] Genius and Manners, the more it is incumbent upon us to make them useful and happy Subjects; and if they are incapable of meriting and enjoying the Freedom of British Laws let us endeavour to leave them the Happiness and Security of their own institutions unviolated.[30]

He was writing in 1785, by when, it seemed, the Bengalis were already 'the happiest Subjects of any great state in India'.

This vision of a benign Raj actively promoting the happiness and prosperity of its subjects went a long way towards satisfying Burke's demand for an Indian empire governed in accordance with British principles of equity and respect for the rights of individuals. Shore spoke with the voice of a new generation of Company servants who were coming into prominence towards the end of the century. They shared with their predecessors, the nabobs, the conviction that the Indians were, in Shore's words, 'wholly devoid of Public Virtue'. The Indian mind was afflicted by a form of mental astigmatism which prevented its owner from ever telling the truth or making an impartial judgement. If this sweeping generalisation was the case, British government could be defended on moral grounds because it was disinterested, just and directed by men of the highest integrity who placed public duty before self-interest.

But these administrators would have to proceed warily, for, as Shore had pointed out, the Company had no mandate to uproot well-established Indian institutions. None would ever have been given, for a conservative British political establishment would have shrunk from interference with the Indian social order which, like that at home, was an organism produced by a gradual historical development based upon practical needs. Old hierarchies were not be dismantled and, wherever possible, the old live-and-let-live approach to local customs would be maintained.

And yet, for all its new and yet-to-be-defined good intentions and hopes that, in the future, the Indian empire might be one based upon goodwill, the Company's Raj still depended ultimately on its formidable war machine. There were still plenty of disaffected Indians within its provinces, and beyond their borders there were hostile Indian states whose rulers were prepared to challenge the Company. No one understood this better than that tough realist Henry Dundas, who became president of the Board of Control in 1793. 'Military men,' he insisted, 'are the best of all governors of India.'

PART TWO

THE CONQUEST OF INDIA: 1784–1856

No Retreat: Grand Strategy and Small Wars, 1784–1826

There was never a masterplan for the conquest of India. No minister in London or governor-general in Calcutta consciously decided that the ultimate goal of British policy was paramountcy throughout the sub-continent. Instead, there was a sequence of tactical decisions made in response to local and sometimes unexpected crises. A backsliding raja who evaded his treaty obligations, a client state in peril from its neighbours, encroachments on British territory, or an independent frontier state making aggressive noises were sufficient justifications for war. When the fighting was over, the Company found itself with additional land, responsibilities and revenues. The upshot was that by the middle of the century it had acquired a monopoly of power in India.

No single genius made this process of conquest and annexation possible. Its course was directed by a handful of individuals most of whom, if pressed on the matter, would have argued that British supremacy in India was the only practical and desirable solution to the problems they faced as commanders and administrators. The most forthright explanation of their principles was delivered by John Malcolm in 1805 as a protest against the recall of the Marquess Wellesley:

> It was a true saying which the great Lord Clive applied to the

progress of the British empire in India – 'To stop is dangerous; to recede ruin.' And if we do recede, either from our right pretentions and claims – nay, if we look as if we thought of receding – we shall have a host of enemies, and thousands who dare not even harbour a thought of opposing the irresistible tide of our success, will hasten to attack a nation which shows by diffidence in its own power that it anticipates its downfall.[1]

This was the gospel of the 'forward' school expressed by one of its most pugnacious members. Malcolm was one of seventeen children of a pious Borders farmer and his entry into the Company's service was a fitting prelude to his career. Presented to the directors in 1781 at the age of twelve, he was asked, 'Why, my little man, what would *you* do if you were to meet Hyder Ali?' 'Do, Sir?' replied Malcolm. 'I would out with my sword, and cut off his head.' 'You will do,' said the astonished questioner. And he did; during the next forty-nine years, Malcolm discovered a flair for Persian, served successively as an assistant resident, Marquess Wellesley's secretary, Ambassador to Persia, a brigade commander and Governor of Bombay. He never diluted his opinions. 'No retreat' was the sole basis for British policy in India, he told a Commons select committee a year before his death. 'The liberality of our government gave grace to conquest,' he added, perhaps sensing that his audience might have been taken aback by his robustness.[2] Malcolm's likeness, as rendered by the fashionable portraitist, Sir George Hayter, is that of a sturdy but genial John Bull, wearing an antique steel gorget which might have done service for Don Quixote, and a huge fur pellise. Were it not for the Order of the Bath round his neck, he might have been some Border chieftain from the pages of Scott.

In India, as on the Anglo-Scottish marches, war had a momentum of its own. Supremacy rested upon fear, and hesitancy would always be interpreted as weakness by a population that needed continual reminders of British invincibility. In March 1804, General James Stuart assured Lord Hobart, the secretary for war, that the defeat of the Marathas would 'give a new Character to the British power, and promote that Superiority of Strength which will be the best means of securing the Tranquility of India'.[3] The psychology of the Indian was such that he saw power solely in terms of winning or losing battles and his memory needed constant jogging.

British prestige soared every time the Company's army beat a native one. If, for some reason, British forces were overcome or forced to retire,

Britain's standing was diminished throughout India. Reverses suffered at the hands of Haidar Ali during the 1780–84 Mysore war severely tarnished the Company's reputation.[4] The final overthrow of his son, Tipu Sultan, in 1799 obliterated at a stroke 'the spirit of insubordination and contempt' which the Marquess Wellesley imagined to be abroad among Muslims.[5] The capture of Delhi and the subsequent victory at Laswari convinced Man Singh, the Maharaja of Jodhpur, to shift his allegiance away from the Maratha prince, Daulat Rao Scindia, and towards the Company.[6] A loss of face in one region might encourage defiance in another. In July 1815, as British forces were plunging into Nepal, the Marquess Hastings told the War Office that more was at stake than teaching the Gurkhas a lesson in civility: 'To be foiled by the Gurkhas, or to make a discreditable accomodation with them, would have led to incalculable mischief.'[7] Even a temporary tactical withdrawal of a small garrison could have dangerous repercussions. 'Any diminution of our forces in Gujarat will diminish our local influence,' a nervous commissioner predicted in 1803.[8]

No chance was ever missed to deliver a condign blow. When a Jat raja ignored his treaty responsibilities by turning his stronghold into a sanctuary for brigands, his misconduct provided what one officer called a 'fair excuse' for war. It was a comparatively minor affair in which a small force 'soon convinced him out of the eloquent mouths of cannons and mortars (how wondrously convincing they are!) of the error of his ways'.[9] The rhetoric of gunfire was not always effective the first time. In May 1800, Arthur Wellesley (the future Duke of Wellington and Marquess Wellesley's younger brother) who was later known for his humanity on the battlefield, ordered the commander of a punitive column in Malabar to burn Mapilla villages and carry off property and livestock. By these measures, he argued: 'The confidence of our Native Troops will be increased and that of their opponents diminished.' The Mapillas proved a stubborn lot; eighteen months later Wellesley was still urging further applications of 'Terror' to bring them to their senses.[10]

Hammering the Company's enemies made good strategic sense if one imagined, as did most Governor-Generals and senior officers, that British paramountcy was precarious. The Company's situation and its inherent perils were summed up by the Governor-General, Lord Hardinge, in 1844:

> In India no man can say what a month may produce in a country of 120 millions of inhabitants governed by an army

which is officered by aliens, whilst the mass of the force under
these foreign officers consents to co-erce their own countrymen, merely for the sake of pay and pension – *mesmerised* as
it were by a handful of officers exhibiting in the working of
the system the greatest phenomenon that the world ever witnessed.[11]

In these circumstances, there was no alternative to taking the offensive
immediately and with the maximum force at the faintest hint of unrest or
defiance. The long arm of the Raj could reach anywhere and its enemies
could expect no respite. Extreme hawkishness had its risks. The Company
could never be strong everywhere, for its forces were always scattered and
outnumbered by those of its potential enemies. Furthermore, the cost of
more or less continual military exertion was stretching the Company's
resources to breaking point. This was one of the reasons why, in May 1803,
Viscount Castlereagh, the president of the Board of Control, advised the
Marquess Wellesley against further offensives. The minister was also nervous about the balance of forces in India. There were 18,000 white soldiers
there, of whom at least one in ten was an invalid of some sort, and roughly
three times that number of sepoys with which to a control a population
then reckoned to be about fifty million.[12] Besides, Britain was preparing to
resist Bonaparte's invasion army and no reinforcements were available.

The Marquess already had the bit between the teeth, and when
Castlereagh's letter reached Calcutta, operations against the Marathas were
already in full swing. They did not proceed as Wellesley would have
wished: after a series of stunning successes, the campaign in northern
India ran out of steam. He had finally overreached himself and the court
of directors were jittery about the £6.5 million loan hurriedly raised by
London markets to pay for the new war. Bankruptcy threatened and
Wellesley was recalled in 1805. He faced a clumsy attempt at impeachment
in the Commons, in which he was charged with, among other things:
breaking treaties, squandering his employer's wealth, exercising power
despotically, and setting up his own statue in Calcutta after consigning that
of Lord Cornwallis to a cellar. If this was true, it had been a symbolic gesture, for Cornwallis had avoided expansionist policies. Aged sixty-seven, he
returned to India as Wellesley's replacement. He died there towards the end
of 1805 and was succeeded by Sir George Barlow and the Earl of Minto,
who followed to the letter pacific and non-interventionist policies dictated
in London.

II

The Marquess had been able to justify his stepping up the pace of con-quest on the grounds that India was a war zone in the global conflict between Britain and France. Robert Clive had predicted that the French would seek to reverse the verdict of 1763 and try to regain their former power in India in coalition with anti-British princes. His prophecy was fulfilled by the alliance between Haidar Ali and France in 1780, and for the next four years the Company had some narrow scrapes. It was saved in this and in later conflicts by British domination of the Atlantic and Indian Oceans, which severely limited the assistance the French could send to their Indian partners. Even so, there were some tricky moments. The Royal Navy's control of home waters and the North Atlantic was uncer-tain for much of 1797, and the French gained a temporary superiority in the western Mediterranean the following year. Victory at Trafalgar in October 1805 brought lasting security and removed for ever the possibil-ity of French seaborne intervention in India. In any case, the odds against this had been considerably lengthened by the occupation of the Cape in 1795 and Mauritius in 1809. Henceforward, the Indian Ocean was a British lake.

From the standpoint of Calcutta, it was not the ambitions of the Paris government, but the activities of several hundred Frenchmen in India which attracted the most concern. Professional soldiers, they had been hired in the 1770s to train the armies of Mysore, Hyderabad and the Maratha polity to fight with muskets and cannon in the European fashion. Modernising the fighting techniques of the Company's potential foes had been accompanied by hurried rearmament programmes. Indian gunsmiths and iron and steel founders began fabricating European-style weaponry to provide firepower for the new armies. While Indian steel matched British in quality, output was limited and gun-making was undertaken on a small scale.[13]

The techniques being developed during Britain's industrial revolution guaranteed that the Company's army would have a steady supply of flint-lock muskets and cannon, the two weapons which now dominated the Indian battlefield. Perhaps in acknowledgement of this, Tipu Sultan sent agents to Paris in 1791 with orders for artillery, muskets and ammunition, which were to be supplied by Dutch arms dealers.[14] Details of their shop-ping list were discovered by Admiralty Intelligence. This information confirmed what was well known from other sources: Tipu was bent on a new trial of strength with the Company which, if he triumphed, would restore the boundaries and fortunes of Mysore.

Tipu had declared himself the tiger prince, a ferocious champion of Islam and the state which his warrior father had seized in 1767. His son kept a menagerie of tigers in his palace at Seringapatam and he surrounded himself with images of that beast. Snarling gold tigers adorned his personal weapons and, in premature celebration of future victories, Tipu had a mechanical tiger fabricated. This massive, brightly painted creature stands astride its prey, a cowering Company officer, complete with tall black hat. The animal roars and the man screams; sounds created by a contraption of clockwork and bellows inside the tiger. This device was among the spoils of war taken when Seringapatam fell, and eventually found its way to the Company's cabinet of curiosities, housed in Leadenhall Street. Today, Tipu's tiger is displayed in the Victoria and Albert Museum and is still capable of making a sound, if somewhat feebly. Sadly, Tipu's real tigers were all shot, for the Company's army could provide no food for them.

The tiger sultan's vanity was balanced by political shrewdness. The restoration of Mysore could only be accomplished through an alliance with France and injections of French help through Mauritius. Tipu went to considerable lengths to cultivate the revolutionary régime in Paris and its offshoot in the Indian Ocean: he wore a cap of liberty when he met French representatives, called himself 'Citizen Tipu' and expressed sympathy for the ideals of Robespierre. Elsewhere in India, French mercenary officers elected their generals, hoisted tricolours and voiced what the Marquess Wellesley called 'the most virulent and notorious principles of Jacobinism'. One alarmist intelligence report claimed that Hyderabad's French officers were planning a revolution, which would overthrow the nizam and establish the Rights of Man in southern India.

These developments frightened the Marquess Wellesley. But they were also a godsend, for they gave him an excuse to invade Mysore and deal once and for all with a persistent and dangerous adversary. Wellesley had carefully read the intelligence summaries from southern India during his voyage from Cape Town to Calcutta and, on his arrival early in 1798, he set in motion policies designed to destroy both Tipu and the Hyderabad mercenaries. As the year unfolded, preparations for war took on a new urgency when news of Napoleon's intended invasion of Egypt reached Calcutta.

On hearing of his destination, Dundas, the president of the Board of Control and secretary for war, had imagined that Bonaparte might use

Egypt as a springboard for an overland offensive against Indian's western frontier. Geographers and travellers were invited to offer opinions and they argued that he could easily attack through Persia or Afghanistan with the connivance and possibly active help of their rulers. Then and later, those who ought to have known better were united in their opinion that large European armies, complete with pack animals, would move swiftly and comfortably across waterless deserts and over mountains in extremes of heat and cold. Having marched thousands of miles to the borders of India, the armies of the French Republic would be welcomed by Tipu and the anti-British princes.

The great 'scare' of 1798 came to nothing. Nelson shattered the French Mediterranean fleet at Abukir bay on 1 August, leaving Bonaparte's army stranded in Egypt. He soon abandoned it and returned to France, where he made himself its dictator. The French officers in Hyderabad and their sepoys had been neutralised by a bloodless coup. Mysore was overrun and Tipu died during the storming of Seringapatam. Shortly after, an Indian contingent was sent to help eliminate the detritus of the French army in Egypt.

The importance of the events of 1798–99 was not in what happened, but what was feared might happen. They offered a blueprint for the possible overthrow of the Raj by a coalition of internal and external forces which it lacked the manpower to withstand. The message was clear: so long as independent and well-armed hostile native states remained in existence, there would be allies for any invader. The Maratha leaders were known to have been following events in Egypt and Europe with great interest. Nonetheless, the War Office imagined that with Tipu dead and Napoleon back in Paris, Calcutta no longer had anyone to fear. In 1802 the Marquess Wellesley was asked to send home surplus troops.[15]

This was the last thing he intended, for his mind was on his next target, the Marathas. It is easy to define the Maratha polity in terms of geography and almost impossible to define it politically, or at least in terms which would have been comprehensible to the Marquess and his staff. The Marathas dominated a broad swathe of land which stretched from the Sutlej in the north across the Deccan to the frontiers of Hyderabad and Mysore. There was no political, legal or fiscal uniformity within this vast region, which was why the government in Calcutta tended to think of it as a ragbag of conflicting anarchies. Kinship held one key to political power and, by the end of the eighteenth century, five Maratha dynasties had come to enjoy considerable power with the polity: the Raos, peshwas of Poona; the Scindias of Gwalior; the Holkars of Indore; the Bhonsles of Nagpur and the Gaikwars of Baroda. There was no head of the Maratha polity, but the peshwa enjoyed a special prestige, which Calcutta mistakenly took to be a form of political overlordship.

Factional struggles and disputed successions intermittently disturbed the Maratha polity. Their prevalence compelled each dynasty to retain large armies, mostly irregular light horsemen, which had recently been stiffened by battalions of Indian infantrymen, drilled and commanded by European and American mercenaries. All Maratha princes faced perpetual insolvency and so their armies were in a permanent state of deliquescence, with unpaid cavalrymen living off the peasantry. Despite a ramshackle military system, the Maratha princes could put enormous armies into the field in an emergency. Intelligence based upon residents' reports estimated that Daulat Rao Scindia could muster 16,000 well-trained infantrymen commanded by a Frenchman, General Pierre Perron, as well as swarms of irregular horse. Perron aroused deep suspicions in Calcutta; from his days in Hyderabad he had a reputation as an extreme republican, and there were well-founded suspicions that he might re-establish a new focus for French power in India by taking full control of the tax districts allocated him by Scindia for the upkeep of his troops. During the brief Anglo-French peace between 1802 and 1803, Perron made approaches to Bonaparte and a shipload of French recruits for Scindia's army turned up at Calcutta, only to be sent packing by Wellesley. This incident and Perron's intrigues made it easy for the Governor-General to resurrect the French bogey when it came to justifying the Maratha war in London.

A welcome chance to meddle in Maratha affairs was presented in 1802, when the peshwa, bedevilled by debts and enemies, threw himself at the Company's feet after his eviction from his capital, Poona (Pune). Baji Rao returned, escorted by an army commanded by Arthur Wellesley (now a major-general) the following year. The price of his restoration was an unequal treaty which transformed him into a Company stooge, guarded by sepoys and under the thumb of a resident. In return, he ceded territory and allocated revenues to pay the wages of his new guardians. The Company now had the means to splinter the Maratha polity and secure control over the fragments. Scindia and Rahugi Bhonsle of Nagpur were the first targets, and by the middle of 1803 they had been temporarily isolated by a brilliant exercise in diplomatic chicanery. A dozen years later, on the eve of Waterloo, the Prussian general Von Gneisenau warned a colleague that

Arthur Wellesley had been schooled in the arts of duplicity in India to the point where he could 'outwit the Nabobs themselves', and was not, therefore, to be trusted.

War broke out towards the end of the south-west monsoon and at the onset of the cool season in 1803. There were two simultaneous offensives by a total of 60,000 men; the smaller in the Deccan under Major-General Wellesley and the larger in the north, under General Sir Gerard (later Viscount) Lake. His was the crucial theatre, for Wellesley had ordered him to deliver lightning attacks which would successively eliminate Perron's force, seize Agra and Delhi and drive a wedge between Scindia's territories and the Sikh state of the Punjab to the north. Both cities were taken. Maratha forces were beaten in a series of hard-fought battles on the southern front (Assaye and Argaum [Argaon]) and in the north (Aligarh, Delhi and Laswari). To everyone's relief, the European-trained battalions were overcome without much difficulty, thanks in large part to the desertion of most of their white officers, who chose not to hazard their lives in what was clearly a lost cause. Among them was James Skinner, the son of a Scottish officer and Rajput lady, who offered his sword to the Company and soon distinguished himself as a commander of irregular Indian cavalry.

The defeated Scindia relinquished all his territory north of the Jumma, including Agra, Delhi and Gujarat, while Bhonsle handed over Orissa and other lands to the east of Nagpur. Various small Jat, Ruhela and Rapjut states, which had previously been within Scindia's orbit, passed into the Company's. Next, Wellesley launched the all but exhausted Company's northern army against the hitherto neutral Jaswant Rao Holkar. It came unstuck, as did the Governor-General, who was called home. The bruised and truncated Maratha polity was given a twelve-year breathing space.

Treaties dictated at bayonet point had left the Maratha princes in a sort of political limbo. Power passed to the Company's residents who, backed by sepoys, were the masters of the state, dictating policy and supervising all aspects of everyday government. Friction was inevitable, especially in Poona where a sulky Baji Rao resented his humiliating dependency. Resistance flared up, more or less spontaneously, in Poona and Nagpur during the autumn and winter of 1817.

This was good news for the Marquess Hastings. He was a phlegmatic, well-meaning soldier in his mid-sixties who had first seen action against the Americans at Bunker Hill. As Governor-General he shared Wellesley's vision of British India as a spreading sea of civilisation which would eventually cover the whole sub-continent for the benefit of all its peoples. He dedicated himself to the promotion of the 'happiness of the vast population of this country', a goal which included the extension of civil peace to areas which had hitherto lacked it.[16] Hastings's aspirations ran against the grain of his instructions, which were to continue the peaceful policies of his immediate predecessors and steer clear of any entanglements with the independent princes. His expansionist inclinations were stiffened by the advice of Wellesley's old acolytes, Malcolm, Montstuart Elphinstone and Charles Metcalfe, all of whom had kept alive the Marquess's aggressive spirit. They persuaded Hastings that it was both foolhardy and impractical to quarantine British India from its jealous and unruly neighbours. Above all, the Company could not afford to allow wounded tigers (i.e. the Marathas) to remain at large. Proof of this assertion was provided by the incursions into British territory of marauding bands of Pindari horsemen during 1815 and 1816.

Pindari temerity was evidence of the ineptitude and malevolence of the Maratha princes. According to the treaties they had unwillingly signed, it was their duty to restrain these freelances whom they occasionally hired, but could rarely afford to pay. The result was that the Pindaris roamed the Deccan, plundering as they went. There were at least 20,000 of these parasites and, once they began causing havoc in British-ruled districts, Hastings was determined to destroy them. His reports of Pindari atrocities provoked the 'warmest indignation' of members of the Board of Control and persuaded them to approve a punitive war in the Deccan. With a massive policing operation as cover, Hastings was now free to extinguish what remained of Maratha power by deposing Baji Rao and Appa Sahib of Nagpur. He foresaw few difficulties in a war which he called 'a temporary evil, with little hazard'.[17]

Save in its scale, the final Maratha war was a rerun of its predecessor. Hastings assembled 91,000 regulars and 24,000 Indian irregulars, the largest army the Company had ever fielded, for a series of synchronised offensives on several fronts. One detachment found itself retracing the steps taken by Arthur Wellesley's force fourteen years before and came across Hindu and Muslim holy men praying for the dead on the battlefield of Assaye. As in the earlier war, the fighting was confined to the cool dry season and lasted from October 1817 to March 1818. There were no hitches, for the Maratha generals chose to fight Hastings on his own terms in open battle rather than wage a partisan war against the British columns and their vulnerable supply lines. Maratha armies were beaten in engagements at Kirki,

Poona, Sitalbi, Nagpur and Mahidpur. As Hastings had predicted, many Marathas and Pindaris defected, lured into the Company's army by the prospect of higher wages, paid regularly.[18] A new pattern of war was emerging: the Company divided, conquered and then recruited. Defeated Gurkhas exchanged brigandage for Company service after 1816 and proved first-rate soldiers. So did the Sikhs who enlisted during the 1850s.

III ·

Hastings had made the last Maratha war acceptable to his superiors in London by the argument that it was necessary for security. Security had many meanings within the Indian context. In its broadest sense it represented protection of the lives, property and trade of the Company's subjects. Expansionists defined it in terms of a universal stability which, once it had been imposed, would transform the whole of India for the better. Progress was impossible without peace, and peace could only be obtained through war. This equation is what Malcolm had in mind when he said that the evils of war were more than compensated for by 'the liberality of our government'. In what was the official history of the 1817–18 Maratha war, Lieutenant-Colonel Valentine Blacker claimed that the extermination of 'useless' Pindaris would prepare the way for the 'blessings of peace and industry' in the Deccan.[19]

The 1814–16 Nepal war was also portrayed in this light; it was the last resort of a patient government which could find no other way to tame a wild race who preyed on their neighbours. After the war the Gurkhas' former victims lived in peace and prospered. By 1824, the annexed districts in the Himalayan foothills had become a new Arcadia, according to a report of the local commissioner, Lieutenant Murray:

> These petty principalities are enjoying the full measure of British protection and are in a state of the most profound tranquility. Murder is seldom committed and robbery unknown, and several Rajas are content and their subjects receiving all the blessings of a mild and happy rule. The cultivation has improved in a fourfold degree, and the mountains are clad in stepped verdure to the base.[20]

Attached to this lyrical testimonial to British rule was the inevitable estimate of the local land-tax yields. Nonetheless, there is no reason to imagine that these people wanted a return to the old order, any more than the Deccan peasantry would have welcomed a return of the Pindaris.

For the public at home, waging war for humane ends was a noble enterprise. This was how Indian wars were represented when Parliament formally congratulated a victorious army and its commanders. Votes of thanks for the Nepal and Burma wars included fulsome tributes to the stamina and gallantry of the troops and, as several speakers noted, were delivered in a bipartisan spirit. Whigs and Tories agreed that the greatest reward a fighting man could seek was the praise of his countrymen, expressed by their representatives in Parliament. At the same time, custom dictated that soldiers were given prize money, collected from the spoils taken during a campaign and officially distributed according to a fixed scale. In 1827 Sir Charles Watkins Wynn, the president of the Board of Control, expressing the nation's gratitude to the army in Burma, drew MPs' attention to the final advance on Ava. The heart of every man was 'glowing in the expectation of pecuniary advantages that soldiers gain from the forcible possession of an enemy's city', but the prize eluded them. Their commander, Sir Archibald Campbell, halted the advance and negotiated and accepted the city's surrender. He had stood to gain the most, but, according to Wynn, 'he had a higher duty than satisfying the personal interest of his soldiers and his own'.[21] The values of public service had triumphed over private gain, as of course they should. Nonetheless, £1 million taken from the compensation paid for the King of Ava was shared among the troops.

The largest beneficiaries from the prize system in India were senior commanders, often the same men who had backed aggressive policies. This fact could have cast doubt on their integrity, which was why Cornwallis refused the £47,000 due to him as the commander-in-chief for the 1790–92 Mysore war. Likewise, the Marquess Wellesley rejected £100,000 offered him after the fall of Seringapatam.[22] Others were not so scrupulous: Viscount Lake received £38,000 from the capture of Agra alone and Hastings, who combined the posts of commander-in-chief and Governor-General but did not take the salary of the former, was given gifts totalling £260,000 by the directors.[23] Little wars also yielded valuable dividends. The reduction of the Raja of Kittur's stronghold in 1824 produced over £100,000 in prize money of which £12,000 was pocketed by the local commander, Lieutenant-Colonel Deacon, much to the irritation of his brother officers, for he had spent only three days in the siege lines,

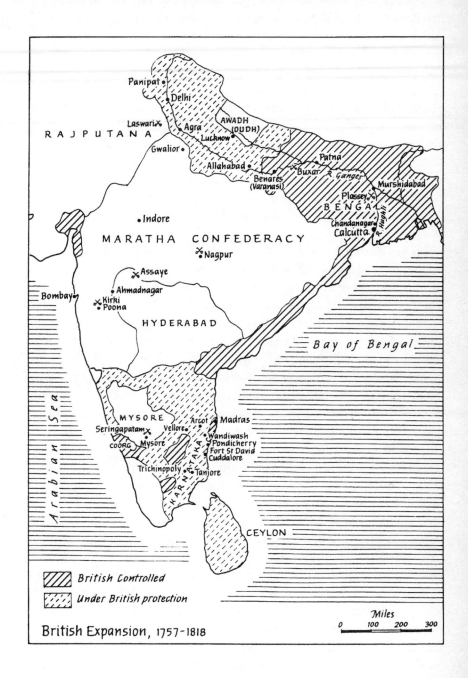

Panipat
Delhi
Laswari
RAJPUTANA
Agra
AWADH
(OUDH)
Gwalior
Lucknow
Allahabad
Patna
Benares
(Varanasi)
Buxar
R. Ganges
Murshidabad
Plassey
Indore
BENGAL
Chandanagar
Calcutta
R. Hughli
MARATHA CONFEDERACY
Nagpur
Assaye
Ahmadnagar
Bombay
Kirki
Poona
HYDERABAD
Bay of Bengal
Arabian Sea
MYSORE
Arcot
Madras
Seringapatam
Vellore
Wandiwash
COORG
Mysore
Pondicherry
Fort St David
Cuddalore
Trichinopoly
KARNATAKA
Tanjore
CEYLON

British Controlled
Under British protection
British Expansion, 1757–1818

Miles
0   100   200   300

directing operations from a palanquin.[24] Six weeks of bush fighting against the Raja of Coorg during the spring of 1834 brought in £29,000, of which the commander, Brigadier-General Patrick Lindsey, was allocated over £9,000.[25]

It was not always easy to discern the line between public service and private advantage. Consider Major Alexander Walker, a humane and fair-minded warrior proconsul. In January 1806 he persuaded the Bombay government to approve a small expedition to the restless Kattiwah district to show the flag and punish bandits. He asked for command and his request was allowed, no doubt on the grounds of his character and previous experience of the region. As commander, he exercised his right to license the liquor, tobacco, *ganja* (cannabis resin) and opium sellers who were attached to the mobile bazaar which accompanied the troops. He received 760 rupees (£76) a month for these licences, as well as the normal additional allowances for active service.[26] Even without prize money, waging war in India was a profitable business.

This was appreciated by everyone involved. In 1813, Lady Hood expected Montstuart Elphinstone, then a rising star in administration, to accumulate at least £20,000 before his retirement. He was less optimistic and imagined that he might return home with about £4,000, a sum which did not include his 1803–05 Maratha war prize money, which had yet to be distributed.[27] His friend John Malcolm had been far luckier. In 1797, his energy and talents secured him the post of secretary to the commander-in-chief with an annual income of just of over £4,000, as much as a general would receive in Britain. Within nine years he had sufficient capital to send £400 annually to his family and, he calculated, to provide him an annual income of £1,500 on his retirement. When he returned to England in 1822 he used his investments to lease an estate in Hertfordshire for £450 a year.[28] Malcolm's rewards were obtained legally and openly and it would be unfair to compare them with the fortunes corruptly acquired by the nabobs of the Clive and Hastings era.

There were objections galore to the overall goal of British supremacy in India. While not questioning the necessity of the 1798 Mysore war, Dundas was full of gloom about its costs which, he rightly feared, would add to the Company's already large burden of debts.[29] Castlereagh had similar misgivings about the 1803–05 Maratha war, and had vainly tried to restrain the Marquess Wellesley. When news of the outbreak of the war reached Britain, the Whig opposition was indignant and looking for a scapegoat. In a series of debates during the spring of 1804, the Marquess was accused of having flouted the 1784 Act by declaring war on the Marathas without the permission of Parliament and having squandered the Company's revenues.[30] By 1806 the Company's debts stood at £28.5 million, of which two-thirds had been run up by the Marquess's wars. Bankruptcy had been staved off by getting Parliament's approval for the adoption of the government's method of raising cash in an emergency: an appeal to the London money markets. As a result of issuing new stock, the East India Company acquired its own version of the National Debt. Nevertheless, the Company had no trouble in getting the capital it needed. It was still a flourishing concern, for, as Wellesley's defenders pointed out, additional territories equalled increased revenues. Their government also required more soldiers and administrators, a fact which tended to be overlooked.

The Marquess may well have overreached himself and behaved with little regard for the exact letter of the law, but his countrymen's disapproval was tempered by the knowledge that the Indian empire was a national asset in terms of prestige and economic potential. The loss of America in 1783 had heightened public interest in India, which was reflected in the abundance of prints which appeared during 1799 and 1800 showing scenes from the recent war in Mysore. Possession of a growing empire in India was a source of patriotic pride, especially in the post-Waterloo years when national self-confidence was soaring. There was also a feeling that India, in common with other parts of the empire, contributed substantially to overall national prosperity. In 1836, William IV observed: 'Now this is a fine country, but it is nothing without its colonial possessions, especially India.'[31]

Sensing the mood of the times, the Marquess Wellesley augmented his family's achievement of arms with a motto of a line from the *Aeneid*: '*Super Indos protenit Imperium*' (He extended the Empire over the Indians).[32] On his death in 1842, one obituarist praised his exertions in India, where he had attempted to 'assume a natural authority which would suffer no rival from the mountains to the sea'.[33] By this date, the Company had acquired paramountcy across the entire sub-continent south of the Sutlej, was encroaching on Burma, and was well on the way to gaining sovereignty over its north-western neighbours, the Sind and the Punjab.

What was astonishing was that this ascendancy was achieved within forty years by a handful of men of determination and foresight with at best lukewarm support from the government in Britain and downright hostility from the directors. To a large extent, the wars of Wellesley and Hastings accelerated a process that had been first set in motion by Clive in Bengal. Pausing or turning back would have been disastrous, for the conquered would have rounded on their adversaries. 'As long as there remains in the country any high-minded independence', Thomas Munro told Lord Hastings in 1817, there would be resistance of some kind. He added, prophetically, 'I have a better opinion of the natives of India than to think that this spirit will ever be completely extinguished.'[34] For the time being there would be tranquillity in India. In 1829, Lord Ellenborough, the president of the Board of Control, considered the era of conquest was over and one of peace was about to begin. Everything still depended on the native army and he wondered how it and its British officers would take to a long period of what was virtual unemployment.[35] The high-blooded and venturesome did not have to kick their heels for long; there were still plenty of wars to be fought as the minds of India's strategists turned from internal consolidation to the establishment of strong frontiers.

2

The Cossack and the Sepoy: Misadventures of an Asian Power, 1826–42

I

Ascendancy in India had made Britain an Asian power without equal. This point was made, with a degree of diplomatically justified hyperbole, by Captain James Abbott in a series of conversations with the Khan of Khiva in the spring of 1840. Asked whether Russia was a greater nation than Britain, Abbott answered, 'By no means. England is first in extent of dominions, number of population and wealth.' It was so rich a country that: 'The house of a labourer in England is far more comfortable than the palace of a nobleman in Persia or Herat.' This may not have surprised the khan, who had already heard how an Englishman needed only look at a hill to know whether it contained gold; a national reputation for seizing the economic main chance had clearly run ahead of Abbott.

He had risked his life on a perilous journey from India to a state which had hitherto been virtually inaccessible to Europeans in order to convince its ruler that Britain, a nation whose empire rested on 'justice and good faith', was the natural ally of all central Asia's Muslims in their struggle against Russia. And what an ally; questioned about the cannon possessed by Britain, Abbott let his eloquence and his imagination run wild:

> The number is too great to be reckoned, and therefore no account is kept of them. The seas are covered with the ships of England, each bearing from twenty to one hundred and twenty guns of the largest size. Her forts are full of cannon, and thousands lie in every magazine. The very posts in our streets [i.e. bollards] are often made of guns which, in Persia and Afghanistan, would be considered excellent. We have more guns than any other nation in the world.

British artillerymen were matchless, being able to fire seven rounds a minute. The khan was unimpressed, remarking that a Persian ambassador had once told him that Russian gunners could manage a dozen shots a minute. 'We count not the number of shots fired, but the number that take effect,' Abbott sharply retorted.[1]

In another audience, Abbott outlined the Indian government's attitude to its Asian neighbours. It wanted only peace and the right to trade freely with them, and it never wavered in its pursuit of justice. To this end, it had recently sent an army to Kabul to restore to power its rightful ruler, Shah Shuja. It was also, and this request was made by Abbott on several occasions, anxious that the khan released his Russian slaves. This was as much a political as a humanitarian gesture, for a Russian army was known to be on its way towards Khiva to liberate the slaves by force, and Abbott had been instructed to deflect it by achieving its purpose through persuasion. He made little headway. Muslims in central Asia were genuinely perplexed by European protests against slavery, particularly those of Russia whose serfs and soldiers were treated little better than slaves.[2] As it was, the Russian force was overcome by a combination of the climate and slipshod logistics. Abbott left Khiva in May and proceeded eastwards to a Russian outpost on the shores of the Caspian, and from there to St Petersburg, where he presented Czar Nicholas I with a letter of friendship from the khan.

It is not known what the khan learned from Abbott about the outside world and Britain's place in it. That mixture of fable, hearsay and rumour which passed for political knowledge in Asia probably rated Britain very highly during 1840. Details of its occupation of Afghanistan had filtered through to Odessa by the summer of 1841 when James Yeames, the British consul, reported that Russian officers were gloomily contrasting their army's misfortunes in the Caucasus with 'the brilliant success achieved by British arms in Asia'.[3]

Yeames was a consummate intelligence gatherer who gained the confidence of several Russian officers who grumbled to him about the incompetence of their superiors and reverses suffered at the hands of tribal guerrillas. The Russians were not bothered with field security, and happily gave Yeames details of the units involved in the campaigns and their deployment. All this information was relayed to the Foreign Office. Over two years spent listening to first-hand accounts of skirmishes on Chechen mountain-sides left Yeames, if not his masters, convinced that Russian endeavours in the Caucasus and Central Asia were doomed to failure. There was not, he concluded, 'sufficient genius' in Russia to carry out the grandiose empire-building schemes dreamed up in St Petersburg, or even the small campaigns of aggrandisement waged by various generals commanding frontier districts.[4] Events were proving him right, but his message was not one which London or Calcutta wanted to hear.

For the past twenty years a handful of ministers, proconsuls, generals and intelligence specialists had been wracking their brains to devise policies and strategies to counter a Russian march across Asia which would end with an invasion of India. For nearly everyone involved, it was not a question of would the Russians come, but when and how.

Before a plan for the defence of India could be framed, it was necessary to discover something about the lands which separated the two great Asian powers. Since the early 1800s individual explorers, usually young army officers with strong nerves, a taste for high adventure and a skill in native languages, had made their way into a previously impenetrable region. They drew maps and prepared exhaustive reports of what they had seen, whom they had met and what they had heard. Not all returned, for the natives were hostile to infidel intruders. James Abbott was one of this succession of spies, and his own and his comrades' exploits in the Himalayas, Persia and Central Asia became known as the Great Game. The phrase was an invention of Captain Arthur Conolly, who was murdered in 1842 by the Khan of Bukhara after a short career during which, among other things, he had wandered across the Caucasus, watched the Russians do battle with the Circassians and, in the company of Muslim holy men, visited Kandahar.

Conolly's excursions confirmed what his superiors in Calcutta had long feared: that it was perfectly feasible for a Russian army to invade India, either following in the footsteps of Alexander the Great through Afghanistan and the Khyber Pass, or else by way of Persia, using Herat, Kandahar and Quetta as staging posts.[5] Like other players of the Great Game,

Conolly published an account of his travels which alerted British readers to the possibility that the lands he had traversed might soon become a battle-field between Britain and Russia. He was not an alarmist and in a calm analysis of the situation pointed out that, while it was wise to undertake preventative measures, Russia's advance across Asia was bound to be slow and ponderous. Besides, any army undertaking a central Asian campaign would face immense logistical problems and stiff resistance from the Muslim states in its path.[6]

Possession of a recondite knowledge of the geography and politics of Central Asia gave players in the Great Game an excessive influence over policy-making. One figure, Alexander Burnes, stood out from the rest. His promotion had been swift and spectacular and owed much to his fluency in Persian, Arabic and Hindustani, an engaging personality and a flair for the sort of flattery which eastern princes adored. On their first meeting, he addressed the Shah of Persia as: 'Centre of the universe, what sight has equalled that which I now behold, the light of your Majesty's countenance, O attraction of the world!'[7]

This arcane skill qualified Burnes for his first mission in 1831, which was to convey six dapple grey drayhorses, a gift from William IV, to Ranjit Singh, the Maharaja of Lahore. Using this gesture of princely goodwill as a cover, Burnes made a careful survey of the Indus and undertook some economic espionage to discover markets for British goods in the Punjab. Burnes regarded the Indus as more than a conduit for Lancashire cottons and Bradford cloth; as he sailed up the river to Lahore, he immediately recognised it as the path for future British conquest. He delivered his horses (one died during the journey and the rest perished later from pampering and unfamilar fodder) and returned to Simla, where he captivated Lord William Bentinck, the Governor-General, with tales of his experiences.

Next, and at his own suggestion, Burnes was sent on an ambitious intelligence-gathering tour. It took him to Kabul, over the Hindu Kush to Bukhara and from there, via the Caspian and Persia, back to India. On his return in 1833 he published a three-decker version of his peregrinations, which became an instant best-seller. It provided readers with a vivid picture of a hitherto unknown region, its colourful races, their customs and religions. Like other early-Victorian travel literature it would certainly have prompted the reaction 'how unlike our own dear country', with descriptions of sadistic tyrants, slavery and tribal feuds. News of Burnes's wanderings reached St Petersburg, where he was accused of acting as an agent of sedition, and fomenting unrest among, and running guns to, the trans-Caspian tribes.[8]

Burnes saw himself as a leading actor in an epic historical drama which would shortly be played out in Central Asia:

> England and Russia will divide Asia between them, and the two empires will enlarge like circles in the water till they are lost in nothing; and future generations will search for both of us in these regions, as we now seek for the remains of Alexander and his Greeks.[9]

Alexander the Great had a special place in the consciousness of everyone engaged in the Great Game. His physical presence, largely imaginary, seemed everywhere in the disputed regions. Burnes encountered a Muslim tribe who had incorporated Alexander into their theology as a prophet of Allah.[10] His colleague, John Wood, met a warrior clan living in the upper reaches of the Oxus who assured him they were descendants of Alexander and his Greeks.[11] These two myths were perhaps the inspiration for Rudyard Kipling's short story 'The Man Who Would Be King'. Staff officers well-versed in the Classics pointed out what they took to be Alexander's camp sites to their comrades during the march to Kabul in 1839.[12]

What was real in the minds of men like Burnes was the spirit of Alexander, above all his indomitable willpower and indifference to the obstacles of nature and climate. Where he had gone, others might follow, and so even the most fanciful scheme for an invasion of India deserved serious attention.

II

Contemporaries had regarded Napoleon as a second Alexander. His descent on Egypt in 1798 had started speculation about an invasion of India. It was revived in 1807 when he had discussed a Franco-Russian overland expedition to India with Czar Alexander I during the Tilsit negotiations. Nothing seemed beyond Bonaparte's reach, for his recent victories in Europe had proved him a 'genius' in the mould of Alexander the Great. It was, therefore, confidently expected that in four months he could assemble an army of 60,000 at Astrakhan and bring it through Persia to the Indian frontier.[13] Faced with such a superhuman adversary, Indian commanders pleaded with the War Office for reinforcements. In 1810 the commander-in-chief at Madras reckoned his troops could beat any native army, but he was less sanguine about how the sepoys would fare against experienced white soldiers when the moment came to repel 'the long threatened Invasion of our Eastern provinces by the combined French and Russian Force'.[14] The phantom of invasion disappeared for the time being in 1812, when Napoleon attacked Russia and for the moment all misgivings about the safety of India's frontiers were suppressed.

These anxieties surfaced again in the late 1820s in a new and more intense form. The Russo-Persian war of 1827–28 and the Russo-Turkish war of 1828–29 revealed that Russia was set upon a new course of expansion in Asia. These conflicts also demonstrated the vulnerability of the two, dilapidated Islamic empires, the Persian and the Ottoman, which stood between Russia and India. Neither could be expected to serve as an obstacle for a modern, European army, although no one was at all clear as to how such an army, with all its baggage train and pack animals, would survive the march across deserts and mountains. Colonel George de Lacy Evans, a veteran of the Peninsular war, the battles of New Orleans and Waterloo and a radical MP, believed that the Russians were up to such a feat of stamina and logistical organisation. In his pamphlet *On the Practicability of an Invasion of British India* (1829) he outlined a hypothetical plan of campaign in which a Russian invasion force thrust east from the Caspian, occupied Khiva and used it as springboard for an army of 30,000 which would cross the Oxus, take Kabul and enter the Khyber Pass. Quoting examples of forced marches during the Napoleonic wars, De Lacy Evans predicted that the Russians would need three months to travel from the bases in the Caspian to the Oxus. Local opposition would be either neutralised or swept aside, as it had been by Alexander the Great.[15]

The very appearance of this army even on the shores of the Caspian, let alone in the Khyber Pass, would be a signal for widespread unrest throughout India. De Lacy Evans had struck a raw nerve, for the Indian government had always been fearful that masses of Indians would turn against the British the moment they were distracted by an external threat. This assumed that the Raj principally rested on force and that Indian goodwill was so brittle that it would snap in a crisis. Britain's swift takeover of the sub-continent had been made possible largely by the willingness of substantial numbers of Indians to follow the path of self-preservation and, for that matter, advancement, and throw in their lot with the conquerors.

If another European power followed suit, then Indians might very well reconsider their loyalties. And they would be free to do so, for the Russian threat would draw the bulk of the Indian army towards the North-West Frontier.

There was some substance in De Lacy Evans's reasoning. In 1815 it was imagined that the Marathas would have welcomed the Russians.[16] The Marquess Hastings had believed that all Indians were indifferent as to who ruled them, and were completely without any sense of patriotism, whatever this might have meant for an occupied people.[17] There was residual Muslim resentment which, according to Hastings, might easily be transformed into a militant movement to restore Mughal power.[18]

If the worst came to the worst, a white man's Raj would be defended by white soldiers. The point was bluntly made by a senior officer after a serious mutiny by units of the Madras army at Vellore in 1806: 'It is true we can only hold our Indian Empire by our European Force, but to save that European Native Troops are absolutely and indispensably necessary.'[19] The Indians understood this, too: not long after the Vellore mutiny a junior Indian officer warned his superiors that no amount of white troops could save the Raj 'when all the Natives shall entertain hostile designs' against it.[20]

In April 1836 there were just over 17,000 British troops in India, of whom over a thousand were utterly unfit for duty and another 1,400 were invalids, most the victims of venereal diseases or chronic alcoholism. Looking over these figures, the Governor-General, Lord Auckland, commented that the Raj would face an unprecedented danger 'if ever the 80 millions of natives by whom they are surrounded should be out of humour or if ever we should have a more formidable enemy [i.e. Russia] to cope with'.[21] The Duke of Wellington, by now a venerated elder statesman, was more level-headed, and his opinion counted for something, for he had seen British and Indian troops in action. He wrote in 1834:

> I believe that if ever we are to come to blows with the Russians in India we must rely on our sepoys, as we have in all our wars there with Europeans as well as native powers. These with our superior knowledge of the art of war in that country and superior equipment, founded upon our knowledge of the resources of the seat of war, the character of the natives and other circumstances, will give us advantages which will more than counter balance the supposed inferiority of our troops.[22]

The sepoys themselves shared the Duke's faith in their courage. During the autumn of 1838, when preparations were in hand for the invasion of Afghanistan, veterans of Lake's campaigns against the Marathas boasted that they had beaten Scindia's Frenchmen and that they would do the same to the Russians if they met them.[23]

There were two views of how the Great Game might develop. De Lacy Evans predicted the bolt from the blue, while men like Conolly and Burnes saw the slow build-up to a collision some time in the distant future. The immediate remedy was to create a *cordon sanitaire* which would block the possible approaches to India. A diplomatic offensive was needed which would bring Persia, the Sind, the Punjab and the Afghan states of Herat, Kandahar and Kabul within Britain's orbit. Simultaneously, and here men like Burnes, Conolly and Abbott were vital, the Indian government had to extend feelers towards the states of central Asia, persuading them that Britain was their friend. Most importantly, the Company would have to get itself accepted as a sort of honest broker, settling the disputes which frequently flared up between these states. Somehow their territorial ambitions would have to be curbed or balanced, for if they were not, Russia would be quick to step in as a patron and source of military assistance.

Relations with the Sind presented few problems. Its amirs were nominally Afghan subjects and they had inclined towards the Company whenever the rulers of Afghanistan showed any sign of re-asserting their sovereignty. By 1830, they were, to all intents and purposes, the Company's allies. The Punjab, under Ranjit Singh, Maharaja of Lahore, was an island of stability and a formidable power with its European-trained and equipped army, the Khalsa. But the 'Lion of Lahore', who had held absolute power since 1799, was ageing and his vigour was impaired by a stroke in 1836 and an addiction to brandy and opium. Burnes believed that on his death the Sikh state would dissolve into anarchy. In the meantime, relations with the Punjab were cordial and here, as in the Sind, were being strengthened by growing economic dependency.

One of the first consequences of De Lacy Evans's scaremongering had been a stepping-up of British commercial activity throughout the region. Lord Ellenborough had been shaken by De Lacy Evans's conclusions, but believed that Russia might be frustrated through an economic offensive which would extend across the Himalayas into central Asia. To this end, he had encouraged Burnes and Conolly to examine the prospects for trade in the area in the hope that Brummagem metalware would soon swamp the bazaars of Bukhara. Free trade was Britain's new economic orthodoxy and its prophets declared that its spread across the globe would lead to universal peace. Lord Auckland believed this would be the case on India's frontiers. In 1836, he predicted that paddle steamers puffing up the Indus with cargoes of British goods would transform the outlook of those who lived on its banks. In future, they would 'look . . . more to our merchants than our soldiers'.[24]

Indo-Persian relations were more complex and fraught with danger since Russia, like Britain, was anxious to assume the role of the shah's protector. Bonaparte had tried, but had been thwarted by an Anglo-Persian treaty signed in 1809, in which the shah pledged to bar the passage of any army bent on invading India in return for an annual subvention of £150,000. During the next twenty years, Persia suffered a series of encroachments on its northern territories, but Czar Nicholas I was unwilling to press his military advantages further. In typical Romanov fashion he allowed dogma to override commonsense, refusing to annex Azerbaijan on the grounds that it was the shah's private property. His local commanders had advised him to take it as a buffer against incursions of Shi'ite fanatics from Persia who were helping Caucasian guerrillas.[25] From the 1820s, the Russian army in the region had its hands full dealing with tribal resistance, and the imperial military budget would not stretch to large-scale campaigns of conquest. What the Czar wanted was a biddable shah who would bring Persia within Russia's sphere of influence.

Extending the hand of friendship to the shah during the 1830s caused panic in Calcutta and London, where Russian diplomatic moves were interpreted as the first stage of the long-expected thrust towards India. It was not; rather, Russia's intrigues in Tehran and later Kabul were a crude and, as it turned it out, clumsy exercise in what would later be called 'destabilisation'. The crisis which unfolded between the end of 1835 and the summer of 1838 revolved round the efforts of Count Ivan Simonich to persuade Shah Muhammad to add Herat, and possibly Kandahar, to his empire. This attempt to engineer a Persian–Afghan war could not have come at a worse time for the Indian government, which was endeavouring to prevent a war between Dost Muhammad, the Amir of Kabul, and Ranjit Singh for possession of Peshawar. Here, too, Russia was fishing in troubled waters. At the very end of 1837, Captain Vitkievitch, a young Cossack officer from the staff of the Governor of Orenburg, arrived in Kabul with messages of goodwill from the Czar to Dost Muhammad. He was also anxious to make contact with Ranjit Singh, who refused to admit him to the Punjab, and with Afghan tribal chiefs. Russia was applying the diplomatic leverage which could easily prise apart the states which formed India's buffer zone and set them at each other's throats.

At first, the British and Indian governments tried to shore it up diplomatically through a series of missions to Tehran and Kabul. The first failed; in the spring of 1838 Shah Muhammad laid siege to Herat with the encouragement of Simonich and the assistance of a Polish officer and a battalion of Russian deserters. They did not, as expected, tip the balance and were badly mauled during an attempt to storm the city's walls on 24 June. From that moment, the shah knew that he could not take Herat, although operations dragged on for several months, adding to the tension in Calcutta.[26]

In the face of British protests, St Petersburg disowned Simonich, claiming that he was acting off his own bat. This puzzled the British and Indian governments, who assumed, not unreasonably, that an autocrat's servants did exactly what they were told. If this was so, then Russia was at best testing the waters or, at worst, provoking a confrontation in Persia which could easily lead to war. 'If we go on at this rate,' Filipp Brunov, the Russian ambassador in London, told Sir Cam Hobhouse, the president of the Board of Control, 'the Cossack and the Sepoy will soon meet on the banks of the Oxus.' 'Very probably,' Hobhouse replied, 'but however much I regret the collision, I should have no fear of the result.'[27]

To a large extent, British and Indian reactions to the events leading up to the Herat crisis had been coloured by the outpourings of men like De Lacy Evans, whose warnings now seemed like prophecies. There was also a powerful strain of Russophobia in British political life, then and for the next eighty or so years. Russia represented the reverse image of Britain: its rulers were tyrants and its masses of serfs automata, who obeyed their masters unthinkingly, which was why it remained a hopelessly backward power. In 1841 a British visitor to Russia contrasted the 'free and sturdy' British with their 'wealth, intelligence and individual enterprise' with that 'great mass of organised and mechanised humanity' who were the Russians.[28] Another tourist wrote of the Russians as 'one machine'.[29] An Indian official predicted in 1838 that if Russia overran India, a 'benevolent' imperialism would be supplanted by an oppressive one which would reduce all Indians to serfs.[30] Despite the ignorance and abjectness of its people and the purblind obscurantism of their Czar, Russia was a country to be feared greatly. Nicholas I commanded 729,000 serf soldiers and tens of thousands of Cossacks, with which, in the words of the soldier and historian Sir William Napier, he could threaten 'freedom and happiness and civilization'.[31]

Russophobia united politicians of all complexions. Those on the left reviled the Czar as the enemy of liberalism and destroyer of liberty in Poland. Right-wingers distrusted him as a devious schemer intent on undermining Britain's position in the Middle East and India. It was, therefore, not difficult for any government to gain public backing for a tough, even combative line against Russia.

Prevailing anxieties about the likelihood of a Russian invasion of India had grossly exaggerated the importance and mischief-making capacity of the Czar's two representatives in Kabul and Herat. The hawks in India were impatient with shilly-shallying and wanted action. All that was needed was for the British to 'stretch forth our arm of power and crush incipient aggression in the place where it is being mustered' insisted Major-General William Nott.[32] In London, the Foreign Secretary, Lord Palmerston, agreed, but hoped to avoid a direct collision with Russia. Rather, what was required was a forceful demonstration of British power on India's frontiers which would convince the local inhabitants and the Russians that Britain would not shrink from defending what it considered to be its vital interests in the area.

Afghanistan was an ideal testing ground for Britain's imperial will. Dost Muhammad was acting in what Burnes thought to be an obstructive and wayward manner by refusing to accept British terms and flirting with Russia. Revealingly, one apologist for the war against him represented the invasion of Afghanistan as a masterstroke equal to that which had overthrown Tipu Sultan forty years before. Dost Muhammad was just another refractory Indian prince. 'Every man at all acquainted with the Oriental mind' knew that the Amir of Kabul had had his head turned by Russians, as Tipu's had been by the French, and in this giddy state might even launch an attack on India. Moreover, appeasing barbarians on its frontiers had accelerated the decline of the Roman empire.[33] Britain had already amply proved itself to be the paramount power within India by the force of arms; the time had come to show that it was an Asian power to be reckoned with.

The decision to invade Afghanistan was taken in May 1838 by Auckland against a background of 'universal panic', prompted by reports of the intrigues of Russian agents in Persia and Kabul and fears that Herat would be captured. While no one seriously expected a Russian army to approach India's frontiers in the near future, there were very real fears that unless the government acted resolutely, Kabul and Persia would be detached from Britain's orbit. Auckland was swayed by a coterie of experts, most notably William Macnaghten, the secretary of the Indian government's secret department. He was a deskbound official with an over-developed sense of his own omniscience and an undeserved reputation for being a diplomatic genius. He proposed that an Anglo-Punjabi army occupy Afghanistan, dethrone Dost Muhammad and replace him with the pro-British Shah Shuja, an exiled pretender then living in India. Details of this plan reached London at the end of October, and were warmly endorsed by the Cabinet and the Duke of Wellington.[34]

The following month, the Russian government finally gave way to British pressure. It repudiated Simonich (his efforts had come to nothing in any case), recalled him and promised to work alongside Britain to promote stability in Persia. Vitkievitch was also summoned back to St Petersburg, where official disapproval drove him to kill himself in May 1839. Having given Britain a nasty shock, the Russians were prepared to back off, and get down to what really mattered, negotiations over the future of the Turkish empire. The disappearance of what had been a largely illusory threat did not change the plans for the march to Kabul. Britain still needed to affirm its power in the traditional way and, with Shah Shuja installed in Kabul, a hitherto wobbly state would be transformed into a firm and submissive ally of the Company. Furthermore, the downfall of Dost Muhammad would serve as a warning to other rulers in the region.

III

Macnaghten's policy was a gamble. It was condemned by Montstuart Elphinstone and Metcalfe, both now retired, and the Tory press in Britain, which considered it a pointless and dangerous adventure. Neither Auckland nor his advisers had considered the reactions of the Afghans to the advance of an infidel army into their country to evict a popular ruler and replace him with a prince whom few of them knew and fewer cared for. Their mood was discovered by General Nott when two 'fine-looking fellows' entered his tent during the first stage of the advance to Kabul. When he explained to them that the army had come to make Shah Shuja their amir, one remarked: 'We prefer Dost Muhammad.' 'He has a right to the throne,' Nott retorted. The Afghan stepped forward, placed his hand on the general's shoulder, and asked, 'What right have you to go to Benares and Delhi? Why, the same right that *our* Dost Muhammad has to Kabul, and he will keep it.'[35] Their preference was understandable. Burnes had written of Shah Shuja: 'His manners and address are highly polished; but his judgement does not rise above mediocrity.'[36] Captain Henry Fane, a staff officer attached to the Kabul army, was impressed by his handsome features, but disturbed to hear that he had a repuation for cutting and running in a crisis.[37] Once in his capital, Shah Shuja did little to endear himself to his new subjects. One of his favourite pastimes was to sit in his palace and peer through a telescope at the wives and daughters of the Kabulis as they took the air on the flat roofs of their houses. Those who excited him were summoned to his presence.[38]

Macnaghten imagined that by throwing large sums of money at the Afghans he could win them over to Shah Shuja.[39] It was a policy which had worked, up to a point, with the Indian princes, but it failed in Afghanistan where religious and national passions were deeper and fiercer. The strength of these feelings was revealed to Macnaghten a fortnight before he entered Kabul when Jubba Khan, Dost Muhammad's brother, came to the British camp seeking terms. The amir was offered exile in India and a jagir of £10,000 a year. Jubba Khan responded with a speech of defiance:

> These proposals are so insulting that I will not even mention them to my brother; for what less could have been offered had you already vanquished him in the field? We have hitherto heard that the English were a just and equitable nation; but on what plea can you found the right of dethroning a monarch and placing on the throne yonder deposed puppet whom I spit at [Shah Shuja was standing nearby]. You have taken our stronghold of Ghazni; you may also, perhaps, overcome the army which my brother had raised to defend himself; but the eyes of all Asia are upon you. . . . May Allah defend the right.[40]

This made the listeners uneasy, and one, Lieutenant Mackinnon, thought Jubba Khan's arguments were unanswerable. Like many other officers he was learning to respect adversaries who, though cruel, were also frank, manly and brave. Afghan defiance remained strong. Refusing payment to allow British forces to retire down the Khyber Pass early in 1842, Afridi elders told a British officer: 'They would not barter their religion for gold, nor incur odium and contempt of their brother Mussulmans by allowing troops to pass.'[41] It proved hard to find Afghans to fight for Shah Shuja and those who did deserted to Dost Muhammad at the first opportunity. Macnaghten had to hire mercenaries, which was not easy; Gurkhas were uncomfortable about the prospect of service in Afghanistan.[42] There were lapses of enthusiasm for Shah Shuja among Indian Muslim troops, reluctant to fight against their co-religionists. During one engagement in November 1840, two squadrons of the 2nd Bengal Cavalry refused to charge and held back while their five British officers galloped into a body of Afghan horse.[43]

At the beginning of the campaign some officers had expected a walk-over, although a few fire-eaters hoped that they might eventually test their mettle against the Russians.[44] The Bengal contingent converged on Firozpur during November, often marching by night to avoid the heat. Cantonments were set up and at the end of the month the troops paraded for Lord Auckland and Ranjit Singh. Gifts and compliments were exchanged and the prince kissed a portrait of Queen Victoria, which everyone thought a gallant gesture. During the subsequent junkettings, General Sir John Fane and the maharaja stumbled over the pile of cannonballs, which Hindu sepoys took to be a bad omen. Sir William Kaye, the official historian of the war, took it to be a good one, reminding his readers that, within ten years, the Sikhs would fall before the fire of British cannon.

The plan of operations was simple. Kabul would be approached by a dog-leg route which would take the Bengali units along southern banks of the Sutlej and Indus to Sukkur, where they met the Bombay contingent which had been carried up river. The combined forces were over 12,000 strong and accompanied by 38,000 camp followers, including sepoys' families, hucksters selling opium, rum and tobacco, prostitutes, officers' servants (some had at least a dozen) and baggage-train attendants. Added to this human mass were pack animals: elephants, bullocks and 38,000 camels, the mainstay of the army's transport system. This ponderous caravan crossed the Indus by a 300-yard-long pontoon bridge, and then headed north for the second stage of the advance. This took it across the Kachchhi desert to the Bolan Pass and Quetta, from where it moved to Kandahar before turning north-east for Kabul. Ahead of the columns rode Burnes with a clutch of political officers whose job it was to induce the Sind and Baluchi amirs to allow the Army of the Indus a free passage and, in the case of the former, to extract £250,000 from them as a contribution to Shah Shuja's war chest. In some quarters it was hoped that the 'politicals' would fail and the Sindians would block the army's passage, which would mean a windfall of prize money if the rich city of Hyderabad were stormed.[45]

The Sindian amirs caved in. 'All I have is theirs [the British], and I am your slave,' the Nawab of Bahawalpur told General Sir Henry Fane, the commander-in-chief. Somewhat embarrassed, Fane changed the subject to the weather, remarking how chilly it was. The nawab agreed, adding 'but at the present moment, I feel neither cold nor damp, whilst basking in the sunshine of your presence'.[46] Not everyone was so accommodating. Once the army left Shikarpur and approached the Bolan Pass, it was under constant pressure from Baluchi and later Afghan tribesmen, who ambushed isolated detachments and stole whatever they could get their hands on. Baluchi horsemen were particularly adept at hijacking strings of baggage camels. A blood-soaked rag was thrust in the face of a bull camel which, incensed, would would rush off in pursuit of its tormentor, dragging along its companions.[47] Stragglers were murdered and their bodies hideously disfigured by the Afghans. An officer of the 3rd Bengal NI (Native Infantry) came across the corpses of a pair of camp followers near Kandahar; one of the woman's breasts had been cut off and placed in her husband's mouth while his penis had been removed and laid in her mouth.[48] When they were caught, robbers were shot out of hand. Once, soon after an affray in which a young officer of the 16th Lancers had been killed while on a fishing trip, Shah Shuja intervened to release four suspect thieves who were about to be hanged as an example. He claimed them as his subjects and was backed by Macnaghten, which added to the tension which was growing between army officers and the 'politicals', who hindered operations by their willingness to go to any length to appease the Afghans.

They were unappeasable. When the army entered Kandahar in April 1839, Shah Shuja was greeted with icy indifference by its inhabitants, a fact which Macnaghten glossed over in his despatches. Opposition was fiercest in Gilzai country between Kandahar and Kabul, where the army learned to respect Afghan snipers, armed with long-barrelled *jezails*, smoothbores with a range of 400 yards, well over twice that of the standard British and Company musket. Antique weapons, bows and matchlocks, were used by the defenders of the fortress at Ghazni. Resembling some awesome creation of Viollet le Duc, this great fort fell to a mediaeval device, a petard made up of sacks of gunpowder which were laid at its main gateway. There was no alternative, since the army's siege guns had been left behind, and Macnaghten was in a hurry to get to Kabul. The storming party of British troops rushed the breech as if they were drunk, according to one eyewitness, even though they had had no liquor for two days. 'Knocking over defenders like bricks', the soldiers surged into the town in search of plunder.[49] Close behind came Henry Fane, who recalled:

> Such a scene of plunder and confusion I never saw: one black–guard of ours had a cooking pot wrapped up in a cashmere shawl; a second was busily employed in ripping up a woman's quilt, and sticking the silk into his pocket or inexpressibles [trousers]; while three or four others had seated themselves on the steps with a huge pot of tamarind paste, of which I took my share.[50]

There was not much left to be distributed in prize money; when it was shared out just over ten years later other ranks got five shillings (25p) each.[51] Order was soon restored by Colonel Sir Robert ('Fighting Bob') Sale and Shah Shuja gave a demonstration of his style of royal justice by ordering the summary execution of a number of captured *ghazis*, Muslim holy warriors of suicidal fearlessness.

On 7 August the Army of the Indus entered Kabul. Dost Muhammad had fled northwards across the Hindu Kush to Bukhara and Shah Shuja was enthroned as his successor. The new state was precarious, resting almost entirely on a network of British political officers, garrisons and hand-outs to malevolently neutral tribal chiefs. But Macnaghten, chief political officer, the power behind the throne and soon to be a baronet, was highly optimistic about the new state's chances of survival. Resistance from the top had been ended in November 1840 when Dost Muhammad surrendered to Macnaghten after a brief uprising. He was sent into exile in India. Opposition from below flickered on with ambushes and raids, which the new régime dismissed as tribal brigandage, just as in the 1980s the Russians referred to all Afghan partisans as '*dushmans*' (bandits). The Russians, as did the British before them, discovered that well-trained troops backed by modern artillery could defeat the rebels whenever they stood their ground and offered battle. Such victories were Pyrrhic; within a month of the British having beaten a force of Gilzais near Qalat in May 1840 the tribesmen were back to their old tricks, interrupting communications between Kandahar and Kabul.[52] Nonetheless, during 1840 and the first nine months of 1841, British garrisons and punitive columns were able to keep the lid down on tribal insurgency, but only just.

IV

Even though the numbers of the army of occupation had been successively reduced, the costs of supporting Shah Shuja remained high. The bill for the Bengali contingent alone was £408,000 a year and additional military and administrative expenses, together with the gratuities scattered among tribal chiefs, made the total annual budget for Afghanistan just over £1 million. It was an increasingly irksome burden and threw into question the purpose behind supporting Shah Shuja indefinitely. Auckland was becoming increasingly nervous and, by June 1841, was wondering whether he had miscalculated the depth of Afghan 'national spirit'.[53] Macnaghten pooh-poohed references to nationalism and persisted, purblindly, in his belief that he and his colleagues were creating a permanent, popular and stable government. In London, the new Tory ministry of Sir Robert Peel was prepared to take him at his word, and during the autumn of 1841 was contemplating a partial evacuation of British and Indian troops, who would be replaced by Afghans under British officers. Macnaghten responded to this new spirit of economy by suggesting cuts in tribal subsidies, that Danegeld upon which the security of Shah Shuja and previous amirs had depended.

This arbitrary removal of traditional subsidies triggered an uprising among the Gilzais of the Khyber Pass at the beginning of October 1841, which became a signal for a national rebellion. This region was called by its peoples 'yaghestan', the land of rebellion. Like the rest of Afghanistan, it was a tribal society in which clans and extended families united in the pursuit of blood feuds or against intruders. Shah Shuja and his British puppet-masters fell into this last category, which explained the persistence of attacks on their forces and outposts for the past two and a half years. The initial disturbances in the region of Khurd Kabul, twenty miles east of Kabul, might have been contained if Sale's brigade had been better prepared. Unable to force well-defended positions, faced with the first falls of winter snow and running low in ammunition, Sale was compelled to fall back to his base at Jalalabad, which he reached on 11 November.[54] Four days later, he found himself cut off from Peshawar and began to prepare for a siege.

What amounted to the seizure of the Khyber Pass encouraged dissidents in Kabul under the leadership of Akbar Khan, Dost Muhammad's son. On 2 November Burnes was assassinated by tribesmen. His death left the entire military and civil command in a state of paralysis from which it never recovered. The 4,500 British and Indian troops in Kabul were commanded by General Sir William Elphinstone, a 59-year-old who had last seen action at Waterloo and whose tendency to dither was made worse by bad health. His second-in-command, Colonel John Shelton of the 44th Regiment, was a gallant Peninsular war veteran whose stupidity and rudeness exasperated everyone. Neither had the ability or stomach to face up to the emergency and their hesitancy and blunders were a bonus for the Afghans, who gained and kept the initiative. Macnaghten's intelligence system had broken down (Lady Sale thought it of little value) and he was at a loss as to what to do, not that he had much choice.[55] Intermittent skirmishing with Kabulis and the tribesmen who were pouring into the city during November made it clear that the cantonment was indefensible. By 20 November Macnaghten realised that he could no longer restrain the Afridis and the road to Kandahar had been blocked by large bodies of guerrillas. The garrison's only hope lay in a negotiated withdrawal down the Khyber Pass. While Macnaghten, Elphinstone and Shelton bickered, morale plummeted, and afterwards there would be rumours of a collapse of discipline among both British and Indian troops, even cowardice.[56]

The final phase in the disintegration of Shah Shuja's artificial state began with the murder of its architect, Macnaghten, during talks with Akbar Khan on 23 December. Experience had taught him no wisdom; in the last hours of his life he was contriving to buy himself and his colleagues out of the crisis by seducing Akbar Khan with a bribe. He was suddenly attacked and stabbed to death by some of Akbar Khan's retainers, acting with their master's approval. After Macnaghten's death, Akbar Khan turned to a captured British officer with a triumphant jeer: 'You'll seize my country, will you? You'll seize my country?' On 6 January 1842, in keeping with the terms Akbar Khan had granted, the detritus of the army and its 12,000 camp followers began its evacuation. Within a week all but a few hundred had perished, killed either by tribesmen, hunger or cold or a combination of all three. Among the last to die were a handful of men from the 44th Regiment who clustered around Captain Souter, who had wrapped the regimental colours around himself to save them from capture. The embroidered silk may have marked him as a rich man, and so he was taken prisoner by the Afghans in the hope that he would be ransomed. His last stand at Gandamak was the subject of a stirring genre painting by W. B. Wollen, in which the dwindling but defiant band was made a symbol of the sort of against-the-odds courage which made the empire.

The strategic situation at the beginning of 1842 was summed up by

Major Henry Havelock, then with the 13th Regiment inside Jalalabad. 'Our only friends on this side of the Sutlej,' he wrote, 'are our own and General Pollock's bayonets.' Jalalabad, Qalat, Kandahar and Ghazni, which was later retaken by the Afghans, 'stand like isolated rocks in the midst of an ocean covered with foam, while against and around them the breakers dash down in wild fury'.[57] But Havelock was undismayed; he was a lion-hearted, God-fearing Baptist who was certain that Divine Providence would favour British arms. Recovery was remarkably swift and helped by the fact that, having partly expelled the intruders, the Afghans began to quarrel among themselves. Much was owed to two good generals, Sir George Pollock, who took charge in the Khyber Pass in the spring, and the acerbic but thorough Nott, who held his position at Kandahar and inflicted defeats on tribes in adjacent districts.

There was a change in political direction. After gentle nudging from London, Auckland had resigned in October, and was replaced by the more martial Lord Ellenborough, who had attempted to persuade the Prime Minister to appoint him Captain as well as Governor-General. On his arrival in Calcutta in March 1842, Ellenborough allowed his bodyguard to exercise their mounts in flower gardens which had been laid out by his predecessor's sister, Emily Eden. She was horrified, but the generals in Afghanistan were pleased to have a Governor-General who was happy to let them transform an evacuation into operations designed to punish the Afghans. Throughout the summer and autumn of 1842, Nott's and Pollock's columns fanned out, engaged Afghan forces, destroyed villages, drove off or slaughtered stock, burned crops and storehouses, and hustled tribesmen and their families into the hills to perish. The severest chastisement fell on the inhabitants of those areas in which the refugees from Kabul had been massacred. The fortress and town of Ghazni were razed to the ground and, during the brief reoccupation of Kabul, its bazaar was demolished. Hostages taken during the Kabul débâcle were rescued or, in some cases, handed back, and 300 captured sepoys enslaved in Ghazni were liberated.

The systematic rampage of what was called the Army of Retribution may have done something to refurbish Britain's reputation as a great power in Asia. To judge by what they wrote of their activities, it satisfied an understandable need for revenge among the soldiers. When their satisfying work had been done, they retired across the Indus. The post-war political settlement restored the status quo: Dost Muhammad returned to Kabul as amir (Shah Shuja had been assassinated in April 1842) and Afghanistan was left to its own devices. The Russian threat had receded; there had been a scare in the spring of 1840 with news that a Russian army was on it way to Khiva, but it failed to reach its objective. For the time being the Russians were prepared to leave Khiva alone. They were having a grim time in the Caucasus during 1841 and 1842, if Yeames's intelligence reports from Odessa were anything to go by. The next ten years saw an Anglo-Russian *rapprochement* during which both nations forgot about what might become of the empty wastes beyond the Oxus.

The Afghan fiasco had serious repercussions. The humiliations inflicted on the army severely damaged Britain's reputation for invincibility in India and beyond. A Baluchi amir may have voiced the thoughts of many when he gloated over 'the English having been turned out of Afghanistan and eaten dirt'.[58] The British official who reported this outburst could only explain it as the consequence of the speaker's intoxication with *bhang* (hemp). But even the sober recognised that damage had been done to Britain's standing everywhere in Asia. The point was made, rather melodramatically, by Wellington:

> There is not a Moslem heart from Peking to Constantinople which will not vibrate when reflecting on the fact that the European ladies and other females attached to the troops at Kabul were made over to the tender mercies of the Moslem Chief who had with his own hand murdered Sir William Macnaghten . . . It is impossible that that fact should not produce a moral effect injurious to British Influence and Power throughout the whole extent of Asia.[59]

The ladies had, in fact, been decently treated, although, like many other captives, they had found Afghan food not to their taste. The Duke was also concerned as to where India's north-western frontier was to be drawn, and whether it should include the Sind and Punjab. The Sindian amirs were restless in the wake of the Afghan disaster, and the Punjab's strong man, Ranjit Singh, had died in the summer of 1839. Within three years the subsequent power struggle had propelled the province into anarchy. Inevitably, the hawks in Calcutta demanded intervention and war, but ministers in London, chastened by the recent misadventures in Afghanistan, were disinclined to listen.

The *cast of a Die*: The Sind and the Sikhs, 1843–49

I

'We were thrashed out of Afghanistan,' observed the Radical MP John Roebuck in February 1844 during the Commons debate on the annexation of the Sind. He was defending the man responsible, General Sir Charles Napier, and like so many MPs on the left, Roebuck never pulled his punches. Every Indian conquest had been an 'injustice', but what he called 'inevitable fate' had dictated that the Sind would be taken over. Roebuck understood the true nature of British expansion better than most of his colleagues, who had been regretting its baleful influence on the national moral character. British India would continue to grow despite all the hand-wringing in Westminster, and he confidently predicted that, 'you will possess the Punjab in less than two years in spite of yourselves'. Members scoffed in disbelief, for after the Afghan fiasco the government had announced an end to military adventures on India's frontiers.[1] Within eighteen months British forces were preparing to fight the Sikhs.

The conquest of the Sind had been one of the first fruits of Lord Ellenborough's governor-generalship. Whereas his predecessor, Auckland, had been a pacific man driven to make war by circumstances beyond his control, Ellenborough was an instinctive hawk under orders to avoid aggression at all costs. He refused to go against the grain of his nature. He warmly encouraged the punitive campaign in Afghanistan in 1842 and, when it was over, sent home a jubilant despatch. Its bombastic tone was mocked by the new satirical journal *Punch*, which, on hearing of his recall in 1844, had him lament in the manner of Othello:

> *Farewell, the plumed troop, and the big wars,*
> *That make ambition virtue.*[2]

Ellenborough had waged two big wars, both in 1843, one against Gwalior and the other against the Sind, states which had hitherto been within the Company's orbit. The first had been forced upon him by a disputed succession in which the rights of the ten-year-old Raja of Gwalior were in danger of being overridden by a clique of anti-British courtiers. There were fears the row might rekindle Maratha resistance, and intelligence reports suggested that the dissidents were secretly soliciting support from other princely states. Calcutta was alarmed by these developments, which were further evidence that the recent humiliations in Kabul and the Khyber Pass had reduced British prestige throughout India. Ellenborough reached for the traditional prescription: at the end of 1843 two powerful armies converged on the city of Gwalior.

The Company's standing was restored by two simultaneous battles at Panniar (near Narwar) and Maharajapur on 29 December. Sir Harry Smith, the newly arrived adjutant-general, was astonished by the bravery of the Maratha gunners at Maharajapur, which he took to be the result of a generation of British training. He and many others were gratified by the steadiness and grit of the two British regiments involved, the 39th and 40th, who advanced through 'grape like hail' to storm the enemy's batteries.[3] The battle was also watched from the backs of elephants by Lady Gough, the wife of the commander-in-chief, Sir Hugh Gough, and Lady Smith, for whom such spectacles were familiar. When she was twelve, her future husband had rescued her from the bloody saturnalia which followed the taking of Badajoz in 1812, and thereafter she had followed him and the army across Spain.

Unlike Gwalior, a princely state previously under the Company's thumb, the Sind still enjoyed a degree of independence. It was an inaccessible region of 50,000 square miles on India's vulnerable north-western frontier and straddled the lower Indus, the river earmarked as a future highway for British commerce. The Sind's million or so inhabitants were predominantly Muslims and were ruled by amirs from the Baluchi Talpur clan, whose government was well liked. The area was said to have been relatively peaceful and free from crime, although the stock-rustling and blood feuds which were the main preoccupations of the Baluchi majority were not regarded as criminal by the Sindians.[4] As relations between the amirs and the British deteriorated, the latter vilified them as wanton despots whose judgement and wits were permanently blurred by an addiction to bhang and opium. As so often in the past, the extension of British rule was portrayed as the replacement of bad government by good. Moreover, and this was useful in whipping up support for the Sind war among humanitarians at home, the amirs tolerated domestic slavery.

In 1843 the Sind was in a precarious political limbo. For the past sixty years it had been slowly penetrated by the Company, first in the name of trade and then in that of strategy. By and large Anglo-Sindian relations had been cordial, largely because the amirs saw the Company's friendship as a bulwark against the claims of their nominal overlord, the Amir of Afghanistan. Matters took a turn for the worse at the end of 1838, when the Company had demanded and obtained passage through the Sind for the Army of the Indus and tribute from the amirs for Shah Shuja. Baluchis living close to the extended British lines of communication regarded the war as a godsend and, following their instincts, raided supply convoys and attacked isolated detachments. By the beginning of 1842, British political agents and troops, often locally-recruited irregular cavalry, were engaged in a small-scale war against the marauders. At the same time, Sindian independence was being eroded by the British seizure of Karachi (a useful base close to the mouth of the Indus) and the establishment of a network of political residents and small garrisons in towns along the route from Sukkur to Quetta.

Once British forces had returned from Afghanistan, the Sind faced two futures. The first was a continuation of the status quo, with the province as a loosely controlled British protectorate in which the amirs upheld Britain's interests in return for their limited independence. The alternative was annexation. This course was favoured by Ellenborough, who believed that the security of a vital frontier zone could no longer be entrusted to resentful princes who might prove political weathercocks and many of whose subjects were openly hostile. Advocates of annexation were backed by sheaves of intelligence reports, many of them based on hearsay, which indicated that the amirs were fomenting disaffection in readiness for a general uprising to avenge Britain's recent intrusions. It went without saying that their truculence was a direct consequence of events in Afghanistan.

The man instructed to forestall the imagined insurrection and settle the problems of the Sind was Major-General Sir Charles Napier, a sixty-year-old veteran of the Peninsular war. He was an eccentric choice for a Tory government and Governor-General, for he was a former Radical MP who had once denounced the East India Company's administrators as leeches sucking the lifeblood of Indians. His features and bearing were those of some early Christian ascetic as conceived by a Renaissance artist; a callotype photograph of 1850 shows a lean, upright man with a commanding brow, aquiline nose and a straggling white beard flowing to his waist. Napier lived up to his appearance, for he saw himself as an instrument of God and constantly sought Divine guidance. On arriving in Karachi on 3 September 1842, he noted that it was the day which had been so decisive in the career of another soldier of the Lord, Oliver Cromwell. The coincidence added to his inner turmoil and he admonished himself in his journal: 'Charles! Charles Napier! Take heed of your ambition for military glory; you had scotched that snake, but this high command will, unless you are careful, give it all its vigour again. Get thee behind me Satan!'[5] Napier's other gospel had been set down by his former commander, Wellington, who insisted that in India a general should never retire in the face of the natives.

A servant of God who never flinched was ideally suited to fulfil Ellenborough's wishes. From the start, Napier was determined to have his way, and he quickly convinced himself that the Sindian amirs were a pack of degenerate tyrants whose word could never be trusted. Nor could his political officers, a breed which he blamed for what had occurred in Afghanistan, where 'the chief cause of our disasters was, that when a smart lad could speak Hindustani and Persian he was deemed a *statesman*, and a *general*, and was made a *political agent*'.[6] Napier soon developed a dislike for one 'smart lad', the highly capable and opinionated Major James Outram, an Aberdonian who had served as a political officer in the Sind since 1839. Basing his judgements on experience and a special insight into the amirs' minds, Outram contested his superior's assumption that they were secretly preparing for war. Rather, he claimed, they were being driven into resistance by the minatory and unyielding diplomacy of Napier, who was bent on fighting, come what may. There was much truth in this. On one occasion, Napier bluntly warned the amir Ali Murad of Khairpur: 'Woe attend those who conspire against the powerful arms of the Company. Behold the fate of Tipu Sultan and the Peshwa, and the Emperor of China [the first Opium War had just ended].'[7]

The purpose behind this hectoring was a political settlement by which Britain would assume complete paramountcy over the Sind. Various towns, including Karachi and Sukkur, were to be surrendered; all local duties on cargoes passing up and down the Indus were to be abolished; and the Company was to be given the right to settle differences between the amirs. As a token of this new sovereignty, Rustum Khan, an amir of suspect loyalty, was ordered to cede some of his territories to the ruler of Bahawalpur, who had been actively helpful during the Afghan war. Ellenborough imagined that this exercise in coercion would discourage future princely backsliding, but in Britain it looked like a gross infringement of the universal rights of property.[8]

Throughout the winter of 1842–43, Napier brushed aside the amirs' efforts towards conciliation and compromise as procrastination. He hoped to flush them out, as it were, before April and the onset of the hot season, during which his British forces would be at a severe disadvantage. At the end of January, with time running out and without a formal declaration of war, Napier forced the issue. He led an army 3,000-strong, supported by two steamers, towards Hyderabad where the amirs had been mustering their followers for some weeks.

Napier was taking a gamble, even though he may have been confident of Divine assistance. If his intelligence reports were anything to go by, there were between 20,000 and 60,000 Baluchis in arms. Everything hung on the performance of his artillery and his one British regiment, the 22nd, which, like so many regiments at the time, consisted mostly of Irishmen. To keep them fit and preserve their stamina, Napier had 300 placed on camels during the cross-country march. Progress was slow, for the region adjacent to the Indus was criss-crossed by dried-up irrigation canals with raised banks through which sappers had to cut passages to allow the artillery to pass. Early on the morning of 18 February, scouting parties from the Sind Irregular Horse discovered the amirs' army in defensive positions close to Miani, seventeen miles south of Hyderabad. Weak in artillery, the bulk of the Sindian army, sword and matchlockmen, was concealed in the bed of the Fuleli river, a tributary of the Indus. A perfunctory reconnaissance revealed that there were 11,000, about half the actual total.

There was no time for a detailed examination of the Sindian dispositions. Napier wanted to strike quickly and hard, and so he drew up his infantry in three sections which advanced in echelon with the 22nd in the lead. The battle opened with an unequal artillery duel, with the Sindian gunners firing high and their opponents answering with grape at close range, which overwhelmed Baluchi matchlockmen on the flank of the main army. As the Anglo-Indian force approached the raised bank of the Fuleli, it was met by matchlock fire and then an onrush by impatient Baluchis armed with swords and bucklers. There followed a scrimmage in which the 22nd handled their bayonets more adroitly than the sepoys, who were driven back. The 12th Bengal NI all but broke before the Baluchi tulwars, but were rallied by an officer and two *havildars* (sergeants), who led a counter-attack. Napier himself rode over to steady the 25th Bombay NI, which had retreated in an 'alarming manner'.[9] The Baluchi onslaught was stemmed and they were pushed back at bayonet point into the river bed. Now was the moment for the Company troops to use their terrible firepower. Volley after volley of close-range musketry poured down into the Baluchis as they crowded into the river bed, and cannon were brought up to enfilade them with grape shot. Trapped, they fought back with 'determined valour' but it was useless; hundreds were killed, some burned to death as their robes were set alight by matchlock fuses. When they finally broke, the Baluchis retired walking in what some onlookers considered a defiant manner. It had been a classic Indian battle, won by a mixture of offensive audacity, superior weaponry and disciplined firepower. British losses were 39 dead and 231 wounded. As at Plassey and so many subsequent battles, nobody bothered to count the enemy casualties, which were estimated to be about 2,000.

The battle of Miani made the Sind a British province. Napier entered Hyderabad, summarily deposed and exiled the defeated amirs, and declared their lands to be under British administration. Two amirs, Sher Muhammad and Muhammad Ali, kept resistance alive for a few months, but were eventually run to earth in a brief campaign which cost the 28th Regiment thirty-nine dead, all the victims of sunstroke.[10] Napier had been right to strike when he did for it was soon clear that British troops would never withstand the hot Sindian summer, when temperatures regularly rose to over 120 degrees.

But had he been right in resorting to war in the first place? Ellenborough, who was delighted by the outcome, had no doubts; nor did Napier, who afterwards claimed his conscience was clear. As details of the origins of the war became known in Britain there was a public outcry. There were allegations, first raised by the *Bombay Times* in May 1843, that British officers had violated the amirs' harems and carried off the most attractive odalisques for their own pleasure. The incident was represented as an insult to all Muslims. Imagining, perhaps ingenuously, that they had entered the harems willingly, the newspaper lamented the misfortunes of women 'who three months since were sharers of a palace and in the enjoyment of the honours of royalty, [and are now] the degraded lemans of the Feringhi [foreigners]'.[11] These allegations were indignantly denied by the officers of Napier's army.

More serious were the charges made by Outram on his return to Britain. He accused Napier of having deliberately engineered the war through intransigence and underhand manoeuvres when it was clear that the amirs wanted a peaceful accommodation with the Company. Defending his attack on Napier in February 1844, Outram argued that the general had in fact destabilised the Sind, where peace now rested on a garrison of 10,000 which the province could not afford. Many soldiers were succumbing to the heat and fevers and the rest only stuck it out for additional allowances. Napier's aggression had driven many Baluchis into Afghanistan and their incursions might eventually compel the Company to mount a second invasion of that country.[12] Outram also had a personal axe to grind; he imagined that Napier had laid a 'stigma' on him by 'shameless misrepresentations' of his conduct, and he wished to clear his name in order to continue what had been a promising career in India.[13]

Outram's case was taken up in the Commons in February 1844 by Lord Ashley, better known as the champion of exploited working children, who depicted the Sind episode as a 'foul stain' on national honour. Sir Robert Peel, the Prime Minister, was obliged to defend Ellenborough, but he did so without much conviction. While ministers might impose a ban on governor-generals annexing territory, 'there was some great principle at work wherever civilisation and refinement come in contact with barbarism' which unavoidably led to the acquisition of land in the interests of security. Some members may have wondered, if this was the case, why Ellenborough had been forbidden to annex territory in the first place.[14] As with Wellesley and the Marathas, the Sind affair was an instance of a ministry being embarrassed by an uncontrollable proconsul. In the end, Ellenborough and Napier were vindicated. The censure motion was rejected by 134 votes, with Disraeli and his precious 'Young England' Tories voting against the government while the Whig Palmerston joined forces with Peel.

The political reverberations of the Sind affair continued for some months. *Punch* made the famous pun in which Napier sends the message '*Peccavi*' (I have sinned) to Ellenborough. The ageing Montstuart Elphinstone likened Ellenborough's behaviour to that of a bully who, having been knocked down in a street brawl (i.e. Afghanistan), returned home to pummel his wife (i.e. attack the Sind), which was a reasonable analogy.[15] Ellenborough had also injured the directors in that area where they were most sensitive, their pockets. He had ignored claims for patronage from their protégés as well as dissipating revenues in the Wellesley manner on wars neither they nor the government had wanted. In April 1844, the board asked for his recall and Peel agreed, much to the amusement of *Punch*, which believed that its members always did what the government told them. A cartoon showed a carriage pulled by 'well-trained hacks' (the directors) running out of control to the horror of the coachmen, Peel and Wellington. Napier survived Ellenborough's recall, remaining in the Sind where he was soon bogged down in one of those protracted 'savage wars of peace' against local bandits.

II

It was commonly but wrongly believed that Ellenborough's replacement, his brother-in-law Lieutenant-General Sir Henry Hardinge (created Viscount Hardinge in 1846), would continue his predecessor's policies, even though Peel had urged him to maintain peace as far as it was possible.[16] Hardinge would have liked to have done this. He was fifty-nine, a high-minded, paternalist Tory who had campaigned in the Peninsula, lost a hand at Ligny and served in several Cabinets. Hardinge arrived in India in September 1844 with his head full of schemes for the regeneration of its peoples; he wanted to open more schools, train more Indian doctors, found universities and invest millions in a network of railways.[17]

His dreams remained largely unfilled. The new Governor-General was quickly distracted from good works by events in the Punjab, the now deliquescent Sikh state which Ellenborough would have liked to have invaded and annexed if he had stayed in office. His reasons for intervention, which were also to be Hardinge's, were a mixture of fear and expediency.

The object of fear was the Khalsa, the Sikh army. It was later described by Hardinge as Britain's 'bravest and most warlike and most disruptive enemy in Asia', which was a fair assessment of its qualities. The Khalsa had been created by Ranjit Singh and a body of European and American professional instructors, many of them veterans of Napoleon's army. They had taught the Khalsa's soldiers to fight and drill in the Western manner, making them the most efficient fighting men in India, next to the Company's troops. There were some who argued that the two were equal; Sir Harry Smith thought Sikh gunners the equal of their French counterparts, whose fire he had encountered as a rifleman in the Peninsula. The Khalsa possessed 376 cannon, but its backbone was 45,000 infantrymen, all dressed in blue turbans and red jackets and armed with modern muskets, manufactured in Lahore. The Punjabi cavalry were less numerous and less impressive. There were about 26,000, of whom at least three-quarters were irregulars, some picturesquely dressed in chain mail, breastplates and helmets.

The death of Ranjit Singh had left the Khalsa the most powerful force in Punjabi politics. But it was muscle without a brain, for no political or military figure emerged to lead it or harness its energies. This deficiency was partly made good when the soldiers created their own command structure, which was akin to that of the soviets adopted by the Russian army in 1917; each battalion elected five representatives who, together, formed a governing committee. Its primary concern was the Khalsa's rights to substantial and regular pay.

While the men of the Khalsa strengthened its internal bonds, the rest of the Punjab drifted into anarchy as various court factions jockeyed for control of Ranjit Singh's heir, the infant Maharaja Dalip Singh. Intelligence of the ever-changing state of play in Lahore regularly reached Hardinge, much of it lurid and all of it disturbing. He heard that the court was 'a hotbed of vice' presided over by Dalip Singh's nymphomaniac mother, the Maharani Jandin. She was, Hardinge discovered, 'a handsome debauched woman of thirty-three, very indiscriminate in her affections, an eater of opium'.[18] Not by any stretch of the imagination an ideal regent, she and her son were the only hope of some future stability, and so the Company made it plain that any attempt to supplant the young prince would invite military intervention. This was the last thing the Governor-General wanted, as it would draw Britain into the racial and religious entanglements of a state where hitherto the Sikh minority had lorded it over the Hindu and Muslim majority. The latter would, he believed, have welcomed British justice and 'a mild administration', but he dreaded a situation arising in which the Company's army was employed to collect the grinding taxation imposed by the Punjab's landowning class.[19]

Events forced Hardinge's hand. During 1844 and the first part of 1845 the Khalsa had been employed against Gulab Singh, the Rajput Raja of Jammu, a warlord who had been secretly offering to deliver the Punjab to the British. During September spies in Lahore were reporting that the Khalsa was inclining towards a giant plundering raid into British territory. It was rumoured that the Maharani Jandin was giving it every encouragement in order to get the soldiers well away from Lahore and the temptation to indulge in Praetorian politics. Hardinge carefully avoided offering any provocation, for he did not want to be branded an aggressor by London or, in his words, get into another 'Sind scrape'. When, in September 1845, a Sikh *vakil* (emissary) abused his position to tempt sepoys to desert from the Firozpur garrison, no action was taken, although he was kept under close surveillance. His efforts did not come to much; thirty sepoys deserted from a garrison of over 10,000.[20]

Hardinge combined a policy of wait-and-see with the prudent and, as far as possible, secret despatch of 5,000 extra troops to the region south of the Sutlej. At the end of September, he set off from Calcutta to join them, making the by now customary Governor-General's progress up the Ganges to Agra and Delhi, from where he intended to travel north to the frontier. On 3 December, he and his entourage reached Ambala, where he heard that a fortnight ago the Khalsa had crossed the Sutlej. Their move was a technical infraction of the 1809 Anglo-Punjabi treaty, and provided Hardinge with a justification for the declaration of war on 13 December.

The British were about to fight their first and only 'modern' war in India against an army of 60,000 who matched them in discipline, training and weaponry. Confronted with this force, Hardinge could not afford to take risks and so, by the beginning of December, he had approximately 54,000 men deployed on the frontier, over a fifth of the entire Indian army. Command was in the hands of Gough, who imagined, as did many others, that the reputation of the Company's soldiers and good, old-fashioned head-on charges with bayonet, sabre and lance were still all that was needed to win battles in India, even against professional soldiers with up-to-date weapons.

Gough's tactical thinking belonged to what might be called the Ritchie–Hook school of warfare: victory came from continually 'biffing' the enemy. He was a 66-year-old Anglo-Irishman who had fought under Wellington but learned little from him, believing that relentless applications of what in his brogue he called 'could steel' would solve every tactical problem. 'He is brave as a lion but has no headpiece' commented one of his officers.[21] Another observed that Gough's tactics were perfect for dealing with opponents such as the Marathas but 'to hasten forward under all disadvantages and attack the enemy' was not the way to beat the Khalsa.[22]

Gough swept aside all criticism and was furious when he was censured, particularly by subordinates.[23] Hardinge, who placed himself under Gough's command, found the old man 'peevish and jealous'. There were awkward moments when he attempted to curb his commander's impetuosity, but, in time, he came to appreciate his bluff good nature.[24] Sir Harry Smith was less charitable; he regarded Gough as a cantankerous dunderhead and relations between the two were strained.[25]

The rank and file warmed to the old war horse, whom they nicknamed 'Tipperary Joe', and believed he was a decent sort who had their welfare at heart. Private George Tookey of the 14th Light Dragoons told his family how Gough had visited him and other wounded men in hospital, speaking to them in a familiar manner as if they had been officers.[26] At the head of his troops, Gough was a splendidly eccentric figure. A watercolour sketch of him with his staff during the battle of Sobraon shows him ginger-whiskered, mounted on a grey, carrying a riding crop and wearing a long white overcoat, which he called his 'fighting coat', and a huge white conical turban.[27] He led from the front and men would die for him. Battle-weary soldiers somehow found fresh energy and courage whenever he appeared among them. Gough's greatest contribution to the war was sustaining the confidence of his army during crises which would have broken the nerve of less resolute generals.

A more imaginative man would have been overwhelmed by the task he faced, for a single defeat would have had dangerous repercussions throughout India. The future of British India was at stake, for the Khalsa posed the last and most formidable challenge to the Company's monopoly of military power. As he travelled to the front, Hardinge was apprehensive about the effect the Punjab crisis might have on restless elements elsewhere in the country. He took special care to cultivate the Raja of Patiala, whose territories lay immediately south of the Sutlej. He remained loyal and was rewarded with £4,000 a year in lands when the war was over. Sir Harry Smith was infected with Hardinge's pessimism, imagining that if the Sikhs captured Ludhiana, the 'general blaze of revolt' would spread across northern India, perhaps beyond.[28]

Gough was lucky in his adversaries. Before crossing the Sutlej, the Khalsa's committees had given absolute command to Tej Singh and Lal Singh, both experienced generals. But their hearts were not in the war, for they were both convinced that sooner or later the Punjab would pass under British control. In that event they hoped to secure senior posts in the new administration, which in fact they did.[29] On the battlefield, their lack of commitment was reflected in a series of operational errors. The two generals threw away their superiority in numbers and artillery, elected to fight a defensive campaign and handed the initiative to their enemies.

The Sikh high command began the campaign with a show of tentative bravado, moving forward to engage Gough at Mudki during the afternoon of 18 December. It was a golden opportunity; British units were still concentrating and the army approaching the fortified village of Mudki was briefly resting after an exhausting forced march. The clouds of dust thrown up by the approaching cavalry alerted Gough and the Sikhs lost the element of surprise. The Sikh cavalry screen was soon dispersed by a combination of British cavalry and horse artillery. They provided time for the infantry to form, which was no easy matter for the surrounding countryside was broken up by clumps of thorn trees. A general advance was ordered by Gough and the battle assumed the pattern that would be followed by its successors, with a mass attack in the teeth of Sikh artillery and musket fire. Shortly after midnight, the Sikhs retired to their fortified positions at Ferozeshah. In what had been an inconclusive contest the British casualties were 848, of whom 52 were officers. It was noted that the Sikh gunners had singled out officers as targets, believing that, once leaderless, the Company's troops would lose the will to fight.[30]

The sheer determination of the British attack had made some impact on the Sikh generals who, thereafter, stuck to the defensive. The war became one of attrition with the Khalsa tied down behind earthworks defended by cannon. Gough, believing that delay launching an attack weakened his men's resolve, pressed ahead with an offensive against Ferozeshah on 21 December. His overall strategy was to break his opponent's nerve by persistent offensives. It paid off, but only just, and at the cost of casualties unparalleled in any previous Indian campaign.

Outnumbered by four to one and outgunned, Gough repeatedly stormed the Ferozeshah defences and took them after a struggle which lasted thirty-six hours. 'This was fighting indeed,' remembered the veteran Sita Ram. 'I had never seen anything like it before.'[31] The 62nd Regiment lost 260 men in ten minutes and were thrown back by the weight of the Sikh cannonade, and stunned sepoys imagined that the all-conquering British army was about to be defeated. Nightfall brought little respite, for it was bitterly cold, and fatigued, hungry, and thirsty survivors slept in the open. A supreme effort was needed the next morning. It was accomplished in splendid style, at least by Sir Harry Smith, who led four British battalions 'as if they were upon Parade' with colours flying towards the Sikh breastworks. The defenders were overwhelmed and driven back beyond their camp. For a dangerous moment, their general Tej Singh considered a cavalry counter-attack that would have swept through the British force, which was low in ammunition and already engaged in looting the Khalsa's baggage. Inexplicably he retired; a stroke of luck which restored the confidence of many sepoys.[32] One British participant believed, with some justice, that the battle of Ferozeshah had decided 'the fate of the British empire in India'.[33]

Mudki and Ferozeshah had upheld the mystique of the Company's army. The price of moral superiority had been very high, with casualties of over 3,000. Some regiments, like the 3rd Light Dragoons, had been reduced to below half strength. Reinforcements were on hand, trudging up from Meerut, and Gough wisely chose to wait for his siege train before attacking the Sikh entrenchments and field works at Sobraon. In the meantime, a new crisis had occurred as a substantial Sikh force under Ranjodh Singh menaced Ludhiana and lines of communication to the east. It was engaged on 28 January 1846 at Aliwal by a detachment of 2,400 under Sir Harry Smith. It was yet another straightforward frontal attack in which the Sikhs were thrust from their positions by what Smith described as 'a bold and intrepid advance' by infantry, cavalry and artillery. The 16th Lancers charged Sikh infantry, who threw down their muskets and surged to meet the horsemen with swords and shields, which may have been why Smith described Aliwal as 'a stand-up gentlemanlike battle'. He was a popular officer of the tough old school who knew how to draw courage and devotion from his men. One recalled fondly how, as he wandered through the camp in the evening, he would call 'Trumpeter, order a round of grog; and not too much water' whenever he encountered a group of soldiers.[34]

Reinforced and now supported by powerful siege guns, Gough began his onslaught against the Sobraon lines on 10 February. The battle became another slogging match and lasted for two days. Discipline and sheer doggedness triumphed again in a fourth collision between shells, round shot, grape and musketry and flesh and bone. According to Smith, it was almost as tough going as Waterloo, 'a brutal bulldog fight' in which British regulars 'laid on like devils'.[35] So did the Gurkhas, who used their kukris 'with unaccountable zeal among the Sikhs'.[36] The British lost 2,000 men, a seventh of their strength; the Sikhs 10,000, about a third of theirs. The greater part died struggling to cross the Sutlej under heavy fire. The British had won the war, but by a narrow margin and after Gough had taken some considerable risks. But then, as Sir Harry Smith wrote afterwards: 'India *runs* on the *cast of a Die*.'[37]

What was left of the Army of the Sutlej entered Lahore in fine style. A band played 'See the Conquering Hero Comes' and a procession of hundreds of captured cannon passed through the streets to remind onlookers that the Khalsa had been scattered and emasculated. But Hardinge was reluctant to press the advantages of the recent victories. A few months before, Peel had allowed him a free hand in dealing with the Punjab, but both Prime Minister and Governor-General were adverse to outright annexation. They were also against the Punjab becoming another Indian 'subsidiary state', which would have permitted a rapacious landlord class to batten down on their tenants with the assistance of Company troops. Hardinge preferred a compromise which would allow the Company a degree of political influence in the Punjab and guarantee a secure border against Afghanistan. The Punjab was stripped of some of its most fertile lands, worth £400,000 a year, on the banks of the Sutlej; forced to pay a £1.5 million indemnity; and Kashmir was handed over to Gulab Singh. Dalip Singh remained maharaja and his mother continued to act as regent under the guidance of a new resident, Sir Henry Lawrence. Political agents were established in other major Punjabi towns supported by British garrisons and locally raised units. It was soon discovered that many former Khalsa men and Pathans from the frontier districts were glad to put their talents to the Company's use in return for regular wages.

Hardinge's Punjabi state was a brittle structure which collapsed during the early summer of 1848. Lieutenant-Colonel Sir Henry Lawrence, the first resident and power behind the throne in Lahore, thought the Punjabis were 'patient and submissive, if not contented and happy' with their new government.[38] This was not a recipe for future tranquillity, although Lawrence and his assistants in the countryside felt sure that, in time, the Sikh, Hindu and Muslim populations would develop an affection for a régime which was just and respected their customs and creeds. The new order was proclaimed by Lieutenant Herbert Edwardes to the tribesmen of Bannu: 'You shall have the best laws that an enlightened people can frame for you; but they will be administered by a Sikh Governor. He cannot oppress you, for the English will be over him. You shall be justly ruled, but you shall be free no more.'[39] In this context, freedom meant the liberty to pursue blood feuds, rustle stock and expel tax-collectors, none of which the frontiersmen felt inclined to abandon. Nonetheless, they were impressed by the force of personality of the new government's 27-year-old representative, who combined the patience and wisdom of Solomon with the warrior vigour of a Joshua.

There were losers under the new system. They gathered around Mul Raj, the former governor of Multan, an administrator with a reputation for justice and honesty, who emerged, probably reluctantly, as the leader of a revolt against British domination.[40] The uprising began at the end of April 1848, when two British officials were assassinated by mutinous soldiers from the Multan garrison. Within the next few months, Mul Raj attracted a variety of discontented souls all of whom had suffered in various ways under the new régime. There were members of Ranjit Singh's extended family, including the Maharani Jandin; thousands of discharged and unpaid Khalsa soldiers; and zamindars and officials who had been sacked or who had had their powers and incomes curbed by the British. Soon after the outbreak, Edward Cust sent out spies to discover the reactions to it in his district. He discovered that many Sikh zamindars, having lost so much that they had held dear (i.e. their power), believed they had nothing to lose in an attempt to regain it.[41] The same was no doubt true of the Ruhela horsemen dimissed by James Abbott for being 'too rapacious', or the ex-Khalsa men who objected to the loss of the freedom to steal food, firewood and fodder from villagers.[42] There were also plenty for whom any breakdown of civil order was a chance for easy pickings. Edwardes came across Baluchis and Pathans 'who, at all times prefer military service to agriculture' taking up arms and joining both sides. Among his own government levies were 3,000 Pathans who were glad to take fifteen rupees a week and a possibility of plunder. 'War is their trade and also their pastime,' he observed, but was worried whether he could restrain them once the fighting had started.[43] Not all war profiteers wielded swords. On the fringes of the Company's army were enterprising Indian traders who exchanged loot for the cash which soldiers needed to buy drink.[44]

Losers outnumbered winners in the war. For most, perhaps the majority of Punjabis, the insurrection was a catastrophe, made worse by a recent drought and the prospect of a famine. The best that these people could do was to avoid trouble. In the hinterland of Multan, Edwardes found the ryots continued to pay their taxes but needed 'the assurance that they are paying to the strongest side'.[45]

During the first three months of the revolt there was no way of knowing which was the stronger side. The events in Multan at the end of April had taken the government by surprise, and for some time intelligence as to

Mul Raj's motives and support was fragmentary. Containment measures were quickly taken, largely thanks to the initiative of junior officers like Edwardes who, in his own words, 'rushed in where Generals feared to tread'. Uncertain of the loyalty of many of his Sikhs, he hurried south from the foothills of the North-West Frontier with as many men as he could muster. He joined an improvised army of irregulars and a contingent from the loyal Raja of Bahawalpur which assembled in the vicinity in May and June under Colonel Cortlandt. Dashingly led, this force of about 5,000 established a blockade around the city and fought a sequence of successful actions which temporarily contained the revolt. The arrival of a 7,000-strong Anglo-Sikh division and a train of heavy artillery under Brigadier William Whish in August made it possible to besiege the city. Within a few weeks the defection of the Sikh contingent under Sher Singh compelled the British to withdraw. This signal humiliation persuaded many Punjabis who had hitherto maintained a wait-and-see neutrality to throw in their lot with the rebels.

Those officers who had done their utmost to act swiftly were dismayed. They had been left in the lurch by a high command which appeared to have forgotten that, in India, military success was the child of decisive action. James Abbott spoke for them all when he complained:

> Delay, when a fearful and instant retribution is everywhere expected, will be attributed to timidity. We hold our position in the Punjab wholly by force of opinion, by the general belief in our superior courage and resources. Our Empire in India has the same foundation, and one or both may pass away if we evince any symptoms of hesistancy.[46]

Implicit in what Abbott and others said was the contrast between the quick thinking of the men on the spot in the Punjab and the Olympian indifference of their masters in Calcutta.

The excuse for this apparent paralysis at the top was simple and unanswerable, given that a commander's duty is always, whenever possible, to preserve the lives of his men. Sending an army into the Punjab during the summer would have been disastrous in terms of losses of British troops from heat exhaustion. Experience, particularly in the arid region of the Sind, showed that sunstroke was as deadly, probably more so, than enemy fire. At best a none-too-healthy creature, the British soldier could not campaign in temperatures of over 100 degrees. Recalling a march across the

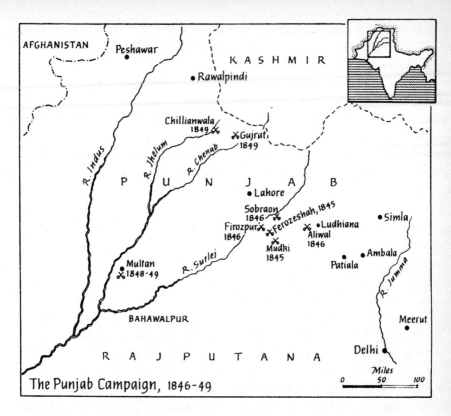

The Punjab Campaign, 1846-49

sandy plain north of Delhi in March 1848, Private Charles Ryder of the 32nd described men fainting from lack of water, others with swollen tongues bursting from mouths and his own collapse with sunstroke and fever. 'I felt very bad. It was a sickly kind of feeling. There the men lay, groaning in the greatest of agony. The doctors and apothecaries were all a bustle, bleeding the men as they lay upon the sand.' One soldier shot himself.[47] Dehydration and attendant disorders cost Ryder's regiment 14 dead and 175 sick. Knowledge of occurrences like this made even such aggressive spirits as Gough and Napier pause. Moreover, as events unfolded during July and August, it appeared that local forces were gaining the upper hand, having confined the uprising to the environs of Multan.

Once it became clear that this was not the case and the insurrection was fanning outwards, the new Governor-General, Lord Dalhousie, took the necessary action. With characteristic vigour, he told his senior commanders: 'Unwarned by precedent, uninfluenced by example, the Sikh nation has called for war; and on my word, sirs, war they shall have and with a vengeance!' Preparations for what was to be a massive punitive expedition were in hand during September and October as two armies assembled. The smaller, including a Bombay contingent, was destined to reopen the siege of Multan, and the larger concentrated at Firozpur for an advance to the second centre of the revolt, the area north of Lahore. Once again, the Sikh commanders had chosen static warfare: Mul Raj stayed inside the walls of Multan and Sher Singh's field army was sitting tight in positions on the northern and southern banks of the Chenab near Gujrat.

Both commanders appealed to religious and racial emotions: Muslims were urged to rally behind the anti-British *jihad*, and Sikhs to fight for their faith, Dalip Singh and independence. This was the message on leaflets which circulated among Edwardes's Pathan troops, but, much to his relief, they spurned them as the outpourings of '*sugs*' (dogs) and '*kaffirs*' (unbelievers).[48] Others were persuaded: there was a trickle of deserters, including Gurkhas, to Multan during the siege.[49]

The encirclement of Multan was completed by the end of December. Its outer wall was breached on 4 January 1849 and British and Indian troopers fought their way through the streets. As in the last war, no quarter was asked or given as the battle resolved itself into hundreds of individual combats. One, between an Irish corporal and a Sikh swordsman, was watched by Private Ryder. 'They closed upon each other, and grappled each other by the throat; when the corporal gave him the foot and threw him upon the floor.' He then cut off his head with his own sword.[50] Mul Raj had withdrawn with 3,000 men into the inner fortress, which was stormed on 22 January. Pandemonium followed as soldiers rushed about looting and killing anyone who resisted, whatever their sex or age. 'All the houses were ransacked, and what could not be carried off was completely destroyed. Temples were broken into, and the brass idols and Korans carried away and sold . . . All our men, European and native, looked for precious metals. They took the rings and chains from every dead man, as well as the living.'[51] Ryder got some idols, a dagger, a carpet and a breastplate. Officers surpassed their men in the free-for-all. 'I was as good a plunderer as the rest,' Captain Alexander Grant told his family a week later, adding that the prize agents had already secured loot worth 2.5 million rupees and were about to begin digging for buried treasure.[52]

The fall of Multan released men for the campaign in eastern Punjab, which was languishing. Gough was again in command and his arrival at Firozpur in December had chilled some hearts, for memories of the last war were still fresh. The disrespectful called him 'Sir Huge Gouk'. Richard Baird Smith, an engineer officer, prophesied that 'our success will be gained by the blood of the officers and men and will owe nought to the genius of the Chief'.[53] The unburied skeletons of men killed at Mudki and around Firozpur were a further, sombre reminder of what had occurred three years ago.[54] In London, the prospect of Gough's generalship also called alarm; his appointment was criticised in *The Times*, where his lack of tactical finesse was attributed to his Irishness.[55] The government decided to replace him with Napier, but the order reached Calcutta after the war had ended.

The new year saw a slow advance of Gough's 14,000-strong army across the Sutlej towards the main Sikh concentration beyond Lahore. Gough was, as ever, keen to get to grips with the enemy and engage them in the bull-at-a-gate manner which his men and their opponents had come to expect. The chance came on the afternoon of 13 January 1849, when he ordered an attack on Sher Singh's extended defensive position in dense bush between Chillianwala and the River Jhelum. Again, British troops advanced headlong into heavy artillery fire and suffered accordingly. The 24th Regiment survived the cannon fire and stormed a battery but were thrown back by intense musketry, losing over half their strength. The remnants of the regiment fled, some men running for two miles, and two adjacent sepoy battalions followed suit. 'How could they stand if the Europeans could not?' asked Sita Ram. Another stunned onlooker, Baird Smith, afterwards told his wife: 'The flight of a Queen's Regiment in India is a sad affair at any time, but it is especially so in a war like this one when our Europeans are our main support.'[56]

Elsewhere, the assailants had mixed fortunes. The 61st captured a battery after two supporting sepoy regiments had fallen back; the 29th gained its objective at a cost of nearly a third of its numbers; and the 3rd Light Dragoons got badly mangled as a result of muddled orders. Behind the lines there was chaos. Treating the wounded of the 29th, Surgeon Stewart was suddenly overwhelmed when a horse artillery battery careered into a struggling mass of retreating infantry, dragoons, lancers and riderless horses.[57] As darkness fell, the battle had become a stalemate.

The Sikhs had been severely shaken, and their commander, Sher Singh, remembering how the Khalsa had been destroyed in the earlier war of attrition, made overtures for negotiations. They were rejected (rebels could only offer unconditional surrender) and he slowly drew his forces away northwards to new positions near Gujrat. Gough did not pursue. Chillian-wala had been a draw in which he had suffered over 2,300 casualties, over a quarter of his force, and he dared not risk another such encounter.

Gough reopened his offensive during the second week of February. The odds were now firmly in his favour: additional forces from Multan had increased his army to 23,000 and he had, in what turned out to be his last battle, decided to follow the textbook rather than instinct. The result was a brilliant *tour de force* in which artillery, cavalry and infantry were co-ordinated in a scientific manner. First, light artillery and skirmishers moved quickly forward to engage the Sikh lines which were drawn up in open country south of Gujrat. A two-hour artillery duel severely damaged the Sikh batteries and enabled the infantry assault to be pressed home without the customary heavy losses. Fractured in many places by the infantry, the Sikh line collapsed and the remnants of the Khalsa fled. Their retreat was turned into a helter-skelter rout by close cavalry pursuit.

In the weeks that followed, those who had survived Gujrat were ordered to lay down their arms. During one act of surrender, Brigadier-General Colin Campbell was struck by the pathos and dignity of one old warrior who put down his musket, placed his hands together in a salute, and cried out, '*Ay Ranjit Singh mar gaya*' (Today Ranjit Singh is dead).'[58] The ritual of the Khalsa's final capitulation was chosen as the image for the obverse of the medal given to all who had fought in the second Sikh War; it showed Sikhs laying down their weapons before a mounted British general in a cocked hat with lines of infantry in the background.

The Punjab was formerly annexed by Dalhousie in March 1849. Even before the campaign was under way, he had decided to bring the province under direct administration and extend British India to its natural frontier, the Indus. The second Sikh War ended the process of piecemeal conquest which Clive had begun; Britain now possessed the whole of India. In a triumphal mood and looking back over nearly ninety years of wars, Gough told his soldiers: 'That which Alexander attempted, the British army have accomplished.'[59]

4

Robust Bodies and Obstinate Minds: An Anatomy of Conquest

I

How had an army which never numbered more than a quarter of a million been able to conquer and subdue 150 millions in less than 100 years? Just as there was no master plan for India's conquest, there was no single explanation for how it had been achieved. Some answered the question in terms of Divinely impelled forces of historical destiny. There was certainly something miraculous about the apparent willingness of the Indians to accept the verdict of a handful of battles and submit to rule by a tiny, alien minority. 'If each black man took up a handful of sand and by united effort cast it upon the white-faced intruders, we should be buried alive,' wrote Hardinge.[1] But no such act of concerted determination occurred. Indians, it was argued, largely by civilian officials, ultimately knew what was good for them, and after initial resistance, had quickly settled down to enjoy the blessings of a mild and humane government.

This was a part of the truth; a small part, according to the army. In 1829, a junior officer of the Bengal army expressed what was both a justification for his profession and a reminder of the realities of power: 'Orators, we know, love to call British India, the "Empire of opinion"; but it is the EMPIRE OF SEPOYS: and woe to its rulers, when they shall venture to neglect this main spring, this too critical secret of its mechanism.'[2] The same message was delivered in 1853 by Gough to a Commons select committee:

> India is a very peculiar country; you do not know the hour
> when some outbreak may take place: and we all know that the
> people of India have their heads up like leeches looking for
> anything that may occur.[3]

Each statement takes it for granted that, were it not for the ever-present
threat of force, a precarious Raj would eventually be toppled by its subjects. Moreover, as Gough indicated, this state of affairs had not been
changed by the recent spectacular victories in the Sind and the Punjab.
Indians still needed to fear the army which had conquered them.

Whatever its future might be, there was no question that the army had
created the Indian empire. Between 1791 and 1849 British forces had
successively defeated the three most powerful and resilient Mughal successor states: Mysore, the Maratha polity and the Punjab. All resisted
tenaciously and each required two hard-fought campaigns before it was
finally overcome. Victory had never come easily. The British were always
outnumbered, possessed no overwhelming technical advantages, and white
soldiers succumbed to unfamiliar distempers and extremes of heat and
cold. There were, however, compensations which proved decisive. The
Company had abundant cash which was transformed into wages,
weaponry, victuals and transport, and an officer corps which somehow
managed to draw the best out of their soldiers in an emergency.
Leadership, combined with steadiness and stubbornness among the rank
and file, gave British forces an edge in every battle.

Throughout this period the Company had the largest fighting force in
India. In 1830 India was garrisoned by 36,400 white soldiers, two-thirds of
them government troops, one-third Company officers, infantry and gunners, and 187,000 Company sepoys and cavalry. Fourteen years later, there
were 33,000 British regulars, 17,000 Company Europeans and 201,300
Indians, including 30,000 irregulars and auxiliary units from the princely
states. This preponderance of manpower was never apparent on individual
battlefields. Logistics and the demands of internal security dictated that
only a limited proportion of the Company's forces could ever be concentrated on one front. British armies were, therefore, always outnumbered,
but not always greatly so. During the 1803–05 Maratha war the Company
deployed 37,000 British and Indian troops against 56,000 Maratha regulars
and an untold number of irregulars, mostly light horse. Aware of the
mishaps that had occurred towards the end of that campaign, Hastings preferred shorter odds when he fought its successor. In 1817 he took the field

with 87,000 white and Indian troops and 20,000 irregulars against enemies whose combined strength was calculated at 137,000 men, a large number of whom were Pindaris.[4] And yet, when it came to pitched battles, the Marathas had the advantage in numbers because the nature of operations compelled Hastings to divide his forces and deploy large detachments to protect his lines of communication. Against the infinitely more formidable Khalsa, the British never committed more than a fifth of the regulars available and were outgunned in every engagement before Gujrat.

By this time, the British high command had become mesmerised by its own military mythology, a combination of racial arrogance and past experience. At its heart was the belief that resolutely led white soldiers would always sweep all before them, regardless of the odds. Quality always mattered far more than quantity, for, since the time of Clive, Indians had developed a terror of white troops and were unnerved whenever they faced them. 'A body of mounted Europeans will produce an excellent effect,' suggested Captain James Carnac, the resident in Baroda, after he had uncovered evidence of local unrest in 1812.[5] The mere appearance of a hundred or so light dragoons would overawe a city of many thousands. According to Cornwallis, British troops were the 'pith and essence' of his army and his adversary, Tipu Sultan, agreed. When he used his few white mercenaries, Tipu had them carried to the battlefield in palanquins, the better to preserve their vitality.[6] He was copying his enemies, who shifted British soldiers to the front in palanquins and bullock carts or on the backs of camels and elephants. When the fighting started, these men had automatic priority at dressing stations and convalescent hospitals.[7]

Every general cherished his white soldiers, whether British rank and file, or the officers who commanded the sepoys. 'It is impossible to do things in a gallant style without Europeans,' Lake told the Marquess Wellesley after the fall of Agra in 1803. His judgement was upheld in the subsequent battle of Laswari and, after casting his eye down the casualty sheets, he warned that his army would lose its punch if European reinforcements were not sent immediately.[8] In this and other campaigns, white troops delivered the hammer blows which won battles.

Sepoys provided the ballast of an army. They provided the weight of an attacking force, but the vanguard were always British soldiers, who were, quite literally, the cutting edge of empire.[9] This was how they were regarded by Lieutenant-Colonel Blacker in his analysis of the 1817–18 Maratha war. British courage, he concluded, had been the key to victories in a countryside where there had been no room for tactical flourishes. This prognosis was illustrated by his account of the battle of Kirki in November 1817, when a Company force of 2,800 attacked a Maratha army believed to contain 10,000 infantry and 25,000 horse. The turning point came when the Bombay European Regiment advanced unflinching into Maratha fire and set an example of steadiness and aggression which inspired the supporting sepoy battalions.[10] The Indians may also have been itching to avenge themselves against an enemy which had recently killed their officers and maltreated their wives after the seizure of the Poona residency.[11]

As described by Blacker, history and legend merged at Kirki. A few hundred British soldiers marched forward, shoulder to shoulder with fixed bayonets. Their officers walked calmly ahead of them, setting the tone of the fight by their jaunty coolness. Close behind came the battalions of sepoys, eager to match the resolve of their British counterparts and, like them, encouraged by officers who seemed impervious to fear. It was an exercise in willpower, an assertion of moral superiority; and it worked. The Maratha sword and spear men shrank from the close-range musket volley and did not stand to face the bayonet charge which came moments later. The Maratha horsemen followed suit, having already suffered from infantry fire when they had made an ill-judged charge. For Indian professional cavalrymen, their horses, harness, armour and weapons were the source of their livelihood and they were reluctant to hazard them in any do-or-die exploits.[12] This understandable prudence was recognised by the British; whenever the Company hired an irregular horse *sowar* (trooper), he was promised compensation if he lost his horse in battle.[13] To judge from the eighty-six British casualties, the Maratha army at Kirki had had little stomach for the fight. Perhaps, like the Company's generals, the Marathas were conditioned to believe that a British advance was irresistible.

Generalship played a limited part in this sort of engagement. This was just as well, for, with the exception of Arthur Wellesley, British commanders in India at this time were not imaginative tacticians. The command 'Level well my lads and then come to the bayonet' was the key to victory. Everything depended upon the peculiar virtues of the British soldier, which were commonly acknowledged as discipline and perseverance in the face of adversity. How far these qualities were revealed in the battlefield depended upon leadership; fearlessness flowed downwards from officers to men. Whatever they lacked in military science, commanders like Combermere, Napier and Gough made up for in gallantry. When battle was under way, they placed themselves at the head of their troops, cheering them on or rallying them when the going got tough. During the street fighting in Multan, Napier led a body of men and, when the way was blocked by two Sikhs who were cutting down all assailants, he drew his pistol (presumably one of the new Colt revolvers) and shot both dead.[14] Sir Colin Campbell rode among the Sikh gunners at Chillianwala and sabred at least one.[15]

With limited tactical control from above, the quick thinking and intrepidity of junior officers could change the course of a battle. At Sitalbi in November 1817, a small force entirely made up of sepoys was in danger of being routed by a larger army of Marathas, supported by cannon and swivel guns mounted on camels. As the tide turned against the British, and in defiance of his commanding officer's orders, Captain Fitzgerald led three troops of his Bengal cavalry against the Maratha horse who were protecting the artillery batteries. It was a desperate manoeuvre, but audacity paid off. The heavily outnumbered sowars sliced through their astonished opponents and captured the guns. Fitzgerald and his brother officers had led the way and suffered accordingly; out of the 318 men who charged, 22 were killed, 5 of them officers, and 22 wounded, 3 of them officers.[16]

This piece of derring-do was a golden example of how every officer should behave. A few years later, the following description of the qualities expected from an officer under fire appeared in a military journal. 'Disregarding death, without despising it', he 'looks cheerfully around, orders and directs everything within his charge, and electrifies his subordinates in that noble spirit that animates him.'[17] This was the spirit which sent Lieutenant Torrens Metje 'dancing on' in front of his company, contemptuously picking up spent shot and throwing it aside, as the 29th advanced on the Sikh batteries at Chillianwala.[18] He was mortally wounded in the groin by grape shot, an example of the sacrifice which was the inevitable price of this type of leadership. Sepoys drawn from warrior castes were instinctively drawn to officers who revealed their courage in hand-to-hand combat. During a tight moment in a fight in the Deccan in 1803, Lieutenant Bryant, outnumbered by Arab mercenaries, saved the life of a brother officer and cut down a standard bearer. His sepoys wavered, so he harangued them and pitched into the fray, breaking his sword on an Arab's skull. He then seized a musket, and using butt and bayonet, knocked down two more adversaries, by which time his sepoys were at his side. In another engagement, an Arab hurled a spear at Lieutenant Langlands of the 74th Highlanders, who plucked it out and threw it back, spitting the thrower through the body. A sepoy grenadier rushed from the ranks and patted him on the back with the words '*Atchah sahib! Bhota atchah Keeah*'

(Well done, sir! Very well done!).[19] This kind of exploit, performed at the right moment, injected fresh heart into men whose will to fight on was flagging.

Casualty returns were a yardstick which measured the importance of European officers. At Delhi in 1803, where a third of those engaged were British, the total European casualties were 208, of whom 11 were officers. Indian losses were proportionally less, with 288 dead and wounded, of whom 35 were white officers and sepoy NCOs. It is worth noting that in each sepoy regiment of 1,840 men there were 45 British officers and 120 Indian NCOs. At Laswari, when 5,500 Company troops were present, 33 officers were among the 824 men killed or wounded. This pattern of losses recurred throughout the Sikh wars: at Ferozeshah, where one in seven of the units was British, Europeans made up half the 2,415 casualties. Of the 700 dead, 115 were officers. 'The British infantry, as usual, carried the day,' concluded one of Gough's staff officers, which was hardly unexpected since the commander had placed them in the vanguard of his advance.[20]

The lists of dead and wounded did not indicate how men died or were injured. There is, however, plenty of anecdotal eyewitness evidence about the effectiveness of Maratha and Sikh musketry and artillery fire. Arthur Wellesley had been forewarned about Maratha fire before Assaye, but even so he was amazed by its accuracy and intensity. He lost a third of his army and, to judge by his and others' recollections, nearly all the casualties were the result of the enemy's bombardment and fusillades. During the assault on Deeg at the end of 1804, Maratha artillery fire was well directed and 'snipe men' (i.e. marksmen) continually picked off men in the siege lines.[21] Maratha artillerymen were always a disciplined, well-trained and brave élite; at Maharajapur (1843) they poured grape and canister into advancing British infantry, pelted them with horse shoes and scrap iron when their ammunition ran out, and died defending their pieces.[22] Sikh gunners displayed the same professionalism and grit.

When an attack was pressed home, a battle was transformed into a mass of individual conflicts between men with bladed weapons. Justifying their often crude offensive tactics, British generals liked to imagine that this was the pivotal moment upon which victory hung. To an extent they were right, in that the defending infantrymen often preferred to fly rather than tackle a line of supermen who had just survived and seemed undaunted by intense artillery and musket fire. This was what happened when storming parties surged through breaches made in small hill forts during the 1791–92 Mysore war. No quarter was given to those who fought back.[23]

And yet, the few first-hand accounts of hand-to-hand contests suggest that British soldiers tended to use firearms rather than bladed weapons. A soldier of the 29th who had lost an arm at Chillianwala boasted to his regimental surgeon that he had shot six Sikhs and bayoneted a seventh, presumably the antagonist who had crippled him.[24] A private of the 11th Light Dragoons, harrying fugitives after the taking of Bharatpur in 1826, remembered how his sergeant had fired his pistol at a Rajput horseman but missed at six yards. The Rajput then raised his carbine, but before he could fire the private had ridden forward and shot him dead with his carbine. Shortly after, the private attacked another mounted Rajput who had refused to surrender, and knocked him out of his saddle with a single sabre stroke. But the turban broke the blow and the Rajput remounted, spat at his assailant (a common gesture of contempt which was also used by Sikh horsemen) and cantered off. The dragoon also rode away to look for the rest of his unit.[25] British cavalrymen at Chillianwala preferred to use pistols rather than sabres because they usually came off worse against Sikh horsemen armed with tulwars. The trouble was that the troopers found it difficult to control their Indian chargers using the traditional British cavalry seat, while the Sikhs were able to turn their horses quickly and deliver a cut to their assailant's skull as he rode past.[26]

Indian armies usually possessed a disproportionate amount of horsemen. Blacker interpreted this as evidence of 'immature civilisation' and, given that a substantial number of the cavalrymen were mercenaries, 'a love of uncontrolled license'. By contrast, the British, whom he revealingly likened to two earlier empire-builders, the Greeks and the Romans, placed their faith in the infantryman, for, 'Infantry best succeeds among a people with robust bodies and obstinate minds.' Indians, he imagined, lacked both. They preferred the outward trappings of power to its substance, which was why they set so much store by masses of horsemen:

> The exterior of cavalry service bears an imposing appearance of grandeur and power, which in the vain, flatters self-love, while it inspires terror among the ignorant. These are particularly moved by whatever affects the eye, as are savages, by brilliant colours.[27]

This sweeping generalisation reduced the conquest of India to a racial conflict, a collision between national stereotypes in which the British were bound to triumph because of their peculiar virtues. A unique distillation of fortitude, individualism and discipline made the British soldier more than a match for a race who were superficial and inconstant. Furthermore, Blacker and other observers believed that, by and large, Indians had no patriotism.[28] No explanation was offered for this, perhaps because it would have been hard to defend in the light of experience. Such attachments made Indians fight courageously, even when the tide of battle was flowing against them. India did not then exist as a nation. The Indian fighting man's loyalty was focused elsewhere: to his religion, his commander, his locality or to whoever fed him and paid his wages.

II

As many British soldiers testified, their Indian opponents often matched them man for man in vigour and skill in handling their weapons. In these circumstances, morale was vital. The Company's army was the sum of its many individual parts and ultimately its success depended on their collective will to win, or, as was commonly the case, refusal to accept defeat. This interior strength was the product of training, discipline, self-confidence, mutual reliance and devotion to officers. These were the ingredients of the regimental spirit of which the British army was proud and which Company officers endeavoured to cultivate among their sepoys.

There were two kinds of British officer in India. The first served in the royal army; he purchased his commission and lived as a gentleman should with the support of a private income. The second served in the Company's army, owed his commission solely to patronage, and endeavoured to live as a gentlemen with the help of more generous pay and campaign allowances. Although bound together by the common tastes, outlook and codes of honour of gentlemen, there was always tension between the King's (or the Queen's) officers and the Company's. Indian warfare was very different from European. The gibe 'sepoy general', once levelled at Wellington, was a reminder that experience and reputation gained on the European battlefield counted for more in the eyes of the world than that gained defeating what were commonly regarded as 'savage' armies. This prejudice died hard, despite the Duke's insistence that all he had ever known about war had been learned in India.

Promotion jealousies added to the friction, with Company officers often feeling affronted when senior and highly-paid Indian posts were given to officers from the government's army who had political leverage in

Britain. In 1807, Colonel Brunton of the Madras army grumbled about '*young lords*' coming out to assume commands and, if they could pull strings in London, shin up the promotion ladder ahead of more experienced men.[29] After a brisk exchange with his commanding officer, Major-General Sir John Keane, during the early phase of the Afghan campaign, the testy Nott wrote: 'The truth is, he is a Queen's officer and I am a Company's; I am decidely of the opinion that a Queen's officer, be he ever so talented, is totally unfit to command the Company's Army.'[30] Among a caste which set a high store by the recognition of honour, even the smallest slight, real or imaginary, could rankle. For instance, men who had fought at Waterloo were given an official medal, a token denied to the veterans of Indian battles until 1842 and a source of irritation to Company officers. In Sir Charles D'Oyly's verse satire *Tom Raw, the Griffin*, a 'dandy warrior', a lancer officer arouses the envy of a Company veteran:

> *The Colonel looks on the well-dressed Lieutenant*
> *With wonder, and the badge of Waterloo,*
> *On his young beast conspicuously pendant,*
> *And sighs that all the battles he'd gone through,*
> *Should not have gained him some distinction too.*

But there were compensations for the colonel: the Company paid well, gave generous campaign allowances, and there was always prize money. These rewards made Company service an attractive proposition for the younger sons of the professional and upper-middle classes, the more so since they did not have to pay for a commission. This was why James Young, the son of a professor of Greek at Glasgow, found himself disconsolate in the siege lines at Deeg at the close of 1804, when he wrote:

> My Father, the most sensible and the best of men – has, like most of the Fathers of Families in Europe – a great prepossession in favour of India – founded on the splendour of the very few who return, from peculiar circumstances with great fortunes to Englands – and *strengthened*, if I may use the expression, by the Ignorance of the far greater number, who perish miserably here.[31]

The spectacular fortunes of Clive and Hastings had made a lasting impression. It was jokingly said that there existed in India a pagoda tree which, when shaken, dropped its fruit of gold coins. This legend and its influence were described in *Tom Raw*:

> *The colonies and foreign governments*
> *Are famous drains for pride and poverty;*
> *For gentlemen deficient in their rents,*
> *Always in India turn a longing eye.*
> *They talk in England of a precious tree*
> *That, but to shake, brings down its fruit, – (pagodas).*

Contemplation of that crop sustained James Young during the dog days in the trenches at Deeg and, when the fortress fell, he took a lively interest in the progress of the prize agents and what they had accumulated.[32] The prospects of prize money animated every officer in India. 'Money, medals and promotion' and 'prize money' lay ahead of Cornet Thomas Pearson of the 11th Light Dragoons, newly landed in India and happy to be part of the army which was about to lay siege to Bharatpur in December 1825.[33] He got what he wanted, but it took time; in 1835 he received his cornet's share of the prize money, £218 16 shillings (£212.80) and sixteen years later an Army of India medal with a clasp for Bharatpur.[34] There were, however, no instant fortunes available, save for senior officers chosen to command expeditions who, according to the official sliding scale, always took the largest sum. The major and captain in charge of the punitive force sent against Cochin in 1795 each received £2,218, while lieutenants got £93 19 shillings (£93.95).[35] Knowledge of these discrepancies made the scramble for promotion more intense.

The best most officers could hope for was a steady acquisition of comparatively small sums augmented by what could be saved from pay and allowances. In 1820 it was estimated that a thrifty ensign might save as much as £120 a year from his salary, but it is unlikely that many managed this, given the temptations which surrounded them.[36] William Home, who had entered the Company's service as an officer in the Bengal European service in 1786, was able to pay £200 a year towards the mortage of the family estate in 1806.[37] Five years later, he asked his brother whether £500 a year was enough to rent an estate in his native Berwickshire.[38] His dreams remained unfulfilled; he died, aged forty-three, in Calcutta in 1816, leaving his house there and £1,500 for the upkeep of his favourite horse, a mare called 'Khoose Khan'. His will included special instructions as to her diet and preference for eating it from a table.[39] Like many others, particularly from Scotland, Home's exile provided his family with the wherewithal to restore its fortunes. Another borderer, Sir Walter Scott, saw India as 'the corn chest for Scotland where we poor gentry must send our youngest sons as we send our black cattle to the South'.[40]

Getting the corn often involved young officers in a lifetime's game of snakes and ladders. Consider James Campbell, who joined the Madras army in 1771 as a subaltern. During the winter of 1773–74 he served on an up-country expedition against brigands, for which he was delighted to get an additional allowance of £10 a month. It failed to cover the costs of his transport and servants and when he returned to Fort St George he complained of a 'very foolish' campaign in which there was no action and 'instead of making a great deal of money which was not expected, we are all greatly out of pocket'.[41] An officer with the wonderful old Puritan name of Goodbehere was forced to borrow £40 at 12 per cent during the 1803–05 Maratha campaign to meet his immediate campaign expenses.[42]

James Campbell quickly recouped his losses when he secured a command in a nawab of Arcot's cavalry in 1774, with a monthly salary of £14. But a year after the Company banned what was, in effect, 'moonlighting' by its officers. Campbell's chance came in January 1787 when he obtained the lucrative contract to supply bullocks to the Madras army. 'I shall have a genteel enrichment,' he told his family, 'and a fair chance of returning to you in a very independent situation.' It did not turn out as he had wished; Cornwallis, with a mandate to eradicate corruption, refused to allow a serving officer to act as a private contractor. Campbell was obliged to resign on the eve of the 1790–92 Maratha war. He was disappointed, but by the time he returned to Scotland as a colonel at the beginning of 1797 he had been able to remit home a total of £25,000. This sum was, he felt, 'poor recompense considering the magnitude of the Concern and the trouble, torment and anguish of mind I underwent'.[43] He retired to Edinburgh's New Town, a minor but eventually contented nabob whose life revolved around convivial evenings in the New Club. He died in 1836.

Campbell had learned his soldiering by experience, but, by the time he left India, his successors were receiving professional training, not least in the languages of the men they commanded. The quality of this education varied. Baraset military college, sixteen miles from Calcutta, was a bear-garden where cadets, not satisfied with their daily allocation of a pint of wine, regularly drunk themselves silly. In or approaching this condition, they fought duels, terrorised the inhabitants of neighbouring villages, and made riotous forays into Calcutta. Their 'ungentlemanlike' conduct was explained by the presence among them of former militia officers from Britain who were often men of humble background – the sort of fellows whom Mrs Bennett wished to keep out of her younger daughters' way. In 1808 the Baraset cadets mutinied, were bloodlessly put down by the Governor-General's bodyguard and reform was set in hand. It failed, and the college was closed three years later.[44]

The faults of the Company's military academy at Addiscombe near Croydon were less glaring, but equally damaging to its army. Founded in 1809 as an Indian army equivalent to the new military college at Marlow (later Sandhurst), its curriculum included Hindustani along with such professional subjects as mathematics, fortification and surveying. Instruction was skimpy and rushed and Hindustani soon languished in the face of student hostility and slipshod teaching. The Hindustani professor appointed in 1829 was then aged nineteen and had never heard the language spoken. Generations of cadets embarked for India better versed in Latin than any native language, and the tendency of lecturers to cram meant that many were hazy about their regimental duties. For this preparation their families paid £65 a term in 1835.

During their voyage out, Addiscombe graduates discovered more of their new life and what was expected from them in a handbook written by a former Company officer. At all times and in all circumstances, they were to behave as gentlemen. Aboard ship, they were free to enjoy the society of its officers, but keep a distance from the crew to whom they were to show a 'pleasant condescending civility'. The rest of the advice was concerned with the expenses of servants, essential items for the wardrobe and the need to conduct themselves decorously. Nothing was said about their military duties or the men they would lead, save that aspirants ought to master Hindustani.[45] In India, the primary duty of the Company officer was 'to uphold the British character'.[46] The mainsprings of his conduct were love of country and the quest for reputation. 'The proper motives of a Soldier are Patriotism and love of Fame,' wrote Blacker. 'Of these excitements, neither can have any valuable operation without constant and attentive study of the Military Profession.'[47] Artillery and engineer officers certainly heeded Blacker's advice as a matter of practical necessity, but few cavalry or infantry officers investigated the arcane mysteries of the science of war or even concerned themselves with the everyday running of their regiments. As a former officer of the Madras army remarked in 1833, the undertaking of 'minor and trifling duties' diminished the standing of British officers in Indian eyes.[48]

Leadership was the chief preoccupation of the officer. The exercise of authority came naturally to a gentleman, whether over the British working classes, who filled the ranks of the white regiments, or sepoys. But the gentleman officer could not rely on instinctive authority alone in the thick of battle, he had to set an example of bravery and strong nerves. Both needed fostering, and this was conveniently and agreeably provided by stalking and shooting game of all kinds, from tigers to partridges. Hunting was the commonest diversion of officers who found time heavy on their hands and it was, as it had been in the Middle Ages, a preparation for war. During his frequent expeditions in pursuit of antelope, hyenas, foxes and wildfowl, Lieutenant Horward of the 13th Bombay NI convinced himself that he was fine-tuning his mettle for the moment when his sepoys would look to him for inspiration on the battlefield. Like his brothers-in-arms, he knew the interior strengths which distinguished the ideal officer: 'Unflinching courage must inspire him, imperturbable coolness must govern him.'[49] He was something of a fire-eater and anxious to make a name for himself, which was why he tried to secure a command in the newly-formed Sind Horse. It was 'the finest corps in India', full of 'rough and ready' tribal cavalry who were 'in action as steady as an old Waterloo man'.[50]

III

There was a tremendous romantic appeal in winning the respect and obedience of such free spirits. Commanding sepoys was a different matter, in so far as their submissiveness and response to authority were seen as inbred. 'It is rare indeed that they desert, and, from their temperate habits, they are easily managed,' wrote a British NCO who was used to the bloody-mindedness of his countrymen.[51] Always a volunteer, the high-caste Hindu or man from a Muslim warrior class was engaging to serve in a profession which had always been honoured in Indian society, even if this involved, as it inevitably did, fighting against his own people. The Indian fighting man had always commanded respect, often fear, and old military customs died hard. On campaign, the soldier was traditionally a law unto himself and, in spite of the threats and punishments delivered by their officers, many sepoys believed this was still so. During operations in Gujarat in

1809, sepoys stole silver bangles, nose rings and necklaces from villagers along the route of march and seized firewood for baking their chapattis.[52] A uniform also gave its wearer the right to throw his weight around: in 1831 Jemadar (junior officer) Ranjit Khan and his nephew, both Company cavalrymen on leave, grabbed two Bhopali villagers and ordered them to carry their baggage. When one refused he was slashed about the head with a tulwar. This high-handed pair had a bad record; they had committed a similar outrage before, were 'turbulent and mutinous' characters, and had beaten up a couple of sowars when their commanding officer had been on leave. For these reasons they were dimissed from the Company's service.[53] It says something for the Company's reputation for disciplining its men that the villagers made a complaint, although many similar cases may probably have passed unnoticed.

Soldiering carried with it dignity and offered a good livelihood and pension. But the rewards of wearing a red coat alone did not make a sepoy brave or steady in battle. This was the task of British officers, according to the conventional wisdom. They enkindled pride in their men, taught them discipline, and trained them to drill and shoot. Most importantly, and in this they had the advantage of working with men who were accustomed to hierarchy, they ruled their sepoys as fathers. Explaining the success of operations in Mysore in 1780–81, an officer remarked that it owed everything to men like himself who 'infuse a martial Spirit' into the sepoys, especially 'those Boys they breed up in their battalions'. The magical formula was an amalgam of impartiality, strictness and 'daily unremitting discipline' as instinctively understood by every Englishman.[54] It helped, the writer added, to get recruits young, which was easy enough since it was the custom in many battalions for sons and nephews to follow their fathers and uncles into the Company's service.

This was how Sita Ram joined up in about 1814. He had been brought into the battalion by his uncle, a jemadar, and was immediately struck by the friendly manner of the British officers. The adjutant warmly greeted the jemadar, enquired how he was, and touched his sword, a gesture of respect. Nearly fifty year later, Sita Ram remembered how the colonel had 'spoke very kindly to me, telling me to be good boy and imitate my uncle in everything'. It was easy to like the colonel; he was a portly, bald, red-faced old buffer who smoked a large hookah. But, as Sita Ram soon discovered, appearances were misleading. His commanding officer had shot nine tigers, a feat which made him a figure of awe among his sepoys.[55] Sita Ram had become part of what was, in effect, an extended family presided over by a benevolent patriarch in which everyone knew his duty and where discipline rested in great part upon the Indians' natural quietism. This ideal was striven after by Captain Charles Christie, who raised and trained the second battalion of the 25th Bengal NI 'with all the fondness of a parent and all the solicitude and pride of a soldier'. A bond of mutual respect and personal attachment was created, which was poignantly illustrated when Christie died on active service in April 1805 as his regiment was marching between Agra and Mathura. His corpse was carried by native officers and NCOs and the battalion followed, many men weeping as he was buried by the banks of the Jumma.[56]

A brother officer composed an encomium in which Christie became a dual paragon, combining the inseparable virtues of his countrymen and the doctrines of Christianity. 'Men, who, by such noble conduct, exalt the character of their nation among foreign Tribes and in distant regions of the globe', whatever other rewards they might receive, had the nobler satisfaction of having 'well fulfilled one great principle of Christian duty, by having considered and treated all mankind as brethren'.[57]

The backbone of every sepoy regiment was its Indian officers (jemadars and subadars) and NCOs. They had the daily supervision of the sepoy lines, were the eyes and ears of their white superiors and enforced discipline. Sepoys were always tried by native courts martial, in which Indian officers heard the evidence, assessed it and passed judgement. Their punishments were the same as those handed down to British miscreants: a sepoy who murdered a woman was sentenced to hang, looters got 500 lashes each, as did a servant who lost his temper and threw water over a British officer.[58] Ties of race and culture gave the Indian officer and NCO an intimate knowledge of the sepoys and an insight into their thinking denied the European. According to an anonymous jemadar petitioner, 'The secrets of the natives are to be learned from natives only' and would always remain hidden from British officers.[59] He was writing soon after the Vellore mutiny of July 1806, in which three battalions of Madras infantry had risen up and killed several of their British officers. It was a bolt from the blue which sent shudders through the entire British community in India, and left behind lingering misgivings about the trustworthiness of the native army.

The Vellore mutiny was a consequence of official ham-handedness coupled with complacency. In November 1805 the Madras commander-in-chief ordained that henceforward all Madras sepoys would shave their whiskers, remove their caste marks and earrings, and wear a European-style cylindrical shako with a leather cockade. At a stroke Hindu and Muslim sensibilities had been trampled on and, when there were objections, two NCOs were made scapegoats and given 900 lashes each. Uncowed by these punishments, the disgruntled soldiers were easy prey to agitators, including the exiled sons of Tipu Sultan and two Indian officers who planned a mass uprising. The conspiracy was exposed by a sepoy informer, Mustafa Beg, but his commanding officer ignored his warning, preferring instead the word of two native officers, both plotters, who assured him all was well in the sepoy lines.[60] The mutiny began in the early hours of 2 July 1806 with the murder of several officers and sleeping soldiers of the only British regiment in Vellore, the 69th. Many of the insurgents were interested only in what they could plunder; two sepoys broke into the bungalow of Colonel St John Fancourt, broke his furniture, but did not harm his wife Amelia and their small children. Later, one returned with some bread for her son, Charles, who was fretful, although afterwards there were lurid rumours that women and children had been slaughtered.[61] At dawn, the terrified Amelia heard the 'Huzzas' of the 19th Light Dragoons who had rushed to Vellore with a horse battery. After a brisk fight, the core of the mutineers had been either killed or disarmed. Some of the survivors were executed by being tied to the mouth of a cannon and blown apart, the punishment once prescribed by the Mughals for disloyalty.

The post-mortem which followed the Vellore mutiny revealed the fragility of the Company's regimental system. Sepoy discontent and intrigues had gone undetected because they had the covert support of Indian officers and NCOs. Many imagined that they were undervalued and they took umbrage easily at real and imagined slights from their British superiors. What was most unbearable, according to the jemadar petitioner, were the discrepancies between the status of the Indian and British junior officers. Better-paid Company officers could procure 'agreeable and beautiful women' as their mistresses, while Indian officers cannot 'obtain the Slave of a handsome woman' and were 'ashamed to show even our faces to fine women'. God had created black and white men equal and alike, and yet within the Company's army, they were divided by a vast gulf:

> Horses, palanquins, carriages, lofty houses, ample tents, couches, pleasure and enjoyment, gratification and delight, whatever yields joy is the portion of the European Officer; pain, wind,

cold and heat, fatigue and hardship, trouble and pain and the sacrifice of life itself is the portion of the Sepoy.[62]

It would be wrong to take this outburst from an embittered but articulate native soldier as a reflection of the mood throughout the Company's native army. At the same time, it would be naïve to imagine that the idealised paternal relationship between white officers and Indian soldiers was universal. Whatever his officers imagined, the sepoy was never an automaton who blindly obeyed. Soldiering might be his profession, but his religious faith remained central to his life and he protested whenever he imagined that it was being ignored or slighted. Hindu and Muslim holy men blessed regimental colours and sent armies into battle with prayers, and when sepoys charged their war-cry was '*Deen!*' (the Faith).[63] The sepoy was also sensitive about his martial honour and did not take kindly to the practice of always placing British troops in positions of the greatest danger. During the 1824–26 Burma war, Madras infantrymen complained of the 'unfair partiality' which deployed British troops in the front line of an attack, for they wanted to take the same risks as Europeans.[64]

Above all, the sepoy was always conscious of his elevated position within Indian society and, as a professional soldier, of the contractual obligations between himself and his employer. He was not easily put upon and had a tradition of collective bargaining. Between 1837 and 1846 there were seventeen mutinies among sepoys of the Madras army.[65] For the most part these were demonstrations about alleged maltreatment by officers and shortfalls in pay and allowances, always preoccupations among men who had wives and families to support. Underlying these outbreaks was a deep-rooted sense of fair play and a belief that it was shared by their officers. On hearing that their *batta* (campaign allowance) had been withdrawn in 1849, sowars of the 6th Madras light cavalry refused to mount, hurled themselves to the ground, scattered dust on their heads and cursed their colonel and his family. He had, as their behaviour indicated, driven them to break their oaths as soldiers and dishonour themselves. Some of their European officers were sympathetic, paying a Eurasian lawyer to represent the accused at the subsequent court martial.[66] The incident caught the eye of the commander-in-chief, the Duke of Wellington. Following the sound maxim that there was no such thing as bad men, only bad officers, he ordered the Madras commander-in-chief, the Marquess of Tweeddale, back to London to explain himself. He was not re-appointed to an Indian command.

Blame in such cases usually passed, directly or indirectly, to officers who had neglected their responsibilities or lost touch with their men. They had also succumbed to 'those feelings of repulsiveness' towards Indian customs and religious observances which the tolerant Major Beaven of the Madras army detected among his colleagues in the 1810s and 1820s.[67] There was also a new coldness and arrogance among younger British officers which was sensed by the jemadar who listed his and his colleagues' grievances after Vellore.[68] Two handbooks produced for junior Company officers in 1820 and 1833 confirm this impression of frosty hauteur, with pages crammed with hints as to how an officer ought to behave among his peers in the isolation of the mess and next to nothing on how to handle the sepoy. Unless he was ambitious and seeking a political post, an officer did not feel impelled to master the language of his men, and early-Victorian, schoolroom evangelical bigotry made him increasingly hostile towards India's religions. Under pressure from missionaries, religious cranks and busybodies in Britain, the Company was forced to ban officers from attending Hindu festivals and withdraw permission for the use of its flags and cannon in these celebrations. This trend towards the segregation of officers and sepoys was regretted by General Sir George Pollock, whose service record stretched from the 1803–05 Maratha war to the 1842 Afghan campaign. In 1853 he told a Commons select committee that the modern officer appeared indifferent to the welfare and customs of the sepoys and, in consequence, enjoyed far less affection than his predecessors.[69]

No one seemed to mind too much, for no remedies were suggested. After all, the sepoy, despite occasional obstreperous outbursts, appeared a docile enough creature, glad to hazard his life for comparatively good wages and a Company pension. And he would continue do so as long as British soldiers showed him the way to win battles.

IV

Conditions of service were far less agreeable for the British ranker. Whether in the Company's or the government's army, he came from the British or Irish working class. Unskilled men predominated; nearly all the 389 men of the 4th Bombay European battalion in 1786 gave their previous occupation as labourer, although there was a sprinkling of craftsmen, including cordwainers and butchers. Most were small by today's standards, with heights of between 5′ 2″ and 5′ 5″, which makes it hard to understand why they had such a presence on a battlefield.[70] Sixty years later, Captain Fane noticed that six-foot sepoy grenadiers dwarfed most British soldiers.[71]

Unlike his officer, the ranker seldom saw soldiering as a vocation. It was a last resort, grasped in moments of economic desperation and in the knowledge that respectable society still saw a red coat as a mark of those without moral backbone. Many recruits were men who dipped in and out of the margins of delinquency. To make sure he did not slip back into his old ways and to keep him biddable and sober, the British soldier was disciplined by the lash. Lieutenant Blackwell was dismayed when confronted with a party of newly-enlisted men from the 47th Regiment, just arrived from England in 1828. 'There is scarcely a sober man at present in the Corps, and drunkenness under every stage and form presents itself to view wherever you turn. Some are crying drunk, some laughing drunk, and some roaring drunk.' These future defenders of the Raj were swearing foully and demanding their 25-rupee allowance, presumably to buy more liquor.[72] Private Ryder of the 32nd, the son of the Waterloo veteran and member of the respectable working class, was appalled by his fellow rookies when they assembled at the Bull Inn in Nottingham in the summer of 1845. 'I was ashamed of being among them, for they were a dirty, ragged lot of blackguards – some of them nearly drunk.' Many would rue having taken the Queen's shilling and, when in India, Ryder 'heard men curse the country and everything in it'.[73]

There was much for Ryder's companions to execrate. During the monsoon season their Chinsurah barrack walls ran with water and cholera was about. The hot season in Meerut brought fresh torments: 'Thousands upon thousands of flies would be continually buzzing about us, so that one has sufficient to do to keep them off, and if one's mouth was open, they would soon fill it, with a great many other insects.' Not everyone was uncomfortable and disgruntled. In 1838, Private Jonathan Cottrill of the 39th told his parents in Birmingham that India was a healthy country where food was cheap and Agra was 'the noblest place in the East'. For all its marvels, soldiering in India was not a perfect life and he was saving up to buy himself out; he died in 1844, having accumulated £8.[74] Another Midlander, George Tookey of the 14th Light Dragoons, was delighted by life in the cavalry barracks at Chinsurah, where native servants were plentiful and duties few. 'We are leading a very easy life here, we take no drill and the blacks clean our boots and spurs and everything else, in short we are gentlemen.' And well-fed gentlemen too, for on Christmas Day 1846 they dined on roast beef, duck and fowl, and were allowed a bottle of wine each.[75]

The coincidence of abundant spare time and the free availability of cheap liquor was a permanent threat to the stamina and, in many cases, the lives of British soldiers. With drill limited to nine hours a week, the soldier was free to roam about his cantonment and its adjacent town. He usually gravitated towards one of his regimental bazaar's three toddy sellers and got drunk. To judge by the court martial statistics, he might steal to raise more cash, quarrel with Indian shopkeepers and brawl with anyone who crossed his path. The drinking soldier's capacity was gargantuan. The 710 men of the 26th Regiment, stationed at Fort William, Calcutta, consumed 5,320 gallons of *arrack* (a locally distilled rice liquor), 220 gallons of brandy and 249 of gin together with 207 hogsheads (each containing fifty-two and a half gallons) of beer during 1833. In 1835, the 674 customers of 49th Regiment's canteen drank 7,216 gallons of arrack, 177 of brandy and 144 of gin. There were eighteen deaths from alcoholism, but the total may have been higher, for cirrhosis and hepatitis were also the price of gross intemperance.[76] The treatment for delirium tremens may also have added to its victims; in 1841 an infantry officer admitted to the Calcutta European Hospital died after thirteen hours during which he was successively prescribed measures of brandy, camphor, tartar emetic, opium and an enema.[77] The pattern of heavy drinking was identical among the Company's European troops. Out of the 357 offences committed by men from the Madras European battalion, two-thirds involved drunkenness and half were committed by men who were officially classified as habitual drunkards.[78]

The military authorities were at their wits' end to cope with an addiction which led to a continual haemorrhage of the very soldiers upon whom the security of the Raj depended. Largely through the efforts of regimental doctors and the slow spread of army temperance societies, the average annual wastage rate was held down to 4 per cent during the 1830s and 1840s. Better could not be hoped for, as it was understood that the army's raw material contained a large share of chronically incontinent men who, like the rest of the class they sprang from, were insensible to reasoned persuasion. Some blame was placed on the cheap rum sold on board India-bound ships which, as it were, converted to spirits men who hitherto had been satisfied by beer. One answer in the 1820s was the substitution of Cape wine for liquor, but this scheme made little headway in spite of

Wellington's blessing.[79] Marriage or regular cohabitation with an Indian or Eurasian girl was seen as a sobering influence, but it created new problems in the form of children who, with their mothers, would have to be shipped back to Britain when a regiment's Indian tour of duty ended.[80]

Monogamy in some form was also a means of preventing another consequence of the common soldier's refusal to moderate his appetites, venereal diseases. Between 1827 and 1833 the infection rate among British soldiers in Bengal fluctuated between 16 and 31 per cent as a consequence of what one official called 'promiscuous and hazardous intercourse with profligate women of the bazaar'.[81] Nearly all infected recovered, but treatment and convalescence took a man out of the ranks for several weeks, which meant that at any given time nearly every British regiment was under-strength by as much as a quarter.

European resistance to indigenous diseases was less than Indian. Sixty-one per cent of the Madras army European soldiers suffered from what was called 'intermittent fever' (i.e. malaria) during the 1840s compared to 28 per cent of sepoys.[82] Cholera did not discriminate and probably accounted for the most fatalities among European troops during this period. They called it Jack Morbus, and in the summer of 1819 it killed sixteen men from the 26th Regiment and forty-four from the 14th. Perhaps the worst outbreak was in Karachi in 1846 when 385 men, women and children attached to the 86th Regiment died in ten days.[83]

No one then knew how cholera was caused or transmitted. As with fevers, it was imagined that contagion was carried in the air, which was why contact with Indian villagers along its route of march was blamed for the epidemic in the 49th Regiment in 1839.[84] The same fiction made army doctors ensure that Indian hospitals were well ventilated, and this was seen as one explanation for the relatively high recovery rate among soldiers.[85] During the 1830s it was between 30 and 40 per cent, which compared well with the 50 per cent achieved by London and provincial hospitals during the 1853–54 epidemic.[86] This success rate owed something to soldiers usually being treated during the first phases of their infection. Among the survivors were a boatload of the 21st Light Dragoons whom an unknown trooper of the 11th Light Dragoons encountered on his way to Cawnpore in 1819. 'They were yellow and fleshless,' he noted. He also heard the latrine rumour which alleged that men who contracted the disease and went on drinking as heavily as before had the best chance of recovery. This self-medication proved as efficacious as any of the hospital remedies, for he later survived an attack by drinking three bottles of Cape wine.[87]

Fevers and excessive drinking sapped a soldier's strength. They made him vulnerable to fatigue and the harsh vagaries of the Indian climate. Temperatures of 110 degrees in the summer of 1804 brought down sepoys as well as British soldiers and, combined with dust storms and typhoons, forced Lake to pull his army back to Cawnpore. Casualties during this march totalled 300, as many as might have been suffered storming a fort or forcing a Maratha position.[88] 'You can form no idea of the misery there is attached to a soldier's life in this country,' Henry Plumb of the 39th told his parents as he trudged across the Punjab in March 1849. Even a night of heavy drinking with comrades of the 29th could not compensate for the cold nights, the dust and makeshift meals of chappatis and raw turnips.[89]

Plumb kept going because he hoped to save enough to buy himself out of the army, a prospect which may have sustained many others. There was also hatred of the enemy and, with it, a sense of racial superiority. There was 'bitter Animosity, or rather Antipathy, at all times, and especially in war times' felt by white troops against the natives, thought James Young during the siege of Deeg.[90] Nonetheless, the British soldier always treated the sepoy as a brother-in-arms and the feeling was warmly reciprocated. Indian soldiers helped drunken British comrades evade provost-marshals' patrols. When a sepoy collapsed with the first stages of cholera during the 1817–18 Maratha war, a private of the 87th, also infected, gave him his palanquin. Both men later died.[91] There was also patriotism. Before an engagement near Multan, Private Ryder thought of England and said the prayers his mother had taught him. He also felt fear, but it evaporated as he went into battle and when it was over he recalled: 'Nothing can be a grander sight than to see a field of victory carried by the point of a British bayonet.'[92] The regimental band of the 52nd Regiment played 'Britons Strike Home' during the assault on a Mysorean fort in 1792 to encourage the storming party to think of their nation and glory.[93]

In all likelihood their minds were probably on what lay in store for them. For most rankers the prospect of prize money meant more than the glory which was the prerogative of their officers. Often with the help of amanuenses, for many were illiterate, veterans tenaciously pursued their rights. Corporal Richard Tolney of the 8th Light Dragoons, a veteran of the 1803–05 Maratha war, was badgering the Company in 1817 for his share:

I ham a poor man and Got a Large family I should Be Glad to

have itt if is ever so little which tis well known by my officers that I fought hard for itt.[94]

Others forewarded the claims of dead kinsmen. 'I am a blind woman of 74 years of age' declared 'the Widow Hamilton' of Glasgow, who asked for what was due to her son, who had fought with the 74th Highlanders under Wellesley in the Deccan. She signed with a cross and her application was endorsed by her minister. James Allen, 'a poor man and present in the workhouse', wrote from Birmingham for the share of his son, a Company gunner who had been drowned in 1813. The amounts involved were tiny by comparison with those allocated to officers, but nonetheless they were welcome windfalls for poor men and women. An infantryman got £4 from the taking of Bharatpur (the equivalent of eight weeks' wages for a labourer), but only five shillings (25p) from the spoils of Ghazni, which had been thoroughly looted before the prize agents got to work.[95] It did, however, take time for the cash to be delivered. The widow and son of Private Bennett of the 39th had to wait twenty years to receive his portion (£4 9 shillings [£4.45p]) of the prize money from the 1834 Coorg campaign.[96]

The wealth of India fell slowly and in droplets to the poor. Many did not bother to wait and snatched every opportunity to loot. After the capture of Bharatpur, British soldiers surged into the town, grabbing whatever they could. It had been a hard-drinking campaign, despite frequent floggings of men found drunk on duty, and plunderers were happy to exchange gold coins worth £2 each for a glass of brandy.[97]

V

For all his moral infirmities, the British soldier was an efficient fighting machine. His officers, NCOs and the flogging triangles saw to that. Against him were Indian armies which ranged from well-disciplined, European-trained units with modern arms to the equivalent of a medi-aeval host. Major Birom was struck by the exotic magnificence of the Maratha army which appeared, as allies, during the march on Seringapatam in 1792. Chiefs rode on elephants preceded by musicians and poets who recited the marvellous exploits of their masters. There were cavalry-men (some in mail), pikemen, banners and a continual barrage of *feux de joie* from matchlockmen and musketeers. 'A spectacle so wild and irregular, yet so grand and interesting, resembled more the visions of romance than any assemblage that can have supposed to have existence in real life.'[98] This fairy-tale assembly of fighting men was, in fact, an army in a state of transition from the mediaeval to the modern, a phase which European forces had passed through in the sixteenth century.

Indian military thought in this period wavered between modernism and conservatism. The modernists were the Maratha princes and Ranjit Singh, who endeavoured to transform their armies into forces which relied wholly on firepower. But they did not jettison the old; the Marathas and Sikhs still fielded the sort of troops which so struck the imagination of Major Birom. The result was a sort of military hybrid, with 'modern' infantrymen and gunners placed alongside traditional mounted and foot units. It was as if Wellington's forces at Waterloo had been substantially filled out with billmen and armoured knights from Henry V's army. What might be called the 'mediaeval' elements of the Indian princely armies proved little more than a liability on the battlefield.

More importantly, the partial adoption of European military technology was not accompanied by a revolution in tactics or the creation of a professional officer corps. Indian princes preferred to direct battles in person rather than place overall command in the hands of their hired European professionals, who understood modern tactics. Time and time again, Indian commanders chose static warfare rather than use their superiority in numbers for offensives. Elaborate and precise battlefield manoeuvres required disciplined troops, and officers who knew their business and were willing to gamble. Only the Sikhs possessed the first two, but they were hamstrung by generals who refused to take risks. Sitting tight and trusting in a numerical superiority of artillery and men made for good morale, up to a point. But once the British, undeterred by the odds and the weight of shot, were on the verge of breaking through their enemy's line, Indian confidence usually dissolved.

In purely technical terms, the Company had two advantages. All its infantrymen were armed with smoothbore, muzzle-loading, flintlock 'Brown Bess' muskets and were trained to fire synchronised volleys at close range at a rate of between three and four rounds per minute. Intensity of fire rather than accuracy was what counted. Tests undertaken in 1838 revealed that only three-quarters of rounds fired from a range of 150 yards hit a target roughly thirty-three feet square. Within the next four years the flintlock mechanism was replaced by the percussion cap, which reduced the numbers of misfires, but the new musket was introduced slowly in

India. With all its defects, the musket was always a better firearm than the traditional Indian matchlock, a cumbersome weapon which had a lower rate of fire and required its user to carry a slow-burning match. It fired slugs and was only effective at close range. Nevertheless, it remained in use for want of anything better throughout this period; some Sikh auxiliary units were still armed with matchlocks in 1848–49. The Company's other advantage was its nimble and adroitly handled six- and nine-pounder horse batteries. Their mobility enabled them to get to within grape-shot range (200–300 yards) and open fire with the quilt-wrapped bundles of shot which were probably the most lethal projectile on the battlefield.

All artillery was still muzzle-loading and at long ranges fired only round shot, although after 1800 some progress was being made with fused, explosive shells (fired from howitzers) and shrapnel which exploded in mid-air. By and large this was not a period of innovation, although Indian artillerymen experimented with muskets mounted side by side on a frame and fired one after another. As well as this primitive machine-gun, there were war rockets fired in quick succession. 'Showers' of these missiles were fired by the Marathas during fighting around Poona at the end of 1817, but appear to have had no effect.[99] Drawings of them in use suggest that they were a variation of the familiar firework-type rocket with a warhead. The British equivalent was the Congreve rocket, a wayward projectile with a fiery tail and an explosive warhead. They were used to considerable effect at Sobraon, where they stampeded Sikh horsemen, but those sent from the Firozpur magazine during the siege of Multan all proved duds.[100]

In the broad terms of military technology the period which witnessed the British conquest of India was one of comparative stagnation. Unlike British forces in Africa or on the North-West Frontier during the last quarter of the century, the Company's army did not benefit from the scientific and technical innovations which were slowly gathering pace in Europe. The Industrial Revolution may have provided the Company with mass-produced weaponry, but it was not markedly superior to that of its enemies. It was only after India had been subdued that the balance of power shifted decisively: in 1851 British troops were equipped with the Minié rifle, which was accurate up to a thousand yards; in 1857 Company gunners were being armed with Colt revolvers, and in 1860 an Anglo-Indian army in China used long-range, shell-firing Armstrong cannon.[101]

The logistics of the Company's army were always superior to its opponents, although human competence being what it was, there were breakdowns in supply during every campaign. The worst example was in

1805, during the first siege of Bharatpur, when there were not enough heavy guns to knock down the walls, forcing Lake to use his men as human battering rams with horrendous results. The strength of the Company's logistics was a ready and ample supply of money. It could always pay its suppliers and labourers in cash drawn from the land revenues from the territories under its control and, as it did, albeit unwillingly, during the 1803–05 Maratha war, raise capital on the London money markets on the security of future income from taxation.

Money was the lubricant of war and without it campaigns ground to a halt. The brave and high-spirited Beema Baee, the twenty-year-old daughter of Jaswant Rao Holkar, rode with lance and tulwar at the head of 2,500 men during the 1817–18 Maratha war. She told a British officer that she was fighting to defend her country and recover her property, but was forced to throw in the sponge because she ran out of money. She and her remaining 200 followers were immediately given 200 rupees a day.[102] War and diplomacy went hand in hand when the Company drew up peace treaties with princes whose military efforts had brought them to the brink of bankruptcy. An Indian ruler might retain what passed for independence, but his future ability to wage war was curtailed by the loss of revenues. During a dearth during the Mysore campaign of 1790–92, Tipu's commissaries took their grain and rice to the Company's lines, where they were paid in hard cash rather than credit notes.[103] His own soldiers must have gone hungry, or else fended for themselves. The lure of ready money attracted the professional military victuallers, the *brinjaris*, to Cornwallis's camp rather than Tipu's. With over 50,000 transport bullocks and access to the grain and rice dealers of Karnataka, the brinjaris supplied most of the army's rations.[104]

Silver rupees purchased the draft bullocks vital for an army's logistics. A six-pounder gun required 35 bullocks to pull it and a further 105 for fodder. A 24-pounder siege cannon and its eight tumbrils of powder and shot were drawn by 155 bullocks with 620 carrying fodder.[105] The wherewithal for horse and rider meant that there were six bullocks for every cavalryman and, in an age when officers required huge tents, their mistresses, servants and every form of creature comfort, their baggage allowance was at least six bullocks.[106] Wastage was enormous: over 14,000 bullocks died during the 1790–92 Mysore war and probably greater numbers of pack camels perished during the 1838–39 invasion of Afghanistan. Camels were restricted to operations in northern India and were attractive to the budget-conscious military authorities because they cost only three rupees a month to feed. It was estimated that four camels could carry the load of one elephant which, while it was more durable and versatile, was far more expensive to maintain. Beasts purchased during the 1848–49 Sikh war cost 515 rupees each, and the cost of their feed was 35 rupees a month.[107] What mattered of course was that in an emergency the Company's representatives could buy as many elephants or anything else that was needed to sustain an army in the field.

The administrative machinery which oversaw the Company army's wartime logistics existed on an *ad hoc* basis, save when it came to auditing accounts. There was no permanent general staff of specialist officers, and the daily business of supplies and victualling were usually handled at a regimental level. There were hints that military contractors and purveyors made fortunes through fraud, but somehow the system worked. For this reason and the instinctive conservatism of the military high command, it was allowed to continue.

The absence of an Indian central intelligence agency was even more remarkable, given the perpetual nervousness about security. Both the military and also the civilian authorities preferred an idiosyncratic system which always managed to deliver what was needed at the right time. In the broadest sense, every Briton abroad in India was a spy, expected to use his eyes and ears and record what he had seen and heard. Surveys of newly-annexed districts give copious details of resources which might be useful in wartime, and roads were judged according to their ability to withstand the passage of artillery and military transport. The same applied to Indian fortifications, which were sketched and measured. Even so, armies sometimes had to march blindly, relying on cavalry patrols to discover the way ahead. At Assaye, the position of the ford by which his army crossed a river was discovered by Wellesley, who rightly guessed that it would be beside a spot where a few houses were visible. It was an intrepid sepoy volunteer, Ramdin Missir, who tested the depth of the fords across the Chenab and spied out the Sikh position on the other bank in December 1848. He was promoted to *naik* (corporal), a somewhat niggardly reward for a dangerous mission.[108]

Every British resident at an Indian court ran his own espionage system. It comprised a network of native spies, informers and 'writers' who compiled newsletters based upon local gossip and their own observation. In 1816–17 Montstuart Elphinstone in Poona employed a 'broker' who collected and collated intelligence from a variety of sources. Disguised agents were sent into Maratha territory to track down Trimbakji Danglia, the focus of anti-British influence in the peshwa's court, after he fled Poona. He was found and kept under surveillance by these spies and various writers.[109] There were also eavesdroppers like the ex-servant of the Gaikwar (literally 'keeper of the cow') of Baroda, who exposed details of his master's covert anti-British activities to the assistant resident in 1812.[110] Intelligence of this kind, provided by agents in a prince's confidence, led to the resident at Nagpur being forewarned of the raja's duplicity in November 1817.[111]

The Baroda informer seems to have been a disgruntled courtier who had been slighted in some way. An Indian court was an open society in which jealousies and tittle-tattle abounded, and princes lived a greater part of their lives under public scrutiny. State secrets were, therefore, if not common knowledge, easily procureable. Field intelligence reports compiled during the summer of 1805 reveal that Company agents had penetrated the inner councils of Jaswant Rao Holkar and the rajas of Bharatpur and Jaipur. There were accounts of conversations between princes, the numbers of soldiers they were mustering, their financial difficulties and secret correspondence.[112] Some of this information came from spies who appear to have been based permanently in the Maratha camps and some from hircarras. Hircarras were professional, freelance secret servicemen, often equipped either with fast horses or camels, who entered the enemy's camp, mingled with the crowds there and snooped around. Wellesley employed them in the Deccan in 1803–04, with Montstuart Elphinstone as his translator. Those who provided verifiable and useful intelligence were well paid, those who concocted tales were whipped. Hircarras faced other dangers; those taken around Deeg in 1804 were mutilated by the Marathas.[113]

Some officers showed a flair for intelligence work. Major Henry Broadfoot learned the trade of spymaster during the Afghan campaign, when he was attached to Sale's brigade based in Jalalabad. 'Through a native channel' he was the first to hear of Macnaghten's murder, but was inclined to treat the story as preposterous until it was confirmed by a more reliable spy from Kabul, whom he identified as a commissary servant. Another informer was an Afghan soldier in Shah Shuja's army whose brother was Broadfoot's jemadar.[114] Given the distances involved and the season of the year, front-line intelligence was circulated with astonishing speed. It took just over six weeks for details of events in Kabul between 9 and 21 November 1841 to reach the Governor of Bombay, who immediately forwarded them to London.[115]

The willingness of hundreds of Indians to collaborate with the British was of immeasurable value to men like Broadfoot. Spying was not considered a disreputable occupation; a Rajasthan villager gave his occupation as 'police spy' for a tax return of 1817.[116] The fickleness of his countrymen when it came to providing intelligence for cash was appreciated by Baji Rao, the fugitive Maratha peshwa, at the end of 1817. Pursued by a British column, he asked village headmen for the best route to follow and, when they told him, took a different path. He knew that these men, all his former subjects, would, when asked, point the British in the direction they believed he had taken.[117]

In defeat, Baji Rao had at last understood the mystery of why the British were conquering India. They could always rely on the active collaboration of thousands of Indians who, for a variety of reasons, were willing to co-operate with those whom seemed destined to become their new masters. And yet, as these new rulers were all too aware, this support was conditional on the knowledge that the Company's army was unbeatable. For both Hindus and Muslims, this success in war was interpreted as a mark of some Divine favour, just it did for those Christians who considered that British paramountcy in India was an expression of God's Providence. Whether or not divinely assisted, the victories won between 1784 and 1856 decided the future of India for the next hundred years, and for that reason alone were among the most outstanding achievements of any army at any time. Gough was right when he congratulated his men for having triumphed where Alexander had failed, but he would have been among the first to admit that there had been some close-run things.

PART THREE

THE RAJ CONSOLIDATED: 1784–1856

1

European Gentlemen: India's New Ruling Class

I

Charles Lord Cornwallis was in every way a model Governor-General. He was an upright, well-intentioned soldier whose interior life had been touched by the ideals of contemporary Evangelical Christianity. These had taught him that the service of God was also the service of mankind, and good done in India could bring personal redemption as well as happiness to others. His successors, Minto, Hastings, Lord William Bentinck, Auckland, Hardinge and the Earl of Dalhousie were all, in different ways, inspired by the same creed. High-principled aristocrats from Britain's political élite, they were, in a sense, on loan to India, where they set the moral and social tone of the administration.

They saw themselves not as India's conquerors but as its emancipators. In one celebrated public gesture, Cornwallis was able to reveal to the world the new spirit which animated him and would, in time, regenerate India. After his victory at Seringapatam in 1792, he took into his custody Tipu Sultan's ten- and eight-year-old sons, welcoming them with a grace and tenderness which moved onlookers. He 'received the boys as if they had been his sons' in a scene which would soon become stamped on the British consciousness. Cornwallis had invited Robert Home, an artist, to accompany him during the Mysore war and make sketches for future publication. Home's most ambitious work showed the surrender of the

boys and was exhibited at the Royal Academy in 1797. The public imagination was stirred by a painting which appealed to the current taste for the
exotic – there were several elephants – and to Romantic sentiment.[1] The
picture was also an allegory; the weak, helpless and bewildered were being
brought under the strong, paternal arm of a government which promised
its subjects peace, justice and enlightenment. The same symbolism appears
on a massive canvas commissioned by Lord Combermere after his capture
of Bharatpur in 1826. The mounted general extends an open hand of
friendship and protection to downcast women, children and elderly men
as his staff look on benevolently.[2] This was not entirely artistic licence, for
a group of well-dressed women had in fact been rescued from marauders
by a party of British cavalrymen soon after the fortress had fallen.[3]

The noble theme of deliverance was taken up by the Marquess Wellesley
when he declared in 1800 that the British governed 'the most opulent,
flourishing part of India, in which property, life, civil order and liberty are
more secure, and the people enjoy a larger proportion of good government
than any other country in this quarter of the globe'.[4] This state of affairs
could only be sustained through the exertions of men who were honest,
fairminded and dedicated. These virtues were the ingredients of what the
Indian administrator Charles Metcalfe once called 'the characteristic excellence of British humanity', a quality which, he was sure, commanded
respect and emulation among Indians.[5] Nonetheless, nobody expected
that ruling India was merely an exercise in lofty altruism. The Marquess
Wellesley, who laid the foundations of the new administration, insisted that
officials should be allowed 'the means of acquiring a competent fortune'
with which they could return home.[6] He had in mind money saved from
generous salaries and allowances, rather than the profits of corruption.

As Governor-General he did all he could to stamp out old habits, but
they died hard and slowly. In 1795, Thomas Munro told his father that it
was common for collectors to collude with Indian tax farmers and pocket
revenues.[7] This explains why, in 1800, Alexander Read confided to a
friend that 'a man is certain to make a fortune' when he is appointed a collector. But he was not immune from the new idealism, for he added as an
afterthought that the post 'is of all others the most satisfying to a humane
mind – to think that you have it in your power constantly to make a multitude of people happy by an attention to their complaints'.[8] William
Brodie, who had entered the Company's service as a magistrate in 1795,
clung to the old ways. He accepted various presents from suitors, including
a diamond ring and an elephant, and was investigated by his superiors, who

suspected graft. Brodie defended himself clumsily, alleging first that the elephant had been borrowed for a hunting trip and then, giving the lie to this, claimed that other officials took similar favours. He was sacked in 1809 with a tart reminder that receiving gifts 'however customary, it is not, we believe, usual, and is not requisite or proper'.[9] Indians thought otherwise and it took time for them to understand the nature of their new rulers. In 1846, James Abbott was given 280 rupees and some food by a Sikh official on the look-out for a favour. Having given the normal fee to the *munshi* (interpreter) who had delivered the bribe, Abbott forwarded the residue to the government coffers in Lahore.[10]

The imposition of integrity had been one of Wellesley's principal objectives. During his first year as Governor-General he had cast his eye over the officials in Bengal and been appalled. 'Sloth, indolence, low debauchery and vulgarity' prevailed everywhere, because of a general relaxation of standards and willingness to embrace native habits. The guilty men were, in theory at least, men from gentlemanly backgrounds, for even the lowliest Company official or officer needed £300–£400 in cash to pay for his passage, kit and setting up a household. What the Marquess had uncovered were lapsed gentlemen. Their undoing was the consequence of the Company's insistence that each new recruit spent some time as a writer, undertaking what Wellesley called the 'menial, laborious, unwholesome and unprofitable duty of a mere copying clerk'.[11] Trade and government did not mix, and when they did, the result was a community of the 'ignorant, rude, familiar and stupid', whom the Marquess treated with disdain.[12]

Wellesley was a man on the move and the direction was upwards. He saw his governor-generalship as a springboard for an illustrious career in British politics. He was an Anglo-Irish peer, and therefore very touchy on all matters of rank and deference, for his kind were below the English and Scottish nobility in precedence. This may explain his exaggerated aloofness and passionate, old guard Toryism, whose principles guided his reorganisation of India's government. Like Britain, it could only be administered properly if authority were concentrated in the hands of gentlemen like himself, who were born to rule. 'I wish India to be ruled from the palace not a counting house, with the ideas of a Prince, not those of a retail dealer in muslins and indigo,' he once wrote. At the same time as pushing back the frontiers of British India, Wellesley threw himself into the reform of its government.

He relied heavily on the ideals he had learned at Eton from its provost, Dr Edward Barnard. During the 1770s, Wellesley had been one of a constellation of extremely able, high-born young men whom Barnard had singled out and cherished as future political leaders.[13] The Marquess wanted to cultivate a similar circle of talented, self-confident and self-possessed gentlemen who would be specially trained for the highest offices of state. The upshot was Fort William College near Calcutta, which was founded by Wellesley in 1800. He framed its curriculum, which included courses in Indian languages, culture and history. Most importantly for Wellesley, the aspirant proconsuls would be instructed in the 'sound and correct principles of religion and government', that is as preached by the Church of England and upheld by the Tory party. Lecturers would instil 'a sense of moral duty, and teach those who fill important stations, that the great public duties which they are called upon to execute in India, are not of a less sacred nature than duties of similar situations in their own country'.[14] There was clearly no longer any place for businessmen in the running of India, and directors objected strenuously to Wellesley's plan. But the Board of Control prevailed and Fort William College went ahead.

Wellesley took a keen interest in his college and the progress of its pupils, whom he admitted into his intimate circle. One so honoured, Charles Metcalfe, noted in his diary that, 'Such civility from Lord Wellesley is no common thing.' The Marquess regularly attended the graduation ceremonies at the college and was no doubt gratified to hear that the subject chosen for the Persian disputation in 1802 was: 'The Natives of India under British Government enjoy a far greater degree of tranquillity, security and happiness, than any former government.'[15] Sadly, he knew no Persian. On these occasions, cash prizes were handed out to outstanding cadets, a practice which was eventually extended to the Company's military academy at Addiscombe and Imperial Service College (now Haileybury school, Hertfordshire), which, by the 1840s, had become a 'feeder' school for the Indian army and civil service.

Thanks to Wellesley, ruling India had become a vocation of an élite. Along with the church, the armed services and the law, it was a profession that could be pursued by gentlemen without loss of dignity or status. Furthermore, the Marquess had created an institution which fostered a powerful sense of purpose, a shared outlook and close personal bonds between its alumni. He had also set a pattern which would be followed by future high-ranking proconsuls, such as Sir Henry Lawrence, who surrounded themselves with young disciples whom they trained as administrators. As in Fort William College, they passed through more than a mere apprenticeship in the techniques of government; they absorbed the ideals of their master and, through his experience, gained a recondite knowledge of the ways of Indians.

Those who learned the arts of government in India were gentlemen. In 1800 the word carried no connotations of gentleness; rather, it denoted birth and upbringing. Both enabled a young man to acquire manners, learning and a sense of his place in the world and what it expected from him. His inner moral code and conduct in society were shaped by a close study of Greek and Roman literature which, for the great part, concerned the deeds of heroes who were men of noble birth like himself. Tales of their perseverance, fearlessness, honour and love of their native land provided models for the gentleman's future behaviour. Rome, in particular, was a shining example of a civilising empire whose achievements rested on the exploits of its natural leaders. It was no accident of fashion that so many eighteenth- and early-nineteenth-century commanders and proconsuls were portrayed on their monuments as Roman senators or generals. This is how General Sir Samuel Auchmuty appears on his marble wall tomb in St Patrick's Cathedral, Dublin. He died in 1824, having commanded armies in North America, India and Ireland, and appears as a second Scipio with imperturbable and imperious features.

Church memorials broadcast the virtues which distinguished a gentleman. In Bath abbey, the epitaph of Colonel Alexander Champion of the Bengal army announces that 'his Zeal, Courage and Success were ever tempered by humanity' and that in his dealings with the world he was 'plain, open and unaffected'. This paragon died in 1793, during a period when the public image of the gentleman was changing. As the Romantic and Evangelical movements were capturing the imaginations and souls of the upper and middle classes, the concept of the gentleman was reappraised. He was now expected to be more than just a gallant dandy with an over-developed sense of his own superiority and personal honour. 'True courage blended with humanity' were the essence of the gentleman, according to Piers Egan, historian of the fashionable sport of boxing. As might be expected, he set great store by manliness and feared that, without a régime of rigorous exercise, 'The English character may get too *refined* and the *thorough-bred* bulldog degenerate into the *whining* puppy.'[16] 'Character for honour' was the inner hallmark of the true gentlemen, an army officer wrote in 1827. Social distinction, he added, brought with it obligations for, 'Society very justly expects from all who move in a certain rank, an amenity of manners, and fair, manly and upright lines of conduct in the general intercourse and transactions of life.'[17]

The public schools tempered the cultivation of these noble qualities with a preparation for the realities of the unkind world. Charles Metcalfe, the son of a nabob, described Eton in the 1790s as a 'humble imitation of the world'. Within this microcosm, he discovered that 'every vice and every virtue which we meet in the world is practised, although in miniature, every deception is triflingly displayed which one would be open to in life.'[18] This experience did not make him or men like him unreceptive to idealism, far from it, but it did make them acutely aware of the darker side of human nature. Passage through a public school was a valuable preparation for the daily tasks of an India administrator.

From the beginning, the Raj placed its faith in men before measures. If the men struck the right note, then the Indians would accept the system they brought with them. This enkindling of trust, even friendship, could only be accomplished by a gentleman. First impressions were vital, according to the resident in Delhi who, in 1807, reminded his subordinates that:

> By bringing European gentlemen into direct and immediate contact with those of our new subjects who are yet unacquainted with our character, their minds would be conciliated and a groundwork laid for the introduction of our financial and judicial system.[19]

The gentleman embodied the humane spirit and integrity of the Raj. In 1847, Herbert Edwardes relied on what he believed to be the reputation of his countrymen when he assured tribesmen from the Bannu region that their taxes would not be crippling. 'You know very well that no "Sahib" ever fixes a heavy revenue. "Sahibs" are at this moment settling the revenue throughout the Punjab, and making all the people happy.'[20]

II

'Sahib', more than any word in the Anglo-Indian lexicon, has come to stand for the relationship between Indians and their British rulers. Its undertones of imperial servility mean that it is now seldom heard in India, where 'sir' has become the everyday expression of deference. In Edwardes's time, 'sahib' meant master and was universally used to all Englishmen, whatever their rank. He thought that this polite usage was also 'an involuntary confession of the master-race energy' of the British race.

Racial arrogance was always hard to avoid in India, even among the most open-minded and sensitive. Prolonged exile in the country transformed the British for the worst, according to Lieutenant-Colonel H. B. Henderson of the 8th Bengal NI. He lived in India for nearly twenty years and published a miscellany of quirky recollections in 1829. His frankness and acerbity made him a revealing chronicler of his countrymen's activities in the midst of what he called, 'The millions of the East . . . happily sunk in their subjection, even as the careless sleep of infancy.'[21] In this position of absolute mastery, natural British pride and independence became contaminated by 'Asiatic' arrogance so that, in time, the exile became 'accustomed to measure his own humanity by the standards of a conquered and degraded race around him'. Among the older, stiff-necked generation of Company men, he discovered a breathtaking arrogance which expressed itself in such statements as:

> No native, however high his rank, ought to approach within a yard of an Englishman; and every time an English shakes hands with a Babu [Indian clerk] he shakes the basis on which our ascendancy in this country stands.[22]

Even those fired with a sense of mission found it hard to repress their inner disdain towards Indians. Consider Captain James McMurdo, who died in 1820 aged thirty-three and who was in many ways the perfect example of the dedicated and hard-working proconsul whom Wellesley hoped would uplift India. According to his encomium, this officer had advanced himself through 'the paths of integrity, industry and knowledge' and had acquired a 'deep insight into all the turnings and wanderings of the Indian character'. In Kathiawar and Kachchh, he suppressed brigandage and won over the natives, having a 'constant interest in their happiness'. And yet, 'The native character was far from standing high in his estimation, but as it was his lot to live and act amongst them this he at all times carefully concealed.'[23] One wonders how many others similarly placed who shared McMurdo's secret distaste for the Indian character masked their feelings, and whether they did so successfully.

It would be impossible to generalise about this subject, but among McMurdo's contemporaries there were officials who believed that the British reserve and exclusiveness handicapped their dealings with Indians. 'The French character is more popular in India than ours,' General James Stuart told Dundas in 1800.[24] Another officer, whose experience was

confined to country stations in the Deccan, wrote in 1808 that he regretted the distance between the British and Indians: 'We do not intermarry
with them, as the Portuguese did; nor do we ever mix with them, in the
common duties of social life on terms of equality.'[25] More starkly, when
Private Ryder tried to calm two frightened camp followers under fire at
Multan in 1849, one said, 'If a ball strikes me, and I am killed, you would
say, "Oh, never mind – it's only a black man."'[26] By this time racial hauteur was more pronounced than ever. The word 'nigger' begins to appear
in private correspondence and its use spread rapidly. A philologist, touring
India on the eve of the 1857 Mutiny, was distressed to find expressions of
racial abuse in common use: '*Now*, one hears ordinarily and from the
mouths of decent folks nothing but contemptuous phrases (nigger &c).'[27]

Early impressions often sowed the seeds of racial contempt. As his ship
sailed up the Hughli, Ensign James Welsh was horrified by the sight of
flotillas of small rowing boats filled with food sellers. They seemed 'a race
of beings seemingly intended by nature to complete the link between
man, the image of his Maker, and the tribe of apes and monkeys'.[28] Similar
thoughts crossed the mind of Lord Hastings after he had disembarked at
Calcutta in 1814. 'The Hindu appears a being nearly limited to mere
animal functions, and even in them indifferent,' he noted in his journal,
adding that they seemed to possess 'no higher intellect than a dog, an elephant or a monkey'.[29] In part, these were reactions to the sheer numbers
of Indians seen along the shores of the river or congregated by the *ghats*
(landing places), which was something no traveller from the West was
ever wholly prepared for. The tinted prints of the city's waterfront and
streets, which became increasingly available in Britain after 1800, showed
nothing of the multitudes who moved along them. The newcomer discovered these for himself, together with the ceaseless bustle of masses of
men and women who were accustomed to prepare food, eat, wash themselves and defecate in public. There were, of course, crowds in the streets
of Regency London and the larger cities, but nothing on the scale of
those seen in India. They were an unfamiliar spectacle which heightened
a sense of isolation and aroused that nervousness so often expressed in the
question 'how could so many be ruled by so few'. Hastings was relieved to
notice that Indian crowds were infinitely more docile than their British
counterparts.

The faceless throng first seen from the deck of a ship soon became individuals as the new arrival established his household and hired servants.
Advice on their duties, how they should be treated and how much they

ought to be paid was plentiful. Ceaseless vigilance and firmness were vital for the smooth running of a household and it helped enormously to have a smattering of the local language. According to John Gilchrist, a former army surgeon who had learned Hindustani through dressing as and mixing with Indians, it was more effective to reprimand 'stupidity, perverseness and chicanery' than to punish them with the usual clout.[30] His Hindustani phrase book, published in 1800, provided the novice with the language of command and rebuke. Among his appendix of useful expressions were: 'Row fast, pull away, don't be lazy'; 'Give me my boots and spurs'; 'Hand me my tooth brush and powder'; 'Give me a clean knife and fork'; 'Brush the curtains well that no mosquitoes may remain'; and 'What! has no one yet told you that bearer is in our tongue a very low word, like a slave or drudge.'[31]

As these imperatives indicate, Indian servants carried, cooked, cleaned and attended to all their master's personal needs. Each had his special status and newcomers were urged to master local religious taboos quickly to avoid misunderstandings. For instance, Hindus would never eat left-overs from a European's plate, or drink from a vessel which he had used and, when asleep on the floor, objected to being stepped over. There were higher-class servants such as the *khidmutgar* (a sort of butler who waited on his master), the *bania* (money agent), *sircar* (cashier) and *munshi* (language instructor and interpreter) who were exempt from manual labour. Household chores were undertaken by menials: the *bhisti* (water carrier), *dhobi* (laundrymen), *hircarra* (messenger), *durwan* (door-keeper), *syce* (groom and collector of grass for a horse), *hookah-burdar* (who prepared a hookah for smoking), *doreah* (dog keeper and walker), *ayah* (nursemaid), cooks and sweepers. The last were from the 'lowest caste', (i.e. Untouchables) and scraped clean the sides of the privy and removed any scorpions or centipedes which had taken refuge beneath its wooden seats.

Servants enabled Europeans to survive in India and provided the commonest contacts between them and Indians. Household management was a constant source of anxiety, although those who kept a native mistress were relieved of most of its burdens, for she would keep an eye on the servants and see that they did not cheat their employer.[32] If the volumes of advice on this subject are to be believed, Indian servants were always seeking ways in which to swindle their masters. Their outward subservience was a mask for what, in 1815, one writer called 'a continual plot to defraud and deceive'.[33] Great care was needed when hiring servants. According to Captain Thomas Williamson, the prissy author of the popular guidebook,

The East India Vade-Mecum (1810), khidmutgars who wore silk 'drawers' were highly suspect. They were the badge of a libidinous, possibly homosexual servant who had learned his 'libertinism' in a harem of a previous European master. A 'jollication' held by the khidmutgar, his friends and some women while Captain James Halket was at a party in Simla proved so engrossing that burglars were able to enter the house undetected and carry off some silver.[34] Williamson also warned that all but a few munshis suffered from permanent bad breath, which must have made daily language lessons an ordeal. Gilchrist complained about servants who spat indoors and doreahs who allowed dogs to foul the house. Retaining a hookah-burdah who turned out to be an opium addict nearly cost Captain Robert Knolles his life in May 1819. The man, heavily under the influence of the drug and claiming he had been fobbed off when he had asked for his wages, tried to murder him and was only prevented with difficulty.[35]

The preparation and service of food involved the greatest traumas. No doubt drawing on his own unhappy experience, Williamson suggested that cooks should be discouraged from straining soup through 'filthy rags'. But compromises had to be made, for he observed that the excellent appearance of a meal had to be allowed to outweigh the 'unpleasantness of preparation', although flies in the sauce could never be tolerated. Dining was obviously full of hazards which, in time, were accepted as unavoidable. 'Good dinner and everything clean . . . which is unusual in India' was the entry in Captain Halket's diary after a meal with Sir Henry Lawrence in August 1851. He had been in India since the beginning of the year and was not yet inured to its discomforts.

How many servants a man had depended on his income. A Company ensign with 100 rupees (£10) a month was expected to run an establishment with a khidmutgar who, each month, was paid eight rupees (80p); a dhobi and a cook who got six apiece; a punkah wallah who got four for operating the fan and a sweeper who got three. Sixteen rupees covered the wages of the syce and fodder for the horse. In all, the ensign was paying out just half his salary on his servants, and once promoted to a lieutenancy with 300 rupees a month, he could expand his household. In 1824, Lieutenant Blackwell employed five servants, and, on his arrival in India, Captain Halket hired thirteen, including a gun bearer for hunting excursions.[36] Travelling required additional staff: Captain Forrest and his six companions needed seven elephants and a hundred servants for their journey from Calcutta to Cawnpore in 1809.[37] Personal servants also accompanied their masters on campaign. Captain Arthur Becher's khidmutgar followed him on a camel during the 1845–46 Sikh war and was on hand to serve him tea before the battle of Ferozeshah.[38]

Everyday travel was by a shaded palanquin, a form of travelling bed or armchair which could cost as much as 250 rupees and was an expensive necessity for the new arrival. Palanquin bearers were normally hired for a specific journey. They worked in teams of eight with four men carrying the passenger and the others following, ready to take over when their colleagues became weary. If the going was good and travel by night, when it was cool, they could jog as much as twenty-five miles in eight hours. Their profession required skill and stamina and they were probably the least biddable of all servants. In the 1790s the Calcutta palanquin carriers set up a trade union to protect wages and maintain a closed shop, but their monopoly collapsed with an influx of bearers from Dacca and Patna, who undercut them. In 1797, when James Cochrane, a Madras customs official, gave his 'palanquin boys' a 'refreshing' (i.e. beating), they retaliated by burgling his house. There were other forms of revenge for disgruntled palanquin bearers, as his friend Alexander Read observed ruefully: 'I would advise *all lads* like *me* who can't swim to keep in with their Palanquin boys in the monsoon time, otherwise they might get a *Dinso* in some of the *nullahs* [streams].'[39]

Moderate physical punishment of disobedient or slack servants was legally tolerated in India, as it was in Britain well into the nineteenth century. Europeans were, however, discouraged from using fist, stick or whip for their use was so incompatible with their moral status. 'Moderation, temper, and kindness' were the distinguishing features of the British officer, according to general orders issued by Sir John Malcolm in 1821.[40] His exhortation was necessary, for in July, Lieutenant Vignolles of the 26th Bengal NI had been tried for flogging his syce with a buggy whip. The victim suffered eighteen strokes and complained to Vignolles's commanding office, a reminder that even the humblest Indian took British claims to moral integrity at their face value. During the subsequent trial for assault, it emerged that the defendant was a sadist who had been previously reprimanded for thrashing his servants, an activity which one witness noticed gave him 'seeming pleasure'. Two other officers had stood by while he delivered the final beating and throughout his examination Vignolles was insouciant. He was cashiered as a warning to others who might feel similarly inclined.[41] The same judgement was delivered against another junior officer who struck two sepoys with a buggy whip in Calcutta in 1824. Between 1835 and 1845 the lash was abolished as a punishment for sepoys on the grounds of their natural tractability and the fact that it was degrading for men from the higher castes, for whom dismissal was shaming enough.

Public humanitarianism was one thing; what happened in private was another. T. W. Webber, who worked in the Indian Forestry Service from 1861, recalled at the end of his forty-year career that many of his contemporaries saw nothing wrong in abusing and 'thrashing' their servants. He confessed to having twice struck a native and considered that in 'courage, high principle, and honourable feeling' many of his servants were equal to 'educated Christian gentlemen'.[42] He was thinking in particular of the *shikaris* (professional huntsmen) and gun bearers who accompanied him in pursuit of game.

Throughout history and across the world, hunting for its own sake has been the prerogative of the rich and powerful with time on their hands. This was so in Britain and India, which made the chase a major source of common interest and everyday contact between Indian noblemen and British gentlemen. The connection was brilliantly shown in John Zoffany's most famous Indian painting, *Colonel Mordaunt's Cock Match*, where sporting Indians mingle with like-minded British officers. This informal but animated scene, executed in 1786, so impressed the Nawab of Awadh that he commissioned Zoffany to make a copy, which hung in the palace at Lucknow until the 1857 Mutiny. The picture is a reminder that shared tastes stimulated mutual respect, even friendship. During the early 1830s the Nawab of Firozpur regularly invited British officials and officers to join him on extended lion and tiger shoots in the countryside west of Delhi. His companions instantly recognised him as a gentleman, with all the virtues of a fox-hunting squire from the pages of Surtees: 'He was enthusiastically fond of hunting and shooting, and naturally of a frank and generous disposition.'[43]

Indian princes frequently entertained high-ranking British visitors by staging contests between fighting elephants, a spectacle they understood would appeal to the sporting tastes of British gentlemen – its near equivalent, bull baiting, was only abolished in Britain in 1835. An elephant fight was presented by the Nawab of Awadh for Colonel Forrester and his party during their stay in Lucknow in 1809. The guests were taken to a verandah overlooking an arena within a bamboo palisade. *Aficionados* explained how the war elephants had been fed on a highly-spiced diet which kept them in a permanent bad humour. This was raised to a pitch of fury when their favourite females were sent ahead into the ring. But sexual tension failed to ignite the first pair of elephants, who gave 'little sport'. There were no disappointments from the second pair, who battled away head to head and had to be separated by fireworks thrown between them.[44]

There was 'nothing very remarkable' about a duel between the Raja of Ladwa's fighting elephants, who went through their paces for Richard Cust in 1844, but he enjoyed 'a capital contest between two deer'.[45] In 1851 the Raja of Bharatpur's elephants performed for Lord Anson, the commander-in-chief and his staff, one of whom heard afterwards that the beasts had had their tusks blunted.[46] Maybe this was a precaution against the loss of a valuable animal, or else an acknowledgement that the sahibs' tastes in blood sports were less robust than formerly. Sporting gentlemen with a sense of history and the stomach to watch these contests wondered whether the show had its origins in the diversions of the Roman circus.

Sport drew British and Indians together in other ways. Villagers were peremptorily pressed to serve as beaters whenever an officer or official paused on his journey and spent a day shooting. Perhaps those summoned welcomed the call as a break in the humdrum routine of their lives, and if they did not, then they dared not say so. The ryots of the Deccan were always accommodating to Major Beaven, revealing to him the haunts of deer, porcupine and hogs. Looking back over many hunting trips during the 1810s and 1820s, he interpreted this co-operation as a token of the greater respect shown to anyone who wore a red coat and cocked hat. The peasantry, he imagined, regarded officers like himself as the natural heirs of the warrior overlords who had so recently dominated the countryside. This sense of deference was finely tuned to the point where a villager could detect the difference between a senior officer ('*burra sahib*') and a junior ('*chota sahib*'), in other words a great and a minor gentleman.[47] There were, of course, plenty of chota sahibs who behaved as burra sahibs. When Tom Raw, the hero of Sir Charles D'Oyly's comic epic, travels up country, he lords it over zamindars and ryots, brandishing his sword and bellowing, '*Hum Comp'ny ke lupteenant! Bhote Khudderdar*' (I'm a Company Lieutenant! Mind what you're about). The phrase does not appear in Gilchrist's compendium, but variations of it, delivered with bluster, must have been many Indians' experience of the British.

Indians were imagined to possess a social sixth sense which made them immediately recognise a gentleman. This facility was notably well-developed among the Indian nobility. Hastings was highly gratified when it was reported that a raja had said of him:

This man knows what to say to us. You ought always to have
a great sirdar [senior officer] at the head of the government.
Sir George Barlow [Governor-General, 1805–07] was of the
weaver caste, and could not flatter us with anything he said.[48]

Barlow had disclosed his middle-class background by his inability to
master that courtly manner which would have struck a chord with princes
who had grown up surrounded by elaborate ceremonial and fulsome
addresses. Hastings, with a noble pedigree that stretched back to the
Middle Ages, knew what to say and said it elegantly. This clearly mattered,
even if some high-born Indians were regrettably unable to detect an
authentic gentleman and treat him accordingly. 'Manners go for nothing in
India,' Montstuart Elphinstone complained to his friend, Lady Hood, in
1814. Nonetheless, his experiences as a soldier and diplomat had taught
him that, when 'handling Indians' it was best to stick to 'the principles of
good breeding'.[49]

It was pleasing to find Indians who appreciated and lived by these principles. Elphinstone, like many others, warmed to the warrior castes of the
Ganges valley, whom he considered to be the 'most warlike and manly of
the Indians'. Colonel James Tod praised the Rajput nobility for their
'courage, patriotism, loyalty, honour, hospitality and simplicity'.[50] 'No
English gentleman could conduct himself with greater propriety and good
breeding' than the elder sons of Sadat Ali, Nawab of Awadh, concluded
Colonel Forrest after having dined with them.[51] Their polish no doubt
derived from their father, who was infatuated by everything British. 'His
breakfasts, dinners, houses are completely English,' remarked another of his
guests, Charles Metcalfe, who also noticed that the nawab employed a
French cook and a band with European instruments. Anand Rao, Raja
and Gaikwar of Baroda, displayed 'the esprit and manners of a gentleman'
on state occasions, but soon forgot himself in private. Then, according to
Brigadier Alexander Walker, the prince acted like a 'common Maratha
horseman', drinking more cherry brandy than was good for him and
smoking too much opium.[52]

The rituals of state required that British gentlemen and Indian aristocrats behaved according to an elaborate code of etiquette. Lord Hastings
gave the required four embraces to the Nawab of Karnataka when they
met in 1814 and gave a further four to each of his sons and a nephew.
Then, the nawab, his hand covered with a handkerchief scented with otto
of roses, handed the Governor-General a betel nut and placed a chaplet of

flowers round his neck. On Hastings's departure, the nawab injected some amusement into the ceremony by uttering what he took to be a warm English farewell: 'How d'ye do, Governor-General.'[53] Before an audience with Bahadur Shah in 1837, Captain Fane and other officers were given muslin robes and asked to bind their cocked hats with scarves. Fane later heard that the Company was strict in enforcing respectful behaviour and that the late resident, William Fraser, had been reprimanded for handing his ceremonial costume to a beggar.[54] Such occasions could be tedious and required considerable self-discipline; Fane's companions found Indian singing 'the most atrocious screaming they ever heard', but as the formal concert proceeded, they became entranced. 'Many of the airs were simple and sweet,' the converted Fane wrote afterwards.

It is not known what the 'principal native Gentlemen and Merchants' made of the tunes played for them during the New Year ball held at the Governor-General's Calcutta residence in 1822. There was dancing from ten until midnight, followed by a firework display which, 'amongst romantic scenery', struck guests as 'most beautiful and picturesque'.[55] The city was now India's metropolis, and its Indian upper classes were drawn into its social life, adopting British manners and social forms. A contemporary invitation card illustrated just how far the process of assimilation had progressed:

> Jamsetjee Jeejeebhoy request the honour of Mr Hyde's Company at a Nautch at his House near the *Mamdadavie Tank*, in celebration of his Son's wedding, on the evening of Monday next at 8 o'clock, 7 February 1822.

There were many British guests and the entertainment was done 'with great splendour', although the bridegroom was only seven. Anglo-Indian social relations were stiffer in Madras despite the efforts of the Governor, Sir John Abercrombie, to introduce the Indian 'higher classes' into European society in 1812. 'Aristocratic feelings' among the Europeans frustrated intimacy and the gulf between the groups actually widened. Observing this, Captain Beaven remarked that this sort of snobbery did not exist in the country districts, where relations were informal and Europeans kept Indian concubines.[56]

III

The world to which Indians were admitted in Calcutta and Madras was one imported from Britain. In many respects, the exiles set about deliberately re-creating Britain, which was why the hillside resort of Simla became so popular from the 1830s onwards. Not only did it offer relief from the heat and dust during the summer, but visitors could actually imagine themselves in Britain. 'Red rhododendron trees in bloom in every direction, and beautiful walks like English shrubberies on all sides of the hill,' wrote Emily Eden in 1838.[57] Others believed themselves transported to the Highlands of Scotland. The serendipity of finding Britain in India or, as was more usually the case, of contriving Britain in India, helped reduce homesickness and recurrent fears that the exile might never return:

> This sigh for Britain, ever in the breast, –
> Of all our pining, panting, exiled train,
> Not one in twenty sees his home again![58]

One of the most striking features of the artificial Britain in India was the tendency of its inhabitants to cling on to attitudes and fashions which had fallen into disuse at home. Duelling, for instance, had all but disappeared from Britain by 1840 under the pressure of public disapproval. It remained popular among the gentlemen of India: 'The duello being pretty nearly as much a matter of recurrence to them, as a dish of curry at the mess table.'[59] Its prevalence was explained by the Indian army officer's overblown sense of personal honour, reckless gambling, heavy drinking and sexual adventures, all of which had been common enough among the aristocracy in Britain twenty or thirty years before. (When Mr Bennett set off to reclaim his eloping daughter, his family assumed that he would challenge her kidnapper to a duel.) Outlawed in Britain, duelling was indirectly condoned by the Indian authorities. In 1836 the young Irish wife of a sixty-year-old Light Dragoon major had been seduced by a young cornet in his regiment. When the husband found the pair in bed, he challenged the junior officer to a duel. The younger man first refused to return his opponent's fire, but when a second round was demanded, he obliged and killed the major. His death was officially attributed to cholera, and the cornet was allowed to enter another regiment.[60] Cholera was again given as the cause of death for another victim of a duel; an Irish Catholic subaltern, who had been driven to fight by the taunts of Protestant brother officers at Poona in 1841.[61]

Nonconformity in the broadest sense was frowned upon by British society in India. Major Havelock was sneered at by his brother officers, for 'his manners are cold while his religious opinions [Baptist] seclude him from society', wrote his friend Henry Broadfoot in 1841.[62] Furthermore, and this was unforgiveable, he treated his profession 'as a science' which needed careful study. Richard Cust, who had passed through Eton, Haileybury and Fort William College and began his official career in 1844, recalled the India of his early years as a land 'where no breath of intellectual air from the outside' was ever felt and where intelligent conversation was impossible to find.[63] The fault lay with the exclusiveness of Indian society, according to Major-General Sir William Sleeman, a distinguished warrior proconsul who died in 1854 after over forty years' service. The trouble was that in Indian provincial cities British society consisted entirely of soldiers, administrators and, by the 1830s, clergymen, all of whom were agents of the government.[64] Unlike British middle- and upper-class society, India possessed no businessmen, manufacturers, landowners, writers or creative artists who could contribute different perspectives to conversations.

Boredom was the recurrent complaint of many exiles. Lieutenant Blackwell spoke for thousands when he described life in the mess of the 13th Regiment at the close of 1823:

> There was nothing but ennui and complaining of the abominable climate from morning to night . . . If a billiard table had not been purchased, I cannot imagine how many would ever have been able to have got through the dreary day.[65]

There were physical discomforts which were so commonplace that sufferers seldom bothered to record them in their journals or letters. James Welsh recalled an airless night when he unwisely discarded his mosquito net and was beset by swarms of the insects, which seemed as 'large as bees'. The following morning he was 'a mass of pimples; his clothes covered with blood' and his eyes closed.[66] The bowels were a constant source of anxiety and tribulation. 'I shall take care of my stern post in the future,' Alexander Read told a friend as he was convalescing from a bout of fever which he had strangely diagnosed as a by-product of constipation.[67] A pickled fish, eaten for breakfast, was blamed by Assistant Surgeon Oswald for a day of vomiting and diarrhoea in January 1858.[68]

Oswald also recorded his occasional hangovers. Among the officer and official classes, drinking was a common antidote to tedium, so much so that every guidebook warned the newcomer against excess. Wines were plentiful and cheap. 'I drink hock, claret, and champagne only, and at dessert malmsey; the others, alleging the coldness of the climate, stick to port, sherry and madeira. I do not recollect having tasted water for the last seven days,' a French visitor reported after a round of Simla dinner parties in the early 1830s. 'Nevertheless,' he added, 'there is no excess.'[69] A wide variety of drink was always available. Madeira, taken on board Company ships during routine stops during the outward journey, was universally popular and cheap, at roughly a rupee a bottle in the early 1800s. Another favourite was 'English' claret, to which brandy had been added to enable it to survive the Indian climate. It cost one and a half rupees a bottle and was infinitely superior to its rival, 'Danish' claret, which, Captain Williamson believed, was the source of 'severe bowel complaints'. The sufferer who followed his advice would take port, which he suggested as an ideal restorative for the victim of diarrhoea.[70] Williamson recommended porter, pale ale and 'table beer' and mild punches. One brew, known as 'brandy shrob paunny' and made up of brandy and water, was to be shunned for it 'never fails to produce that sottishness at all times despicable, but particularly unsuited to Oriental Society, in which at least the better half are men of very liberal education, and all are gentlemen'.

Mild intoxication could be obtained from the soothing and highly addictive hookah. A good hookah man could earn up to fifteen rupees a month, often more, for his arcane skills and, above all, a formula for a satisfying smoke. The hookah bowl required a blend of local tobaccos, some laced with molasses, ground fine, and the addition of minute quantities of plaintain leaves, raw sugar, cinnamon and other aromatics. Some gentlemen's tastes ran to opium or cannabis, although Europeans usually consumed the latter in sweetmeats.[71] According to Williamson, taken in this form it produced instant gaiety followed by nausea and headaches. Smoking hookahs (there were small ones for use in palanquins) went out of fashion in the 1820s, when they were supplanted by cheroots.

Indulgence of any kind had to be balanced by exercise if an exile was not to succumb to distempers. Those who took medical advice seriously, and most did, lived their lives according to a routine which included a time set aside for riding. In the hot season men rode for an hour after dawn, or in the cold, two. Williamson then suggested a moderate breakfast without ghee or salted foods followed by an hour of language study. The hours set aside for work varied according to a man's responsibilities. In 1811, William Home, an officer, worked between nine and three when he took 'a capital collation . . . called tiffin' which might take up to two hours to consume. Afterwards he played billiards. Lieutenant Blackwell's day in Calcutta in 1823 was even more leisurely: he rose at five, rode as the sun came over the horizon and then ate breakfast. Then he 'lounged or idled the time away till tiffin, and did what he could to kill the enemy [tedium] from tiffin to evening parade'. Richard Cust, an official, followed a more rigorous regime in the Punjab during 1846. He was up by six, worked at his papers until midday, when he had breakfast. He read for the next three hours and then spent the next three going through his official correspondence. His main meal, dinner, was at eight. At Rangoon in 1854, Assistant Surgeon Oswald also began work at six, making his morning visit to the hospital. He breakfasted at nine and then read or shot crows or kites. At noon he made his second round of the wards, leaving an afternoon which was free until his final inspection of his patients at seven.[72] One consequence of this abundant leisure and, of course, plenty of servants, was that military men and civilian officials had time in which to keep journals and write to their families and friends.

Service in India offered unlimited time and opportunities for gentlemen to indulge in their ruling passion, hunting. In 1799, that compulsive huntsman, Arthur Wellesley, annexed Tipu Sultan's cheetahs and leopards and hunted deer with them in the Mysorean fashion. An instinctive conservative in all things, he preferred to ride to hounds like an English squire, and so he had some foxhounds imported. Unused to the climate, they fell sick and died. The pack of the 16th Lancers survived and, with a spirit which would have delighted Jorrocks, officers of the regiment arrived in Kabul in 1839 with their hounds. The drainage ditches which criss-crossed the countryside provided a stiff test for men and horses and several 'gentlemen sportsmen' took a tumble as they pursued Afghan jackals.[73]

War was never allowed to interrupt a gentleman's sport. Off-duty officers during the siege of Bharatpur soon discovered that the shallow lakes and marshland south of the city abounded in game and wildfowl. On one occasion, fifteen elephants were borrowed from the army for a 'grand shooting party' which was joined by Gurkhas, who were welcomed, for they had a reputation for marksmanship.[74] Elephants were essential for shooting in countryside where tall grass and low bushes made it all but impossible for the guns to see their targets. Beaters were hauled in from nearby villages (they were joined by pariah dogs during the fruitless pursuit of a rhinoceros in Awadh in 1809) and, directed by local shikaris, they fanned out through the bush. Behind came the line of elephants with howdahs on their backs which contained the huntsmen. As deer and wild pigs were flushed out and birds took flight, the guns opened up.

Up-country hunting excursions had other attractions. In April 1857, Lieutenant Alexander Lindsay of the Bengal Horse Artillery reckoned that by undertaking a six-month hunting and fishing trip in Kashmir he could save enough to pay off all his debts. His must have been an expensive mess or else he was living beyond his means. In Calcutta, Madras, Bombay and the larger garrison towns and administrative centres there was a social life which in every respect mirrored that of British provincial cities. The diary of Lady Chambers, the wife of a judge, for 1784 might easily have been that of a gentlewoman taking the waters in contemporary Bath. She attended dinners and balls, took tea with her friends, worshipped on Sundays, went on boat trips on the Hughli and watched a production of *Hamlet* in the city's playhouse.[75]

The climate, particularly in the hot season, prevented the exact reproduction of the British social round. In turn-of-the-century Calcutta, formal dinner was eaten between four and five and afterwards ladies and gentlemen went abroad in their carriages until ten. There were after-dinner receptions, with cards for older guests and dancing for younger, and a handful were invited to remain behind for late supper. Customs changed by the 1840s, when the formal evening dinner became the focus of social life. Bachelor officers dined in their messes in the evening, as in Britain, and hostesses gave dinner parties. These were often something of an endurance test, according to the fastidious Sleeman. In the hot season, and he must have been writing from experience, 'a table covered with animal food is sickening to any person without a keen appetite, and stupefying to those who have it'. If dinner was followed by a ball, the prospect was grim, for the entertainments would continue until early morning, which did not suit Sleeman, who liked to be in bed by ten. The Indian dinner party had other drawbacks, which were noted by Captain Williamson. It was the custom for each guest to bring his khidmutgar and maybe other servants, who stood behind his chair while he ate and flicked away the flies. These attendants formed 'a living enclosure' within the dining room, 'tending by its own exhalations, added to those from their masters and from the viands' to cause nausea.[76]

British society in India was always narrow and exclusive. Newcomers would not be admitted easily without a friend, for as Captain Williamson noted, 'he who knows nobody, him will nobody know'.[77] It could also be stultifying and there was inevitably tetchiness among men and women thrown together by chance and with little or no relief from each other's company. Trivial incidents would get blown up out of all proportion. One May morning in 1809, Captain Joseph Gordon of the 22nd Light Dragoons was about to inspect some lame horses on the parade ground at Arcot when he saw his dog being attacked by two or three others. Immediately he hurled some stones at the assailants, which fled. Soon after, Cornet Charles Ellis accosted Gordon with the words, 'I'd thank you Sir, not to throw at my dog.' 'If your dog attacks mine, Sir, I shall knock him down if I can,' answered Gordon. Enraged, Ellis spat back at his superior, 'Then I shall knock yours down, and something else too. I can tell you that I will not allow you to throw at my dog or any man like you.' Gordon rebuked him, 'Mr Ellis, you are very violent this morning.' Ellis stumped off, muttering. There was bad blood between him and Gordon, he admitted, when he excused his conduct to a court martial. He had heard his dog howl when hit by one of the captain's stones and was determined to avenge what he imagined to be an insult, 'from a gentleman with whom I have not been on an intimate footing for some time, who had slighted my acquaintance'.[78] Not surprisingly, the army encouraged young officers to expend surplus energy in 'manly' games, such as cricket and fives.[79]

And yet British society in India possessed a remarkable cohesiveness. It had to, if the Raj was to be preserved. The strongest ties were those of social background, shared attitudes and pastimes and a sense of common purpose. This was the widest possible advertisement of the superior virtues of British 'character', or, to be precise, the character of the gentleman. It was because of his interior strengths that the gentleman had found it possible to step naturally into the role of the Indian lord. The ease with which this authority was assumed struck Lieutenant Godfrey Pearse when he received the ceremonial oaths and homage of the frontier horsemen he was about to command in 1849:

> There is something very pleasing in their feudatory customs: to see a young scion of the Blood Royal of Afghanistan, a Suddozye [Suddozai], and the oldest Sikh general of the Khalsa army swear allegiance to a young boy and a foreigner is certainly an odd sight.[80]

Such an experience was reassuring, for it reaffirmed the belief that the common culture of gentlemen warriors transcended race. By this date, and in large measure through the endeavours of the Marquess Wellesley, the tenor of the Raj was aristocratic. Its underlying philosophy was a form of romantic Toryism which imagined that every Indian had an almost mystical respect for the authority of a sahib, whom he knew instinctively would treat him fairly. It was a self-perpetuating dogma: in 1907, the governor of the United Provinces (now Uttar Pradesh) assured the Viceroy, Lord Minto, that the Indian had always admired a true gentleman and despised 'the lower-class, non-official European'.[81]

2

Utility and Beneficence: British Visions and Indian Realities

At some date in the 1770s, an English gentleman and child of the Enlightenment presented one of its instruments, a microscope, to a 'liberal minded-Brahmin' with whom he had become friendly. The Indian peered through the eyepiece at a piece of fruit and was astonished by the 'innumerable animaliculae' which he saw. Pleased by his curiosity, the Englishman gave him the microscope. Soon after, the Brahmin destroyed it, telling his friend that what he had seen had left him 'tormented by doubt, and perplexed by mystery' to the point where he imagined his soul was imperilled.[1] Seventy years later, a Baptist missionary was exasperated by Indians who insisted that the earth rested on either the back of a tortoise or serpent, and refused to be persuaded that the world was round and had been circumnavigated by European sailors.[2] The Hindus' attachment to their ancient cosmography was a well-known example of their stubborn refusal to open their minds to the revelations of modern science and reason.

Anecdotes like these became part of the folklore of British India. They illustrated the unwillingness of the Indian to comprehend, let alone engage with, the modern world, and the intellectual gulf between rulers and ruled. This widened as Indians came into contact with the marvels of British science and technology. New inventions appeared with a bewildering swiftness: in 1824 the paddle-steamer *Diane* chugged up the Irrawaddy, spreading terror among the Burmese; four years later a Company passenger and mail steamer appeared on the Hughli; and by 1836 four iron-hulled tugs were hauling boats up the Ganges as far as Allahabad.[3] Within the next decade steamships became a familiar sight on the Ganges and the Indus and in every major port. The early 1850s witnessed the arrival of fresh tokens of Britain's inventive genius: the telegraph and the railways. Indians were alternately impressed and apprehensive; a passenger travelling on the Calcutta line in 1860 noticed how villagers rushed out to see the engine and carriages pass by, looking on 'in ignorant admiration'.[4]

The steamship, railway train and the telegraph epitomised progress, that historical force which seemed to have been gathering momentum since the intellectual and scientific revolutions of the eighteenth century. Britain was in the forefront of progress, indeed the first industrial nation found no difficulty in identifying itself as the banner-bearer of civilisation, destined to transform the world for the better. India represented a stagnant nation, where progress had long ago ground to a halt and where minds closed to reason were filled with fairy tales. In theory, it could have remained in this condition, for the system of government set up in 1784 confined the activities of the state to defence, internal security and the collection of revenue. The Company possessed no mandate to act as a universal dispenser of improving knowledge, rather it existed to promote what successive governors called the 'happiness' of its subjects.

In reality, the Company could not distance itself from the moral and intellectual welfare of its subjects. On a purely practical level its operations required a body of educated Indians to serve in junior administrative posts. More importantly, there was something within the contemporary British temperament which rendered it impossible for them to perpetuate a status quo in which the mass of Indians languished in a state of cataleptic contentment.

The impulse to reform and elevate had various sources. Perhaps the most powerful was the Protestant tradition which regarded all ignorance as evil, if only on the grounds that it prevented men and women from understanding the word of God. The vast majority of Indians were Hindus and, therefore, pagans in need of conversion which, according to Evangelical orthodoxy was one of the highest duties set a Christian. From the beginning, the ultimate goal of all programmes for spreading Western education throughout India was the conversion of the Hindus. As the mythology of Hinduism withered under the blast of science and reason, its former adherents would automatically turn to the one, living God. 'No Hindu, who has received an English education, ever remains sincerely attached to his religion,' asserted Thomas Macaulay in 1837. A junior member of the Board of Control who had been seconded to the Governor-General's council in 1834, he was a man of immense influence who drew up the blueprint for ambitious legal and educational reforms. The latter, he hoped, would eliminate Hinduism among the Bengali educated classes within thirty years. Indian civil servant and fellow reformer Charles Trevelyan predicted that technology would accelerate the decline of Hinduism. 'Railways will also be the great destroyer of caste, and the greatest missionary of all,' he told a Commons committee in 1853.[5]

Evangelical ideals also contributed to Britain's swelling self-esteem. After 1815, the British increasingly saw themselves as the inheritors of over two hundred years of scientific and intellectual enlightenment which they had been remarkably adept in harnessing to practical ends. The achievements of the Industrial Revolution, which had been gathering pace during the last quarter of the eighteenth century, together with the patriotic pride kindled by victories in the Revolutionary and Napoleonic wars, created a powerful sense of national destiny. A godly, virtuous and industrious people appeared to be marked out for a special greatness which might easily exceed that of Rome and the empires of the Classical age.

All these elements fused in an appeal, delivered in 1846, by a former Indian postal official in favour of a rail network across the sub-continent:

> The honour, the dignity, and the glory of Imperial Britain are concerned in it . . . a magnificent system of railway communications would present a series of public monuments vastly surpassing in real grandeur, the aqueducts of Rome, the pyramids of Egypt, the great wall of China, the temples, palaces and mausoleums of the Great Moguls – monuments not merely of intelligence and power, but of utility and benificence.[6]

National greatness lay in the fulfilment of great tasks for the physical and moral regeneration of mankind. This concept of Britain as the engine of universal progress permeated the minds of politicians and administrators in London and Calcutta from the 1820s onwards. Indians were, in the words of Lord Auckland, 'a people conquered and not yet reclaimed'.[7] Their redemption was not just an exercise in lofty-minded altruism. The resuscitation of India made good commercial sense, for it would create customers for British imports and boost local industry and agriculture, creating additional income for the Company. Among those clamouring for an Indian railway network in the 1840s were British businessmen who saw the new lines thrusting inland as levers opening up new markets and sources of raw materials.

II

The British were confident that they were ideally fitted to supervise the rebirth of India, but they disagreed as to how it might be best accomplished. Opinion was divided over the pace of reform and how far the government could go in interfering with indigenous creeds and customs. There was also a profound difference of approach: those of a liberal frame of mind tended to diagnose India and prescribe often cathartic remedies for its ailments, while conservatives chose to engage with the country and its peoples. Both factions recognised the abundant features of decay, but the conservatives never allowed this knowledge to blind them to the virtues of Indian society, religion and institutions.

The conservative attitude to India was grounded in the experience of the French Revolution of 1789, which had demonstrated how high-minded experiments in remaking entire societies in the name of reason could go horribly awry. This had been the warning contained in Edmund Burke's *Reflections on the Revolution in France*, which first appeared in Calcutta early in 1792 and was well received. His account of how France had been thrown into chaos by rationalist reformers and giddy Utopians struck a chord with administrators confronted with the job of ruling a people who had developed an ordered society and strong traditions. Burke reminded them that, like all societies, the Indian was a living organism which, however imperfect and irrational it seemed to outsiders, had evolved in response to special human needs. His veneration for the past and respect for whatever was rooted in it was shared by the Marquess Wellesley and the knot of young proconsuls who enjoyed his patronage – Charles Metcalfe, Montstuart Elphinstone and John Malcolm.

All were also touched by contemporary Romanticism, which made them highly susceptible to the wonders of Indian architecture, history and literature. As in Britain, ruins attracted Romantics and stimulated their imagination. Looking over a dilapidated Muslim graveyard in 1802, Metcalfe fell into a melancholy reverie on the Mughals and those shifts of fortune that had led to 'the fallen state of this race of beings who but half a century back ruled everywhere supreme'.[8] Most of the picturesque Indian 'scenes' which were now being reproduced and sold by British print-sellers showed ruined temples and palaces, often half-covered in foliage, but still conveying a sense of past grandeur. Colonel James Tod, surveying Rajasthan during the 1810s, was often overcome by flights of Romantic fancy when he came across Rajput strongholds. His first sight of the fort of Ajmer brought to mind lines from Byron's *Childe Harolde* and its vision of, 'Banner on high, and battles passed below'.[9] Reciting the region's history, he transformed the Rajput warlords into Indian Peverils of the Peak, complete with castles, armoured retainers, feudal hosts, heraldic pennants and bards reciting ancient deeds of glory. The colourful and idealised Gothic past of Sir Walter Scott seemed to have survived in India. Scott himself wrote a novel set in India, *The Surgeon's Daughter* (1827), with a plot set against the background of the struggle between the Company and Mysore forty years before. The sultan, Haidar Ali, is invested with the virtues of an ideal mediaeval king, displaying many instances of 'princely generosity and, what was more surprising, of even-handed generosity'.

Conservatives found much in India to admire and cherish. The caste system appeared a natural and ordered hierarchy and a valuable social cement. Metcalfe was particularly struck by the resilience of the Indian village, which had so miraculously survived the catastrophes of drought and civil war. He called these communities 'village republics' and wanted them to become the bedrock of the British Raj. They had proved their usefulness by standing the test of time, and for this reason deserved every encouragement. India's aristocracy also needed to be preserved and persuaded to become active partners with the Company. Elphinstone regretted the decline of the Bengali zamindars after the government had stripped them of their judicial powers and given them to callow Englishmen who knew nothing of local languages or culture.[10] In 1821, he was willing to perpetuate the fiscal privileges and legal powers to the Kathiawar nobility in return for their future co-operation with the administration. Another conservative, Alexander Walker, predicted that a dispossessed and dishonoured Indian nobility was bound to chafe against what he called the 'British Yoke'.[11]

Walker held the classic conservative view that gradual assimilation was far preferable to the imposition of change by decree. He believed history supported him:

> It is now upwards of 2,000 years since Alexander proposed to civilise the wild tribes he subdued, by building cities among them and reclaiming them from their savage customs by induc-ing them to relish the comforts of Social Intercourse. The same plan was followed by the Romans in Gaul and Britain.[12]

Assimilation required a degree of tolerance which many officials, includ-ing Walker, found all but impossible. He was rightly repelled by the Hindu custom of killing new-born baby girls and, in 1807, started a one-man campaign against it in Gujarat. Using moral persuasion, the force of his own personality and promises wrung from local chiefs, he made some headway. Success came slowly, although when he rode through the region in 1809 he was gratified to be greeted by mothers who stood by his stir-rup and presented their infant daughters to him.[13] Montstuart Elphinstone kept up the pressure, but found that in many areas religious prejudices remained strong. In 1828 he regretted the persistence of this abhorrent custom, but like Walker shrank from direct 'intrusion' into what he described as the 'private lives of the superior castes'. In time, the spread of 'tranquillity and good order' would, he believed, make the people amenable to 'reason and morality'.[14]

At the heart of the conservative view on how India should be governed was the acknowledgement that its religions and culture were sacrosanct. In its extreme form, this opinion was expressed by Wellington during the Lords debate on the 1833 India Bill. Calling for the rejection of the clause which banned slavery throughout the sub-continent, the Duke argued that it was the supreme duty of the British administration to 'uphold the ancient laws, customs and religion of the country'. All sanctioned slavery and he knew from experience that slaves were decently treated by their owners. 'Violent innovations' such as the abolition of slavery would inflame Indians and possibly provoke an uprising. None occurred, but Wellington was right when he predicted that the abandonment of a live-and-let-live policy towards certain Hindu rites was bound to provoke resentment and possibly rebellion.

1. The spoils of conquest: Robert Clive, whose victory at Plassey in 1757 set the stage for British domination of India.

2. Vision without integrity: Warren Hastings, the Governor-General who enlarged the East India Company's influence – and, his enemies claimed, his own fortune.

3. *Colonel Mordaunt's Cock Match*, by John Zoffany – 'At Lucknow in the Province of Oude [Awadh] in the Year 1786, at which were present several High and Distinguished personages.'

4. The Tiger Sultan: a likeness of Tipu Sultan of Mysore, who was killed when his capital Seringapatam fell in 1799. A hundred and forty years later, he would become a hero for Jinnah's Muslim League.

5. Fortunes to be made: a poster from about 1810 offers adventure and advancement in the East India Company's army.

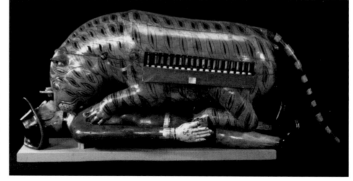

6. The Company overthrown: Tipu Sultan's mechanical tiger tears at the throat of a prostrate East India Company officer. The former roared and the latter howled in agony.

7. Trouble with tradesmen: a young Company officer considers an unpaid bill in about 1818, to the amusement of a sepoy and the distress of his wife. Indian ayahs calm the children.

8. Gentleman conqueror: the Marquess Wellesley, who determined that gentlemen should rule India, overthrew Mysore and then overstepped himself in a war against the Maratha Confederacy.

13. Images of conquest: the reverse of the Indian Mutiny medal (left) shows Britannia presenting laurels to the vengeful British lion. The 1848–49 Sikh War medal shows Khalsa warriors laying their arms at Lord Gough's feet. The recipient of this medal, an Irish lancer, charged twice against the Sikhs and was flogged during the campaign for being drunk on duty.

14. Apprentice to the Raj: Henry Vibart, Addiscombe cadet, in about 1850.

15. Khalsa general: although clad in armour, Raja Lal Singh was a commander of one of the most modern armies in Asia.

16. Colonel Samshur Bahadur Singh, grandson of Lal Singh, saw active service with Patiala states forces in Egypt during the First World War.

17. Rajput warriors, 1855. They carry tulwars, a shield and a matchlock musket, typical of the weaponry of Indian armies of the eighteenth and early-nineteenth centuries.

18. A centurion of the Raj: an officer of the Bengal Horse Artillery in full dress, with a helmet in the Graeco-Roman style, 1856.

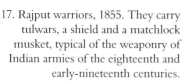

19. A model proconsul: Major Herbert Edwardes was one of a band of high-minded and resourceful young officers who served under Sir Henry Lawrence in the Punjab.

III

Policies based upon patience and a faith in the gradual mutation of Indian society and habits of mind were less easy to apply after 1832. A profound political upheaval in Britain had brought to power men of liberal views. They were reformers who believed that the tests of reason and usefulness should be applied to all institutions and that nothing could be justified solely on the grounds of antiquity and tradition. There was no fixed liberal ideology; rather its exponents blended their own doctrines from contemporary theories of individualism, Evangelical Christianity, Free-Trade and Laissez-Faire economic theories and that Utilitarian philosophy which pronounced good whatever promoted the happiness of the majority. Liberals took a systematic and rational approach to politics: first investigate and then legislate on the basis of thorough knowledge.

India was already undergoing a close examination. It had begun in the 1780s when the Company initiated the first of many surveys to discover and record the races and castes in its possession: their languages, religions, history and culture. Knowledge equalled power since the more the government knew about its subjects, the better it could exercise authority over them. For instance, in 1855 a district magistrate with an intimate understanding of purification rituals was able to detect vital inconsistencies in the testimony of several Hindus accused of murdering a woman and throwing her corpse in the Ganges.[15] Widespread misgivings about the honesty of munshis, *babus* (clerks) and courtroom advisers on Hindu and Muslim law made it imperative that British officials mastered Sanskrit, the language of the law and literature, and Persian, the language of diplomacy.

There was also a need to uncover the sources of India's wealth, its potential for development as well as its natural features. In 1784, a group of 'curious and learned men' gathered in Calcutta to found the Asiatick Society of Bengal. In imitation of the Royal Society, its members collected, exchanged and published their research on Indian tongues, history, science, mathematics, zoology and meteorology. Their work supplemented that of government officers, like Major Colin Mackenzie, who traversed Mysore in 1800 with instructions to catalogue its human and natural resources. Geography became the servant of altruistic paternalism, for he was told that what he discovered would assist 'the amelioration of the state of the Native Subjects' and deliver 'the means of conciliating their minds, of exciting habits of industry, and cultivate the Arts of Peace under the milder influence of a fixed rule'.[16]

The expanding encyclopaedia of India provided the raw material for liberal theorists. The most influential was James Mill, a philosopher and political economist, who became an examiner of official correspondence in the Company's London office in 1819. A year before, he had produced a lengthy, plodding and unimaginative history of British India, in which nearly everything Indian from religion to farming methods was either condemned or given the thinnest praise. Today, Mill's judgements on India appear presumptuous, for they rested upon an assumption that the Britain of his time represented a perfect model of a civilisation on course for perfection and infinitely superior to that of India. Indians had failed to move up what Mill called 'the scale of civilisation' because their minds were shackled by superstition and an exaggerated veneration for the past. Moreover, in one characteristically condescending passage, he observes that while 'our ancestors, however, though rough, were sincere, but, under the glosing exterior of the Hindu, lies a general disposition to deceit and perfidy'. The Muslim was another moral delinquent, possessing, 'The same insincerity and perfidy; the same indifference to the feeling of others, the same prostitution and venality.'[17]

Nothing short of a complete educational and moral reformation could rescue India from continued degradation was Mill's conclusion. Macaulay agreed both with this analysis and the cure. Like his mentor, Macaulay was intellectually conceited to the point of arrogance, once observing that the entire literature of the Middle East and India were not worth 'a single shelf in a good European library'. But the Indian mind was not beyond redemption, as he explained to the Commons during the debate on the India Bill in the summer of 1833. India, he predicted, would be transformed into 'the imperishable empire of our art and morals, our literature and laws'. Its dismal present would be replaced by the glowing future:

> I see bloody and degrading superstitions gradually losing their power. I see the morality, the philosophy, the taste of Europe beginning to produce a salutary effect on the hearts and understanding of our subjects. I see the public mind of India, that public mind which we found debased and contracted by the worst forms of political and religious tyranny, expanding itself to just and noble views of the ends of government and of the social duties of man.

In essence, this was the liberal view of how India could be reborn, or, to be more exact, how Indians might be moulded into liberal Englishmen. The agent for this metamorphosis was the Company, which Parliament deprived of the last vestiges of its trading monopoly, making generous allowance for stockholders and subscribers to its loans. Henceforward, the East India Company was to devote itself solely to the government and improvement of its subjects along the lines suggested by Macaulay.

An autocratic state like the Company's was superficially well suited to undertake what was, in effect, a revolution from above. No one imagined that the process would be speedy or that reform could be achieved by a sheaf of edicts. In 1832, James Mill, who had now learned something of the realities of Indian administration behind his desk in Leadenhall Street, warned a Commons committee of the risks involved in pressing ahead with reform too quickly. High-caste Brahmins found the British concept of equality before the law distasteful and so its introduction would have to be gradual and piecemeal.[18] Nonetheless, he and Macaulay had provided the moral justification for the Company to interfere with, even forbid ancient customs and rites.

The political mandate had been given by the 1833 India Bill, and there were plenty of keen, *bien pensant* young officials on hand to fulfil it. One of them, Charles Trevelyan, was approvingly described by his future brother-in-law, Macaulay, after their first meeting in 1834:

> He has no small talk. His mind is full of schemes of moral and political improvement, and his zeal boils over in his talk. His topics, even in courtship, are steam navigation, the education of the natives, and the equalisation of the sugar duties, the substitution of the Roman for the Arabic alphabet in the Oriental languages.[19]

India was about to be engulfed in a tide of progress and swept forward. But what was its eventual destination? Macaulay imagined that, at some distant date, its emancipated people would announce themselves as qualified for self-government and claim Britain's birthright of individual freedom and democracy for themselves. The prospect pleased him, as it did the conservative Alexander Walker, who also believed that when Indians had absorbed the morality and sense of responsibility of their rulers, they would be qualified to rule themselves 'with fidelity'.[20]

III

For all their enthusiasm and faith in scientific methodology, men of Trevelyan's stamp were bound to have limited success. Their zeal was not shared by all their colleagues, many of whom inclined towards cautious pragmatism. Indians understood despotism and welcomed it, if it was sensitive and worked in their best interests. This was why Sir Henry Lawrence sent his magistrates across the Punjab, holding impromptu, open-air courts in the villages and delivering rough and ready judgements which were firm and seen to be fair. For these men, the elaborate codes contrived by men like Macaulay were of little value.

And yet, even if everyone concerned with the administration of India was inspired by uniform dreams of reform and renewal, they would have found it well-nigh impossible to surmount the hurdles which stood in their way.

To start with, there were two British Indias. There were the annexed areas, such as Bengal, which were directly under Company rule and where the laws were made by governor-generals and their councils under the supervision of Parliament. This strictly British India was in many ways suited to the social and political experiments planned by the reformers, for the government enjoyed absolute power and could overrule objections from those who failed to recognise what was in their best interests. In other words, conditions were ideal for a benevolent despotism. But, as Mill appreciated and regretted, there were also large swathes of India ruled by hereditary native princes, who were technically 'allies' of the Company and bound to it by what were called 'subsidiary' treaties. In 1830 the largest were Travancore, Hyderabad, Baroda, Awadh, Gwalior, Indore and the Rajput states of present-day Rajasthan. The population of all the princely states was estimated at about 181 million in 1857, while that of British India was just over 23 million.

In theory, Britain as the paramount power could exert pressure over the princes through official residents, even to the point of deposing a recidivist raja. This was what happened to Bharmalji, the Rao of Kachchh, who was dethroned in 1819 for persistently making war on his neighbours. The laws of inheritance were upheld and he was replaced by his infant son, who would presumably learn how to govern in a manner acceptable to the Company.[21] This procedure was a final resort, undertaken reluctantly and rarely. Alexander Walker had warned in 1810 that the princes would not be bridled by 'intolerable' restraints on their power and could easily be turned into active enemies the Raj could do without.[22] Provoking the princes was a foolhardy enterprise when, at least before the final defeat of Sikhs, they were needed as allies. During the first Sikh campaign, the Company was specially indebted to the Maharaja of Patiala, whose lands were adjacent to the Punjab. His friendship and refusal to get drawn into any anti-government plots was rewarded with a grant of land worth £4,000.[23] Religious and political figureheads for millions of Indians, the princes were a power to be reckoned with, as Bengali Hindus reminded the government in 1850, when they protested against changes in the law which were 'odious' to their beliefs.[24]

This point was understood by Lord Auckland who, in 1836, shrank from over-zealous meddling in Awadh, where the day-to-day administration was in a parlous state thanks to an idle and dissolute king. This merry sybarite had told the resident 'that nothing in the treaties stopped him from having "Hip, hip Hworah" as he pleased', which was right, according to the letter of law. The Governor-General had to agree, and prescribed a policy of 'moderation and respect for right', rather than one of 'ambitious appropriation and the extinction of the last spark of Mahomedan splendour and power in India'. Unseating this powerful prince would arouse the hatred of what was left of the 'native power'.[25] Likewise, everything possible was done to avoid a head-on collision with Man Singh, the Raja of Jodhpur, when he refused to co-operate wholeheartedly with the government's campaigns against *thagi* (ritual robbery and murder) and *dakaiti* (armed robbery) in 1833. After six years of obstruction, Calcutta's patience was exhausted and a small force was sent to Jodhpur to compel the raja to do as he was told or face deposition.[26] He chose to toe the line.

Well-intentioned reforms were by and large unwelcome in the princely states. They were unasked for and often appeared to both rulers and their subjects as interference from above which threatened popular customs and rituals. Such objections were dismissed out of hand by impatient officials. One, reporting on the progress of administrative reorganisation in Awadh during 1836, blamed opposition on prejudice and what he took to be ingrained hostility to any form of innovation.[27] He may well have been right, but it was unwise to awake too many sleeping dogs. Many were allowed to slumber for years to come; in the early 1870s an investigation into the affairs of the Gaikwar of Baroda revealed the prevalence of the official use of torture, abduction and illegal imprisonment.[28]

There were also severe financial constraints on what the government could do. The total revenue for the year 1852–53 was £20.4 million, of which £13.8 million came from Bengal and the north-western provinces, £3.27 million from Madras and £2.8 million from Bombay. The biggest charges on the presidencies' budgets were military expenses, and there were additional charges for Company pensions, the bill for regular British troops and interest on the Company's debts (£2.7 million), which totalled £5.3 million. The overall surplus for the year was £424,200, with Bombay having a deficit of £113,000. There was no escaping the outlay for security, between a third and a half of the annual budget, more in war-time. This left the narrowest margin for those public works and educational measures which were vital if India was to be regenerated. The allocation for non-English schools in Bengal during the early 1850s was £15,000, while the annual military expenditure was over £5 million.

Funding large-scale public projects was difficult. The Company had to operate within boundaries laid down by current economic dogma. This excluded government agencies from capitalist enterprises, such as railways, but permitted official investment in public works which would augment revenues or facilitate administration. Within this framework, it was possible for the Company to fund the construction of the roads and telegraph lines which linked the three presidencies. The latter, undertaken during the early 1850s, cost £110,250. Road-building costs in the 1840s consumed an average of £400,000 a year from the public works allocations, with the largest sums on the great trunk road between Calcutta and Delhi. It had, unsually for India at the time, a Tarmac surface, cost £1,000 a mile and required £50,000 a year to maintain.[29] Metalled roads had an obvious military value, and they also facilitated and expedited internal trade. Purely economic advantages flowed from the Ganges and Punjab irrigation canals, for which £2 million was set aside in the 1840s. Both increased the amount of land available for cultivation and protected farmers from the vagaries of the monsoon, benefits that were translated into higher revenues from land taxes.

Railways were a different matter. Their champions agreed that they might, at a stroke, transform India for better and, as in Britain, provide an upsurge in economic growth. According to one lobbyist, railways would inject an 'entirely new element of civilisation' into the sub-continent and prove a 'regenerating influence' over its entire population.[30] Another promised that the rail network would be welcomed by 'the growing class of intelligent natives', although they would be condemned by 'a few, old, antiquated Hindus, who look upon every innovation with a feeling of horror'.[31] Their sulking could be discounted. Railways were a blessing and travel would widen Indian horizons and bring caste barriers tumbling down.

The trouble was how to pay for them. In 1845, when Indian railway mania was getting under way, Lord Hardinge hoped that they might be financed by an allocation of £4–5 million of public money.[32] The first Sikh war scuppered an idea which, in any case, ran counter to prevailing economic doctrines. These were formally upheld when Parliament insisted that the capital for Indian railways would come from private sources. Nonetheless, the Company was free to lure investors by offering its own funds as a guarantee for a very generous annual return of 5 per cent on all railway stock, irrespective of the company's profitability. Shareholders were being given the equivalent of gilt-edged stocks, and the Indian railway companies were able to secure the cash needed for the initially heavy outlay on engines, rolling stock and construction. The East India Railway Company, established in 1849 to build the Calcutta–Agra–Delhi line, raised £10 million, and the smaller Great Indian Peninsular Railway Company secured £3.4 million for a network designed to open up the hinterland of Bombay. In the case of the former, the hidden subsidy was paid until 1866, after which the firm could afford to pay the full dividend from its profits.[33]

An appeal for investment in Indian railways delivered in 1849 by one of General Napier's aides-de-camp regretted that the Company had made 'so little progress in the physical improvment of India'.[34] He was repeating the complaint made by another railway enthusiast, four years before:

> Brilliant as is the prestige which hangs over our Indian empire, it must be confessed that it is still in a state of helpless and discreditable barbarism, many, many, centuries behind the example set by any other nation in civilised history.[35]

This was a source of national shame, but it was unavoidable.

None of those concerned with the remoulding of India had ever seriously calculated the intensity of popular attachment to familiar habits. They assumed that Indians would bow before superior reason and gladly accept what was for their own good. Nor did they take much account of the resistance to change, or, most important of all, the connection in the Indian mind between innovation and conversion. 'The bigotry of Mussalman maulavis [Muslim lawyers and theologians]' was an obstacle to filling places in English schools in Bengal, where a fear of possible Christian indoctrination often outweighed the urge to learn the language, which would assure a pupil a post in the administration.[36] Attempts by the Madras government to introduce agricultural shows of the kind which had so helped British farming foundered in 1856 because some peasants feared their cows' milk yields might fall as a result of a journey. In one district, the ryots suspected that offers of prizes for the best rice was a government trick, contrived to compel everyone to eat boiled rice, a diet which would somehow lead to mass conversion.[37]

No doubt the officials who read these reports either sighed or shook with laughter. But Indian credulity was not as far-fetched as it might have seemed, for the eventual dominance of Christianity was widely seen by reformers as an objective which was both inevitable and desirable. As it was, the rehabilitation of India always had to take second place to the mundane but essential duties of the Company, the collection of taxes and the imposition of civil order.

3

Gradual and Mild Correction: Taxing and Policing India

I

Thomas Fortescue was a diligent, fair-minded and generous-spirited official attached to the Delhi residency, and a man ideally fitted to discover whether the Company's system of revenue assessment and collection was working.[1] In the late spring of 1819 he left Delhi for a lengthy tour of the villages to the north and west of the city. His employers were acutely conscious that they were the heirs general of the Mughal emperors whose most valuable legacy were the rights to tax their subjects. Their methods were far from perfect, and in many areas exactions were iniquitous. But the system could be improved through the labours of men like Fortescue, whose task was to balance the ability of the peasantry to pay with the needs of the Company.

Aware of the delicacy of his mission, he went to great lengths to put people at their ease, speaking directly and in their own language to zamindars, headmen and peasants. He and his party of servants and sepoys traversed a gently rolling countryside of fertile soil where the predominant ochre is broken by the dark greens of scattered trees, mostly thorn, shrubs and growing crops. Here and there are stretches of close bush, known as jungle, which still harbour game of all kinds and a few tigers. It was an area favoured by Indian and British sportsmen.

Following in his footsteps, one can still share his pleasure at the sight of small towns and villages with well-built houses which, together with the wells, tanks (reservoirs) and acqueducts, he took to be signs of 'former abundance, population, security and happiness'. Fortescue was greeted by effusive Rajput zamindars full of praise for the 'all-powerful government' which, in less than twenty years, had eliminated banditry and the extortions of their former Maratha overlords. This was an overstatement, for Fortescue noticed that the Gujars still divided their time equally between farming and marauding, but believed that 'gradual and mild correction' would make them change their ways for the better. He was somewhat over-optimistic; the next generation of revenue officials was ordered to coax the Gujars into good habits by generous assessments and, when necessary, the seizure of the defaulter's lands.[2] Taxation was always a valuable means of social and political control.

Zamindari flattery turned to evasiveness and concealment of records whenever Fortescue or any other official attempted to obtain exact definitions of who held what and how much they owed the government. When the region's revenue obligations had first been estimated eleven years before, the assessors found themselves stumbling through a maze of ancient tenures, obligations, usages and immunities. Everywhere, there was an understandable unwillingness to tell the truth, for to do so would burden a community with a tax liability for the next few years, or, in some regions, for ever. Alexander Read relied on a translator when he made his enquiries in the northern part of Kanara in 1800, but was certain that its inhabitants 'play tricks and make a false settlement'. His colleague, Thomas Munro, was of like mind, and relied on spies to collect precise information.[3]

Often in exasperation, tax surveyors were driven to rely on the advice of local men of substance, landowners or village headmen. This was both a dangerous and a naïve expedient, for such men inevitably looked to their own interests and misled investigators. As an official guide to tax assessment of 1844 put it: 'There is a great tendency amongst natives especially, to assess heavily the poor and industrious classes of cultivators and be more lenient to the powerful.'[4] Quite so; and the results were calamitous for the ryots. Disparities abounded in many areas and came to light once the system was in operation. In one extreme case it was discovered in 1894 that the charge per acre for rice-growing lands in Malabar varied between less than one (8p) and 40 rupees (£3.20) an acre. This was not surprising since the original assessment of Malabar had been undertaken a hundred years before with the assistance of local landlords, whom the Company's agents considered worth cultivating because of their influence. This made political sense, but the cost of such alliances of convenience was born by the Malabar peasantry whose holdings were highly taxed. Wealthier men, self-assessed, as it were, paid less and sometimes appeared to have exempted themselves from all liability.[5]

The most formidable barrier between tax assessor and tax payer was the difference between British and Indian legal and philosophical perceptions of the rights of property. Like everyone else engaged in this field, Fortescue's mind was filled with peculiarly British concepts of proprietary rights and obligations. In many respects his and his colleagues' enquiries can be compared to those undertaken for that earlier, exhaustive catalogue of national resources, the Domesday Book. But there was one, highly significant difference. When William the Conqueror's agents asked their questions, they did so in the knowledge that they and the Saxons shared many common ideas about the nature of land ownership.

No meeting of minds occurred between the Company's inquisitors and Indians; instead there was confusion and mutual misunderstanding. Merely occupying and tilling land gave an Indian peasant a legitimate right to it, something which was unthinkable in Britain. Moreover, at this period, it was common for entire communities to migrate and set up new villages on unbroken land. And then there was the barrier of language. What, for instance, did Fortescue understand by a '*bigha*', a unit of land he encountered many times during his journey. It could not be measured, nor could its owner's title be defined in terms comprehensible to any British jurist. But an Indian understood what the word conveyed: it was an allocation of land whose produce could support a family, according to the needs of its caste.[6] Likewise, Fortescue would have been puzzled by the frequent absence of the paraphernalia of deeds and tenancy agreements which were essential for anyone who occupied land in Britain. Indians could manage without them, but they had an elaborate language of land occupation; there were 162 different words and phrases classifying tenure in Bengal alone.[7]

Where earlier, Mughal tax returns existed, they were frequently found to have been mislaid, often deliberately. In 1850, bundles of old tax assessments were found being used for firework manufacture in Poona. In this area, Company officials endeavouring to find out exactly the tax burden on the deposed peshwa's lands resorted to raids on the homes of landowners to uncover hidden files. Doggedness paid dividends: in 1848 the Bombay presidency could proudly claim that over £6,000 spent on fiscal sleuthing was yielding £20,000 a year.[8] Not everyone was so patient and painstaking. The pressure on surveyors to reach a settlement was always strong, for the Company had to meet bills for conquest and administration and justify the argument that aggressive wars eventually paid for themselves in tax dividends. It was, therefore, easy for assessment officers to succumb to frustration and fall back either on the dubious advice of local landowners or cut through the tangle of unintelligible terms and customs.

Misunderstanding was common, and injustice inevitably followed. Nevertheless, experience taught men like Fortescue to be flexible. Faced with 400 or so villages which had sprung up in the past few years, he reported to his superiors that, despite the absence of title deeds, it was 'pretty well understood' that the newly cultivated lands belonged to the families who were farming them. Above all, he knew that the Company needed to foster what he called 'the small Republics' in their self-sufficiency and productiveness. The commissioner was enchanted by their inhabitants, who entertained him with songs and stories of past triumphs and independence. He believed that the tax settlement was to their ultimate advantage and rather hoped that the coming of British rule would mark a revival of the peace and plenty they had known long ago. He urged the Company to use these people kindly and, remembering that he was a civil servant, added that their prosperity would ensure a handsome tax return.

II

Past and present analysts of the various settlements made across India agree that their consequences were far-reaching and, by and large, hurtful to millions of the poorest classes. There were winners and losers, and in many instances what was hoped to be an equitable system of raising revenue had unlooked-for and unwanted consequences. This gap between intention and result was most glaring wherever the Bengal Settlement was adopted.

The Bengal Settlement was introduced in 1793 and eventually extended to the north-western provinces, the Punjab, Awadh, some southern districts and various parts of the former Maratha territories in the Deccan. It presumed the existence of a landowning class, which would serve as collectors of revenue from the peasantry on their lands and repay official recognition of their titles with loyalty. Those who framed and applied this system imagined that it would accelerate the creation of a stable stratum of landowners who, in the British fashion, would combine support for the government with the economic development of their estates. The zamindars and *taluqdars* (landowners) of northern India would, in time, become the counterparts of the English squire and Scottish laird – a benevolent, improving landlord with a stake in the country.

Things did not turn out as expected. To start with, the newly elevated zamindars of Bengal were a mixed bunch of varying wealth and status, ranging from rajas with sizeable territories to revenue farmers and tax collectors whose connections with the lands they happened to occupy when the settlement was being drawn up were tenuous. Collectively, this artificial Indian squirearchy did not behave as predicted. Deprived of any judicial powers over their tenants, they saw themselves merely as cogs in the Company's tax-gathering machine and free to squeeze as much profit from their lands as possible. They were helped by a government which, having created a hierarchy, found itself obliged to back it. Between 1799 and 1812 ordinances were issued which whittled away the remaining rights of the ryots and empowered the zamindars to raise rents as they pleased. Land was transformed into a highly lucrative source of investment which was swiftly exploited by those with spare capital. Among those who did well from the settlement was Rammothan Ray, a Calcutta businessman who, between 1799 and 1810, purchased four zamindar's estates worth £1,000 a year.[9] He was not one of those whom the settlement had been designed to benefit; nor were the speculators who used the profits of banking and rural money-lending to purchase estates, often of tax defaulters, in the Benares (Varanasi) region.[10]

Indian folklore commonly portrays the zamindar as an oppressive figure, and he is second only to the Raj in the demonology of the mainly Marxist historians of India's peasantry. In most instances, the zamindars' worst crime was to protect their property, rights and interests with the same determination as the ryots, and usually with greater success. In the collection, as well as the assessment of taxation, they were certainly capable of deceit, often on a large scale. In the Sherpur district, close to the present-day border between India and Bangladesh, local zamindars were alleged in 1820 to have collected 20,000 rupees from an area assessed at 12,000.[11]

This is creditable, if not credible, and it was certainly not new. There is nothing to suggest that fraud was not commonplace under the Mughals. The Company also found itself the embarrassed inheritor of severe Mughal methods of tax extraction which were still being employed in the middle of the century. Herbert Edwardes noticed how Punjabi tax gatherers 'screwed' the zamindars and ryots on the North-West Frontier in 1847, something he hoped would cease as British law was established. It did not; a Parliamentary report of 1855 revealed that ryots who could not or would not pay their dues were sometimes tortured by zamindars' servants. Torments included beatings, starvation, thumb-screws and inserting chillies or peppers into the eyes and genitalia of victims.[12] Between 1871 and 1873 there were several incidents in which the Raja of Baroda's police thrashed and abused alleged defaulters, of whom four died from their injuries.[13]

Superficially, the ryotwari system of revenue collection appeared less likely to be a source of oppression. It was seen as an extension of Mughal custom, and was widely adopted in the annexed districts of the Madras presidency at the turn of the eighteenth century. Assessments of each village were made, first on a three-year and then a ten-year basis, and the taxes were paid by an agent, usually the *patel* (headman). Despite considerable efforts, the rate of taxation was as variable at that under the zamindar system.

This unevenness was, perhaps, the worst feature of the Company's revenue system. Under the Mughals, an average of between 40 and 50 per cent of a ryot's produce was taken from him, but the proportion was occasionally as high as 65 to 80 per cent.[14] There was no uniform rate under the Company, with as much as 83 per cent being extracted in Orissa, an amount which was progressively lowered to 60 per cent by 1840. At this time, a two-thirds deduction was considered as an equitable mean and exactions of 50 to 60 per cent were widespread.[15] In the Madras presidency, the ryot's annual income was officially broken down as follows: 40 per cent for costs of cultivation, including seed for the next year's sowing, and 14 per cent for the sustenance of his family, which left 46 per cent for the government. This estimate, which made no provision for the vagaries of climate, condemned the ryot and his descendants to exist perpetually at a subsistence level without the opportunity to save or acquire additional land.

Official arithmetic took no account of the human tragedies brought about by a system which, at its most generous, demanded half a family's income every year. Complaints were plentiful, especially in times of drought. In 1819 a petition from the peasantry of Malabar described the bodies of destitute men and women lying by the roadsides where they had fallen, overcome by starvation as they moved away from areas of severe taxation.[16] The view from the top was often as grim. In 1853 the collectors of Trichinopoly, Bellary and Tanjore reported that the ryots were compelled to accept the lowest prices for their produce just to meet their tax demands.[17] This also occurred in the Punjab during the early 1850s when, for the same reason, farmers were forced to sell their crops when the market was glutted and prices were dropping. Matters here were made worse by an excessive assessment, based upon abstracts drawn up by Ranjit Singh's Treasury officials which bore no relation to the actual sums collected in the countryside.[18]

The Raj always insisted on prompt payment of taxes. Its demands for immediate quittance created an annual crisis in millions of ryots' households. In some desperate instances, it was resolved by the sale of seed corn, cattle, household utensils and clothes. More commonly, the ryot plunged himself and his family into debt. Borrowing to settle a tax bill was the only alternative to eviction, but it placed a ryot and his descendants in permanent bondage to moneylenders of one kind or another. The rates of interest were savage; typically, a patel or village *marwari* (moneylender) might loan cash at between 12 and 18 per cent interest, although rates of up to 25 per cent were not exceptional.[19] Huge sections of the rural population were shackled to steadily accumulating debts without any hope of ever paying off the original loan. If they defaulted on the interest, moneylenders foreclosed using distraints obtained from the growing number of British courts: 2,900 ryots were sued in the Ahmadnagar court in 1835, over twice that number four years later.[20]

Investigations of rural indebtedness in Awadh during 1868–69 revealed that in most districts between 60 and 80 per cent of peasant families owed money. In some areas the total was as high as 90 per cent, and many debtors were compelled to surrender their surplus crops as interest payments.[21] The average ryot holding was between three and four acres and the burden of tax and interest payments ruled out investment in extra land, stock and tools. Again, the courts were the handmaidens of the usurers. In the Punjab 45,000 were arrested for debt and 5,000 locked up between 1880 and 1884. In the latter year, there were 103,000 recovery suits brought by moneylenders against peasants. It was calculated that one in twenty families was embroiled in debt litigation.[22]

Agricultural stagnation, investment paralysis and social tension were the direct results of the Company's land taxation. By taking an excessive cut from the farmer's crops, the government was starving rural communities of capital which could have been used to increase production, particularly improvements in irrigation. It was noticed that in the Coimbatore district, where the ryotwari assessment was relatively low, farmers had spare cash for irrigation projects and the population rose. Economic growth generally was stifled because anyone with capital channelled it into high-interest loans to the poorest classes who were unable to pay their taxes on time.

Peasant riots and uprisings were an unavoidable result of the system. They were sporadic and localised outbursts of desperate rage, often first triggered by drought and religious and ethnic tensions. The Muslim Mapillas were at the bottom of the social and economic pile in Malabar, and their intermittent, violent protests against the predominantly Hindu landlord class had a sectarian edge. After an outbreak of disorder in 1851, a local magistrate discovered that a holy man had promised Mapillas 'religious merit' if they murdered a Hindu landlord who had evicted a poor tenant.[23] There was also a desire to lash out blindly against moneylenders. During the 1854–55 uprising by the Santals of the Midnapur district, insurgents hacked off the limbs and head of a zamindar moneylender, chanting 'Four Annas', 'Eight Annas', 'Twelve Annas' and, at the final stroke, 'Farkatti [quittance]'.[24]

These rural jacqueries presented very few problems for the authorities. In 1833 Company forces easily overcame a millennialist, anti-zamindar and anti-government revolt in the Sherpur district of northern Bengal. The rebels were armed with spears, bows, poisoned arrows, a few matchlocks and the belief that if their faith in their messianic leader was strong they would be immune to musket balls.[25] No doubt the many casualties were warriors of shallow convictions. Troops deployed against the Santals in 1855 were moved for part of their journey by the new railway line between Calcutta and Burdwan, and help was forthcoming from local landowners, including the Raja of Murshidabad, who loaned transport elephants. This co-operation was a reminder that men of property would rally to the government whenever the social order was challenged. Loyalty was always well rewarded; a landowner who helped in the suppression of the 1838 Coorg revolt was given a remission of taxes.[26] It is not known whether he passed on his good fortune to the local ryots.

The many faults in the tax system were recognised by those responsible for its everyday operation. Collectors expressed their misgivings, suggested adjustments and sometimes offered relief on their own intiative. After severe flooding in the Guntur district in 1849 and 1850, Mr Stokes the collector admitted to the ryots that he had been unduly strict and made concessions of up to two-thirds on the demands for 1851.[27] This sort of tinkering with the machine was frowned on by the Company; in 1805 the Madras government turned down pleas from subordinate officials for tax reductions during a famine on the grounds that it might be interpreted by Indians as weakness.[28]

Whenever major alterations to the tax system were proposed, expediency overruled compassion. The Company could not afford to change the system: like the Mughal empire, it rested on the exploitation of India's main source of wealth, the land. There were no comparable alternate sources of income. The 1813 and 1833 India acts had imposed prevailing free-trade doctrines on the Company, which compelled it to relinquish most of its commercial monopolies. For the same reason, the Company abolished internal tarrifs that had once been a standby for the Mughals. Besides, a fundamental reorganisation and rationalisation of the land-tax system might antagonise the princes and zamindars who enforced and often profited from it. Responding to a critic of the system in 1837, Lord Auckland told him: 'Were you yourself to become a real autocrat of India, you would of course not endanger so vital a portion of its existing resources as is the land resource.'[29] There was, however, some lowering of the proportion of their income extracted from the ryots, largely because of pressure from London, where commercial lobbyists were anxious not to deprive potential Indian consumers of the wherewithal to buy British goods. By 1856, the average rate lay somewhere between 50 and 60 per cent, but it was not universal and in many regions the ryots' liabilities stayed unrealistically high.

III

Stiff taxes which fell heavily on the poorest were defended on the grounds that the payers got public order and personal security in return for their outlay. In peace, as in war, the Company's self-image was one of a bringer of peace to a country that had hitherto been convulsed by chronic disorder and crime. As the agencies of the law extended into the Indian interior, underworlds of crime were exposed just beneath the surface of societies which appeared tranquil. Officials began to discover what they imagined to be castes of bold, resourceful and ruthless professional criminals who roamed the countryside, preying on its inhabitants. These robber bands were, one civil servant wrote in 1855, 'like an infernal machine beneath the keel of the good ship government' and they had to be extirpated.[30] There were other, equally disturbing revelations of crimes that were part of religous rituals and social customs, including the sacrifice of children by the Konds and the burying alive of lepers by their kinsfolk.[31]

As the Company's servants accumulated intelligence about the nature of Indian crime and attempted, in the manner of bureaucrats, to classify it, they came to believe that they were exploring a hideous moral wilderness. They were penetrating what an army doctor and forensic pathologist, Major Norman Chevers, called in 1854 the 'darker recesses of the Bengali and Hindustani nature'. Once this had been understood, 'an European can learn how strange a combination of sensuality, jealousy, wild and ineradicable superstition, absolute untruthfulness, and ruthless disregard of the value of human life, lie below the placid, timid, forbearing exterior of the Indian'.[32] The old racial stereotype of the docile Indian gave way to a new one, of a creature whose mildness was a façade behind which lay a morally flawed character. He was, in short, a natural deceiver.

Deception was the trade of India's most notorious criminals, the *thagi* (thugs). Since 1810, the British had collected fragments of intelligence about bands of criminals who murdered and robbed travellers in central and northern India. Their activities came into sharper focus when William Sleeman, the magistrate at Nursingpur, gathered confessions from thugs between 1822 and 1824. This trickle of information became a torrent during the next dozen years, revealing the existence of between forty and fifty gangs who were calculated to be killing between 20,000 and 40,000 victims each year.

Perhaps the most vivid insight into the secret world of the thugs comes from the confessions made to James Paton, the assistant resident at Lucknow, during the autumn of 1836. The principal informer, Rumrati, had grown up in the Awadh village of Kothdi, the home of at least eighty thugs who, in return for a cut from their spoils, enjoyed the protection of the local zamindar. As a youth he was introduced into the fellowship of thugs by his uncle and, at some date between 1829 and 1834, joined a 24-strong expedition. It started with a sequence of purification rituals in which the thugs fasted, washed themselves and their clothes, consecrated their strangling cloths and the pick that was used to dig their victims' graves. Then a goat was beheaded as a sacrifice to the goddess Kali, the thugs looking closely at its head to see if its mouth was open. It was and this was a good omen, indicating Kali's blessing on the enterprise. Other portents were needed before the thugs set off. An ass braying on their left was a good sign, someone sneezing foretold misfortune, as did the cries of kites, owls and partridges. Given the numbers of these birds in rural India, thousands of expeditions must have been called off at the last moment.

Heartened by favourable omens, Rumrati's party moved southwards, once meeting another gang of thugs. After thirteen days, they encountered four palanquin bearers with two bullocks travelling northwards to Lahore, and decoyed them off their road by claiming that if they continued on their route they would be forced to pay a heavy tax. The bearers were led to a spot already chosen for their murder, persuaded to sit down and share a hookah. At the signal '*Sussul Khan Chulo*' the stranglers pounced. According to Paton, Rumrati snapped his fingers to indicate the swiftness with which death came. Some of the spoils were sent home to the thugs' families, and then they shifted westwards. They continued for at least four weeks and finally ended up at Benares, having strangled and plundered thirteen travellers, including four soldiers.

The pattern of murder was always the same. The site of the killing was selected in advance and the 'inveiglers' lured the victims to it by shows of friendship. Twice an inveigler offered to massage the limbs of men suffering from rheumatism. The corpses were stabbed, a ritual which linked the slaughter to sacrifices once made by thugs to their protectoress, Kali. The bodies were then squeezed into narrow graves which had been previously dug, or, in one instance, thrown down a well.[33]

Paton heard from other approvers that they regarded their crimes as a trade. One told him: 'I have followed the trade of murder. I have seen at a guess some four or five hundred men strangled and I have strangled about one hundred with my own hands.' A man of Evangelical inclinations, Paton was shocked by the 'relish and pleasure' with which the murderers confessed, and their obvious pride in following their kinsmen into a profession which was often hereditary. They punctuated their narratives with laughter, and one approver was highly amused when the corpse of one of his victims was snatched by a Ganges *mugur nutah* (crocodile), which had become, as it were, the thugs' accomplice. 'The crocodile knew that we were murdering and came for his prey.' This assassin claimed 'the love of money' was the thugs' motive, but others described rituals and taboos (women were never killed), which linked thagi to Kali.[34] This connection did not prevent Muslims from occasionally joining thug gangs. And yet bonds of religious brotherhood were brittle, for there were plenty of captured thugs who broke faith with their comrades, displaying the same devil-may-care spirit they did when they befriended and then killed their victims.

Paton was one of the eighteen officers attached to the Thagi and Dakaiti Department, which had been set up by Lord Bentinck in 1829 under Sleeman's direction. It worked through informers whose intelligence enabled troops and police to intercept parties of thugs and excavate their burial grounds. By 1837, the department had acquired 483 informers who, their work over, were employed at Jabalpur gaol weaving carpets and tents. This manufactory was called The House of Industry, a title which reflected the current faith in honest labour as both corrective and cure for criminality. In 1857, four thugs-turned-weavers posed for the photographer Felice Beato, demonstrating how they had strangled their victims; they had not forgotten their old skills. Convicted thugs were either hanged or transported to the penal labour colonies on the Andaman islands. Sleeman believed that the executions deterred the thugs' close relatives from taking up the family calling. The thugs were unmoved by their fate; in one instance several under sentence of death sung cheerily on their way to the scaffold and hung themselves rather than die at the polluted hands of an executioner who was a leather dresser.[35]

It is highly likely that Sleeman and his staff often mistook *dacoits*, who were straightforward armed robbers, for thugs, who had loose religious connections. *Dakaiti* (armed robbery by gangs) was a far commoner crime than thagi. There was an average of 1,500 dakaitis committed in Bengal in the early 1800s, but the number reported to the police had fallen to 169 by 1828. This downward trend was soon reversed. In the early 1850s there was an upsurge in dakaiti, and one magistrate admitted that no man of property could sleep easily at night in the Calcutta district.[36] Dacoit bands were mobile, well-organised and often worked hand-in-glove with village *chowkidahs* (watchmen) and even the Company's police.[37] In Awadh in 1840 there were an estimated 1,500–2,000 dacoits, all *Bhudduks* (peasant mercenaries hired by landowners), who enjoyed zamindar patronage and, like the thugs, had their own argot. The wandered far and wide, sometimes straying on to Company territory disguised as faqirs and pilgrims, and robbed taluqdars, bankers and tax officers.[38]

The typical dacoit was never a Robin Hood figure, although he and his exploits have been romanticised by Indian balladeers, story tellers, and, more recently, left-wing fantasists, for whom he was a class warrior, fighting inequality and oppression. This is sentimental nonsense. In reality, the dacoit was a vicious brute who robbed the poor more often than the better-protected rich. One case of dakaiti from 1809 may stand for many more as testimony of the nature of the crime and its perpetrators. Juggernath Ghose, aged seventeen and a cow driver, described to the magistrate how a party of dacoits came to his parents' house at midnight, armed with swords, spears and a gun. They tore straw from the roof and made torches with which they tortured the couple in an attempt to force them to reveal where they had hidden their money. Burning hemp impregnated with *ghi* (butter) was also used, and the pair later died from their injuries. The dacoits fled with some trinkets.[39] Torture, usually involving fire, was used whenever dacoits wanted to discover the whereabouts of hidden cash or treasure. All of the 148 charged with dakaiti in the Nuddea district in 1848 had burned their victims, at least one of whom, an old man, died from his wounds.[40]

Whilst greed was invariably the mainspring behind Indian brigandage, there were bandits who were glamourised as local heroes because they led the authorities a merry dance and terrorised its more unpopular representatives. Maharashtra folk songs still recall the exploits of Raghu Bhanagre, a resourceful and elusive bandit chief active in the early 1840s:

> *Raghu raised his revolt,*
> *He stayed in the deep hollows of the Konkan,*
> *Hid in the mangrove groves,*
> *There was a big gun battle.*
> *The rebels fought until they were victorious,*
> *And the goda's [white man's] face was besmeared with blood.*[41]

Raghu was the son of a Bhil chieftain who, like so many figures with local power, was persuaded to serve the Raj. Appointed a police jemadar, he soon quarrelled with his masters over his salary and his son fell foul of the new jemadar, a Brahmin, who suspected him of leading a raid on a neighbouring village. Police investigating this incident tortured members of Raghu's family by attaching 'clipping horns' to their breasts and testicles. This outrage started a war of personal vengeance which soon became a random campaign against everyone associated with the government: policemen were murdered, their wives raped, moneylenders had their noses sliced off and Indian revenue officials were robbed. Early in 1845 a detachment of the Bhil irregular corps under British officers was ordered to restore order. Raghu's followers were dispersed and he was taken, tried and hanged.

The Bhils were one of those ethnic groups whom an official report of

1804 described as 'thieves by profession', stealing whenever the opportunity arose.[42] They were, quite literally, a 'caste' of well-organised,
peripatetic delinquents who posed a permanent threat to the peace of
their districts. As a result of analyses of criminal intelligence made by the
Thagi and Dakaiti Department, the Bhils, together with the Gujars, the
Kolis, and the Bhudduks, were officially lumped together as members of an
incorrigible and hereditary criminal class. Together, they presented a problem as vast as the country they ranged over. The remedy lay in vigilance
and a prescription, which was first applied in 1856 by the Punjabi and
Awadh administrations. Henceforward, there were officially defined 'criminal tribes', whose members were made subject to a strict régime of
registration and surveillance.[43] Another disciplinary formula, already well
tested and tried, was applied to the Bhils. From 1841 onwards, they were
recruited into the Company's army as members of various Bhil corps.
They proved excellent soldiers, loyal to the Raj during the 1857 Mutiny,
and always willing to suppress disorders among their own people.

Nevertheless, the Bhils tenaciously clung to their old ways. In 1883, Sir
Lepel Griffin, the resident at the Central Indian princely courts, reported
a spate of Bhil outrages including peppering a bania with arrows when he
unwisely appeared to recover a loan. 'The true Bhil,' he wrote, 'is the child
of the forest and will avoid hot work or plough if he can steal enough to
get drunk upon,' he told the Viceroy, Lord Ripon. As for the luckless
bania, Sir Lepel added: 'His Excellency remembers the old ballads of
Sherwood.'[44]

Catching and chastising organised criminals required the co-operation of
the princes. Many were lethargic and others refused to collaborate. Man
Singh, Raja of Jodhpur, was reluctant to throw his weight behind Bentinck's campaign against the thugs, or permit the extradition of suspected
thugs from the ancient Hindu sanctuary at Marwar.[45] The Gaikwar of
Baroda's officials turned a blind eye to Bhil outrages in the early 1830s, and
servants of the Maharaja of Bikaner were suspected of helping a notorious
bandit chief, Doongur Singh, after his escape from Agra gaol in 1845.[46] To
prevent such backsliding, British officers often took charge of operations
against dacoit bands in the princely states.

This was one of the tasks of James Paton at Lucknow. In 1834 he masterminded an attack by Awadh cavalry on a gang of 500 or so dacoits who
had a base in the Bheera forest. The bandits were taken by surprise and
sixty were cut down for the loss of one dead and sixteen wounded. Over
200 men, women and children were sent for punishment in Lucknow,

including Rorki, the widow of the dacoit chief. Smiling, she told Paton that, 'The troops got great spoils amongst us – all our Ornaments &c. I wore [jewels and clothes worth] about 1,000 rupees – My petticoat alone cost 60 rupees.'[47] Like others, before and after, Paton discovered that Indian gamekeepers often had poachers' instincts.

Company officers frequently found themselves in regions where the machinery for enforcing the law was either ramshackle or non-existent. Mughal authority had never run in these areas, which had been largely left to their own devices. One such district was the remote uplands of southern Orissa, where the Konds had lived a semi-nomadic life for centuries, undisturbed by the local rajas, who were notable for their 'imbecility and feebleness of character'. This was the verdict of John Campbell, the Company official responsible for extending civil order to the region. His greatest problems were female infanticide and *meriah* (child sacrifice), a ritual used by the Konds to placate their gods, bring good fortune, and make the soil fertile. Kidnapped children were sold for a religious ceremony in which they were drugged and cut to pieces. Campbell was horrified by this custom, but he realised that the practice could only be eliminated slowly through patient persuasion. 'The superstition of ages cannot be eradicated in a day, the people with whom we have to deal have become known to us only within the last few months,' he wrote in 1837. 'Any increase of coercion would arouse the jealousy of the whole race.'[48] This was also the opinion of Viscount Hardinge, who believed that a minatory approach would drive the custom underground among a race with 'a jealous love of liberty'.[49]

Campbell, a man of outstanding perseverance and humanity, proceeded with forebearance, always explaining rather than condemning. Seated alongside Kond chieftains on a tiger skin, he would tell them that the British had once sacrificed humans ('we were then fools and ignorant') and then ask them to renounce it for ever by making a traditional oath. Each held a handful of rice, water and soil and intoned: 'May the earth refuse its produce, rice choke me, water drown me, and tiger devour me and my children if I break the oath which I now take for myself and my people to abstain from sacrifice of human beings.'[50] By the late 1840s, his methods were bearing fruit; female infanticide had vanished and incidents of meriah were declining rapidly.

Legends of the coming of Campbell lingered in Kond folk memory. In one version, current at the turn of the century, he appears as a saviour:

At the time of the great Kiabon [Campbell] Sahib's coming the country was in darkness; it was enveloped in mist.

And how was the country enveloped in mist? – there was murder and bloodshed; conflagration of villages; destruction of rice and crops.

Brothers and uncles sat together and deliberated how they were to act.

While they were discussing whether they would live or die the great Kiabon Sahib came.

All the people fled in terror; the Sahib said, 'Brothers, uncles, fear not; Maliko [headman] Kuaro, come to me.'

Having caught the Meriah sacrificers, they brought them; and again they went and caught the evil councillors [who supplied victims].

Having seen the chains and shackles, the people were afraid; bloodshed and murder were quelled.[51]

Not the least of Campbell's achievements was his ability to overcome natural moral outrage.

Loathing and fear were commoner reactions to Indian crime. Both were understandable, given the attitudes which prevailed in contemporary Britain. This was the age in which proto-psychologists, jurists and philosophers were endeavouring to define the criminal class and peer into its mind. Their efforts concentrated on discovering the nature of crime and the characteristics of what was called 'criminal man'. Like the thug or dacoit, once his secrets were revealed, he could be deterred and restrained. It was thought likely that his moral deficiences were mirrored by his physical appearance, a theory which appealed at a time when phrenology had captured the popular and scientific imagination. While agents of the Thagi and Dakaiti Department were cataloguing the 'criminal tribes', phrenologist Hubert Lavergue was systematically examining his patients in Toulon gaol for facial signs of inner depravity.[52] The theory that moral character, or the lack of it, was reflected in human features was given an academic imprimatur by Cesare Lombroso, the Italian doctor whose *L'Uomo Deliquente* appeared in 1876, a few years after the Indian government had issued laws that classified the so-called 'criminal tribes'. Both the scientist and the legislators agreed that there were 'born criminals'.[53]

How such creatures behaved and the world they lived in were vividly and disturbingly revealed by Charles Dickens in *Oliver Twist* (1838) and

Victor Hugo in *Les Misérables* (1861). Both described what today is called the 'underclass', a body of people who, from time to time, had made menacing appearances as the 'mob' in the principal cities of Britain and the Continent from 1789 onwards. Such a class clearly existed in India, or so the Company's officers came to believe during the 1830s and 1840s. It endangered state and individual equally, for it was parasitical and capable of flourishing, hidden from the rest of society. Its members inhabited a deviant moral universe in which their delinquency was determined by birth. It was no accident that Indian delinquency was associated with vagrancy; for hundreds of years British law-makers had issued codes designed to coerce those whose lack of a fixed dwelling made them hard to control and, therefore, 'natural' miscreants.

These may have been exaggerated reactions to the phenomena of organised crime, but they were understandable. Given residual apprehensions that the Raj was precarious and depended upon the passive goodwill of its subjects, knowledge of the secretive and well-organised criminal clans was disconcerting. Most worrying of all was the Indian's apparently unlimited capacity for dissembling. Were the external goodwill and obsequiousness of the thousands of Indians who worked for the British merely masks for malevolence and viciousness? What did British officers at Meerut make of the fact that, in 1845, two mess servants who handled their water and food were found to be datura (a species of poisonous plant) poisoners? The proximity to hidden crime must have been particularly unnerving. Another datura poisoner, a woman, was employed as a cook in an Indian household where she managed to drug and rob her master.[54]

Datura poisoners usually hung around public highways on the look-out for victims. They approached travellers, gained their confidence and then laced their food with narcotic datura seeds. Since they copied the thugs' methods of ingratiation, the authorities leapt to the conclusion that they were part of another, vast clandestine confederacy. They were not, but most supported themselves solely by murder and robbery. In 1853, three men journeying from Calcutta to Cuttack were joined by a poisoner who, noting that they were of the same castes, offered to share travelling expenses. He added datura seeds to their rice and all fell ill, eventually recovering to testify against him. The court heard he was a professional poisoner with several previous convictions and sentenced him to spend the rest of his life in a penal settlement.[55]

IV

Catching Indian criminals was very much a hit-or-miss affair. As Sleeman once wryly remarked, the government devoted more cash and energy to taxing Indians than to policing them. A collector was marginally better paid than a district magistrate and, if salaries were anything to go by, Indian police *darogas* (inspectors) and constables counted for nothing in the Company's scheme of things. Professional – and the word signified little in this context – policemen were rare. Throughout princely India and in large swathes of the annexed territories, arrangements for law enforcement were makeshift and based upon the imagined goodwill and energy of local grandees and village headmen.

Rights of justice and punishment were exercised 'by each man according to his power and influence' in the Maratha districts occupied after the 1817–18 war. After a close examination of legal practices in this region, Montstuart Elphinstone failed to detect any system or consistency. There was 'no prescribed form of trial' – suspects were whipped to obtain confessions and 'notoriety' was enough to condemn a bandit to death. Patels had the power to flog wrongdoers, high-ranking Maratha noblemen could impose capital punishment, which included being blown from a cannon and trampling to death by a tethered elephant, the last a penalty for rebellion.[56] It was confusing, but at least legal authority was vested in men of substance and standing, which Elphinstone thought best.

They had ordered things differently in Bengal and simultaneously managed to undermine the zamindar class's influence and create a police force that was corrupt and incompetent. The 1793 police regulations had abolished the zamindars' judicial and policing powers and replaced them with Company magistrates and constabulary. They were thinly spread. In the early 1850s, when the population of Bengal was between 25 and 35 million, there was one police superintendent, 400 darogas and 10,000 policemen. They were assisted by 180,000 chowkidahs and the zamindari police which had been reinstituted in 1805. It was usual for the local zamindar and daroga to work together, not always in the public interest. A novice magistrate was warned by an experienced colleague in 1816: 'You may depend on it, that against a combination of Zamindars and corrupt Darogas you can do nothing.'[57] Dishonest darogas abounded: in Midnapur one was a salt smuggler and, in one year alone, thirteen out of the eighteen serving in the Hughli district were sacked for misdemeanours, including neglect of duty, suppressing evidence of a crime, bribery and torture.

Torture, a hand-me-down of Mughal policing, was discreetly permitted by some British officials as, in the frequent absence of efficient detective work, it offered a sure way of procuring evidence and confessions. According to Major Chevers's investigations, torture was normal practice in the Madras presidency, where a native police officer would command his men to treat a suspect '*cayidah procaurum*' (according to custom). Presidency custom included crushing the testicles. During the early 1850s a variety of euphemisms for torture were in everyday use in Bengal police stations. The expressions '*Bhalaharo bhajoy*' (make him understand well), '*Kala ghora miaghoy*' (take him to the back room) and '*Patkara ana*' (Bring him back after he has been well prepared) all had one painful meaning for a man under interrogation. Immersion to the point of drowning, suspension by the arms, insertion of a chewing insect into the prisoner's navel and the rape of his wife or a kinswoman were among the common torments.[58]

Elsewhere, police discipline was slack. There were 551 allegations of misconduct against the village and district police in the Madras presidency in 1848, of which 191 cases were proved; and a further 726 the following year, when 128 were upheld. The magistrate in North Arcot was disappointed by the performance of the local zamindari police and feared that most village watchmen were thieves. In other districts a lack of arrests was interpreted as evidence of police laziness or collusion with criminals.[59] Remedial action was not taken, simply because of the effort involved and a reluctance to tamper with rural institutions. Slipshod policing by village headmen and indifferent zamindars was better than none at all. In these conditions, the only direction was downwards and, by the mid-1850s, the Madras police system was on the point of collapse. It was the same story in Bengal, where the 1857 Mutiny interrupted long overdue reform measures.

It was hardly surprising that few Indian criminals were caught and punished. There were 178,000 crimes reported in the Madras presidency during 1848, of which 164,000 were some kind of assault. Just under 30 per cent of offenders arrested were found guilty and punished.[60] These figures may be deceptive, for cases occasionally came to light of wrongdoers being summarily killed. Chevers recorded instances of burglars caught in the act of being hacked to death by the tulwars of indignant villagers, a chowkidah charged in 1857 with beating a robber to death, and suspected thieves being hanged by their victims.[61] Much wrongdoing went unreported. It was suspected that among the thousand or so suicides in Madras were wives driven to take their lives by the continual violence of their husbands. Others were feared to be undetected murders.

The level of crime was directly linked to economic conditions. It fell in Kanara during 1851, a year of good harvests, cheap food and a high demand for labour. Shortages and rising prices were blamed for a sharp increase in thefts in the Rajahmundry district in 1853 and in Masulipatnam the following year, when granaries were broken into and plundered.

Avarice and jealousy, rather than the desperation of hunger, were the usual mainsprings for Indian crime, as they were and are everywhere. Marital tensions, real or imaginary infidelity, and an older husband's insistence on sexual relations with an unwilling child bride – sometimes as young as ten or eleven – led to many murders. So too did the golden and silver armlets and jewellery, part ornament and part advertisement of status, worn by young children. In one instance of this common crime at Bareilly in 1853, the murderer was a boy of between ten and twelve, his victim a three-year-old.[62]

Confronted with horrifying reports of such outrages, and conveniently ignoring the extent and nature of crime in Britain, it was easy for officials to agree with the conclusion of one district magistrate: human life was of little or no value in India.[63] Moreover, its people seemed to be in the grip of a powerful recidivism. Dismissing optimistic forecasts made during the late 1840s that thagi and female infanticide were decreasing, Major Chevers believed that both were still flourishing. How was it that one official, travelling through Rajput villages in 1846, noticed that in twenty-six villages notorious for female infanticide there was not a girl under the age of six? They were in very short supply elsewhere, leading him to wonder how much passed in India unnoticed by and against the wishes of its rulers.[64]

He was certainly right. Whilst the Company boasted that its government was promoting peace and individual security throughout India, it failed to create the policing apparatus necessary. Nor was there a coherent policy towards law enforcement: Macaulay's proposals for a uniform code of laws for the whole sub-continent were quietly shelved in 1835. The Raj was, however, good at accumulating crime statistics and, when confronted by something as widespread, organised and threatening as thagi, it moved decisively. But then, more was involved than the safety of travellers on India's roads, for the thugs, dacoits and the so-called criminal tribes were seen as dangers to the state.

4

A Hearty Desire: Sex,
Religion and the Raj

'I now commenced a regular course of fucking with native women,'
wrote Edward Sellon, recalling his arrival in India as a sixteen-year-old
Company cadet in 1834.[1] A brother officer, Lieutenant John Daniels, also
new to India, was infected with a different passion. 'I have this day,' he
wrote in his diary on 30 May 1836, 'been deeply impressed with the culpability of not proclaiming the glad tidings of the Gospel to the Heathen
around and I have had a hearty desire created within me to impart instruction to the Natives.'[2] Both young men were, in their ways, typical of their
background and times. India offered each the opportunity to indulge their
passions freely; its native population providing the raw material for unlimited debauchery or conversion to Christianity.

India offered the libertine abundant and varied sexual experiences, as
Sellon soon found out. His exploration of Indian sexuality was not, however, a case of a young Englishman losing his home-grown inhibitions and
being seduced by the legendary sensuality of the tropics. Sellon had left
behind a country where the sexual culture was rich and diverse, although
less exuberant and open than it had been twenty years before. The forces
of what today we call Victorian 'sexual repression' were just beginning to
muster for their systematic campaigns against the vice and depravity they
feared would undermine the nation. The purity campaigners, Evangelical
churchmen, public school headmasters and self-appointed champions of
public morality faced an uphill struggle and would only start counting their

gains in the early 1880s. There was no sudden revolution in morals either in Britain or in India.

Sellon and other young men of his generation were still free to follow a well-established pattern of sexual indulgence which stretched back beyond the days of Clive. Creating a seraglio in the Indian style had been one of Sir Matthew Mite's daydreams in *The Nabob*, and at least one of his kind actually did so. He rented a house in Soho Square, where he lived with his wife and six imported Indian concubines. All shared a common bedroom with the beds in a circle, allowing the nabob to make nocturnal tours. Fearful that his exotic concubines might fire the lusts of London's rakes, he forbade them to walk the streets unchaperoned.[3] His wife was extraordinarily accommodating, as was the Marquess Wellesley's wife, Hyacinthe, who had rejected her husband's request to accompany him to India. Soon after his arrival in Calcutta, he wrote to her pleading for permission to acquire a lover, on the grounds that the climate had so aroused his appetites that he could not live without sex. She replied: 'Prélaque [their code-word for intercourse] if you are absolutely forced to, with all the honour, prudence and tenderness you have shown me.'[4] The Marquess's example was followed by his protégé, Charles Metcalfe, after a sequence of rebuffs from eligible European ladies in Calcutta, which he blamed on his unattractive features. His well-born Sikh mistress provided him the affection he needed and three sons.[5]

Sir David Ochterlony, the conqueror of Nepal and agent for Rajputana, was alleged to have kept a harem of thirteen odalisques.[6] A native of Boston, Massachusetts, he had first come to India in 1777 and stayed attached to the flamboyant, princely style of the old nabobs of the Warren Hastings era. Not long before his death in 1825, he briefly met Reginald Heber, the hymn-writer and Evangelical bishop of Calcutta, who was impressed by Ochterlony's train of elephants and servants, but dismayed by his lack of morals. The bishop deplored the keeping of mistresses by Company officers and officials and hoped, mistakenly as it turned out, that it was fast disappearing.

Sexual liaisons of the sort which Metcalfe, Ochterlony and hundreds of others found necessary and enjoyable were a moral affront for Heber. They broke not only the laws of God, but the new codes of gentlemanly conduct. Whilst the working-class soldiery were naturally incontinent in all things, gentlemen possessed finer characters and the self-discipline to resist temptation. By keeping concubines or consorting with Indian prostitutes, they debased themselves, their Christian faith and the prestige of their nation. By keeping chaste they elevated themselves above the pagan Indians, who knew no better, and their feckless countrymen. Abstinence was the course chosen by the narrator in Tennyson's 'Locksley Hall' (1842). Orphaned by the death of his father in 'a wild Mahratte battle', the young man contemplates taking a native wife 'who shall rear my dusky race'. He rejects the notion, for to do so would make him: 'Like a beast with lower pleasure, like a beast with lower pains.'

Such high-mindedness was still exceptional. The licentiousness of the eighteenth century survived well into the nineteenth, and was proving remarkably resilient in face of the growing assaults by the Evangelical movement and its various offshoots dedicated to the reform of public morals. 'Sexual intercourse', which only began for Philip Larkin in 1963 after an unspecified period of suspension, was still flourishing as late as the 1840s. Oxford and Cambridge undergraduates seduced housemaids and kept mistresses with an abandon which shocked strait-laced American youths. In 1848 Emerson heard from Dickens and Carlyle that male chastity scarcely existed among middle- and upper-class young men in Britain. They confirmed what the American had already seen in Liverpool and central London, where he had been horrified by the numbers and brazenness of the streetwalkers.[7] No one counted them, nor was it possible since many were part-timers, underpaid seamstresses and milliners driven by poverty to solicit. An estimate of 1850 suggested that there were about 50,000 prostitutes in the whole country, with the largest concentrations in London (8–10,000), Liverpool (2,900) and Glasgow (1,800) and, inevitably, the provincial garrison towns and ports.[8]

In 1840 there were thought to be at least a thousand brothels in London, catering for every taste, including flagellation (always popular) and pederasty.[9] There was also a thriving trade in erotic prints and books, often conducted by dealers who were radicals and freethinkers, like George Cooper who did business from various premises in the Covent Garden area of London. When his shop was raided by the police in 1853, they discovered over 2,000 erotic prints and 81 indecent books.[10] Among these may have been copies of *The Randy Songster* and *The Nobby Songster*, anthologies of music-hall lyrics of the 1840s. Individual items in this genre included: 'Oh, Miss Tabitha Ticklecock!!!', 'The Height of Impudence, or the Turd in the Muffin' and 'The Lost Cow!!! or, the Bulling Match Under the Tree', all first published between 1815 and 1835.[11] Old strains of ribald humour remained strong and may be detected, often reading between the lines, in the novels of R. S. Surtees, who depicts the essentially

Georgian and Regency world of the hard-drinking, coarse-grained, hunting squires surviving well into the 1850s.

On the whole, early-Victorian novelists succumbed to the pressure of the new respectability and did not present their growing middle-class readership with anything which might cause a blush. The emotional entanglements, frustrations and reverses of courtship were staple fictional themes, but writers steered clear of describing the physical impulses which accompanied them or actual love-making. Readers were free to exercise their imaginations in this area, a task which was imagined to be easier for men than women. The nature of female sexuality and the possibility that women might enjoy sex as much as men were taboo subjects. *The Battle of Venus* (1760) had suggested that women might have more intense sexual feelings than men, as did *Fanny Hill*, but the erotic literature of a far less inhibited age played no part in shaping Victorian attitudes. The consensus on this fissile subject was contained in an article on prostitution which appeared in the *Westminster and Foreign Quarterly* in July 1850. The anonymous author defined male sexual urges as 'inherent and spontaneous', but argued that in women they were, 'dormant, if not non-existent, till excited; always till excited by undue familiarities; almost always till excited by actual intercourse'. For a woman to enjoy sex for solely physical reasons was 'against nature', for the sensations would be divorced from 'all feelings of love that which was meant by nature as the last and intensest expression of passionate love'.[12]

For these reasons, prostitutes were creatures who were driven by desperation to follow what they often recognised as a shameful and unnatural occupation and were sustained in it by frequent draughts of gin. It was impossible for them to find any pleasure in sex, the author concluded, a verdict which was extended to women in general during the second half of the century. It was as a mother, not as a bedmate, that the mid-Victorian wife fulfilled what society took to be her highest duty.

II

And yet, Indian prostitutes clearly enjoyed sex for its own sake and their status, like that of mistresses, carried no social opprobrium. Or so Edward Sellon discovered. Remembering his ten years of philandering, he recalled two kinds of prostitutes: one charging two rupees (10p) for her services, the other, an infinitely superior creature, five. He recalled:

The 'fivers' are a very different set of people from their sister-hood in European countries; they do not drink, they are scrupulously cleanly in their persons, they are sumptuously dressed, they wear the most costly jewels in profusion, they are well educated and sing sweetly, accompany their voices on the viol de gambe, a sort of guitar, they generally decorate their hair with clusters of clematis, or sweetly scented bilwa flowers entwined with pearls and diamonds.[13]

The contrast between British and Indian prostitutes was stark; Mrs Theresa Berkley, a celebrated madame who died in 1836, was praised for having 'the first grand requisite of a courtesan, viz lewdness'.[14] Her Indian counterpart cultivated a sophisticated sensuality.

At the heart of this difference in the approach to sexuality lay the Indian attitude towards sex. The Indian courtesan saw herself as a sharer in a legitimate pleasure which men and women naturally desired and to which no guilt was attached. Understanding the nature of this pleasure, and how best it could be achieved, required not only a belief that its fulfilment was worthwhile, but training. In the early eighteenth century, Alexander Hamilton had reported the existence near Calcutta of what he called a 'Seminary of female Lewdness where Numbers of Girls are trained up for the Destruction of unwary Youths'.[15] He had heard of and rendered in crude terms which were familiar to his British readers one of those Hindu temples to which families brought daughters to be prepared for what they considered an honourable profession. At the age of seven or eight the girl began training as a dancer and singer, and at the onset of puberty was initiated into sexual activity by the temple priests. The 'coming of age' of these *kasbis* or *deva-dasis* (entertainers) was publicly celebrated with a feast and a religious festival.[16]

Among the accomplishments of the Hindu kasbis and their Muslim equivalents, the *taiwaifs*, was an amazing range of gymnastic love-making positions which, carved in stone, decorate many Hindu temples. They were, as now, a popular tourist attraction, at least for male officers and officials. Captain Halket made a special excursion to see some erotic paintings on the walls of a tank near Bharatpur in 1851. He was specially struck by a scene in which a naked woman tempted three naked men, one in the 'excited state . . . of one about to forfeit the reward of years of abstinence', whatever that might have been.[17] For many British onlookers, Indian erotic art was a revelation of practices which were all but unheard of in their homeland, or condemned as deviant and depraved. There was group sex, oral sex, sex in every conceivable position, buggery and masturbation, a pastime which was already being described by clergymen, dominies and quacks as the cause of debility.

Temple reliefs were a confirmation of that eighteenth- and nineteenth-century European commonplace which assumed that the Orient was a place where men could freely sample fruits that were either rare or forbidden at home. As Sellon noted, India was a country where erotic fantasies could be fulfiled with impunity, for he came across many courtesans who shaved their pudenda 'so that until you glance at their hard, full and enchanting breasts, handsome beyond compare, you fancy you have got hold of some unfledged girl'.[18] Back in Britain, rich men spent large sums on procuring pubescent virgins.[19]

Homosexuals were also free to satisfy their fancies in India, whereas in Britain they were widely despised and buggery was a capital crime until 1861. There was a strong antipathy towards homosexuality, especially among the working classes and those who satisfied heterosexual clients. London streetwalkers were in the forefront of the mob which vigorously pelted a group of homosexuals arrested and pilloried in 1810. Public rage was further inflamed by the knowledge that some of the accused had engaged in such outwardly 'manly' occupations as coal-heaver, butcher and blacksmith.[20] Regency 'Margeries' and 'Pooffs' also trampled on national self-esteem by indulging in what was known as the 'Italian vice', a perversion which had its origins among the notoriously degenerate Turks. There was a similar working-class revulsion against lesbianism, which enjoyed a vogue at the turn of the century among actresses and aristocratic ladies.[21] Class feelings erupted again in 1822 when Percy Jocelyn, Bishop of Clogher, was caught *in flagrante* buggering a dragoon. A contemporary cartoon by Cruikshank nicely captioned 'The Arse Bishop Joslin a Soldier' showed the pair and indignant onlookers shouting out 'Hang them in Chains', 'The Pillory, The Pillory' and 'Hang the Dogs'. The cleric escaped the gallows by flight, but between 1800 and 1835 fifty men were hanged for sodomy.[22]

There were no such risks in India, so long as a homosexual was careful. Major Chevers noted disapprovingly in 1852 evidence which recently came to light of what he called 'a very extensive and abominable trade of unnatural prostitution carried on by eunuchs'.[23] They dressed as women, were strikingly effeminate and kept brothels in which transvestite *nautchs* (musical and dancing entertainments) were held for patrons. In 1786 one

British officer, not satisfied with his Hindu mistress, made a lunge at what he took to be a pretty young lady to discover that 'she' was a Eurasian drummer boy in women's clothes, presumably looking for custom.[24] Rumours that three British officers were regular clients at a male brothel in Karachi in 1845 led General Napier to send Richard Burton, then a junior officer on his staff, on a clandestine mission to investigate these places. Masquerading as a native, Burton reported with minute clinical detail the practices he had witnessed and perhaps participated in, noting that several senior amirs were among his fellow customers.[25]

Whilst the homosexual in India had greater opportunity than in Britain, he could not rid himself of his countrymen's aversion to his conduct, nor their laws against it. Lieutenant-Colonel Edward Smythe of the 5th Madras Cavalry found himself at the centre of an acrimonious scandal in December 1831 when he was posted to take command of his old regiment, the 8th Madras Cavalry. For many years there had been rumours that he had been 'addicted to sodomy' and had practised it regularly with troopers of the 8th. One, Muhammad Lal, had attempted to murder Smythe after he had made advances, an excuse which the regiment's commander had dismissed as nonsense. Another officer, Captain Garton, was also accused of being an active homosexual by Indian NCOs. Nothing was proved, but the charges were said to have contributed to the captain's display of symptoms of insanity, although some contemporaries would have readily believed that these might well have been a consequence of his vice.

Matters subsided when Smythe left the regiment, but surfaced again when it was known he would return. A havildar and jemadar major repeated old stories about him to the adjutant, Major John Watkins, claiming that he had favoured his catemites for promotion. Those sowars 'who wish to do their duty like honest men' hoped that Watson would remain in command. Meanwhile, Smythe was facing ridicule from officers of the 5th Cavalry: 'It was currently said among the Mess of the Regiment that there were still more men to be buggered and that it had fallen Colonel Smythe's lot to commit sodomy on them.'[26] The subsequent official enquiries exonerated Smythe, who was then urged to retire, which he did. Invariably in such cases, where there is smoke there is also fire, and no doubt the Company was glad to see the back of a source of embarrassment. Watson was also asked to leave the service for encouraging the rumours and failing to tell his superior about them, which together constituted ungentlemanly conduct.

It would be impossible to draw any far-reaching conclusions from an unusual scandal save that there was a strong suggestion that Smythe used his authority to indulge his passions. Not all of his partners appear to have objected and some may have been of his inclination. Homosexuality seems to have been rare among British other ranks, at least according to the court-martial returns.

What is perhaps most interesting about Colonel Smythe's case is that it supports the contention that the British in India commonly asserted their power to force Indians, mostly women, to submit to their embraces. What might be called 'sexual imperialism' was nothing more than a form of rape, because the master race somehow compelled Indian prostitutes and mistresses to cohabit with them against their will.[27] Genuine rape certainly did occur in wartime, although it was very rarely mentioned in diaries and letters home. An exception to this rule was Private Ryder, who recorded a horrific example after the storming of Multan in 1849:

> A man of the 3rd company of my regiment [the 32nd], an Irish Roman Catholic, named B_____, went into a room, and took a young girl from her mother's side, and perpetrated the offence, for which he has to answer before God who heard that poor girl's cries and petitions.[28]

Ryder added that had he been present, he would have shot the man. It is impossible to know how many similar offences were committed by British and Company troops during other Indian campaigns. Nor was rape a crime confined to the conquerors; the wives of sepoys were violated by Marathas after the cantonments near Poona had been overrun in November 1817.[29]

These outrages occurred in brutal circumstances when the normal disciplines of human conduct had been suspended which, to a great extent, explains, without, of course, condoning. The same was never true of everyday sexual relations between British men and Indian women. If, as some nationalist and feminist historians have claimed, these were always the outcome of aggression on one side and were unwelcome on the other, then the same was true of the sexual relations between many Indian men and women. Frequent consorting with temple prostitutes was a mark of their superior status for men of the Indian upper classes, and low-caste girls and women were regularly abducted for sale as wives. Moreover, caste taboos on remarriage often drove young Hindu widows into the margins of society and prostitution.[30] The British did not invent and import into India the concept of rich and powerful men asserting sexual prerogatives over women; of that we can be sure. Nor were they innovators in the sexual exploitation of women. A guest at a nautch in Peshawar early in 1842, Lieutenant Trower of the Bengal army, was attracted to a very young girl singer. He had never before seen her 'equal beauty' and he contrived the means to speak with her as the party progressed. The pair talked until daybreak and Trower discovered that her name was Kareemun, that she was thirteen years of age and had been recently purchased by a Sikh for 112 rupees (£11.20). She appears to have accepted her lot, not that she could have changed it.[31] By our standards, and no doubt those of Trower's enlightened contemporaries, Kareemun was a victim of oppression.

When British officials and officers took Indian lovers or sought out prostitutes, they were conforming to well-established local customs. Indians did not question their right to do so; when, in 1807, an anonymous Madras NCO complained that white officers always got the prettiest women, his sole concern was the discrepancies in pay which prevented him from competing for their charms.[32] Obviously the wealth and status of British administrators and officers made them attractive to Indian women, who found being 'under the protection of a European' advantageous.[33] There were benefits too for the British officer, as Richard Burton recalled:

> She [the mistress] keeps house for him, never allowing him to save money, or if possible to waste it. She keeps the servants in order. She has an infallible recipe to prevent maternity, especially if her tenure of office depends on such compact. She looks after him in sickness, and is one of the best of nurses, and, as it is not good for man to live alone, she makes him a manner of a home.[34]

It is extremely hard to trace the emotional relationships between the British and their Indian mistresses. Burton believed that for the woman the union was always one of convenience rather than passion. He blamed the absence of love on the lack of art or imagination in his countrymen's approach to sex. Their love-making was rough and over-hasty, at least by the standards of Indian youths who had learned how to prolong foreplay and intercourse. Hindu women, therefore, likened British soldiers to 'village cocks' and their sexual abruptness rendered it impossible for them to be 'truly loved by a native girl'.[35] His views may reflect either hearsay or his own performance and, therefore, cannot be taken as universal.

There was a conspicuous candour about sexual matters among the British community in India, at least during the earlier part of the nineteenth century. In 1813, Poona was home to an odd European club in which new members underwent a pseudo-masonic initiation which involved, among other things, the 'frank confession of all the principle sins' of the novitiate. Recording one rumbustious session, Montstuart Elphinstone told Lady Hood how a certain Captain Campbell, 'a grave and respectable and orderly figure', had confessed to being the father of three 'innocent black babies'. Members thought it a great joke to convey this news surreptitiously to Mrs Campbell. Major Warren admitted that he had opened the curtains of Mrs Smith's palanquin, chased her into the bedroom of her house and kissed her. There may have been more, but Elphinstone forebore to tell it.[36] Even less inhibited was the 'Rajah Nob Kissen's nautch' an allegedly fictional diversion for officers described by Captain Henderson who, one assumes, knew what he was talking about. At one stage an infatuated subaltern composes a poem about one of the dancers. It opens:

> *A dove-like bosom, where a mimic load*
> *Of swelling ripeness rears its twin abode.*[37]

This occasion, or one like it, may have been one of the 'lascivious orgies' held by temple nautch girls which, according to Sellon's *Annotations on the Sacred Writings of the Hindus*, could set a young officer back 150 rupees (£15).[38]

Not all nautches were sex parties. A formal nautch dance was no more indecent than the Italian ballet he had seen in England, thought Captain Beaven, who added that this was the opinion of Anglican clergymen who had attended them. But then, Georgian clergymen were more worldly than their successors. Reflecting on a nautch he had just witnessed at the palace of the Raja of Bharatpur, Captain Halket concluded that it had not been 'indecent', but 'of course one can have an indecent nautch as well as an indecent dance at home, but it is not usual'.[39] Again, it would appear that Indian sexual diversions paralleled those in Britain in form if not embellishments.

Erotic dances, Hindu phallus worship, sculptures and paintings, together with an abundance of attractive young women expert in making love for its own sake, gave the overwhelming impression that the Indians were a lascivious people, dedicated to sensuality and undisturbed by any sense of shame. Additional evidence of licentiousness was provided by Muslim polygamy and Hindu child marriages, in which the bride was expected to have intercourse on or even before her twelfth birthday, a custom which shocked some commentators. In this and much else that was said and written on this subject, disapproval involved the application of double standards; in England twelve was the age of female consent until 1885.

Evangelicals found evidence of depravity everywhere. A journey down a Ludhiana street in 1847 was a sequence of distasteful encounters for the prim and pious Mrs Colin Mackenzie. 'You may imagine,' she wrote, 'the degraded condition of the people here, when I tell you we constantly pass women in the open street bare down to the hips, little children have generally no clothing at all, and many of the men have the smallest possible quantity. They do not seem to have the least sense of decency.' On another occasion she passed 'a pretty little girl, singing at the top of her voice' and asked her husband, an army officer, the meaning of the words. He replied saying that they 'were so utterly detestable and vile, that hardly any man among the worst in London would sing such, unless previously intoxicated'.[40] The singer must have been a prostitute tempting potential clients, but whether Mrs Mackenzie inferred this from her husband's explanation she did not say.

Youthful promiscuity was blamed for the prevalence of syphilis in the north-western districts in an official medical report of 1840–42, which noted, disapprovingly, that Indian boys in Delhi 'lose their virility' quickly and were consequently driven to pester Company dispensaries for aphrodisiacs.[41] An all-pervading and contagious licentiousness was the explanation for the fact that British soldiers in India had higher rates of syphilis than those stationed in the West Indies. This was the conclusion reached in 1829 by an army surgeon, who added that in India the rate of infection rose during periods of famine.[42] Was it perhaps that, as in Britain when times were hard, poor women were driven to prostitution to keep themselves and their families alive?

III

The ordinary soldiers' addiction to Indian prostitutes was a moral and logistical headache for the Company. Statistics collected between 1816 and 1818 showed that an infected soldier spent between twenty-one and forty-five days in hospital recovering if he was treated with emollients, including magnesia in fennel water, and a diet strong in vegetables. If, however, he underwent the more usual medication by which mercury ointment was applied to the sores on his penis, he would expect to spend between thirty-three and fifty-days as an invalid.[43] For the next half-century, between an eighth and a third of the British garrison in India was infected with syphilis each year. Various experiments were tried to eliminate this wastage of men and money. The obvious practical solution was supervision of the prostitutes in the regimental bazaars through what were called Lock hospitals. The bazaar and army medical authorities identified infected women and compelled them to undergo treatment in quarantine. This form of control, with variations, was adopted in each presidency after 1800, or, at a local level, by regimental commanders. It worked after a fashion, although it was never possible to restrain those reckless spirits who wandered off into the native quarter in search of whores. But what, on one level, made good clinical and economic sense was, on another, an official endorsement of promiscuity. Spasms of conscience among the men at the top led to periods in which the Lock hospitals were abandoned.

The problem was not confined to India and it is certain that many sol-diers carried the infection with them when they were posted there. Assistant Surgeon Frederick Robinson of the 74th Highlanders noted that the worst outbreak in his regiment occurred when it was stationed in Limerick. Interestingly, what he described as a near epidemic of syphilis occurred throughout Ireland during 1849–50 in the aftermath of the potato famine.[44] One sure way to keep men out of the syphilis ward was to encourage individual soldiers to stick with one woman. This was diffi-cult because military regulations severely limited the numbers of men who could be married and whose wives and families could live with them in barracks. This hurdle was overcome in India where, with their colonel's approval, soldiers were free to make semi-permanent liaisons with native or Eurasian women.

In 1804 the Company decreed that those half-caste wives of British sol-diers who had been educated were entitled to half the allowance given to British spouses. It was argued, with breathtaking pomposity and arro-gance, that having been 'born in India and habituated to live chiefly on rice, the wants and wishes of the Half Caste are much more confined than those of a European woman'. In consequence, the latter received eight rupees (80p) a month, the former, four.[45] The emotional needs of the non-European wife were also less; they and their children were forbidden to follow their husbands back to Britain. It was callously suggested that once there, they would become destitute and seek poor relief, which was a common destiny for soldiers and their dependents. Since 'they have no parish to support them', it was best that they remained in India. In 1819, the commander-in-chief, the Duke of York, was displeased when he heard that men from the 66th Regiment had brought large numbers of native wives with them when they transferred from Ceylon to Bengal. He refused these women passage to Britain and, rather then leave them stranded in Bengal where they were bound to 'obtain a livelihood by vice', they were to be returned to Ceylon. Those of their children born in wedlock would be supported by army funds.[46] The Duke, one of George III's more lumpish younger sons, had kept a mistress for many years who had once got him into a scrape for peddling officers' commissions.

The children abandoned when the 66th embarked for Britain were part of a growing Eurasian community which occupied a social and racial no-man's-land, spurned by Indians and shunned by Europeans. In 1791 the directors excluded Anglo-Indians from senior administrative and military posts on the grounds that Indians would never look up to them in the same way as they did to the British. The ban was never absolute; James Metcalfe, Charles's son by his Sikh mistress, became a Company cadet in 1836 and an aide-de-camp to the Governor-General, Lord Dalhousie, in 1848.[47] His advancement may have owed much to his father's influence, while that of Colonel Sir Robert Warburton was the result of his knack with frontier tribesmen. Warburton was born in 1842, the son of an Anglo-Irish gunner officer and a niece of the Afghan amir, Dost Muhammad. He was educated in India and at Kensington Grammar School before passing through Woolwich and Addiscombe. In the 1870s he found his niche on the North-West Frontier thanks to his knowledge of local languages and customs and a rare ability to command respect and affection among the Raj's most turbulent subjects.[48]

Warburton and Metcalfe were exceptional. Most other Eurasians could expect only junior posts, placing them alongside the Indian babu in the Company's hierarchy. Nor were they admitted into British society. The prevailing convention was set down in a manual for cadets written in 1820, which warned new arrivals to be on their guard against the enticements of Eurasian girls, who had been confined by their fathers in Calcutta's boarding schools. If he was ensnared by their 'insinuating manners and fascinating beauty', the officer would make 'a matrimonial connexion which he might all his life-time regret'. He and his Anglo-Indian wife would be socially ostracised.[49] An illicit union, one assumes, was unlikely to blight the young man's prospects. Where no institutions existed for the care of Anglo-Indian children, and if the father had a conscience, he provided a modest income for the support of his offspring. In 1810 Lieutenant Good-behere left £200 for the maintenance of his child by his Indian mistress, appointing a brother officer its trustee.[50]

What treatment this infant might have expected when it grew older is described in one of a sequence of short stories by 'a Lady' set in India during the 1820s. The hero, Walter, is the half-caste son of General Vane of the Madras army, who has sent him to Britain to be educated. In Britain he was never made aware of his mixed race or status until a cavalry officer told him that his colour disqualified him from a commission in the Company's army, although it would not stop him from obtaining a command in a princely army. On Walter's return to India, Mrs Vane shows him 'cold politeness', while her daughters are downright rude. 'You are a *half-caste* – that is *blacky* – and mamma says, you always show black *blood*,' he is told by one, who continues, 'and you have no proper mamma, like ours, and *your* mother is a blacky, like our Ayah, and it is not proper for Europe children like us to talk to half-castes too much, mamma tell us.'[51] When he protests to his father that what he has learned in England had stirred in him 'such feelings and aspirations' that made his humiliations doubly hurtful, he is brusquely informed that the alternative had been an upbringing with 'yonder half-savage Indians'.

Walter's miseries multiply. His birth prevents him for marrying the English girl with whom he falls in love and his Hindu mother, now living on General Vane's monthly allowance of twenty rupees, rejects him as a foreigner and infidel. He has some consolation in the knowledge that no shame attaches to her among her own people. Unable to be part of their world or that of his father, his only escape is to return to England where, he imagines, he may be accepted. For all its melodrama, this tale has the ring of truth, not least in its portrayal of the British women as more racially intolerant than men. Only Arthur Vane, Walter's half-brother, treats him decently.

This was understandable since British women were bound to be jealous of Indian mistresses, with their rumoured sexual virtuosity, and offended by reminders of their husbands' infidelities. At the same time, the philanderer's pursuit of the erotic and exotic damaged the prestige of his race and imperilled his soul. Much to her disgust, Mrs Mackenzie heard that in the past British officers under the sway of their mistresses had gone so far as to paint themselves and publicly perform Hindu rituals. She saw India as a source of profound moral corruption for her countrymen, and, in July 1850, she was pleased to record in her diary that they were learning how to resist its temptations: 'The recent improvement in the religious and moral standard at home causes a marked difference between the majority of men under fifty and those above it.'[52] This was a premature judgement, for in 1858 Colonel Garnet Wolseley, then aged twenty-five, told his brother that he had acquired a native mistress who fulfilled 'all the purposes of a wife without giving any of the bother'.[53]

Nonetheless, and in spite of many exceptions, there was a change in the moral climate of British India after 1850. It has partly been explained in terms of the influx of more and more European women, the wives of officers and administrators and those seeking husbands among them. Certainly the numbers who travelled to India rose steadily. They were taking considerable risks and flying in the face of current medical wisdom, which held that the female constitution was more fragile than the male, and therefore more likely to suffer from the Indian climate and those 'miasmas' which were imagined to disperse fever.[54] Moreover, India was a dangerous place in which to conceive and have children. An 1829 medical guide listed the hazards, which included births attended by native midwives or the wives of British soldiers and ayahs whose diet of ghi, garlic and 'sour and acrid vegetables' produced milk that was thin and unnourishing. A shortage of doctors, especially in country districts, compelled the mother to become an amateur physician, and the book included a list of infantile symptoms and remedies.[55]

As the doctors predicted, losses of wives and children were high. Richard Cust, whose wife followed him to India in the early 1850s, wrote on her death an epitaph which would have served for many others:

> *Far in that Orient land, whose annals show*
> *The price paid yearly of domestic woe;*
> *Where many a blooming wife and mother lie*
> *Who left their native country but to die.*[56]

Whole families were all but extinguished, and the very young were always the most vulnerable. The memorial to Captain Joseph Haydock of the 53rd Regiment in Bath abbey records that he died, aged forty-one, of the effects of 'exposure' suffered during the 1857 Mutiny. His son, Francis, died aged one at Karachi in 1849, his daughters Mabel and Maud during their sea voyage home in 1860, aged fifteen and four months. The graveyards of cantonment churches across India tell similar, melancholy stories.

Wilting wives and children flocked to the temperate hill resorts at the onset of the hot season. In the spring of 1839, there were twelve gentlemen staying in Simla and forty-six ladies, including the sixteen-year-old Betty James, the recent bride of Lieutenant Thomas James of the 22nd Bengal NI.[57] She soon divorced him, gained notoriety three years later on the London stage as Lola Montez, Spanish dancer, and then capered about Europe as mistress to various rich and famous men. No doubt she added some frisson to Simla's social scene. Wherever they went, European women were always a welcome novelty:

> . . . *the fair of Britain's isle.*
> *When wafted to Indostan's strand,*
> *Amidst the sable nations smile*
> *Like angels from a fairy-land.*[58]

This exiled poet had in mind those young ladies, in their late teens, whose families despatched them to India with letters of introduction into those circles where they might find husbands, preferably well-paid officers and officials. Theirs was a precarious existence, for when visited by suitors they had to steer a course between over-accommodation and stand-offishness at the same time as always keeping an eye open for a profitable opportunity. These 'debutantes', as they were half-mockingly called, had a year in which to find their husbands, a task which was easier up-country than in the three presidency capitals where most congregated. If they did not succeed, they went home either with a reputation for being a 'jilt', or, sadly, as failures in what was effectively a seller's market.[59]

Working-class women came to India as soldiers' wives. Lieutenant Horward contemptuously described them as 'heavy baggage' in a letter of 1840 to his sister, Harriet. He also called them 'milliners and dressmakers', a choice of words which indicates that, as in Britain, they were easily corrupted.[60] Sergeant John Ramsbottom from Sheffield, who had enlisted in the Bombay Fusiliers in 1854 after a quarrel with his sweetheart ('as for Emma Bromhead her be buggered I have forgotten her'), found more than enough women in Karachi. He told a friend: 'As for going among married women or any single I just get amongst them, as many as I can both black and white. I can assure you we have got some very fine blacks and they pass off very well.'[61] Rankers reacted like their superiors if their wives committed adultery which, as Horward and Ramsbottom hint, they often did. At some date in the 1830s, a light dragoon private discovered that his wife had become the lover of a corporal in the same regiment, and challenged him to a duel. Neither was punished, although the regiment thought it prudent to expel the source of the row and so the errant wife was sent home.[62]

Outside the regimental cantonments, the moral tone of British India was being transformed, although the pace of change was gradual and its impact uneven. Some of the impetus was provided by a growing body of middle- and upper-middle class European women like Mrs Mackenzie. Their presence was most strongly felt in the conduct of social life: husbands were constrained by the presence of their wives and families and a pattern of off-duty entertainment which revolved around mixed formal dinner parties. The memsahib ousted the native concubine as bedmate and mistress of the household – a guide to Indian kitchen management and recipes appeared in 1860.[63] Bachelor officers and civil servants ran the risk of social disapproval and isolation if they openly lived with Indian women.

IV

It was the missionaries and their allies in Britain who assumed the roles of moral watchdogs in India and they did as much, if not more than the memsahibs to restrict sexual contact between British men and Indian women. In the early stages of the Company's rule, Christian missions were regarded as divisive, mischievous and capable of sowing discord among Hindus and Muslims. If, as was widely believed, British authority in India was never absolutely secure, then it would have been foolhardy to do anything which might arouse the religious passions of its people. Support for this commonsense view came from rumours that one of the causes of the 1807 Vellore mutiny had been fears that plans were in hand for the conversion of sepoys.[64]

The Company always strove to show even-handedness in all religious matters. The pattern was set when Admiral Watson was formally introduced to the Nawab of Arcot in 1756. The admiral presented his chaplain, dressed in Anglican canonicals, and, as a matter of courtesy, the nawab brought forward his faqir who was 'wild and staring in his looks'. Brought together, 'The two holy men congratulated each other on their respective office.'[65] There were undertones of current Deist thinking in this meeting, for it assumed a kind of equality between the two religions and their gods. Such a juxtaposition would have been an anathema to most Christians. While it was possible for contemporary scholars who studied Hinduism to appreciate the metaphysical and ethical truths contained in their sacred texts, they had no choice but to condemn a form of spirituality which existed without reference to Jesus Christ and His redemption of the world. Whatever the Hindus might own concerning the supreme being and the immortality of the soul, and however learned men might present contemporary Hinduism as priestly distortion of pure beliefs, for Christians it was a false and pagan creed. In the words of Britain's most influential Evangelical, the anti-slavery crusader William Wilberforce: 'Our religion is sublime, pure and beneficent. Theirs is mean, licentious and cruel.'[66]

Wilberforce was addressing the Commons in 1813 in support of a clause in the India Bill by which the Company would remove all obstructions to Christian missions. Its arguments were wholly pragmatic: commerce, government and harmony between rulers and ruled would be disrupted once missionaries were allowed to wander freely, found schools, set up churches and chapels and, if they were Dissenters, preach by the wayside and in the markets. These objections made no headway against the heavy guns of the Evangelical movement which thundered in the Commons and during meetings of shareholders and directors. Conversion of the heathen Indian was both a Christian and imperial duty. For those of Wilberforce's mind, the Protestant faith was part and parcel of the civilisation that Britain was then spreading across the world. Enlightened Protestantism was the essential ingredient in Britain's greatness; it provided the cement which held the nation together and released the genius and industry of its people. It was the partner of all human progress. According to the Evangelical vision, the conversion of India would bring unlimited benefits, for it would liberate the Indian mind and make it receptive to all the fruits of human reason. With a head purged of superstition and fancy, and applying newly acquired knowledge and patterns of thought, the Hindu would inevitably accept the truths of Christianity. Or so the Evangelicals believed.

The Evangelical lobby swept all before it in the Commons and the Lords. From 1813 missionaries of all denominations were free to trawl for converts throughout the Company's territories so long as they possessed an official licence. Twenty years later, and after further intense lobbying, the Company forfeited the right to license missionaries and was bound by Parliament to gave the Indian Christian the same civil and employment rights as those enjoyed by Muslims and Hindus. The various missions were quick off the mark and well funded by their British sympathisers, whether the philanthropic businessman or the Sunday School pupil with his or her weekly penny. By 1846, the major missionary societies had an annual budget of £425,000, nearly half of which was spent by the Anglicans and Methodists.[67] Denominational rivalries were fierce and were imported into India: when, in 1815, the Church of Scotland began building a church in Bombay, there was a prolonged and vinegary row over whether or not it should have a steeple. The local Anglican bishop weighed in with an objection on the grounds that Scottish churches in London managed without these adornments. Prestige was at stake and the Scots got their steeple.[68]

Unable to agree over steeples and much else, the various denominations were united in their abhorrence of Hinduism. Letters home and journals brimmed with expressions or revulsion. Andrew Leslie, a Baptist, denounced 'the horrors and abominations of Hinduism' in 1825, and his contemporary, Elijah Hoole, a Wesleyan, was appalled by the 'abominable figures' which decorated the temples of southern India.[69] Equally disturbing were the Hindu holy men, like those encountered by a traveller at Jaganeth early in 1814:

> You see some standing for half a day on their heads, barking all the while for alms; some with their heads entirely covered with earth; some with their eyes filled with mud, and their mouths with straw; some lying in puddles of water; one man with his foot tied to his neck, and another with a pot of fire on his belly; and a third enveloped in a net made of rope.[70]

These reactions were transmitted back to Britain and became the staple of missionary tracts and sermons and a source of indignation. One church journal spoke for all when it declared in 1846 that India was 'sunk in ignorance, idolatry and vice'.[71] But remedy was at hand through the reforming work of the Company, which was complemented by that of the missionaries. Some had reservations about this stark view of India and Hinduism. Reginald Heber, appointed Bishop of Calcutta in 1822, was a humane and decent man who detected elements of spirituality among Hindu holy men and virtue among the Hindus. He advised missionaries against blanket condemnations and suggested that Hindus and their rites should always be treated with respect and courtesy.[72]

Many missionaries found restraint impossible and were inclined to aggressive evangelising. A Hindu holy man on a pilgrimage was accosted in 1823 by Elijah Hoole, who asked him the identity of a temple idol. 'It is the image of God,' answered the Hindu. 'Impossible,' retorted Hoole. 'All adoration rendered to idols is an insult to God; by pursuing your present intention, you will provoke his anger.' He then gave a tract to the pilgrim and went on his way. Another confrontation, this time with a zamindar, ended with Hoole being told that all gods were the same, whatever their names.[73] A Baptist missionary at Santipur in 1843 spotted a crowd listening attentively to a pandit in a market place, and moved in to address the 'stragglers'. His impromptu sermon provoked hoots of derision from an audience stirred up by a youth who insulted the preacher 'with indecent gestures'. In 1850 another Baptist, asked by an 'upstart lad' to remove his shoes before entering a temple, told him and the other worshippers that 'God's curse would rest on their temples; and that their idols would soon be destroyed.'[74]

Such an outburst must have reinforced growing fears that the Company, in alliance with the missions, was secretly planning the mass and forcible conversion of all Indians. This was preposterous, but understandable in the light not only of the vehemence of individual missionaries but also of official Company policy. In 1827 Bentinck, after consulting with Hindu sacred writings, outlawed the custom of *sati*, claiming that it had no sound theological basis. The end of the voluntary burning or burial of Hindu widows was the first, direct affront to Indian religious beliefs and gave credence to misgivings about the imposition of Christianity.

Just how dangerous this apprehension might prove was shown by the Bangalore conspiracy of the winter of 1831–32. At the heart of the plot were men whom the Raj had made into losers: unpaid troops of the Raja of Mysore, deserters from his army and former members of his household. They were joined, alarmingly, by fifty Company sepoys. Other footloose characters were easily drawn in, for, according to the investigation later undertaken by the local superintendent of police, 'every markam, chaultry, and other Public Building in the pettah was literally filled with the discharged, unemployed, and discontented spirits in the country'. At the time, an 'unaccountable excitement pervaded the minds of the lower classes of Muslims that their religion was in some danger, and that it was intended to convert them to Christianity'. Support was expected from Hindus in Mysore and Coorg once the uprising had begun. It was to be triggered by a contrived outrage in which a mosque would be defiled by placing in front of it a pig's head surmounted by a cross. The plot misfired and the ringleaders were arrested, thanks to informers. Severely shaken, the Madras government dismissed the incident as another example of fanaticism by the 'ignorant, bigotted and disaffected'. Terror influenced such minds and so the execution of the main culprits was contrived as piece of grand guignol. In the presence of huge crowds and a large contingent of troops, and against the resonance of the Dead March from Handel's *Saul*, the condemned men were led to an open space where some were shot, some hanged and some blown from cannon.[75]

V

The theatre of retribution did not allay Indian misgivings about religion. Friction increased when the Company found itself unable to ward off demands for its official disengagement from the Hindu and Muslim faiths. Until 1833, holy men of both religions had blessed sepoy regimental colours, British officers had joined in Hindu ceremonies and, as a gesture of goodwill, troops and cannon had been loaned for festivals. As successors to the Mughals and various native princes, Company officials found themselves involved as trustees for temple funds and collected pilgrim taxes. In Britain, Evangelicals were incensed; by associating with idolatry, the Company and its employees diminished the Christian religion in Indian eyes, even to the point where it might appear to be equal with Islam and Hinduism. Again the meddlers got their way. The directors were bulldozed into issuing instructions for the immediate severance of all official links with the two faiths.

The men-on-the-spot were uneasy and attempted to bypass these unwelcome orders. Compliance with them would distance the government from its subjects, and the sensible Tory pragmatist Ellenborough argued that if the Raj was universally perceived as a Christian government then it would alienate the Indian masses who were already perturbed by the activities of the missionaries. Many officers and administrators privately agreed and discreetly continued to show favours to Muslims and Hindus. Stories were soon circulating in Britain about British troops being kept from church by compulsory attendance at a Hindu festival, and of Company funds dispensed for repainting idols and repairing their carriages.[76] In the end, officials were compelled to toe the line, although in Baroda government troops were still participating in Hindu ceremonies as late as 1875.[77] During the 1840s, the Evangelical lobby turned its attention to the legal disabilities of Christian converts who, under the Hindu law upheld by the Company, were compelled to forfeit their inheritance when they forswore their religion. In March 1848 it was reported that a zamindar had evicted twenty-nine families from their holdings after they had converted.[78] The law was amended in 1850, after considerable Hindu protests. Higher-caste Hindus had their customs overturned again six years later, when the Company legalised second marriages by Hindu widows and legitimised the offspring of such unions.

Seen from a Hindu perspective, this legislation appeared to be Christian-inspired and the result of external pressures by the implacable enemies of their faith. 'Missionaries in India and their friends in England may be more worth conciliating than the Hindu population of the country,' claimed a pamphlet directed against the change in the inheritance law.[79] Muslims were also full of trepidation. Islam, once the faith of India's ruling dynasty, was under a systematic assault in its northern Indian strongholds, and there were fears that unlettered Muslims might easily succumb. Particularly obnoxious was the spread of English-language mission schools, their extension of education to women, and the missionaries' adoption and conversion of abandoned orphans.[80]

The mission schools were regarded as dangerous Trojan horses, even though many freely admitted non-Christian pupils. Visiting one in Calcutta at the end of 1847, Mrs Mackenzie was delighted to find that its Hindu and Muslim boys, once they had mastered the English language, were 'instructed *exactly* as Christian boys would be'. This instruction was the crassest propaganda:

> Dr Duff asked them who several of their Gods were? and how they were represented? 'The God of War is represented riding upon a pig.' 'A pig! – that is a very warlike animal,' said Dr Duff right merrily, whereupon there was such a display of white teeth, and such mirthful looks, as showed they had wonderfully small respect for the warlike deity. He then made them describe Durga, the consort of Shiva and Goddess of Destruction.
>
> 'A very sweet and merciful goddess, was she not?' This they denied laughingly . . .[81]

Earlier these astonishingly good-natured schoolboys had had an hour of

Christian indoctrination which included minute examination of 'Mundy's Christianity and Hinduism Contrasted'.

These crude methods of conversion were adopted to compensate for the failure of more conventional evangelising. Missionaries were alternately dismayed by the immensity of their task and the resistance of the Indians. Elijah Hoole, reviewing thirty years' work in 1844, calculated that he and his fellow Wesleyans had just under 4,000 'hearers' (i.e. church attenders) and 342 communicants in India. The Anglican Church Missionary Society had fared much better, and had just under 19,000 'hearers' and 1,639 communicants. The schools of both denominations were flourishing, with just under 7,000 pupils between them.[82] Opponents of missions claimed that the mass of their converts were Untouchables, for whom any faith was preferable to one which condemned them to the bottom of the pile. Among Hoole's first converts in 1822 were the Tamil wives of soldiers of the 69th Regiment. One wonders what they thought of Christianity when they and their children heard that they were forbidden to follow their husbands to Christian Britain on account of their colour.[83] There was always the fear of apostasy; young Bengali and Eurasian girls visited by Mrs Mackenzie in a Presbyterian orphanage near Calcutta were not sent into domestic service for fear that they might be contaminated by the 'heathen servants they would be obliged to mingle with'.

The popularity of their schools was one of the missionaries' greatest advantage, and one that they imagined would eventually tell in their favour. By 1850 India appeared in the middle of massive, far-reaching changes and, while the pace of conversion was still slow, it was gathering momentum. This was the message preached in 1846 by William Wilberforce's son, Samuel ('Soapy Sam'), the Bishop of Oxford. He also, and this struck at the roots of the caste system (and, for that matter, the racial hierarchy which was being established by the British in India), saw Christianity as a force for human equality. 'Am I,' he asked, 'the keeper of the Hindu, the Indian, the Hottentot? . . . Is the savage my brother? If all have sprung from the same parents then the wild wanderer, the painted barbarian, is thy brother, though civilisation may have separated you by so wide an interval that you can scarcely seem to belong to the same race.'[84]

The bishop was convinced that progress in India was unstoppable and the gap of enlightenment was narrowing thanks to dedicated men and women working busily in missions and schools across India. Whether or not the Indians wanted it to be closed was another matter which, when it was considered, was dismissed by references to their inability to know what was good for them. In many troubled Indian minds, eventual conversion appeared an integral part of the Company's relentless programme of reform. The result was widespread suspicion and fear, combined with a feeling that the British were becoming less sympathetic and more distant in their everyday relations with Indians. Officers and officials may have lost more than sexual satisfaction when they began to drop their native mistresses.

PART FOUR

THE MUTINY:
1857–59

1

The Sahib
Paid No Attention:
The Raj Imperilled,
January–July 1857

I

Nemesis overtook the Raj in 1857, but it came slowly and its approach was hardly noticed. Wise and experienced officials like Sir Henry Lawrence sensed that something was wrong, although they could not say exactly what.[1] Perhaps the passion for reform and change was out of control and Indians had had more change than they could absorb. 'I am afraid the enlightenment of Calcutta and other presidencies is going too fast for our Upper Provinces and Central India,' commented one administrator.[2] Others felt that everything was normal and behaved accordingly. On 26 January the officers of the Ambala garrison challenged their Meerut colleagues to a cricket match, and for the next three months both cantonments enjoyed the weekly rituals of balls and horse races. At the beginning of May, Lieutenant Alexander Lindsay of the Bengal Horse Artillery said goodbye to what had proved an expensive social life and set off from Meerut for a six-month shooting and fishing trip in the hills of Kashmir.[3]

He left behind him a country full of murmurs. The grumbling had begun during the winter and continued, gathering intensity, as the new year unfolded. Indians were the hosts to a tangle of grievances: economic, religious, political, tangible and intangible. A few were old, but most were new, which was why they were more bitterly felt. At the top, and kept at the government's expense in relative comfort, there were great men and women whose fortunes had been reversed by the Raj. Wajid Ali Shah, the ex-king of Awadh, grumbled in Calcutta where he and a reduced court had been exiled after the Governor-General, Lord Dalhousie, had deposed him for misrule. Another victim of the new order was Nana Sahib, a Maratha nobleman, who held court at Bithur on the outskirts of Cawnpore. Despite official objections, he styled himself maharaja and would have liked to call himself peshwa, for he was the adopted heir of the last peshwa, Baji Rao. He had been refused this title and, after a six-year battle in the courts, had failed to secure the £80,000 annuity that the government had paid his adoptive father. Nana Sahib had fallen foul of Dalhousie's doctrine of 'lapse', which overruled Hindu customs of adoption, and insisted that a state whose ruler died without a direct male heir was forfeit to the Company. Between 1847 and 1856, when he left India, the Governor-General had acquired Satara, Sambalpur, the Punjab, Jhansi and Nagpur by this legal stratagem. The kin of their former rulers were naturally disgruntled and, like Lakshmi Bai, the Rani of Jhansi, had tried to assert their rights in the courts in Calcutta and London, but without success. Henceforward, there would be no dynastic security for any prince, however loyal and accommodating.

The fall of princes had repercussions throughout their states. When Awadh had been taken over in February 1856, the royal household was severely reduced, the 200,000-strong royal army was dispersed and those who maintained it, including 12,000 armourers, were thrown out of work.[4] The numbers of unemployed rose further when the new government ordered the taluqdars to dismiss their armed retainers. Jobless and discontented men drifted towards the big cities, and they may have been among the crowds whose foul-mouthed incivilities distressed Mrs Amy Haines whenever she went abroad in Lucknow.[5]

Rural grudges were long-standing and directed in equal parts against the government which extracted taxes and the moneylenders who supplied the peasantry with the wherewithal to pay. In some districts in north-western India there was a largely artificial sense of foreboding caused by the appearance of strangers in villages. The visitor would seek out the chowkidah, present him with four small chapattis, instruct him to bake four more and have them delivered to neighbouring villages. Officials were perplexed and the best explanation they could offer was that the rigmarole had been contrived to ward off some unspecified but imminent catastrophe.[6] In Baroda, a pariah dog was guided from village to village with a basket of food which was shared among local dogs and then replenished. Bewildered magistrates dug into local mythology and discovered that the Maratha god of the sword was a dog, which suggested the dissemination of restlessness and violence. As for the food, eating it might be some form of sacrament, rather like the ritual taking of sugar which bound the thugs together.[7]

Indians interpreted these phenomena differently. They saw the distribution of food as a token that in the near future the Company would end all distinctions of caste and religion and that everyone would share a common diet.[8] Sepoys of the 2nd Bengal NI told their colonel that now: 'Rajas, Thakurs [Rajput landlords], Zamindars, Maharajas and Ryots all eat together and English bread has been sent to them.' This prediction was a variation on an old but persistent theme: the Company's secret plans to impose Christianity on India. 'The Lord Sahib [the Governor-General, Lord Canning] has given orders to all commanding officers which he has received from the Company to destroy the religion of the country,' the sepoys continued. The signs were unmistakable; why, they asked, had a law been passed to allow Hindu widows to remarry? Now the Company was contaminating the salt, ghi and sugar of its sepoys with the bones of pigs and cows and, as every soldier knew, the cartridge for the new Enfield rifle had been lubricated with the mixture of pig and cow fat. A government which had just demonstrated its absolute supremacy by dethroning the most powerful prince in India, the Nawab of Awadh, would stop at nothing to gets its way.

Evidence for this official conspiracy was everywhere. The 34th Bengal NI listened uneasily to sermons from Colonel G. S. Wheler, whom, they imagined, regularly went to Calcutta to consult with Lord Canning on the regiment's conversion. In fact, the Governor-General considered Wheler's preaching made him unfit for command.[9] Routine movements of European soldiers were regarded in the same sinister light. Reports that British artillery and infantry units were being posted to Barrackpur in March were immediately seen as evidence that some measure of coercion was about to be applied to the sepoys. In the middle of the month, latrine rumours of the 2nd Bengal NI predicted the imminent arrival of 5,000 white soldiers who would compel the sepoys to use the cartridges for the new rifle which was then coming into service.[10]

Sepoys groused more than anyone else in 1857, mostly in that secret world of the regimental lines, cantonment bazaars, grog shops, and street corners where few Europeans went and none were welcomed. One night towards the end of April, a private of the 9th Lancers stumbled across three sepoys gathered in a garden at Ambala and was manhandled by them, spat at and thrown out.[11] Such was the mood of the times that he reported the incident to an officer who thought the information worth passing on to his superior. No one knew exactly what the sepoys were saying or imagined that their complaints might be translated into a massive insurrection. Even when the mutinies were under way, there was a degree of lassitude when it came to uncovering precisely what the sepoys were planning. Major-General Hearsey, the local commander in Calcutta, in many respects a vigilant officer, found spying on his men distasteful. On 20 May, he admitted that it would be impossible to get 'secret information' from his soldiers, adding, 'It would not be proper for me to do it.'[12] Where the intelligence-gathering machinery was in place, it was quickly activated. On 12 May, Captain Richard Lawrence of the Thagi and Dakaiti Department based at Lahore sent a Brahmin agent into the sepoy lines to discover their mood. When he returned, he told Lawrence, 'Sahib, they are full of fissad [sedition].'[13]

During the first five months of 1857 sedition meant tales about cartridges and their potential to defile the Muslim and break the Hindu's caste. No number of perfectly true official statements that the cartridges were untainted could persuade the sepoys otherwise. Nor were they mollified by suggestions that the cartridge paper could be torn rather than bitten. Moreover, there was the legendary remark of an untouchable labourer at the Dum Dum arsenal who, on being refused water by a Brahmin sepoy, told him that soon there would be no barriers of caste, for the army was grinding pig and cow bones into the sepoys' flour. The Company was suspected of a similar trick in Gujarat, where it was using its salt monopoly to destroy the caste system. Cow's blood was being surreptitiously added to the salt, which was why it had a curious reddish tinge.[14] The discolouration actually came from the red ochre dye on the sacks, but this explanation convinced no one.

As rumours and complaints proliferated, it was clear that the Raj was suffering a gigantic loss of credibility among its most valuable collaborators, the Bengali sepoys. On every occasion, they believed the worst of their officers and the Company. Not only did they share their countrymen's apprehension at the quickening tempo of change and reform, they felt individually endangered, for their social and religious status appeared to be under a systematic assault. Gurkhas and Sikhs were making their way into an army which had hitherto been the exclusive preserve of Rajputs,

Brahmins and well-born Muslims. The pursuit of efficiency was sweeping away old privileges such as the right of Hindus to refuse foreign service on the grounds that they would be polluted if they crossed the sea. And then there were the recent laws against Hindu inheritance and marriage customs, preaching officers who favoured Christian sepoys, and the meddling arrogance of the missionaries whose schools taught young Indians to scoff at their parents' creeds.

These anxieties might have been allayed had the Company's officers been more patient and understanding. Many, especially younger men, were out of touch with their sepoys, preferring the society of the officers' mess and leaving regimental chores to Indian junior officers and NCOs. Martin Gubbins, the financial commissioner for Awadh, was struck by the aloofness of Company officers. 'How can you expect devotion on the field,' he once asked some subalterns, 'when you are a stranger to your men in cantonment?'[15] This detachment might not have mattered too much if native officers and NCOs had faithfully carried out their customary duty of being the eyes and ears of their British superiors. In many, perhaps the majority of instances, they were swept along by the same misgivings as their men with whom they made common cause. 'The Native Officers, Subadars, Jemadars are all good men in the whole brigade except two whose faces are like pigs: the Subadar Major of the 70th Regiment who is Christian and Thakur Mizra of the 43rd Light Infantry,' the 2nd NI told their commanding officer.[16] Interestingly both men were Christians, for the latter is later described as a man who 'has lost his religion' and the respect of his men, since Brahmin sepoys refused to salute him. Faced with this sort of statement and those of informers, British officers retreated behind a barrier of prejudices: the ruckus was no more than another, exasperating example of Indian naiveté and gullibility, and would soon pass.

Treating the unrest with impatience and disdain made matters worse. Dismissing the the 19th and 34th regiments' apprehensions about the cartridges as absurd deepened disquiet. Violence erupted on 29 March with the one-man mutiny of Mangal Pande of the 34th. He may have expected assistance for he was discovered on the Barrackpur parade ground, armed with a loaded musket, calling on his fellow soldiers to join him. 'Come out, you *banchuts* [sister-fuckers] . . . Why aren't we getting ready? It's for our religion! From biting these cartridges we shall become infidels. Get ready! Turn out all of you! You have incited me to do this and now you banchuts, you will not follow me!' A British NCO and subaltern hurried to the scene and were wounded by Pande. A bloody tussle followed which involved his colonel and General Hearsey. Much to their consternation, the British officers were hindered by all but one of the nearby sepoys, who was afterwards promoted. After a desperate resistance – he had been taking bhang, as he later admitted – Pande tried to shoot himself. Just over a week later, and still recovering from a wound in the neck, he was tried by a court martial of Brahmin and Muslim NCOs and sentenced to be shot. It was thought prudent to have a detachment of British regulars present during the execution.

The day after Pande's defiance, the 19th Bengal NI was disbanded, and since it was all too clear that the 34th was wobbling, it too was disarmed in the presence of a strong British force, including artillery. These punishments were designed to deter and humiliate: the sepoys were disgraced, deprived of their livelihood and pensions and sent back to communities where they would no longer enjoy any special standing. The same procedure was followed at Lucknow at the beginning of May after Sir Henry Lawrence had detected evidence of sedition among sowars of the 7th Awadh irregulars. They were cowed by the 32nd Regiment and a battery of loaded cannon and disarmed. As they surrendered in their muskets, the sepoys gave no hint of their emotions; a few were heard to mutter, '*Jai Company Bahadur Ki* [Long Live the Illustrious Company].'[17] Whether this was loyalty or irony, no one knew.

The pattern had been set; once a regiment showed signs of sullenness or intractability, the authorities would move pre-emptively and break it up in the hope that its fate might concentrate the minds of others inclined to disobedience. The psychological effect was not always as predicted. Fear of disarmament and perhaps being shot down by British musketry and grape shot panicked sepoys who were already the hosts to terrifying phantoms. Rather than submit and hand over their muskets, they would make the first move.

At Meerut, Colonel Edward Carmichael Smyth of the 3rd Bengal Light Cavalry was prepared to face trouble head-on in a characteristically bullish manner. Stiff and short-tempered, he was disliked by his sowars who, in the same circumstances and handled by another officer, might well have done as they were told. The temper of his men was sulky and he was determined to put them to the test. On 24 April Carmichael Smyth ordered a special parade for the regiment's eighty-five skirmishers, lectured them about the new ammunition, and ordered them to load their carbines with the suspect cartridges, tearing the paper with their fingers. They refused, even though they had fired the carbines previously, and were immediately arrested. 'The real case is that they hate Smyth,' one of his subalterns commented.[18] The mutineers were tried by a native court martial, found guilty and each sentenced to ten years' hard labour. But first they had to undergo a ritual humiliation designed to intimidate their colleagues and the sepoys of the 11th and 20th Bengal NI On 9 May the convicted men were marched to a parade ground where they were stripped of their uniforms and shackled, a process which took several hours. Among the onlookers were the 60th Rifles with loaded guns, the 6th Dragoon Guards with drawn sabres and a battery of artillery – Major-General William ('Bloody Bill') Hewitt, the divisional commander, was taking no risks. It was a sombre spectacle with old soldiers weeping at their shame and pleading for mercy. One cried out: 'I was a good sepoy, and would have gone anywhere for the service, but I could not forsake my religion.'

Nor would his brothers-in-arms. On the evening of 10 May, a Sunday, the cavalrymen broke into the gaol and rescued their comrades. Horsemen then galloped through the town, calling civilians to join them. The mob, swelled by sepoys from the two infantry regiments, attacked off-duty British soldiers in the bazaar and rampaged through the cantonments, burning bungalows and murdering every European man, woman and child they encountered. It was a frenzied, almost suicidal gesture, for everyone involved knew that Meerut had the largest British garrison in the region and they would surely take fearsome revenge. There was, bizarrely, a purpose behind this and later massacres. Killing men and women of a race which had hitherto represented authority and demanded obedience destroyed the mystique of British supremacy. It was almost an act of sacrilege; even the thugs had shrunk from attacking Europeans. Furthermore, the rebels were forging a sort of unity, for murdering Europeans made them men apart, cut off for ever from any chance of reconciliation and mercy. There was only one way forward: to fight and find friends. It was a desperate and irreversible course which many sepoys refused to take, then or later. At Meerut a handful of sowars and sepoys stayed loyal and did what they could to rescue Europeans.

There was a guiding political hand behind the wanton fury of the Meerut uprising, although it was never definitely identified. It had used violence to give the mutineers cohesion and a common cause, and somehow persuaded them that their only future course lay in an alliance with the old Muslim ruling dynasty, the Mughals. To stay in Meerut would mean annihilation by the 1,700 European troops who, thanks to the nerveless incompetents in command, had not yet been ordered into action. At some time during the night, a body of cavalry sowars set off for Delhi, thirty-six miles to the south-west, and were followed by the remants of the infantry who had been persuaded not to scurry off to their homes with their loot. The first horsemen galloped across the bridge of boats over the Jumma two or so hours after daybreak on 11 May. They then rode into the great open-air audience hall of the Red Fort, swords drawn, and demanded that Bahadur Shah, King of Delhi, appoint one of his sons their general. One of them, the seventeen-year-old Mirza Jiwan Bakht, thought the Russians had come![19] An 82-year-old poet, somewhat gaga and addicted to opium, Bahadur Shah was an unlikely leader for what was about to become a revolution. But he had one invaluable asset: he was the heir of the Mughals, and as such was a figure of legitimate authority whom the insurgents needed as a focus for what they were beginning to perceive as a popular movement that would defend their faiths and expel the British. As they later pointed out, Bahadur Shah was the legal ruler of India and the British were in fact traitors and rebels.

The coup took the British in Delhi completely by surprise. The events of the next few hours followed the same awful pattern as those in Meerut. Europeans were killed at random and attempts by their officers to rally the city's garrison, the 38th, the 54th and the 74th Bengal NI, ended with mutiny and murder. A handful of gallant officers rose above the chaos and forestalled the seizure of the Delhi magazine by blowing it up. As their assailants rushed the building their warcry was the same as that uttered by sepoys when they had fought for the British: 'Deen' (the Faith). Antipathy towards Christianity united Hindus and Muslims, as the leaders hoped it would, and mobs desecrated churches and cemeteries and murdered Indian and Eurasian converts. There were many hair-breadth escapes, but fifty British, Indian Christian and Eurasian prisoners, mostly women and children, were taken and confined within a dungeon in the Red Fort. On 16 May, and at the instigation of the original mutineers, they were brought into a courtyard and slaughtered in the presence of Bahadur Shah and his family. They were now accomplices in the uprising and had no choice but to act the parts assigned to them by the Meerut mutineers. Not long afterwards the new emperor composed a couplet on the events which had so suddenly elevated him to his throne:

> Na Iran, ne kiya, ne Shah Russe ne, –
> Angrez ko tabah kiya Kartoosh ne.

The English who conquered Persia and defeated the Czar of Russia had been overthrown in India by a simple cartridge.[20]

II

The situation in north-western India was extremely dangerous, but it did not yet represent a calamity. There were perhaps five or six thousand mutinous professional troops in Delhi, together with the poor-quality ceremonial troops of the emperor. There were also potential friends in the region to the north of the city where there had been a wave of peasant insurrections under leaders who were willing to assist what they saw as the new Raj.[21] But to make real headway, the rebels needed more trained soldiers. Scattered across the Punjab, the Ganges plain and Bengal were a further 130,000 sepoys of the Bengal army who, in various degrees, shared the anxieties of their colleagues at Meerut and Delhi.

News of the uprisings there travelled by word of mouth at a speed which amazed the British. In some cases it was accelerated by agents; two were arrested at Allahabad on 24 May after they had been discovered attempting to suborn sepoys on the eve of a Muslim festival.[22] The job of agitators was made easy by prevailing fears of the immediate disbandment of regiments and possibly chastisement.[23] After their officers had attempted to stifle unrest at Firozpur on 12 May, the 45th and 61st Bengal NI rebelled and hurried south to Delhi, and eight days later several companies of the 9th Bengal NI rose at Aligarh. Here the catalyst was the execution of a sepoy for inciting a mutiny, and news of his fate led to outlying detachments of the 9th rebelling in the next few days. In response to proclamations in the new emperor's name they too fled to Delhi, where they had the safety of numbers and protection against retribution.

The insurgents made no systematic attempt to disrupt the telegraph. Wires were cut for a time between Meerut and Agra (possibly by Gujars), but communications remained open across north-western India for most of May. This was a godsend for administrators and commanders, who were able to trace the course of the unrest and make preparations. Forewarned, they could either appeal directly for loyalty or disarm the sepoys. This was the wisest and most popular response for, as Sir John Lawrence, the commissioner for the Punjab, told Calcutta on 13 May, no faith could now be placed in any Bengali regiment.[24]

Colonel Thomas Pierce still trusted his 6th Light Cavalry and appealed to them to charge mutineers from the 15th Bengal NI, who had risen at Nasirabad on 28 May.

> Men of the 6th corps, listen to me, I have every confidence in you, I beg of you keep order in the ranks and listen to no commands but mine, which I know you obey. When the moment arrives, behave like Heroes, and I will answer that conspicuous gallantry shall not pass unrewarded – if the worst comes to the worst, I am ready to die with you.

His words were enthusiastically received, and Pierce decided to demonstrate his faith in the troopers by sending his wife, Isabella, then eight months pregnant, to the quarters of the native officers' families.[25] After a bloody skirmish with the insurgents, who had seized a cannon, Pierce's men switched sides. They did not, however, harm their officers or Mrs Pierce. Likewise, Europeans in Nimach were allowed to leave unmolested after the garrison mutinied. Officers there had endeavoured to extract oaths of loyalty from their men, sworn on Ganges water and the Koran, and had demonstrated their confidence in them by sleeping in the sepoy lines.[26]

In the recently annexed Punjab, Sir John Lawrence and his administrators would pander to no one. He and his judicial commissioner, Robert Montgomery, were Protestant Ulstermen and, in the words of the semi-official historian of the Mutiny, Sir William Kaye, were 'familiar with the stirring watch-words of Derry: "No Surrender".'[27] They took that same rigorous line with actual and potential mutineers as their ancestors had done with the Catholic, Gaelic Irish. Immediately the first baleful telegram reached Lahore, Montgomery ordered European civilians to take refuge inside the fort and stopped the issue of arms and percussion caps to the sepoys. There were 6,000 native troops garrisoned near the city and intelligence revealed that they were in a perverse mood. Montgomery acted decisively and swiftly: while a ball was in progress, preparations were secretly put in hand to disarm the entire Indian force. On the morning of 13 May, three regiments of sepoy infantry and one of cavalry were summoned to a special parade where, according to military practice, they would be formally told of the disbandment of the 19th and 34th Bengal NI at Barrackpur six weeks before.

There were six cannon, all loaded with grape shot, and six companies of the 81st Regiment, who were deployed where they could rake the native lines with fire. A junior officer commanded the sepoys to lay down their muskets, an order that was being given, he assured them, 'not so much for the peace of the country, which the British would maintain, as for the sake of preserving untarnished the names of the regiments'. No one was fooled; but the command, 'Eighty-first, load!', followed by the 'ominous ring of each ramrod as it drove hard the ball-cartridge, carried conviction to the hearts of the waverers'. So too did the gunners standing with lighted linstocks above the touch holes.[28] Montgomery had every reason to congratulate himself: his bluff had saved Lahore and with it communications between the Punjab and the rest of India.

Civilians were soon sucked into what had begun as a purely military revolt. Gujars from the hinterland of Meerut joined its inhabitants during the looting of the British cantonments, and once the government's authority had dissolved there were plenty in Delhi who snatched the opportunity to do the same. These plunderers, and thousands more who emerged as anarchy spread in towns and countryside, were purely self-interested. Officials described them all as *badmashes* (ruffians and petty crooks), but many, perhaps the majority, were probably poor and glad to turn a public emergency to their own advantage. In Azamgarh the mutiny of the 17th Bengal NI was preceded by three weeks of civilian unrest triggered by news of events in Meerut. The tax assessment on the ryots was heavy, urban weavers suffered from a local impost and a grain shortage was forcing up food prices. As he rode through the countryside during the third week of May, the magistrate Charles Horne found the villagers insolent, and inside the city shopkeepers offered to pay for armed guards on the bazaar.[29]

Just as there were Indians with much to gain from the collapse of civil order, there were those with much to lose. Their interest lay in the preservation and restoration of British government and they were ready to do all in their power to assist the Raj. After the revolts by the Nasirabad and Nimach garrisons, Takht Singh, the Maharaja of Jodhpur, who depended heavily on British support, immediately offered his own troops to help crush the mutineers. The Jodhpur Legion deserted to the mutineers and provided the cue for one of the maharaja's local political enemies, Thakur Kushai Singh, to join them, bringing with him 2,000 armed retainers.[30] Maharaja Jaijii Rao Scindia of Gwalior also stuck by the Raj, but his confidence in its survival was not shared by the largely Bengali Gwalior contingent, a force which he financed. On 14 June the Gwalior contingent mutinied and murdered its British officers. It did not, however, join the Delhi mutineers or march to the front, which was opening up along the Ganges, thanks to Jaijii Rao's willingness to keep paying its wages. The regent of Bharatpur also stayed true to the government, although his subjects favoured the mutineers. In both instances, princely fidelity rested in large part on an unwillingness to exchange the Governor-General in Calcutta for an emperor in Delhi.[31]

There was no mistaking the temper of the ordinary people of Gwalior. By 19 May the shock waves from Meerut and Delhi had reached the city and they convinced many that the Raj was tottering. The time was ripe for the venting of long suppressed resentments. Servants were impertinent and some looked as though they might cut the throats of their masters and mistresses. The Reverend George Coopland, a zealous Company chaplain, noted 'a scowl on every native's face' and blamed his employers for 'weak tampering with idolatry and flattering vile superstition'.[32] Elsewhere sahibs were perplexed and dismayed by the frailty of their servants' loyalty. Colonel Pierce was upset by the sudden departure of his bhisti and washerwoman, who had served him for between twenty and thirty years. There was some consolation in the fidelity of his orderly, who had been at his side throughout the Afghan and Sikh wars and remained in Nasirabad to guard Pierce's property.[33]

In areas where British authority had either vanished or was on the point of disintegration, the peasantry moved quickly to settle old scores. Within days of the Meerut revolt, there were upheavals in the adjacent Saharanpur and Muzaffarnagar districts in which zamindars and ryots attacked their creditors. The Gujars, a semi-nomadic pastoral tribe prone to banditry, were prominent in the revolt against what they called the 'bania ka raj' (the rule of the moneylenders) and they and their account books were favourite targets. Overnight, thousands of debts were unilaterally repudiated. These disturbances temporarily subsided after swift action by two local magistrates, backed by police and a detachment of cavalry from Ambala. R. Spankie, the 'gallant and active' magistrate of Saharanpur, was horrified by how brittle the Raj's authority had proved. 'The people of this district,' he wrote after they had been brought to heel, 'and in all others in this country I suppose, have no sympathy with the Government, British or Native. Separate castes and communities have separate ends and desires to attain, and the weakness of Government is their strength.'[34]

In these early days, it was far from clear whether or not the mutineers would forge a permanent alliance with the rural insurgents. What was beyond question was that attacks on property, pillaging and assaults on bankers and businessmen convinced men of substance that they had a common cause with the British. The mutineers at Nasirabad had extorted between two and three thousand rupees from each of the town's money-lenders and merchants.[35] Inside Delhi, Mohan Lal, a munshi and British agent, noticed that many rich and influential Hindu and Muslim business-men, who had prospered under British rule and had used 'British laws and courts' to their advantage, realised that a rebel victory would be their undoing.[36] At Mathura, 115 miles south of the city, the powerful Seth banking family were happy to supply the embattled magistrate Mark Thornton with information from their own extensive intelligence network and loan him two nine-pounder cannon which they kept for festivals.[37] What had begun as a soldiers' insurrection had become a civil war from which Indians could not escape. They were confronted with three equally perilous choices: neutrality, support for the Raj, or rebellion.

III

How they would make up their minds depended on the government's chances of crushing the insurrection swiftly and decisively. During May and early June 1857 most Indians, however deep their grievances, preferred to wait and watch rather than throw themselves behind one side or the other. Old habits of obedience were hard to shake off and the mystique of the Raj still lingered; Mirza Jiwan Bakht spoke for many when he later recalled, 'I was always afraid of the Company's government.'[38] If past example was anything to go by, Indians might expect the Company's response to the rebellion to be speedy, aggressive and overwhelming. It was none of these things.

The government had been caught off balance with its military resources stretched to breaking point. Sir John Lawrence exposed its vulnerability in his analysis of the strategic situation on 19 May: 'Between Meerut and Calcutta we have but five regiments of Europeans scattered over the coun-try at wide intervals. What is to become of them and all our countrymen, if we hold our own at points where we are strong?'[39] European troops were isolated and bottled up in key bases, protecting civilians, women and chil-dren and defending government property and treasure. The five British regiments immediately available for action in May were strung out along the 750 miles between Delhi and Calcutta: the 53rd and the 84th cover-ing that city, the 10th at Dinajpur, the 32nd at Lucknow, and the 3rd Bengal Europeans at Agra. Priority had been given to holding these strongpoints and, at the latter three, neutralising their sepoy garrisons.

This left approximately 3,800 British and trustworthy Indian troops at Ambala and Meerut who were earmarked for the blockade of Delhi at the end of May. The only strategic reserve of Europeans was scattered across the Punjab, temporarily tied down, as it were, by 36,000 Bengali troops whose loyalty was fragile. By the final fortnight in July more than half had been disarmed by British, Sikh and Gurkha troops. By this time, Sir John Lawrence could no longer resist pressure to reinforce the army besieging Delhi. He gave way grudgingly on 21 July after his arm had been twisted by the commander at Delhi, Brigadier-General Archdale Wilson, who threatened to abandon the siege if he was not sent additional men. Many of the 4,200 soldiers ordered south were withdrawn from the Punjab fron-tier garrison, a gamble which Lawrence was forced to accept. As one of his subordinates wired Calcutta: 'It will be vain to attempt to retain the Trans-Indus border while we lose the interior of the Punjab.' As it was, luck favoured the British. On the whole, the notoriously volatile tribesmen remained quiet, and thousands were happy to join improvised detach-ments which Lawrence was raising for service against the mutineers.

Like Sir John, Canning had identified the weaknesses of the British strategic position. He also guessed that there was more trouble ahead and, on 19 May, had summoned reinforcements. Four days later the 1st Madras Fusiliers began disembarking at Calcutta and were immediately hurried up country piecemeal, shortly followed by the 35th which had been recalled from Burma. The 64th and the 78th Highlanders, whose kilts, red beards and tanned faces unnerved the Indians, returned from the Persian expedi-tion during the first week of June and were immediately rushed to the front. Canning could also count on another Scottish regiment, the 90th, which had been on its way to Hong Kong as the advance guard of an army sent to force the Chinese government to accept a free trade in opium. Its troopships were intercepted at sea and diverted. The 90th reached Calcutta at the beginning of August and was later joined by the 5th from Mauritius. News of the mutiny reached Cape Town on 9 August and the 93rd Highlanders, then heading for China, were immediately ordered to Calcutta, which they reached thirty-eight days later.[40] Further reinforce-ments, the 48th, 57th and 71st Highlanders, were hurrying from Malta, carried by steamships and via the overland route across the Suez isthmus.

This route was a godsend which considerably accelerated the flow of manpower to India. The 8th Hussars who sailed from Southampton on 20 October arrived at Bombay on 24 November.[41]

Over 4,000 British troops were rushed up from Calcutta to the Benares/Allahabad region during June and a further 4,000 were expected within the next six weeks.[42] They were just enough to tip the balance in the fighting around those two cities and forestall the spread of unrest to districts between them and Calcutta. Little help could be expected from the other two presidencies, at least for the time being. The commander-in-chief in Madras was nervous about disaffection among his forces, and his counterpart in Bombay had been taking precautionary measures since 12 May. They were needed, for, on 14 June, seditious correspondence between the mutineers and Bombay sepoys was discovered.[43]

There was just enough manpower for holding operations and a counter-attack towards Cawnpore, but insufficient for the creation of a mobile field force when it was most needed during the last fortnight of May and the first of June. As predicted, the crisis worsened during the first week of June with a second wave of mutinies at Lucknow, Cawnpore, Azamgarh, Allahabad and Bareilly. Awadh and the greater part of the north-western provinces passed out of the Company's control and much of central India appeared to be in jeopardy after mutinies at Gwalior and Jhansi. The government's authority evaporated, its servants and remaining soldiers, mostly white, were driven behind hastily constructed fieldworks at Cawnpore and Lucknow and at Agra into the massive Mughal fortress palace, overlooking the Jumma. Beyond these embattled enclaves there was anarchy.

The situation was most perilous in Cawnpore, 260 miles south-east of Delhi. Command was in the hands of General Sir Hugh Wheeler, a veteran of nearly every Indian campaign since 1805. He commanded 200 European soldiers and was responsible for nearly a thousand fugitives, over a third of them women and children, whom he had placed behind makeshift defences close to his house. After a fortnight of alarums, the 2nd Bengal Light Cavalry mutinied on the night of 4–5 May and attempted to subvert the rest of the Cawnpore garrison. The 1st Bengal NI broke immediately, but the 53rd and 56th were less than enthusiastic. Their minds were made up on the morning of 5 June when, in a moment of confusion, they were fired upon from Wheeler's trenches. Even so, many sepoys and cavalrymen stayed loyal and made their way to the British lines during the next few days.

Within hours of the first rising at Cawnpore, a large body of mutineers made their way to Bithur to plead with Nana Sahib, whose grievances against the British made him a natural ally. Although after the Mutiny there were allegations that Nana had been at the heart of a vast conspiracy and was said to have had secret contacts with Russian agents, Wheeler and many others believed that he would remain loyal and were astounded by his defection. Nana and those close to him claimed afterwards, and when he was a fugitive, that he had been compelled to join the insurgents, not least by threats that they would plunder his property.[44] A more likely explanation for his conduct was that he was part trimmer, part political gambler. Recent experience had taught him that he could expect nothing from the British, however hard he tried to ingratiate himself with them. The sepoys offered him a chance to fulfil his ambitions and he snatched at it in the belief that British power was on the verge of disintegration throughout India. On 6 June he appeared with his artillery and armed retainers in front of Wheeler's fortifications and the siege began.

At Lucknow, Sir Henry Lawrence had been victualling and fortifying the residency since 23 May. He was cautiously optimistic, for he had the 32nd Regiment as part of the garrison, but did not feel confident enough to disarm the four Bengal regiments who showed no hints of restlessness. As in so many towns and cities at this time, the European mood was one of outward calm and inner foreboding and, as gruesome details became known of the massacres in Meerut, Delhi and some of the smaller stations, hysteria occasionally broke surface. Everyone expected the sepoys would mutiny, but no one could say when or how. When they did, on 11 June, the disturbances began, as at Meerut and elsewhere, among the cavalry-men. After a brisk fight, the mutineers were expelled from the city and set off towards Delhi. Interestingly, on the eve of the uprising, a loyal sepoy for the 13th Bengal NI warned the authorities of what was about to occur, but was ignored.[45] Twelve days later, when a mounted police control discovered a substantial force of mutineers advancing on Lucknow, Martin Gubbins refused take the matter seriously. 'The sahib paid no attention,' remembered his informant, who later joined the mutineers.[46] This phrase might easily have been the epitaph for a crumbling Raj.

IV

The events of May and early June dictated the first phase of British operations in northern India. The mutineer command had everywhere opted

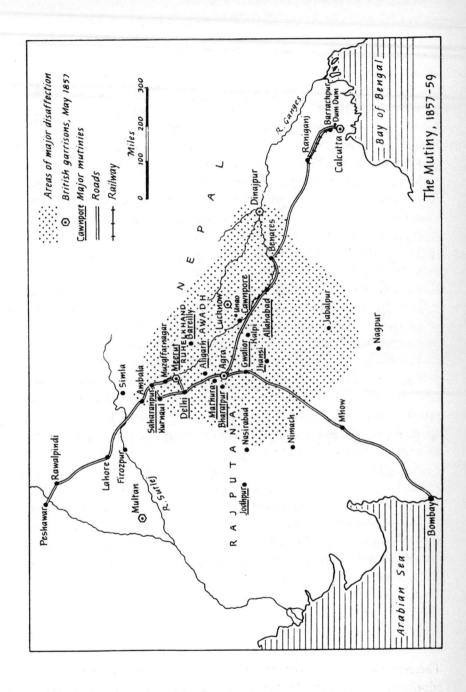

The Mutiny, 1857-59

Areas of major disaffection

◉ British garrisons, May 1857

Cawnpore Major mutinies

═══ Roads

━┼━ Railway

Miles

0 100 200 300

for static warfare: a growing body of insurgents poured into Delhi and sat tight, while other forces encircled Cawnpore and Lucknow. This timidness made containment easier, allowing a small force to blockade Delhi and another, successively commanded by Colonel James Neill, Major-General Sir Henry Havelock and Lieutenant-General Sir James Outram to push along the Great Trunk road from Benares towards Cawnpore and Lucknow. It was a messy campaign during which commanders were restricted by a lack of manpower. Reinforcements arrived in penny packages, units had to be detached to cope with rural uprisings, and, since this was the hot season, men succumbed in hundreds to sunstroke and fevers.

Much, therefore, hung on leadership. Neill and Havelock were not master strategists, but they possessed in abundance the qualities that were vital: stamina, tenacity and steadiness. Both men might easily have stepped from the ranks of Cromwell's Ironsides; they read their Bibles regularly and saw themselves as agents of a stern Providence, chosen by God to chastise, avenge and pacify. Neither flinched from the use of terror in a cause which they believed had Divine approval and against an enemy who were, in Havelock's words, 'devils incarnate'. Lucifer was loose in India and he had to be checked with fire and sword. Both were applied ruthlessly and promiscuously by Neill. 'I trust for forgiveness,' he wrote, 'I have done all for the good of my country, to re-establish its prestige and power, and put down this most barbarous, inhuman insurrection.' If his conscience quivered, he stiffened it by the knowledge that his victims had raped and tortured women at Delhi.[47] Havelock too saw himself as an avenging angel. He was sixty-two years of age, just over five feet tall, proud, austere, as brave as a lion and loved by his men. For his countrymen in India and Britain, he was the ideal Christian warrior, a perfect hero for his times.

Neill led the advance on Benares, which he entered on 9 June, just in time to impose order. Two days later he was pressing on towards Allahabad, all too aware that with less than 2,000 men he had to restore the authority of the Raj in a region where it had been dramatically overthrown. Unable to intimidate with weight of numbers, he fell back on systematic terror, backed by the mandate of martial law. During the next five weeks, small parties fanned out from his column with instructions to inflict condign punishment on all suspected of insurrection. The laws of evidence were suspended, age and sex ignored, and those who carried out the killings were proud of their deeds, which they justified as revenge for the atrocities at Meerut and Delhi. In one grotesque incident, an officer arranged to have prisoners hanged from trees so that their swinging corpses formed a figure of eight, something he found rather droll.[48] Looking back with distaste on this episode, Sir William Kaye wrote:

> . . . in Native histories, or, history being wanting, in Native legends and traditions, it may be recorded against our people, that mothers and wives and children . . . fell miserable victims to the first swoop of English vengeance; and these stories may have as deep a pathos as any that rend our own hearts.[49]

Neill did not invent the concept of ruthless, indiscriminate revenge. At the end of May, British forces burned Gujar villages between Delhi and Meerut and suspected rebels were massacred wherever they were found.[50] In one village, where it was feared that three fugitives from Delhi, a doctor, his wife and child, had been murdered, eleven suspects were rounded up. One boasted that he had raped the woman and killed the child; each was coated with pork fat and had pork thrust down his throat before being hanged.[51]

Both sides adopted mass murder as an instrument of policy. It was used most infamously by Nana Sahib after General Wheeler had abandoned the unequal struggle to defend the lines at Cawnpore. He had accepted terms under which the British would be allowed passage by boat down river to Allahabad. On 27 June, at Nana Sahib's orders, a detachments of sepoys ambushed the refugees as they embarked from the Sati Chaura ghat and many were shot down or drowned. There were a handful of miraculous escapes and 125 women and children were seized and incarcerated in the bibighar, which was, significantly, a small bungalow where a British officer had once housed his Indian mistress. Many of the captives were suffering from dysentery and cholera and, as if to symbolise the reversal of fortune brought about by the rebellion, British women were forced to grind corn. Nana Sahib proclaimed the massacre by the ghat a victory and celebrated it accordingly, inviting 'all the peasants and landed proprietors of every district to rejoice at the thought that the Christians have been sent to hell, and both the Hindu and Mahomedan religions have been confirmed'.[52]

This was empty bravado, for his forces had been unable to deflect Neill. On 30 June, the day Havelock assumed command, an advance guard of 820 hurried forward from Allahabad, and, by 14 July, the main army was within striking distance of Cawnpore. Havelock commanded just under 2,000 men, of whom nearly 1,300 were British, and in every engagement got the better of his opponents, largely thanks to the superior range of the new Enfield rifle. Nana Sahib had about 5,000 effective troops whose morale was drooping in the face of constant setbacks. Faced with the collapse of his power and beset by panic, Nana ordered the slaughter of the surviving women and children, which was undertaken by local butchers on the night of 15–16 July. Their bodies were then thrown down a well. There is no direct evidence to suggest that Nana Sahib ordered this or the earlier massacre as deliberate retaliation for Neill's terror. Rather, they appear to have been atrocities contrived to demonstrate that the power of the British had been destroyed for good and that a new era had dawned. In all likelihood, this had also been the motive behind the horrific public massacre of Europeans in Jhansi by sepoys and townspeople. Interestingly, when fugitives from villages close to Delhi arrived in the city early in July with claims that women had been raped by British troops, there was no call for tit-for-tat retaliation. According to the spy who reported this news, the mutineers pledged to fight to the death to avenge these wrongs.[53]

Killing white women and children had not made Nana's soldiers any braver. On the morning of the 16th, they fled from their defensive positions outside Cawnpore and Nana abandoned the city. It was occupied by Havelock the following morning, native spies having informed him that the women and children had been slain. The sight of the place of slaughter, blood-stained and littered with ladies' dresses, children's clothing and locks of hair, provoked an explosion of anguished rage among the soldiers. Havelock pressed on to Lucknow, leaving Neill to exact retribution on the inhabitants of a city who, for him and his soldiers, were all guilty by association. He did so with a characteristic thoroughness and a refinement designed simultaneously to satisfy the craving for vengeance and spread fear. Condemned men were made to lick the blood from the floors under threat of a lashing and then Muslims were be forced to swallow pork and Hindus beef. After defilement and often more dead than alive, they were hung before parties of jeering soldiers.

The bibighar became a sort of shrine, to which soldiers were taken as they passed through Cawnpore on their way to the front and where, as it were, they consecrated themselves to the task of retribution. A Pathan guide, who claimed to have been a veteran of the 1838–42 Afghan war, showed visitors the detritus of mass murder and retold the harrowing story. What the fighting men heard and saw transformed then into Furies, determined to pursue and kill without pity any Indians tainted with disloyalty. 'I felt as if my heart was stone and my brain fire,' Lieutenant Arthur Lang told his family.[54] He had killed a dozen during the fighting in Delhi and, after Cawnpore, looked forward to killing more. Highlanders swore the ancient oaths of vengeance of their race which pledged a hundred deaths for one. 'Remember Cawnpore!' became a battle-cry, and soldiers with a taste for gallows humour renamed the regulation, twelve-inch spike bayonet a 'Cawnpore Dinner', a deadly repast which went straight to the stomach. By an act which was as pointless as it was cruel, Nana Sahib had made every Indian rebel an accessory to his crime and condemned many who were innocent to humiliation and death. The opportunities for immediate vengeance were not great in mid-July. Lucknow still held out, and would have to for some time to come, for Havelock's force, reduced by sickness and exhaustion to less than 700 effectives, was compelled to fall back on Cawnpore. The invasion of Awadh had to be postponed until fresh troops arrived from Calcutta. No decision was yet possible at Delhi where the besiegers had no difficulty in holding their lines, but lacked the manpower and siege guns for an assault.

There were, however, plenty of grounds for optimism. Whenever they had fought mutineers in open battle, the British triumphed, although hitherto the engagements had been on a small scale. Moreover, their opponents showed a marked and, as it turned out, fatal preference for immobile warfare, whether inside one stronghold or besieging others. Large areas of north-western and northern central India had slipped from Britain's grasp, but their inhabitants were, by and large, distracted by the pursuit of private vendettas or internecine squabbles. During the crucial first two months of the uprising, no co-ordinated, concerted anti-British front emerged. Despite encouraging signs of mass rural and urban antipathy to the Raj, the rebel leadership failed to devise and implement any sort of guerrilla campaign against the British. This mistake had lost them the numbers game; from the first days of the crisis, British reinforcements and supplies were free to pass to the front from Calcutta without hindrance. In time, the government would be able to concentrate their growing armies where the mutineers were strongest, confident that their lines of communication were safe. The Raj would be revived.

Very Harrowing Work: The Raj Resurgent, August 1857– January 1859

I

It took eighteen months of hard fighting to restore the British Raj. There were two, loosely connected wars. The largest was a contest between the British and their Indian auxiliaries, chiefly Punjabis and Gurkhas, and the Bengal sepoys who, at various times, were augmented by units from the princely armies and civilian rebels. The other war comprised subsidiary counter-insurgency operations undertaken by comparatively small detachments against bodies of fugitives and rural rebels.

The problem of numbers, which had constrained commanders during the early months of the war, had disappeared by the end of 1857. In the following year, British commanders in Bengal had at their disposal 46,400 British troops and 58,000 Indian, including 10,000 Punjabis. Overall losses from enemy action were small, at least by the standards of the later Franco-Austrian and American Civil Wars: 2,600 British other ranks were killed in battle, 2.7 per cent of those engaged, and 157 officers, 4 per cent of their total.[1] Even regiments involved in the hardest fighting came off relatively lightly. The 93rd Highlanders, engaged in nearly every action on the Lucknow front between Sepetmber 1857 and March 1858, lost 49 from enemy action and 129 from wounds and sickness out of 1,392. The

Highlanders' experience was repeated throughout British units. Over 8,000 British soldiers died from sunstroke and diseases, and a further 3,000 had to be discharged and sent home as invalids.[2]

Intense heat, fatigue, boils, smallpox, dysentery and recurrent outbreaks of cholera wiped out more men than the rebels. The severely under-manned medical department used chloroform for amputations whenever it was available, but large numbers died from trauma and infection.[3] By far the greatest number of wounds were the consequence of enemy fire, rather than hand–to–hand fighting in which quarter was seldom given by either side.[4] Doctors argued that many lives could have been saved if the army had provided more suitable light cotton clothing during the hot season, when some regiments advanced to the front in red serge tunics with leather stocks around the mens' necks and stiff, felt shakos on their heads. During a three-day march near Jaipur in July 1858 twenty-two British soldiers collapsed and died from sunstroke.[5] An oversight sent the 1st Dragoon Guards into battle at Lucknow in heavy brass helmets which, in temperatures of over 100 degrees, became so hot that they seared flesh, and troopers claimed that they could toast bread inside them.[6]

Precious British lives could be saved if soldiers were spared the debili-tating exertion of cross–country marches. Troops who disembarked at Calcutta travelled by train to the railhead at Raniganj, where they were transferred to convoys of carts pulled by teams of bullocks which were changed at regular intervals. These wagon trains covered between thirty and thirty-six miles a day and were supplemented by elephants, camels with panniers and Ganges river steamers hauling barges. Much of this transport had to be commandeered or borrowed from friendly princes and landowners, for the department normally responsible had been run down in the interests of economy and was poorly managed. A makeshift system inevitably suffered breakdowns and then soldiers marched, rising before dawn to avoid the midday and afternoon heat, but still enduring what one officer described as the 'furnace wind' of the Indian plains which was 'as pungent as dry snuff'.[7] In favourable conditions and moving by night, reg-iments could make up to twenty-four miles a day, but it was always 'very harrowing work'.[8]

Men pushed to the limits of endurance in extremes of climate needed iron willpower and a sense of purpose to sustain them. Morale under-pinned stamina and for most of the war it was very high. There had been a few pockets of paralysis and panic during the first phases. Old colonels refused to entertain the possibility that men they had commanded for years might be disloyal and delayed their disarmament, sometimes fatally. There were a few outbreaks of funk. Bachelor officers galloped out of Gwalior the moment trouble seemed imminent and, in the Punjab, Brigadier-General Halifax proposed a mass evacuation of British forces down the Indus to Karachi, where they would take ship for home.[9] These spasms of premature despair were exceptional, and even when it faltered, morale was quickly rekindled as tales of sepoy atrocities spread through camps and cantonments.

Outrage at the horrifying and invariably exaggerated stories of women raped, children tortured and, in one persistent tale, roasted alive and fed to their parents roused the British soldier to a pitch of fury. Few armies have ever been infected with such a powerful urge to beat its enemies. 'The Lion hearts of our soldiers yearned for revenge upon these blood-thirsty villains,' wrote Private Potiphar of the 9th Lancers.[10] Such passions helped fighting men survive the overpowering heat, flies, fevers, thin rations, thirst, and the stench from unburied corpses which comprised the common experience of soldiering during 1857 and 1858.

Interior impulses, largely vindictive, made the British fight with a demonic energy and contempt for the odds which were often stacked against them. It mattered little that the more gruesome details of the atrocities were inventions; those shocked by them went into battle in the belief they were fighting a foe who had forfeited his humanity and was capable of unlimited evil. For this reason, many officers and men were convinced that God was truly on their side and, when the war had ended, regarded victory as a manifestation of Divine justice.[11] Similar emotions similarly animated the allies of the Raj, although their antipathy towards the rebels was ancestral and sectarian. Sikh hatred for Muslims mirrored that of British soldiers towards the sepoys.[12] In one incident during the capture of Lucknow in March 1858, a band of Muslim fanatics, wearing green scarves, defended a bungalow to the last man, killing a British officer from a Sikh unit. The Sikhs snatched the survivor and stabbed and burned him to death as British officers and men stood by, untouched by his screams for mercy.[13] Elsewhere, Sikhs protested that their co-religionists had been tortured and murdered whenever they had fallen into the mutineers' hands.

One bonus was the shambling rebel leadership, which was largely drawn from sepoy NCOs and junior officers. It seldom showed imagination or initiative, and failed to evolve either an effective command structure or a grand strategy. One capable general did emerge, Tanti Topi, who, revealingly, had had no previous military experience. He learned the arts of war in the field and, by the midsummer of 1858, had appreciated his adversaries' weakness. The result was a fast-moving guerrilla campaign in Gwalior and Nagpur which kept the British on their toes. But this display of tactical brilliance was too late to influence the outcome of a war which had already been decided by British victories in Delhi and Awadh. Given the nature of the uprisings and the diversity of the rebels' interests and objectives, it would have been well-nigh impossible to pull together all the participants and co-ordinate them through a master plan.

British generals were, therefore, free to exploit their opponents' errors, which was just as well for none was an outstanding strategist, although all were good at improvisation. The deaths from cholera in June and early July of the commander-in-chief, Anson, and General Sir Harry Barnard were a stroke of luck, for neither enjoyed the confidence of their officers and men and the former made no effort to hide his dislike for Indian soldiers.[14] The new commander-in-chief, Sir Colin Campbell, who took over the Lucknow front in October 1857, proved to be just what the circumstances required. He was a cautious but stout-hearted 65-year-old who had fought in the Peninsula, against the Sikhs and in the Crimea. Above all, he had the knack of getting the best from his men, particularly his fellow Scots of the Highland regiments, whom he cherished – some said too much.

Perhaps the most telling advantage which the armies of the Raj possessed was a cadre of younger, energetic and dashing career officers who embodied that peculiar British 'pluck' which was widely accepted as the key to winning battles. The most celebrated was Brigadier-General John Nicholson, commander of the Punjab contingent at Delhi, a 36-year-old Dubliner who had made his reputation in the Afghan and Sikh wars. Untouched by his colleagues' religious zeal, he was a pugnacious professional whom the soldiers loved for his fearlessness. At Delhi, Nicholson was 'their general' and his ardour was contagious; he was mortally wounded leading the assault on the city, but characteristically refused to accept treatment until he knew the attack had succeeded.[15] Another darling of the rank and file was William Hodson, a devil-may-care ex-infantry officer who ran field intelligence for the Delhi Field Force and commanded a regiment of irregular horse, whose 300 Punjabi and Pathan troopers were known as 'Plungers'. Hodson was one of those instinctive warriors whose life found its highest expression in facing danger and who believed that wars were won by getting to grips with the enemy and killing him. During a skirmish near Delhi he burned twenty-three sepoys alive after they had fled to a building, and he was rumoured to be a consummate looter, but in the eyes of those who fought alongside him he was exactly the sort of officer the times demanded.[16] At the middle and junior levels of command, men of Nicholson's and Hodson's stamp were worth their weight in gold, and there were plenty of them. They played the usual price for leading from the front; of the 122 men killed during Campbell's entry into Lucknow, 10 were officers, and they amounted to 35 of the 414 wounded.

II

The war against the sepoys was fought on three main fronts: in and around Delhi; along the road which passed through Cawnpore and Lucknow and into southern Awadh; and in central India.

The Delhi theatre was crucial. It was the base of the largest professional mutineer army, which had congregated there during June and July, and it contained their figurehead and counterweight to the authority of the Raj, Bahadur Shah. Delhi had been a magnet for all mutineers, drawing first the fugitives from Meerut who were augmented by men from the city's garrison and, on 17–18 June, by sepoys from Nasirabad. The flow continued: the 6,000-strong Bareilly contingent arrived on 1 July, a force from Jhansi appeared on 18 July, followed by a troops from the Jullundur garrison on the 22nd, and 4,000 men from Nimach four days later. By the beginning of August, there were probably between 30,000 and 40,000 former Bengali sepoys in Delhi. This formidable and potentially dangerous army chose to squander its energies on the defence of a position which was of greater symbolic than strategic value. In doing so, it allowed itself to be checkmated by the Delhi Field Force, which appeared outside the north-western wall of the city in June and refused to budge. At its largest, at the beginning of September, it contained 7,000 men, although at any one time up to a quarter of its strength was laid up, either sick or exhausted.

The siege of Delhi was a campaign of attrition in which nerve and sticking power ultimately mattered more than numbers. British forces were camped on the lee of the Delhi ridge, out of range of the superior rebel artillery. The conflict resolved itself into a series of assaults on British positions, all of which were repelled, but with losses which the defenders could ill afford. And yet, by successfully holding their ground against greater numbers, the Delhi Field Force gained a vital moral victory. The sepoys fought with a raw courage which impressed their adversaries, but, time and time again, they flinched when the moment came to press home the bayonet charge in the face of intense artillery and rifle fire. Here and elsewhere the mutineers were handicapped by their old-fashioned smooth-bore muskets, which were outranged by the more accurate new Enfield rifles now in use by many British units.

The unbroken sequence of reverses during July and August fostered defeatism among both soldiers and civilians inside Delhi. It could be detected in a letter sent on 3 August by Bahadur Shah turning down an offer of help from 6,000 ghazis (Muslim warriors). How could they dislodge the British, the emperor asked, when ten times their number of sepoys had failed?[17] This sense of hopelessness permeated the rest of the city and, within three weeks, substantial numbers of mutineers were voting with their feet. Between 21 and 25 August the Jhansi, Bareilly and Nimach brigades abandoned the city and headed into the countryside, reducing its defenders by over 10,000.

The fugitives guessed that they were about to lose the safety of Delhi's walls. On 4 September, a formidable siege train arrived in the British camp and a bombardment was soon in progress. All who heard the big guns knew that once the city fell, everyone inside faced retribution. One form it might take was revealed by British newspapers which had been obtained by the mutineers, containing reports that the former Governor-General, Lord Ellenborough, had proposed mass castration of the city's males and its appropriate re-naming as 'Eunuchabad'.[18] Morale suddenly rallied and, on 12 September, a British spy reported: 'The soldiery are ready to fight to the last. None now desert.'[19] Given the temper of their opponents, there was no alternative.

The city was stormed on 14 September and, after six days of fierce house-to-house fighting, it was finally subdued at a cost of over a thousand casualties. At one stage, during the night of the 15th–16th, a large body of British and Sikh soldiers temporarily fell out of the battle, lured by the untouched cellars of a city's liquor dealer. Men collapsed drunk and others spread their good fortune by offering bottles of champagne and brandy to their comrades for a few pennies each. In exasperation, the commander, Brigadier-General Archdale Wilson, ordered the wholesale destruction of what was left of the bottles.

The battle for Delhi was marked by random massacres of sepoys and civilians, for all within the city were held responsible for the murders of

Europeans four months before, even if they had been passive onlookers. Bahadur Shah had taken refuge five miles beyond the walls in the Hamayun, one of those elaborate mausoleums which his Mughal ancestors had erected to advertise their power. His sanctuary was revealed by his eldest son's father-in-law, Mirza Ali Bakht, whom a grateful government rewarded with his life and, later, an annual pension of 25,000 rupees for himself and ten rupees a day for the seventy-six of his kinsfolk who were dependent on him.[20] The prince's information led Hodson to Bahadur Shah's final refuge, a gloomy anteroom now disfigured by graffiti, on 19 September. The emperor was taken prisoner and returned to his palace to be tried for treason against a government which had once claimed that its powers derived from his forefathers. He was found guilty and sent into comfortable exile in Rangoon with his wife, Zinat Mahal.

The next day, Hodson and his sowars returned to the Hamayun to arrest two of Bahadur's sons, Mirza Mughal and Mirza Khizr Sultan, and his grandson, Mirza Abu Bakr. Arthur Lang heard that 'orders had been given that no princes are to be brought in alive', which was understandable, given that Delhi had only just been pacified and there were plenty of Mughal retainers and ghazis hanging around the Hamayun.[21] The three youths were siezed by Hodson who, alarmed by the menacing crowd which threatened to overwhelm his small detachment, ordered them to strip. They accepted their fate without any show of emotion and were shot by Hodson, who then had their corpses thrown into a cart. No onlooker intervened. The murders were applauded by Hodson's brother officers, who believed he had despatched three potential rebel leaders, each of whom had been an accomplice to the slaughter of their countrymen and women. The story ran through the army that each time Hodson pulled the trigger his mind had been convulsed by the image of a distraught English girl who, it was said, had been chained to a Delhi parapet by the mutineers and had been killed by British fire.[22]

Other minds were full of visions of wealth. Delhi suffered a systematic and thorough sacking, as later did Lucknow. The treasure-seekers' methods were brutal. Lieutenant Lindsay told his family how 'a very nice fat-looking sleek Hindu' had been taken down to the cellar of his house where pistols were fired at him in the dark to make him reveal where he had buried 90,000 rupees. 'Another corpulent nigger' had knives thrown at him 'after the manner of the Chinese jugglers'.[23] It was highly likely that both these unfortunates may have been among the rich banias and merchants from whom the sepoys and emperor had extorted cash during the siege. The Delhi looters shared the common belief that their recent exertions justified special rewards. 'Rode into Kotah and did a little plundering,' Veterinary Surgeon Edward Grey of the 8th Hussars casually noted in his diary for 6 April 1858. He ordered Indian regimental servants to kick in the door of a temple where, to their horror, he pulled down some statues before stealing one, 'a small female idol in marble tricked out in tinsel finery'.[24] Wherever the armies marched in India during 1857 and 1858 there were similar acts by men for whom personal profit was a compensation for weeks of discomfort and peril. All through the final Lucknow campaign, *The Times*'s correspondent, William Howard Russell, heard men say, 'If it were not for the rupees I would not stay in the confounded country for an hour.'[25]

The fall of Delhi was a signal catastrophe for the mutineers. Their principal army had been fragmented, many fugitives heading south-east towards Awadh, which had now become the main centre for resistance. There had been a stalemate in this region after Havelock's severely weakened forces had failed to break through to Lucknow. His successor, Outram, felt strong enough to resume the advance and reached the residency on 26 September after heavy losses. Trapped inside the city, his army and what was left of the original defenders faced a second siege, which lasted until 14 November when Campbell cut his way through with 3,400 men. They included sailors from the frigate *Shannon*, with sixty eight-pounder guns and war rockets under the command of Captain Sir William Peel, the son of the former Prime Minister. Still not strong enough to overcome the besieging forces nominally led by Nana Sahib, Campbell prudently decided to evacuate the city and retire to his base near Unao to await reinforcements.

It turned out to be a tricky operation, and there were some nervous moments when Tanti Topi approached the isolated detachment holding Cawnpore at the head of the 15,000-strong Gwalior contingent. Hitherto malevolent neutrals, the Gwalior force had kept out of the fighting, living off subsidies from the pro-British Baijii Rao. It played its hand too late and was defeated by Campbell on 6 December and fell back on Kalpi. Although not decisive, the actions around Cawnpore and Lucknow at the end of 1857 confirmed the verdict at Delhi: the tide of the conflict had turned irreversibly against the mutineers.

The final knock-out blow was delivered on 28 February 1858, when Campbell renewed his offensive against Lucknow. He now commanded 31,000 men, the largest army yet fielded by the Company, including reinforcements from Britain, the Punjab and Nepal which had joined him during the winter. The big push was first directed against Lucknow, which fell on 15 March after savage street fighting, something which Campbell had hoped to avoid. He was then free to proceed at leisure into Awadh and pick off the fragments of Nana Sahib's army and, simultaneously, pacify the province and adjacent areas which were still defiant. The war now became what one officer called 'manhunting', a term which was as accurate as any in describing the many cross-country chases after fugitives who either sought safety in strongholds or tried to throw back their pursuers by rear-guard actions. It was a type of warfare that strongly appealed to the sporting officer of the Hodson mould. One, on discovering that a party of mutineers had hidden in a cornfield, ordered it to be beaten as if for partridges, while his soldiers shot at the game and men who were flushed out. The 'best sport', he warmly recalled, was provided by the running sepoys.[26]

There were more opportunities for this grim diversion during operations in central India. Early in 1858, Sir Hugh Rose ordered a two-pronged invasion of the disaffected districts by columns based at Mhow and Jabalpur. He encountered fierce resistance during his march on Jhansi, which was taken early in March, and afterwards from the combined forces of its rani, Lakshmi Bai, and Tanti Topi. They suddenly entered Gwalior, where the bulk of the raja's army defected to them, and then began what turned out to be a nine-month, 3,000-mile peregrination through parts of Gwalior, Indore and Nagpur. Lakshmi Bai was killed early on, displaying the same reckless spirit which now animated so many engaged in what they must have known was an unwinnable last-ditch campaign. On 24 June, dressed as a Maratha horseman, she was wounded and knocked from her horse by a trooper of the 8th Hussars during a skirmish. As the British horsemen retired from the action, she spotted her assailant and fired at him with her carbine. She missed and he shot her dead, only realising who she was from the jewels she was wearing which, like so much else of value found during this war, soon disappeared.[27]

Tanti Topi fought on, avoiding pitched battles and, in classic partisan fashion, utilising the goodwill of local sympathisers. An officer who trailed him through forests and over hills noted how he could always call on local chiefs for reinforcements. In the end, Tanti Topi fell to the Raj's money-bags rather than its bullets, after one of his close associates, Man Singh, accepted a bribe to betray him. He was hanged in March 1859.

Man Singh's duplicity was a striking reminder that the suppression of the Indian Mutiny had been a civil war in which large numbers of Indians had made common cause with the British. It would be impossible to under-emphasise the value of these collaborators in filling the ranks of armies and supplying them with cash, victuals, transport, and, perhaps most important of all, intelligence. Knowledge of the enemy's capacities, dispositions, plans and morale was crucial throughout a conflict in which British commanders had to assess as precisely as possible the odds they were facing. This infor-mation could only be obtained by native spies, for with a few, very rare exceptions, Europeans could never successfully pass themselves off as Indians. Natives were also essential to maintain communications between isolated outposts and armies wherever and whenever the *dak* post (relays of camel- or horse-mounted messengers) or electric telegraph had been disrupted.

The task of creating a messenger and espionage network from scratch was allocated to a handful of younger men, most notably the magistrate William Muir in Agra and Major Herbert Bruce, formerly of the Punjab police, who worked under Neill, Havelock and Campbell. They recruited loyal and venal Indians like Raja Nahr Singh, Delhi spymaster, who paid his men ten rupees a day for information, which he had secretly conveyed to Muir at Agra.[28] Muir also had his own agents inside the city within a few days of the mutiny there, and they supplemented what soon became a steady flow of intelligence on the state of the rebels' morale, stocks of ammunition and reserves of cash. Some of these snoopers were amateurs, tempted by the rewards, but there were also a few professionals who had worked for business houses, like the Seths of Mathura. Mukdum Baksh appears to have been one of this class, for after the fall of Delhi he moved across country to Bareilly, where he was detected and executed at Nana Sahib's orders.[29] He appears, not surprisingly given his occupation, to have been an elusive figure, even to his masters who found it hard to find anything about him and his activities after the war, when his family were asking for compensation. There was also at least one gentleman spy, Khan Jehan Khan, a nephew of the Raja of Jorhat and 'a first-rate English scholar', who worked in Delhi during the siege. His expenses claim was subsequently rejected by the Punjab government which, after reconsider-ation of his services, gave him, as fitted his rank, a horse and fine robes worth 1,500 rupees.[30]

Major Herbert's spies penetrated the camp of the Gwalior force and brought back intelligence that revealed its movements and Tanti Topi's intentions and, during December 1857, provided forewarnings of mutineer offensives from Lucknow. His agents may have been among those arrested in Lucknow during the second siege, some carrying letters in English, and interrogated by Wajid Ali, a former police officer.[31]

Obtaining such information seems to have been easier in Delhi, for what today would be called field security was easy-going or non-existent. On 2 July, Mabub Khan, a Guides trooper in mufti, was able to pass through the Lahore gate into Delhi where he wandered through the lines of the Bareilly and Ruhelkhand contingents and gossiped with the mutineers. He then left the city by way of the Ajmer gate and made his way back to the headquarters of the Delhi Field Force where he reported what he had heard. Given that the camps of both sides were open to the world and filled with men and women of every caste, race and tribe it was not hard for the spy to come and go as he pleased. Sir Colin Campbell understood this and warned Willam Howard Russell against unguarded chatter. 'You will be among a set of fellows here, surrounded as all of us are, by natives who understand all that is going on better than we think. They talk about what is happening, or what is going to take place; and that gets to the ears of the enemy. So that our best plans may be frustrated. It is most essential for us to preserve secrecy in war, especially in a country like this.'[32]

Since eavesdroppers were paid for what they had overheard or uncovered, there was an unavoidable tendency for them to say what they knew would satisfy their employers. Mutineers inside Delhi heard of British privations and cash crises and similar revelations about conditions within the city reached British ears. Invention may also have played a part in the intelligence war. In Rajasthan, Colonel Pierce was faced with so many conflicting reports that he suspected he was being fed fables and only accepted as genuine intelligence that which was confirmed by at least two sources.[33]

The mutineers developed a counter-intelligence service which was on the look-out for British *cossids* (messengers). A pair, caught by patrols between Delhi and Agra, were beheaded and another two, Sikhs, were blown from cannon. As a precaution against their letters falling into enemy hands, commanders set down sensitive information in French or used the Greek alphabet which, they assumed, would not be understood. These missives were carried by professional carriers who, when the hazards were greatest, commanded their own price. During the dire days of mid-May

1857, a cossid charged fifty rupees for taking a letter from Kurnaul to Mathura, ten times the normal rate.[34]

Money or the prospect of it commanded allegiance during the Mutiny, as it had in every Indian conflict for the past hundred years. This fact of life was immediately recognised by the British who, whenever faced with signs of unrest, always took measures to safeguard district treasuries. Attempts to remove stockpiled taxes from Mathura and Azamgarh acted at catalysts for mutinies, with sepoys trying to stop the departure of carts crammed with rupees. At Azamgarh, a native officer complained to Charles Horne that the British had slighted Indian religions. Pointing to the bags of coins, Horne sharply riposted: 'Here's your caste, faith and religion.'[35]

He was right, for while the sepoys would declare that they were in arms to protect their faiths, they never forgot that they were paid professional soldiers. Everywhere they mutinied, one of their first objectives was the district treasury. At Mathura some of the spoils were handed out to rioting townsfolk, but the Bareilly mutineers carried their silver rupees, the equivalent of six months' wages, with them to Delhi. Once there, they spurned suggestions that it ought to be added to the general kitty.[36] Those directing Bahadur Shah's propaganda recognised that the Bengal sepoys remained at heart hireling soldiers when they issued proclamations which offered twelve rupees a month to infantrymen and thirty to cavalry, more than the Company paid. Generosity was not matched by resources so that, by the final fortnight of the siege, many sepoys inside Delhi were unpaid. There were cash-flow problems for Nana Sahib, despite the usual expedient of forced loans and outright theft. Some of his soldiers turned to private enterprise money-raising in the traditional manner, forcing rich men to excavate their cellars for concealed cash.[37]

The Company had more money to throw around. Sir Henry Lawrence offered a bribe of 200,000 rupees to one nobleman and a jagir of 100,000 rupees a year to another if they remained constant. Four sepoys received 500 rupees each and promotion after they refused to join the Azamgarh mutineers, and the same sum was distributed among the Multan Irregular Horse after they had helped expel rebels from the city. Old Mughal precedents were resurrected and lands and a 200-rupee jagir were given to two loyal NCOs from the 4th NI. Those who helped fugitives were duly rewarded for their kindness and courage: a zamindar from Pulri received 200 rupees and a land grant, and a blacksmith from Badli got 200 rupees.[38] In July 1857 the government proclaimed a fifty-rupee reward to anyone who captured an armed mutineer and thirty for an unarmed one.

The price of rebellion was high. A proclamation of 5 September 1857 warned the taluqdars of Awadh that their estates would be reduced to 'deserts' and their families obliterated if they succoured the rebels. This was too severe even for Neill, who suggested that it might be wiser to entice men of property into the government's camp by pledges of future favours, a policy which was later adopted. Nonetheless, in many areas rebels' lands were seized and their heirs evicted. Once back in the saddle, the government could afford some relaxation of its penalties. In 1859 the wives and children of executed mutineers from the Hisar district were allowed to enter their inheritances, although the widow of one 'Abdullah', shot in Delhi at the orders of Mr Clifford, was refused permission to acquire her husband's land. Despite her protests to the contrary, 'a man having been shot for rebellion by order of a competent authority . . . was a rebel', and that was that.[39]

In the war of inducements, victory was bound to go to the side with the larger purse or better credit. Here, the mutineers were at a severe disadvantage, for they never secured the breathing space in which to reactivate effectively the tax-collecting machinery in those regions they controlled. Initial windfalls from looting were quickly used up in Delhi, where Bahadur Shah's officials were forced to borrow with menaces. Between fifty and sixty less-than-compliant bankers and banias were locked up and 40,000 rupees extracted from Punjabi merchants at the end of August. In the meantime, the emperor had been able to seize cash abandoned by the collector of Gurgaon and had received offers of taxes from zamindars in the Doab district, but endeavours to proceed with regular collections elsewhere were resisted.[40] Peasants who had been celebrating the end of one Raj could hardly have been expected to welcome tax collectors from its replacement. Abdul Rahman Khan, the rebel Nawab of Jhajjar, offered to pay his dues to Bahadur Shah, but it was considered prudent to send a force of cavalry with cannon to collect them. During their progress through eastern Rajasthan, the sowars wrested 2,200 rupees from various zamindars and banias they encountered, presumably for the Delhi government. The nawab delivered 60,000 rupees at the end of August, when it was desperately needed; it might have been more, but he had recently been fleeced of 160,000 by Hodson and his 'Plungers'.[41]

The mutinies and rural uprisings meant a temporary loss of income for the Raj. Tax revenues slumped in the Agra region and, at the end of August, its treasury contained 735,000 rupees, just enough to keep ahead of day-to-day expenses, including paying the wages of native levies. The moment Delhi was recaptured, collections restarted, as they did in the Meerut district in mid-October.[42] It was noticed in areas where there had been peasant insurrections that the ryots were abnormally accommodating when it came to paying up, no doubt well aware of how officials would react to even the slightest hint of reluctance or disrespect.[43] The Punjab had reserves to cover expenses until September, but its government took the precaution of seeking loans at between 4 and 5 per cent from the friendly rajas of Patiala and Nabha.[44] Appeals for money from the commercial community in Peshawar had a frosty reception at the end of July, understandably since the money men had no way of knowing how events would turn out at Delhi and Lucknow.[45]

There was no hestitation among local tribesmen when appeals were made for troops to help suppress the rebellion or replace garrisons sent south. 'Friends were as thick as summer flies' Herbert Edwardes reported from the frontier districts, and the call to arms in the Peshawar valley was warmly welcomed by 'all the idlers and adventurers' for whom a war in the rich plains of Hindustan was a dream come true.[46] What amounted to an official invitation to sack Delhi, for this must have been how the call to arms was interpreted, brought in thousands of volunteers from all over the Punjab. Those who could not join the armies heading for Delhi, attacked and killed fugitives from disbanded Bengali regiments and were officially commended.

Among the Punjabis who attached themselves to the British were many former Khalsa soldiers who had not quite forgotten their old loyalties. The warcry '*Jai Khalsa Ji!*' (victory to the Khalsa) was heard when Sikhs charged during the fighting around Cawnpore at the end of 1857.[47] Lieutenant-Colonel Chardin Johnson of the 9th Lancers thought Sikh loyalty was superficial and temporary:

> The Sikhs don't love us one bit, but hate sepoys like poison . . . Moreover, they are the lastly conquered of the Indian races and have not forgotten what British Pluck can do. They like the cause now, for the sepoys have mutilated and tortured their men . . . and their blood is up on our side at the present – but, this business over, they may play us the same trick as the sepoy ruffians, anyday. There is no sympathy between us – we despise niggers, they hate us.[48]

He was mistaken; when the war was over Sikhs, as it were, stepped into the shoes of the Bengali sepoys and became the mainstay of the new Indian army. They also got on well with British troops. There was a warm and intimate camaraderie between them and the Highlanders, another warrior race, during the Lucknow campaign. Its echoes may be heard today as Indian and Pakistani regiments parade with bagpipes playing.

Experts in comparative martial virtues rated Sikhs the equal to British troops in combat and more resilient during hot-weather campaigning. They were also a match for anyone when it came to plundering; after the capture of Delhi, Sikhs had to be dissuaded from returning home with their bundles of loot.[49] Their conduct was part of that deeply-rooted convention of Indian warfare by which fighting men, native and British, considered themselves professionals for whom war was a legitimate source of personal enrichment.

The ruthless pursuit of private gain was a constant feature of the Mutiny. The cities, towns and villages and the camps of beaten armies were prizes to be taken and stripped bare by soldiers who went to war in the hope that they would emerge from it better off. Everyone, on both sides, was convinced they were entitled to rewards and, in the case of official British prize money, pursued their claims relentlessly and sometimes dishonestly. Men who had remained at Meerut during the siege of Delhi thought that they deserved a share of the spoils and put in false applications.[50] Even small-scale operations paid a dividend; the personal belongings of the dispossessed rebel Ali Bahadur, Nawab of Banda, were assessed by the prize agents at over a million rupees and included old Roman, Venetian and Portuguese coins and four elephants which fetched 700 rupees each at the prize auction.[51] Seen from the perspective of the prize auction or through those letters and diaries which contain detailed accounts of the plunderers' exploits, the Mutiny appears as a huge free-for-all in which risk-takers prospered. Private advantage was, therefore, uppermost in many Indian minds when they made the choice of which side to support, or whether or not to become entangled in the conflict.

IV

Nonetheless, large bodies of sepoys rebelled without weighing the odds, swept along by a knot of ringleaders and, at the time, with little idea as to what the consequences of their actions might be. Many of the original Meerut mutineers, having parcelled up their plunder, threw away their muskets and ammunition pouches and headed for their homes in Awadh. Some reached their villages where they were later discovered by Havelock's forces, but the majority were persuaded to stick together and set off for Delhi.

At this level, it is hard to look into the sepoy's mind and discern his motives. What amounted to an anatomy of an individual mutiny was undertaken by officers attached to Rose's army after the Bhopal contingent had been captured at the close of 1857. It was realised that many of the mutineers had been passive or secretly loyal and might be re-admitted to the Company's service. All the sepoys were interrogated and then placed in three categories: active mutineer, weathercocks who swayed either way, and loyal. Of the 657 infantrymen, 166 were found to have been the instigators of the revolt, 96 to have been sympathetic, 223 wavering and 37 steadfast. Among the 220 cavalry sowars there were 130 loyal men (who re-joined the army), 47 hostile trimmers and 23 mutineers.[52] So, in one regiment, it only required the participation of less than half the strength to effect a successful mutiny and in another, just over a tenth. This attempt at a scientific analysis bore out the judgement of a loyal native officer who observed that each mutiny was the work of one knave and nine fools. The rogue encouraged the others and, once they had crossed the boundary which separated obedience from rebellion, told them there was no going back.[53]

There was no unanimity of purpose among the Bengal army either before or after the first mutinies. Collectively, it was the victim of the equivalent of the Grande Peur which infected the French countryside during the summer of 1789, during which men and women fell victim to spasms of irrational and often paranoiac dread. At the heart of India's great fear was the conviction that in the future, probably sooner rather than later as all the signs indicated, the Company would mount an assault on Hinduism and Islam as a preparation for mass conversion. Every examination of the events of 1857 comes back to this fact: that the rank and file of the Bengal army imagined that they were about to be made Christians. At Delhi in May, they implored their countrymen to join them in a war for India's faiths, even if this meant fighting under a Muslim emperor. Sir Henry Lawrence realised the importance of the binding power of religion when he undertook an exercise in black propaganda by spreading rumours that Muslim mutineers had desecrated Hindu temples.[54]

In the atmosphere generated by the all-pervasive dread, soldiers feared the worst and prepared for it. At the end of May, and a fortnight before they rose, sepoys at Bareilly were said to be disheartened by 'a great depression of spirits caused by the fear of some heavy punishment they imagined the government was about to inflict upon them'.[55] The frightening paraphernalia of disarmament with lines of British troops and batteries of loaded cannon must have added immeasurably to the sepoys' apprehension. Foreboding was the father of panic, and this was the common reaction when disbandment was threatened or individual soldiers had been found guilty of acts of defiance. 'You hanged five sepoys lately,' a sowar of the 12th Irregular Cavalry shouted at his commanding officer before he shot him. The murderer, a Muslim, announced that he had acted under the orders of God.[56]

All Muslim mutineers imagined that they were fulfilling a holy duty. The Mutiny was a jihad, a holy war for their faith and the restoration of an Islamic, Mughal Raj in India. Jihadic recruiting officers, usually holy men, and jihadic propaganda were found throughout northern India and beyond once the Mutiny was under way. A number of Muslim missionaries from Delhi, including a *maulavi* (religious teacher) from Bareilly, were apprehended preaching holy war and calling for ghazis in the foothills of the North-West Frontier in July 1857.[57] Muhammad Husain, another maulavi, was one of the figures behind a rebellion which miscarried at Belgaum, one of the very few instances of an attempted mutiny by Bombay sepoys. Local intelligence had been vigilant and intercepted correspondence between mutineers and Bombay troops. One anonymous Bombay soldier had written ominously:

> We are your children, do with us as it may seem best to you.
> We are all of one mind, on your intimation, we shall come run-
> ning. You are the servant of Raymath [the God Man].

Shape and direction for this unrest was provided by the maulavi and sub-adar Thakur Singh, who hoped to use the jihadic mutiny to make himself 'chief ruler in these parts' in the manner of a Mughal warlord of the previous century. The conspirators and their plot were exposed by a Christian sepoy on 14 July, and the two ringleaders were tried and executed by being blown from cannon.[58]

Further north, two charismatic maulavis, Liaquat Ali and Ahmad Ullah Shah, assumed spiritual and military leadership of rebels during the campaigns around Lucknow. Ahmad Ullah Shah was a well-educated and travelled teacher who had fallen foul of the authorities by preaching an anti-British jihad in Rajasthan and Awadh during 1856, and was one of those released by prison by the Faizabad mutineers. He gained command through sheer force of personality and alleged supernatural powers, which included an immunity from bullets. He was a populist, adored by the men he led into battle and, like other Muslim holy-men-turned-political-leaders, he was uncompromising, falling out with the factious aristocratic clique which had taken control of the rebellion in southern Awadh. His war was one for the annihilation of the British in India, and he once boasted that he would beat his drum in London. He was killed in the fighting near Lucknow in February 1858.[59]

Equally unwavering in his faith and hostility to Christianity was Dr Wazir Khan of Agra hospital, lecturer in Pharmacology at the local medical college. Educated at the Murshidabad English school, Calcutta Medical College and in Britain, he was appointed Governor of Agra by Bahadur Shah after the British had withdrawn into the fort. Very much a Westernised Indian in terms of learning, he was one of many Muslims who had been offended by the encroachments on Islamic law by the British; the spread of Christian missions; and what were considered underhand means of gaining converts through orphanages and preaching to the illiterate.[60] For Dr Khan, active support of the régime in Delhi was a contribution towards the regeneration of Islam within India and the expulsion of an alien faith promoted by its rulers. Only through the eviction of the British would Islam be secure.

Did this then make him or any of the mutineers nationalists in a modern sense? Probably not, although Indian historians have endeavoured to present the 1857 Mutiny as a proto-war of national independence, despite its confinement to the northern regions of the country. Even though the Awadh mutineers once referred to themselves as 'the Army of India', there is nothing in what they said or did to suggest that they could have comprehended, let alone wanted, an equivalent to the Indian state that emerged during the twentieth century. Rather, wherever they were free to create systems of government, the tendency was towards restoration and particularism. This was attractive, in so far as the process of reinstatement favoured those like Nana Sahib and Lakshmi Bai, who had been losers under the Raj. Lower down the scale, efforts by Begum Hazral Mahal to revive the former Awadh court in Lucknow resulted in some brief reversals of fortune. Mismur Ali, who had spent between twelve and thirteen years as a munshi in the old king's service, hurried back to Lucknow on hearing a summons for all his servants to resume their posts. So too did

Abdul Duleep, who arrived to find his house had been looted by muti-neers. One ex-Mughal servant declared himself delighted to wear again his forefathers' 'ring of slavery' and to have the emperor's 'saddle cloth on his shoulders'.[61]

The old ways returned in the district around Mathura almost the moment British authority dissolved. 'No one regretted the loss of our rule,' remembered Mark Thornhill, the local magistrate, 'and with the exception of the Banias who suffered by it, all classes enjoyed the confusion.'[62] Zamindars were glad to do as they pleased: some declared themselves independent, some pledged allegiance to Bahadur Shah and several went raiding. In some places, domestic slavery and sati made a comeback.

There was also a widespread release of pent-up social tension in which peasants attacked the estates of new proprietors, as often as not hard-grinding financiers for whom villages were investments. Leadership came from below in the form of Devi Singh, a peasant who seems to have dis-tinguished himself during the days of paying off old scores. By an ancient Jat custom he was elected raja of fourteen villages and established his state in Tappa Raya, a market town, where he held court and set up formal rev-enue and legal departments. Wearing yellow robes, as was the custom for Hindu royalty, he sat in judgement over the local banias who, after some rough usage, were compelled to surrender their mortgage deeds and bonds. Raja Devi Singh also kept his electorate happy by letting the peasants strip bare the banias' shops and houses. His reign ended abruptly on 15 June, when Thornhill appeared at Tappa Raya with a small force and a howitzer. Two shells were fired; one exploded over the town, the other inside, and the inhabitants scattered into the countryside. Devi Singh was taken and faced the mockery of his former subjects' ironic salaams before his execution.[63] In some respects he was an Indian Jack Cade, but he obviously possessed some qualities of leadership and might, had things turned out differently, have founded a dynasty in the fashion of those men-on-the-make who had flourished during the disorders which had accompanied the decline of the Mughals. But by no stretch of the imagi-nation was he a nationalist in any modern sense.

Individually and collectively Indians were not bent upon the creation of a unified nation state. Instead, what came out of the Mutiny was a frag-mentation which would have gathered momentum if more men like Devi Singh had been free to emerge. And yet, in the eyes of Lieutenant Majendie, who fought against him around Lucknow, the Indian civilian in arms was 'simply taking advantage of a great revolt to strike for a country which had been taken from him'.[64] It was an exceptional view for the time, but one which few Indians would have understood, although they might not have shared a young Englishman's concept of national identity and the power of the sovereign state. Shah Mal, an insurgent leader in the region north of Delhi in June 1857, insisted that he was defending the Chowrasee Des, eighty or so villages bound together by traditions of independence and clan kinship, against 'pale-faced invaders'. But his attachment was to a location and its peculiar customs, not a nation, and not all the Jats and Gujars to whom he appealed were prepared to follow him. Some sided with the government.[65]

Where national consciousness was evident among the rebels, it was defined in terms of a loathing for the British which, at times, seemed so intense that it appeared that they were waging a racial war of extermination.[66] This animus was often expressed by the wholesale destruction of all things British, including railway engines which were shattered by cannonfire at the orders of rioters in Allahabad.[67] Intelligent Indians would have shared the British horror at this manic Luddism, and understood that many recent innovations had been beneficial. But their value was diminished for many educated Indians by 'the distant and contemptible manner in which they are treated by the generality of English gentlemen' which 'wounds their hearts and compels them to forget the blessings of British rule'.[68]

British racial aloofness drove Muhammad Ali Khan into the arms of the mutineers, according to a confession he made to his gaoler, Sergeant William Forbes-Mitchell, on the eve of his execution. A native of Ruhelkhand, Muhammad Ali Khan had been trained as an engineer in the colleges at Bareilly and Roorkee and became a jemadar engineer in the Company's service. But he found himself subordinate to a British NCO who, 'like most ignorant man in authority . . . exhibited all the faults of the Europeans which irritate and disgust us, arrogance, insolence and selfishness'. Muhammad Ali Khan was later employed by the King of Awadh and then the Nepalese ruler Jung Bahadur, with whom he travelled to Britain in 1853. It was sad and ironic that in his last hours he discovered that some Europeans were capable of kindness and decency; the Scottish sergeant forbade his men to smear Muhammad Ali Khan with pig fat, or have him and his fellow prisoners flogged by sweepers, and he provided all with a good meal at his own expense.[69]

The barriers and prejudices created by religion, caste, clan and tribes were still too strong to allow the cultivation of national sentiment or cohesion, even had the rebels attempted to do so. They naturally tried to find allies within the Madras and Bombay armies. In July and September 1857 two agents were turned in to the authorities by Madras soldiers whom they had tried to subvert.[70] Both the Madras and Bombay armies had a wider range of castes and races than the Bengal, including many who were not so jealous of their status. Nonetheless, there were 11,700 British soldiers in the Madras presidency during 1858 as an insurance against any unrest. They were moved at even the slightest hint of trouble; in November a detachment of the 60th Rifles and an artillery battery were rushed to Mysore after noisy gatherings there of the local 'disorderly rabble' and 'strangers and foreigners' from the countryside.[71]

The arrival of the white soldiers was also an earnest of British backing for the Maharaja of Mysore, who had been loyal throughout the troubles. Like his counterparts in Gwalior, Indore and Nepal, who had visited England and knew its potential strength, the princes were unwilling to commit themselves to a rebellion. In some cases this may have been sitting on the fence, something which made political sense when the balance of power was as unclear as it was during the summer and early autumn of 1857. Once the war began to swing Britain's way, it was prudent to show active support. It took some time for the reverberations of events in the north to reach much of southern India. The Bombay presidency suffered an upsurge in internecine disturbances during the back end of the year and 1858, but these were firmly suppressed without difficulty. The authorities there were reassured by additional British troops, including the 89th Regiment at Ahmadabad, which was thought to have had a calming effect in a district which had been notably restless.[72]

V

Wherever British authority disappeared, however briefly, there were peasant insurrections. They presented no serious long-term threat largely because they were localised and, even in the most turbulent areas, the leadership found it an uphill struggle to impose solidarity or sustain momentum in the face of counter-insurgency forces which were better armed and disciplined. The sudden eruption of what horrified local officials saw as rural anarchy and its persistence throughout the Mutiny was, however, an uncomfortable reminder of how superficial their influence had been.

At times, conflict in the countryside overlapped with the larger-scale struggle between the sepoys and the British. Among the defenders of Lucknow were peasant bowmen whose arrow showers reminded Sergeant Forbes-Mitchell of *Chevy Chase*.[73] Shah Mal, the leader of Jat and Gujar insurgents in the Baraut district to the north of Meerut during May, June and July 1857, declared himself a subject of Bahadur Shah and promised him assistance. His uprising seems to have been spontaneous and began with a sequence of thefts from passing merchants, a tax official and bazaar traders, which may have been why escapees from Meerut gaol hurried to join Shah Mal's band.[74] In the same area there were zamindars who were making themselves rajas, and, like Shah Mal, hoped to make their elevation legal through the sanction of the new emperor. Unlike Shah Mal, Wallidad Khan of Bulandshahr was a man of respected family whose inheritance had been pruned by the British authorities which made him a natural, although at times hesitant rebel figurehead. He too sought legitimacy and perhaps future rewards by an alliance with Bahadur Shah, who gave him a jagir and official powers.[75]

The collapse of British power around Allahabad in early June 1857 was the signal for Udwant Singh, backed by close kinsmen and about a thousand of his clan, to bid for independence from his overlord, the Raja of Benares. Udwant Singh proclaimed himself Raja of Bhadolu and began collecting taxes, but was snared and delivered to the British for execution by the Benares raja's agents. What was turning into a rebellion against the raja continued under the leadership of Jhuni Singh until the middle of 1858, when his adherents were defeated by the forces of local zamindars, no doubt keen to show their zeal for a Raj which was fast regaining control everywhere.[76]

In the absence of British constraint, the petty jealousies and rivalries of different tribes, castes and races had free rein. For the greater part, alignment was decided on purely local grounds; most notably whether a village or a caste had suffered losses through an oppressive tax assessment or new land-owning arrangements introduced by the British. It went without saying that wherever taxes had been high or imposed unevenly there were disorders. Past injustices were remembered and old vendettas re-opened, processes which meant that those who had benefited from the Raj tended to support it, for its enemies were now theirs. Those whom their British masters believed mixed husbandry with banditry for a living were in the forefront of any disturbances. Around Meerut, the Gujars and Rangars lived up to a reputation contained in a local proverb:

The dog and the cat are two, the Rangar and Gujar are two.
If it were not for these four, one could sleep at night with an
open door.[77]

Both castes were accused of robberies and, of course, outrages against
banias, but they were equally happy to place their energies at the disposal
of the government. Three hundred Rangars formed an *ad hoc* detachment
raised by the district magistrate, which kept order in Kurnaul during the
unquiet days of May and June 1857.[78] Several hundred miles to the south
in Agra, E. J. Churcher was able to collect a scratch force of Gujars with
which to restore order in Etah. He had 5,000 rupees from the Agra treasury in his pocket and this brought him Bahadur Singh and 140 Gujars, all
'of fine physique, and regular dare-devils'. He guessed some had been
dacoits, but this did not matter in an emergency, and they were, as he soon
discovered, more than satisifed with their generous wages. As his small
expedition progressed through the countryside, Churcher encountered a
party of Sikhs, all suspected rebels, whom he promptly enlisted with a
promise of ten rupees each for a few hours' work storming a fort.[79]

Co-operation was also secured through fear. Engagements between
rural insurgents and British forces were invariably one-sided; Gujar
matchlocks were no match for Enfield rifles, and during a fight between
Kol archers and matchlockmen in the Cuttack district, native losses were
thirty dead against one British soldier wounded.[80] Villages near Meerut
which had been up in arms or had harboured rebels, whether local men or
fugitive sepoys, were burnt as a matter of course. Richard Dunlop, who
served with a volunteer force during these operations, recorded that in
some instances men of military age were dragged from their villages and
shot.[81] Those who assisted the government were compensated, sometimes
much later. In 1859, Indians who had unsuccessfully tried to fend off an
attack by Meos on the treasury at Noh, not far from Mathura, were given
portions of land confiscated from their former adversaries.[82]

Around Lucknow at the end of October 1857, wretched villagers found
themselves squeezed between two predatory armies, competing for their
allegiance. 'The population is so timid and stands in such awe of the
possible return of the Mutineers,' reported William Muir, 'that even a
momentary disadvantage gained by them would probably unsettle our
hold on the people again.'[83] British victories along the road to Jhansi in
February 1858 swung local villagers behind the Raj and made them willing to reveal the route and battle positions of a body of mutineers pursuing

British cavalrymen.[84] Obsequiousness and accommodation were obviously the only policy for the weak, but they did not guarantee safety. Two months later in this campaign, Edward Grey noted in his diary how villagers fled whenever British soldiers approached. On 18 May, he explained why: 'Four men hanged this morning selected from a dozen poor devils taken at Mugrah and tried yesterday. They were probably as innocent of mutiny as most other villagers.'[85] It was small wonder that there were pockets of peasant resistance which held out in remote districts well into the following year, even when it was clear to their countrymen that the Raj had been fully restored.

3

Like Elephants on Heat: Anglo-Indian Reactions to the Mutiny

I

Garbled news of the mutiny at Meerut and the seizure of Delhi reached Britain on 27 June 1857. Even in fragmentary form, these tidings disturbed the public, which waited uneasily for the official telegrams due to reach London on 12 July. Speculation flourished and the mood was pessimistic. The *Saturday Review* suspected that the causes of the disturbances were deep-rooted and the massacres of Europeans indicated that India might be on the verge of a bloody racial conflict like that between the slaves and their masters in Haiti sixty years before.[1] In the correspondence columns of *The Times*, a retired Indian officer warned that, 'without India, Great Britain would subside into a third-rate state', a fact which, he thought, was not widely understood. Two days later, on 8 July, the same newspaper hinted at the source of the trouble by reporting a speech recently delivered to Addiscombe cadets by another India veteran, Major-General Tucker. The old soldier had exhorted his listeners to treat their sepoys with kindness and respect and praised those of his generation who had known and loved their men. By implication, today's officers were less in touch with and sympathetic towards the Indian soldier.

Government telegrams from India, carried by sea and transmitted in haste from the Italian port of Cagliari, were released by the Board of

Control on 13 July. The India mail, comprising over 20,000 letters, arrived in London on the night of the 11th, and was delivered the next day. By 14 July, the worst fears of the public were confirmed as national and provincial papers were filled with reports of a revolt by at least 30,000 sepoys, the slaughter of Europeans and the loss of Delhi. Recipients of private letters from India passed them to newspapers for immediate publication. There was now no doubt as to the scale of the insurrection or its implications for Britain and India, where the Raj appeared to be on the brink of collapse. 'The civilisation of fifty-three years has been destroyed in three hours' concluded a Bombay resident, whose verdict on the calamities in Delhi was published by *The Times* on 14 July. As the crisis unfolded and deepened, news from India, mostly baleful, dominated the British press.

Few who read the startling reports of mutinous sepoys, mass murders and episodes of heroism which filled the newspapers during the summer of 1857 knew much about India or its people. Where it existed, public knowledge was either superficial or distorted. This was the opinion of William Thackeray, who had been born in India in 1811 and whose family bonds with the country had remained strong. In 1841 he had outlined the three commonplace images of India then current in Britain. The romantically inclined continued to regard it as 'the region of fable and marvel, the gorgeous East', a fairy-tale land where sultans sat on ivory thrones, 'fanned by peacocks' wings' in 'palaces paved with jasper and onyx'. Prosaic minds imagined India as full of 'feeble and unwarlike people', who were backward and in thrall to cunning priestcraft. For the middle and upper classes, India was still 'a country where younger brothers are sent to make their fortune'.[2]

There were, Thackeray added, a handful of learned men who possessed a deep understanding of Indian languages, literature, cosmology and philosophy, subjects which were notably unpopular with British publishers and readers. Scholarship in these areas was largely directed towards uncovering links between ancient Indian tongues and Greek, Latin and Hebrew. It was assumed that there had been exchanges between the highly sophisticated culture of India and its counterparts on the shores of the Mediterranean and that, for this reason alone, Indians might be considered as an 'Eastern Division of the Indo-European race'. It went without saying, even among the most sympathetic Indophiles, that whilst the European branch of this race had flourished, the Indian had withered. Celtic philologists detected similarities between Welsh and Sanskrit. The remote possibility of distant ties, even kinship between the ancient Celts and the

Indians, persuaded Welsh scholars to invite Dwarkanath Tagore, a celebrated Bengali businessman and philanthropist, to be their guest of honour at the 1842 Eisteddfod.[3]

Tagore had been effusively welcomed throughout Britain. He had chatted to Queen Victoria and been made a freeman of London and Edinburgh. Although he wore Indian costume and smoked a hookah, Tagore was recognised by his hosts as living proof of how British enlightenment could transform India for the better. Educated at a British school in Calcutta, he was successively a tax official, cotton merchant, newspaper proprietor and entrepreneur with interests in coal, sugar and commercial docks. Men of his stamp could be found running businesses in London, Birmingham, Manchester and Glasgow, where they devoted their spare time and money to works of improvement. Tagare too had a well-developed sense of his public obligations, for he had diverted some of his profits to charity, founding a medical college. He was also, in a distinctly middle-class, British manner, a man of humane and liberal persuasions, having been among those who had advised Bentinck to proceed with the abolition of sati. Tagore, a high-principled anglophile (he chose to retire to Surrey, where he died in 1846) demonstrated that the Indian mind could be recast in a British mould.

Thackeray was sceptical about Indians ever cultivating 'the sterling virtues of our middle classes', which, he thought, were a peculiar product of Protestantism and liberalism, both of which were lacking in India. He did, however, praise the villagers of India who were 'a gentle, social and amiable race; in contrast to the British urban masses, who were slaves to drunkenness and gross debauchery'.[4] The hackneyed stereotype of the quietist Indian was trotted out in *Chamber's Information for the People*, published weekly during 1842 at one and a half pence (less than 1p) and designed for working-class readers in search of self-improvement. Indians were 'a simple race, and little inclined to war and unconcerned as to who ruled them. Presently a "more or less barbarous people", they had once manifested the symptoms of civilisation, and even a knowledge of some science.' The British Raj was a blend of altruism and selfishness: 'The only advantages which we receive from our occupation of these immense countries are control over trade, which can be developed by cultivation of order and peace.' This commerce was worth nearly £4 million a year and, thanks to land taxes, India needed no subsidies, unlike other colonies.[5] These facts, augmented by sheaves of statistics drawn from Company reports, formed the British working man's picture of India. There were also the propaganda tracts of the missionary societies which, predictably, painted a bleak picture of a people beguiled by priests and sunk in depravity.

Ignorance about India was matched by popular unconcern as to what happened there, argued Thackeray. This indifference was briefly interrupted by the two Sikh wars, which suddenly thrust India into the public consciousness. The simultaneous development of the fast overland route, cheap postage and the spread of national newspapers, particularly the weekly *Illustrated London News*, made it possible for these wars to be reported with a fullness, immediacy and intimacy not found in the official despatches of commanding officers. Using on-the-spot sketches and letters sent home by officers, the *Illustrated London News* provided a vivid coverage of the 1845–46 campaign, with engravings of commanders, Sikh soldiers and dramatic battle scenes. There was no censorship of press reports and correspondence, either in India or Britain, so soldiers writing home were free to castigate their superiors and include unflattering material in letters which their families passed on to newspapers. Describing Chillianwala, one officer observed that: 'The loss of our guns was owing to the cowardice of —— [a cavalry regiment], who, you will hardly believe this, ran away from a party of [Sikh] cavalry.' Home-letters were often the vehicle for political statements. One officer, after condemning Gough and the cheese-paring economies of the directors, urged his family to get his letter published: 'I would like the good folks at home to be enlightened in regard to matters out here, and show them how India is governed.'[6]

No editor shrank from printing the most harrowing details of the fighting, which is not surprising since the peacetime stock-in-trade of the press were gruesome accounts of coroners' inquests and murder trials. The predominantly middle-class newspaper readership were treated to the same brutal realism when it came to reporting battles. One officer's letter, printed in *The Times* and reproduced in the provincial press, graphically described how exhausted, thirst-crazed men had swilled water stained with the blood of Sikhs, whose bayonetted bodies lay by a well. It was a striking feature of early and mid-Victorian journalism that papers could print grim eyewitness accounts of the miseries of war alongside bellicose appeals to patriotic pride. The capacity of British soldiers to endure and overcome privation were proof of superior mettle. As for the wars, they were, ultimately, tests of national superiority, a conceit which underlay verses published during the first Sikh war.

We lately tamed the Afghan's pride,
And now rolls down a fiercer blood.
The clarion sounds, the cannons boom –
Unfurl the banner of St George!
Proudly the Punjab's bandits come,
Grim Havoc's joyful maw to gorge!
Their cry blasphemes the name of God –
'Allah! Il Allah! Wild hurrahs
Respond . . .[7]

There were warlike alarums, war cries, the thunder of cannon, bugle calls and British hurrahs in plenty for audiences at Astley's Amphitheatre, which staged *The War in the Punjab* during Whitsun week, 1846. These spectacular reconstructions of scenes from imperial campaigns were the equivalent of newsreels, and were an exciting and immensely popular entertainment for Londoners and their families until the end of the century. India, as seen from the stalls at Astley's, was a remote, exotic land where the British triumphed over wild-eyed savages, whose images were familiar from the illustrated papers.

Of considerably less interest were the public affairs of India which, when debated by Parliament, rarely attracted much interest or, for that matter, many MPs and peers. Neither they nor the government could ignore the concerns of businessmen, particularly the cotton manufacturers of Lancashire for whom India was a major market, or the pressure from the church lobbies, who were always displeased by the way in which the Company treated missions. Both groups had to be pandered to, for they exerted considerable influence over a largely middle-class electorate which was particularly susceptible to political arguments which had religious overtones.

II

Public indifference towards India vanished in the summer of 1857. The dramatic events there had a compelling fascination which was amply catered for by the press. By mid-July, the news from Meerut and Delhi had supplanted the trial of Madeleine Smith as the main story in every national and provincial paper. The saga of the Indian Mutiny was related to the British public in a sequence of episodes which made it, in many ways, like a contemporary novel by Dickens or Thackeray, whose parts were published monthly. Every two to three weeks, a new batch of telegrams and private letters would arrive from India and be swiftly disseminated through the sheets. As relaid through the newspapers, the Indian Mutiny was part penny dreadful, with plenty of grisly murders and massacres, and part cliffhanger, for reports of the sieges at Delhi and Lucknow kept readers on tenterhooks for over three months. To this mixture of melodrama and expectation was added a powerful series of images provided by the *Illustrated London News*. Not surprisingly, the public's reaction ranged across the whole emotional spectrum; according to the nature of the reports and in quick succession, Britain was convulsed by anguish, despair, trepidation, fury and elation.

Rage dominated during the summer and autumn of 1857 as news poured in of the wholesale defection of the sepoys and the massacres of women and children at Meerut, Delhi, Jhansi and Cawnpore. 'I wish I were commander-in-chief in India,' wrote Charles Dickens on 4 October. 'I should do my utmost to exterminate the Race upon whom the stain of the late cruelties rested.' He spoke for millions outraged by the betrayal and murder of their countrymen and women which, so the stories ran, had been accompanied by rape and lingering tortures. Nothing less than extermination of the Hindus would have satisfied Dickens, who was disgusted by reports in October that Canning had offered an amnesty to mutineers not directly involved in the killings.[8] The clamour for promiscuous revenge became so strident in both Britain and India that Sir John Lawrence feared it would hinder operations, driving Indians to wage a defensive guerrilla war against vengeful armies. Such a war, he imagined, would be protracted and debilitating.[9] In the midst of the hysteria, the voice of reason was not quite drowned. Disturbed by reports of Neill's activities around Benares and Allahabad, an anonymous poet warned the British soldier not to embrace his adversaries' habits:

> *Upon the wretched slave they vengeance feast;*
> *There stop; let not his guilt they manhood stain,*
> *But spare the Indian mother and her child.*[10]

The defilement of innocence, whether of children or women, had sent collective shudders through Britain. What the *Manchester Guardian* called 'outrages fouler than our pens can describe' left the British people stunned and burning for vengeance.[11] Invented atrocities jostled with real ones in the newspaper columns, including a tale of a colonel's wife sawn in half, which appeared at the end of September in Dublin and Edinburgh.[12] A fortnight later, the *Illustrated London News* offered what was one of the most compelling icons of the Mutiny, an imaginative engraving of the last moments of Miss Wheeler during the first Cawnpore massacre. Distraught, she points a pistol at her head as fiendish sepoys approach. The message is clear: she will take her own life rather than suffer violation. This was universally regarded as the fate of any European women at the hands of the mutineers, a fact which drove Alexander Skene to shoot his wife and then himself after an unequal fight with mutineers at Jhansi. An imaginative reconstruction of the incident also appeared in the *Illustrated London News*.

This poignant scene deeply moved Christina Rossetti who, within a few days, had composed a poem in tribute to a love which was so deeply shared, compassionate and noble:

> *A hundred, a thousand to one; even so;*
> *Not a hope in the world remained;*
> *The swarming howling wretches below,*
> *Gained, and gained, and gained.*
>
> *Skene look'd at his pale young wife: –*
> *'Is the time come?' 'The time is come!'*
> *Young, strong, and so full of life;*
> *The agony struck them dumb.*
>
> *'Will it hurt much?' 'No, mine own:*
> *I wish I could bear the pang for both.'*
> *'I wish I could bear the pang alone:*
> *Courage, dear! I am not loth.'*
>
> *Kiss and kiss: 'It is no pain*
> *Thus to kiss and die.*
> *One kiss more,' 'And yet one again.'*
> *'Good bye! Good bye!'*

The sum of such acts of individual self-sacrifice and heroism combined with national pride made Tennyson contemplate writing an epic of the siege of Delhi. In 1879 he produced a shorter work, *The Defence of Lucknow*, which extols the endurance of the defenders and repeats in every stanza a reference to the 'banner of England' which remains flying over the residency.

The Indian popular muse was stimulated by the Mutiny. Forty years after, Gujar women in the countryside around Saharanpur were singing the lament of a wife whose husband had proved an inefficient thief:

> *People got shawls, large and small; my love get a kerchief.*
> *There is a great bazaar in Meerut; my love did not know how to plunder.*
> *People got dishes and cups; my love got a glass.*
> *There is a great bazaar in Meerut; my love did not know how to plunder.*
> *People got coconuts and dates; my love got an almond.*
> *There is a great bazaar in Meerut; my love did not know how to plunder.*
> *People got coins of gold; my love got a half-penny.*
> *There is a great bazaar in Meerut; my love did not know how to plunder.*

In answer, as it were, to Tennyson's heroic account of Lucknow, was a song in praise of the exploits of Lakshmi Bai, the Rani of Jhansi:

> *Well fought the brave rani; Oh, the rani of Jhansi.*
> *The guns were placed in the towers, the heavenly balls were fired.*
> *Oh, the rani of Jhansi, well fought the brave one.*
> *All the soldiers were fed with sweets; she herself had treacle and rice.*
> *Oh, the rani of Jhansi, well fought the brave one.*
> *Leaving Morcha, she fled to the army; where she searched and found no water*
> *Oh, the rani of Jhansi, well fought the brave one.*

Unlike their British counterparts, Indian balladeers were ready to honour the gallantry of their adversaries, and did so in this song about the relief and second defence of Lucknow:

> *Time upon time, the sepoys struck their blows,*
> *Digging in about them, the white warriors fought well.*
> *On their feet they wore boots, on their bodies kilts.*
> *Tassels of silk on their hats and trembling aigrettes*
> *The white warriors went into battle like elephants on heat*
> *With no fear of death, they set their faces to the front.*[13]

As the British had long imagined, the kilts, feathered bonnets and cockades of the Highlanders unnerved their enemies.

British artists were also inspired by episodes in the Mutiny. It offered perfect subjects for that school of genre painters who sought to capture a dramatic moment which, according to the viewer's imagination, could be interpreted as a turning point in a broader narrative. Edward Hopley's *Alarm in India*, exhibited in February 1858, shows a nocturnal scene in which a fraught officer looks from a window across an Indian townscape, illuminated by distant fires. He grasps a revolver while his wife reaches for another; whether to defend herself, or to hand to her husband we do not know. She might even, like Miss Wheeler, be preparing to take her own life rather than die dishonoured. There was no ambiguity about Edward Armstrong's *Retribution*, displayed at the same time. A stalwart Britannia thrusts a sword into the breast of a tiger, whose recent prey, a dead mother and child, lies in the foreground. This painting derives from an earlier *Punch* cartoon of 22 August 1857, in which a snarling British lion leaps on a crouching tiger, again disturbed by the bodies of a woman and infant.

An atmosphere of terror pervades Joseph Noel Paton's *In Memoriam*, which was shown at the Royal Academy's 1858 summer exhibition. A group of fearful women and children are huddled in a room in what must be Cawnpore, for the severed hand of a child lies on the floor. One woman clasps an infant to her while another holds a Bible; beyond, at the end of a narrow corridor, a door is being opened by a villainous sepoy. There is no question what is about to happen, and the frightening implications of the picture made some argue that it should never have been displayed. It was said that one young lady fainted contemplating the scene. Bowing to pressure, Paton withdrew the study and hastily repainted it, replacing the mutineer with a reassuring bearded Highlander to give his story a 'happy ending'. It was re-titled *In Memoriam, Henry Havelock*.[14]

The artists had responded to the stories that were circulating during 1857 and early 1858 which alleged that women had been raped, sometimes tortured by the mutineers. These tales had a disturbing effect on public opinion; the mutiny was more than a violation of trust, it was a brutal assault on national ideals of womanhood and it placed the perpetrators beyond the pale of mercy. The violation of women, more than anything else, justified the retribution which was being handed out and reported throughout the press. On 31 October the *Illustrated London News* showed pictures of mutineers being hanged (executions were still public in Britain and drew large crowds in London and the provinces), and of others being blown from cannon with flying limbs clearly visible amid the smoke. Such vignettes and lurid eyewitness accounts of shootings and hangings whetted the public appetite for more. The voice from the pulpit was stern and echoed those many Old Testament demands for mass slaughter delivered by Jehovah to the Israelites. The Bishop of Carlisle demanded severe punishments in a sermon on 7 October, a day designated by Queen Victoria as one in which her church-going subjects should fast, consider the nation's sins and pray for God's assistance in India. Anglican wrath was matched by Presbyterian. In Edinburgh, Dr Cumming forthrightly denounced the 'whining sentimentalism' of anyone who dared question the rightness or severity of retribution then being served out by Britain's soldiers.[15]

In India, careful enquiries revealed that rape and torture had not been the prelude to the murder of European women.[16] This information, one official noted, was of some comfort to those who had lost wives, sisters and daughters, but there were many in Britain who refused to accept it. In February 1858, Lord Malmesbury told the Lords that he had private information that women had been raped and tormented, but refused to give either details or sources.[17] By then the public mood was less frenzied and horror stories were treated with a degree of scepticism. One Scottish journal felt obliged to prefix a letter describing the mutiny of the 34th Bengal NI in Chittagong as from 'a perfectly trustworthy source', which suggests that the public was becoming wary of hair-raising horror stories.[18] Investigation into the fate of Miss Wheeler, who had preferred to die unsullied, revealed that she had made no such choice, but had, it appeared, been abducted by a Muslim with whom she was later found to be living.[19] Nonetheless, it was deemed prudent for women to carry revolvers when they accompanied their husbands on campaign.[20]

Given the choice between telling the truth or repeating the legend, James Grant took the latter course in his novel *First Love and Last Love: A Tale of the Indian Mutiny*. Although it appeared ten years after the suppression of mutiny, it contains many passages which shed a revealing light on contemporary attitudes towards women and their sexual maltreatment. Its author was born in 1822 and served as an ensign in the 62nd Regiment until 1843, when he turned to writing, producing over sixty history books and novels during the next forty-seven years. In many respects, *First Love and Last Love* was a conventional romance in which two eminently eligible young officers set their caps towards two pretty young ladies, Magdalene and Kate Weston, the daughters of a clergyman. The course of love is more than usually convoluted and full of adventures, for the background is Delhi in the spring and summer of 1857.

The two girls and their younger sister, Polly, have other, sinister admirers, Mirza Mughal and Mirza Ali Bakht, the son and grandson of Bahadur Shah, then King of Delhi. The two men follow the sisters through the streets of Delhi, provoking one of the heroes, Jack Harrower, to rail against them as: 'A couple of d___d impertinent niggers.' Inside their father's palace, the two princes are plotting a rebellion which, one says, will 'fill our tents with gold mohurs, and the white-skinned girls of the Europeans'. Grant explains the roots of this desire:

> To the brutal Mussulman [Muslim] and the sensual Hindu, the position occupied by an English lady, or any Christian woman, seems absurd and incomprehensible; hence came the mad desire to insult, degrade and torture, ere they slay them.[21]

This is the fate of the European women in Delhi once the mutiny is under way. In passages which, for the period, were extraordinarily explicit, white women 'were outraged again and again before they were slaughtered', or forced to suffer 'every indignity that the singularly fiendish invention of the Oriental mind could suggest'. Polly, the youngest Weston sister, falls into the hands of Babu Singh, who strips her to the waist before delivering her to Mirza's *zenana* (ladies' quarters), where she rejects his advances and is thrown, naked, into the streets. When Delhi has fallen and her tormentor has been shot, she is found, crucified.

For all its elements of *grand guignol*, and there are plenty of them, *First Love and Last Love* presents a picture which would have been understandable to those who were appalled by what had apparently happened in India. Whereas the young officers regard women as creatures to be set on a pedestal and treated with honour and Christian chivalry, the Indians see them as playthings without feelings. Moreover, as Polly's steadfastness suggests, no truly pure women could ever be raped entirely against their will, a foolish contemporary assumption that largely explains why English courts often handed out light sentences to rapists.

Equally realistic, but in different ways, is the vivid novel *My Escape from the Mutineers in Oudh*. It was also from the pen of a soldier, Captain Gibney, who preferred to remain anonymous, and was published in September 1858. It claims to be autobiographical and some of its material prompted the *Atheneum* to wonder where fact began and fiction ended. The appearance of 'irascible, ignorant and tyrannical commanding officers and slang-talking, smoking, drinking and dissatisfied subalterns' indicated to the priggish reviewer that the book was fabrication; he obviously knew nothing of India or the Indian army.[22]

The actual mutiny plays a relatively small part in what is an exciting picaresque novel full of well-observed local colour, frank comment and convincing dialogue. The Company's officers embrace all the vices listed by the reviewer and petty snobbery is endemic. In one mess, a drunken young officer asks a poor colleague: "'How did you come to India? Did the parish send you?'" The hero and narrator, Phillip Villars, also encounters his countrymen's attitude towards the Indians, who are everywhere referred to as 'niggers'. On arrival, he hears from an old hand of the curative and punitive values of 'a fearful kick', which he termed a 'lifter', on the natives. There is warm praise for Sir John Lawrence and his knot of young administrators in the Punjab, who made decisions and dispensed justice swiftly, winning respect and affection, unlike the 'rich old civilians choaking with pride and satisfaction at their position and immunity from censure' who ruled Bengal. Missionaries were depicted as overfed creatures whose self-indulgence set the natives a poor example.

There is sympathy for the ryots, expressed in a round-about way in a passage during which one character relates the story of a hard-dealing collector:

> . . . often did the poor ryot sigh for the day back again when he was taxed by the Mussulman, he at any rate spent his exactions among them, and planted trees, sunk wells, and allowed they were better than beasts.

Contradicting this, Villars later observes of Muslim-ruled Oudh (Awadh) that the peasantry were 'victimised by those devils in human forms, native civil officials'. In the end, the author comes down very strongly in favour of British rule which, for all its faults, is just and incorruptible. 'From the sahib . . . justice is obtainable, but from our own people just the reverse. From the native magistrate to the jail daroga, all take bribes.'[23]

This justification of the Raj prepares readers for Villars's dinner-party confrontation with Mr Jones, the local Liberal MP and a 'vulgar brute'. He stands for John Bright, the Birmingham MP and self-appointed voice of the non-conformist conscience, and his opinions echo those expressed by Bright during the Commons India debate in July 1858. Like Bright, Jones is solely concerned with how much Lancashire cotton the Indians will purchase and he dismisses its government as overbearing and belligerent.

Villars defends the Raj as humane and honest, but fails to change a low commercial mind which sees the world only in terms of profits and losses. The row gives Villars the chance to take a side-swipe at recent press criticisms of the Indian government, its officials and generals. 'So long as we govern India,' he insists, 'it is improper for England to let the ruled know that their rulers are infamous.'

III

The intensity of public agitation rendered it impossible for editors and politicians not to seek scapegoats. When it was not demanding Indian blood, the public was casting about for someone to blame for a calamity which had taken everyone in India and Britain unawares. There was a close analysis of the actions of individuals, in which the Meerut commanders, Carmichael Smyth and Hewitt, came off badly, and rightly so. Thinly disguised, they appeared in a mocking verse in *Punch*:

> *The idiots stood gazing while cities were blazing,*
> *And all they could do was gibber and gape.*[24]

It was less than a year since the end of the Crimean war and memories were fresh of the chapter of blunders which had marked its opening stages. It was still open-season for ageing, slow-witted generals and Company bureaucrats bound in red tape. *The Times* had some wicked fun at the expense of General Lloyd, the 'gouty old general' who mismanaged the disarmament of sepoys at Dinajpur. Lloyd indignantly riposted that gout had not impaired his judgement and that a bandaged foot was no impediment to active command.[25]

There was much political mileage in the Mutiny for the Tory opposition. This was the era of the Whig–Liberal ascendancy which stretched from 1846, when the Tories had split over the Corn Laws, until 1874, when they won their first general election for over thirty years. Stuck in the wilderness, the Tories were grateful for any opportunity to discountenance the government, and the Mutiny offered one. The former Governor-General, Lord Ellenborough, opened the assault on the government on 13 July, accusing ministers of an ostrich-like complacency over the news from India. The following day, Disraeli pressed the Prime Minister, Palmerston, for details of the revolt and hinted that the Cabinet was deliberately withholding embarrassing information.[26]

A full-scale attack on the government's policy was launched by Disraeli in a three-hour speech delivered on 27 July. It was a characteristically sharp-edged performance, which began with a challenge to government to declare publicly whether the Mutiny was a soldiers' rebellion or a national insurrection. Disraeli plumped for the latter and claimed that the sepoys were the 'exponents of general discontent'. Its sources were obvious: the abandonment of sound, practical policies and the misapplication of the principles of Whiggery to the government of India:

> In olden days, and for a considerable time – indeed, until, I would say the last ten years – the principle of our government of India, if I may venture to describe it in a sentence, was to respect Nationality.[27]

This had gone by the board. Reforms had been thrust upon the Indians, irrespective of whether they needed or wanted them. The authority of the princes had been devalued and their lands and privileges had been snatched from them by Dalhousie's policies of lapse and annexation. Having trampled on the rights of property, the reformers tampered with religion and had offended the sensibilities of Hindus with laws which overturned their customs of inheritance. The Company had forfeited its right to rule India and its place should be taken by the Queen, who would publicly pledge that her government would safeguard property, uphold established traditions, protect native faiths and honour treaties. It went unsaid that the Tory approach to India, with its respect for ancient and well-loved hierarchies and usages, would not have brought the Company to its present position. Disraeli's charges were lamely rebutted by Robert Vernon Smith, a mediocre hack who held the presidency of the Board of Control, who insisted that there was no widespread disaffection in India. The lobby fodder then did as they were bid and the government emerged with a majority of 124.

The damage had been done, although Disraeli was accused of scoring political points from a catastrophe whose exact compass was not yet fully known. Nonetheless, his indictment had been convincing and the Company's reputation had been indelibly tarnished. On 15 August, *Punch* published a cartoon which showed 'John Company' being fired from a cannon, mutineer-style, with fragments labelled 'Avarice', 'Misgovernment', 'Nepotism', 'Blundering', and 'Supineness'. Press criticism gathered momentum as reports of the setbacks during the summer and autumn began to reach Britain. The Company became the scapegoat for the Mutiny and would soon undergo a metamorphosis into a sacrificial calf. Its 'extravagantly centralising policy' and reforms which had pleased the high-minded in Britain and looked good on paper had been a recipe for disaster, according to the conservative *Saturday Review*. Furthermore, great harm had been done by the religious zeal of officers' wives, especially 'a Scottish Free-Kirk woman', presumably the Mrs Mackenzie whose memoirs had appeared three years before.[28]

The churches defended themselves by a series of offensives designed to show that there had been too few Christian influences in India rather than too many. This theme was woven into many of the sermons preached on 7 October, with robust claims that the Company's misfortunes owed everything to its even-handedness in religious matters. Canon J. G. Miller detected God's will behind the conquest of India and regretted that the government had not attempted to convert the sepoys. Praising the humanity of British government, Canon Stowell hoped that when the Mutiny had been crushed, mass conversion would follow:

> This is the revenge I covet – that every idol should be caste to the moles and the bats, every pagoda changed into a house of prayer, every Mahommedan mosque into a temple of the living God.[29]

An anonymous hymnist had the same vision, and portrayed those who had been killed in the war as proto-martyrs:

> *O may their blood, by Satan shed,*
> *Our Holy watchword be,*
> *In turning, by Thy Spirit led,*
> *A pagan race to Thee!*[30]

The religious establishment held its ground, as might be expected in an age which believed that Christianity and civilisation were inseparable, and when few would dare suggest that there were admirable elements of spirituality within Islam and Hinduism. The Company was unable either to stifle or resist the growing criticism of its record. At the end of 1857, Palmerston had decided to end the Company's government and replace it by the Crown. His Indian legislation died with his ministry on 18 February

1858, after a Commons defeat on an anti-terrorist measure which the John Bullish majority regarded as appeasement of the French.

A minority Tory ministry succeeded, headed by the Earl of Derby, with Disraeli as Chancellor of the Exchequer. It was quick to restore old principles to the Indian administration: Canning was sharply and publicly rebuked for his seizure of taluqdar estates in Awadh, which both infringed the rights of property and made bad political sense, for in future the Raj would need the friendship of the land-owning classes. Henceforward, the British government 'desired to see British authority in India rest upon a willing obedience of a contented people. There cannot be contentment where there is general confiscation.'

Public opinion was now behind measures to terminate Company rule and re-order the government of India. This was accomplished by the India Act, which was passed during the spring and early summer, guided through the Commons by Disraeli. Henceforward, there were two sources of executive power: the Secretary of State for India, who answered to Parliament, and the Viceroy, who oversaw everyday administration and law-making in Calcutta. Here, he presided over a sort of cabinet, comprising the heads of the Indian departments of states such as finance, and co-opted councillors, including Indian princes. Under the Viceroy was the familiar, layered pyramid of Indian government, with its hierarchy of presidency and provincial governors, collectors, commissioners, deputy commissioners, assistant commissioners, judges, magistrates, assistant magistrates, police superintendents and inspectors and the legion of Indian clerks and tax gatherers. All were now servants of the Crown and, in theory, their every action was subject to Parliamentary scrutiny, although Indian business was usually conducted before an all-but-empty chamber.

The new order would continue the work in the spirit of the old, but with a greater sensitivity to the feelings of its subjects. On 1 November 1858 the temper and aims of the new state was made known to Indians through the Queen's proclamation, which was read aloud, in various languages, in all the main cities and towns. Queen Victoria promised that her government would treat all its subjects equally, uphold the rights of the princes and respect all the religions of India. Rebels who surrendered before 1 January 1859 would be automatically pardoned unless they had been involved in massacres. A line was being drawn between the past and future. The Raj may have been severely jolted by the mutiny, but its servants' ideals were as strong as ever. Programmes of reform in education and recruitment (by competitive examination) begun in 1854 and 1856 went ahead. In a statement which could have been made at any time during the past fifty years and would be repeated, in various forms, for the next fifty, the *Edinburgh Review* reminded its readers that it was 'the glorious destiny of England to govern, to civilise, to educate and to improve the innumerable tribes and races whom Providence had placed beneath her sceptre'.[31]

The Mutiny had been a dire warning as to what might occur when that sceptre disappeared. As the Whig Lord Brougham had told an audience of working men in the Leeds Mechanics Institute in November 1857, if India was ever lost, Britain would 'abandon millions to the most cruel of fates – the anarchy, the rapine, and the bloodshed of their contending chiefs and tyrants'.[32] He had in mind an aspect of the Mutiny which was less well known in Britain: the outbreaks of rural insurgency that had followed the disappearance of British authority. The mass of first-hand accounts, histories and commentaries which poured from the presses during 1858 and 1859 said little about the disorders in the countryside. Where they were mentioned, they were ascribed to the recidivism of the Indian equivalent of the British criminal underclass, a mob which, in India, would break loose 'when the hangman's whip no longer menaces them'.[33] Military men were the chief historians of the Mutiny and they stuck to the thesis that it had been a war between the Company and its former soldiers. This convinced large sections of the public who, like the editor of the *National Review*, insisted that the Indian peasantry had been unwavering in their loyalty because they understood that the Raj protected them.[34]

This had not been the case, but few realised it. 'This is no mutiny now we are contending with, but a desperate rebellion,' Richard Cust wrote in his diary as he traversed southern Awadh in March 1858.[35] A few months later, an indigo planter from Aligarh told a Commons select committee that Indians 'look on our hold of the country as ephemeral'. Another witness, a former magistrate from eastern Bengal, remarked sadly that 'the Europeans were most popular in those parts where they were least known'.[36] Coupled with the evidence of the upheavals that followed the collapse of the Raj's civil authority, these comments indicated that the government was not universally loved and that its temporary departure had been welcomed by sections of a peasantry whom it had expressly claimed to safeguard.

This message had penetrated the sub-conscious of the official mind. What might be called the subsidiary, civil uprisings served as a warning which was well understood by India's rulers for the next ninety years. Even in tranquil times, the Raj could not be strong everywhere. There was a constant fear that failure to act swiftly and vigorously whenever trouble threatened was to invite more, perhaps on a scale which might prove unmanageable. This nervousness lay behind the Punjabi government's reactions to the disturbances in the province during the spring of 1919, when force was applied with the utmost ferocity. Throughout the emergency and afterwards, everyone in authority cited the Mutiny as an example of what might follow inertia or half measures. Neither was apparent in the Punjab where, under the orders of its governor, Sir Michael O'Dwyer, rioters were strafed and bombed by aircraft and fired on by soldiers – most infamously at Amritsar, where 379 were killed and several hundreds wounded.

In justification of these measures, the Viceroy, Lord Chelmsford, later wrote:

> At any moment the trouble might have spread to the United Provinces and the remaining provinces; at any moment the Army might have gone, and once they had gone we should have had a state of things which would have been infinitely more serious than the Mutiny of 1857. *You must remember that it was the initial indecision in the Mutiny which led to its widespread nature.* [My italics.][37]

As to the nature of the unrest, Chelmsford believed that, again as in 1857, it would prove impossible to uncover the 'real truth'.[38] Be that as it may, the Mutiny had left behind a legacy of paranoia which, in the passage of time, lost nothing of its power to make the flesh creep. In 1918, young British subalterns, fresh to India, were given a solemn lecture on the Mutiny by a senior officer which ended with a warning that history might repeat itself if they were not vigilant. One in the audience wondered whether the speaker had heard the same talk many years before, perhaps from an eyewitness.[39]

Conspiracy theories offered a comforting explanation as to why the British, like the Americans at Pearl Harbor, had been taken by surprise and briefly humiliated. The credulous, including Disraeli, wondered whether the Russians had had a hand in preparing the ground for the rebellion, but speculation along these lines collapsed for lack of evidence. Another blind alley was the theory that the Mutiny had been the product of a vast Muslim plot. This was superficially attractive; after all, the mutineers had restored the Mughal emperor and had been egged on by various maulavis who had preached anti-British and anti-Christian jihads. Reluctant and ambiguous confessions made after the event by a handful of Indians convinced the Mutiny historian Colonel G. B. Malleson that there had been a secret, countrywide masterplan for simultaneous uprising across India. It went awry, so he was told, when the Meerut mutineers jumped the gun.[40]

This was implausible on the grounds that, like everyone else in India, the Muslims were divided by the Mutiny. A *wahabi*, member of a strict Islamic sect, forewarned the authorities of imminent unrest in Patna in July 1857.[41] Defiantly anti-British Muslim communities in the foothills of the North-West Frontier refused to make common cause with mutineers from the 55th NI, whom they expelled from their villages.[42] Muslim cavalrymen in the Madras army were reported as solidly behind the government in August 1857, and that their 'good treatment secures the loyalty of a large number of Mahomedan families' who were glad for their sons to secure well-paid and honourable employment.[43] The Mutiny had not been the product of Muslim intrigue, but this has not prevented historians in modern Pakistan from attempting to portray it as a Muslim national uprising.[44]

It was inevitable that twentieth-century Indian nationalists looked back to the Mutiny for inspiration, a process which involved transforming widespread rejection of the Raj into a positive affirmation of a national will. In 1908, a Bengali nationalist called on his fellows to celebrate 10 May, the anniversary of the Meerut disturbances, as a reminder of the first campaign of the war of Independence. *Oh! Martyrs*, a pamphlet then current, invoked the ghost of Bahadur Shah and promised him that '*your Diamond Jubilee* [1917] *shall not pass* without seeing your wishes fulfilled and the Raj overthrown'.[45] In 1942 the first women's regiment of the Indian National Army was named after the Rani of Jhansi, no doubt in the hope that its members would be enthused with her Amazonian spirit.

There was a British as well as Indian mythology of the Mutiny. Even before it had ended it had become fixed in the national psyche as an epic struggle between good and evil, with the good, often surrounded and outnumbered, sustained by courage and Christian faith. The Union Jack which had fluttered over the Lucknow residency was both a token of national willpower and a beacon of civilisation. It was transformed into a token of British determination to rule India, and its successors flew over the residency until 15 August 1947, when, after a row with local nationalists, it was finally hauled down. Havelock, Nicholson, Sir Henry and Sir

John Lawrence and Campbell, ennobled in 1858 as Lord Clyde, took their places in the pantheon of imperial superheroes. Their perfect blend of Christian manliness, love of country and willingness to persevere against the odds made them ideal models for future generations of empire-builders.

There was a sinister side to the British memory of the Mutiny, and one which would have repercussions in India and in other parts of the empire. Racial arrogance had been on the increase in India for at least a decade before the Mutiny, its spread being reflected in the everyday use of the word 'nigger' for Indian, a term which, during the Mutiny, regularly appeared in print. From what they had read in the newspapers, supplemented by the more-or-less instantaneous memoirs and histories of the Mutiny, the British were presented with a story in which a people, hitherto believed capable of improvement, turned against their helpers in the most vicious manner imaginable. It was not just the Raj which been attacked; the revolt was an onslaught against everything the mid–Victorians cherished. Firing cannon balls at railway engines symbolised a wilful and irrational rejection of technical progress. The killing of women and children was a calculated assault on national moral values. Both suggested, at least to the cynical, that efforts at uplifting Indians had been misguided and were doomed, if not to failure, then to very limited success. 'The CHILD and the SAVAGE lie very deep at the foundations of their being,' one commentator observed. 'The varnish of civilisation is very thin, and is put off as promptly as a garment,' he continued, placing Indians in roughly the same evolutionary place as had been occupied by the English in the Dark Ages.[46]

But the work of the civilising had to go forward. Two alternatives offered themselves. One was to 'rule our Asiatic subjects with strict and generous justice, wisely and beneficently, as their natural indefeasible superiors, by virtue of our purer religion, our sterner energies, our subtler intellect, our more creative faculties, our more commanding and indomitable will.' The other was to shed the mantle of omniscience and accept Indians as what they had now become, subjects of the Queen, 'fellow citizens' who could be tutored in the arts of government in preparation for ruling themselves. In this they were, in many respects, like the British working class, who were slowly moving towards enfranchisement.[47] Not everyone subscribed to this patronising view of Indians. In 1868 the *Spectator* broke ranks from the consensus and reminded its readers that the Indians were a sophisticated people with much to be proud about. 'They say they have governed a continent for three thousand years, have filled it with beautiful cities, have erected buildings which European architects regard with longing admiration, have covered provinces with works of irrigation, have organised armies, carried out policies, invented arts . . .'[48] A race with such achievements and memories was not likely to be contented with 'permanent degradation'.

PART FIVE

TRIUMPHS AND TREMORS: 1860–1914

1

Low and Steady
Pressure: The Exercise
of Absolute Power

I

Twenty-two railway carriages conveyed various dignitaries and their entourages to the gala opening of the Empress bridge across the Sutlej in June 1878. It was an occasion for fulsome self-congratulation. Sir Andrew Clarke, representing the lieutenant-governor of the Punjab, declared that the iron bridge would have astonished Alexander the Great, whose armies had been halted by the Sutlej. No obstacles could stand in the way of British willpower and genius. Next, the Bishop of Lahore hailed the bridge as 'a temple of science', a monument to the Christian virtues of faith, patience and hard work. Those who had undertaken much of the latter, between five and six thousand Indian labourers, were then treated to a feast of sweetmeats. Afterwards, the Allahabad *Pioneer* described the bridge as 'exactly the kind of work that makes the natives look up to and feel the superiority of the English, who are able to control and bridge the wildest rivers'.[1]

The bridge over the Sutlej was a perfect metaphor for the new Raj. It was chosen and elaborated upon by Rudyard Kipling in his short story 'The Bridge Builders' (1898), which describes the completion of 'the great Kashi Bridge over the Ganges'. It has been the creation of a hierarchy presided over by Findlayson, a government civil engineer and absolute master of the project. Immediately below him is Hitchcock, another engineer who has recently arrived from Britain, and for whom the construction work is an apprenticeship and an immersion in the ways of India, for he is also temporary magistrate, ruler of the thousands of Indian labourers and their families. He handles outbreaks of cholera and smallpox and is distracted by the day-to-day headaches of every junior official: 'Death in every manner and shape, violent and awful rage against red tape frenzying a mind that knows it should be busy on other things; drought, starvation, finance; birth, weddings, burial, and riot in the village of twenty warring castes.' Findlayson and Hitchcock represent the brains and will of the Raj, applying superior wisdom, common sense and forebearance to the physical and moral problems of India. Working under them as foreman and major domo is Peroo, an intelligent Hindu seaman, who has seen something of the world which has made him more sceptical than the rest of his countrymen who dig and carry. Rivetting the girders and other skilled work is done by a gang of European artisans, borrowed from the railway workshops.

Building the bridge involves overcoming primordial India. This is the river, which has to be dammed and channelled, and its deity, Mother Gunga. The natural and the supernatural combine to produce a great flood which threatens to sweep away the earthen banks and shatter the piles that support the bridge's ironwork. Forewarned in the nick of time by a telegram, Findlayson and his team hurriedly prepare for the onrush. Peroo offers the engineer some opium to ward off fever and, in a trance, the two men witness a nocturnal gathering of the Hindu gods. Mother Gunga, a Ganges mugger, supported by Kali, demands that this affront to her power is destroyed, for every conquest of nature weakens the gods' hold over men's minds. In a lively exchange, Ganesh, the elephant-headed diety of wisdom, defends the railways: 'I know only that my people grow rich and praise me.' The debonair Krishna, who moves among ordinary Indians and can 'read the hearts', tells his audience to bow to the inevitable. The old cosmography dominated by him and his fellow gods is doomed; they cannot survive in the world of the 'fire-carriages' and will, very slowly, disappear from the Indian consciousness, leaving only Brahma, the eternal god spirit.

The bridge is saved, thanks to the assistance of a steam yacht of the local prince, Rao Sahib. He represents a hybrid India, suspended between the traditional past and the modern future with his 'tweed shooting-suit and a seven-hued turban'. He prefers to spend time with Findlayson rather than attend a temple dedication – 'They are dam-bore, these religious ceremonies.'

'The Bridge Builders' is a revealing parable. Natural barriers to human progress are overcome by tough, single-minded men using modern technology. In the process, the more formidable obstacles of prejudice and ignorance are being eroded; the old gods know that they and their lore will disappear. For Kipling, who accepted wholesale the values and aspirations of those who ran the Raj in India and did all within his power to make them comprehensible to their countrymen at home, the bridge stood for a future that was infinitely better than the past. What mattered above all was the dynamism and energy of men like Findlayson and Hitchcock, who made possible the spanning of rivers. Writing to his sister from Lahore at the beginning of 1886, he insisted that in India 'every thing is done by personal influence – the personal influence of Englishmen'. Whenever there was a crisis, every Indian looked for and to the nearest Englishman.[2] He repeated the point in his short story 'His Chance in Life' (1888) in which a Eurasian telegrapher outfaces a mob in the remote Bengali township of Tibasu after two Indian functionaries, a police inspector and a babu have scurried off. For Kipling it is the man's 'white blood' which makes him bold and, for a few vital moments, 'the Government of India in Tibasu'. In 'The Head of the District' (1891) a Bengali babu, Grish Chunder Dé, MA, deserts his post as a magistrate and precipitates a crisis. Kipling's opinion of Indian shortcomings in government was widespread; in 1900, the Viceroy, Lord Curzon, argued that from his experience native officials commanded little respect and were prone to absent themselves whenever there was an emergency.[3]

There was very little that was novel in Kipling's exposition of the philosophy of the new Raj. It derived in considerable part from those principles which had been current during the closing years of the Company's rule and rested upon a faith in the British way of doing things and its superiority to the Indian. The process of transformation and enlightenment was carried with a new vigour and sense of mission. Bridges, real or imaginary, were, therefore, fitting symbols for its purpose and achievements.

Overcoming obstacles like the Sutlej and the Ganges was part of a wider struggle against nature. Together, the bridges and the railways they carried were part of an ambitious programme to free India from those accidents of climate which brought periodic droughts, crop failures and famines. Like the floods which nearly swept away Findlayson's bridge and much else in India, monsoon failure could not be predicted, but, with foresight and ingenuity, its impact could be lessened. How this might be accomplished was a matter of the greatest urgency at the time of the opening of the Empress bridge. In 1876 and 1877 there had been two successive seasons of inadequate rainfall which had affected a swathe of the country, stretching from Mysore to the Punjab, in which 58 million people faced chronic food shortages. The government's efforts to cope with this disaster had failed, partly because of under-funding, partly because of current *laissez-faire* dogma which forbade interference with market mechanisms, and partly because there were not enough railway lines to convey foodstuffs from unaffected regions to those of dearth.

There had also been administrative myopia and bungling. It was worst in Madras, where the authorities had adopted a system devised by Sir Richard Temple, a Bengal official, who had calculated that every man receiving official relief could survive on one pound of grain a day, the ration per prisoner in Bengali gaols. On this thin and imbalanced diet, a destitute man was expected to undertake heavy labour, digging and carrying soil as part of a programme of public works financed by the government. The work camps were often sited far from the areas of greatest scarcity, and thousands collapsed and died as they tried to reach them. In all, between 3.5 and 4 million perished in the Madras presidency alone, over a quarter in Mysore, where the relief arrangements were the most slipshod.[4] Disease went hand in hand with malnutrition: in Mysore the death rates from cholera, malaria and intestinal distempers rose from 41,000 in 1876 to 189,000 the following year.[5] The actual totals were probably far higher, for uncounted thousands died unrecorded where they fell by roadsides.

This catastrophe could have been avoided by technology, planning and cash. This was a conclusion of a committee of officials and experts who analysed the disasters of 1876–78 and suggested ways in which they might be prevented. Irrigation schemes and accelerated railway building offered the best long-term solutions to famine and, incidentally, to the slow but steady growth in India's population. Despite intermittent droughts, this increased from 255 million in 1871 to 285 million in 1901, although infant mortality rates remained stable at between 50 and 55 per cent. Railway building was stepped up and, by 1900, the network had almost doubled in size to 25,000 miles, of which 5,000 had been laid in the past five years. Irrigation projects also went ahead swiftly and, by 1891, it was estimated that new canal systems had made over 10 million acres available for cultivation and an eighth of the population was dependent on them for survival.[6] In the short term, the government allocated emergency funds and prepared a blueprint for a public works programme in which the hungry would be paid in return for labour on roads, wells and tanks (reservoirs). On no account was the administration to resort to handing out cash; a policy which would create overnight a class of paupers wholly dependent on state hand-outs and, therefore, unwilling ever to seek work. The social and economic orthodoxies which had given Britain the workhouse and transformed the Irish potato famine into a human catastrophe were upheld in India.

The test of these measures came with the delayed and sparse monsoons of 1895 and 1896. The scale of the calamity was marginally greater than that of twenty years before: 53 million Indians faced starvation and, in April 1897, 33 million were being kept alive at government labour camps.[7] Here the indigent gathered, were given spades, hoes and baskets to carry earth and stones, and then set to work, for which they were given grain with which to make chapattis. There were difficulties in persuading those in remote, jungle districts to leave their homes and epidemics spread rapidly in the crowded camps. Sixty-eight million rupees were available to finance the relief programme and there were contributions from charities in India, Britain, America and Russia. Revenue collections, even if reduced according to circumstances, continued; in Kashmir the ryots lamented:

> *Batta Batta*
> *Tah piyada patta.*
> *[We are crying for food*
> *And the tax collector is after us.]*

Ultimate responsibility for directing this operation lay with the Viceroy, the ninth Earl of Elgin, a lustreless administrator noted for his silences, which some, perhaps unkindly, took to be an indication that he had little worth saying. He was, however, very voluble when it came to resisting pressure from Queen Victoria and others who urged the government to buy up local supplies of grain and supplement them with imports. Elgin repeatedly argued with some passion that state interference in the free market was an 'extreme measure' which no emergency could ever justify. Nor was he willing to forbid the hoarding of supplies, claiming that dealers would not cling to their stocks for ever. He forgot, of course, that many were only prepared to open their granaries after the shortages had driven up prices to the highest possible level.[8] In spite of Elgin's unshakeable faith in the market, his management of the crisis had some success, although the annual death-rate in Awadh more than doubled and at least 90,000 of the Queen Empress's 'poor Indian subjects' succumbed in the Central Provinces, many of them in the relief camps.[9]

The shift from centralised work camps to relief distributed through villages cut the spread of infections and losses during the 1899–1900 drought in central India. In western areas, where there was a good rail network, the local official response was tardy and half-hearted. There was also an unbelievable complacency; the chief commissioner for Gujarat blamed the high death-rate there on the 'soft' habits of its people which prevented them from subsisting on a reduced diet.[10] Despite the efforts of the Viceroy, Lord Curzon, to inject large sums into the relief programme and ginger into those managing it, about 800,000 died in the Bombay presidency. Matters improved considerably after the failure of the monsoon in the Punjab in 1907, thanks to a willingness of local officials to jettison the rule books and economic dogma and adopt flexible methods tailored to local conditions. Losses were far less than had been expected. From then until 1942 nature was kind to India and there were no further large-scale droughts.

How the Raj treated the famines of the 1870s and 1890s says much about its character. Original prognoses about railway and canal expansion were probably correct, although there is no exact method of calculating precisely the numbers saved by food distributed by rail. Many more would have died if there had been no extension of the rail network; of this we can be certain. Likewise, as Curzon appreciated in 1903 when he initiated a new, ambitious policy of digging more canals, artificial irrigation saved lives. But humanitarianism was always balanced by pragmatism and the Raj never lost sight of the need to pay its way. Technical improvements which made Indians less vulnerable to the wayward forces of nature were also contrived to enrich them and, through taxation, the government. The waterways which rendered hitherto arid regions of the Sind and the Punjab fruitful added to the government's revenue. A Punjabi district which had been assessed at £15,000 annually before irrigation was rated at £24,000 afterwards.[11]

Increasing acreage of land under cultivation involved elements of political and social engineering as well as hydraulics. The £3 million Chenab canal scheme, begun in 1887, was designed to make fertile an arid region, relieve population pressure in the cities of the Punjab and produce a model agricultural community which would inspire imitation. Its members, largely Muslims and Sikhs, were selected for their quietism and loyalty.[12]

The settlements were intended to provide a prosperous bedrock of support for the government and a valuable recruiting ground for its army. Moreover, this and similar projects served to strengthen ties between the Raj and local men of influence. Day-to-day supervision of the canals and collection of fees for their use were undertaken by an *amin*, who wore a distinctive uniform and was paid between five and ten rupees (35–70p) a month. According to regulations, he had to be 'an intelligent peasant' who was literate, numerate and approved by the local headman, which offered plenty of opportunities for nepotism.[13] The corruption of low-ranking native officials employed in the Chenab settlements contributed towards unrest there in 1907, and there was a tendency to blame the breakdown of famine-relief operations on the venality and slackness of Indian staff.[14]

II

The anecdotal shortcomings of the tens of thousands of Indians who served the Raj as clerks, policemen, and petty functionaries were well understood by Rudyard Kipling. As a young journalist between 1882 and 1889, he absorbed the gossip and the tales of the Raj, which he shaped into highly successful short stories, and he believed that he knew better than most its inner mechanisms and secrets. The value of the Eurasians and Indians in government offices was one. In 'Wressley of the Foreign Office', a Eurasian clerk at the Pay Office announces that, if he removed one line from a document, he would 'disorganise the whole of the Treasury payments' for an entire presidency. Possibly so; but he was a cog in a machine whose engine was driven by British officials.

The white man's omniscience was not just a matter of administrative capability, although this was obviously important. It was his mystique which sustained the Raj. 'Prestige of race' alone upheld British rule, thought William Horne, who served in the Madras government between 1882 and 1914. How else, he reasoned, could millions whom had never seen a British soldier and rarely a sepoy submit so passively to alien rule? Unwittingly he provides a part of the answer in his description of how police shot down over thirty spear- and lathi-armed tribesmen, the followers of a messianic swami, after an uprising in a remote district in 1899. Nevertheless, for Horne it was the British character, not the force which lay behind it, which underpinned the Raj. Indians responded to their immediate master, the Collector or his equivalent – 'the ruler whom most of India knows, the man whom, if he is worth his salt, she fears and respects, often even loves'. His and the Raj's prestige were easily bruised. In the early 1880s it was considered 'unthinkable' in Madras for ladies to appear on stage and dance in an amateur Gilbert and Sullivan production. If skirts went up, prestige would drop.[15]

Prestige involved more than outward dignity. Sir Michael O'Dwyer, whose Indian career began in 1885, believed that he and his kind were revered by the masses as 'protectors of the poor', perpetually defending them from the rich.[16] It was a self-image which particularly appealed to O'Dwyer, the son of a Catholic Irish squire and an instinctive paternalist. He and others like him provided Indians with 'peace, security, good government, and orderly progress'. By temperament they were autocrats but, as Horne recalled: 'We were trained to rule, not to serve, though in ruling we served.' This might easily have served as the motto for their caste, the Indian Civil Service (ICS), an élite of about 1,000 mandarins. They enjoyed a monopoly of all the senior administrative posts within India and, according to one member, formed 'one vast club'.[17]

Since 1854, admission to this club had been by competitive examination. To start with, the examination syllabus, framed by Macaulay, was contrived to select young men with a liberal education and a broad understanding of the world, gained from wide reading. This concept did not suit current academic fashions and was soon abandoned in favour of tests, which measured what was then being taught in public schools and universities. By 1890 the assessors were allocating a mere 500 marks to English language and literature, the subjects Macaulay had cherished, and 1,150 to Classical subjects, with a heavy emphasis on style rather than textual content. These changes opened the way for what Macaulay had dreaded, cramming, and success went to those who could memorise, retain and regurgitate knowledge. Inevitably, the ICS came to be dominated by men more at home with facts than ideas, and whose intellectual strengths were an ability to collect data and argue from it convincingly. As a result what the ICS did best was the compilation of vast, thorough official reports which examined in minute detail every aspect of a problem and the possibilities of action. Statistics became an obsession, perhaps because they offered irrefutable evidence of progress, and time was no object: the famines of the 1870s had spanned two years, but it took three to investigate them.

A fee of £5 was charged for the two-week examination which ensured that the bulk of applicants were public schoolboys from professional and upper-middle-class families. Of the 333 successful entrants between 1874 and 1884, 227 were the sons of landowners, army and navy officers, home and Indian civil servants, clergymen, lawyers and doctors, and 84 came from commercial and farming backgrounds.[18] Originally, applicants were expected to be under nineteen, but the age limit was extended to include university graduates. Over half the graduate entrants between 1880 and 1883 were from Scottish universities and five from Oxford and Cambridge. As with all public examinations, there was an element of chance which hung on the numbers of candidates and available places; between 1854 and 1874 the odds varied from three to eight to one.[19]

From 1878 onwards, apprentice administrators undertook a two-year course at Balliol College, Oxford, where they studied Indian vernacular languages and culture in preparation for a second test, which was taken after their arrival in India. An Indian Institute was set up in Oxford in 1884 which, it was hoped, would become both a powerhouse for Indian studies and a hall of residence for Indian students. Instead, it became a rather musty museum of Indian artefacts. It was also hoped that the future ICS men at Oxford would develop a keen sense of their responsibilities, something which was cultivated by the master of Balliol, Benjamin Jowett. He once, revealingly, told his acolytes that they had a far greater opportunity to do good in India 'than in any department of administration in England'. Moreover, the salaries were far higher than at home: the lowest grade of the ICS, assistant commissioner, got £300 a year; judges and collectors £2,700; and a lieutenant-governor, £8,000. After twenty-five years' service, every official qualified for an official pension of £1,000.

Too much philosophy and any kind of intellectual flair were generally frowned upon in India, where character counted more than brains. When he was commissioner for the Punjab, Sir John Lawrence had threatened to break in pieces a piano which was owned by a newly appointed young official. Playing an instrument of any kind did not accord with Lawrence's view of an ideal administrator, because it was an indication of the lack of the 'grit' which he expected from his acolytes. 'We want well-educated gentlemen rather than first-rate scholars,' he wrote in 1858.[20] When scholars or intellectuals set foot in India, they faced a dusty welcome from colleagues and superiors. 'All head, no physique and a hundred theories' was how Kipling summed up the hero of his 'The Conversion of Aurelian McGoggin', a brilliant young ICS greenhorn who talked about Comte and Spencer in the club. He gets his come-uppance and is told that: 'His business was to obey orders and keep abreast of files.' William Horne concurred; he believed that the muscular, sporting official mixed easily with Indians and was the sort of fellow who 'gets into the minds of the country people'.[21] This was just as well, for ICS men were invariably the products of an education system which went to extraordinary lengths to promote the cult of athleticism.

The post-Arnoldian boys' public schools and their imitators were the nursery of the ICS. The late-Victorian and Edwardian public schoolboy was relentlessly urged to take on board a code of values which exalted self-lessness and loyalty to team and institutions. Dogged perseverance was more laudable than cleverness, playing the game well mattered more than winning and displays of emotion were to be avoided at all costs. To its credit, this creed encouraged a sense of fair play, chivalry and altruism; to its discredit it fostered philistinism, conformity, the suppression of individuality, a reverence for rules and an unthinking obedience to authority. As Sir Walter Lawrence, a senior ICS mandarin, observed, the virtues prized in a school prefect or captain of games and those of an ideal Indian administrator were interchangeable.[22] And yet, in many respects, these qualities were similar to those which the Marquess Wellesley had wanted to instil in his embryo proconsuls at Fort William College at the beginning of the century. But there were significant differences: the late-Victorian administrator tended to lack imagination and flexibility of mind. Intellectually unadventurous, he was happiest following lines laid down by those above him or those who had gone before, and distrusted innovation.

This is the impression given by Horne and O'Dwyer, the former resigning in 1914 rather than continue service in a country where the natives were being allowed more say in the government. He, O'Dwyer and other officials of the same generation were inclined to look back on their time as a golden age of the sahibs' rule over a contented people. Each was, in Sir Walter's Lawrence's phrase, 'a sun-dried bureaucrat', over-free with advice for the newly disembarked official and, as it were, a curator of the Raj's tradition of government. Of course, there were recruits who refused to conform to antique codes and dismissed some or all of the wisdom of their elders. Malcolm Darling, who joined the ICS in 1905, quickly realised that he and his blue-stocking wife, Josie, were outsiders in a turgid, self-centred community where life revolved around sport outside and games of bridge and billiards indoors. Conversation was confined to gossip and banality. The memsahibs were worse, almost universally disgruntled and hostile to the Indians. Once, over the teacups, Mrs Darling told one matron that she looked forward to her husband's posting in Rajasthan, which was 'real old

India'. 'Then I hope I'll never go there [if] it means meeting natives. Hate the brutes!' her hostess snapped back.[23] Malcolm Darling's new position in a distant, desert region was in fact a form of punishment for his refusal to conform to the mores and habits of his colleagues.

A product of Eton (where Arnoldian cant was less prevalent) and King's College, Cambridge, Darling was a sophisticated aesthete and high churchman who was deeply disturbed by the racial aloofness of his countrymen. It was at his house that his friend, the novelist E. M. Forster, found it possible to have close contact with educated Indians during his 1912–13 tour. Darling dreamed that he might, almost single-handedly as it turned out, bridge the many gaps between cultured Indians and British. An earlier generation believed such an undertaking was impossible and futile. In Kipling's imaginary poetic dialogue between two viceroys, Lords Dufferin and Lansdowne, the former remarks:

> *You'll never plumb the Oriental mind*
> *And if you did, it isn't worth the toil.*[24]

Sir Walter Lawrence agreed: 'No one can boast that he really understands the Indian. The more that is learned about him, the more the student is aware of his ignorance.' Nevertheless, Lawrence told potential ICS recruits that they should always master the languages and customs of their district and take care never to undermine an Indian's self-respect. It was 'a fatal mistake to be satirical or superior'. Part demi-god and part godfather to his charges, the ideal official was sympathetic without inviting intimacy. If his club was exclusive, and in fairness not all were, it was because he, his colleagues and womenfolk preferred to relax in their own company.

This apartness was emphasised by what Lilian Ricketts, the wife of an Indian army colonel, saw as the exaggerated Englishness of the decorations and pastimes of the club. It was a temporary sanctuary for a community whose members were perpetually moving from station to station which, Kipling believed, was why casual flirtation was so common in India. There was, however, more to the ritual of balls, bridge parties, evening drinks, racquets, badminton and cricket matches. Mrs Ricketts believed that these helped to keep 'men and women upright and hard-conditioned' and 'in training for all eventualities'.[25] A contemporary, reviewing Kipling's *Kim* in 1902, detected another reason for this obsessive drive to re-create England in India. The English, he wrote, 'defend themselves from the magic of the land by sport, games, clubs, the chatter of fresh-imported girls, and by fairly regular attendance at church', because, if they did not, 'the empire would be lost'.[26]

This was a trifle far-fetched, although a reminder of the power and durability of the belief in India's capacity to seduce the unwary. A more plausible explanation of British exclusiveness lay in the philosophy which guided every white servant of the Raj. They were, the élite of the ICS in particular, the equivalents of Plato's philosopher princes, men of education, integrity and wisdom whose talents fitted them to rule fairly and honestly. Distant and dispassionate, these men convinced themselves that they alone could maintain peace and impartial justice in a land where Hindu and Muslim mistrusted each other and where there were more than 2,000 castes and over 200 languages. Moreover, there was the ever-present sense that the British were genetically and temperamentally a master race. During his voyage to Bombay in 1876, the newly appointed Viceroy, the second Lord Lytton, was struck by the warlike appearance of Sikh and Pathan cavalrymen whom he met with their commander, General Probyn. Afterwards, he wrote: 'You felt that the Englishman was the finest man of the three, fitted in all respects to command these stalwart hill-men, not only *par droite de conquête*, but also *par droit de naissance*.'[27]

III

As Viceroy of India, Lytton was, superficially, one of the greatest autocrats on earth. In fact, he was ultimately responsible to Parliament through the Secretary of State for India. In theory the two men worked in tandem, but, if one had a stronger personality, he was, in effect, master of India. As in the time of the Company, Parliament's interest in India was perfunctory, with routine debates taking place in a sparsely attended house. When things went spectacularly wrong, as they did for Lytton in Afghanistan in 1879, or, when the tempo of nationalist agitation increased, as it did after 1905, then the interest of MPs was aroused.

Furthermore, changes in the British franchise in 1885, which extended the vote to the bulk of the working classes, produced a breed of radical Liberal and, later, Socialist politicians keen to expose what they took to be injustices in the daily administration of India and reprimand those responsible. Some made it their business to tour India in search of iniquities, and they and their stay-at-home brothers were bitterly resented. In 'Pagett, M.P.' (1897), Kipling adopts the persona of a district officer who is host to one of these Parliamentary tourists ('travelled idiots who duly misgovern the land') and relishes his miseries during the hot season:

> *Pagett was dear to mosquitoes, sandflies found him a treat,*
> *He grew speckled and lumpy – hammered, I grieve to say,*
> *Aryan [Indian] brothers who fanned him, in an illiberal way.*

At the end of the 1911 Abor frontier campaign, Colonel Alban Wilson chuckled to himself about how furious left-wing MPs would have been had they known that 'sticks and opprobrium' had been used to force tribesmen to erect a monument to a murdered officer.[28] Had the incident been reported, there would certainly have been a Parliamentary rumpus and trouble from above for the Viceroy.

Mischief could also come from below, stirred up by the elder statesmen of ICS, the specialist departmental heads who sat on the viceroy's council. With the authority of experience, they imagined they always knew best, as Kipling recognised:

> *You've seen your Council? Yes, they'll try to rule,*
> *And prize their Reputations.*[29]

The collective influence of the executive council was appreciated in London, which was why the government preferred to select viceroys from politicians with a sound administrative record. They had to be prepared for what the cosmopolitan diplomat Lytton called 'the incessant grind' of a daily routine that involved poring over sheaves of telegrams, reports, statistics, committee minutes and memoranda. These were spewed out by subordinate secretariats which generated an average of least 100,000 separate documents a year, many of them lengthy. Besides, the Viceroy had to correspond with the Queen, the Secretary of State, his councillors, provincial governors and residents. Before the general introduction of the typewriter in the 1890s, these exchanges were handwritten. When not in his residences at Calcutta, or, during the hot summer season, Simla, the Viceroy was undertaking cross-country progresses.

Common-sense and custom dictated that he saw as much of India as possible and met his servants at every level to find out about their work and encourage them. The bland viceregal public face was recalled to E. M. Forster by Sir Clement Hindley, who worked for the railways: 'All Viceroys are alike – all affable: Curzon, Hardinge, Minto – if I shut my eyes I shouldn't know which I was listening to.'[30] It was a hard act to sustain and, in private at least, Lansdowne let the mask slip. He moaned about princely durbars in which he was 'smeared with their [Indian] attar of roses', listened to the National Anthem played off-key and once, during a state visit to the Raja of Bharatpur, being badgered by photographers. A valetudinarian, he was perturbed by tours of the Bombay leper asylum ('ghastly array of noseless faces and feet and hands without toes and fingers'), a veterinary clinic and a hospital. 'I ought to pick up something unpleasant as a souvenir of my visit,' he complained afterwards.[31] But, as an aristocrat he had, like Trollope's Duke of Omnium (who would have made an ideal viceroy), to suppress private feelings and perform his public duty.

Stamina was a further viceregal qualification. Hard work in an unkind climate was debilitating, more so for vicereines than their husbands. Lady Canning died in India while her husband was in office, as did Curzon's first wife. Lady Elgin's frail health deteriorated during her husband's viceroyalty and local distempers contributed to the premature death of Lady Hardinge. On her arrival in Bombay at the end of 1888, Lady Lansdowne was overwhelmed by the heat. In her first moment of privacy, she stripped to her underwear and flopped on to a sofa, where she was fanned by a native woman who told her she was too thin!

Those who accepted the viceroyalty, Curzon apart, had no illusions about what they were letting themselves in for, nor were they tempted by the glamour of riding on elephants and being fêted by princes. Hard work and plenty of it was all they could expect. 'Labour steadily,' Gladstone advised the Marquess of Ripon on his appointment in 1880. His successor, Lord Dufferin, told an audience of his fellow Ulstermen in 1884 that, 'The days when great reputations are to be made are, happily perhaps, as completely past as those in which great fortunes are made.' He prayed for an 'uneventful' time in office and hoped all he needed to do was maintain a 'low and steady pressure' on the engine of government.[32] On the eve of his departure in 1888, the next Viceroy, Lord Lansdowne, told his ambitious mother that he was about to take a 'responsible and honourable' post which presented a chance to undertake 'useful work for my country and improving the prospects of my children'. Moreover, and this had helped persuade him to take the position, what he could save from his salary would help pay off mortgages on his estates. He would return with 'something to my credit' that would further his political career.

Lansdowne did prosper and became successively Minister for War and Foreign Secretary under Lord Salisbury and Arthur Balfour, who had once been his fag at Eton. He and Curzon, who also got the Foreign Office, were exceptional. For everyone else, the viceroyalty was a political terminus. Lytton, Dufferin and Hardinge resumed their diplomatic careers, the former two eventually obtaining the prestigious Paris embassy. Ripon and Elgin had to be satisfied with what was then a minor ministry, the Colonial Office.

This was not surprising; viceroys were not expected to be initiators of policy or men of decision. Memories of Wellesley and Ellenborough made British governments nervous about sending out men with strong wills and expansive visions. The outlines of policy making had been laid down shortly after the Mutiny and deviations were unwelcome in London and Calcutta. India was held by Britain in trusteeship and the Raj existed for the betterment of its subjects, which was to be accomplished through slow but steady progress in education, farming, communications and the generation of wealth through cash crops and industry. Above all, the Viceroy and his councillors had to submit to current financial disciplines and ensure a balanced budget. There was also the perennial problems of defence and security which revolved around keeping the Russians to their side of Afghanistan and the Himalayas and cracking down on sedition inside India. Progress and stability could only be achieved with the collaboration of the Indian population, in particular the princes and land-owning classes. As before, these were believed to be susceptible to men of their own kind, which was why viceroys were always aristocrats.

A system whose ends were virtuous was beset by vices, most of them bureaucratic and racial. They were uncovered and vigorously dealt with by Lord Curzon, who arrived in Calcutta in January 1899. He was a man of vision who, unlike his predecessors, had wanted his position and came to it with an unequalled knowledge of Asian affairs. Curzon was certainly the most attractive and intelligent Viceroy, and India's best ruler under the British Raj. He was not an easy master in that he recognised and upbraided incompetence and procrastination. He found plenty of both in the upper ranks of the ICS, where nearly every pair of safe hands was also arthritic. The government was läocooned in red tape, there was an exaggerated respect for every bureaucrat's opinion and the day-to-day administration crept forward at a snail's pace. It said everything for Indian officials that when Curzon began to shake up their procedures they threatened to retaliate by having him 'paper-logged in three months'. They had done the same to his predecessor Elgin, whom, Curzon discovered, had not taken a single policy decision in over four years.[33] A minor, but overdue revolution followed in which procedures were accelerated, but, as he understood too well, it required considerable energy and a thick skin to make officialdom change its ways. Old habits returned after his departure in 1905.

IV

Curzon also gave much attention to what some previous viceroys had considered a chore, the state pageantry of India. Sound, benevolent and even-handed administration alone could not captivate the imagination and win hearts in a country where the exercise of power had always been associated with outward magnificence. This had been understood by Lytton, a Tory with Bohemian inclinations, who had decided to revive Mughal traditions in the grand manner for the formal declaration of Queen Victoria as Empress of India in January 1877.

At his invitation, over 400 Indian princes and their retinues converged on Delhi during the closing weeks of 1876 for a dazzling display of impe-rial theatre, devised to show them the majesty, permanence and sheer strength of the Raj. There were 15,000 red-coated British soldiers, the muscle of empire, and its brains, the immaculately uniformed, plumed and bemedalled British officials and officers. The Delhi durbar emphasised the new unity of India as well as resurrecting the grandeur of the Mughals. Indians were impressed: Sir Dinkur Rao, chief minister of the Maharaja of Gwalior, was overwhelmed by the size and organisation of the great camp beside the Jumma. It represented 'the epitome of every title to command and govern which one race can possess over others' he told Lytton. The Maharaja of Indore saw the durbar as a symbol of a new national cohesion. 'India has been until now a vast heap of stones, some of them small,' he informed the Viceroy. 'Now the house is built and from the roof to the basement each stone of it is in its right place.'[34]

These were heart-warming reactions to a political *coup de théâtre* which had been masterminded by Disraeli, now Prime Minister and keen to show the world the solidity of the Raj and the permanence of Britain's power in India. His Jewishness and former wanderings in the Middle East had convinced him that he possessed a special insight into that mysterious creation of Western imagination, the Oriental mind. According to his reckoning, it revered tradition; accepted hierarchy as both natural and desirable, associating magnificence with authority; and was mesmerised by flamboyant exhibitions of power. By identifying the new Queen Empress with the illustrious Mughal past, Disraeli and Lytton were deliberately appealing to Indian atavism. Besides, Indians were reminded that their country was again united and that the present Raj was a continuation of an ancient and glorious tradition.

Stunning displays of state pageantry made good political sense. An empire which claimed sovereignty over a myriad of different races, religions and castes needed strong bonds if it was to remain intact. Loyalty to the Crown was a bond which transcended India's divisions and was carefully cultivated, as it had been in during the Renaissance when Austrian Habsburg emperors tried to keep control over their multi-racial European empire. In Europe and later in India, the government spent considerable energy on theatrical displays of power designed to win respect and allegiance. Both took trouble to emphasise continuity: the sixteenth-century Habsburgs presented themselves as the heirs of the Roman emperors, the Queen Empress Victoria and her successors revealed themselves in public displays as the heirs of the Mughals.

The value of such shows was appreciated by Curzon, who was the moving force behind the Delhi durbar of December 1902, which simultaneously celebrated the coronation of the new King Emperor, Edward VII, and the achievements of the Raj. It was an ambitious project which Curzon hoped would be more than just another lavish public spectacle. At his direction, elements of India's past would blend with its present and future to give participants and onlookers the sense that they were making history. In his words, they were permitted 'a glimpse of a higher ideal, an appreciation of the hidden laws that regulate the march of nations and the destinies of men'. The genius and progress of India were revealed through an exhibition of carpets, jewellery, paintings and gold and silverware. The dignity and omnipotence of the Raj were conveyed by the grand procession in which Curzon rode in place of the King Emperor, raised above the crowds on an elephant, seated in a golden howdah and shaded by the golden parasol. Afterwards, the Viceroy exchanged a placid elephant for a rather wilful horse and took the salute as thousands of imperial troops marched and cantered past. Most striking of all were the Indian cavalry men – big, bearded soldiers carrying pennoned lances and wearing ochre, green and blue tunics and brightly coloured cummerbunds and turbans. No one who saw them could have doubted that India's martial traditions were flourishing and vibrant under the Raj.

At the heart of India's theatre of power was the monarchy. The first royal tour of India had been made in 1875–76 by the Prince of Wales, and was a prelude to the announcement of his mother as Queen Empress. It was vital in this and future royal progresses that representatives of the house of Saxe-Coburg-Gotha conducted themselves in ways which would win the admiration of the Indian aristocracy. They had to display prowess as sportsmen, ritually shooting tigers from the backs of elephants, potting deer, buffaloes and wild fowl, sticking pigs with lances and riding to hounds. Fine horsemanship, nerve and marksmanship were evidence of noble birth and manhood, as was informed enthusiasm at polo matches and race meetings.

The future Edward VII excelled in these activities, or so ran the reports of his tour. His bluff affability touched the right chord with many; a journalist noted approvingly how the boy Maharaja of Gwalior who 'delights in manly sports became at once the friend of the Prince who took to him greatly'.[35] He found Indian officialdom less engaging, and privately reported to his mother the widespread use of the word 'nigger' among Europeans. She too was appalled and prodded Lytton into issuing an unwelcome rebuke to his staff. The prince's eldest son, the Duke of Clarence, also possessed winning ways, at least with the independent-minded warriors of the Khyber Pass, who instinctively recognised an authentic sahib when they met one. Clarence fell into this category, for, during his 1890 tour of the frontier, he shook the hand of Ayub Khan, the exiled Afghan prince who had led resistance against the British ten years before. This encounter between 'the grandson of the Queen Empress' and one of her most persistent foes delighted tribal headmen. Overwhelmed by this display of chivalry, one exclaimed: 'No wonder the Sirkar [government] is always victorious.'[36] Whether this revelation induced the speaker to forgo rustling his neighbours' flocks or renounce blood feuds is unrecorded. Nonetheless, officials were pleased with the favourable impression the royal visit had had on some of the Queen Empress's most reluctant subjects.

So much sycophancy surrounded official and unofficial accounts of the various royal peregrinations in India that it is impossible to measure exactly what the Queen Empress's Indian subjects thought about her. Sir Walter Lawrence, Curzon's future secretary, recalled that in Kashmir during the 1880s Victoria was a cult figure: her image on the coins was revered and many Hindu homes contained her portrait, an icon of benevolence often similar in style and execution to those in temples. A goddess in all but name, it was widely said that she asked every Viceroy to treat her Indian subjects with tenderness.[37] Soon after the Queen Empress's death early in 1901, Curzon claimed that every class was warmly attached to her and wholeheartedly backed his plan for a Victoria Memorial Hall in Calcutta.

He would have liked some counterpart to the Taj Mahal, but there were no artists alive who could match its craftsmanship, and so the hall would be an art gallery filled with portraits and carvings of such heroes of the Raj as Clive and Elphinstone.[38]

The concept of the Queen Empress as a distant, benign goddess owed something to her attempts to learn Hindustani as well as her intense interest in Indian affairs. In 1887 she took a munshi, Abdul Karim, into her court where he made himself an unofficial adviser on India. Ministers and viceroys found the interference of the son of an Agra prison pharmacist tiresome, but impossible to prevent, for the Queen grew very fond of Karim. A Muslim, he may have prompted the Queen Empress's partisan remarks to Lord Elgin after Hindu–Muslim clashes in Bombay in 1894. 'Mahommedans should be protected, and their worship not disturbed,' she demanded, for, 'They are the real supporters of the British government.' Brahmins were at the root of the trouble and Muslims needed to be 'protected from insults and disturbance in their peaceful and quiet worship which is so opposed to idolatory'.[39] Elgin was then asked to deliver his respects to Karim's father in Agra, as Lansdowne and her grandson had done. Not surprisingly, there was much alarm some years after when an official printer leaked some copies of the Queen's letters to the Viceroy, mercifully not those which referred to her subjects' faiths.

Of all Indians, soldiers found it easiest to give their unreserved loyalty to the Crown. 'I have taken up service for my king,' wrote an Indian soldier in France in 1915, adding that he and his brothers-in-arms 'must be true to our salt and he who is faithful will win paradise'.[40] There were plenty more, often moving statements of fidelity to George V in other letters home from the front. Among the traditional warrior castes and classes, personal attachment to a great king was natural and honourable; a soldier who served a great and illustrious emperor shared some of his master's glory and respect. Moreover, as the soldiers serving in Europe knew, the King Emperor regularly visited them in their Brighton hospital or at the front line. On the other hand, the still minute body of nationalists had only distaste for the figurehead of an alien régime: in 1907 one of their journals, clearly aware of some aspects of his private life, called Edward VII 'drunken, careless, sinful and tyrannical'.[41]

The Raj also forged bonds of loyalty by creating its own titles. From 1860 onwards, the pseudo-chivalric paraphernalia of the British honours system was imported into India and adapted to meet local requirements. These were roughly the same in each country: the need to flatter those to whom the government looked to for support and goodwill and to reward public service at little expense. This was the age which witnessed the self-conscious revival of the exclusive mediaeval orders of the knighthood by which the monarchy bound itself by elaborate rituals and oaths to its richest and most influential subjects who, in turn, received distinct tokens of favour. During his 1876 progress, the Prince of Wales presided over the neo-Gothic ritual of the new Order of the Star of India, a knightly brotherhood of Indian princes. He invested its latest member, the Raja of Jhind, with a pale blue mantle and the order's badge set with a cameo profile of Queen Victoria.

Indian orders and titles proliferated during the next forty years. There was the Order of the Crown of India, the Order of British India, the Indian Order of Merit, the Kaisar-in-Hind medal for services in the Raj (gold for outstanding work and silver for run-of-the-mill duties undertaken efficiently) and sundry police decorations. Soldiers were well catered for. Even the smallest expedition to chastise frontier tribesmen merited a special clasp to the handsome silver general service medals and, from 1907, Indian NCOs and rankers were entitled to their own gallantry award, the Indian Distinguished Service Medal. All the chivalric orders were split into grades: the Order of the Indian Empire had a first and second class (Knights Grand Commanders and Knights Commanders), and also a third, Commanders. The former two wore exotic regalia with a purple mantle and a gold chain decorated with elephants, peacocks and lotus flowers.

These baubles mattered greatly in a stratified society. They satisfied civil servants and soldiers whose place in the hierarchy was officially recognised, and also the princes, whose local status was enhanced. Despite his independent views and flirtation with nationalist politics, Sayagi Rao, the Gaikwar of Baroda, was very peeved to see that he had not been made a knight of the Indian empire in the 1919 honours list.[42] His omission seemed inexplicable because he had recently given 35,000 rupees to the government's war fund – he obviously understood the secret mechanism behind political honours in Britain.

The gaikwar's generosity could not, however, compensate for the dent he had made in the façade of the Raj during George V's Delhi durbar in December 1911. The only visit to India by a reigning King Emperor was commemorated by a durbar of unprecedented scale and extravagance. It began with a cascade of decorations and orders for princes and proconsuls, including elevating the status of the Maharaja of Gwalior so that he received a twenty-one rather than a nineteen-gun salute. This mark of esteem meant much to Indian princes, for it was, as it were, an aural recognition of their rank and importance to the Raj. The highlight of the celebrations came when the King and Queen, wearing their crowns and ermine-lined robes of imperial purple, received the homage of the princes. The pair sat on golden thrones within a crimson pavilion topped with a golden canopy. Elevated above the 100,000 or so spectators, they were, in the words of *The Times* correspondent, 'remote but beneficent, raised far above the multitude but visible to all'. One by one the Indian princes approached the dias, each dressed in his full regalia and festooned with jewels, halted, bowed three times and stepped backwards. The Gaikwar of Baroda, second in line and in a simple white outfit, walked forward, inclined his head once and then turned about. Onlookers were scandalised and, worse still, the incident had been filmed by newsreel cameramen – the Raj's moment of supreme glory was later shown in British cinemas. Sayagi Rao's 'perfunctory' bow was clearly shown on the footage which, according to *The Times*, revealed very little of the 'picturesque' Indian crowds.[43]

Lord Hardinge, the Viceroy, played down the snub and claimed that no disrespect had been intended by the gaikwar, which was not what spectators thought. When Henry Cobb, the Baroda president, tried to extract an explanation, the prince showed signs of extreme tension and his words lost coherence. After a headmasterly dressing down from Cobb, the gaikwar set off for Europe and medical treatment.[44] His misconduct, if such it was, had been obviated by a royal solecism: George V had ignored precedent and entered Delhi on horseback rather than the traditional imperial elephant. He made amends by mounting one when he went to receive homage from the princes and again when he went hunting in Nepal over the New Year. He claimed twenty-four of the thirty-nine tigers killed and, fittingly for an emperor, managed to shoot one with one barrel and a bear with another. Other casualties of this excursion included eighteen rhinoceroses, which were plainly more numerous than today.

In many ways the late-Victorian and Edwardian Raj resembled the spectacles it staged so splendidly. It was stately and moved with the firm, deliberate tread of the principle prop of Indian state pageantry, the elephant. The direction was always forwards, but the pace was unhurried, which was fortunate, for no one was certain as to the ultimate goal, or when it would be reached. There was also something distinctly elephantine about the government itself. It was a complex and ponderous organism, fundamentally good-natured, but capable of frightening tantrums when its patience was exhausted.

2

Not as Relics but as Rulers: India's Princes

The great durbars of Nripendra Narayan, Maharaja of Cooch Behar (Koch Bihar), matched any viceregal show for richness and spectacle. One, held at the beginning of the century, left Major Gordon Casserly spellbound. A local garrison commander, he had been invited to witness the maharaja's eldest son pay homage to his father in a glittering ceremony which simultaneously proclaimed the prince's status, loyalty to the Crown and love of all things British. Outside the palace there were lines of elephants, painted and caparisoned with cloth of gold, and legions of white-coated servants carrying flambeaux. Inside and illuminated by electric light were the maharaja's red-jacketed bodyguard, carrying swords, spears and antique muskets, and his aides who wore British-style white uniforms and pith helmets with spikes. The maharaja was traditionally dressed in a pale blue tunic with a diamond-studded aigrette pinned to his turban. He sat on a gilded throne behind which was hung his banner, embroidered with elephants and tigers, a present from Queen Victoria.

It was proper that the Queen Empress should have made such a gift, for Nripendra Narayan was one of her most steadfast subjects and a favourite guest at Windsor and Sandringham. A few years before he had served as a cavalry officer during the Tirah campaign on the North-West Frontier. Later in the evening, he remarked to Casserly that: 'If ever, during [his] lifetime, the British quitted India, my departure would precede theirs,' for this would be no country to live. 'Chaos, bloodshed and confusion would be its lot.'[1] Exile would not have proved too tiresome for him, as he preferred England to India and spent as much time there as possible. Nripendra Narayan was not, however, an absentee landlord, indifferent to his subjects' well-being. He had paid for a hospital and a gaol in which, Casserly noticed, the convicts were better fed and employed than in the prisons of British India. A manly, public-school spirit pervaded the maharaja's boys' college where the major was delighted to see playing fields crowded with 'native youngsters competing in sprint, hurdle and long-distance races and doing high and broad jumps just like their contemporaries in England'.

The maharaja's eldest son and heir, Rajendra ('Raji'), had played the same games at Eton. At the durbar he appeared in the scarlet coat of a British cavalry officer and presented his sword to his father with the customary supplication, 'I place my life and my sword in your hand.' 'I accept the gift and give you back your life,' the maharaja answered. His younger sons also rendered their homage, each dressed in the gala uniform of the Imperial Cadet Corps. One, Prince Victor, a godson of the Queen Empress, was destined to study economics and plantation management at an American university, the better to develop his family's assets when he returned to Cooch Behar. After the ceremonies, Nripendra and his guests withdrew along corridors hung with the heads of bison, deer, and buffaloes, all of which he had shot. Tiger skins in the billiard room were further evidence that the maharaja was a consummate sportsman, happiest with a gun in his hand. He had a good eye for bloodstock, too; in the dining room there were cups won at the Calcutta races.

Before and during dinner, Casserly chatted with the maharaja's daughters, who had learned their manners and small talk from English governesses and in the salons of London and Paris, whose dressmakers and perfumiers had provided their wardrobes and scents. The major also talked familiarly with the young princes, discussing shooting, polo and 'London theatrical gossip'. This subject may have held Raji's attention more than the others, since he had fallen in love with an English actress, to the horror of his family, who forbade marriage. Piqued, he later took a bizarre form of revenge by drinking himself to death with champagne.[2] The durbar ended with a rather tedious nautch, after which Raji and Casserly revived their spirits and cleared their heads by a moonlight drive in one of the young prince's motor cars.

All that passed during that night fits almost too neatly into a familiar, romantic stereotype of princely India during the heyday of the Raj. There is the hospitable prince whose passionate loyalty to the Crown is matched only by his mania for sport, and whose object in life is to make himself into a benign English aristocrat, caring for his game and tenantry with equal diligence. His cosmopolitan and sophisticated offspring, entranced by the *beau monde* of Europe, lead lives which revolve around a relentless and expensive pursuit of fizz and fun. Given that ostentation and uninhibited behaviour had always been distinguishing features of India's princes, their novel pastimes did not cause much stir among their subjects. There was, however, censure from the nationalist press and the Foreign Office in Calcutta, whose job it was to oversee relations with what were pointedly called the 'subordinate states'.

High-living and over-spending princes were a permanent headache for officials whose taste tended towards the Spartan. The government wanted the princes to visit Britain, where they would be received by the monarch and, perhaps, find inspiration for modernising projects in their states. At the same time they would see for themselves the wonders of the imperial metropolis and leave suitably impressed, although not all were. After a visit to London's East End in the 1890s, the younger brother of the Maharaja of Jodhpur, Sir Pratab Singh, expressed amazement at the poverty he had seen there. He and probably many others from his background had imagined that Britain's population consisted of 'Sahibs', that is the equivalent to the British soldier, or 'Chota Sahibs', the counterparts of their officers and high-ranking officials. Puzzled by the slums, Sir Pratab suggested that London's paupers and workless might emigrate to Jodhpur, where there was plenty of untilled land.[3] Nearly every other Indian prince abroad mixed exclusively with Burra Sahibs and were lionised by high society in London and on the Continent. Regardless of their local means and status, they were universally regarded as exotic, powerful and fabulously rich, fancies which they did nothing to dispel. Rather, many were flattered by the treatment they received and did all in their power to live up to their imagined reputation. One consequence was, in Curzon's words, that the playboy princes were better known 'on the polo ground, or on the race course, or in a European hotel' than in their own states. Conspicuous consumption in Europe and a taste for its luxuries played havoc with noble bank balances: between 1898 and 1903 the Maharaja of Jodhpur ran up debts of over £250,000.

It was impossible to prevent over-indulgence, although the Raj tried as hard as it could. A secret report of 1908 that detailed princely misdemeanours over the previous ten years was a catalogue of every form of

addiction and delinquency. The young Maharaja of Alwar combined the
vices of Toad of Toad Hall with those of Oscar Wilde, with his taste for
'new palaces, motor cars' and boys. Other homosexual princes included
Shivaji Rao Holkar of Indore, who was officially forbidden trips abroad in
1900, and the Maharaja of Patiala, who kept the company of 'stablemen,
jockeys, and panders of every description'.[4] His excesses represented a fall
from grace, for, until recently, he had been under the tutelage of 'a most
worthy and high-minded' British officer. Curzon was appalled by such
goings-on, which he blamed on early marriage, a suggestion dismissed by
the Secretary of State for India, Lord George Hamilton, who reminded the
Viceroy that for the Indian upper classes homosexuality was 'a natural
pleasure'.[5] At least it could not be blamed on contact with Europe.
Another victim of 'physical and moral disease', the spendthrift Maharaja of
Jodhpur, was encouraged in his drinking and pursuit of young men by his
wife. The 21-year-old Raja of Jhind rejected his two Sikh wives, and
Curzon's injunction to produce a son and heir, in favour of 'the daughter
of a European professional aeronaut of low character' whom, allegedly, he
had purchased from her father.[6] 'European women of bad character' hung
around the court of the Nawab of Bahawalpur who, in defiance of his
faith, consumed large amounts of alcohol as well as chloral and opium.

The hard-drinking prince was a recurring official problem. In 1881, the
Maharaja of Gwalior told Sir Lepel Griffin, the senior political agent in
central India, that he had reduced his drinking by four-fifths and was now
down to a bottle of brandy a day, which he believed was a 'fair allowance'
for a diabetic. In Rewah, the Raja was at loggerheads with his mother, 'a
high-born virago' who sheltered mischief-makers and criminals in the
zenana (ladies' quarters).[7] When the Maharaja of Vizagapatam, a keen
polo, tennis and cricket player, was mildly reproved by William Horne for
his intake of gin, champagne and pilsener lager, he confessed, 'I know, sir.
I am an idle, drunken fellow . . . But what can I do?' He added, 'Your Pax
Britannica has robbed me of my hereditary occupation. What is my hereditary occupation? It is fighting.' He died in 1897, sadly aware that he was
the third generation of his family to die in bed rather than on the battlefield.[8] His summary of his and his fellow princes' predicament was largely
correct; they were the proud descendants of a *noblesse d'épée* who were now
forbidden to wield the sword by a government which had robbed their
ancestors of their independence. Although they were revered by their subjects, the princes' status and power ultimately rested upon their ability to
keep on the right side of the Foreign Department. Intemperance, unpaid

bills, attachments to stableboys or disreputable white women, indeed all the vices of their European counterparts, were impediments to what Calcutta wanted: hard-working partners in government. 'You should reflect that you have the honour to be a unit of the great British Empire,' the local political agent told the young Raja of Kolhapur on the day of his installation in 1910.[9] It was a privilege which he and the rest of the princes were never allowed to forget.

II

And yet the Raj needed the goodwill and co-operation of the princes. At the beginning of the twentieth century there were 675 of them, who ruled over an area of 822,000 square miles which contained just over 72.5 million inhabitants, roughly a fifth of India's population. They were clustered in the north-western part of the country and on the north-eastern frontier with a couple of substantial outliers, Hyderabad and Mysore, in the south. They ranged in size from Hyderabad with 83,000 square miles and Jammu and Kashmir with 80,000, to pocket-sized states such as Jalia, Mengni and Kuba, all in Kathiawar and each of under five square miles. Another of Kathiawar's tessera of mini-states, Dedan, was so tiny and obscure that it got lost from official sight. In 1906, after being requested by Calcutta for a report on Dedan, the Bombay administration admitted to knowing nothing whatsoever about the place.[10] Like every other Indian state, great and small, Dedan's political status was the result of treaties between its rulers and the East India Company. These agreements acknowledged Britain as the paramount power with control over the state's defence and relations with its neighbours. In return for protection, the prince was expected to govern even-handedly and humanely with the guidance of a British resident or, in the lesser states, a peripatetic political agent. If a prince or chief broke faith, usually by making war on another state, or, less commonly, by gross misrule, he could be unseated by the Raj, which also insisted upon having the final say in any disputed succession. Calcutta also determined the standing of the prince among his peers by fixing the number of guns to be fired whenever he received an official salute, which was no trifling matter among an élite that set a high store by protocol.

Successive Governor-Generals had turned a blind eye to the internal affairs of the princely states and were reluctant to intervene if abuses occurred. Only in 1860 did the rulers of Patiala, Nabha and Jhind formally agree to outlaw sati, slavery and female infanticide. The old live-and-let-live attitude survived in the new Raj and in a handful of seldom-inspected corners bad old ways lingered on.[11] Slavery persisted in the remote north-eastern state of Manipur until 1891. The maharaja possessed over a thousand slaves, some of whom he occasionally gave as presents to his favourites, and his subjects were permitted to buy and sell them. And yet Sur Chandra Kirti Singh, Manipur's ruler from 1851 to 1886, was considered a congenial ruler, more perhaps for his loyalty during the Mutiny than his enlightenment, although he was considered more progressive than most of his contemporaries.[12]

In Calcutta it was hoped that princes of Sur Chandra's sort would die out one day and be succeeded by heirs who had been carefully tutored in their moral and political responsibilities in British-run colleges. In the meantime, living Sur Chandras presented the Raj with a dilemma. Were they to be coerced into changing for the better, or were they to be subjected to continual, gentle pressure? In general, and because it preferred a quiet time, the government chose the carrot rather than the stick, which made sense since this policy avoided confrontations and kept friends. This was why princes were allowed to maintain their armed retinues even though, in some instances, they were bands of part-time robbers. In 1881, Sir Lepel Griffin complained to the Viceroy, Lord Ripon, that: 'The swaggering ruffians who form the bodyguards of the smaller chiefs and Thakurs in Central India and Rajputana are a terror to the countryside.' A large number were 'fanatical' Muslims, Afghan and Baluchi mercenaries whom, he guessed, were dacoits during their abundant off-duty hours.[13] A few years after, a British officer, called in to assess their martial usefulness, calculated that there were at least 74,000 of these 'riff raff' in Rajputana alone. Armed with old muskets, matchlocks, spears, bows and arrows, swords and some 'worn out and dangerous cannon', they menaced no one save those who had the misfortune to live near them.[14] Political agents coaxed the Rajputana chiefs to whittle down their private forces which, by 1900, mustered 29,000 men. The eventual solution to this problem was a masterstroke of pragmatism: the surviving men-at-arms were converted into a police force, the first the region had known.[15] It is of more than passing interest that that powerful arm of law and order, the Thagi and Dakaiti Department, was only allowed to operate in Rajputana in 1896.[16]

Cutting down and re-employing princely retinues was a delicate business. The decorative fighting men, some of whom, Griffin noted, wore fine gold-inlaid armour, were a source of pride and a token of a ruler's ancient rights and power. In a sense they were as much a symbol as the Union Jack which flew over every residency as a reminder of Britain's supremacy, or the Indian army lancers who escorted political agents when they attended durbars in the smaller states. Convincing a prince he no longer needed or could not afford the customary trappings of authority required tact and patience. Moreover, in the case of the Rajput rajas and chiefs, British officials were disinclined to meddle too zealously in the affairs of men whose frank manliness made them honorary public school-boys. Reporting in 1907 on relations between British officials and the local princes, the president of Rajputana told the Viceroy, Lord Minto, that for decades there had always been 'a sympathy between Rajputs and Englishmen'. 'Towards the old-fashioned native gentleman the attitude is unchanged; towards the leaders of the younger generation, educated in English methods and frequently adopting our customs, relations have become more friendly than before.'[17] This was understandable if the experience of Sir Walter Lawrence is anything to go by. Offered champagne by a Rajput raja, he was urged by his host to 'drink until your head goes turning, or you will never appreciate the nautch we are going to have in the Palace tonight; until your head goes turning round and round you will not like our dancing'.[18]

There was rarely any scrimping on hospitality when British officials made their routine visits to the Raj's princely clients. These duties were undertaken by political agents, who were either seconded army officers with a good command of native languages or 'uncovenanted' civil servants, occupying the grade just below that of the ICS. The political officer investigated how a state was being run and reported on the character and abilities of its rulers. He attended durbars, where he observed a prince at work and tried to sense the prevailing atmosphere in the state, and, where they existed, inspected public utilities. This last was often difficult, for, when a prince feared that these were not up to scratch, he might deflect the agent in the manner of the slack functionaries in Gogol's *The Government Inspector*. Every agent was assisted by a small staff of Indian clerks, the most important of whom was the *daftardar* (supervisor), who undertook much of the day-to-day business. These officials needed careful watching. One who might have stepped straight from Gogol's play, Venkalesh Manjekar, native agent in Kolhapur, made 75,000 rupees from bribery and extortion during the ten years before his arrest in 1897.[19]

Princely government was personal government. Residents and agents therefore needed to know everything they could about the ruler's private

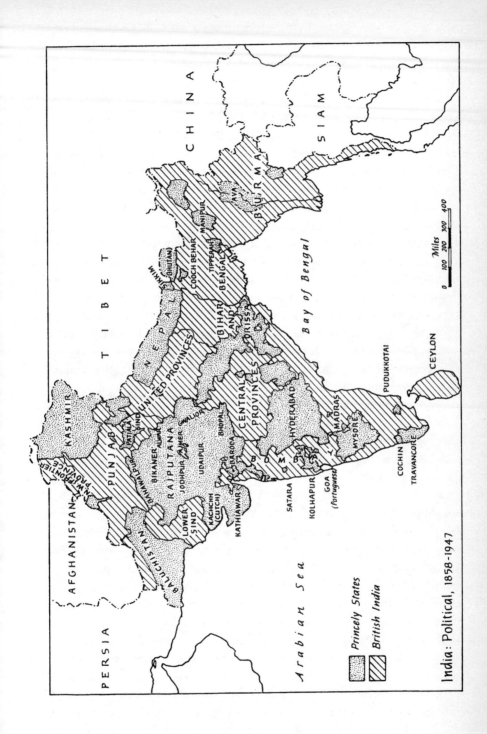

India: Political, 1858-1947

Princely States
British India

life, intrigue among his often extended family and court factions. From their reports it is clear that those responsible for overseeing native rulers ran their own intelligence networks, which picked up hearsay and gossip. These varied in efficiency. In 1884, informers told the Hyderabad resident that his departure from a tiger shoot had been the signal for 'a drunken and disgraceful orgy' by the eighteen-year-old nizam and his companions. The disturbed official investigated the matter closely and was glad to discover that the affair had merely been 'boyish larking'. This vindication of his moral soundness was complemented by signs of political wisdom; at durbars, the young prince and his ministers listened to the complaints of extortion made by ryots against state officials and had sacked several of the culprits.[20]

Vigilance was vital, even though it was physically impossible to keep a close eye on the inner workings of every state. Extremes of watchfulness and supervision of the sort practised by twentieth-century dictatorships would have been deemed unnecessary and unwelcome by a government proud of its respect for law and precedence. So long as the princes complied with the guidelines laid down by the Foreign Department and heeded the advice of its agents in the field, they and their inheritances were safe. Nevertheless, the government's antennae were always highly sensitive to any development or incident within a native state which might injure its prestige or infringe its rights. If a threat was perceived, then intimidation followed, even to the point of enforcing treaty clauses which assigned to the Raj the right to depose a prince or appoint a successor.

This is what occurred in Manipur in 1891, with disastrous consequences. Hitherto, relations between Calcutta and the state had been cordial; at the end of 1885, its ruler had provided useful assistance in operations against neighbouring Burma and, by way of thanks, had been presented with a handful of breech-loading rifles for him and his family and four rifled cannon for his army. A palace coup in September 1890 replaced Sur Chandra Singh by his brother, Kula Chandra Singh, with real power in the hands of their sibling, Tikendrajit Singh, who was also commander-in-chief of the army. Frank Grimwood, the political agent, saw no cause for alarm, informing his superiors the the new régime was sound and widely based, for Tikendrajit Singh enjoyed great popularity. Furthermore, he quickly proved an energetic administrator, launching a programme to repair roads and bridges throughout the state.[21] Tikendrajit was distrusted in Calcutta, where he had a reputation for cruelty and anti-British sentiments.[22]

After some debate, the Foreign Office decided to recognise the new raja, but, invoking a well-used law of 1818, insisted on Tikendrajit's arrest and exile as a subversive influence. The Raj might condone a palace revolution, but it could never tolerate an alternative source of power within a native state, especially when it enjoyed the backing of the people. An ultimatum was delivered to Kula Chandra Singh by J. W. Quinton, the Chief Commissioner for Assam, backed by over 400 Gurkha riflemen. He was confident that there would be no resistance and so he did not bother with the added insurance of a battery of mountain guns. The column reached Manipur on 22 March 1891, and the raja and his brother were immediately summoned to a durbar at the residency. Both turned up and, after a wait, Tikendrajit went away. He may have heard rumours that Quinton intended to flout hallowed custom and arrest him at the durbar. The following day Quinton called another durbar, insisting on Tikendrajit's presence. When he did not appear, a detachment of a hundred Gurkhas were ordered to storm his house and seize him. The attack went awry, and the badly-mauled unit was forced to withdraw to the wooden, thatched residency, which was now under siege by between five and six thousand Manipuri troops and the recently-acquired modern cannon.

Faced with an unequal fight, Quinton, Grimwood and four British officers accepted Tikendrajit's offer of negotiation. Decoyed into the palace, Grimwood was speared by a soldier and the rest beheaded. Afterwards, their blood was sprinkled on stone dragon idols in the palace forecourt and their dismembered bodies displayed in the city; there were gruesome tales that they had been tortured, but these turned out to be untrue. Believing their position untenable, the 270 survivors abandoned the burning residency and, accompanied by Mrs Grimwood, made their way across rough, wooded country to find safety in the form of a small British column. Tikendrajit, having slain the representatives of British power, turned his attention to a ritual purge of all British influence from Manipur. A procession marched through the streets to what what was left of the residency, which was demolished. Telegraph offices and lines were destroyed, telegraphists murdered, a sanitorium burned down, and British graves desecrated.[23]

The machinery of retribution was soon in action. Within a fortnight, British forces, mainly Gurkhas, were converging on Manipur. Resistance was hopeless against mountain guns and disciplined firepower. In one fight close to the city, 80 Gurkhas threw back 3,000 Manipuri troops for the loss of one man killed. Manipur was occupied on 27 April and those responsible for the outrages were rounded up, tried and executed. The raja's palace was looted before it and the citadel were razed to the ground to make way for a permanent military camp. The final act in this reversal of fortune was the public hanging of Tikendrajit on a scaffold erected on his polo field. The execution of a prince, albeit a villainous one, upset Queen Victoria, who protested to Lansdowne, suggesting that, in general, residents and political agents were overbearing. The Viceroy was adamant on the matter, believing with good reason that the Queen had obtained her opinion from her munshi, Abdul Karim. There were further reverberations of the Manipur affair in the Commons where the government faced charges of perfidy, for it was widely believed that the original durbar had been a device to abduct Tikendrajit. The allegations were strenuously denied both in London and Calcutta, but the mud stuck, as it usually does when it has been thrown with good reason. One officer who had taken part in the campaign remarked afterwards: 'Because this man was a useless rogue is no reason why we should have resorted to underhand trickery; it never pays.'[24] Not only had the Raj's integrity been called into question, its reputation for unflinching resolution had been compromised. This was to some extent restored by the courts martial and subsequent cashiering of the two officers who had advised retreat from the ruined residency. As usual when governments blunder, scapegoats were selected from among the middle and lower ranks.

The sequel to the Manipur incident gave the Raj an opportunity to restate its faith in princely government. Annexation was ruled out, wisely perhaps for there was strong evidence that the British connection was disliked by a wide section of the population. A new maharaja, Chura Chand Singh, was chosen and given the status of a ruling chief with entitlement to an eleven-gun salute. He was the nephew of his predecessor (who had been exiled) and six years old, which gave the resident the opportunity to guide the affairs of Manipur for the next sixteen years. During part of this regency, Chura Chand was groomed for his future role at Mayo College, a government academy for princes.

The twists and turns of court in-fighting always needed to be monitored, and princes needed occasional reminders that they were not above the criminal law. Allegations that Madhava Singh, Maharaja of Panna, had been party to the murder of his uncle, Rao Raja Singh, led to swift and decisive action during the late summer of 1901. The source of these charges was the dead man's two widows, who had written to Curzon with an account of the events leading up to their husband's death. It appeared that three years before, the Hindu maharaja had become infatuated with a Muslim prostitute, Hydree Jan, who became his mistress. He was thirty, childless and, in April 1901, his wife died. Soon after, his mistress was found to be pregnant and he prepared to marry her. His uncle, who had already condemned his nephew's dissolute way of life, objected strongly. At the end of June, Rao Raja became seriously ill and feared, rightly, that he and his three sons were being poisoned by food prepared by the maharaja's cook, Shimbu. Rao Raja's death at the end of the month, the cook's flight and forensic evidence confirmed his family's suspicions.

The weight of evidence compelled the government to intervene. On 12 September, Captain Beville, the political agent in Bundelkhund, rode to Panna with a small force, assumed control over the government and arrested the maharaja. Investigations were undertaken by an officer of the Thagi and Dakaiti Department, which uncovered a conspiracy involving the maharaja, who had tested the efficacy of the arsenic and strychnine on hunting dogs, a courtier and the fugitive cook. The courtier was executed, the maharaja deposed and imprisoned. His former income had been £50,000 a year and, to make incarceration bearable, he was given an annual allowance of £2,400. Jadrendra Singh, the eldest son of the murdered Rao, was nominated maharaja and packed off to a princes' college, leaving the government in the hands of the political agent.[25]

III

Curzon had dreamed of making men like the Maharaja of Panna 'a colleague and partner', which was why the Viceroy was so disheartened by instances of princely immorality and indolence. At the end of his viceroyalty, he explained to an audience in London's Guildhall that he wished the princes to be treated 'not as relics, but as rulers; not as puppets, but as living factors in the administration'.[26] He was repeating a well-established principle of Indian government which had always been attractive to Conservatives like himself, who saw aristocracies as a natural governing class. In India they were something more: natural allies of a government dedicated to stability and the sanctity of property. This had been proved during the Mutiny when the loyalty of the majority of princes had been one of the decisive factors in ensuring the restoration of the Raj. Their trust was amply rewarded: in December 1860 Baijii Rao, the Maharaja of Gwalior, received a grant of lands worth 30,000 rupees a year and assignments on the revenues of Jhansi, whose rani had joined the rebels.[27] Most important of all, Dalhousie's ill-judged doctrine of lapse was jettisoned and the right of princes to adopt heirs discreetly restored.

The shift in official thinking was also felt in Awadh. In the summer of 1858 the Tory Secretary of State, Lord Ellenborough, halted the confiscations of taluqdar estates on the grounds that, in the future, stable government would depend on their co-operation. Owners of two-thirds of the land in Awadh, their interests were accommodated, even at the expense of the peasantry. The 1868 Awadh Rent Act gave them the power to raise rent at will, which they did, causing enormous hardship. Nearly forty years later, a senior civil servant, Sir Thomas Holderness, described the landowners of Awadh as 'a natural aristocracy' and 'a most useful auxiliary to an alien government such as ours'.[28] Their support was more and more valuable as nationalist agitation was gaining momentum, and with it undercurrents of protest against the land-owning class in general. In 1907 many Bengali zamindars were disturbed by the lack of a firm crack-down on dissidents.[29]

Transforming the princes into active and effective props to the government demanded a revolution in their collective outlook. Partnership, as defined by Curzon and the Foreign Office, involved sharing the objectives of the Raj. Translated into action this meant the princes had to devote themselves to the betterment of their subjects, ploughing back into their states some of taxes they collected. The metamorphosis was cynically described in Kipling's poem 'A Legend of the Foreign Office' (1897), in which a prince plunges into a far-reaching programme of reform spurred on by the hope of a reward:

> *Rustum Beg of Kolazai – slightly backward Native State –*
> *Lusted for a C.S.I. – so began to santitate,*
> *Built a Gaol and Hospital – nearly built a City drain –*
> *Till his faithful subjects all thought their ruler was insane.*

> *Strange departures made he then – yea, Departments stranger still,*
> *Half a dozen Englishmen helped the Rajah with a will,*
> *Talked of noble aims and high, hinted of a future fine*
> *For the State of Kolazai in strictly Western line.*

Unhappily for Rustum Beg, toeing the government line yields an inferior honour and, in a spleen, he commands all innovation to cease. Down come the new police stations, the hospital is turned into a zenana for his wives and concubines and he reverts to his old ways – over-taxing his subjects and over-straining his liver. Rustum's recidivism receives Kipling's implicit approval, for he had a romantic attachment to the old India.

The new India would be created by new Indians, princes educated in the British manner with a strong emphasis on the development of character. Nothing less than the complete remoulding of the aristocracy was the aim of a constellation of officially subsidised, Indian public schools, scattered across the country for the education of the sons of the landowning classes. At the opening of one of the first, Rajkumar College, Rajkot (Kathiawar), in 1870, the local political agent predicted that its alumni would be a 'manly set of youths . . . burning with emulation to outstrip each other in the glorious task of elevating humanity'.[30] In another speech that day, Sir James Peile, director of public instruction within the Bombay presidency, gave pupils a hint of what lay in store for them: 'We shall discipline their bodies in the manliness and hardihood of the English public schoolboy.'[31] His words were taken seriously by Chester Macnaghten, the first headmaster, who believed that muscle and character were best hardened by relentless games playing. He would frequently read to the princes that chapter in *Tom Brown's Schooldays* in which Tom, captain of the cricket XI, sustained his team through a match crisis and saved the day. At the end, there was a homily: 'In hours so spent you will learn lessons such as no school instruction can give – the lessons of self-reliance, calmness and courage, and of many other excellent qualities, which will better fit you to discharge the duties and face the difficulties, which the future must bring.'[32] In other words, they would pass through that mill which produced the sahibs who ruled British India and, it was hoped, would have absorbed their values and codes of behaviour. In time, all of India's rulers, native and British, would share a common attitude.

The same message with slight variations was preached at Mayo College, Ajmer, which served Rajputana, and other colleges which sprang up during the 1870s and 1880s. It was not one which was particularly welcomed; at Rajkumar College Macnaghten found his pupils initially recalcitrant and unreceptive. Matters were not helped by their habit of bringing with them trains of armed servants and old family animosities. But Macnaghten battled on, as had Dr Arnold at Rugby, and in the end the boys knuckled down and absorbed the physical and moral benefits of cricket, which became very popular. Elsewhere, the prospect of long hours in the nets proved unappealing both to fathers and sons, and they voted with their feet, chosing traditional Hindu and Muslim schools where the curriculum was centred on literature, logic, law and, in the latter, Persian and Arabic. The intake of the pseudo-public schools remained disappointingly low; in 1894–95 only 68 of the 150 places at Mayo College had been taken, which was about average, and in 1902 only twelve of Kathiawar's thirty-two chiefs had passed through Rajkumar College. Characteristically, Curzon took action. He re-organised the colleges and made them more attractive by revising syllabuses to include politics and economics and introducing a leaving examination. More British masters were recruited and boarding houses set up under European housemasters. Thereafter, the colleges began to flourish, with Mayo College becoming particularly fashionable among the Indian aristocracy.

Behind these efforts to produce Indian versions of Tom Brown was a desire to wean the princes away from domestic influences, which Victorian and Edwardian officials imagined to be morally corrosive. Consider the illuminating tale of Miss Moxon, governess to the young rajas of Akalkot and Sawantvadi during the first years of this century. In the words of the governor of Bombay she gave the boys 'what is, I believe, almost unique, namely the associations of a pure, wholesome, refined British home, and all the tenderness, watchfulness and care of a good British mother'. This was accomplished despite the 'intrigues' of 'ill-disposed relatives and corrupt and corrupting servants' who sought to mislead the boys. But the high and single-minded Miss Moxon got her way, so that when the Raja of Akalkot entered Rajkumar College he was found to be 'much better equipped intellectually and *morally* than many British boys who proceed to public school'.[33] A high accolade which earned Miss Moxon the Kaisar-in-Hind medal, second class.

IV

Another, larger-scale triumph in princely regeneration was achieved in Baroda, although its sequel proved embarrassing for the Raj. It was a middle-sized state whose two million population was highly taxed, paying £2 million each year into the gaikwar's treasury in the early 1870s. The people of Baroda were also misruled; investigations undertaken by the resident exposed cases of murder, torture and extortion which were sufficiently outrageous to force the Viceroy to unthrone Mahhar Roy, the gaikwar, in 1874.[34] He had no direct heir and so, according to custom, the dowager maharani was instructed to 'adopt' a successor. She chose Sayagi

Rao, the twelve-year-old son of a village headman who was a distant kinsman of the ruling dynasty. He was provided with an English tutor and an enlightened diwan (chief minister), Sir Madawah Rao, a former university lecturer in Mathematics and Philosophy.

In 1882, when the young gaikwar was on the eve of his majority, the resident reported enthusiastically to the Viceroy about a progressive government which was reforming the state with the help of Indian professional administrators hired from outside. The diwan explained that the objective of his government was to be 'like the English without the sahibs'.[35] Sayagi Rao developed into a humane, cultivated and conscientious prince. His day began at six in the morning with prayers, after which he spent a few hours reading; his favourite authors included Bentham, De Tocqueville, J. S. Mill and Shakespeare. At eleven he took breakfast with his family, a meal which, like dinner, consisted of English and Indian dishes. At the time of their arranged marriage, his wife had been fourteen and illiterate. Her husband immediately arranged for her education so that they could enjoy an equal partnership; many years later he wrote: 'An educated lady in the house is more able to shed the light of happiness than one who is ignorant.'[36] During the afternoon, the gaikwar proceeded to state affairs, examining files, consulting with his ministers and considering appeals from his courts. As the evening approached, he would make his daily excursion through Baroda city, travelling in a carriage escorted by a bodyguard of lancers. During these drives and his twice-weekly open audiences with his subjects the gaikwar accepted petitions and pleas. By the standards of his peers, Sayagi Rao was not unduly reckless with money, although he had spent £1.5 million on a new palace, named with unintentional irony, 'The White Elephant Palace'. He also possessed a troop of performing parrots who had been trained, among other things, to walk tightropes and ride miniature silver bicycles.

A sufferer from neurasthenia, the gaikwar had made visits to Europe for treatment in 1884 and 1899 and intended his sons to go to Eton and Balliol, for he had the highest regard for English education. This plan was not to Curzon's liking; he was convinced that at public school and university an Indian would develop a contempt for his own people and possibly be tempted to neglect them by remaining in England. This is what had happened to Ranjitsinjhi Vibhaji, Maharaja of Nawanagar, although his reason for staying was entirely innocent; after leaving Cambridge in 1895 he spent the next nine years playing cricket for Sussex and England and was twice champion batsman of All England. However laudable this

4. A loyal prince: the young Maharaja of Bharatpur poses in 1860 with his courtiers, ministers and zamindars.

5. The backbone of India: peasant farmers in about 1870, with their implements and a yoke for oxen. They paid for the Raj through land taxes and were considered the beneficiaries of the peace it brought.

6. Famine: victims of the 1876–77 famine await death.

7. Soldiers of the Queen: aides-de-camp to the Viceroy, Lord Elgin, in 1896.
Colonel Mortimer Durand (front row, fourth from left) was an experienced player of the
Great Game, an explorer and map-maker who decided the line of the Indo-Afghan frontier.

8. Famine relief, 1897: peasant men and women gather
baskets of rocks which are pounded into a bank.
When completed, the bank will surround a reservoir.

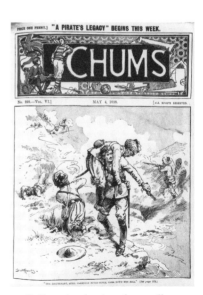

9. Frontier derring-do: a gallant
subaltern saves a wounded sepoy
during a North-West Frontier
ambush in this illustration from
Chums, May 1898.

10. Fighting the plague: a sanitary detachment sprays tenements with limewash as part of the measures against the outbreak of bubonic plague in Bombay in 1896. Well-intentioned, such precautions provoked resentment and anger among the ignorant.

11. The power and the glory: Lord Curzon, the Duke of Connaught and Indian princes ride on elephants from Delhi to the 1903 durbar.

12. Crown imperial: the King Emperor, George V, rides out from Delhi's Red Fort during the 1911 durbar.

13. Starve or fight: a First World War German view of the Raj.
The sahib tells the Indians they can either stay at home and die,
or join their countrymen in France – and die there instead.

14. Jihad! A German cartoon of 1914 declares that
the Turkish declaration of a holy war would strike
terror into British hearts.

15. Mesopotamian misadventures:
a German cartoon celebrates the fall of Kut
in 1916, mistakenly claiming it as an Arab
rather than a Turkish victory.

SAHIBS AND MEMSAHIBS RELAXING

16. Hard playing, South India, in about 1915: the Mysore pack in full cry.

17. Shikari: a pause for refreshment as beaters and bearers look on.

18. General Sir John Burnett-Stuart with trophy – a water buffalo.

19. Polo chukka.

20. The day's bag: conclusion of tiger hunt in about 1910.

21. The gateway to India: the Khyber Pass seen from the air.

22. The avenging arm of the Raj: Hawker Hart bombers patrolling the North-West Frontier. Aircraft were regularly deployed to chastise rebellious Pathans from 1917 onwards.

durbar, and instruct his diwan, B. L. Gupta, to dimiss all state employees who were hostile to the British government or associated with clandestine presses. With the approval of the resident, the mail of known Baroda dissidents was intercepted and opened, and two Baroda teachers were tracked by Madras police officers when they made a journey through India during which they made contact with Aurobindo Ghose. The gaikwar refused to sack them and procrastinated over the imposition of the gagging laws, but in the end he buckled under sustained pressure.[39] In 1913 he was allowed to visit Europe again, ostensibly for medical treatment, but with a stern warning not to make contact with those exiled nationalists he had met on a previous tour.[40] Instead, he had an audience with George V, confirming the official view that he ran with the hare and the hounds. At the end of April 1914 the resident reported that sedition in Baroda was on the wane. When he returned home in December, the gaikwar dutifully made cash contributions to the government's war effort, but kept his views on the conflict to himself.[41]

Neither the gaikwar nor the officials who chivvied him seemed to have been aware of the irony of their situation. Here was an Indian prince who had lived up to the ideal set by the British and made himself an active partner with the Raj, ruling over what a British journalist described in 1902 as a 'thoroughly well-governed Native state'.[42] But Sayagi Rao's concept of modernisation was not confined to the provision of proper drainage or funding a public museum, it embraced new ways of looking at India. This placed him beyond the pale as far as the British were concerned, for he was, after all, a 'subordinate prince', He was also exceptional; all but a tiny handful of princes remained aloof from the nationalist movement that was emerging during the 1880s and 1890s. As its nature became clearer, the great majority became apprehensive and drew closer to the government, often doing all in their power to quarantine their states from nationalist agitation.

Princely conservatism was welcomed by many of their subjects. When Jafar Ali Khan, the young Nawab of Cambay, and his diwan, a Brahmin lawyer, plunged into a programme of improvement in the 1880s the result was a peasant insurrection. Elementary public utilities cost money and taxes had to be increased. The rising was suppressed with the help of troops hurried from Bombay.[43] Elsewhere, the pace of change was measured, sometimes to the point where it was scarcely noticeable. In turn-of-the-century Sirohi, a Rajput state of 2,000 square miles, the inhabitants 'generally go abroad armed'. There was one school, one gaol and one dispensary for its population of 191,000, nearly all of whom were poor. As elsewhere in Rajputana, the most striking indication of British rule was a widespread enthusiasm for cricket.[44]

3

We are British Subjects: Loyalty and Dissent, 1860–1905

I

One of the greatest puzzles about British India was the extent to which Indians felt affection for their rulers. There were strong bonds of attachment between Indian soldiers and their British officers; of this there can be no doubt. Men from warrior castes and martial races were instinctively drawn towards gallant officers who respected their traditions and cared for their welfare. But what about the great mass of Indians? Of course many rarely saw a European of any kind, and knew of them only by reputation. At any one time during this period there were seldom more than 100,000 of them scattered among a population of over 250 million, and most were British soldiers who lived in cantonments concentrated in the northern half of the country. In any case, as British officials frequently pointed out, there was no such thing as public opinion in India, despite rapid spread of the telegraph, railways and postal system and an explosion in the number and circulation of newspapers. Not that this mattered greatly; by 1900 total newspaper circulation was 150,000, serving a literate population of between four and five million. The remaining 298 million Indians could not read and had no way to make their collective feelings known, a fact which did not prevent British administrators and Indian nationalists from claiming that they were the authentic voice of India.

There was some anecdotal evidence as to how Indians felt about their white rulers, and it was not comforting. They 'like our laws but hate *us* and would like to be independent', Lieutenant James Whitton noted in his diary after he and his brother officers of the Royal Scots had spent an evening discussing the virtues of the Raj with the Nawab of Trimulgharry and his guests in December 1867. There was some consolation in that one of the nawab's kinsmen had observed that British rule was infinitely preferable to Russian, which he feared might prove too 'harsh'.[1] George Yule, a Calcutta businessman sympathetic to Indian aspirations (he was unanimously elected president of the Indian National Congress for 1888–89), was convinced the natives had no attachment at all for the Raj: 'It creates in them no enthusiasm, evokes no warmth of liking, produces no healthy desire for permanence or good fortune.'[2] According to Man Ghose, a Calcutta barrister, the fault lay with individuals. Presumably writing from experience, he claimed in 1868 that ICS recruits 'hate and despise the natives with all the true "damned nigger" fervour of speech and energy of action'.[3] One man's generalisation cannot stand as an indictment of an entire community, but in 1876 Lord Salisbury, the Secretary of State for India, cited British 'arrogance' as the main obstacle to warmer relations with the princes.[4]

The above judgements reflected directly or indirectly the view of well-to-do Indians who nursed private grudges against the British. Within princely circles there was residual resentment against a race which had curtailed the independence of the states, and a member of Bengal's extremely touchy educated élite was bitter because the British denied him and his kind what they believed was their proper place in the administration. But what of the masses, the rural peasantry of India?

As might be expected, Sir Michael O'Dwyer, the voice of the old-guard ICS, claimed that all British officials were revered by the people of the countryside as 'the protectors of the poor', a phrase he had heard them use many times.[5] This was not just the wishful thinking of an old man looking back to an imagined golden past. Peasants in arms against their landlords at Pabna in Bengal in 1873 described themselves as 'ryots of the Queen of England' and believed that the government would defend them from grasping landlords. Two years later, peasants in the Deccan imagined that the lady who appeared on the silver rupees, Queen Victoria, would come to their assistance against local moneylenders.[6] This simple faith in a benevolent authority which, once it knew of injustice, would move to eradicate it was not exceptional, although it must have been hard to preserve in the face of annual tax demands. But then, under the infinitely more oppressive régime in contemporary Russia, the peasantry believed that the Czar was their friend and would act immediately to reduce their suffering – that is, if he knew of it. During the next century their descendants would say exactly the same of Stalin.

The official mind imagined that the masses would render loyalty in return for good government. Lord Lytton rejected this contract, believing that the peasantry was an 'inert mass' which could only be stirred by its natural overlords, the princes. 'The only political representatives of native opinion are the Baboos, whom we have educated to write semi-seditious articles in the native Press,' he told Salisbury in 1876. The minister concurred, and warned Lytton that the babus, a term with undertones of condescension which embraced all educated Bengalis, were a potential threat. They would, he predicted, act as 'the opposition in quiet times [and] rebels in times of trouble'.[7] Not long after, he observed, 'I can imagine no more terrible future for India than that of being governed by Competition Baboos.' Indians, lettered or otherwise, were psychologically and temperamentally unfit to rule themselves. In 1892, when he was Prime Minister, Salisbury insisted that: 'The principle of election or government by representation is not an eastern idea, it does not fit eastern tradition or eastern minds.'[8] This doctrine was accepted by Conservatives and formed the bedrock of their policy towards India for the next generation. As for the Raj, it would flourish so long as it never faltered. Indians, Salisbury believed, were capable of asking only one political question, 'Which is likely to win?' If it was the government, then they would support it.[9]

In so far as it represented the collective views of a tiny educated class, Indian opinion could either be treated with cordial condescension or overlooked. British public opinion could not be ignored. In 1888, John Gorst, the Conservative Under-Secretary of State for India, asked Lansdowne to send him vital reports as quickly as possible so that he was always prepared to answer any awkward Commons questions on India. Secretaries of State had now to tread warily and project an image of the Raj as 'progressive and reforming', if they were to keep Parliamentary confidence.[10] Criticism and needling queries came almost exclusively from the Liberal and Irish Home Rule party benches, where there were always MPs ready to expose an Indian injustice or administrative anomaly. During the spring session of 1901, Swift McNeil, the member for Donegal South, wryly exposed the utter lack of Indian experience of the newly appointed Governor of Madras, Lord Ampthill, and expressed outrage against Curzon's restrictions on the princes' foreign travel. In the same spirit, W. S. Caine, the Liberal MP for Camborne, asked why 85 per cent of the land revenue from Surat had been paid by moneylenders and not the famine-stricken ryots? He also suggested that India's memorial to Queen Victoria might take the form 'of some permanent benefit upon the suffering masses in India'.[11] The implications of these and many other similar enquiries was that India was a far-from-benevolent despotism in which the impoverished masses suffered from hunger and over-taxation.

Interest in Indian affairs had grown steadily since the 1870s. This increase was paralleled by the emergence of Gladstonian Liberalism as a force in British political life. Its backbone and chief beneficiary was the middle class, for it was a creed which prized men who had raised themselves through hard work and natural talent, qualities which also marked them out for political responsibility. Liberals were, therefore, susceptible to appeals from the nascent Indian middle class which, in large part, shared their outlook. There was also within Gladstonian Liberalism a strong vein of libertarianism that made it deeply distrustful of imperialism and all forms of autocratic government. If India was to have this type of government, then it should acknowledge the promise of equal rights for all made by the Queen in 1858. As for the Irish Home Rule party, its members instinctively opposed British imperialism and equated the denial of political rights in Ireland with their suppression in India.

II

Indian political consciousness was the direct result of an educational revolution in India which had been under way since 1860. In 1855 there had been 47 English schools in Bengal, in 1882 there were 209 and in 1902, 1,481. In that year there were roughly 250,000 pupils taught by 12,000 teachers. One third of these schools were private, enjoying no government subsidy and sometimes employing badly-qualified staff. Nonetheless, these and the other schools were enthusiastically patronised by prosperous families keen for their sons to move on in the world. In his parents' eyes, the 'good boy' was a pupil who dutifully walked to and from school and devoted all his time and energy to his studies.[12] His introduction to the English language and, through it, the literature, science and philosophy of Europe, would provide him with what one senior civil servant called 'the priceless intellectual gift of Rome . . . the conception of law as the governing power'.[13] Another official, of the muscular persuasion, feared that the Indian schoolboy suffered from a dangerous obsession with book-learning. Long hours of reading deprived him of 'public school manliness', with the result that many educated Indians were 'without true strength, character and with ill-balanced minds'.[14]

Very few girls joined this quest for knowledge and qualifications. In 1870 the government was spending £5,645 on their education out of a total budget of £316,500. These figures reflected the numbers involved: out of 1.1 million Indians (0.5 per cent of the population) undergoing secondary schooling, only 50,000 were girls. Six women graduated from Indian universities in 1881–82 and they, in common with other educated Indian women, had got where had through unusually enlightened parents rather than official policy. Even among the more Westernised Hindu and Muslim families, old shibboleths about the ornamental and domestic role of women still held true.

Five universities had been founded in 1857 and they grew swiftly, planting 'colonies' in the form of outlying colleges in the manner of London University, which had been the model for Indian higher education. Calcutta led the way, becoming by 1900 the largest university in the world with over 8,000 students, just over a third of all those in India. Entry was not easy and depended on a mastery of English as well as a knowledge of Greek, Latin, History, Indian Geography, Geometry, Algebra and Arithmetic. In 1865 Calcutta's entry paper required candidates to explain such phrases as 'Aonion Muses', 'Elijah's burning wheels' and the meaning of words like 'talisman', 'polyglot' and 'laity'. The following year entrants were expected to know the meaning of the vernacular statement: 'German horses are weak and washy, they are inferior in bottom.'[15]

University study was intense and failure rates high. Nearly all students lived in cramped lodgings, ate poor food and were married, which, their lecturers thought, prevented them from philandering.[16] Study was often undertaken in gloomy rooms and there was excessive cramming. One Calcutta tutor observed:

> Examinations exercise a tyranny over the lives of most college students. The extraordinary prevalence of 'keys', with model questions and answers and such like meretricious aids to a degree, sold by every bookseller and advertised by every post.[17]

Arts subjects predominated at Indian universities. Between 1857 and 1882

Calcutta produced 1,589 arts graduates and 176 doctors of medicine. Of the arts graduates, 581 entered the law and 526 public service, which were the ultimate goals of all students.[18] The system responded to students' aspirations, but whether at the time India needed a plethora of lawyers and arts graduates is open to question. Medicine certainly lagged behind. In 1912 there were only 269 doctors within the Central India Agency, an area with a population of 9.3 million. In that year they treated 1.72 million patients. Matters were improving thanks to a new regional medical college, largely financed by local princes, which had just under a hundred students.[19]

What appears with hindsight to have been a neglect of scientific and technical subjects with a practical value was a reflection on the nature of the Raj. It was strong on vision, but weak when it came to turning dreams into reality. Financial considerations always outweighed all others, which was why India, unlike Britain after 1870, lacked a system of universal education. English-language schools were confined to cities and towns and they, like the universities, were allowed to develop their own curriculums which reflected the career hopes of students rather than national needs. Most important of all, there was never an attempt to create a nationwide primary education programme of the sort which was being introduced in contemporary Japan.[20] Instead, the government transferred available funds to urban secondary schools where places were taken by boys whose parents were rich. As a result, India's peasantry remained untouched by the new learning.

The chief beneficiaries from the educational revolution were its most zealous supporters, the *bhadralok*. It was a term used for the Bengali upper and middle classes and indicated a combination of eminence, wealth and respectability. From the beginning of the century its members had recog- nised the value of European knowledge and the part it could play in a Bengali renaissance. Then and for many years to come bhadralok loyalty tended to focus on their province rather than India as a whole. In the 1820s, Rammohan Roy claimed 'the greater our intercourse with Europeans, the greater will be our improvement in literary, social and political affairs'.[21] When this process of regeneration had been accom- plished, Indians might be free to take control of their destiny. Twenty or so years later, when the Governor-General Lord Ellenborough was discussing Macaulay's plans for Indian education with the Calcutta businessman and philanthropist, Dwarkaneth Tagore, he remarked: 'You know if these gen- tlemen succeed in educating the natives of India, to the utmost of their utmost desire, we should not remain in the country for three months.' 'Not three weeks,' answered Tagore.[22] No one then or for many years to come could foretell when this might occur.

What the education system did produce was a body of men, all from prosperous backgrounds, who, by the last quarter of the century, were chafing against what they conceived as intolerable official constraints on their ambitions. The glittering prize for the Indian graduate was passing the examination for the ICS. Even failure carried a certain status: in 1912 a newspaper job advertisement asked for 'a B.A., or Failed Civil'.[23] Man Ghose believed that, to compete successfully, it was imperative for an Indian to study in Britain, where he would 'acquire that refinement and independence of thought and action that alone can place them on an equal footing with Englishmen'.[24] For a time in the late 1860s, the government contemplated awarding scholarships for Indians to study at British universities, but rejected the idea on the grounds that it would favour Bengalis. There was some consolation; the authorities decided that they would appoint a number to middle-ranking posts without a prior examination. Indian penetration of the higher echelons of the government remained difficult and progress was slow; in 1909 there were 65 out of the 1,244 members of the ICS were Indian.

Behind this measure and all the Raj's dealings with the educated Indian classes was a profound feeling that they were a tiny minority whose ambitions had to be actively discouraged. Most were high-caste Bengalis whose advancement to positions of authority over other Indians would exacerbate existing caste and religious divisions, for the official mind was convinced that, however many examinations a native passed, he could never shed his religious prejudices. These were indelible and rendered their owner incapable of strict impartiality. Besides, the educated Bengali was imagined to be the host to a number of moral shortcomings which disbarred him from the highest offices: he preferred words to action, lacked natural authority, was prone to venality and crumpled in a crisis. Dufferin detected in the 'Bengali babu' an affinity with the Irish nationalist, with both possessing 'perverseness, vivacity and cunning'.

The educated Indian was sometimes a comic figure on account of his occasional malapropisms, known as 'babuisms'. Lytton found them delightful and relayed them home for the amusement of, among others, Queen Victoria. One, selected by him, may serve as an example of others. It concerned an English judge who enquired why an Indian barrister's female client was not in court. 'I beg your pardon, Mr Chunder [Chandra] Ram, but is your client an adult?' 'No, my Lord,' was the reply. 'She is an adultress.' Underlying this mockery was the feeling that the babu acquired knowledge without ever understanding it properly.

British prejudices were as ingrained as Indian were supposed to be, and were mirrored in a widespread antipathy towards the bhadralok, individually and *en masse*. The servants of the Raj found it all but impossible to regard an educated Bengali as an equal, something which the latter found genuinely bewildering. The barriers were sensed by Bolanath Chandra, a Calcutta graduate and son of a Hindu bania, who was full of admiration for the British and the way in which they were modernising India. Travelling in Awadh in the mid-1860s he detected an unofficial colour bar which excluded him from the company of Europeans:

> A native may read Bacon, Shakespeare, get over his religious prejudices, form political associations, and aspire to a seat in the legislature – he may do all these and many things more, but he cannot make up his mind to board at an English hotel.[25]

Nonetheless, Chandra saw India moving towards a better future. Hitherto incapable of 'the construction of a civil polity' which was not despotic, his countrymen were on the threshold of doing so. The 'political science' which men like himself were learning would eventually create a sense of national coherence and purpose among a people who still lacked 'any patriotism or philanthropy'. And yet, Chandra could not quite shake off his private feelings, for an antagonism towards Islam colours his writing. 'The fusion of the Mahomedan element to form a national Indian mass requires the melting point of granite' he observed, unintentionally adding to British doubts about the ultimate judicial and bureaucratic impartiality of even the most sophisticated Hindu.[26]

British political thought and systems and their adoption in India were among the range of scientific, religious and philosophical subjects debated and discussed by the many associations of educated Indians which had been springing up since the middle of the century. Members of these bodies investigated India's past, examined the foundations of its faiths and contrived ways in which to synthesise Indian traditions of thought with such new European ideas as liberalism and utilitarianism. Like Chandra, they were searching for the intellectual basis for an Indian renaissance, and a few became convinced that this would culminate with self-rule and the adoption of representative government in the British fashion. Members of these associations were well–off, educated professional and business men, the nucleus of India's middle class. Under the Raj they enjoyed complete freedom to assemble and there was never any official attempt to interfere with or restrict what passed during their meetings. Many members were in active public life, serving on the committee which ran Calcutta university, the Calcutta bar association and on the handful of municipal councils. These earnest, well–intentioned men comprised an embryonic political class.

III

These Indian societies might have continued with common goals but separate existences for many years, but for the viceroyalty of Lord Ripon. He replaced Lytton in 1880 and was welcomed by educated Indians, who hoped that he would bring with him the fresh and reforming air of Gladstonian Liberalism. Indians who had followed British politics closely were well aware that the Liberal leader had denounced the 1878 invasion of Afghanistan and had pledged himself to defend the rights of oppressed peoples everywhere. One of Ripon's first measures was the repeal of Lytton's Vernacular Press Act which restrained political comment in native-language newspapers. The time seemed full of promise for India's educated classes. Two of them, Behari Lal Gupta and Romesh Chandra Dutt, then a district officer, proposed that Indian judges and magistrates should be given the right to try Europeans who, hitherto, could insist on trial by a British justice.[27] The suggestion was taken up by Sir Courteney Ilbert, the law member of the viceregal council, who put forward the appropriate amendment to the Indian legal code in February 1883.[28]

For Indians the change was greeted as a gesture towards equality under the law. The European community was horrified and erupted in fury. The reverberations reached Kipling in Lahore and he told his sister that, 'Old stagers say that race feeling has never been so high since the Mutiny.'[29] Something of the heat and passion of the British reaction to this proposal can be seen in one outburst:

> Would you like to live in a country where at any moment your wife would be liable to be sentenced on a false charge of slapping an Ayah to three days' imprisonment, the Magistrate being a copper-coloured Pagan who probably worships the

Linga, and certainly exults in any opportunity of showing that
he can insult white persons with impunity.[30]

This simultaneous appeal to racial, religious and sexual prejudice was typical of the hundreds which poured from India's European community
during 1883 and early 1884 and from those sections of the British press
which championed their cause.

The most strident clamour came from the least attractive section of the
white community in India, the non-official Europeans. In 1883 this class
totalled 29,000, and it contained professional men, entrepreneurs, railway
employees and indigo and tea planters and their wives and children. Their
numbers had grown during the past twenty years as a consequence of
increased investment in plantations and transport. They possessed a strong
sense of solidarity and were very prickly about their standing in a hierarchy which was dominated, socially if not numerically, by government
servants and army officers. Whatever their place in the white man's pecking order, the non-official Indians had no doubts about their superiority
over the natives.

In terms of racial arrogance, the tea and indigo planters had a shameful reputation; like plantation owners and managers in every corner of the
world, the Indian planters believed that they had the right to do as they
pleased with their labour force and exercised it in defiance of the letter of
the law. Consider Gerald Meares, an indigo factory manager from near
Jessore, against whom Panchu Hakara, a *dak* (post) runner, lodged a complaint for assault in April 1874. Meares took revenge by getting his
servants to seize Hakara, bind him and deliver him to their master for
second thrashing. During the beating Meares told his victim, 'If I murder
a man like you what will happen to me?' As both men knew, the answer
was probably nothing. But Meares was found guilty of assault and imprisoned in spite of false alibi evidence provided by three other Europeans,
including his two brothers, both indigo planters.[31] The non-official community was vociferous in its support for Meares and indignant at his
punishment.[32] They believed in a world in which some men were
ordained to deliver blows and some to receive them: during his tour of
India during 1866 and 1867, the politician Sir Charles Dilke noticed
how British station masters kicked and cuffed Indian crowds on railway
platforms.[33] Men of this stamp cared nothing for law, save when it looked
after their interests, and they howled loudest against the Ilbert amendment. If it became law, Indian magistrates might not turn a blind eye to

or deal leniently with planters and managers who mistreated their work-force.

An Anglo-Indian and European Defence Association was formed and held noisy meetings across India. It found powerful and equally strident allies among the London newspapers and journals, with *The Times* and *Daily Telegraph* making the running. There were predictions that planta-tions would collapse in ruin and that every European who ventured into those country areas where Indian magistrates operated would be in danger. Behind the rant were undercurrents of fear that the government was going too far in its efforts to assimilate Indians into the administration. The 62,000-strong Eurasian community feared for its monopoly of railway jobs when a policy of reserving a fixed number of Public Works Depart-ment posts for Indians was introduced. Businessmen were angry about recent factory legislation which protected Indian workers. Together, the disgruntled swung almost the entire white community in India against the government.

By the end of 1883 feelings were running high. Ripon, dismayed by a surge of personal attacks, thought the atmosphere in Calcutta 'electric'. His councillors were divided and nervous, fearing that European emotions might lead to violence which could not be contained by the largely Indian police force. The government caved in; a compromise was cobbled together by which whites facing trial could opt for a British judge and demand juries with at least six of their countrymen. The Anglo-Indian and European Association was jubilant; the Indians bitterly disappointed.

There were several lessons from the Ilbert affair. First, the Raj's boast that all were equal before the law was mere rhetoric and that attempts to enforce it would be strenuously resisted by Europeans. Many high-ranking officials, particularly among the judiciary, were openly hostile to the Ilbert bill. Most important of all, a relatively small body of men and women had deflected the government from its purpose. In doing so they had given Indians a signal demonstration of how to organise politically and enlist out-side support for a single end. Such concerted activities had been a feature of British political life for most of the century: there had been the mass movements for the extension of the franchise, the Anti-Corn Law League and, currently, the Irish Home Rule party. Indians realised that they might do likewise, especially as they had been united in favour of the Ilbert amendment, although lacking an organisation to channel their feelings. In May 1883, the Lahore *Tribune* declared that: 'The Ilbert bill . . . has brought together the people of India of different races and creeds into one common bond of union . . . the growing feeling of national unity which otherwise would have taken us years to form, suddenly developed into strong sentiments.'[34] Inevitably there were demands that like-minded Indians should copy the Europeans and unite under a single umbrella organisation that would represent their national feeling.

The result was the formation of the Indian National Congress, which held its first annual meeting in Calcutta in December 1885. In essence it represented a fusing of many smaller societies from all parts of India. Its overall objective was to hold Britain to its word, which was that the Raj existed for the benefit of Indians who, under its guidance, would advance to a state in which they could manage their own affairs. No one at the time had the slightest idea of how long this process would take, and some members argued that Congress would overreach itself by aiming at home rule. They would have been quite satisfied with a greater share in the day-to-day administration of their country. There was agreement on one issue: Congress was the voice of all India. The reason why was explained by one of its leading members, Romesh Chandra Dutt, in 1898:

> The English-educated Indians represented the brains and con-science of the country, and were the legitimate spokesmen of the illiterate masses – the natural custodians of their interests, and those who think must govern them.[35]

At heart, Congress was fundamentally loyal. At its annual meetings the Queen Empress was referred to as 'Mother' and her name cheered. Such displays were genuine and represented a widespread anglophilia among the organisation's founding fathers. It was rather touchingly expressed during the 1900 session by Achut Sitaran Sathe:

> The educated Indian is loyal by instinct and contented through interest. The English flag is his physical shelter, the English philosopher has become his spiritual consolation. The English renaissance has so far permeated the educated Indian that it is no longer possible for him to be otherwise than loyal and affec-tionate towards the rulers of his choice. He is the vanguard of a new civilisation whose banner is love, charity and equality.[36]

But what about India's old civilisation and religions, whose tenets still held sway over the minds of nearly every other Indian? Here the early nationalists were tormented by the same problem which confronted the Raj. How could modernity in all its forms be reconciled to deep-rooted customs and creeds, many of which, in the light of Western reason, appeared to be brakes on progress? The past need not be a shackle; it could, if properly interpreted, serve as a springboard for the new India. Romesh Chandra Dutt believed that, by discovering their roots, Indians would develop a sense of national pride which would encourage them to achieve greatness again. National pride was essential if Indians were to create national unity. It was a theme which permeated Dutt's histories and historical novels, written in between his duties as an administrator and judge. His history textbook for Bengali schoolchildren, published in 1892, exalted a heroic past and his investigations of ancient Hinduism led him to conclude that roughly between 1000 and 320 BC India had passed through a golden age when art, literature and philosophy had flourished.

Re-evaluating history fostered self-confidence and a novel sense of national identity. It also posed a dilemma for educated Indians. How long could tradition and progress exist before there was a collision? Social reform was necessary, but the price might be excessively high if it led to the uprooting of beliefs and customs which the mass of Indians cherished and, as the British experience proved, would defend. Whatever shape it might take, a programme of enlightened social reform was bound to encounter enormous difficulties, for it could never avoid intrusion into such sensitive areas as caste and the position of women. These were hornets' nests best left undisturbed, for, if agitated, they might reveal the gulf which separated the educated Indian from the masses for whom he claimed to speak. Dabhadi Naoroji, a Parsi businessman and powerful force within Congress, recognised the danger and warned the inaugural session to avoid social reform and stick to purely political objectives.

It was impossible to ignore social issues completely. After a death from haemorrhage of a very young Hindu bride after sex with her husband, the government introduced a law to raise the age of consent from ten to twelve in 1890. The measure provoked a passionate debate among the Indian intelligentsia which spilled over into Congress's annual meeting at Nagpur. A minority favoured the change, but the majority objected on the grounds that it was an intrusion into family life and interference with religion. The police would receive the right to force their way into bedrooms and a troop of obscurantist Hindu clerics claimed that ancient scriptures endorsed the violation of pre-pubescent girls. Muslim clergymen concurred, stating that Muhammad had lain with Ayesha when she was nine.[37]

In the end, Congress came down on the side of custom rather than humanity. Its attitude gave ammunition to its enemies, who invoked James Mill's observation: 'Among a rude people, the women are generally degraded; among a civilized people they are exalted.' According to Kipling, divergent views on the treatment of women would always ensure 'an immeasurable gulf' between his countrymen and Indians.[38] One Indian editor responded by printing reports of sexual misbehaviour in Europe, forgetting that such behaviour was not universally condoned or defended by the religious authorities.[39] Interestingly, the Age of Consent Act proved to be a piece of token liberalism, for there were no prosecutions for the next thirty years.[40]

Putting aside potentially tendentious issues of social reform, Congress turned its attention exclusively to securing a say in India's government. It had two main functions: as a lobby exercising pressure in Calcutta and London, and as a forum for Indian opinion – or, in the words of one Congressman, 'the germ of a Native Parliament'. 'We are British subjects,' insisted Naoroji, and if the Raj denied Indians their rights as such, it was no more than another Asiatic despotism.[41] The quest for these rights was pursued along conventional political lines through resolutions, petitions and lobbying. During the past thirty years Indians who had visited Britain found that there was a knot of British MPs who sympathised with their aspirations and were willing to promote them. Naoroji, whose business regularly took him to London, was among the first to cultivate these friends. Converts were drawn from radical Liberals and Irish nationalists who agreed that Indian interests would be best served if an Indian could speak for them in the Commons.

In 1884 Naoroji was offered an Irish constituency and in July 1886 he contested the London seat of Finsbury (Holborn) as a Gladstonian Liberal. He lost heavily, a casualty of the public reaction against the former Prime Minister's conversion to Irish Home Rule. Naoroji tried again in the July 1892 general election, this time as candidate for Finsbury Central, and won by three votes. His Conservative opponent alleged he had illegally hired cabs to convey his supporters to the polls and demanded a recount. The charges were repudiated and after the second count Naoroji's majority was raised to six![42] He lost his seat in the 1895 general election, as a result of the national swing to the Conservatives. Naoroji had made his point; henceforward, Congress would conduct one part of its campaign within the House of Commons. Its support there was growing, thanks in large part to its London branch which had been started by a former ICS official,

Sir Charles Wedderburn. Through newspaper and journal articles and lobbying MPs, he estimated that after the January 1906 general election there were at least 200 members sympathetic to Congress.[43]

Congress carefully nurtured its British allies. Charles Bradlaugh, the notorious atheist MP for Northampton, who had invited Naoroji and another prominent Congressmen to address his constituents on the misfortunes of India, was, by way of return, asked to attend the 1890 annual meeting of Congress. Proud of his honorary title as 'the member for India', he visited the country. 'The poor Hindoo folk', he wrote afterwards, 'seem to worship me', but he noticed that Rajputs, Parsis and Marathas appeared hostile to Congress.[44] Four years later, Congress invited the firebrand Irish MP, Michael Davitt, to become its president for a year, but he declined. There were also a small group of British Congress supporters, most notably Wedderburn and another retired ICS member, Allan Octavian Hume. They added their weight to a systematic propaganda campaign in India and Britain which was designed to outline Congress's campaign for political reform and highlight the shortcomings of the Raj.

IV

The failures of the government and the misdeeds of its servants were the stock-in-trade of the Indian newspapers. When, in 1883, Hume had urged Ripon to stick by the Ilbert bill because it had the backing of 'public opinion', he had in mind the burgeoning Indian press. It was one of the most remarkable by-products of British rule and, as it turned out, one of its most influential gravediggers. Newspapers in India had a long history which stretched back to the 1790s, and there was an equally long history of official attempts to control them. The Marquess Wellesley had done so, as a wartime measure, and restrictions remained until the 1830s, when the Whig Governor-General Bentinck removed them. In Britain a free press was regarded as the cornerstone of national liberty and an unfree press was the hallmark of tyranny. This laudable application of a principle of British freedom to India was part of that wider Whig programme of uplift and liberalisation. It had unforeseen repercussions.

From the 1860s Indian newspapers and journals proliferated. Most were in native languages with small print-runs and a local circulation, although the expanding rail network and an efficient postal system made it possible for weekly journals to command an extensive readership. By 1885 there were 319 vernacular titles with a total circulation of 150,000, and 96 English language papers with a circulation of 59,000. Most of the native papers were cheap weeklies costing a quarter of anna (less than ½p). Setting up and running such a newspaper was inexpensive, with 2,000 rupees (£160) covering the costs of a hand-operated press and other essentials. Muhammad Ismail Khan, whose Moradabad news-sheet had a circulation of 200, made sixty rupees a month from his enterprise, paying his printer nine.[45] There were a handful of journals with a big readership; in 1895 the Bengali edition of the Calcutta *Bangabasi* was selling 20,000 copies a week and the *Hindi* 10,000, putting them far ahead of their rivals.

Like its competitors, the ultra-nationalist *Bangabasi* depended heavily on stories taken from other journals and comment, most of it knockabout polemic against the government, although, in its case, shafts were also launched against Congress for its lack of spirit. Typical was the following from another Calcutta paper, *Sahachar*, of 25 August 1890:

> PUPIL: Sir, in what relation do Englishmen stand to the people of India?
> TEACHER: The same in which a tiger stands to a lamb . . . the Englishman broke the necks and drank the blood of immeasurable Indians.[46]

Personal abuse of officials was commonplace and usually crude. In 1889 the Punjabi *Hasicher Patrika* described the province's Lieutenant-Governor, Sir George Campbell, as: 'The baboon Campbell with a hairy body . . . His eyes flash forth in anger and his tail is all in flames.'[47] The English language press with a predominantly European readership answered in kind. Kipling's old paper, the Lahore *Pioneer* (circulation 5,000) and the Simla *Civil and Military Gazette* (circulation 4,000), both mouthpieces for British and official opinion, never missed a chance to slate Congress. When Naoroji stood for Parliament, the former quoted Sir Lepel Griffin's comment that he 'no more speaks for Indians than a Polish jew settled in Whitechapel represents the people of England'.[48]

A robust, adversarial press had an enormous impact on Indian politics since the educated classes were avid newspaper readers and, like their counterparts elsewhere in the world, tended to believe what they saw in print. Unrelenting criticism of government policy, jeers at officials and allegations of abuses (several papers claimed that Tikendrajit Singh had been tortured before his trial in Manipur) were corrosive and undermined the prestige of the Raj. It had no choice but to live with this evil. Any attempt to fetter the press would have caused a ruckus inside India and in Westminster. There was, however, an Official Secrets Act in 1888 which forbade the unauthorised publication of government papers.

A waspish native press made it less and less easy for the Raj to implement policies which impinged on Indian sensibilities. Moreover, and this added immeasurably to the government's difficulties, the telegraph carried news fast from one part of the country to another and was impossible to control. The new official predicament was illustrated by reactions to the measures adopted by the Bombay authorities to stem an epidemic of bubonic plague which began in the autumn of 1896. Science had not yet identified the precise cause of an infection which passed into the human bloodstream by way of fleas whose normal hosts were rats. Nevertheless, informed medical opinion believed disease could be arrested by a strict quarantine of the plague-ridden areas, the isolation of victims and disinfecting their homes with limewash. This was extraordinarily difficult in Bombay, where the centres of contagion were tenement blocks of between five and seven storeys which housed as many as 1,000 people, and the city's three public and thirty private hospitals were overwhelmed by the numbers of patients. Interestingly, the best was one of the latter, run by the Parsi community.[49]

At first, the official handling of the epidemic had been feeble. A jittery Elgin feared that over-zealous implementation of the anti-plague code would antagonise Hindus and Muslims, but as the death toll rose and under pressure from Hamilton, the Secretary of State, a more rigorous approach was adopted.[50] In February 1897 a ban was imposed on the annual *haj* (the Muslim pilgrimage to Mecca) and railway passengers were forced to take disinfectant baths at stations. Existing procedures were stringently enforced and tension increased as search parties, often including British troops, scoured Bombay looking for fresh victims. Purdah was disregarded and Hindu women were distressed by being forced to strip to the waist so that their armpits could be examined for the swellings which were the first symptom of infection. Across the country there was an outcry which was taken up by the press. In May, Bal Gangadhai Tilak, the owner-editor of the local Maratha weekly *Kesari* (circulation 13,000), denounced W. C. Rand, one of the co-ordinators of the anti-plague measures, as 'suspicious, sullen and tyrannical'. Seven weeks later, Rand and Lieutenant C. E. Ayerst were shot dead by a pair of Hindu youths in Poona.

The murders shocked the British community and many Congress supporters, including Romesh Chandra Dutt. No senior British official had
been assassinated since 1872 when the Viceroy, Lord Mayo, had been killed
by a Muslim fanatic during a tour of the Andaman islands penal colony. In
London, Hamilton believed that the outrage was directly linked to the
anti-government press which, he believed, was encouraging terrorism as it
had done in Ireland in the 1870s and 1880s.[51] His apprehension had some
substance. Tilak was a Maratha, a *chitpavan* (high-caste Hindu) and militant
nationalist. A member of Congress, his nationalism looked back for inspiration to Hindu resistance against the Mughals and forward to complete
swaraj (self-rule). Violence justified this end and Tilak had been the moving
force behind the revival of Hindu festivals and the cult of Shivaji, a seven-
teenth-century Maratha warrior hero who had fought for independence
against the Mughal empire. His association with the Hindu past had brought
him into contact with local militant Hindu secret societies. This underground movement had been the nursery for the assassins, the Chapekar
brothers, who were subsequently arrested, tried and hanged. Chitpavan
Brahmins, they represented a new, violent strand in Indian nationalism, for
they cast themselves in the mould of the old heroes whom Tilak had
exalted. Damodar Chapekar had once written: 'We shall risk our lives on
the battlefield in national war, we shall spill upon the earth the life-blood of
the enemies [who] destroy [our] religion.'[52] The brothers soon attracted a
cult following among young Hindus. Tilak was charged with sedition on
the grounds that his attack on Rand had been an incitement to violence,
found guilty and given eighteen months. The three Indians on the jury
dissented from the verdict but were outvoted by their European colleagues.

The Bombay plague measures led to further trouble. There was a *hartal*
(strike and closure of all shops and businesses) against them and in October
a crowd of Muslim mill-workers attacked an army doctor, murdered two
British soldiers and burned down a hospital. With or without the encouragement of a hostile press, the Indian peasantry became suspicious of all
efforts to improve their health. There were rumours that inmates were tortured in hospitals, that innoculation would make a Muslim abandon his
faith, and in Cawnpore in 1900 a mob demolished a hospital, killing
several attendants.[53] For the men striving to combat disease and the
English-language press, these acts were manifestations of gross ignorance
and bigotry. In Indian eyes they were gestures whose roots lay in a sense of
powerlessness in the face of an authority which could ride roughshod
over them whenever it chose.

V

When Curzon disembarked at Bombay on the very last day of 1898 he was determined to reassert British power in India and revitalise the Raj. He was approaching his fortieth birthday and possessed a self-confidence and intelligence which marked him out from his immediate predecessors. Unlike them, he had welcomed an appointment which he had been seeking for the past nine years, for he believed his intelligence, vision and temperament made him an ideal Viceroy. His career had followed the almost natural path of a talented young grandee: Eton, Balliol, a seat on the Conservative backbenches, Under-Secretary of State for India and then, in 1895, an under-secretaryship at the Foreign Office. In between his public duties, Curzon had travelled. Between 1887 and 1890 he had toured Canada, the United States, the Far East, India, Persia and Russia, where he visited its newly subdued Central Asian provinces. In 1894–95 he undertook a more ambitious and dangerous excursion which took him into the heart of that remote and turbulent region where the frontiers of the British, Russian and Chinese empire met amid the Pamirs. He then passed through Afghanistan to Kabul for an audience with the amir, for which he purchased a pair of gold epaulettes and some foreign orders and borrowed a large sword.

What he saw of the empire strengthened Curzon's imperialism and taught him to respect the character and work of the proconsuls who ruled in Britain's name. He detected the hand of Divine Providence behind the creation and expansion of an empire which was a supreme force for good in the world. The forces of destiny which had given Britain the mastery of India also demanded that the British remake and uplift its people. It was a duty that could only be performed properly by men of Curzon's patrician cast of mind. Recent experiments with diluted Gladstonian Liberalism had been a recipe for drift and confusion in a country where there was no internal coherence beyond that provided by the state. Essays in democracy would bring chaos; to be effective, power had to flow downwards in India.

Before his departure, Curzon had been urged by the Queen Empress to treat her Indian subjects with tenderness, listen to their grievances and do all in his power to remedy them.[54] He needed no such instructions for he saw himself as a model of an enlightened autocrat and possessed what one of Congress's founding fathers, Surendraneth Banerjea, believed was a genuine love for the Indian people. They did not reciprocate this affection because, in Banerjea's words, it took forms that 'they did not appreciate

[and] which excited their resentment'.[55] Nonetheless, there was applause for Curzon's release of the Natu brothers, who had been detained without trial under a regulation of 1827 for unproven association with terrorism. Injustice of another sort regularly attracted Curzon's attention and aroused his anger: the impunity which British subjects appeared to enjoy whenever they assaulted Indians. So long as Europeans who attacked and even murdered natives got off scot-free or with minimal sentences, Indians would dismiss the Raj's boast that its courts were impartial.

Early in his viceroyalty Curzon's attention was called to two horrific cases which received considerable coverage in the Indian press. The first involved the mass rape of an elderly Burmese woman by a party of soldiers from the West Kent regiment in Rangoon. Their officers did nothing to apprehend the culprits and so Curzon stepped in and had the regiment posted to 'the barren rocks of Aden' for two years, with home leave banned. A second outrage occurred at Sialkot in April 1901, when a pair of drunken privates of the 9th Lancers kicked to death an Indian cook after he had failed to procure them prostitutes. Before dying, he identified his assailants, but the regiment refused to charge them. The commander-in-chief ordered the regiment's winter leave to be cancelled, a mild rebuke for the calculated obstruction of justice. The lancers, who fancied themselves as an élite corps, blamed Curzon and mobilised their friends in the army's high command and at court. But the facts of the case spoke for themselves and Curzon was vindicated, although not by diehards. When the 9th Lancers rode past the Viceroy during the 1902 Delhi durbar they were wildly cheered by a sympathetic crowd of Europeans. Curzon was philosophical about this demonstration, which said so much about the attitudes of his countrymen. Unperturbed, he recalled feeling 'a certain gloomy pride in having dared to the right'. A few days later, after seven Welsh soldiers had murdered an Indian policeman on the Delhi ridge, Curzon remarked: 'It is a pity we cannot have another Review for them to receive a popular ovation.'[56]

In fairness to the military authorities, they were not universally lax in dealing with soldiers who maltreated Indians. A gunner found guilty of striking an Indian woman and using insurbordinate language in 1878 was given just under a year's detention, and two soldiers who assaulted natives during 1884 received sentences of 14 and 112 days' hard labour. All the accused were drunk at the time of their offences.[57] Casual violence of this kind seems to have been common on the railways, where a passenger's ability to pay rather than the colour of his skin dictated which compartment he occupied. Racial friction was the result; in April 1896 a Punjabi entered a carriage to be greeted by a shout of 'Out, you nigger' from a Eurasian. A fight followed, which spilled on to the platform, where a European station master joined in, repeatedly thumping the Eurasian.[58] Incidents like this, and the often exaggerated tokens of respect demanded by some Europeans, were reported in the native-language press, adding to a general impression that the British considered themselves a master race.

And some clearly did. Describing one of his many tiger shoots, Colonel Alban Wilson recalled how he demanded the services of a cowherd. The man refused, claiming that if his beasts were unattended they might be attacked by a leopard. Wilson then summoned another cowherd, ordered him to watch over both herds and warned, 'If any of them are killed, I will send a big man from my camp who will beat your head into a jelly with his shoe.'[59] Another keen sportsman, T. W. Webber, who joined the Forestry Department in 1861, remembered that some of his contemporaries regularly used the word 'nigger' and beat natives. He confessed to having twice struck an Indian and may have regretted it.[60] Curzon imagined that such tolerance was rare among Europeans and blamed what today we call 'racism' for the fact that there was 'no justice in this country in cases where Europeans and Natives are concerned'.[61]

This blemish might in part be wiped away by fair government. Curzon's programme of reform embraced every public institution and was dictated by what he judged to be in the best interests of the natives. Nowadays he is best remembered for his efforts to rescue from dereliction and refurbish the masterpieces of India's ancient monuments, most famously the Taj Mahal. Less well-known was his timely intervention to save the Indian lion from extinction and his refusal to allow the Bombay government to take water from the Gorshoppa falls 'for the sake of some miserable cotton mills'.

Enlightened, far-sighted measures would, Curzon hoped, restore Indian faith in the Raj and, in the process, Congress would wither. 'The Congress is tottering to its fall,' he claimed in November 1900, 'and one of my greatest ambitions while in India is to assist it to a peaceful demise.' By withholding concessions demanded by a minority, the government would show its firmness. India would continue to be guided by British officials, because, in Curzon's judgement, they 'possess partly by heredity, partly by upbringing, and partly by education, the habits of mind and vigour of character which are essential for the task'.[62] Unbending in his adherence to the principles of the Raj, Curzon was also willing to take the offensive against Congress in its heartland, Bengal. At the very end of 1903 the government mooted a plan for the division of the province into East and West Bengal. This made administrative sense, given that the province covered 189,000 square miles and contained 78.5 million inhabitants, but, as Curzon had expected, there was a clamour from the Bengali educated class. One Dacca newspaper claimed that Bengalis in the new western state would be thrown into the company of 'naked barbarians' from Assam (racism in India was not just a British disease), but most protests centred on the notion that Bengal was some kind of political entity rather than the creation of administrative conveniences, which in fact it was. Curzon dimissed this uproar as nothing more than typical Bengali rhetoric which would soon burn itself out. Its intensity was an unmistakable sign that he had taken the right decision.

The issue of the partition of Bengal breathed some life into Congress, which had been flagging, but its influence over the national movement has been exaggerated. The preoccupations of the 1904 Congress were Curzon's recent closing the door to further Indianisation of the civil service and preparations for a campaign of intense lobbying in Britain, where a general election was approaching. However, once Bengal had been sundered, its treatment was singled out as a symbol of Indian impotence and British despotism by militant nationalists who were exasperated by Congress's reliance on persuasion and petition. Neither had yielded very much and Curzon's viceroyalty had revealed a Raj which seemed as strong as ever.

Curzon was recalled in the autumn of 1905, the victim of a campaign of deviousness and political string-pulling engineered by the commander-in-chief of the Indian army, Lord Kitchener. Differences over departmental responsibilities and arrangements for India's defences had swollen into a row and then become a trial of strength. A vain, amoral self-seeker, Kitchener used a wide range of political chicanes: he bullied, intrigued, threatened resignation and used his toadies in the press and the Conservative party.

Within two years of Curzon's departure, Sir Denzil Ibbetson, the Lieutenant-Governor of the Punjab, remarked disapprovingly that: 'The native felt that he had the Viceroy at his back, and under such circumstances the Indian tends to presume and become impatient.'[63] This was ironic, for Curzon had hoped that the sure-handed and humane exercise of absolute power would have satisfied the Raj's subjects and swept away for ever incipient nationalism. This and the demand for more Indians taking decisions remained, and, henceforward, the Raj was forced to find ways in which to come to terms with its greatest contradiction. How could its sub-jects be called 'British' and yet be governed by a system of government which was un-British. The problem was bound to worsen, for those most troubled by the question, the Indian educated class, was growing year by year. Pressure for change would only increase and, as events had already shown, could easily take frightening forms. 'The Extremists of today will Moderate tomorrow,' predicted Tilak, 'just as the Moderates of today are the Extremists of yesterday.'

4

Not Worth the Candle: Wars, Real and Imaginary, 1854–1914

There is a Russian chess manoeuvre known as a 'Maskirovka' which can be adapted for war and diplomacy. It involves a sequence of moves contrived to convince an opponent that certain of his vital pieces are at risk. He reacts by preparing for an offensive which never materialises; instead, his adversary strikes elsewhere, as he had first intended.

During the second half of the nineteenth century, successive Russian statesmen and soldiers employed the Maskirovka strategem against Britain. Through a mixture of diplomatic intrigue, disinformation, railway building and parading armies on frontiers, they persuaded their British counterparts that one day Russia would invade India, either through Persia or Afghanistan, or both. A reservoir of anxiety was created which the Russians tapped whenever it suited them, for it was the only way in which they could harm or exert pressure on a nation which consistently frustrated what they considered to be their rightful ambitions: possession of Constantinople and a free hand in the Balkans. If India was even remotely menaced, Britain had no choice but to strain every nerve and muscle to defend it because, as the Russians knew, it was a vital source of political and economic power. Britain had invested pride, energy and cash in India. Its possession underpinned Britain's status as a world power and, by the end of the century, British investments there totalled £270 million. In a more and more fiercely competitive world market, India was a valuable customer, taking a fifth of all British exports. Popular and press responses to the Indian Mutiny were proof that British public opinion sensed that the loss of India would be a national catastrophe which had to be prevented whatever the cost.

All this was appreciated in St Petersburg which was why, whenever Anglo-Russian relations took a turn for the worse, there were unofficial hints to the effect that British rule in India was precarious and unlikely to survive a hard knock from outside. This was the message of Colonel Terentiev, whose *Russia and England in the Struggle for the Markets of Central Asia* was translated and published in Calcutta in 1875. It was designed to make the flesh creep, with the prophecy that if Russia ever mounted a serious military challenge to the Raj, the Indian army would turn on its masters and the masses would follow suit.[1] General K. P. von Kaufman, the Russian commander in Turkmenistan, struck a raw nerve when, in 1876, he made the 'impudent prediction' that the British would soon plead for his troops to protect them from their Indian subjects.[2] This rankled at a time when reports were filtering through to Calcutta which indicated that many Indians, including some princes, believed that Britain was frightened of the Russians and lacked the will to fight them. In the Madras presidency, disgruntled peasants told tax officials: 'Well, the Russians will be here before long and then we shall see!'[3] This theme of the deep-rooted Indian discontent was revived during the 1884–85 Anglo-Russian confrontation, when an article in a Moscow newspaper claimed that Britain's grip on India would dissolve once a Russian army appeared on its borders and the Cossacks would be welcomed as liberators. The author was supposed to be General Leonid Sobolev, a former chief of the Asian section of the Foreign Ministry, which suggested that the piece reflected official thinking.[4] The notion of the Raj's fragility soon became commonplace; during dinner in an outpost in the Pamirs in 1897 a Russian army doctor assured Captain Ralph Cobbold that the British garrison in India was 'pampered', and that the Cossack would prove no match for the sepoy who, when put to the test, would refuse to fight for his rulers.[5]

London and Calcutta reluctantly agreed with these forecasts. When plans were being prepared for India's defence in 1885 a substantial force was earmarked for internal security.[6] In 1901 it was estimated that at least 129,000 British and Indian troops would have to be kept in reserve for police duties and guarding lines of communications to prevent religious strife, a crime wave and sabotage, all of which would be triggered by a

Russian invasion.[7] Field Marshal Lord Roberts of Kandahar, India's most illustrious soldier, agreed with this bleak prognosis. Always a Cassandra when it came to discussion of the Russian menace, he expected 'grave unrest' the moment the Russians entered Kabul, with worse to follow if they advanced any further.[8] Forgetting for a moment the rough handling his army had received at the hands of the Afghans in 1879–80, he imagined that once the Russians had taken Kabul the whole country would swing behind them. He spoke loudly, often and with authority for the 'Forward' school of strategic thought, which insisted that any Russian threat to India, however indirect, had to be instantly countered by an offensive across the Afghan and Persian frontiers. Political considerations outweighed military, for if an Anglo-Indian army waited on the borders and passed the initiative to its adversaries, British prestige would slump. It would plummet beyond recovery if, by some mischance of arms, that army retreated on to Indian soil.

Roberts's views became the dogma of a small but highly influential knot of senior officers and ministers. Their strength and persuasiveness lay in their knowledge of men and conditions in previously inaccessible regions. Some, mostly soldiers, had at great personal risk traversed deserts and mountains and knew intimately the tribesmen who lived there and the outposts and passes which had not yet appeared on the War and Foreign Office maps. Such knowledge had to be taken seriously by those who shaped policy, and its possessors were, almost to a man, Russophobes whose travels had strengthened their conviction that Russia intended to invade India when the time was right.

There was something in the heady, pure air of the Hindu Kush and Pamirs which infected explorers with a sense of foreboding and opened their minds to all kinds of phantoms. 'No man,' wrote Colonel Algernon Durand, 'in his senses ever believed that the Russian *army* would cross the Pamirs and attack India by the passes of Hunza and Chitral, but we could not overlook the fact that in 1885 when war was in balance, some thousands of troops were moved towards the Pamirs.'[9] He did not ask what might have happened when men and mountains met, nor did he look too closely at the transport and logistical problems which faced even small detachments in this region. A distinguished explorer and cartographer, Durand had led a small force into the Hunza valley in 1892 in a brief campaign of pacification, so he knew exactly what the Russians would be up against. Practical considerations were secondary in such matters; all that counted was the psychological effect of the appearance of Russian soldiers

on India's frontier. Durand and others of his mind had inherited the orthodoxy of the age when India was still being conquered. Then, aggression
and audacity had won fear and respect in equal parts, and this reputation
could only be preserved by attacking Russia without hesitation and with
overwhelming force. So, by a strange paradox, the hawks in London,
Calcutta and St Petersburg concurred: the Raj was brittle and its subjects'
allegiance depended on its capacity to engage its enemies impetuously and
with vigour. Britain's greatest source of strength was also its greatest weakness, and this made it easy for the Russians to play the Maskirovka gambit.

But to what purpose? The move was used on a chess-board that extended from the Balkans and the eastern Mediterranean to the Chinese
borderlands. It encompassed one, over-extended Muslim empire, the
Turkish, and a decrepit one, the Persian. Beyond and to the east lay the
decayed khanates of Khiva, Kokand and Bukhara, Afghanistan and a scattering of tribal entities whose semi-nomadic inhabitants never recognised
frontiers and were a law unto themselves. Seen from the perspective of a
ministerial desk in St Petersburg, this region represented a vast vacuum to
be filled by Russia which had, during the eighteenth century, slowly built
up a momentum of conquest whose direction lay southwards and eastwards. The pace of war and annexation was dictated by a small body of
bored frontier commanders in search of glory and promotion, ultra-
nationalists preaching doctrines of imperial destiny, Orthodox zealots
hoping to reverse centuries of Muslim encroachments, and businessmen
seeking fresh markets.

Their motives were blended into an intoxicating imperialist cocktail
which was served as an aperitif before any new campaign to push back the
frontier, and, it went without saying, advance civilisation. When Tashkent
was stormed in 1865, a regimental chaplain exhorted his men to remember they were Christian warriors avenging hundreds of years of Muslim
occupation of sacred Russian soil.[10] Their commander, Colonel M. G.
Cherniave, a Russian Clive, had defied orders by attacking the city with an
army outnumbered fifteen to one, but when it had fallen he and his men
were given decorations and cash for what Czar Alexander II called 'a glorious affair'.[11] Behind the armies came the railway engineers and entrepreneurs in search of customers and raw materials.

Fulfilling national destiny in Asia was always secondary to the quest for
security in Europe. Geography had been unkind to Russia, confining its
seaboard to the Baltic and Black Sea and giving it a land frontier that
stretched from one to the other with no natural barriers. In the eighteenth

and early nineteeth centuries this border had pushed steadily westwards until it embraced the Baltic States, Poland, and the Ukraine. There was room for further growth at the expense of Turkey, whose Balkan provinces would provide access to the Mediterranean and a position on the flank of the Austrian empire. To this end, Russian forces invaded what is now eastern Romania in the summer of 1853 and soon became unstuck.

Any infringement of Turkish sovereignty was a challenge to Britain. Ever since Napoleon's invasion of Egypt, British regional policy had been guided by the need to create as cheaply as possible a vast buffer zone stretching from the eastern Mediterranean to Afghanistan, which would serve as India's defensive glacis. Its perimeter encompassed the Turkish provinces of Egypt (then more-or-less independent), Lebanon, Syria, Palestine, Arabia and Iraq, Persia and Afghanistan. A web of discreet power had been spread across this area. Its strands were treaties in which petty potentates exchanged subsidies for privileges; a string of consulates in major ports and cities; and a flotilla of warships which cruised in the Red Sea, the Persian Gulf and on the Tigris and Euphrates. There was a naval base and Anglo-Indian garrison at Aden and the Mediterranean fleet which, among other things, was an earnest of Britain's intention to support the Turkish sultan and preserve the integrity of his empire. By these devices, India was protected by a cordon of weak states which Britain was pledged to uphold. If she failed to do so, the area was sure to be parcelled out by the European powers, most notably Russia which had already stripped Persia of its Caucasian territories and most of the Caspian shoreline.

India's safety would be jeopardised if Russia were allowed to proceed with the dismemberment of the Turkish empire. This argument was invoked in 1853 and set Britain on a collision course with Russia, which culminated with the Anglo-French invasion of the Crimea in the later summer of 1854. The war which followed was a salutary humiliation for Russia; in less than eighteen months its armies suffered four defeats and it was forced to scuttle its Black Sea fleet and abandon the fortified base at Sebastopol. Furthermore, during 1854 and 1855 a British squadron had entered the Baltic, sailed at will and bombarded various shore installations. Worst of all, the war had revealed that the Russian army was hopelessly backward and its government lacked friends in Europe. On the other hand, Britain secured a French alliance and Austrian co-operation, which together tipped the military and political balance decisively against Russia. Fears that Britain might revive this coalition in the future made Russian diplomats extremely cautious in pressing claims in the Turkish Balkans or Persia.

A skilfully played Maskirovka gambit against India offered Russia its only chance to neutralise Britain. During the Crimean war there had been some high-level consideration given to a diversionary blow against India, but it was no more than wishful thinking since 1,800 miles of steppe, desert and mountains separated Russian outposts from the Indian frontier. Nonetheless, the Russian staff officers imagined that their own and, for that matter, the British army could overcome geography without too much trouble. Soon after the end of the Crimean war, it was feared in St Petersburg that the British might follow up their victory with a two-pronged offensive from the Persian Gulf and Afghanistan against Russia's fledgling colonies east of the Caspian. The result would be another catastrophe for Russia: 'The appearance of the British flag in the Caspian Sea would be a death-blow not only to our influence in the East and to our external trade, but would jeopardise the political independence of the Empire.'[12] The only defence against this hypothetical attack was a counter-stroke against India, but this was overruled by the Foreign Minister, Prince Gorchakov; with an exhausted army and 800 million roubles of outstanding debts from the Crimean war, Russia was in no position to fight anyone anywhere.

Whenever British and Russian military planners contemplated wars yet to be waged across the expanses of Asia, they were afflicted with a peculiar giddiness. Imaginations ran wild and each side attributed to the other unlimited ambition, grandiose masterplans and the capacity and willpower to see them through. The process of poring over maps, shifting make-believe armies, exploring unknown regions, discovering the temper of their inhabitants and everyday espionage was an extension on a larger scale of the Great Game of the 1830s and 1840s. The pace of play varied and results were hard to judge, although the conclusion of each round was marked by demands in Calcutta, London and St Petersburg for an increased military budget.

II

Contrary to what was conjectured in St Petersburg, Britain had no desire to push India's frontiers into Central Asia. Admittedly there were a few bold spirits, still unchastened by the Afghan débâcle of 1838–42, who contemplated penetration of the region. In 1853 emissaries from the Khan of Kokand had asked Lord Dalhousie for modern guns, ammunition and British officers to prepare his army for a defensive war against Russia. The Governor-General was sympathetic on the grounds that nothing but good could result from making life uncomfortable for a rival Asian power. Sir John Lawrence disagreed violently and persuaded him to reject the khan's pleas, which, if accepted, would draw Britain into an unnecessary and unwinnable conflict.[13]

Lawrence was exceptionally level-headed when it came to the question of how to handle Russia's Asian ambitions. As Viceroy between 1863 and 1869, he adopted the policy of what he called 'masterly inactivity' in the regions beyond India's frontiers. Combining experience and common-sense, he argued that it was military and political folly to imagine that India was best defended by an invasion of Afghanistan. Memories of the last incursion into their country had created a passionate loathing for Britain which would make it impossible for an Anglo-Indian army to hold the Kabul–Kandahar line which, the generals insisted, was the only way to repel a Russian attack. Lines of communication would be dangerously extended in a hostile region where service was unpopular with Sikh and Hindu troops. If Russia chose to occupy her Asian back yard, so be it. She would, Lawrence believed, be a welcome neighbour whose presence would bring civilisation to the region and keep the lid down on its endemic Islamic extremism. As for alleged schemes for the invasion of India, Lawrence was sceptical: it would prove an enterprise more hazardous and debilitating for the Russians than the British. Furthermore, Lawrence suspected that such plans were no more than the bluster of a handful of ultra-nationalist journalists and generals whose rhetoric was ignored by the Czar's ministers. There was nothing to fear and the Russians had nothing to hide. During 1862–63 and at the request of the Indian Survey Department, one of its officers, Colonel J. T. Walker, was sent to St Petersburg for data needed to compile a map of Central Asia. He was warmly received by ministers and geographers who gave him every assistance and, when the map was published in 1866, the Russians forwarded amendments.[14]

Colonel Walker's new map no doubt helped British officials and officers trace the path of the Russian armies which undertook the piecemeal conquest of Central Asia between 1865 and 1885. There were many parallels between these campaigns and those conducted by the British in India. The men-on-the-spot disregarded orders from distant St Petersburg and pressed ahead, justifying themselves with the excuse that they were stabilising a frontier. As in India, the forces employed were comparatively small, well-disciplined, armed with the most up-to-date weaponry, and irresistible. After a few one-sided engagements, their adversaries were left with the choice of annihilation or submission. The khans of Bukhara and Kokand chose the latter and were permitted to rule as Russian puppets. The toughest and most persistent resistance came from below and took the form of jihadic uprisings; there were four in Kokand between 1873 and 1916, and all were crushed in the khan's name by Russian troops.[15] The new régime promised not to tamper with Muslim customs, but Russian governors, like their equivalents in India, soon faced trouble from deeply conservative and devout communities. There were riots during the Tashkent cholera epidemic of 1892 after Russian doctors insisted on the examination of Muslim women, an incident which mirrored the disturbances in Bombay five years later.

Russia's frontier wars attracted many adventurers with a nose for personal profit. E. O'Donovan, a British war correspondent attached to the Russian army in Turkmenistan between 1879 and 1881, discovered many former Circassian and Caucasian brigands among the irregular forces. There were promises of advancement for the rank-and-file conscripts. On the eve of one sortie, General Lazarev recited tales of past glories to the men of his former regiment, pointed to the stars on his uniform, reminded his listeners that he had once been an NCO and pledged promotion for those who performed their duty well. He was cheered and afterwards vodka was distributed.[16] In the wake of the soldiers came Russian peasant settlers from over-crowded and under-productive lands in the west; by 1911 these *irodtsky* (aliens) totalled 1.54 million.[17] Tension between them and the four to five million indigenous inhabitants was inevitable, and clashes were frequent.

In the hope that they might mislead the suspicious British, the Russians took steps to disguise the reality of power by claiming that the former Muslim states were dependencies rather than conquered provinces. No one was fooled: a War Office report of 1882 noted that the Khan of Bukhara's army now wore Russian uniforms and was commanded by Russian officers.[18] The flow of settlers added to the impression that, to all intents and purposes, the region was as much a part of the Russian empire as, say, Poland or Latvia. Obviously, Russian expansion disturbed those in London and Calcutta already predisposed to believe that Russia would not be satisfied with an eventual frontier on the Oxus or the Pamirs. But there was nothing to indicate that the campaigns in Central Asia were a preliminary to more ambitious enterprises which, if allowed to proceed, would endanger India. Indeed, the Russians went to considerable diplomatic lengths to dispel suspicions that their activities were a threat to India. Nor was this window-dressing. A secret agent sent by the Maharaja of Kashmir to Tashkent in 1865 was sent packing by the authorities there with an emphatic denial that Russia was considering an invasion of India, and the same treatment was given to another emissary five years later.[19] Neither mission was known to the Indian government.

The era of 'masterly inactivity' and tolerance of Russia's Central Asian ambitions ended in the winter of 1877–78. It was terminated by the crisis in Europe which followed Russia's armed intervention in favour of assorted Balkan nationalists who had rebelled against Turkish rule. What Russian nationalists hailed as a war of liberation was interpreted by Disraeli's government as a flagrant attempt to infiltrate south-eastern Europe and possibly seize the Straits. Opinion in Britain was bitterly divided: Conservatives favoured propping up Turkey for the traditional reason of Indian security, while Liberals and Radicals, led by Gladstone, backed Russia as the champion of maltreated and misgoverned peoples fighting for their freedom. Realpolitik gained ground over sentiment at the beginning of 1878, when Russian forces approached the northern shores of the Bosphorus and came within sight of Constantinople's skyline. They also saw the battleships of the Mediterranean fleet, ordered to the Straits by Disraeli as a token of Britain's determination to defend Turkey.

War seemed imminent, and in April orders were sent from London to Calcutta for Indian reinforcements to be shipped to Malta in all haste. The response was heartening. Lytton informed London that 'all the best fight-ing elements in our native army in every part of India' were clamouring for a chance to fight against Russia.[20] Many of these ardent volunteers – Pathans, Baluchis, and Afridis – were Muslims, for whom Turkey was the chief guardian of Islam and whose ruler, the sultan, was also the hereditary khalifa, successor to the Prophet and spiritual leader of all Sunni Muslims. For them the forthcoming war was a jihad. Russia now faced not only a possible holy war but an alliance between Britain and Austria which, as in 1854–55, was unwilling to permit a Russian sphere of influence extend-ing across the Balkans to the Adriatic. Given the combination of powers ranged against her, and the heavy losses of men and treasure incurred during the recent Turkish war, Russia was forced to back down and accept political defeat at the Congress of Berlin in July 1878.

In an attempt to stave off the inevitable, the Russian government played a Maskirovka move designed to weaken British resolve and secure more favourable terms at the conference table. India was the intended target of this feint. At the outset of the war and in anticipation of British hostility, General Mikhail Skobelev had proposed a limited advance to Kabul. Its occupation would be temporary for, he argued, 'our presence can only be justified by the urge towards contributing to the solution of the Eastern Question in our favour, otherwise the game is not worth the candle and expenditure in Turkestan would be a waste'. In January 1878, with an exhausted Russian army checkmated outside Constantinople, General Kryjhanovsky, the governor of Orenburg, suggested a diversionary expedition into Persia. The War Ministry rejected this plan because funds were short and all available troops had to be concentrated in the Near East to face a possible Anglo-Austrian counter-offensive. The only alternative left was a small-scale demonstration on the Oxus and a well-publicised political mission to Kabul.[21] During May General von Kaufman mobilised his entire force of 20,000 men and declared that he was ready to establish a Russian sphere of influence over Afghanistan. One of his more indiscreet officers boasted: 'Now we march to India and drive out the English.'[22] At the same time, General Leonid Stoletov rode to Kabul, brushing aside Afghan protests, and delivered the Czar's terms to the amir, Sher Ali. He was too late; the Berlin agreement was signed in July and he was immediately recalled to St Petersburg.

Von Kaufman's sabre-rattling on the Oxus and Stoletov's brief appearance at Kabul had far-reaching repercussions. As predicted, they created consternation in Calcutta, where Lytton was already considering ways to bring Afghanistan more closely into Britain's orbit. He was also perturbed by what he imagined to be a decline in Britain's standing throughout India. These preoccupations made him susceptible to the advice of two advocates of the Forward policy: the up-and-coming General Roberts, Quartermaster-General of the Indian army with responsibility for intelligence and operational planning, and Major Louis Cavignari, the deputy commissioner at Peshawar. They presented the Viceroy with the means to show Sher Ali that Britain and not Russia was the paramount power in the region and, at the same time, restore British prestige. The formula was simple: an outraged Calcutta would send an agent to Kabul with powers to negotiate the terms of future Anglo-Afghan relations and if, unlike Stoletov, he was rebuffed, the big stick would be wielded. In August General Sir Neville Chamberlain (the inventor of snooker) was ordered to Kabul on a mission to secure a partial surrender of Afghan sovereignty.

As expected, Sher Ali refused permission for the commissioner and his escort to enter his country, fearing with good reason that Chamberlain would demand a partial surrender of Afghan sovereignty. An ultimatum followed which expired in November, by which time preparations for war were well advanced. Once the fighting had begun there were rumours that the Russians had become involved and had taken Kabul and Herat.[23]

In many respects the second Afghan war resembled the first. The most striking similarity was the hubris which infected proconsuls and commanders. It was less excusable in 1878 since Lytton, his advisers and generals should have been aware of what had happened to their predecessors and why. Superior weaponry naturally engendered self-confidence. The past forty years had witnessed a revolution in military technology, which had opened a vast gap between the Anglo-Indian and Afghan armies. British troops were armed with the breech-loading Martini-Henry rifle, Indian with the obsolescent Snider, another breech-loader. Both were accurate to over 1,000 yards and fired soft-nosed bullets, which inflicted hideous wounds. There were also rifled cannon, which fired shells at ranges of over 5,000 yards against which no Afghan mountain fort could stand. A few British units were equipped with the new Gatling machine-guns, which fired 600 rounds a minute for up to mile, although they proved a disappointment. The pair deployed during the battle of Charasiah jammed like the one in Sir Henry Newbolt's poem after a few seconds.[24] Communications between units were facilitated and speeded up by field-telegraph lines and, when the sun shined, heliographs which flashed messages from hillside to hillside. Despite a number of Snider rifles scattered among the tribesmen, the Afghans still relied on their traditional muzzle-loading jezails. As in 1838, the Afghans initially proved incapable of concerted resistance, confirming the official belief that they were an instinctively anarchic race riven by feuds. In Roberts's words, for the past sixty years, 'Disintegration had been the normal condition of Afghanistan.'[25] Dividing and ruling it seemed to present few difficulties.

The objectives of both wars were also similar. Afghanistan was to be transformed from a neutral buffer state into a British satellite, with an amir firmly under the thumb of the British resident in Kabul. In 1878 this arrangement ideally fitted the plans advocated by apostles of the 'Forward Policy', for it would guarantee free access to those two pivots upon which India's defences would ultimately rest: Kandahar and Kabul. The non-military mind, undisturbed by nightmares of Cossack hordes riding down Afghan passes, was sceptical. Disraeli's Cabinet was apprehensive and urged

Lytton not to get too deeply entangled in Afghan politics and to keep
annexations to a minium. The Liberal opposition denounced the war as
immoral; the lives, property and freedom of the Afghan people were being
sacrificed merely to prepare for a war which might never occur. Gladstone,
for whom politics was a series of moral choices, condemned the war as an
example of reckless aggression unworthy of a high-principled, Christian
nation. His pulpit oratory and appeals to the national conscience touched
the right chord, both in his Midlothian campaign during the autumn of
1879 and in the general election which swept the Liberals to power the
following spring.

Public unease about the war was aroused by the press. War correspondents cabled home disquieting reports of atrocities which provoked
questions in the Commons. Maurice Macpherson of the *Standard*, attached
to General Roberts's Kurram Valley column, described the burning of villages, the killing of captives and an occasion when the general had ordered
Indian cavalrymen to take no prisoners. Roberts considered him an
'unmitigated cad' whose stories were distortions, and ordered his expulsion
from Afghanistan at the beginning of February 1879.[26] It was probably a
popular decision with the army. Gilbert Elliot, the future Lord Minto, then
attached to Roberts's staff, expressed a widespread exasperation when he
wrote to his mother: 'I long to encamp the British public in a place like Ali
Khey for a night with Gladstone, Chamberlain, Dilke [both Radical MPs]
and a few others on outpost duty.' Soon after, he complained about the
way in which the newspapers were swaying public opinion from one emotional peak to another. The British public 'is the most sensational ass I
know. Capable either of preaching humanity towards brutes like these
people here, or losing their head and going into lightstrikes when the
savage gives them the worst of it.'[27]

The opening stage of the campaign gave cause for celebration and, in
Calcutta, sighs of relief. The one-armed Mutiny veteran General Sir Sam
Browne VC (designer of the belt which took his name) forced the Khyber
Pass by taking Ali Musjid on 21 November 1878. A month later, Roberts's
column won the battle of Peiwar Kotal. The way to Kabul was opened and
Sher Ali prepared to flee to Turkmenistan, but was refused entry by the
Russians who had enough on their plate with frontier-pacification oper-
ations and had no wish to antagonise Britain. He died in February 1879,
leaving the British free to play kingmaker. With their support, Sher Ali's
elder son, Yakub Khan, became amir and in May he signed the treaty of
Gandamak. Under its terms, he accepted Cavignari as resident in Kabul

and an annual subvention of £60,000 in return for which the British were given control over the Khyber Pass and allowed to annex various frontier districts. Henceforward, Russian influence would be totally excluded from Afghanistan, for its foreign policy was to be decided in Calcutta. In the next few months, nearly all the captains and their armies returned to their cantonments in India, leaving Cavignari and his small escort in the residency in Kabul. On 5 September he and his guards were killed after the building had been stormed by a mob largely made up of unpaid and mutinous soldiers.

Like Sir Alexander Burnes over thirty years before, Cavignari had been the victim of his own over-confidence. Both men mistook endemic Afghan disorder for a lack of national feeling and failed to appreciate the depth of hatred felt against the alien, infidel power which had usurped the government. Lytton's policy was in shreds and it was imperative that British prestige was restored swiftly and decisively. Roberts was ordered to take command of the only substantial force left in Afghanistan, the Kurram Valley force, and lead it to Kabul. Once there, in accordance with Lytton's instructions, 'Your objects should be to strike terror and strike it swiftly and deeply; but to avoid a "*Reign of Terror*".'[28] Those implicated in what Lytton called a 'national crime' were to be 'promptly executed in the manner most likely to impress the popualtion'. Roberts followed his orders with the utmost zeal; sweeping aside Afghan resistance at Charasiah on 6 October, he occupied Kabul after a fortnight's fighting at the end of December. There were punitive demolitions of public buildings, and eighty-seven men convicted by drum-head courts-martial of involvement in the attack on the residency were publicly hanged.

Roberts was now master of Afghanistan, or at least those parts of it which could be reached by British troops. Kipling's self-effacing but highly efficient General 'Bobs' was a short, pugnacious careerist officer with a reputation for kindliness towards his men ('Bobs your uncle') and deep affection for the Indian soldier. Gilbert Elliot found him 'full of go' and he appears to have tolerated heavy drinking among his staff officers.[29] As military ruler of Afghanistan for the first six months of 1880, Roberts ruthlessly applied martial law and stoutly defended himself against charges of inhumanity. Tough measures were the only way to hold down a people who detested their new overlords:

> In addition to the natural hatred which every Afghan feels towards a foreign invader, there is a strong underlying current of

fanaticism which, unless promptly checked, becomes at times, and especially against a Christian enemy, uncontrollable.[30]

The same might have been written by a Russian general a hundred or so years after. For the time being, Roberts's task was to hold the lid down on popular passion by punitive campaigns. The season for these began in the spring, and so his soldiers relaxed in their cantonments; the *Illustrated London News*'s war artist sent home lively sketches of a tug of war between an elephant and various British and Indian soldiers and a race between native *dhooly* (palanquin) bearers.[31]

In London and Calcutta ministers were endeavouring to cobble together a policy that would salvage something from the disaster, preferably a neutral and neutered Afghanistan. Roberts's recent victories had raised hopes that the country might be partitioned, with Herat given to Persia, Kandahar placed under a British stooge and Kabul under a new amir. Yakub Khan had been dethroned and exiled for suspected collusion in Cavignari's murder, and feelers were being put out to two candidates: his younger brother, Ayub Khan, the Governor of Herat, and his nephew, Abdul Rahman Khan, who was living in Samarkand. Whoever was selected would inherit an undivided state, for, in May, the new Liberal government recalled Lytton and replaced him with Ripon, who had instructions to bring all troops out of Afghanistan. It was a setback for supporters of the Forward policy, but Roberts felt sure that in any emergency a British army would be able to re-occupy Kabul and Kandahar without difficulty.

Plans for the evacuation were upset by Ayub Khan, who had stirred up an anti-British jihad to unite the tribes around Herat. Vague details of his activities had been reaching the local commander and political officer in Kandahar since the turn of the year, but had caused little concern. Early in June he sallied out of Herat with, according to intelligence estimates, between 6,000 and 8,000 followers; in fact he had well over 10,000. Counter-measures were taken and a brigade of 1,500 British and Indian troops together with Afghan levies raised by Sher Ali Khan, the puppet *wali* (governor) of Kandahar, was sent to intercept Ayub Khan. The Afghans soon switched sides, having no desire to fight for unbelievers against their countrymen. Command of this detachment was given to Brigadier George Burrows, an unusual choice since he was sixty-three years old and had never seen active service. He was a man of great charm with a tenderness towards animals and, as it turned out, enormous reserves of courage.[32] True to the traditions of Indian warfare, Burrows was determined to take the offensive, even though he had no indication of Ayub Khan's strength or movements.

On 27 July the armies met at Maiwand, forty-six miles from Kandahar. Burrows trusted to superior firepower, particularly the volleys of the 66th Regiment, the backbone of his force. The Afghan attacks were persistent and their artillery was well-handled, so well that it was imagined that European officers were directing fire.[33] Many of the Indian troops were new recruits, inadequately trained, who crumpled under pressure and began to desert. The tide turned against the British, despite a heroic last-ditch stand by the remnants of the 66th, which lost two-thirds of its strength. Burrows gave his horse to a wounded colleague, but was later rescued by an Indian sowar. He had lost nearly half his men, having inflicted over 2,500 casualties on a determined and well-led adversary. The Afghans murdered their prisoners and a soldier was wise to heed Kipling's advice:

> When you're wounded and left on Afghanistan's plains,
> And the women come out to cut up what remains,
> Jest roll to you rifle and blow out your brains
> An' you'll go to yor Gawd like a soldier, . . .

The defeat at Maiwand was followed by the siege of Kandahar. Roberts, with 10,000 men, two-thirds of them Indian, rushed to the relief of the city in an epic march from Kabul which was also a masterpiece of logistical planning. His forces covered 313 miles in twenty-two days in temperatures which ranged from freezing to 100 degrees. On 1 September he engaged Ayub Khan's forces and beat them with slight losses, avenging Maiwand, restoring British prestige and ensuring that the war ended with a flourish. Many years after, Roberts's heroic march was magnificently commemorated by a statue in Glasgow's Kelvingrove Park. The general sits firmly astride his horse on a plinth around which there are strongly carved panels showing Indian and British troops on the march in full kit.

The second Afghan war achieved very little beyond adding significantly to local anglophobia. The new amir, Abdul Rahman Khan, proved a shrewd prince who ruled independently but without upsetting Calcutta too much. Politically, Afghanistan was restored to what it had been at the outset of the war: a neutral buffer state. Roberts and the Forward camp still clung to their belief that an Anglo-Russian war was unavoidable, and it would be best for Britain if it was fought on Afghan and Persian soil. Its outcome filled him with foreboding, for he imagined that the sepoy would prove no match for the Russian conscript. In 1884, on the eve of his appointment as commander-in-chief of the Indian army, he wrote, 'Only a limited number of our native troops could be depended upon to fight against a European enemy, and unless we show a bold front, and let it be clearly seen that we intend to win, even these few would most assuredly question the policy of remaining faithful.' The only hope lay in recruiting more of the naturally warlike 'martial' races and castes such as Gurkhas, Sikhs and Dogras.[34]

III

After 1880 the local military initiative passed to Russia. For the next four years its forces fought a series of campaigns which put the finishing touches to the conquest of Turkmenistan. In January 1881 General Skobelev took the fortress of Gek Tepe, and in February 1884 Merv was occupied, bringing the Russian frontier to within 600 miles of the Indian. During the next few months, General Komarov's pacification operations took a new turn as Russian units probed southwards into the ill-defined borders between Turkmeni tribal lands and Afghanistan. What appeared to be a reconnaissance force came at a bad time for Britain, whose army was heavily committed to a campaign in the Sudan to rescue General Gordon from Khartoum, where he was besieged by the Mahdi. It failed, and in February 1885 Gladstone's government was reluctantly compelled to mount full-scale war to reconquer the Sudan. The Russians had carefully followed the course of events there and sensed that the time might be right to snatch an advantage in Central Asia.

On 11 February the Foreign Office received an account of conversations which Colonel Chevenix Trench, the military attaché in St Petersburg, had recently had with some Russian officers. They had told him that, once the military position around Merv had been consolidated, Russian forces would pounce on Herat. Chevenix Trench suspected that this *coup de main* would be delivered 'a month or two hence, as soon as a large portion of our Forces are locked up in Egypt and the Sudan and are fairly committed to a somewhat lengthened campaign'.[35] His prognosis confirmed intelligence reports which had been reaching London during the past six months.

A new round in the Great Game was about to be played and, for the first time, the British could rely on an intelligence network that provided solid evidence of what the Russians were doing. One, possibly the only, positive result of the second Afghan war had been an overdue overhaul of British political and military intelligence. Before the invasion of Afghanistan, efforts to map the frontier districts had been desultory, partly for fear of antagonising local tribes. When a section of the Kandahar Field Force had returned to India by way of the Peshun valley, it had been marching blindly.[36] A systematic programme of map-making was started and native agents were recruited and trained for espionage in Afghanistan and Central Asia. Colonel T. E. Gordon, who joined the newly founded Indian Army's Intelligence Department at Simla in 1879, recalled one volunteer, Nur ad-Din, a former Guides sowar, who adopted the appearance of a *diwana* (imbecile). This masquerade placed him under Allah's special protection and allowed him to travel as far as the Oxus to investigate Russian activities. Like other recruits, he had served in the army and had to be taught to read and write.[37] Mashad, the capital of the Persian province of Khorassan and conveniently close to the Russian border, was, from 1881, the centre for a network of native spies under the direction of the consular agent, Mirza Abbas Khan, and Colonel C. E. Stewart, the consul.[38] The town possessed a telegraph office that linked it to Tehran, which was invaluable, although, like other Persian public services, it often broke down. A further source of information was General Sir Peter Lumsden, who had been sent with a sizeable military escort to Sarakhs as part of a commission enpowered by the British and Russian governments to establish a Russo-Persian boundary. He arrived at his destination on 31 October 1884 to find that the Russian commissioners would not appear until the spring.[39]

From these sources came a steady flow of intelligence during the winter of 1884–85 which strongly indicated that the Russian pacification of Turkmenistan had been a prelude to large-scale incursion into what, even in the absence of a formal frontier, was assumed to be Afghan territory. Lumsden and the Mashad-based spies uncovered indications that the Russian thrust would be directed against Pandjeh.[40] Local tribesmen believed that there were at least 3,000 Russian soldiers in the vicinity, but as usual with such sources it was very hard to sift fact from rumour. The latter was running wild throughout the region: Turkmeni tribesmen imagined that there were 12,000 British troops in Herat, on hand to help them expel the Russians, and the Afghans were convinced the boundary commission was a cover for an Anglo-Russian partition of their country. This, so the tale went, would lead to the corruption of women and the over-throw of Islam.[41] According to one report received by military intelligence in Peshawar, the Russian invasion was already in progress, with 25,000 soldiers moving towards Herat and a further 35,000 on their way from St Petersburg. In December Peshawar's spies brought stories of heavy concentrations of men in Kokand, Tashkent and Samarkand.[42] At the same time, what purported to be a Russian proclamation to the Afghan people came into British hands. It read as if it had been written for distribution as the Russian army advanced: 'What will the British Government do for Amir Abdul Rahman? They will do for him what they did for Amir Sher Ali. Every ruler who wishes to retain his country should submit to Russian rule, otherwise he will be deprived of it.'[43] This was hardly reassuring for the Afghans and added to British fears that an offensive was imminent.

Matters were clarified in the new year. Early in February the Russian government expressed an interest in negotiating a frontier with Afghanistan and, at the same time, began to occupy Afghan outposts.[44] Under Foreign Office instructions, Lumsden and his escort withdrew towards Herat as a precaution against an accidental clash with the Russians which might lead to war.[45] The Russian big push came on 31 March when a force stormed and captured Pandjeh, killing over 300 of its defenders. Assuming, as nearly everyone in the India, War and Foreign Offices did, that Russia was capable of any infamy when it came to expanding its empire, two alternatives emerged. The Czar's army was going to draw the border with its bayonets or else it was about to creep forward into Herat, 100 miles to the south of Pandjeh. If it did either, Britain would declare war.

The stand-off was in many ways like an extended 1962 Cuban missile crisis. Gladstone's ministry and its successor under Salisbury (which came to power in June) declared that India's security was non-negotiable. Armies were mobilised in Britain and India and plans were drawn up in Simla for an advance to Kandahar. Russia was in an awkward position; it had made a maladroit attempt to snatch Afghan territory, had come unstuck and was faced with a war it had never intended to fight. In February 1884 Cherniaiev, the hero of Tashkent, had been rebuked and recalled after he had put forward a scheme for the invasion of India. Even if it had wanted to fight such a war, Russia lacked the money and the muscle; in the middle of the 1886 Bulgarian crisis, its high command were forced to admit that they lacked the resources to withstand an Austrian invasion.[46]

Britain's scope for action was also limited because it lacked potential allies. This was the period in which the great European powers were embarking on their often acrimonious partition of Africa, and international tension was high. France was bitter at the recent British occupation of Egypt, and Germany used Britain's embarrassment in Central Asia to secure concessions in Africa and the Pacific. As the German Chancellor, Bismarck, rightly guessed, Britain would need friends if it chose to fight Russia. None were forthcoming, nor a convincing strategy. During the spring and summer statesmen and generals scrutinised maps and devised stratagems, none of which was very practical. Turkey, still sore about the takeover of Egypt, would resist the navy's passage through the Straits, which ruled out an attack on Russia's Black Sea coast. Turkey's arm might be twisted by a landing on the Gallipoli peninsula, but this scheme was wisely shelved. Another forlorn hope was an alliance with China.[47]

Without any clear means to injure each other, the two powers came to terms. In September it was agreed that the Russo-Afghan border should be settled by an Anglo-Russian commission. It completed its task within two years. The work appears to have been most congenial as British and Russian officers with common interests enjoyed each others' company. Colonel Holdich later recalled pheasant shoots, disappointing camel fights and relaxing evenings around campfires during which he developed a taste for rye bread, caviare, salt fish and vodka. The last, he discovered, was a less efficacious restorative than whisky and ginger.[48] Cheerful relations between British and Russian officers were a constant feature of the Great Game and whenever their wandering paths met there were impromptu parties. Crossing the Pamirs on a quest for the *mir* (ruler) of Hunza in 1889, Francis Younghusband and his Gurkha riflemen encountered another explorer, Colonel Grombtchevski. The Polish officer was 'a thorough gentleman' who made no bones about his mission and its implications. 'We are both playing at a big game,' he told Younghusband, 'and we should not be one jot better off for not trying to conceal the fact.' Grombtchevski boasted that half a million Russian soldiers were ready to invade India, and his Cossacks cheered when he asked them whether they wished to join this enterprise. A convivial evening ended with brandy.[49]

Grombtchevski's talk was disinformation, as Younghusband probably guessed. The intelligence services of the British and Indian armies knew more or less exactly how many troops were stationed in Russian Central Asia, their movements and their operational efficiency. An unpublicised (many details were not realised until this decade) but vital aspect of the

Great Game was systematic espionage by native agents scattered between the Caspian and the Chinese frontier. At the hub of these operations was Colonel Charles Maclean, a Mutiny and Afghan war veteran, who was consul-general in Mashad from 1885 to 1891. He was an ideal spymaster in that he was diligent, untrusting and a good judge of character. His expenses, together with funding for running repairs on the telegraph lines which linked him with Tehran and ultimately London, were paid by the Treasury, which in those days was keen to get value for money.[50]

Maclean's spies were recruited locally from natives who needed his rupees. At one level there was a handful of venal Persian and Afghan officials anxious to supplement their incomes. A Mashad telegraph clerk supplied copies of the telegrams sent by the Russian consul, although it is not clear whether they were in cipher and, if they were, whether the British possessed the key. Nonetheless, he was paid 100 rupees ($£8$) a month for 'running a great risk'. Russian consulates were kept under close surveillance through spies on their staff, including Mirza, a servant of the Russian consul in Mashad. There was also the postmaster-general of Khorassan province, who was instrumental in placing a valuable agent in Merv. Another fruitful contact was one of Abdul Rahman's news collectors, who forwarded letters and telegrams which were worth 400 rupees a month.[51] Field agents were of two kinds: men specially chosen for a task and professional intelligence gatherers based in Russian towns and outposts. Among the former were Muhammad Reza, who, although illiterate, managed to secure photographs from Turkmenistan in 1886, and Reza Beg, who was sent to check up on permanent agents over the border in March 1887. According to Maclean, he had been 'for many years a hand aboard a Russian steamer in the Caspian' and therefore knew Russian. 'A promising man', he might, the colonel feared, be a double agent.[52]

The full-time spies in Bukhara, Merv, Samarkand, Iolantan, Chardzhou and Pandjeh were of varying reliability in all matters save collecting their pay. In January 1887 Maclean reported that: 'Either owing to snow, or treachery or fear of discovery they have not acted up to their agreements. They will be kept for another month and discharged thereafter if they show no improvement.'[53] The turnover at this level appears to have been high, which suggests that either the agents were slack or Russian counter-intelligence good. In 1889 a fresh attempt had to be made to establish spies in Bukhara, Ashkhabad, Chardzhou, Merv and Pandjeh, who were known by the letters A, B, C and D. Agent B and two of his colleagues were collared in March 1891, after the Russians had discovered secret correspondence in the packs carried by mules on the road between Ashkhabad and Quchan. What happened to them or the unlucky muleteer may only be guessed. In the future, agents were encouraged to write in invisible ink. A fourth spy was sacked that year after he had demanded extra pay.[54]

Maclean's secret service delivered detailed information about Russian strength and dispositions. In November 1887 he was able to forward to the Foreign Office an analysis of Russian frontier garrisons which totalled 11,000 infantry and 2,800 cavalry. He also sent on those snippets of hearsay which were the small change of espionage: in February 1888 there were rumours that a French Hussar officer, the Vicomte Sabran, was about to make a tour of Central Asia for some unknown but doubtless sinister purpose.[55]

A Frenchman accompanied by a Russian were encountered by Kimball O'Hara, the Tibetan lama and Hurry Chunder Mookerjee in the Himalayas towards the end of Kipling's *Kim*. This richly detailed, finely observed novel is probably the best-known account of the Great Game as played. It was also profoundly misleading, endowing the Great Game with a glamour it never possessed, in much the same way as James Bond's derring-do romanticised the intelligence activities of the Cold War. The Indian government's intelligence services were never as omniscient as Kipling imagined, and, while it did employ some resourceful agents, most of its information came by way of the sort of venal informers Colonel Maclean hired in Mashad. There was also an element of propaganda in *Kim*; as might be expected, for Kipling was an admirer of Roberts and the book reflects his fears that 'a friendly northern power' was bent on subversion in India. The novel appeared in 1901, and closely reflected contemporary events; there are references to mischief on the frontiers (there had been a sequence of tribal uprisings on the North–West Frontier in 1897–98), Russian penetration of the Pamirs and possible meddling in the affairs of Tibet.

IV

All were uppermost in the minds of Indian strategic planners at the turn of the century. From the mid-1880s British and Indian intelligence services had become increasingly obsessed with the progress of Russian railway construction in this region. Superficially, it provided the means for economic development, particularly cotton cultivation, and the move-ment of colonists. In Simla and Whitehall the new tracks had one purpose: shifting troops and their supplies. The Russian railway programme began in 1880 with the Caspian line, which ran from from the port of Krasno-vodsk to Merv, which was reached by 1886. It then continued to Samar-kand and terminated uncomfortably close to the foothills of the Pamirs at Andijan in 1899. Branch lines snaked out to Tashkent (1898), Kushk (1900) and Bukhara (1906), where the inhabitants had long objected to railways on the grounds that they were instruments of the devil. A fast line which linked Orenburg with Tashkent was completed in great haste in 1906.

Together these lines represented a fresh danger to India's security. Steps were immediately taken to assess their military efficiency by army officers who posed as travellers. Among the first was Colonel A. Le Mesurier, who went as far as he then could into Central Asia in 1887 and published an account of his journey. There was plenty about engines and rolling stock, which he counted, the speed of trains and Russian habits, most notably women smoking in public.[56] His travelogue is a reminder that, while the Great Game was ostensibly a duel of secret services, the players never mis-sed the chance to rush into print the moment their adventures were over.

Like *Kim*, the publications of men like Le Mesurier, Francis Young-husband and Curzon kept the Russian threat and the Great Game in the forefront of public consciousness. They were also constant reminders that Russia was a rapacious power with its eyes on India. There were dis-senters who both questioned this interpretation of Russian policy and the notion that India could only be saved by a hypothetical war waged some-where in the Afghan passes or the Persian plains. Reviewing Simla's plans for the defence of India in 1889, Sir Garnet Wolseley, the Adjutant-General, wondered whether sending 30,000 reinforcements to India was playing Russia's game. As in 1854 and 1877, its real aim was Constan-tinople, and in consequence the main theatre of war was bound to be in the Near East, or possibly Europe. He had nothing but scorn for any Indian counter-attack:

> Offensive operations against Russia on the Oxus, or in Central Asia, from a base in India, is in my opinion, the dream of a madman, whose head is filled with military theories from the time of Xerxes or Alexander the Great.[57]

Lord Salisbury shared his view of Russian objectives. Any upsurge in Russian military activity in Central Asia was a smokescreen behind which its rulers prepared for an attack on the prize they really wanted: Constantinople. His judgement was upheld when he met Czar Nicholas II at Balmoral at the end of September 1897. A few years before, when he had been Czarevitch, Nicholas had toured India where he and his entourage had raised eyebrows by shooting rather than sticking pigs, and had been discreetly watched by Indian officials fearful as to their real purpose.[58] The emperor fondly remembered his visit for, as he told the Prime Minister, 'it had convinced him of the absurdity of Russia every trying to obtain it'. He added, 'A few Russians had been induced to express a wish for an attack on India by the folly of our newspapers and public men, who were always talking of it; but no Russian Emperor could ever dream of it.'[59]

This was true. But it did not silence the expansionist editors and the generals in St Petersburg, nor calm the Russophobes who were always on the look-out for the tell-tale signs of some new manoeuvre directed towards India. And in any case, Nicholas II did not have a reputation for firmness. By 1890 there were signs that Russia was again on the move, this time towards the Pamirs and Chinese Turkestan. Part of this area had been crossed by Francis Younghusband some years before and, like every British sportsman, explorer and adventurer who found himself in remote lands of possible strategic value, he filed his report with the Foreign Office. What was a 'no-man's-land' between Russia, India, Afghanistan and China appeared to Younghusband to be in China's possession; the British government hoped that things would stay that way.[60]

The frontier, in so far as the word meant anything in the Himalayas, was finally settled by an Anglo-Russian commission in the summer of 1895. The British were led by Captain E. F. Swiney DSO, an Indian cavalry-turned-intelligence officer, and two native NCOs, one of whom had accompanied Francis Younghusband on his trek though this region. Dressed in local padded clothing, balaclavas and tinted snow goggles, they were agreeably entertained by their Russian opposite numbers. Everyone stuck to the rules of the game; at one outpost Russian officers had discreetly covered the perimeter field-pieces so that Swiney could not tell whether they were cannon or machine-guns, and he celebrated Queen Victoria's birthday by presenting a keg of rum to a detachment of Cossacks. Sensitive to all matters of prestige, he was peeved when he noticed that the Czar Nicholas II range of mountains were higher than their opposite numbers on the British side of the border, the Queen Victoria range.[61]

Central Asia

Russian goodwill was bogus; or so Captain Ralph Cobbold believed when he entered the Pamirs two years after. He captured the spirit of the Great Game when he digressed on what animated its players:

> The British officer, jaded with his work in the heat of the plains, is, like a keen sportsman, prepared to rough with the best. He will willingly for a time do without his luxuries, and live, as a Russian officer lives, on what he can get. A month of native chapattis is fully compensated by the mountain air and fine sport available amongst the Himalayas.[62]

Cobbold not only had mountain ibex in his sights. He inspected Russian positions in the Pamirs, counted their garrisons and noted their armaments, for he feared that the region would become a springboard for an offensive southwards. Not surprisingly, he was briefly arrested as a spy, which he indignantly denied. He had lied, for back in London, he duly delivered an account of what he had seen and heard to the Foreign Office. His ears had pricked up when he heard Russian officers praising the new War Minister, Prince A. N. Kuropatkin, whom they hoped would adopt a more pugnacious frontier policy.[63] Most of the speakers were in debt and saw a war as a means to achieve solvency, as Cobbold knew.[64]

Nothing was further from the truth. Kuropatkin was preoccupied with the modernisation of the Russian army and wanted to avoid any entanglement with Britain in Asia. If it occurred, Russia could only afford a half-hearted Maskirovka move by local units which would advance into Khorassan and towards Kabul. According to Russian estimates they would be outnumbered two to one by a combination of Anglo-Indian troops and Afghans whom, it was believed, would resist Russian incursions as fiercely as they had British.[65] A different picture of Russia's military capacity was being drawn in London and Simla, where the recent extension of the railway to Kushk on the Persian frontier, coupled with vague reports of troop movements east of the Caspian, provided the ingredients for a new war scare at the beginning of 1900.

As in 1885, Britain was militarily over-stretched. The Boer war had broken out in October 1899 and the greater part of the British army was concentrated in South Africa, and making heavy weather of the campaign there. Stories of Russian forces in transit across Central Asia added to a general jitteriness, although no one was sure of how many were involved or their destination. The focus of the Great Game shifted to the Caspian and new players were hastily recruited. In April 1900 the military attaché in Vienna approached Major-General Sir John Ardagh of the Intelligence Division of the General Staff with an offer from a 'hard-up' senior Russian officer. He provided details of Russian numbers and dispositions east of the Caspian, but was dismayed by the niggardly payments he received in return. His information tallied with other reports which may explain the value placed on it. A Mr White, 'an educated, observant and reliable man' based in Petrovsk and involved in oil exploration, was hired in July to report on the transport of men and equipment across the Caspian. It all came to nothing: at the end of September the consul in Batumi reported that there had been no further troop movements and that 'things appear to be very quiet'.[66]

A phantom Maskirovka gambit had produced an astonishing attack of nerves and, in turn, led to a re-examination of how India could be protected from a sudden attack. A committee duly went to work and concluded that, as things now stood, the balance of power in Asia had shifted decisively away from Britain.[67] It was calculated that Russians could deploy up to 180,000 men in Central Asia within four or five months using its new railways, and many more once the Orenburg–Tashkent line had been finished. Moreover, there was the possibility that the navies of Russia and its ally, France, would combine in the Mediterranean to disrupt communications with India. Whether or not this occurred, Britain's initial response would have to be defensive. Sitting tight on India's frontiers would undermine the Indian soldier's morale, and reinforcements, including Australian and New Zealand troops, might take as long as nine months to reach the front.[68] The bleak possibility that Britain no longer possessed the capacity to defend India adequately prompted a radical revision of its foreign policy, which, hitherto, had been characterised as 'splendid isolation'. One result was the defensive alliance with Japan in 1902 and approaches to France for an *entente* the following year.

V

At the beginning of the twentieth century the manic element in Russophobia became more and more pronounced, perhaps as a consequence of wider and deeper anxieties about the future and security of the British empire. The Russian menace became more ominous when it was added to the threat of the expanding German navy and the persistent colonial grudges of France. Furthermore, there were signs of increasing restlessness inside India. The nationalist, vernacular press had always seen the twists and turns of Anglo-Russian relations as an opportunity to put pressure on a discomposed Raj. At times, newspapers expressed a muted sympathy for Russia, even claiming with the authority of ignorance that Czarist government was more humane and less racist than British.[69] Journalistic license and nascent nationalism were undermining the Raj, according to General Sir Robert Low, a North-West Frontier veteran and backer of the Forward policy. 'Orientals have not the Commonsense of the Englishmen' he told a *Daily Graphic* reporter in 1897, and were therefore unable to distinguish truth from fiction. 'We have for many years allowed treason to be spoken and published not only by natives but occasionally by our own people,' and now Indians believed the Raj had become soft.[70]

Fears that the public image of the government was one of feebleness, together with a wider mood of apprehension, explains the absurd response to a ragbag of rumours current during 1901 and 1902, which suggested that Russia was about to use Tibet as a base for making mischief in neighbouring Sikkim and Bhutan. The evidence for this was based upon two visits to St Petersburg undertaken by a will-o'-the-wisp called Agvan Dorzhiev, a Buddhist monk. He had proposed closer ties between Russia and Tibet and had been officially rebuffed. Neither the Tibetan theocracy nor the Russian government wanted such an association and, as the latter pointed out, Tibet was legally a Chinese province. But, as in Alice's Wonderland, nothing was what it seemed in Russia, and alarmists immediately sensed that something underhand was being plotted. One veteran Russophobe, Sir Henry Drummond-Wolff, warned Lord Lansdowne (now Foreign Secretary) in January 1902 that trouble lay ahead. The 'Chauvinist military party' in St Petersburg was now calling the tune and the Czar could be discounted, for he was always 'a very weak factor in the formation of important decisions'.[71]

Like Afghanistan, Tibet was a thorn in the Indian government's side, although much less painful. It was a remote, virtually inaccessible state ruled by the Dalai Lama and Buddhist monks, who treated the Indian government with a galling indifference. In Calcutta it was believed that these clerics deliberately kept Tibetans ignorant of the outside world and did all within their power to exclude foreigners and foreign influences. Western knowledge of Tibet was imprecise and confined to descriptions written by a handful of European explorers and reports compiled by the pundits of the Indian Survey Department. Since the 1860s these Indian mapmakers had placed remote regions within and beyond India's frontiers, and memorised what they saw and measured with a remarkable precision. Two Tibet experts, who might have stepped from *Kim*, the pundit, Sarat Chandra Das and Sherab Gyatso, Lama of Ghoon, were asked by the Indian government what they knew about Russians in Lhasa. Neither knew anything whatsoever, as there were none.[72]

Lack of exact knowledge had never been an impediment to Russophobe scaremongers in the past, and it did not stop Curzon from believing that Russian influence was permeating Tibet. He invoked that principle of the Great Game which was to act rather than wait and see. As Lansdowne told the Russian ambassador in February 1903:

> We are much more closely interested than Russia in Tibet, it followed that, should there be any display of Russian activity in

that country, we should be obliged to reply by a display of activity not only equivalent to, but exceeding that made by Russia. If they sent a mission or an expedition, we should have to do the same, but in greater strength.[73]

Prestige tipped the balance in favour of a war which, as it turned out, was as much about frightening the Tibetans as it was about expelling imaginary Russians. For the past twenty years, Tibet's rulers had stubbornly refused to co-operate with the Indian government over matters of trade and cross-border incursions into Sikkim and Bhutan. Niggling rows about answering viceregal letters or whether or not Tibetan yaks could graze in Sikkimese meadows added up to what Curzon considered a gross affront to the King Emperor. As with Afghanistan in the past, the antidote to insolent indifference was a well-armed mission enpowered to force the miscreant to the conference table. The Cabinet in London was unhappy, but acquiesced to a demonstration of force which would penetrate a short distance into Tibet in order to bring the Dalai Lama to his senses. Command of the small force was given to Colonel Francis Younghusband, the explorer, who was on the look-out for promotion and whose chief qualification was his agreement with Curzon's policy.

The 1903–04 invasion of Tibet has been very well chronicled.[74] True to established form, the men-on-the-spot bulldozed the British government into a frontier war which it had tried to avoid. Every instance of Tibetan cussedness, and there were many, was used as an excuse to edge forward a little further until the army reached Lhasa. Edmund Candler, the *Daily Mail*'s war correspondent, was astonished how the primitively-armed Tibetans faced up to machine-gun and artillery fire. Trusting in their own talismans and faith, they were 'unterrified by the resources of modern science and war, the magic, the demons, the unseen, unimagined messengers of death'. The result was a number of massacres, and the campaign was denounced in the Indian native press and in the Commons, where Winston Churchill, then a Liberal, spoke up for the right of Tibetans to defend their homeland. After the war, Younghusband found the avenues of advancement closed, and set off along new paths which led to dotty religious mysticism.

Needless to say, when he reached Lhasa there was no trace of any Russians. It says much for the mentality of the war's promoters that, whereas in 1878 there had at least been a Russian emissary in Kabul, none had ever ventured to Lhasa with messages from the Czar. Interestingly, what turned out to the final round of the Great Game was marked by a novel intelligence ploy: in March 1904 the Treasury's secret service fund paid £400 to a Russian journalist specialising in Asian affairs for articles supporting British policy.[75]

What he had to say would have had little interest for Russian readers, whose minds were now focused on events in the Far East. In February 1904, four months before Younghusband rode into Lhasa, Japanese warships had attacked and destroyed the Russian fleet at Port Arthur. Contrary to what the sibyls of the Great Game had been saying for the past fifty years, the Russian army proved not to be invincible. In spite of its swift and decisive defeat, Anglo-Indian agents continued the close surveillance of rail traffic across Central Asia.[76] The content of intelligence summaries changed dramatically during the early months of 1906, with reports of riots, strikes, mutinies and native unrest, all by-products of the revolution which had broken out in St Petersburg the previous December.[77] As Ralph Cobbold had percipiently predicted a few years before, the Russian bogeyman would succumb to wounds inflicted by internal revolution.[78]

Like the Cold War, the Great Game ended with the implosion of Russia. In August 1907 and under French pressure, the Russian government settled its outstanding differences with Britain. It promised to respect India's frontiers and agreed a partition of Persia by which it enjoyed a sphere of influence in the north and Britain one in the south and east. This was a *rapprochement* based on temporary convenience rather than mutual trust. While the diplomats bargained, Indian intelligence officers were intercepting official Russian telegrams which passed along Indian lines. By September 1907 the Russian code had been broken and messages from the Russian consul in Mashad and the Governor of Manchuria were being read in Simla.[79] This proved a wise precaution. By 1912, when Russia's military revival was well under way, its consul in Mashad was covertly encouraging anti-government dissidents in the city, and familar reports were reaching Simla and London of clandestine Russian activity in Tibet and Chinese Turkestan.[80]

The war against Germany intervened and no Maskirovka gambit materialised. To judge by the events of the past sixty years, had one appeared, the rulers of India would have suffered panic or paralysis, or a mixture of both. These were the reactions of men whom one North-West Frontier veteran, Sir George Robertson, called 'hard funkers', because they spread despondency everywhere, in particular to the Indian population, which was credulous and easily lost confidence in the government.[81] His verdict was correct; players of the Great Game did more harm than good and had much to answer for in terms of squandered lives and treasure. All that can be said in their favour is that they were true to that code which had guided them from their schooldays: they played the game for its own sake.

5

Never at Peace:
India's Frontiers and
Armies

I

The people who lived in the desolate hills and valleys of India's north-western marches called their homeland 'Yaghestan', which translates as 'the land of rebellion'. Fighting was in their blood and they were proud of their independence and pugnacity. Two of their proverbs ran:

> Of course we are brave warriors
> Have not we sucked the milk of Pukhtun mothers?

and,

> The Pukhtun is never at peace
> Except when he is at war.

Their most persistent adversary, the British Raj, which, in theory more often than practice, was also their overlord, collectively called them Pathans. Seen from the parapet of a frontier fort, they were a troublesome, untameable miscellany of tribes and invariably at odds with each other; or, when united by a fierce Islamic faith, with the British. On the battle-field, the Pathan commanded respect and fear in equal parts. His legendary cruelty was redeemed to some extent by his manliness and sense of personal honour, which made him, in the eyes of romantics at least, one of nature's gentlemen.

The Pathan's warrior code had chivalric undertones which appear in Kipling's splendid narrative poem 'The Ballad of East and West'. It is the story of Kamal, a Pathan chieftain, who steals a mare belonging to a colonel of the Guides, a crack frontier cavalry regiment. The colonel's son, a subaltern, sets out in hot pursuit, but his horse collapses from exhaustion. He becomes Kamal's prisoner and learns that his captor's followers have had him in their sights from the start of the race:

> *There was not a rock for twenty mile, there was not a clump of tree,*
> *But covered a man of my own men with his rifle cocked on his knee.*

The young officer is defiant, warning the chieftain that his demise would be avenged by 'a thousand swords' who would bring death and destruction to his kinsfolk, their crops and homes. But there will be no retribution in the customary frontier manner. In an assay of stamina and nerve, each man has recognised his own virtues in the other. A shared pride, sense of honour, recklessness and indifference to death are the bonds of a freemasonry of warriors to which each belongs.

> *'Give me my father's mare again, and I'll fight my own way back!'*
> *Kamal has gripped him by the hand and set him upon his feet.*
> *No talk shall be of dogs,' said he, 'when wolf and grey wolf meet.*
> *May I eat dirt if thou has hurt of me in deed or breath;*
> *What dame of lances brought thee forth to jest at the dawn with Death?'*
> *Lightly answered the Colonel's son; 'I hold by the blood of my clan:*
> *Take up the mare for my father's gift – by God, she has carried a man!'*
> *The red mare ran to the Colonel's son, and nuzzled against his breast;*
> *'We be two strong men,' said Kamal then, 'but she loveth the younger best.'*

He hands the subaltern his jewelled saddlery and by return is given his second pistol: '"Ye have taken the one from foe," said he. "Will ye take the mate from a friend?"' The ritual exchange of gifts ends when Kamal presents his son who, in the manner of a mediaeval squire, will learn his father's soldierly code from a mentor whom he must also protect:

> *'Now here is thy master,' Kamal said, 'who leads a troop of the Guides,*

And thou must ride at his left side as shield on the shoulder rides.
Till Death or I cut loose the tie, at camp and board and bed,
Thy life is his — thy fate it is to guard him with thy head.
So, thou must eat the White Queen's meat, and all her foes are thine,
And thou must harry thy father's hold for the peace of the Border-line.
And thou must make a trooper tough and hack thy way to power —
Belike they will raise thee to Ressaldar when I am hanged at Peshawur!'

The young man then passed from one world to another in the which the Queen's peace is supreme, overruling the customs of his race. He learns this as he enters the fort:

And when they drew near to the Quarter-Guard, full twenty swords flew clear —
There was not a man but carried his feud with the blood of the mountaineer.
'Ha' done! ha' done!' said the Colonel's son. 'Put up the steel at your sides!
Last night ye had struck at a Border thief — tonight 'tis a man of the
  Guides!'

Kipling concludes the ballad with lines which make the encounter between two fighting men into a metaphor of empire:

Oh, East is East and West is West, and never the twain shall meet,
Till Earth and Sky stand presently at God's great Judgement Seat;
But there is neither East nor West, Border, nor Breed, nor Birth,
When two strong men stand face to face, though they come from the ends of
  the earth!

The young subaltern represents an imperial ideal: his character and courage win respect, even affection, from an enemy with whom he has an inner kinship. Sure displays of moral and physical strength had, according to the soldier's lore, won India for Britain and would tame the frontier tribes.

As so often, Kipling was using his genius to elaborate the commonplaces of British India. The theme of 'The Ballad of East and West' was expressed prosaically by officers of the Indian army who, like George Younghusband, believed themselves born leaders with a mystique which enabled them to capture the hearts of 'alien troops'. Such natural leaders instilled self-confidence into their men, showed them how to fight and the results were 'brilliant and dashing exploits' on the frontier, a theatre of war where individual leadership counted for everything.[1]

Kipling's poem of frontier adventure appeared in 1889 and would be followed by many more, real and imaginary in verse and prose. The North-West Frontier was about to enter the public consciousness as an increasing number of punitive expeditions criss-crossed its mountains and valleys. Each campaign was marked by a crop of 'brilliant deeds and dashing exploits' by young officers out to make a name for themselves, and there were war correspondents on hand to see that their daring was publicly recognised. Entry into a new battleground coincided with a period during which imperialists at home were deliberately fostering among the young that cult of the noble warrior that lay at the heart of 'The Ballad of East and West'. In this and his short stories, Kipling set the tone for future writers, endowing the region and its conflicts with a romance that it never lost and which, in time, would be taken up by film-makers in Britain and Hollywood.

Fact and fiction were constantly being blended, as they were by Sir Henry Newbolt in his poem 'He Fell Among Thieves'. The subject, George Hayward, was a young officer who was murdered by robbers during an expedition in the Pamirs at the end of 1870.[2] It was said that he had asked his killers to allow him a night's rest, after which he would meet his death facing the sun as it rose over the mountains. In Newbolt's poem he dreams of the country house which had been his home, the church where he had prayed as a boy, the races he had run at school and his days at university among 'faces merry and keen'. He confronts death with serenity:

> *Light on the Laspur hills was broadening fast,*
> *The blood-red snow peaks chilled to a dazzling white:*
> *He turned, and saw the golden circle at last,*
> *Cut by the Eastern height.*
>
> *'O glorious Life, Who dwellest in the earth and sun,*
> *I have lived, I praise and adore Thee.'*
> *A sword swept.*
> *Over the pass the voices one by one*
> *Faded, and the hill slept.*

This tribute to self-sacrifice, the highest imperial virtue, was, like much else from Newbolt's muse, directed towards the young. For boys who grew to manhood in the 1890s and 1900s the North-West Frontier and its wars were a source of thrilling yarns, written to entertain and inspire. In 'Cut off by Afridis', which appeared in *Chums* towards the end of the extended frontier campaigns of 1897–98, the hero, Lieutenant Vassall of the 'Diehards', rallies a party of English, Scottish, Irish and Indian soldiers for a desperate last-ditch stand against Afridis, whose 'foaming host plunged right among the dripping bayonets'. The pace is fast, and the style breezy. An Irish private rallies his mates with:

> 'I say, bhoys, we're cut off,' yelled Pat O'Mahary. 'Niver moind! On to blood and glory, ye murthering, spalpeens an' the saints 'av mercy on yer!'

A fighting Irishman was more than a match for a fighting Pathan and, after some dicey moments, the band are saved and the young officer wins the Victoria Cross.[3] As ever, it was a simple them-and-us contest in which the 'them' deserved whatever they got. In another short story, 'When Afghan Bullets were Flying', readers heard how if an Afghan mutilated an Englishman he secured the key to Paradise. The Pathan marksman caught by a resourceful young Tommy in 'Stalking a Midnight Sniper' is afterwards hanged – 'the example was enough to deter the tribesmen'.[4] Each yarn was accompanied by an animated pen-and-ink drawing illustrating a tense moment in the plot.

Frontier derring-do and instruction as to why it was required mingle in G. A. Henty's *Through Three Campaigns*, which covers the relief of Chitral in 1895 and the Malakand expedition of 1897. It is a picaresque tale in which Lisle Bullen, the sixteen-year-old son of a captain in the 32nd Pioneers, masquerades as a sepoy in order to get to grips with the Pathans who are blocking the passes along the road to Chitral. An old Indian soldier reassures him and Henty's readers that the Indian army is in good shape thanks to men like Bullen's father: 'They are good men the white officers . . . they are like fathers to us, and we will follow them anywhere.'[5] Bullen's steadiness under fire, his accurate shooting and willingness to take command in a tight spot after his *havildar* is wounded earn him the nickname 'young sahib'. True breeding cannot be hidden on the frontier; far from it, and Bullen's identity is soon unveiled. Commissioned on the spot, he proceeds to another regiment and further adventures, including a spell as the prisoner of a chieftain from whom he escapes intact.

Reminscences delivered to the mess by Bullen's brother officers give Henty the opportunity to retell the tales of other frontier campaigns. It's tough work, and one says he would rather fight the Russians than the Pathans, reminding readers that there are other threats to the peace of India.

There were opportunities for beating the political drum of empire in Henty's *A Soldier's Daughter* (1906), set on the contemporary North-West Frontier. The heroine, Nita Ackworth, is the daughter of Major Ackworth who tells her that her:

> . . . accomplishments are not strictly feminine in their charac-
> ter. You are a good shot as there is in the regiment both with
> rifle and revolver, you can fence very fairly, and you have a
> good idea of cricket, but you know nothing of music.

If these skills were not enough to qualify her as an honorary male in the true Henty mould, she has been having boxing lessons. It falls to her to inject some ginger into Charlie Carter, a subaltern to whom the fort is entrusted after Ackworth and most of his men have been lured away by Pathans. In between beating off attacks, he advises her to keep the last bullet for herself and offers some general instruction on the nature of command on the frontier. 'All savage races love fighting and certainly our own people do,' which explains why British officers enjoy such a rapport with Sikhs, Punjabis and Gurkhas. And it is this martial spirit which makes Indian troops led by British officers a match for the Pathans.[6] It does not, however, prevent the fort from falling and Nita and Charlie being captured by a chief who enslaves them. They escape and, in due time, marry, and one feels she will prove a very stalwart memsahib.

At one penny a week, *Chums* was well within the reach of all middle-class boys and many from the more prosperous working classes. Henty's 'lads', as he called his readers, were from all classes, for his yarns were regularly given as prizes for achievement in Board and Sunday schools – many found in second-hand bookshops today still contain the inscription plates. Together with the poems of Kipling and Newbolt, these juvenile stories gave the North-West Frontier a special place in the popular imagination. Among the last compositions of that robust patriot William McGonagall, Dundee's weaver-turned-balladeer, was 'The Storming of the Dargai Heights'. It described, as only he could, a famous incident during the 1897–98 Tirah campaign:

In that famous charge it was a most beautiful sight

To see the regimental pipers playing with all their might;
But, alas! one of them was shot through both ankles, and fell to the ground,
But still he played away while bullets fell on every side around.

II

McGonagall derived his version of the engagement from newspaper reports. Frontier wars were a staple of the late-Victorian press. Editors rightly believed that readers of all classes relished accounts of distant wars in which imperial armies subdued savage but recklessly brave adversaries. Reporters and war artists concentrated on thrilling incidents and, where comment intruded, the wars were presented as affirmations of national superiority and imperial destiny.

The issues behind Indian frontier campaigns were given relatively few column inches compared to the space allocated for accounts of fighting, on-the-spot photographs and sketches, and imaginary scenes of action drawn by staff artists at home. On 31 August 1897 the *Daily Graphic*, a tabloid with a predominantly lower-middle and working-class readership, summed up the purpose of current operations on the North-West Frontier in one sentence: 'The power which is not seen, is, for the Oriental, non-existent.' This message was repeated later in a letter from a serving officer: 'Never do anything by halves with Orientals. They don't understand it.' The wider implications of the campaign were conveyed in an interview with the explorer, Captain Francis Younghusband, who explained that it was foolhardy for the government to permit the continued existence of native states in an area where the frontiers of the British, Russian and Chinese empires met.[7]

The Times gave prominence to a speech by General Sir George White, the commander-in-chief in India, who insisted that civilisation and barbarism could no longer co-exist on India's frontier. As it was pushed back, civilisation advanced. It was militarily unthinkable that the Indian government could tolerate on its borders 200,000 'of the most turbulent and finest fighting material in the world, unrestrained by civilised government and fired by fanaticism'.[8] The theme of civilisation pressing ahead, which was also being applied to the contemporary campaign in the Sudan, was taken up in the *Graphic*, an illustrated weekly. A sketch of a native tailor using a sewing machine was captioned: 'The Advance of Civilisation in the Tochi valley'. Another drawing which spoke for itself showed doctors testing the eyes of frontier tribesmen at a dispensary in Bannu.[9]

By far the greater part of press coverage of frontier operations concerned the progress of the armies. New printing techniques enabled
photographs to be reproduced, giving a new verisimilitude to campaign
reports, with portraits of generals, men decorated for gallantry or killed in
action. The camera also revealed the landscape which was being fought
over, and off-duty troops and their equipment. The *Illustrated London News*
reproduced a posed photograph of a Maxim machine-gun detachment
during the Chitral campaign. The everyday realities of frontier warfare
appear on a photograph taken by an officer which shows sepoys digging a
drinking-water channel. In the foreground is a sign in Hindi, Nepalese and
English with the order: 'Pakkal Mules not to stand in water'.[10]

Officers' eyewitness sketches, either reproduced direct or re-drawn to
give additional dramatic effect, remained the standard illustrations in weeklies and dailies. They were supplemented by the first-hand material sent
home by professional war artists. The experienced Melton Prior, who
accompanied the Tirah punitive column on behalf of the *Illustrated London
News*, knew what his audience liked most and provided vivid scenes of
hand-to-hand combat. In one, a line of Sikh infantrymen withstand an
Afridi charge while, just behind the mêlée, a doctor gives first aid to a man
wounded in the arm, and nearby a soldier, his face in agony, collapses with
a chest wound.[11]

Most popular of all were representations of extraordinary acts of courage.
The storming of the Dargai ridge on 20 October 1897 provided the raw
material for artists to show their patriotic mettle and give the public what
it wanted. After five hours of inconclusive fighting on the lower slopes, the
3rd Sikhs and the Gordon Highlanders were ordered to advance. They
surged uphill to the sound of 'The Cock o' the North' and Piper Findlater,
although shot in both legs, played on until the position was taken. He won
the Victoria Cross for his part in what the *Daily Graphic* called 'a splendid
piece of pluck'.[12] Specially commissioned pictures soon appeared in the
papers which showed kilted Highlanders bounding up the hillside past the
wounded Findlater; one in full colour was given away free to readers of
Chums.[13] Newbolt commemorated the battle in 'The Gay Gordons':

> *There are bullets by the hundred buzzing in the air;*
> *There are bonny lads lying on the hillside bare;*
> *But the Gordons know what the Gordons dare*
> *When they hear the pipers playing!*

Frontier derring-do was also celebrated in the Music Halls with the stirring song, 'Bravo, Gordon Highlanders':

> *A deafening cheer – a rush of men – a glint of deadly steel,*
> *On dash the Gordons, though the bullets rain.*[14]

Public eulogy for the Highlanders left a sour taste in the mouths of some English soldiers on the frontier, who complained that their achievements never drew such applause.[15] There was some truth in this; but adulation of the Highlanders owed as much to romantic Victorian images of them and their homeland as to their wild prowess on the battlefield. It was somehow appropriate that these kilted clansmen, natural soldiers from a rugged land, should overcome Afridis who, like them, were men of the mountains bred to war. This may have been why Findlater caught the public imagination. After receiving his VC from the Queen Empress, he was discharged from the army and offered a job by a Music Hall proprietor, who wanted him to play his pipes in a spectacular stage re-creation of the battle. The War Office considered this attempt at theatrical authenticity vulgar, and disapproved strongly.[16]

Every fictional version of the wars on India's frontiers drew heavily on the reports sent by war correspondents. They were either professional journalists or army officers with literary talent and a need for extra income, like George Younghusband, who was briefly *The Times's* correspondent during the Chitral campaign. After the storming of the Malakand Pass, he came across a soldier setting up a telegraph line some way back from the front and had the presence of mind to wire his story. The telegram reached London within twenty-four hours and provided his employers with a scoop.[17] Winston Churchill, then a 23-year-old Hussar subaltern, used personal influence to get himself attached as the *Daily Telegraph's* correspondent to General Sir Bindon Blood's force during the 1897 Malakand campaign.

As he admitted to his mother, he was hungry for glory and delighted to be placed temporarily in charge of a company of Punjabis. 'It means the medal and also that the next time I go into action I shall command a hundred men – and possibly I may bring off some "*coup*".'[18] There was something distinctly Hentyesque about this enthusiasm for a scrap on the frontier, and today it may strike a jarring note. But Henty wrote and Churchill went to war in the twilight of that age when the field of battle was still regarded as the field of honour, rather than the killing ground of

mass, technological warfare which it became in the next century. Moreover, there were many actual soldiers who corresponded closely with
Henty's stereotypes. Consider this contemporary description of Surgeon-
Lieutenant James 'Jimmy' Hugo of the 31st Punjabis, who won the DSO
during frontier operations in 1897. He was: 'Captain of school, and also of
the Hammersmith Rugby Football Club; a thick-set, red-headed and very
popular fellow; as strong as a bull, a good athlete, and a steady worker at
"Barts".'[19]

Churchill's chance for fame came not on the battlefield, although he
distinguished himself in some scrimmages, but from his account of the
campaign, *The Malakand Field Force*, which appeared in 1898. It contained
a vivid evocation of what made this kind of warfare so appealing to the
keen young officers with a sense of adventure and a name to make:

> . . . on the frontier, in the clear light of morning, when the
> mountain side is dotted with smoke puffs, and every ridge
> sparkles with bright sword blades, the spectator may observe
> and accurately appreciate all grades of human courage. He may
> remark occasions of devotion and self-sacrifice, of cool cyni-
> cism and stern resolve. He may participate in moments of wild
> enthusiasm, or savage anger or dismay.[20]

III

Behind the adventure and glamour of the frontier wars which so captivated
the public were hard political realities. The land where Kipling's brave men
met and fought each other was also witnessing a far greater collision,
between two societies and cultures which were irreconcilable. The romantic image of the frontier masked one of the greatest headaches which
faced the Indian government. At the conclusion of their account of the
1897 Malakand campaign, two of Churchill's brother officers remarked
that the recent victories over the Pathans had achieved little beyond
demonstrating the muscle of the Raj: 'The frontier remains a source of
perpetual joy to the soldier, but to the politician a problem yet to be
solved.'[21] Even the unprecedented show of military might ultimately
proved of limited benefit; between 1899 and 1906 local intelligence catalogued 602 raids and disturbances in the frontier districts.[22]

The political problem of the North-West Frontier was part geographical and part human. It was a mountainous and, even at the turn of century, largely uncharted region which stretched from the Pamirs in the north to Baluchistan in the south. It included all the major passes which connected Afghanistan with India. Of these the most important were the Khyber Pass, the country of the Mohmands, and to the south, the Kurram Valley, home to the Afridis. Far to the north and close to the borders with Russia and China were the passes which led into Chitral and northern Kashmir. All, even the most inaccessible, were considered as potential 'gateways' to India by disciples of Forward frontier policies and therefore of immense strategic significance. The physical features of the area are best appreciated from a high-flying modern airliner, from which its appears like the wrinkled skin of elephant. From below and the perspective of the soldiers who periodically entered it, the frontier was a succession of physical obstacles. 'Valley walls rise steeply five or six thousand feet on every side,' recalled Churchill. 'The columns crawl through a maze of giant corridors down which the snow-fed torrents foam under skies of brass.'[23] The breathtaking vistas and sudden changes of light and weather were intoxicating, and gave an added zest to frontier warfare.

No one knew for certain how many people lived within the frontier districts. In 1898 the army estimated that there were at least 200,000 fighting men there, of whom a quarter were Afridis and Orakzais.[24] They were well armed; according to intelligence calculations there were 48,000 rifles distributed among the tribesmen, including 7,700 breech-loaders. Ownership of a modern weapon gave a tribesman status among his own people and the capacity to fight as a guerrilla in a countryside he knew infinitely better than his enemies. He moved deftly and was a master of all the arts of ambush. During the 1894–95 expedition into Waziristan, Mahsuds armed with swords and led by a mullah on a white horse made a night attack on a camp, swept through the pickets and slaughtered servants and pack animals.[25]

The wild tribal charge, so beloved of war artists, was becoming a thing of the past as the Pathans took steps to procure modern rifles. More and more were being smuggled across the Afghan and Persian borders; between 1900 and 1907 at least 94,000 Martini-Henry breech-loaders reached the tribesmen from sources in Arabia and the Persian Gulf. The profits of this clandestine trade were enormous, with a Lee Metfold magazine rifle of the sort becoming redundant in the British army costing £6 in Muscat and being sold for £80 on the frontier.[26] New firepower meant new mayhem as outposts built when a tribesman's gun carried no more than 400 yards were enfiladed from hillsides a thousand or more yards away.[27] In 1909 a belated attempt was made to stem the flow of modern weapons when the Royal Navy mounted a blockade of the Persian Gulf, intercepting ships and searching their holds for guns.

The possession of good weapons and the ability to use them were vital for every tribesman who lived by the ancestral code of *puhktunwali*, which demanded that he took vengeance for any injury or slight to his own or his clan's honour. The obligations of the blood feud passed from generation to generation and were pursued relentlessly by warriors who had no other occupation. 'Our women make bread and children,' the Pathan would boast. 'They need do no more. They are like cows.'[28] This one-sided division of labour left men free to fight for profit, honour or the defence of Islam and their land. They did so with a courage and ferocity that astonished British officers. During an engagement in the Sandul valley in August 1895, a large body advanced into the combined fire of the new magazine rifles and Maxim machine-guns and were wiped out to a man.[29] The onlookers did not say whether these men were Ghazis, holy warriors dedicated to killing all enemies of Islam, whom the British called 'Hindustani Fanatics'. Over 180 Ghazis joined the tribesmen who opposed the 1888 Black Mountain expedition and eighty-eight were counted among the dead after one futile headlong charge.[30] They were identified by a red cord tied round the right arm.

Islam was the only force which ever united the Pathans. In its frontier mutation it taught the tribesmen that their land was in purdah, like their women: hidden from the view of unbelievers and sacrosanct. If purdah was violated, then the victim's menfolk were obliged to kill the perpetrator. By this token, gradual British penetration of the frontier appeared as a sort of blasphemy, and demanded retribution. This was among the messages preached by various charismatic clerics who, from time to time, drew tribes and clans together in a jihad. In British official papers they were near-anonymous creatures to whom the adjective 'mad' was frequently attached. Those who followed them respected them as men of outstanding piety, often with supernatural powers. Saddullah, known to the British as the 'Mad Mullah' or the 'Mullah of Mastan', had a revelation that angels would destroy Malakand fort and owned a miraculous pot which contained an inexhaustible supply of ghi and rice. Active in the lower Swat valley during the summer of 1897, he raised 20,000 men within a few days and led them in attacks on the Malakand and Chakdara forts, taking the British by surprise.[31] The resonance of events around Malakand was quickly felt elsewhere and contributed to a wave of anti-British jihads in Afridi and Mohmand territories. All owed their origins and fervour to messianic holy men, about whom the authorities could discover little.[32] Thereafter, military intelligence endeavoured to keep track of all mendicant mullahs and find out what they were preaching.[33]

Spiritual merit was offered to all who joined the jihads; in the case of those who stormed the Malakand fort, equal in value to a pilgrimage to Mecca. Such inducements were valuable, but the real source of Pathan resistance lay in fears that incursions into their country were the forerunners of permanent British military occupation. The warning signs were more or less the same: the construction of telegraph lines, police and military posts, road building and the appearance of political agents attached to the courts of local rulers. The passage through the Swat valley of the sizeable force sent to rescue the resident in Chitral in 1895, followed by the establishment of the base at Malakand, made it easy for Sadullah to convince the tribesmen that their independence and religion were imperilled. Religous passion had also been aroused by reports to the effect that Britain was no longer the protector of the Turkish sultan and was in the process of invading the Islamic state of the Sudan. Both stories were true, but this did not prevent some officers from detecting the malign influence of the nationalist press behind the upsurge in restlessness in the 1890s: 'The unemployed loafer, who twenty years ago might have listened to the seditious preaching of a stump orator now hears the latest news . . . being read out from the papers, framed with the embellishments of a disloyal editor.'[34]

Pathan resistance to British encroachments posed a dilemma for the government. Two options offered themselves, each fraught with danger. There was the deliberate extension of direct control to the Afghan frontier, which most Pathans did not acknowledge, or the adoption of a live-and-let-live approach. This involved reaching an accommodation with the representatives of secular authority, hereditary rulers, *maliks* (village headmen) and *jirgas* (councils of elders), by which they agreed to co-operate with permanent British agents and residents in return for subsidies. Regional security would depend upon locally-recruited police and militia under British officers. It was hoped that such arrangements would, in time, eradicate disorder and finally lead to the area's integration with more settled regions. It was a classic imperial policy which was summed up and gently mocked by the contemporary Muslim poet, Akbar Illahabad:

We of the East break our opponents' heads
They of the West change their opponents' nature . . .[35]

Remoulding the Pathan's character was the task of political officers. Their job required perseverance, courage and, above all, immense reserves of patience. Most were former soldiers with a knowledge of local languages and a willingness to see things through the eyes of the Pathans, which made 'politicals' unpopular with regular officers. The distinctive white tabs on the political officer's uniform were resented by soldiers on campaign, for whom the only policy worth following was that of hammering the tribesmen rather than coming to terms with them.[36] This was understandable, but when the armies had finished their chastisement of the tribesmen, the political officers remained behind to continue the work of conciliation.

This was never easy among a people whose upbringing and religion made them inherently suspicious of all outsiders. Overcoming this distrust ultimately depended on the character of the individual officer. It was achieved with remarkable success by Sir Robert Warburton, who was assistant commissioner in Peshawar from 1879 and 1896. His mother was an Afghan and his father Anglo-Irish, which must have helped considerably in that he was less high-handed and more aware of tribal sensibilities than men from conventional military or civil service backgrounds. He believed that courtesy was the vital ingredient in winning confidence, for, if one was 'kind in words' to an Afridi, 'he will repay you by great devotion, and he will put up with any punishment you like to give except abuse'. It was an approach which paid dividends:

> It took me years to get through this thick crust of mistrust, but what was the after-result? For upwards of fifteen years I went about unarmed amongst these people. My camp, wherever it happened to be pitched, was always guarded and protected by them. The deadliest enemies of the Khyber Range, with a long record of blood-feuds, dropped these feuds for the time when they were in my camp.

He left the region at the onset of a large-scale war of the sort he had endeavoured to prevent. Before his departure, tearful old warriors expressed the hope that he would come to no harm in the fighting. This show of affection was all the more touching because they knew that in a few weeks punitive columns would be burning their villages, slaughtering their livestock and carrying off their stores of grain.[37]

Looking back on his life's work, Warburton believed that he had brought a degree of stability into the Tirah and gained a deep under-standing of its inhabitants. Progress would continue if they remained in contact with upright British officers who passed freely among them, dispensing 'rough and ready' justice. Instinctively querulous people appre-ciated dispassionate mediation from a figure from beyond their world of mutually jealous extended families and vendettas. Warburton maintained his reputation for impartiality by warmly accepting baksheesh from a native and then handing it back with the polite request to keep it for his use at some later date. This was the tack adopted by Sir Michael O'Dwyer when-ever he was presented with 'a fat-tailed sheep' by a friendly malik, telling him to keep it and fatten it up for his next visit. A degree of open-mindedness was also invaluable, but it was often hard to sustain. George Robertson, successively agent in Gilgit and Chitral, was enchanted by the 'Arabian nights' entertainments he was offered, which included perfor-mances by 'beautiful but unspeakable dancing boys'. His hosts' moral universe repelled him:

> Sensuality of the grossest kind, and murder, abominable cruelty, treachery or violent death, are never long absent from the thoughts of a people than whom no more in the world are more delightful companions, or of simpler, gentler appear-ance.[38]

Turning a blind eye to Pathan vices was essential if men like Robertson were to cultivate allies from among their men of influence. Political accommodations with rulers like the *akhund* (messenger of God) of Swat, the *mehtar* of Chitral and maliks were the foundation of British authority in the region. There were also lesser collaborators, the tribesmen who enlisted in Indian regiments or joined the tribal police forces and militias which formed the first and sometimes unreliable resort whenever trouble got out of hand. They could show exceptional courage in the service of their new masters, but when, as in 1897, they had to choose between their faith and their officers, they tended to plump for the former. Many could never completely cut themselves off from the life they had left; at least one Pathan soldier in France in 1915 was keeping in touch with the progress of local blood-feuds by post.[39] Some were willing to play the spy, like two men from the Guides who were detached from the Chitral relief force to make charts of valleys in the Swat region where Europeans would have been attacked. One was given 100 rupees for his work.[40] Espionage did not trouble the Pathan conscience, for in 1927 one army intelligence officer discovered that his Mahsud 'stool pigeons' were boasting to their villages that they were now government employees.[41]

As in earlier phases of Indian history, cultivation of high-ranking collaborators drew the Raj into serpentine family rivalries. The death in 1892 of Aman-ul-Mulk, the co-operative if amoral mehtar of Chitral, was followed by a bloody family power struggle which ended with the accession of Sher Afuz at the beginning of 1895. From Calcutta's standpoint he was an unsuitable candidate who owed his throne to Afghan intrigue and the intervention of Umrah Khan, the anti-British, self-made ruler of neighbouring Dir. George Robertson, the resident, refused to recognise Sher Afuz and withdrew into the residency with his 400-strong bodyguard, two-thirds of them Kashmiri levies. The siege lasted seven weeks and, after the arrival of a relieving force, a more tractable mehtar was found, Shuja-ul-Mulk, whom the British Tommies called 'sugar and milk'. A garrison with two machine-guns was left behind to ensure his safety and Chitral's tranquillity. Its communications with the south were defended by new forts in the Swat valley.

This heavily-armed penetration of this region directly triggered widespead uprisings of 1897–98 and the heaviest fighting the region had yet seen. When it was over the total bill was £4.5 million. In an unlikely alliance, the Indian nationalist press and the new Viceroy, Curzon, condemned the campaigns as wasteful; there were no indications whatsoever that the tribesmen were cowed or ready to mend their ways. Indeed, as the stepping up of arms purchases indicate, they were preparing for a return match.

The answer was a revision of frontier policy undertaken by Curzon in 1901. It was largely an exercise in cost-cutting, with the replacement of Anglo-Indian garrisons by a locally-recruited tribal militia and gendarmerie under British command. The region became the North-West Frontier province and was split between a 'settled' area to the north and east, and a tribal, adjacent to the Afghan frontier. Overall political control was in the hands of a commissioner in Peshawar who led a team of political officers. As before, their mandate was to prevent the pot from boiling over through a mixture of firmness, forebearance and strength of character. Short-term tranquillity would lay the foundation for a metamorphosis which would allow the region to be assimilated fully into the Raj. Sir Michael O'Dwyer, who worked in the area between 1901 and 1908, believed that, as in the Punjab, its everyday government was best undertaken by soldiers who naturally understood how to handle 'a virile and martial population'.

Old habits died hard, and British and Indian troops still had to be summoned to deliver the occasional clout. In 1901–02 they were employed to extract unpaid fines from the Mahsuds and destroy the fort of a persistent robber, Sailgi. He died during the fighting, and afterwards O'Dwyer, who had watched the siege, heard how he had considered shooting down a British officer with whom he was negotiating. He was forestalled by his mother, who told Sailgi, 'The sahib has given you no cause. He has spoken to you fair.' 'He was a brave man and not without a sense of honour,' O'Dwyer concluded, and Kipling would have agreed. There was romance even in the reality of the frontier.

There was also a dark side to the frontier, although it was kept out of the papers. After the 1877–78 punitive campaign against the Jowaki Afridis, there were mess rumours that irregular troops had burned alive some women during the destruction of one village.[42] During another expedition in 1888, houses were looted before they burned, although this was officially forbidden.[43] Fears that the new .303 ammunition was less effective against charging fanatics than its predecessor, the .457, led to a series of secret tests during the Chitral operations. Captured mullahs were executed by firing squads using the two types of bullet and comparative post mortems were then undertaken; the army thought it advisable that this investigation was kept out of the press.[44] The use of Dum Dum bullets in the Tirah campaign was made public, prompting questions from Irish MPs who pressed the government on the precise nature of the wounds they caused.[45]

The Indian vernacular press and Liberal and Irish anti-imperialists were always on the look-out for some incident which could be used to tarnish the army and the Indian government. The frontier *cause célèbre* was that of Colonel Hooper, Provost Marshal in Mandalay during pacification operations there at the end of 1885 and a zealous photographer. According to an eyewitness report in *The Times* of 21 January 1886, he had been responsible for 'ghastly scenes' during executions, when he had set up his tripod and camera to take pictures of condemned men the moment they were struck by bullets. He did, in fact, photograph firing squads, but none of his surviving images show men dying. The report outraged Liberal and Irish

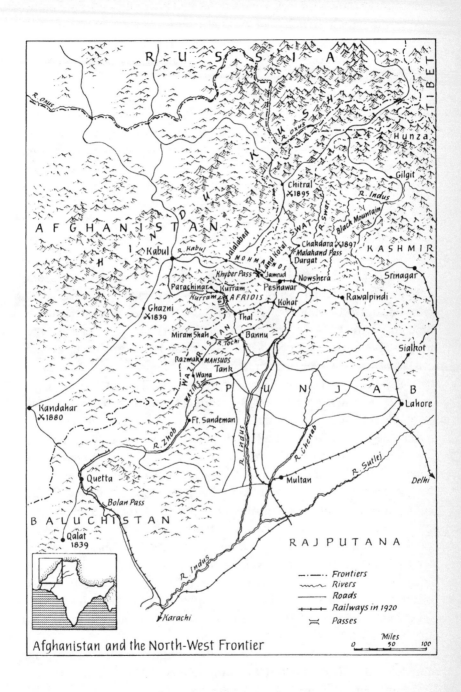

Afghanistan and the North-West Frontier

MPs, who demanded an explanation from the Secretary of State for India, Lord Randolph Churchill. The local authorities quickly responded and Hooper was obliged to resign from the army. There were other Parliamentary questions about the extension of martial law and intimidation of prisoners, who were offered a choice between becoming informers or facing the firing squad.[46] Thereafter, officers in Burma trod carefully. In November the local commander, Colonel Sir George White, warned his subordinates to avoid 'anything repugant to public opinion' during sorties against rebels.[47] His caveat was probably unnecessary, for press interest in Burma had waned; there were few exciting stories to be found in what had become a tedious war of attrition.

IV

India's largest north-eastern campaigns were directed against the kingdom of Burma for familiar reasons: infractions of treaties and its rulers' mistreatment of British subjects. Conquest was undertaken piecemeal and in three phases. In 1824–26 and 1853 expeditionary forces nibbled away at the coastal regions and, in November 1885, the British soldier first came to Mandalay. He was virtually unopposed, for the rump of the Burmese state fell apart from the top downwards, with King Theebaw quietly going into exile. Resistance in central and northern Burma flared up spontaneously in the following months among jobless soldiers and other sections of a racially fragmented society. They had no 'national' programme beyond an antipathy towards an alien régime, and no central leadership. The British called the insurgents 'dacoits', but perversely the Burmese regarded them as freedom fighters, even though they preyed on their villages. Local sentiment and fear of reprisals made finding collaborators difficult. White complained that: 'It is evidently against the instincts of the Burmese, as it is against the feelings of the Irish, to turn informers.' The only answer was to hit them hard, and column commanders were ordered to 'kill as many of them as you can', particularly the leaders.[48] It was grinding work in a countryside of rain forest criss-crossed by rivers, and losses from fever were high, with over 1,700 soldiers being invalided home during the first eight months of 1887.

Matters got so bad that Roberts, the commander-in-chief, spent some time in Rangoon sorting them out during the winter of 1886–87. He recommended more cash for spies and native trackers and a special gendarmerie, largely recruited from the Punjab, to take over from soldiers for whom the climate was too much.[49] Operations dragged on until 1892, after which the Burmese hinterland was officially declared pacified. Thirty years after, George Orwell, on joining the Burmese police, discovered that the old antipathy towards the British was as strong as ever.

Resistance, or rather a refusal to renounce ancient customs, persisted among the tribes who lived along the Indo-Burmese border. Like the Burmese, they were confident that high hills and dense jungle gave them an immunity from punishment, and they were correct up to a point. The going was so rough and the climate so unkind that only Indian troops, mainly Gurkhas, could be deployed for pacification, with, of course, British officers, who were expected to be fit and undeterred by geography. The latter had hindered all attempts to extend administrative control over the Lushai hills in north-eastern Bengal until 1888, when the government's interest was involuntarily aroused by the murder of two British officers attached to a survey party. It was alleged that they had been killed by a chief who required their heads as ransom for his wife, who was being held hostage by a neighbour.[50] Two campaigns were needed to subdue tribal opposition and there were two uprisings in 1892 and 1895–96. Thereafter, government was minimal, with district officers co-operating with the headmen of nomadic tribes who were, in effect, the sole representatives of the Raj.

The Raj had made virtually no impact on the Abor country, by the headwaters of the Brahmaputra, north-east of Assam. It was a wilderness of narrow, wooded gorges and bamboo undergrowth, heavy rainfall and determined leeches which slid through soldiers' bootlace holes or dropped from trees and slithered down their shirts. To these obstacles were added malaria, dysentery and the Abor tribesmen, who were good bowmen and skilled at rolling down rocks on their enemies' heads. There were four attempts to bring them within the Raj's pale between 1858 and 1894, and each failed. A fifth was ordered in July 1911 after they had murdered Noel Williamson, an assistant political officer, and his bearers. He believed that he had won the Abors' trust and had, therefore, gone on his tour without an escort.

The 2,000-strong detachment, as usual nearly all Gurkhas, was well dosed with quinine before and during the campaign, and each man carried an antidote to the aconite poison with which the Abors tipped their arrows. After a few days in their homeland, Major A. B. Lindsay told his grandmother, 'Personally I would give the frontier to the Chinese if they want it, I have never seen a more awful spot.' He saw very few Abors, who hid deep in the bush, occasionally emerging for an ambush. After one, Lindsay observed: 'I hate shooting a man who is on the run and that is what they are. They are curs of the first water, but extraordinarily adept at concealing themselves.' Others were less squeamish. One Gurkha officer was 'so determined to kill his man' that he chased him into the bush, firing his revolver and momentarily masking his own platoon's fire. Deprived of a stand-up scrap, the troops looted and then burned abandoned villages – Abor goats and chickens providing welcome fresh meat.[51]

The Abor expedition's baggage had been carried by hundreds of Naga coolies, each carrying a spear and hoping to return home with an opponent's head as well as his pay. Another north-east border tribe, and clearly no friends of the Abors, they also had a remarkable record for keeping the British at bay. A year before the Abor campaign, they had required 'severe punishment' for continuing to practise domestic slavery and making slave raids on their neighbours.[52] Official policy towards the Nagas was the traditional one adopted for backward and isolated animists: gradual conversion to more settled, civilised habits.

It was a painfully slow, uphill task and recidivism was all too common. As late as 1926–28 political officers accompanied by small parties of troops were travelling from village to village, freeing slaves and extracting promises from chiefs to abandon the sacrifice of children. Each chief bit on a tiger's tooth and declared that, if he broke his vow, he would be eaten by a tiger. The senior political agent, H. E. Mitchell, altered the ceremony by substituting a bullet, after having given the oath-taker and his warriors a demonstration of Lewis machine-gun fire. It was, he claimed, a valuable 'eye-opener' for people whose only firearms were flintlock muskets. In one village, a priest who sacrificed children was encountered and told that 'he might be clever enough to play on the imagination of his ignorant, opium-sodden villagers, but he could not succeed with the government'.[53] Coaxing and coercing in this manner had some effect, for in 1928 only two human sacrifices were reported. There may well have been more, for many Naga villages had yet to be included on official maps and had never been visited by a white man.

It is still surprising that, within twenty years of its demise, the Raj had made only the slightest impact on some areas of India. Admittedly they were all but inaccessible and, thanks to the nature of their inhabitants, needed cautious treatment. The frontier tribes were never in any sense a political danger, for their suspicion of the Raj was based upon a defence of tradition and a desire to keep Britain at arm's length. Indeed, when the government began to make concessions to Indian nationalism, Pathans were puzzled and asked, 'Who but the weak would wish to abdicate power?'[54] All these men wanted were favourable terms which acknowledged their way of life, and the Raj was prepared to offer them in return for relative tranquillity. Total peace was unobtainable when, as Lord Salisbury observed, 'A barbarous mountain population [exists] by the side of a civilised population dwelling in the plains.' The best and only policy was a mixture of persuasion and chastisement, never overdoing the latter: 'We must gradually convert to our way of thinking in matters of civilisation these splendid tribes.'[55]

This approach fitted well with the broad philosophy of a Raj which saw itself as paternal and benevolent, preferring reasoned argument to intimidation. Moreover, it liked to think of itself occupying a moral universe superior to that of its subjects. This was why Curzon was appalled when a senior officer suggested that the problem of illicit rifles on the frontier could be solved by covertly flooding the area with doctored ammunition which, when fired, would explode in a tribesman's face.[56] The alternative to the carrot and stick was outright conquest, and with it the prospect of extended operations of the sort which had been seen in Burma. The cost would be unbearable, the chances of success on the North-West Frontier very slim and, in any case, civilians were never happy devolving power to soldiers. Nor would the British government back such a course; there were fears that frontier operations in 1895 and 1897–98 had got out of hand and their value had been criticised in the Commons.

Henceforward extreme caution was the order of the day. When Lord Minto, the Viceroy, visited the frontier in April 1906, he found the tribesmen calm. His wife noted in her diary that they 'fight for the love of fighting, and though at the moment they they are contented and peaceful, they say openly that they must soon relieve the monotony by having a rising'.[57] The tedium soon proved too much and during 1907 the Mohmands stepped up their raids on their neighbours. Official patience snapped early in the following year, and a punitive force was ordered into their country with strict instructions from London not to stay too long and avoid annexation at all costs. General Sir James Willcocks, an old hand at this sort of business, took command and delivered the necessary blows within a few weeks, much to the relief of Lord Morley, the Liberal Secretary of State, who had an aversion to warfare of any kind.[58] But there was more fighting in the offing; of this Willcocks was sure. After watching eight swordsmen engage a party of sepoys and kill and injure five before being wiped out, he commented: 'Surely a religion which breeds such men can never perish!' Nor, it appears, could the way of life of the frontier tribesman.

6

Conciliatory Sugar Plums: Compromise and Coercion, 1906–14

Curzon's departure for home at the close of 1905 had marked the end of an era in Indian history. Henceforward, the Raj he had tried so hard to strengthen was thrown on to the defensive against mounting pressure from a growing minority of its own subjects and left-wing politicians in London, whose natural sympathies lay with underdogs of all kinds and for whom empires, however benevolent their intentions, were essentially despotic. The tempo of political activity within India increased and found new channels, most significantly the enlistment of the masses. The geography of dissent was also changing; hitherto confined to Bengal and the hinterland of Bombay, it spread to the United Provinces, now Uttar Pradesh (Awadh and Agra), and the Punjab. At the same time, the impatient, mostly young men and women, discarded the constraints of the older generation of nationalists who had always kept their activities within the letter of the law. The strain proved too much for Congress, which split in December 1907 between moderates and extremists, the latter led by Tilak, who wanted to extend the Bengal boycott of British goods to the rest of India. He also urged a campaign of non-co-operation, designed to hinder day-to-day administration.

The task of coping with this rising discontent fell to a new Secretary of State, John Morley, and a new Viceroy, Gilbert Elliot, the fourth Earl of

Minto. Both were appointments of the Liberal government that had won a landslide election victory in January 1906. Congress applauded its success in the expectation of concessions from the party that backed Irish Home Rule, many of whose members were sympathetic to Indian aspirations. Twenty years of Conservative rigour tempered by kindness were over, and a period of far-reaching reform appeared imminent. Morley's arrival at the India Office was particularly welcomed; he was a Liberal of the old school, who took his philosophy from J. S. Mill and his political ideals from his old mentor, Gladstone. Like him, Morley was 'an old man in a hurry', for he was sixty-seven and anxious to make his political mark in what was his first senior ministerial post. Like many intellectuals in politics, he was vain, willful and determined that his ideas would prevail come what may. From the start, he behaved like a master of India, and for the next four years he was.

Minto was, therefore, nudged into the role of a junior partner, which peeved him greatly. He was an open-minded paternalist, a Whig grandee who, like so many of his kind, had fallen out of love with Liberalism when it had embraced Irish Home Rule. He was an experienced and diligent proconsul who had served in the 1878–80 Afghan war, and had been a successful Governor-General of Canada. By no means blind to the faults of his underlings, he was prepared to stand by them when the going got hard, a loyalty which set him on a collision course with Morley. The Secretary of State distrusted India's men on the spot, whom he suspected were Caesarian by instinct and prone to regard coercion as the only solution to political restlessness. In his autobiography he recalled an exchange with one of his staff about the flogging of 'political offenders'. The official explained that 'the great executive officers never like or trust lawyers'. 'I tell you why,' snapped Morley, *''tis because they don't like or trust law: they in their hearts believe before all else the virtues of will and abitrary power.'* Like Edmund Burke over a century before, Morley feared that his countrymen succumbed easily to the virus of authoritarianism the moment they landed in India. There was, he once wrote, 'a great risk of our contact with barbarous races reducing our methods to theirs'. On another occasion he confessed that he thought it would have been better for his countrymen's souls if Clive had lost Plassey.[1]

History could not be reversed, and so Morley saw his duty as promoting in India the principles cherished by the great Whig–Liberal luminaries seventy years before. 'Slowly, prudently, judiciously', the Raj would spread 'those ideals of justice, law, humanity, which are the foundations of our

own civilization'.[2] What India needed was an end to the British monopoly of power which ensured that Europeans dominated every area of
administration from the running of the railways and post office to the
provincial and viceregal councils. Admission of qualified Indians to these
enclaves would eliminate the sense of racial humiliation so deeply felt by
the better educated, and quicken the pace of progress. Democracy was not
part of the way forward for Morley, who believed that it was a system
which flourished only in temperate climes inhabited by Anglo-Saxons.[3]
This was not racial arrogance but an admission that it was impractical, possibly dangerous to apply democratic principles to a people fragmented by
religion, race and caste. If they were, minority groups and interests might
be overridden and a large section of the population could find itself perpetually alienated from the government. When the time came for framing
reform, both Morley and Minto took deliberate steps to see that peculiar
interests were specially catered for. Of these, the largest was the 62 million-
strong Muslim community, which was already becoming anxious about its
future.

Safeguarding Muslims' interests and representing their views were the
principle aims of the Muslim League, which was founded in 1906. It represented the better-off Muslims and aimed to seek guarantees from the
government that their interests would be upheld in the event of greater
popular representation in government. Minto and Morley welcomed the
League and promised to take cognisance of its views when framing
reforms. In the light of subsequent events, the creation of the League and
its warm reception by the Raj have been seen as the beginning of the
process which ended with India's partition forty-one years later. Furthermore, official reaction to the League has been interpreted as the
implementation of a policy of divide and rule, devised to drive a religious
wedge into the nationalist movement. It is, however, hard to imagine how
the viceroy and minister could have responded otherwise to the early
approaches of the League. They were friendly and it represented a substantial community whose members were disproportionately represented in
the army and police. The League was also willing to distance itself from the
largely Hindu protests against the partition of Bengal and the boycott of
British wares, both of which were condemned at its 1908 conference.

Undercurrents of Hindu–Muslim antipathy were always present in
India. Outbreaks of sectarian violence did occur, although they were rare
and localised. In East Bengal, Hindu attempts to enforce the boycott of
British goods between 1905 and 1907 led to clashes with Muslim traders.[4]

A commoner source of friction was the slaughter of cows. Hindus rated it as matricide, believing that the cow represented a universal mother, deserving the protection of the devout. The law, as laid down in 1886, excluded the cow from the blanket protection given to all religious buildings and objects, and the result was the emergence of the Cow-Protection movement. There followed a number of sporadic, localised disturbances in which bands of rioters fought pitched battles, defiled mosques and temples, and threatened, beat or plundered those guilty either of selling cows for slaughter or killing them.

Most were small eruptions, but in 1916–17 there were large-scale riots in the Shahabad district, south-west of Patna, which involved murder and looting. Prior to the upheavals, *patias* (chain letters) passed from village to village in a manner reminiscent of the distribution of chapattis on the eve of the Mutiny. One missive ordered Hindus to 'loot the houses of Muslims, kill the Muslims and distribute five patias'. Failure to perform these acts would brand a man as one willing to violate his own daughter or sell his mother as a bride for a Muslim.[5] Incidents like this reinforced the British belief that only they could keep order even-handedly in a country where religious passions were strong and violence always close to the surface.

Muslims had always been welcomed in Congress which, despite its Hindu majority, wished to create a secular, pluralist India. In 1906 its ultimate goal was still a liberal state whose people were capable of ruling themselves, thanks to the spread of Western education and political systems. This could only be accomplished through co-operation with the British, who, according to the moderate leader Gopal Khrishna Gokhale, still had much to teach the Indians:

> Man for man they are better men than ourselves, they have a higher standard of duty, higher notions of patriotism, higher notions of loyalty to each other, higher notions of organised work and discipline, and they know how to make a stand for the privileges of which they are in possession.[6]

There was no reason why Hindus, with their concepts of *dharna* (duty) and *varna* (caste), could not cultivate these qualities and, in doing so, shake off that sense of inferiority which so troubled men like Gokhale. Asked by the Prince of Wales in 1906 whether Indians would be happier if they ran their own country, he answered: 'No, Sir. I do not say they would be happier, but they would have more self-respect.'[7] Self-respect went with responsibility, and this seemed within Indians' grasp with Morley's arrival in the India Office. The arid years of pleading with viceroys and canvassing in London had finally yielded a harvest.

II

The first sign of a new attitude at the top came from Bengal. Here, the agitation against partition was gathering momentum, with university students and older schoolboys taking the lead in the *swadeshi* (economic self-sufficiency) campaign. Many who took part did so for the sheer joy of kicking over the traces in what appeared to be a good cause, although many were unclear as to what exactly it was. Consider the letter, written in 1907, to the revolutionary journal *Yugantar* (New Era) and intercepted by the police:

> I, a schoolboy living in the hilly country, don't feel the oppression of the *Feringhi* [foreigner], and I give way before people for want of information. I am, therefore, in need of *Yugantar*, for it acquaints us to a great extent with the desire of driving away the *Feringhis*, and also make us alive to wrongs. I am in straitened circumstances, hardly able to procure one meal a day; nevertheless my desire for newspaper reading is extemely strong.[8]

If he ever received it, the extremist magazine *Yugantar* would have soon alerted this politically naïve youth to the alleged oppression of the Raj and how to oppose it. He would have thrown himself into the campaign against the sale of British wares and joined the processions of young people chanting '*Bande Mataram*' (Hail to the Motherland), the title of a patriotic verse which exhorted Bengalis to stand up for themselves. In one demonstration protesters held aloft a figure of Kali dancing on the corpse of an Englishman.

The Lieutenant-Governor of East Bengal, Sir Bampfylde Fuller, was an iron-willed Irishman in his early fifties who possessed great charm and an ever greater determination not to allow the province to slip into the hands of mobs of giddy schoolboys. Above all, he was resolved to do everything within his power to uphold the prestige of the Raj which, he feared, was wilting. Looking back on the situation, he wrote: 'The glory of England is dropping from us. There is no Englishman who should not blush for shame to know that in many places our women cannot venture outside their houses without fear of insult.'[9] Fuller banned anti-partition marches, forbade the slogan 'Bande Mataram' and used armed police to disperse a Congress conference at Barisal in April 1906. Those undeterred were warned that agitators and their well-wishers would be excluded from government posts. After an incident in which Hindu schoolboys overturned the carts of Muslim traders selling British cloth and assaulted a British bank manager, Fuller warned that in future schools which could not control their pupils would find Calcutta university closed to their alumni. In this and other cases, he believed that the masters had connived at, even encouraged, their students' misbehaviour.

Fuller's unbending line embarrassed Minto, who considered him 'hysterical and absolutely unsuited' for his post.[10] When the Lieutenant-Governor, sensing he was not getting the support he wanted, offered his resignation, the Viceroy accepted unhesitatingly. Morley concurred, giving the distinct impression that the government was delighted by Fuller's departure. A shock wave ran through the upper echelons of the ICS. Sir Denzil Ibbetson, a close friend of Fuller and soon to be appointed Lieutenant-Governor of Bengal, spoke for many when he asked whether 'the Bengali agitator, or the Government of India, is to run the country?'[11] *The Times* commented that Fuller had been undone by 'agitation and intrigue' and the 'native mind' would take heed of the fate of a man who had resisted both. A retired Indian civil servant with long experience agreed, adding that: 'In England . . . the impudent young politicians and progressives would have been subjected to the wholesome and effective discipline so often resorted to by the celebrated Dr Keate.'[12] Quite so; but had the miscreants got a caning, the matter would have been raised in the Commons by those Liberal, Labour and Irish Home Rule MPs who kept an eye open for reports of high-handedness by servants of the Raj. Between June and November 1906 there were three Parliamentary questions specifically on the treatment of disorderly Bengali schoolboys, including a protest about a pair who had been given thirty strokes each for obstructing a policeman.[13]

Henceforward, any official who acted firmly and with rigour ran the risk of Parliamentary censure and the possibility that his superiors would buckle under it. Indian Civil Service morale had been struck a severe blow; no official could rely on wholehearted support from his superiors.

Furthermore, the rightness or wrongness of decisions made hastily in a crisis were liable for close scrutiny in Parliament, where party political prejudices clouded judgement. The everyday administration of India was now the small change of domestic political debate.

At the close of 1906 the focus for agitation shifted to the Punjab. The trouble centred on proposals for higher charges and stricter regulations for settlers in the 'canal colonies', those areas irrigated by government-financed waterways. The measures were an additional burden for already hard-pressed farmers, and provoked an unforeseen wave of agitation which united zamindars and peasants, the classes which, according to the new Lieutenant-Governor, Ibbetson, 'owe everything they possess to the government'.[14] Newspapers protested and there were meetings attended by thousands and addressed by political leaders from within and beyond the province. For the first time since 1857, the government was confronted by a widespread popular movement that, and this was deeply alarming, was gaining ground among the peasantry, which the government had always regarded as its staunchest ally. Moreover, Punjabi Muslims, Sikhs and Hindus from the traditional warrior classes made up over a quarter of the Indian army. Indignation against Ibbetson's new laws soon spread to serving Punjabi soldiers, who were naturally distressed about a possible fall in their families' incomes.

During the first quarter of 1907 reports reached army headquarters in Simla which indicated that the army had been disturbed by the agitation. A Eurasian informer claimed that two Punjabi junior officers had approached Gokhale after a meeting and promised him that the army would rise against the government if necessary. The Congressman spurned their offer. Other sepoys were attending political rallies in the United Provinces; Sikhs returning from home leave grumbled about higher taxes and less water in their villages; and in a conversation in a waiting room on Delhi station, a cavalry sowar told a plain-clothes CID officer that his comrades would fight for their countrymen rather than the government. Some agitators reminded soldiers of their long-standing service grievances – lack of promotion beyond a fixed point and poor travel facilities for men on leave.[15]

Not surprisingly, the recipients of these scraps of intelligence imagined that another mutiny was in the offing. So too did those orators who reminded the Sikhs how they had betrayed India in 1857 but now had the chance to redeem themselves.[16] Hoti Lal of Mathura and other like-minded Hindu holy men were prophesying the fall of the Raj within the next six years and, interestingly, an end to cow-killing.[17] There were also persistent rumours that the government was behind the current epidemic of bubonic plague in the Punjab and elsewhere, and that Europeans were contaminating wells. In August 1907 an audience fled during a lecture on innoculation, believing that the sterilisation equipment was a device to spread the plague.[18] Foreign visitors, in whom politically-minded Indians sometimes confided, passed on to the authorities stories they had heard of a secret underground movement ready to rise suddenly against the British. Most scaring of all was the tale that, when the uprising began, servants would murder their masters and mistresses.[19] Unrest continued to simmer in East Bengal where the Lieutenant-Governor, Sir Lancelot Hare, noticed that agitators were now appealing to the peasantry by playing on their grudges against the zamindars.[20] Tension was so high in Calcutta during May that plans were concocted for the police and army to take control of the city if matters looked like getting out of hand.[21]

Ibbetson blamed the Punjabi unrest on Lahore lawyers whom, he believed, had turned the heads of the peasantry with their slogans. Two, Lajpat Ral and Ajit Singh, had taken the lead and had spoken passionately at many mass meetings. The former insisted that the Punjab belonged to the King Emperor and was not a fief of Ibbetson and the ICS and that, united, its people would force the bureaucrats to abandon the new regulations. Ajit Singh was a firebrand whose rhetoric was that of action designed to make the Punjab ungovernable. He invited all Punjabis to withhold rents and taxes and boycott British imports; those who refused were to be treated as outcasts.

Ibbetson, reading through transcripts of speeches and police intelligence reports, concluded that he was facing something more sinister than a protest movement against an unpopular new law. The tenor of what was being said strongly indicated that protests in the Punjab were the façade for a massive conspiracy, whose ultimate goal was a major uprising against the Raj. Indians already sensed that its prestige was waning; why else were sahibs and memsahibs hooted at in the streets of Lahore?[22] Strong measures alone would forestall more trouble and serve as a reminder to the Punjab that the government's nerve was as strong as ever. At the beginning of May and against a background of near panic in Lahore, Ibbetson reached for the apparatus of coercion. He asked Minto for permission to deport the leading agitators, Ajit Singh and Hoti Lal, and impose press censorship.

The Viceroy agreed; he too had read the reports and tended to share Ibbetson's apprehension about a conspiracy. Morley was not so easily persuaded; he imagined that the whole business had been exaggerated by jittery officials who mistook all legitimate political activity for sedition. Nonetheless, and against his better judgement, he backed Minto. Soon after, Ibbetson left for England and medical treatment. Before he left, Kitchener had ordered an enquiry into the loyalty of Punjabi soldiers which revealed that they had been considerably swayed by the agitation. Some had been urged to strike to gain redress of such grievances as pay and promotion prospects.[23]

The potential danger to the loyalty and discipline of his men convinced the commander-in-chief that it was imperative for Minto to veto the Punjabi legislation. The Viceroy agreed and quashed the regulations on 26 May, to the delight of thousands of Punjabis, who were effusive in their expressions of loyalty to a government which had heard their complaints and given them justice. Ignorant of the machinery of local and central government, some imagined that Ibbetson had been the instrument of their deliverance and contributed to a fund for a statue to him.[24]

The Punjabi unrest had been a severe shock for the Raj. Hitherto, the province had been regarded as its greatest success story, both in terms of the quality of the local administration and the steadfast allegiance of the Punjabis. The former had miscalculated the temper of its subjects and their loyalty had suddenly evaporated. The fault lay in the underlying philosophy of the Punjabi government, which stressed the personal authority of an individual officer and his rapport with those beneath him. He was a patriarch who, true to the traditions of Sir John Lawrence and his acolytes, governed through a combination of fairness and firmness, never shrinking from meting out punishment when it was deserved. Above all, he knew what was best for those he ruled and they trusted his judgement. In accordance with this unwritten code, the administration had made no attempt to discover what the Punjabis felt about the new arrangements for the canal colonies. The lesson to be learned from the unquiet months in Punjab was that the Raj could no longer take for granted the passive acquiescence of those thought to be its most faithful supporters. Given the right circumstances, they could become disenchanted and fall under the spell of the agitators who had previously been dismissed as a noisy minority of malcontents. The masses were not as inert as had been imagined.

In East Bengal the unrest which had forced Fuller's resignation continued and had recently taken on a frightening form – terrorism. The years 1906 and 1907 witnessed the growth of small terrorist cells, known as *samiti*, each of which contained a handful of ardent young men, mostly of good family and from the higher Hindu castes. Often, as in the IRA today, the typical terrorist was a youth whose ambitions outstripped his capacities and education. Entering the secret brotherhood of the terrorists was an escape from the boredom and frustration of an unfulfilled life into a world full of excitement and risks, in which he enjoyed considerable power, even adulation. On the day when the assassins of Mrs and Miss Kennedy were hanged in 1908, 'every school that dares, in the seclusion of the jungle or the slums' celebrated their executions with processions and the singing of nationalist songs.[25] Icons of the murderers were sold in the streets, despite the fact the pair had killed two harmless civilians whose carriage they had mistaken for that of a judge.

Political terrorism therefore attracted plenty of failed university graduates and ill-taught pupils from indifferent schools who had drifted from job to job, succeeding in none. Perverted patriotism was their last resort, and it was expressed through the murders of officials, policemen and informers, and armed robberies whose proceeds topped up the terrorists' war chest. Once admitted to a cell, the terrorist recruit became a man apart in a hidden pseudo-monastic world. He passed through initiation rites, bound himself by oath to his cause and his fellow fighters, dieted, followed a severe regimen of physical exercise, and repudiated smoking, alcohol and all sexual activity.

Extremes of physical and mental self-discipline tempered the terrorists' idealism. It had two main roots: Hindu tradition and the recent activities of Russian revolutionaries, to whom Bengalis looked for models of their own organisations. Consider Aurobindo and Barindra Kumar Ghose, both prominent in the Bengali terrorist movement during the early 1900s. They were the sons of an Aberdeen University-educated physician, who practised for a time in Norwood before becoming a government medical officer. His offspring did not flourish: the younger, Barindra, made no headway in business and his elder brother, having failed the ICS entrance exam, took posts in the Baroda government. By 1901 they were active in Bengali politics, founding the newspapers *Yugantar* and *Bande Mataram*. Strongly influenced by Tilak, they became convinced that Indian self-government could only be achieved by violent revolution and began to collect weapons. They sent agents to Paris for instruction in bomb-making from exiled Russian anarchists; lacking specialist knowledge in this arcane technology, the Bengalis had been forced to improvise their bombs from ballcocks and hollow knobs from brass bedsteads.

Aurobindo was a mystic whose nationalism was metaphysical. Indian self-government was an essential part of a process of spiritual advancement which would transform the country into a moral force capable of influencing the entire human race. His philosophy was rooted in a study of Hindu scriptures which had taught him that the individual soul's quest for perfection was paralleled by the struggle for nationhood. Both were inseparable and highly desirable ends. Above all, India's journey towards self-government had to be undertaken on purely Indian terms, rather than those of her rulers. Western concepts of reason, scientific rationality, the supremacy of law and the pursuit of power were rejected in favour of ancient Indian ideals. Inner harmony, oneness with the universe, human intuition and a consciousness of the cosmic presence of God were the ingredients of what Aurobindo and his disciples believed to be a peculiarly Indian nationalism.

The boycotts of British goods became a soul-enhancing act of self-denial and, in 1908, *Bande Mataram* interpreted an upsurge in strikes in Bengal as the will of God. Aurobindo came to envisage India's politics as a cataclysmic contest between the forces of good and evil, in which those who fought for the former were comforted by the presence of Krishna. 'What is there that you can fear when you are conscious of Him who is within you.' Or, in the words of Aurobindo's poem 'Vidula':

> O my son, believe me, he whose victory brings the common gain
> And a nation conquers with him, cannot fail; his goal is plain
> And his feet divinely guided, for his steps to Fate belong.[26]

The terrorist became sanctified as an instrument of a supernatural purpose which was wholly good. 'We never believed that political murder will bring independence,' one declared at his trial. 'We do it because we believe the people want it.' In this assumption, the Bengali terrorists had much in common with the contemporary Russian counterparts to whom they looked for technical help. Awaiting trial in 1908–09, Aurobindo allegedly had a vision of Krishna which confirmed his faith in himself as a warrior pilgrim, whose path to redemption lay in war against a government whose existence was an affront to the gods. A further source of encouragement for young terrorists was the defeat of Russia by Japan in 1905, which dramatically proved that Asians were not destined forever to be overcome by Europeans.

The mystical element in the terrorist creed represented a new departure for Indian political protest. Indian nationalists could now regard themselves as heirs of a Hindu tradition of resistance, like Tilak's hero, the Maratha leader Shivaji, who had fought the Mughals. Hindu theology rather than Western political thought offered a basis for national identity and the struggle against an alien and, it was stressed, unholy government. Violent opposition to the Raj, even the murder of its officials, was justified because it was a tyranny which violated the motherland.

The rhetoric of the new nationalists was that of revolution and war. 'Despotism reigns in India at this hour' where an 'incompetent government' relied upon 'Muscovite methods' to hold down its subjects. 'The plague and the famine are manufactured by British rule.' The phrases were those of a British Socialist, H. M. Hyndman, and were approvingly quoted in Tilak's *Mahratta* of 22 December 1907. Under these conditions, fighting back was the only way of gaining respite. For Tilak and those who hung on his words, the British were predators and the Indians their prey, a relationship which justified political assassination as a form of self-defence. This casuistry was employed by Tilak soon after the Kennedy murders in Muzaffarpur. Writing in *Kesari*, Tilak likened the terrorist to a deer which attacked a hunter, regardless of the odds, in order to save its own life. What happened at Muzaffarpur, or rather what should have happened if the terrorists had not bungled their attack, would serve as a warning for all Indian bureaucrats, whom Tilak saw as pitiless raptors.

Tilak was arrested on 22 July 1908 for this outburst, which was interpreted by the Bombay government as an incitement to further murders. The Governor, Sir George Clark, believed he was taking a risk, but that it was worth it, for the 'violent movement' would suffer a reverse if Tilak was found guilty.[27] His trial coincided with a period of local economic distress and Clark, fearing popular unrest, moved additional troops into the city. They were soon needed, for Tilak's adherents appealed to the masses, in particular workers in the cotton mills, for support on the streets. Between 17 and 29 July there was a sequences of strikes, riots and stonings of Europeans which gave the authorities a foretaste of the mass political protests which would convulse India for the next thirty-nine years. The disturbances started with factory walk-outs, in which Hindus who hesitated were told that they would lose caste and be considered as killers of cattle, or the offspring of sweepers, or Europeans. In one instance, when religious persuasion failed, a mill which remained working was attacked by rioters. There was also a hartal in which all work ceased, shops closed and crowds took to the streets bearing portraits of Tilak. Europeans were attacked and pelted during every demonstration. Limited force was used to keep order; no easy task when women and children were employed to shield crowds. Troops opened fire on several occasions when things got out of hand, and a marksman from the Northamptonshire regiment deliberately picked off the ringleaders of a mob.[28] The trouble died down after Tilak's conviction and six-year gaol sentence, but Clark regretted that the agitators had proved 'too clever' for the local police. Tension remained high for some weeks after the attempted rape and murder of a British nurse at Poona, and the governor feared that there might be further attacks on Europeans in remote districts.

A fresh novelty on the Indian political scene was the emergence by 1908 of networks of revolutionary cells in London, Paris and among Sikh immigrants in Canada and the west coast of the United States. The London cell was financed by a follower of Tilak, Shyamiji Khrishavarma, a businessman who funded an Indian students' hostel, India House, in Highgate, which became a powerhouse for every kind of sedition, including smuggling guns into India. He also financed a newspaper, the *Indian Sociologist*, whose student readers were regularly inflamed by accounts of terrorism in India, the government's measures to contain it and the punishment of convicted terrorists. In all likelihood, one of these reports inspired an engineering student, Madan Lal Dhingra, to purchase a revolver from a London department store (all that was required was a license from a post office, which cost £3 5 shillings [£3.25]) and improve his marksmanship at a shooting range on the Tottenham Court Road. On the evening of 1 July 1909, Dhingra shot dead Sir William Curzon Wyllie, a senior official at the India Office, as he left a meeting at the Imperial Institute, and mortally wounded a Parsi doctor who had attempted to administer first aid.

At his trial, Dhingra excused himself as an Indian patriot whose action was no different from that of an English patriot who fought Germans. In a garbled speech, he alleged that the British had murdered 80 million Indians during the past fifty years and had stolen £100 million from India. He also blamed 'the Englishman who goes out to India and gets, say, £100 a month that simply means that he passes sentence of death on a thousand of my poor countrymen, because these thousand people could

easily live on this £100, which the Englishman spends mostly on his friv-
olities and pleasure'.[29] Revealingly, in October 1907, the *Indian Sociologist*
had singled out Curzon Wyllie as one of the 'old unrepentant foes of
India who had fattened on the misery of the Indian peasant'.[30] After refusing to acknowledge the jurisdiction of the court, Dhingra hoped for a
death sentence which would be avenged by his countrymen. He got what
he wanted and was hanged at Pentonville a month later.

IV

The activists of India House disturbed the Indian government. 'We *cannot*
control the spread of sedition in India,' until its London connection had
been eliminated, Sir George Clark admitted at the beginning of 1910.[31]
Minto was worried that not enough was being done to keep track of the
London plotters, fearing that Scotland Yard's Special Branch, whom he cast
in the Inspector Lestrange mould, would easily be outwitted by 'wily
Asiatics'.[32] The problems of surveillance and detection were even greater
in India, for resources were slimmer and not designed to counter a well-
organised, underground terror movement.

The Raj's coercive power over its 303 million subjects was limited. If,
as Morley once suggested, the British government was confronted by a
choice between political concessions or 'Martial Law and no damned
nonsense', it would have to plump for the former because it lacked the
wherewithal for the latter. The total garrison in 1911 was 231,000, of
whom 156,000 were Indian troops. Of these, over 80,000 were recruited
from the so-called 'martial races' of the north: Punjabi Muslims, Sikhs,
Rajputs, Jats, Dogras and other Punjabi Hindus. There were 200,000
civilian policemen, who were often thinly spread in the countryside; there
were just 21,000 spread across the Punjab which had an area of 99,000
square miles and a population of 24 million. In 1908, the turbulent Dacca
district of East Bengal had one policeman to every 88,500 inhabitants.[33]
Unable for lack of numbers to govern by naked force, the Raj lacked the
apparatus to rule by stealth and fear. Before 1905, the agencies for under-
cover surveillance of dissidents were few, scattered, undermanned and in
some areas such as East Bengal, non-existent. Police special branches
expanded quickly during the next ten years, but in Bengal their growth
failed to match the increase in terrorist crime. Arrests and convictions did
not keep pace with outrages and, from 1911, detectives and informers

became terrorist targets. Efforts to step up police recruitment failed, and serving policemen often found themselves under pressure from friends and kinsfolk who sympathised with the nationalist movement. An over-stretched police force managed just to contain political violence; between 1909 and 1914 there were an average of twenty-four political crimes each year, mostly armed robberies. Thereafter, the number rose so that by the end of 1915 'no fortnight passed in Calcutta without some anarchist crime committed by the revolutionaries'.[34]

There was at least one display of military muscle which, it was hoped, might cool Bengali tempers. A cavalry officer recalled that in 1913 his squadron was ordered to ride through villages near Dacca, since, 'The Bengalis had been getting rather uppish and, as we had had no troops in Eastern Bengal for many years, it was thought to be a good thing to show the flag there.' The cavalcade was warmly welcomed, and even when, as instructed, the soldiers visited those hotbeds of sedition, secondary schools, they were garlanded with flowers.[35] More stringent measures demanded by the Bengal governments were denied by Morley, who was determined not to heap summary powers on those 'hot-headed, high-handed folk, full of alarms and swagger, and clamour for more force'. He did, however, consent to exempting some offences from trial by jury, since too often Indian jurymen were unduly swayed by their political feelings rather than evidence.

The rapid growth of political terrorism and the discovery that the masses were susceptible to political agitation presented the Raj with its greatest challenge since the Mutiny. It responded with that characteristic blend of flexibility, pragmatism and cunning which had served it so well in the past. It had survived and flourished by convincing influential Indians that its interests were their own, and had reached a series of political accommodations with them. These arrangements were ideal in a multi-layered society split by race, religion, caste and sub-caste, and enabled power to be exercised unobtrusively. Wherever possible, the British had trod carefully, preferring to preserve old structures such as the princely states and systems such as revenue collection, even when they were far from perfect. There was also that legacy of the Mutiny which taught offi-cials never to intrude into Indian religious life.

The Raj had amassed an army of collaborators: the princes and their administrations, the Indian army, the native police force and a cadre of such junior officials as deputy collectors and assistant magistrates, who were often its chief link with the masses. The cautious pragmatism and common-sense which guided the Raj made it inevitable that at some stage it would seek an accommodation with the small but growing 'political class' of educated Indians. A tentative move had been made in 1892 with the creation of Indian municipal authorities, elected by rate-payers and with councils carefully balanced so as not to exclude non-Hindu minorities. By 1911 there were 715 of these urban local authorities with a combined budget of £2.5 million, which was spent on public works.

By 1908 the question was how far to extend this principle of Indian participation in government. It was an urgent matter since recent developments in Bengal, the Punjab and Bombay had indicated that the Indian political class could in certain circumstances swing the masses behind them. The answer formulated by Morley was reforms contrived to detach members of the moderate wing of the nationalist movement and admit them to the inner corridors of power. The instrument of assimilation was the Indian Councils Act, more commonly known as the Morley–Minto reforms, which were announced in November 1908 on the fiftieth anniversary of Queen Victoria's proclamation, a pointed reminder that ultimately it was the Crown in Parliament which decided India's destinies. Sixty Indian representatives were to be elected to the Viceroy's executive council, and between thirty and fifty to the provincial legislative councils, where they would contribute to the framing of laws and policy. Indian admission into these enclaves marked an end to their domination by senior members of the ICS, who had always claimed that they spoke for the silent masses of India. Electoral procedures were deliberately designed to achieve a balance of all minority interests, much to the regret of Congress, which otherwise welcomed the measures. No one was disbarred from standing for election, even extremist agitators such as Tilak.[36] A further concession to Indian opinion was made at George V's coronation durbar in December 1911, where it was proclaimed that Bengal was to be reunited.

The 1908 reforms were in keeping with the spirit of enlightenment and progress which the British believed lay at the heart of their government. Educated Indians en masse did not become collaborators overnight, but in time a substantial number did enter the legislative councils, where they believed that they could work for the interests of their countrymen. Opening the door for liberal nationalists isolated the extremists of all complexions, for whom the reforms were a cynical piece of legerdemain by an unnerved Raj. Co-operation equalled surrender; the struggle for full self-government on Indian terms continued, as did terrorism.

Many British administrators were disheartened by the changes, which diluted their power and introduced a democratic element into the government. Sir Bampfylde Fuller took up the cudgels for them when he dismissed Morley's measures as 'conciliatory sugar plums'.[37] The future integrity of the Raj was at stake, for Fuller, along with many present and former Indian officials, believed that it was to them alone that the ordinary Indian looked for the fair play and honest government which his countrymen could never provide. Dispassionate judgement was beyond the capacity of an Indian who was unable to shake off completely ties of family and faith. The British alone guaranteed the peace and security of India; if ever they left or even contemplated leaving, anarchy would follow with inter-state and religious conflicts. The hillmen from the northern frontiers would sweep down from the plains and, in the phrase commonly employed by diehards then and afterwards, there would not be a rupee or a virgin between the Indus and Cape Comorin. Fuller's views were typical and important, for they would be repeated in various forms during the next thirty years by those who considered that the sahibs and not India's self-appointed tribunes knew what was best for the Indian people.

V

Adjustments to Indian government at the highest level had only the slightest impact on the everyday running of a country where more than nine-tenths of the population knew nothing of high politics. They were not, as some civil servants liked to think, utterly apathetic. The wave of protest against the Punjab settlements law proved beyond doubt that Indians would stand up for themselves if their immediate interests were imperilled. The same point was dramatically proved elsewhere. There were regular explosions of fury by railway and factory workers whenever management attempted to reduce wages, increase hours or introduce disciplinary measures. In 1898 strikers on the Madras railways tried to derail a train, and in 1913 factory hands attacked Europeans with sledgehammers, smashed windows and destroyed furniture after the introduction of fines for lateness.[38] Forestry laws which removed ancestral rights to slash-and-burn cultivators were also violently resisted. The docile Indian was a creature of myth, and in the future the government would have to strive to keep his loyalty in the face of nationalist agitation. The age when the Raj could depend upon what Lord Curzon called 'the mute acquiescence of the governed' had passed for ever by 1914.

On the other hand, political turmoil in India was still the exception rather than the rule. It was largely absent from the princely states, and even in East Bengal the mass of population seemed satisfied with the government. Recalling the first stage of his journey home in 1913, Major Casserly wrote:

> Although I was in so-called disaffected Eastern Bengal I met no rudeness or black looks; for the sedition carefully fostered among the feather-headed young Bengali students has not affected the simple cultivators of the soil, who still respect the white man and look confidently to the Sahibs for justice.[39]

It was an almost impossible task to fathom Indian opinion, and some believed the task not worth undertaking, given the vastness of the country and its heterogeneous population. In 1916 an invalided army officer, attached to the staff of Sir Archdale Earle, Chief Commissioner for Assam, kept a record of his superior's routine, six-month tour of his district.[40] It was an arduous trek made easier by a train equipped with offices and a kitchen, a steam yacht which carried the official party up the Brahmaputra and, a recent innovation, motor cars. Nevertheless, Sir Archdale still had to rely upon hill ponies and elephants to reach inaccessible districts, just as his predecessors had done.

The changes of scenery and the variety of people encountered reminded the army officer that crossing India was the same as traversing Europe from the Spanish coast to the steppes of Russia. Britain was the master of what was in all but name a continent which contained a jumble of races, languages, religions, customs, different social and economic hierarchies, and extremes of wealth and poverty. This diversity had, of course, been long recognised and had never prevented the British and educated Indians from making generalisations which treated the country and its people as one.

The officer on Earle's staff was no exception. Reflecting on the different races he had encountered, he fell back on familiar stereotypes: the 'laughter-loving Pathans, the dignified Sikh, or the courteous Rajput of the old military school'. Along the journey there were also reminders that large areas of India had been scarcely affected by the Raj. Head-hunting Naga chiefs appeared before the Commissioner, one knowing enough English to ask him for some whisky. By contrast, there were the sophisticated, educated Bengalis with whom it was less easy to gain rapport:

The less courteous are the younger gentlemen, mostly of the legal profession, who affect patent leather boots, talk pedantic English, and know more about the Cosmic Experience than God ever intended them to.

Many of these educated and talkative fellows were Bengali office-seekers who presented their cards to the commissioner ('Mr Das Dutta, Pleader [failed MA], living opposite the Medical Hall') and begged for government posts for themselves and their kinsfolk. Making friendly contact and establishing relations with this sort of Indian presented considerable problems for the British official class which, by and large, prized moral character above learning. According to Major-General Sir Robert Baden-Powell, the founder of the Boy Scout movement, the trouble was that the Indian schools had not bothered to instil into their pupils 'a sense of honour, of fair play, of honesty, truth and self-discipline'. Mere 'Scholastic education' encouraged 'priggishness and swelled the head'.[41]

Baden-Powell's views on Indian education were shaped by his experience there in the 1880s, when he had been a cavalry subaltern. By 1914 this period had acquired the lustre of a golden age, at least in the minds of those who compared it with the present. Then the Raj had been firm and strong and Indians knew their places in the scheme of things, as Baden-Powell told his mother:

I like my native servants, but as a rule niggers seem to me cringing villains. As you ride or walk along the middle of the road, every cart or carriage has to get out of your way, and every native, as he passes you, gives a salute . . . If you meet a man in the road and tell him to dust your boots, he does it.

These public tokens of subjection did not trouble Baden-Powell, whose mind-set then and for the rest of his life was that of a not-very-bright captain of a public-school First XV, but it disturbed others, who realised how it could poison relations between British and Indians. The 'brusqueness of manner' and 'harshness of command' of many officials upset Indians of all classes, according to Sir Bampfylde Fuller.[42] His opinion was echoed by a younger member of the ICS, Malcolm Darling, who believed that, 'This absurd chosen-race complex of the British is one of our worst characteristics,' and impeded the development of friendships between the races.[43]

But, as with India itself, it is impossible to make generalisations.

Isolation among a population which could never be wholly trusted bred arrogance and a feeling that any form of concession would be interpreted as appeasement and weakness. Prestige mattered at every level and had to be carefully preserved. While Fuller may have been aware of the harm done by his countrymen's sharpness of manner, he was also conscious that allowing Indians to mix socially with white women disparaged the latter. After all, Indian men refused their womenfolk the same freedom, keeping them from British company. One commentator doubted whether 'more intimate contacts' would change much and, if pursued, would lead to a familiarity which would dilute British prestige.[44] On the other hand, there were those like Darling who convinced themselves that a relaxation of his countrymen's aloofness would improve relations between them and those Indians who, to a large extent, shared in British culture.

In 1914, the gulf between rulers and ruled appeared as wide as ever and unbridgeable:

> All the concrete and tangible blessings that British rule has ever conferred on India are as dust when weighed against the incontrovertible fact that we are not of their blood, and do not look out upon the world with their eyes.[45]

Terrorist outrages, an irresponsible and hostile popular press, and the emergence of a body of nationalists who wished to wrest power violently from the British, added up to an impression that in 1914 the Raj was more unsafe than at any time since the Mutiny. A form of representative government had been grafted on to a paternal bureaucracy, and observers were already seriously discussing the possibility that the British might leave India, although no one could predict when or in what circumstances.

Uncertainty as to India's future could not have come at a worse time for Britain, whose self-confidence was wavering. Ever since the 1880s, its hitherto unrivalled position as an industrial and global power had been called into question. Its naval supremacy challenged by Germany, and with a stagnant economy, early-twentieth-century Britain looked out on a world full of virile competitors jockeying for colonies, markets and influence. Never before had India been so important; it was the keystone of the empire and, if it was lost, the rest of the empire would quickly dissolve – and with it, Britain's status as a global power.

PART SIX

DISTURBANCES AND DEPARTURES: 1914–48

1

True to Our Salt: India and the First World War, 1914–18

India was never so united as it was in August 1914. Old tensions and animosities were suspended and representatives of every race, religion and caste publicly declared their loyalty to the King Emperor and willingness to join the struggle against Germany. In the spirited words of *The Times*, 'the swords of the martial Princes leapt from the scabbard' and there was a heartening response from the middle classes. Even Tilak, lately released from prison, added his voice to the chorus, insisting that henceforward 'our sense of loyalty . . . is inherent and unswerving'.[1] Mohandas Gandhi, then little-known in India, rallied his countrymen in London, who pledged themselves to render such 'humble assistance as we may be considered capable of performing as an earnest of our desire to share the responsibilities of membership of a great Empire, if we would share its privileges'.[2] The implication was clear: if India took its share and more of the imperial war effort, it would prove itself worthy of self-government. Other Indian interests were involved in the war. It was, for better or worse, an integral part of the British empire and would face unknown repercussions if Britain was defeated. Better the devil you know . . .

The nationalists were right in their assessment of the war: it was a struggle in which the future of the British empire was at stake. As the European crisis unfolded during the second half of July 1914, Britain was cramped for manouevre, for whichever way events led, the empire was imperilled. Imperial interests ruled out British neutrality since an Austro-German victory over France and Russia would lead to a shift in the balance of naval power against Britain, and a redistribution of overseas colonies in Germany's favour. Moreover, in defeat France and Russia might easily revive old antagonisms against a power which had left them in the lurch. This point was made by the Russian government, which hinted that one consequence of British non-intervention would be fresh confrontations in Central Asia and Persia. The security and preservation of the empire dictated that Britain fought alongside the Dual Alliance, and German infraction of Belgian neutrality on 1 August gave the Cabinet both the excuse for entering the conflict and a bonus in the form of a moral cause which would win support at home and throughout the empire.

India was about to take a journey into a dark, unknown world. As in Europe, no one as yet had any clear idea of the nature of modern war, let alone its capacity to shake and transform societies and economies. In theory, India's contribution to the imperial war effort was manpower. In 1911 the Committee for Imperial defence had proposed the dispatch of two Indian infantry divisions and one cavalry brigade to Europe, where they would be deployed alongside the British Expeditionary Force in defence of the Franco-Belgian border. Thereafter, an enlarged Indian army would act as a strategic reserve and, if they materialised, would be deployed on new fronts as well as undertaking its usual duties on India's frontiers. Substantial Indian forces in France presented no logistical problems as they could rely on Britain for arms, ammunition, rations, transport and medical facilities.

This was fortunate, for any large Indian force dependent on India for its supplies was bound to find itself in trouble. In 1914, India was primarily a producer of raw materials, principally cotton, jute, rice, tea, wheat and hides. It could manufacture uniforms and clothing and small quantities of rifle and low-calibre artillery ammunition, but its metal output was low and it possessed no engineering, machine-tool or chemical industries. All were vital for a modern army which needed heavy artillery, high-explosive shells, precision fuses and limitless supplies of machine-gun and small-arms ammunition. As the war progressed, there was an increasing need for motor transport, and here India was woefully deficient; in 1914 there was just one motor ambulance available for the Mesopotamian campaign. Lorries had to be imported from Britain, as did all wireless, telephone and telegraph equipment. All these items were desperately needed by British forces on the Western Front, where their enemy was strongest, and so it was inevitable that India's demands were a low priority. Moreover, the dominant strategic doctrine favoured a concentration of resources for the war against Germany rather than their dispersal to those subsidiary Middle Eastern and East African theatres where Indian troops were deployed in large numbers.

Short of war materials and the wherewithal to make them, India was strong in manpower and, at the beginning at least, there was a steady flow of recruits to the colours. For the Indian professional soldier going to war was a simple matter of adherence to ancestral tradition and fulfilling his obligations to the King Emperor. Writing from the trenches of north-western France in September 1915, Havildar Hirram Singh told his family: 'If I die I go to Paradise. It is a fine thing to die in battle. We must honour him who feeds us. Our dear government's rule is very good and gracious.' If he survived, he would return with 'prizes, land, medals [and] distinctions'. The same ideals inspired Pirhan Dyal, also serving in France, who wrote home, 'We must be true to our salt and he who is faithful will go to paradise.' Traditions of caste and clan mingled with loyalty to George V. 'Who remembers a man who dies in his bed?' asked a Jat havildar, then recovering from wounds. 'But it is our duty as Khastris to kill the enemy and then a man becomes a hero.' 'It is the duty of the Rajputs to show courage,' one assured his kinsmen. In June 1915 an Afridi sepoy, ashamed by reports that over 100 men from his tribe had deserted from the Bannu garrison, lamented: 'It is the business of men to fight. Now the Afridis have become like women.'[3] Like their sisters in Britain, Indian women urged their menfolk to fight bravely. Three brothers, stationed in Egypt at the end of 1914, were reminded by their sister of what was expected from them. 'War is the task of young men, to sport with death upon the field of battle, to be as a tiger and to draw the sword of honour and daring.'[4]

Ancient martial instincts were as strong as ever and the heart of the Indian soldier appeared sound. The Indian army's muscles and brain were less healthy, and not up to the exertion demanded by modern warfare. This was unsurprising, for the Indian military machine had been developed over the past fifty years with one end in mind: defending and policing the frontier. For this reason, recruitment had been confined to the 'martial races' who were more than a match for their counterparts in the borderlands and might possibly stand up to Russian troops, although senior officers from Roberts downwards had misgivings about this. Fighting efficiency had been maintained by periodic reforms, including the merging of the old presidency armies and the introduction of modern weaponry.

As in the Company days, great emphasis was laid on the leadership of British officers, who alone possessed that strength of character which commanded the respect of Indian soldiers and gave them the will to fight. As the Mutiny had been judged in large part the consequence of officers having lost touch with their men, their successors were made to master their languages, religious customs and culture. Whereas the Company officer had survived with a vocabulary full of expressions which ensured his own physical comfort and the obedience of his servants, the modern officer learned the idiom of practical command and his men's welfare. Among the phrases which Lieutenant W. L. Maxwell of the 10th Bengal Lancers had to translate for an exam in 1884 were: 'Has there been any cholera in that station lately?' and 'I hear that a woman of the suddar bazaar fell into a well and was drowned.'[5]

Some things did not change. The British officer still had abundant time for arduous athletic relaxation in the manner of his predecessors, and Maxwell's diaries and letters are crammed with references to hunting trips, exercising his horses and the social rituals of cantonment life. Polo was an obsession with all cavalry regiments (and many infantry) and was played enthusiastically at every opportunity. Nothing stood in the way of a *chukka* (polo round); once, when Maxwell's regimental pitch was waterlogged, the players took over, and presumably churned up, the brigade parade ground. What very quickly had become the most popular game among British officers was an adaptation of the 'wild mêlée' of horsemen witnessed by Colonel Durand in the Hunza valley in 1892. Riders dismounted and picked up the ball after a goal for it to count and, in the process, the opposing team were free to knock down or ride down the scorer. After a chukka, the losing side was obliged to dance in front of the winners, adding to their humiliation.[6] These robust features were dropped from the game by British officers and rules were drawn up which formalised the chaos of its Indian prototype. Team colours were introduced, with Maxwell's 10th Lancers appearing in purple, black, red and yellow jerseys. Gear, harness and a string of polo ponies made the game a costly and therefore exclusive pastime, confined to the richer officers, a fact reflected in a contemporary doggerel:

> *There's a regiment in Poona,*
> *That would far rather sooner*

Play single-handed polo,
A sort of 'solo polo'
Than play a single chukka
With a chap that wasn't pukka.

Rules of conduct ossified into arcane mysteries characterised the milieu of the Indian officers' mess, although this was changing by 1914, much to the regret of General Sir George Younghusband. In the old days when an officer wished to share a drink with another, he ordered the mess sergeant to take a bottle and glass to him. Now, officers stood each other drinks, 'for all the world as if one of His Majesty's Officers' Messes was a public house, or American bar'. Some taboos survived; officers never smoked in uniform when on duty, even though Younghusband generously conceded that a 'matter of life or death' cigarette might occasionally be permitted. Subalterns and captains continued to address each other by their surnames, the major as 'major' and the colonel as 'sir' or 'colonel'. As in the public schools, from which they derived, these codes served to purge what Younghusband called 'priggishness' and 'caddishness' of the newcomer, but could never cure the 'bad hat or untameable bounder' who was usually encouraged to leave his regiment quietly.[7]

Absurd as they may seem to modern eyes, polo mania and mess conventions had their value. The latter generated a tight cohesion among officers and the former kept them fit and improved their horsemanship; Indian cavalrymen charged many times during frontier campaigns and did so again between 1914 and 1918, but with far less effect. Prowess in energetic sports had now become part of the imperial mystique, according to one visitor to India, who believed that 'the innate love of sport' was 'equally necessary for the life of Englishmen and for supremacy over the natives'.[8]

II

When put to the test, the qualities fostered by the Indian army had more than proved themselves on the frontier, but it was mentally and physically unprepared for the modern war it was asked to fight in Mesopotamia. The invasion of this outlying Turkish province had been suggested by the Committee for Imperial Defence in 1906 and again five years later. The strategic objective was Basra, at the confluence of the Tigris and Euphrates rivers, but there was a knot of imperialists inside the Indian government who looked further towards large-scale Indian immigration into southern Mesopotamia, where agricultural colonies would be established.[9] This ambitious scheme ran counter to Delhi's regional policy and was temporarily shelved.

As ever, the Indian government regarded the integrity of the Turkish empire as the key to its security. Not only did Mesopotamia, the Persian Gulf and Arabia form a barrier on India's western flank, but their overlord, the Ottoman sultan, Abdul Hamid V, was the Caliph (khalifa), acknowledged by India's Sunni Muslims as spiritual successor to Muhammad and empowered to declare a jihad in defence of Islam. His well-being and that of his empire were concerns close to the hearts of Indian Muslims, who had expressed strong disapproval of the lack of British support for Turkey during the Graeco-Turkish war of 1897 and more recent Balkan conflicts. On each occasion, European aggression against the last remaining Muslim power was interpreted as a threat to Islam. And yet, while wishing to be seen as Abdul Hamid V's friend, the Indian Foreign Department was taking out an insurance policy against war with Turkey by making covert approaches to his Arab rulers in Arabia and the Gulf.

While Delhi's political officers were intriguing with malcontent sheiks in an Arabian version of the Great Game, German diplomats were coaxing Turkey's rulers into a partnership. For some years the German Foreign Ministry had recognised the potential of a jihad for making mischief among Muslims in the Russian Caucasus, Egypt and India. In the event of war, Muslim uprisings in their respective empires would compel Britain and Russia to withdraw troops from the European fronts. During August and September 1914 German diplomats intensified their efforts, warning the Sultan's ministers that Turkey's survival depended upon Germany. They were backed by Enver Pasha, the Minister for War, who pinned his hopes on a quick German victory as Turkey's only hope of survival. And rightly so, for France and Russia were keen to acquire Ottoman provinces and, if they won, were certain to embark on a partition of the empire. France in particular was deeply interested in acquiring the oil reserves around Mosul in northern Mesopotamia. Britain could not afford to upset its allies by supporting Turkey and so, reluctantly, had to stand by and watch it slip into the German camp. By early September it was clear which way the Turks would jump, but not when.

The likelihood of war with Turkey caused despondency in Delhi. A large proportion of Indian soldiers were Muslims and were bound to be exposed to seditious, Pan-Islamic propaganda, calling on them to abandon the King Emperor and fight for their faith. Furthermore, the call for the holy war would revive unrest in Afghanistan and on the North-West Frontier.

The solution lay, as it always did when such difficulties surfaced, in a massive affirmation of British power, designed to impress and coerce. The old doctrine of the pre-emptive, aggressive masterstroke was resuscitated by General Sir Edmund Barrow, the military secretary at the India Office. On 26 September he proposed a *coup de main* against the vulnerable Abadan oil fields and the possible seizure of Basra. A veteran of the second Afghan war and sundry North-West Frontier campaigns, Barrow was convinced that shaking the mailed fist would have the right effect. 'So startling and un-expected a sign of our power to strike' would instantly convert all the discontented local rulers to Britain's cause and considerably hamper a jihad.[10] This audacious plan was quickly endorsed by the Secretary of State, Lord Crewe, and Kitchener, the Minister for War. Orders were wired to India where, on the 29th, the Sixth Division, then earmarked for France, was placed in readiness for embarkation for the Persian Gulf.

A campaign marked by awesome muddle and mishaps began as it con-tinued, with hitches in procuring shipping. There was confusion too as to the expedition's purpose. Its commander, Lieutenant-General Sir Walter Delamain, was instructed to land at Abadan in the knowledge that politi-cal officers had forewarned the local Arabs. Yet he was to do nothing which might offend either Turkish or Arab opinion and avoid any pre-emptive action that could upset what the Viceroy, Lord Hardinge, called the 'Muhammedan masses' in India and Afghanistan.[11] On the 26th the invasion force anchored off Bahrain, and after three days aboard the stifling transports the troops had to be put ashore for sake of their health, preceded by a declaration that Britain had no aggressive intentions in the area. Nonetheless, Delamain had been told to treat Bahrain as a *de facto* British protectorate. The following day the former German battlecruiser *Goeben*, now flying the Ottoman flag, shelled Odessa. In November, Delamain was ordered to attack Al-Faw at the southern tip of the Shatt al-Arab, land and advance on Basra.[12] So began a campaign which, when it ended almost exactly four years later, represented India's major war effort.

Basra fell on 23 November, justifying earlier predictions that Turkish resistance would prove feeble. From then on, the war gained an impetus of its own with an advance northwards along the Tigris through Al-Qurnah to Amarah, which was taken in June 1915. What had begun as a minor campaign was transformed into a full-scale conquest of Mesopotamia, with the great Islamic city of Baghdad acting as a magnet. Over-optimistic generals dictated strategy, convincing waverers in London and Delhi that the contest would be a walkover and that once Baghdad was captured British prestige would soar in every bazaar from Beirut to Bangalore. As the front crept forward, local commanders presented their political masters with a well-worn formula. Hardinge was informed during his tour of the front in February 1915 that Basra would only be safe when Nasiriyah and Amarah had been captured. Sir Percy Cox, the senior political officer, agreed. Like all his breed, he imagined that he could penetrate the inner-most recesses of the native mind. It worshipped success, and so a few victories would bring the neighbouring Arab tribes into the British camp.[13]

So far, Arab support had been disappointing. Just before the outbreak of war, Abdal Azi Ibn Saud (the future founder of the Saudi royal dynasty) had hedged his bets by a reaffirmation of loyalty to the Sultan after a period of flirting with Britain. Once hostilities were under way, Arab participation fell far short of what Cox had airily predicted. What he lacked the imagination to understand was that, while Arab sheiks were glad to be rid of their Turkish masters, this did not predispose them to welcome British ones. As it was, a substantial body of Arabs stayed loyal to the Sultan and even more were malevolently neutral, plundering the supply lines of both armies indiscriminately.

Hardinge was seduced by the patter of the generals and his political advisers. His confidence helped persuade the Cabinet to sanction fresh offensives and new objectives. In July the ministers agreed an advance to Kut-al-Amarah (Al-Kut) and in September approved an offensive against Baghdad itself. Not everyone was content; Kitchener, Curzon and Sir Austen Chamberlain, the Secretary of State, expressed misgivings, but these were dispelled by the local commander, General Sir John Nixon. As cocksure as he was incompetent, Nixon was mesmerised by prestige and repeatedly lied to his superiors about the state of his forces, which were deteriorating rapidly.

The Mesopotamian bubble burst on 22 November, when Major-General Charles Townshend's outnumbered Sixth Division was trounced at Ctesiphon and driven back down river to Kut-al-Amarah, where it was encircled. After the battle, it was discovered that Nixon's intelligence staff had under-estimated the size of the Turkish forces engaged by 6,000.[14]

Further, equally disturbing revelations of slovenly staff work and mismanagement came to light during the next six months as the tide of the war
turned against the Anglo-Indian army. The scandals of what was now
called the 'Mess pot' campaign proved that the Indian army lacked the
capacity to fight a modern war; the strain was too much and systems
which might just have worked during a frontier campaign buckled and fell
apart.

Disintegration started at the top. In abler, more versatile hands the army
might have fared better, but the muster roll of the Indian high command
in Mesopotamia was a register of the infirm, myopic and bewildered. The
commander-in-chief, General Sir Beauchamp Duff, was sixty and had
spent the past thirty years pushing a pen in Canada. Nixon was fifty-
eight, ailing, out of his depth, and indifferent to the welfare of his men: in
June he rejected a suggestion that fitted ambulance motor boats should
replace slower, converted native craft for shipping wounded men to the
base hospital in Basra.[15] He resigned early in 1916 and Duff replaced him
with an older mediocrity, Lieutenant-General Sir Percy Lake, who had not
heard a shot fired anger for thirty years. In London, the Chief of the
Imperial Staff, General Sir William ('Wully') Robertson, was appalled by
the appointment of a general who was 'too old and tired' for command,
although Duff assured him that Lake still played games, but did not spec-
ify which.[16] Robertson persisted, sending Lake a pointed telegram which
suggested that some of his brigade commanders were 'too old and tired for
the conditions of modern war'.[17] Lake was not too weary to intercept and
impound critical telegrams sent by the embattled Townshend to his friend,
The Times's military correspondent.[18]

What particularly irritated Robertson was that Mesopotamian blunders
were driving him to divert scarce men and material from the Western
Front to what he considered a strategically valueless sideshow. Furthermore, operations had been allowed to continue after it was clear that India
lacked the wherewithal to support them unaided. 'Our military resources
have been reduced to bedrock,' Hardinge had admitted in March 1915.[19]
This was just part of the story; the truth was that the Mesopotamian army
had been the victim of serious material deficiencies from the very beginning. Only in March 1915 did the army receive its first reconnaissance aircraft, and these and their pilots had been loaned by the Australian and New
Zealand governments. Hitherto, and for some time to come, basic field
intelligence about the enemy's strength and positions was gathered by
cavalry patrols. Communications were primitive thanks to a dearth of

wirelesses, telephone and telegraphic equipment and signallers. Hasty efforts to train Indian signallers resulted in the appearance at the front of men who were slow at transmitting and receiving messages, not that this mattered, for their handwriting was 'execrable'. Transport arrangements broke down under the burdens imposed on them, vital ice-making machines had to be purchased second-hand in India, and, unforgiveably at the onset the summer hot season, supplies of beer ran out.[20]

Most tragic in terms of human suffering were the poor medical facilities, which added immeasurably to the miseries of British and Indian wounded. Springless wooden carts carried injured men from the front to under-staffed hospitals where they were cared for by untrained orderlies, including laundrymen. No nurses appeared in Mesopotamia until April 1916. Before then, no one had bothered to sterilise drinking water because prevailing medical wisdom insisted that cholera, dysentery and diarrhoea were transmitted by flies, which was why three divisions suffered a cholera epidemic during the spring of 1916.[21] The local senior medical officer opposed sending convalescents to Karachi as it would encourage malingering, and there was abundant evidence that men sent back to India would desert rather than return to Mesopotamia.[22] Faced with crumbling morale, Lake's only reaction was to demand the death penalty for men with self-inflicted wounds. It is revealing that a British army medical officer, Surgeon-General F. H. Treharne, with Western Front experience, was ordered to Mesopotamia to take charge of overdue reform and re-organisation.

An army on its last legs was asked to perform superhuman feats during the first three months of 1916, when relief forces tried to break the Turkish grip on Kut. They failed, with heavy losses. In desperation and to the amazement of his superiors in London, Lake adopted a stratagem originally suggested by Townshend and offered a £2 million ransom for Kut's defenders. The Turkish commander contemptuously spurned what looked like a bribe and Kut's defenders were forced to surrender at the end of April. Their capitulation was a reverse equal in scale and damage to prestige of the Kabul débâcle of 1841–42, and a severe blow to the reputation not only of the Indian army but also the Indian government.

This signal catastrophe was followed by an official investigation into the events which had brought it about, and, in turn, a thorough overhaul of the administration and command of the Indian army. The offensive against Baghdad was renewed, and the city fell the following year as part of a general advance which, when Turkey surrendered at the end of October

1918, had put the Indian government in charge of what is today Iraq. There was no agreement as to its political future. On one hand, a faction within the Indian government, most notably Sir Alexander Hitrzel of the India Office political department, and a handful of officials on the spot, wished to retain the province under Indian administration with an open invitation to Indian settlers. On the other, there was a band of Foreign Office Arabophiles who wanted Iraq to become a British satellite under an Arab prince. This made sense in terms of political consistency, for since 1916 Britain had sponsored the Arab nationalist revolt which had spread northwards from Mecca into Palestine and Syria. The British government had promised the Arab leadership post-war self-determination, although nothing had been clarified as to the exact borders of the new Arab states or their form of government. Hardinge and many Indian officials had been horrified by British involvement in the Arab Revolt which, while it dulled the edge of jihadic propaganda, was bound to have repercussions in India. How was it that the British encouraged the aspirations of one people and frowned on those of another? Moreover, by the beginning of 1919 there were clear indications that many Iraqi Arabs and all the Kurds had no desire to become an outlying dependency of India, paying higher taxes to meet the expenses of an administration staffed by overbearing ex-Indian army officers. Those who felt this way placed naïve faith in the contents of President Woodrow Wilson's Fourteen Points, which proclaimed that the Allies were waging war for the rights of small nations to self-government.

III

Indian soldiers serving in France faced as great hardships as their brothers-in-arms in Iraq, but were fortunate in that their ancillary services, largely managed by the British army, were superior. Home letters from the front convey a universal astonishment at the intensity of the fighting and the huge casualties caused by German artillery fire. Early in 1915 one sepoy spoke for all when he wrote: 'The whole world is being brought to destruction. One cannot think about it. He will be a very lucky man who returns to India.' 'It is the ending of the world,' claimed another. 'It is not war.'[23] During two days' fighting on the Ypres perimeter at the end of October 1914, the 57th Gharwalis lost 314 dead, including all their officers, more than half their strength.[24] Death and the bitter winter's cold were endured with a stoicism which owed everything to a faith in the inexorable dispositions of Providence. Like British soldiers, some Indians turned to writing verse, a development which perturbed Captain Evelyn Howell of the ICS, who ran the censorship department. His report for January 1915 warned of a 'tendency to break into poetry which I am inclined to regard as a rather ominous sign of mental disquietude'.[25]

There was reassurance in the repeated praise for the army's medical and welfare services and regular visits by George V and Queen Mary to the Indian convalescent hospitals at Brighton (the converted Pavilion) and Netley. Both offered Indian soldiers the chance to sample what they called 'fruit', their code word for women. One reported that the girls in Brighton were 'no better than the girls of the Adda Bazaar of Indore'. Another, a Lancer duffadar, sent a friend some saucy French postcards in January 1916, which the prissy Howell extracted from the letter, no doubt to the disappointment of the recipient.[26] Possible sexual liaisons between Indian soldiers and English women were a constant headache for the authorities. General Sir James Willcocks, commander of the Indian contingent, while publicly praising his men's courage in the field, privately regretted that they had to be invalided to Brighton. He also objected strongly to Indian wounded being tended by white nurses, as did Sir John French, the commander of the British Expeditionary Force, who was indignant at a *Daily Mail* photograph which showed an Indian convalescent and an English nurse.[27]

Caste barriers proved as strong as sexual. In the behind-the-lines rest camps in France, the YMCA endeavoured to obtain better treatment for the 'untouchable' sweepers and servants from the lower castes. Traditional barriers proved resilient. In one hospital during the summer of 1915, a sepoy asked a Hindu babu for some milk and was told: 'After placing your backside at the disposal of the Germans, you come here to drink milk.' This insult enraged a Muslim invalid, Havildar Karum Ullah Khan, who grabbed a stick and thrashed the babu. Fearing a court martial, he appealed to his colonel: 'Huzur, have we been fighting Germans or getting [buggered] by them?' The officer shared Ullah Khan's indignation at this affront to a member of the martial races, gave him ten rupees and ordered that 'no black babu' was to enter the ward where NCOs were convalescing.[28]

Accounts of incidents like this broke the monotony of the censors' routine. Their major duty was to monitor war-weariness, which grew steadily among the Indians as it did in all armies during the latter half of 1916 and 1917, and keep an eye open for signs of sedition. Its commonest form was the repetition of those Pan-Islamic sentiments contained in the jihadic propaganda leaflets which found their way into Indian trenches. Details of the jihad, the astonishing claim that Kaiser Wilhelm II had converted to Islam and rumours that Enver Pasha was leading a Turkish army to Kabul cropped up in soldiers' correspondence during the spring of 1915, which suggested a few believed enemy propaganda. More worrying for their effect on recruitment in India were letters home that reported heavy losses and replies which described the grief as news of casualties spread through Indian towns and villages.[29]

Eye-witness accounts of the death toll on the Western Front which had reached men serving in the 5th Light Infantry, stationed at Singapore, contributed to their mutiny in February 1915. What seems to have been a spontaneous uprising was triggered by rumours that the regiment was about to embark for France, although its actual destination was Hong Kong. Several officers were murdered and parties of mutineers fanned out into the city, killing Europeans at random. For a time there was panic as refugees fled to ships in the harbour; one woman recalled: 'The Indian Mutiny flashed into my mind; also that we had no white troops.'[30] A scratch force was hastily gathered, including Japanese, Russian and British sailors, and after some nail-biting days, every mutineer had been killed, imprisoned or was a fugitive. The suppression was easier than it might have been, for the insurgents lacked any organisation and an overall plan. After courts martial, eighty-nine were imprisoned and thirty-seven publicly shot by firing squad. Investigation into the causes of the outbreak revealed faults among the officers, factions among the men and undercurrents of religious fervour. Unusually, the 5th Light Infantry was an all-Muslim regiment and anxieties about fighting the Caliph had been exacerbated by two Pan-Islamic preachers, one of whom was later hanged. One sepoy believed that Algerian Muslims had refused to fight the Germans because they were allies of the Turks, and another was troubled by what he had heard from men serving in France: 'We receive letters and we know real feelings.'[31]

The official explanation shared the blame for the insurrection between the regiment's internal problems and Turko-German intrigue, which was convenient for the authorities, but untrue. Religious apprehension lay at the heart of the mutiny, made worse by fears of service in France, sentiments which were self-generated and indicated that the sepoys thought for themselves. Pathans, always highly receptive to Pan-Islamic appeals, were responsible for two mutinies of the 130th Baluchis during the winter of 1914–15, both sparked off by fears of being forced to follow Muslims.

Distress at having to fight in what was considered a sacred land led to murmurs among the 15th Lancers at Basra and when NCOs reported the
men's disquiet firm action was immediately taken. An artillery battery and
British troops surrounded the lancers' camp, the cavalrymen were disarmed, and, according to the maulavi attached to the regiment, their
belongings were plundered.[32]

The gravest unrest in India was generated by the underground Ghadr
(Revolt) party during the winter and early spring of 1914–15. The Ghadr
movement had been active for seven years, was based in the Punjab, and
drew its strongest support from the Sikh émigré communities which had
settled on the west coast of Canada and the United States. Its primary aim
was to kindle a mutiny among the Punjab garrison, which would begin a
mass uprising in which Europeans would be massacred and Lahore and
Delhi seized. To this end, hundreds of Sikhs from North America and the
Far East began converging on India during September 1914. Forewarned
and armed with the recent legislation which allowed them to intern
returned emigrants whose politics were suspect, the authorities prepared to
intercept the returning emigrants as they disembarked. They had limited
success; some militants were killed in gun battles and some arrested, but a
significant number escaped the net and proceeded to the Punjab. Here,
they initiated a campaign of assassinations and dakaiti during the winter of
1914–15 under the overall direction of Rash Behari Bose, a slippery and
experienced terrorist wanted for his part in the bomb attack on Lord
Hardinge two years before. The climax of the Ghadrite campaign was to
have been a series of mutinies by Punjabi troops which would signal a general insurrection. Informers, undercover police work and the energy of Sir
Michael O'Dwyer, the Governor of the Punjab, frustrated the conspiracy
in the nick of time. The subsequent clampdown shattered the Ghadrite
leadership, with some in detention and the rest on the run. Among them
was Rash Behari Bose, who finally surfaced in Japan, from where the
authorities failed to extradite him. The ambivalent attitude of the Japanese
towards India's most notorious terrorist, together with other incidents,
aroused suspicions that its government was dangerously sympathetic to
Asian nationalism.[33]

What is striking about all these outbreaks is that they were, so to speak,
home-grown enterprises, although some rebellious troops had certainly
been exposed to unofficial jihadic propaganda. Nonetheless, Delhi had
been given an unpleasant shock, even though the Ghadrites had had very
little popular support. In March 1915 an Indian version of the British

Defence of the Realm act was passed, with strong backing from O'Dwyer. It allowed for the internment of political agitators and the suspension of trial by jury in cases of sedition and terrorism. To the apparatus of the law was added that of the expanded intelligence services, in India and abroad, and the provincial police CIDs.

These measures began to take effect the moment that Turko-German plans for Indian subversion were coalescing. They owed their genesis to the German chancellor, Von Bethmann Hollweg, who was convinced that India could be set alight by the astute use of Islamic fervour, Ghadrites and Bengali terrorists. Exiled revolutionaries of all these persuasions had made their way to Berlin by the beginning of 1915. The Intelligence Bureau for the East could call upon the Ghadrite Hal Dayal, Virendranath Chatto-padhaya, a Bengali terrorist who had been based in London and Paris, various fanatical Muslim clerics and a trickle of Indian deserters, mostly frontier tribesmen. An exotic addition to this band was Kunwar Mahendra Pratap, a dethroned minor Muslim raja of a Walter-Mittyish disposition, who fancied himself as India's future ruler. Like all political exiles, they were hosts to daydreams which led them and their German accomplices to imagine that a single, spectacular masterstroke would simultaneously over-throw the Raj and arouse the masses. They also shared a tendency to disregard the considerable physical obstacles which lay in their way. A successful Indian revolution required arms and a cadre of dedicated lead-ers, both of which would have to be smuggled into India. Two routes were open and each was perilous. Britain controlled the world's seaways, Ger-many and its allies were under close blockade, and the 1,500-mile overland route to India from Turkey ran across Persia, which was then under the thumbs of Britain and Russia.

If, by some means, an Indian uprising was engineered, it could not rely on any close support from either Turkey or Germany. By contrast the 1916 Arab Revolt, masterminded by the Foreign Office and military intelligence agencies, was kept alive by regular injections of cash, arms, aircraft and troops, which were delivered by sea. It was also helped by the advice of British and French specialist officers, most famously T. E. Lawrence. Any Turko-German inspired movement in Afghanistan, Persia or India could not expect such crucial technical back-up. This was why the endeavours of Wilhelm Wassmuss to lead an anti-British and anti-Russian rebellion in Persia came to nothing.

The Germans and their collaborators optimistically believed they would overcome these handicaps by a two-pronged secret offensive. The aim of the first was to secure a base in Afghanistan or, better still, persuade its ruler, the Amir Habibullah, to declare war on Britain in the name of Islam. After a secret and risky journey across northern Persia, a Turko-German mission reached Kabul in October 1915, but found Habibullah obdurate in his neutrality. Promises of arms shipments and cash did not shift him, understandably given the problems of transporting them across hostile territory. He was, however, prepared to give house room to Pratap who, in December 1916, declared himself head of the 'Provisional Government of India'. Although he hoped to find allies among non-Muslim Punjabi and Bengali revolutionaries, Pratap's most promising source of support was among Muslim extremists, the so-called 'Hindustani Fanatics'. Some of these holy warriors were implicated in the 'Silk Letter Plot', uncovered at the end of 1916, which indicated the existence of vague plans for the formation of an 'Army of God' in India. It proved to be a will-o'-the-wisp, but gave the authorities some nervous moments.

If German artifices worked according to plan, Habibullah's invasion would have coincided with a mass insurrection in Bengal, spear-headed by local nationalists under German direction and armed with weapons purchased in the United States and smuggled through Siam. Procurement of the rebel arsenal was in the hands of the German military attaché in Washington, the foxy Franz von Papen, who later become the last chancellor of Weimar Germany before Hitler's coup. He contrived to buy 11,000 rifles and 500 revolvers but, after a series of blunders in the shipping arrangements, they were impounded by the United States government. A second consignment failed to leave port thanks to the vigilance of local British intelligence agents who alerted the American authorities.

Just how these weapons might have been used was revealed by Vincent Kraft, a German spy, who offered himself as a double agent to the British in Singapore in August 1915. Anxious to ingratiate himself with his new employers and earn his £2 a day, he outlined the amazingly ambitious plan which the Germans then had in hand. An 'extensive organisation' for 'stirring up revolution' was already in place and, to date, it had run 8,000 rifles into Siam, where German officers were waiting to take command of a Bengali uprising scheduled for October.[34] In his new guise and still enjoying the trust of his masters in Berlin, Kraft made fresh contacts in China, from where he returned with a hair-raising tale of a coup planned in Calcutta for Christmas Day, 1915. German agents in the Dutch East Indies were to hire a ship, fill it with arms, land on the Andaman Islands, liberate the convicts and convey them to Calcutta for a surprise revolt, which would catch the sahibs unawares as they celebrated Christmas.[35] Hardinge, who was naturally jumpy, believed him, but there is very little evidence to substantiate Kraft's tale, although it eventually helped him and his family to begin an anonymous life in America, financed by Britain.[36]

The Viceroy ought to have had more faith in his intelligence services, which were well abreast of their adversaries in India, the Far East and North America. Newly re-united Bengal proved the exception as terrorism increased, with a stepping-up of the murders of informers, detectives and senior policemen during 1915. Effective counter-measures were hindered by the Governor, Lord Carmichael, who was temperamentally unfitted to rule a turbulent province. A Lowland laird of strong Liberal views, 'Tom' Carmichael loved art, kept bees and, in his youth, had written a monograph on centipedes. He spoke slowly and took care never to offend anyone's feelings, save those of policemen, whom he instinctively mistrusted. For this reason, he was extremely unwilling to implement the Defence of India act and intern suspected terrorists. Just as it seemed that they were getting the upper hand, Carmichael retired and moved to the relative tranquillity of the world of the company boardroom. His place was taken by the more robust Lord Ronaldshay, who dealt rigorously with terrorism. An augmented and reorganised police intelligence department returned to the fray with fresh heart, and, by the end of 1918, the number of outrages was falling and the number of convictions increasing.

If the Germans had adopted the policy of backing small sabotage units, as the Japanese did in 1942, rather than attempting John Buchanesque conspiracies designed to topple the Raj at a stroke, they might have done greater damage to their enemies. Nevertheless, the Turko-German propaganda campaign caused some nervous moments – at one stage in 1916 there were only eight British battalions in India, all of them guarding the North-West Frontier, and Hardinge was pleading with the War Office for more. His alarm, like that shown by his predecessors at moments of crisis, rested on the assumption that in a dire emergency white troops alone could save the Raj. By early 1917, it was clear that the Germans had failed, overcome by geography, the prudence of the Afghan amir, Anglo-Indian counter-measures and the sheer impossibility of co-ordinating Indian subversion from centres as far apart as Constantinople and San Francisco. Pan-Islamic propaganda had made few converts, thanks in large part to the Aga Khan's proclamation of loyalty to the King Emperor and the fact that Indian pilgrims were free to visit Mecca after it had fallen to the forces of the Arab revolt.

IV

For non-violent nationalists, the war was a period of immense hope. Unstinting Indian participation demonstrated to Britain their fitness for running their own affairs. Tilak argued in 1917 that: 'If you want Home Rule be prepared to defend your Home. Had it not been for my age I would have been the first to volunteer. You cannot reasonably say that the ruling will be done by you and the fighting for you.'[37] Gandhi, speaking at the time of the great German offensive in France in July 1918, insisted that India's future was now in the balance:

> An Empire that has been defending India and of which India aspires to be the equal partner is in great peril, and it ill befits India to stand aloof at the hour of its destiny. . . . India would be nowhere without Englishmen. If the British do not win, whom shall we go for claiming equal partnership? Shall we go to the victorious German or the Turk or the Afghan for it? We shall have no right to do so; the victorious nation will set its mind on imposing taxes, or repressing, harassing and tyrannizing over the vanquished. Only after making its position secure will it listen to our demands, whereas the liberty-loving English will surely yield, when they have seen that we have laid down our lives for them.[38]

By this time Congress had set Home Rule within a federal empire as India's first priority. Its conversion owed much to the labours of Mrs Annie Besant, the sometime wife of a Lincolnshire parson and champion of what were, for a middle-class Englishwoman and most of her contemporaries, outrageous causes. In succession, she had been a militant atheist and accomplice of Bradlaugh, an advocate of free love, a trade union organiser and a Fabian socialist. Her final resort was the murky and manic world of occult religiosity which offered unlimited outlets for her energy and preoccupations. In 1893 she arrived in India, aged forty-six and intent on exploring Hinduism which, she imagined, was highly compatible with her own Theosophy. She was not disappointed; one of her first revelations was that the daughter of a Hindu mathematics professor was a reincarnation of the founding mother of Theosophy, Madame Blavatsky. India also offered new causes for adoption and she soon found herself immersed in the current Hindu renaissance, helping to found the new

Hindu university at Benares (Varanasi). She was also the sponsor of Khrisnamurti, a young Madrasi whom she presented to the world as a messianic prophet, in which role he gathered a considerable congregation in Europe, mostly female and well-heeled. He died in 1986, having lived to see a revival of the vogue for Indian gurus uttering portentous platitudes.[39]

Mrs Besant entered Indian national politics with a supernatural revelation. There existed what she called the 'Great Plan or World Drama', whose scenario was divinely written and aimed at the wholesale elevation of mankind.[40] The individual could only climb this ladder of perfection through an acute awareness of God, and the Indian nation by the readoption of ancient Hindu virtues. This was not a new programme; Tilak and the Bengali nationalists had long advocated a Hindu revival as the foundation for national resurgence. What Mrs Besant offered was an enticing blend of the spiritual and the secular, and it was a recipe which appealed to the educated classes. Her *Wake Up India!* appeared in 1913, and subsequently she embarked on lecture tours across the country on behalf of her All-India Home Rule League. Her message closely coincided with that of Tilak, now the head of the Home Rule League. Neither impeded the war effort in any way, and Mrs Besant went to great lengths to emphasise India's huge debt to Britain and repeatedly urged Indians to imitate British patriotism and public spiritedness. In December 1918 she was elected chairman of a Congress which had been converted to her political goal of home rule.

Patriotic nationalism presented the British government with a dilemma. It could not ignore the sacrifices made by Indians which were growing heavier as the war proceeded, nor disregard the war-weariness which infected India as it did every other combatant nation. Government expenditure was steadily rising and recruits were flowing into the army; by 1918 half a million men had enlisted, a fifth of them from the Punjab, and 400,000 had been recruited for behind-the-lines labour; all at little cost to the British government. Political India was interpreting the news that the Russian autocracy, which nationalists had sometimes likened to the Raj, had been overthrown and replaced by a popular government as a sign that a new spirit was abroad in the world. Above all, they were looking for rewards for loyalty. Facing the third year of the war, and aware that it would demand further, almost superhuman efforts from the empire's population, Lloyd George's coalition Cabinet agreed that Indian political progress would have to be accelerated. Its direction, if not its exact pace, was outlined in August 1917 by the new Secretary of State, Edwin Montagu. Henceforward, Britain's overall objective was

> the increasing association of Indians in every branch of the administration and the gradual development of self-governing institutions with a view to the progressive realisation of responsible government in India as part of the British Empire.

'Responsible government' had been inserted by Curzon during Cabinet discussions as a replacement for 'self-government', but, nonetheless, many Indians imagined that the goal was dominion status and that it would be achieved swiftly.

Transforming a declaration of intent into action was the job of Montagu. He was thirty-eight, a passionate Liberal who had worked under Morley in the India Office before the war, and a member of a Jewish banking family. Jewishness was an asset, he believed, when it came to gaining the confidence and friendship of Indians. 'I am an Oriental,' he wrote in his diary of the Indian tour. 'Certainly that social relationship which English people seem to find so difficult comes quite easy to me; and we shall go from bad to worse, until we are hounded out of India, unless something is done to correct this sort of thing.' He had in mind the frostiness of the new Viceroy, Lord Chelmsford, whom he found 'thoroughly nice, but unfortunately cold, aloof and reserved'. He acted true to form when he refused to be draped with a floral garland by Mrs Besant, while Montagu accepted his from Tilak, who, in any case, did not ask his permission.[41]

Encounters with Mrs Besant and Tilak were part of Montagu's peregrinations across India which lasted from November 1917 to May 1918. He was there to sound Indian opinion for clues as to how best to reshape their government and, like Morley, he felt that India offered him the chance to make his mark on history. He dreamt of accomplishing 'something big' and 'epoch-making' and was worried by it. Still, there were many diversions laid on by the government and the princes. A keen ornithologist and egg-collector, he watched birds and indulged another passion, shooting game. Montagu saw new birds, which delighted him, but had old prejudices confirmed, which did not. After the publication of the Mesopotamian enquiry the previous July, he had roused some hackles, by alleging in the Commons that the Indian administration was 'too wooden, too iron, too inelastic, too antediluvian to be of any use for the modern purposes we have in mind'. In India he found that 'the dead hand' of

Olympian officials was everywhere, and he feared that Chelmsford would easily succumb to the persuasions of 'reactionaries' among his staff. One, O'Dwyer, who struck Montagu as a 'rough Irishman', was particularly vehement in denouncing any further Indian participation in government.

The outcome of Montagu's excursions and deliberations was the Montagu–Chelmsford reform proposals, which were first published in July 1918 and became law a year later. Two levels of elected government were established. The lower comprised eight provincial assemblies in which Indian ministers took charge of education, health, agriculture and the state budget; and the higher, a viceregal legislative assembly whose role was largely advisory. Both bodies operated under considerable restraints. The Viceroy and the provincial governors kept ultimate control over taxation and all security matters, and they could nominate a fifth of the membership of the assemblies and veto legislation. Indian representatives were chosen by an all-male electorate of five million, selected by property ownership, and officers and NCOs of the Indian army.[42]

The system was known as dyarchy and, in essence, was a natural extension of the Morley–Minto reforms, for, like them, it was contrived as a means of securing the co-operation of India's middle classes. It was noted during the Commons debate on the measure that the property hurdle excluded five million literate Indians and nearly all ex-servicemen, both classes considered worthy by the left and the right respectively. Much decision-making was shifted from the centre to the regions and dyarchy further reduced the the power of the ICS. Montagu saw his act as a step towards Indian self-government, and so did his critics, who found the prospect alarming. The *Spectator* greeted the new arrangements as a 'kind of Bolshevism' and feared that the government was about to embark on a new and disastrous version of its Irish policy, which had placated a noisy minority by sacrificing the interests of the silent masses. In India the winners would be the Brahmins and the losers everyone else, including the peasantry who were deeply attached to the Raj.[43] The *Saturday Review* lamented the replacement of the old pattern of authority with 'debating societies', and predicted fresh calamities would follow, for Labour MPs had been admitted to Parliamentary committees which overlooked Indian affairs.[44]

The Montagu–Chelmsford reforms opened up a rift in British political life. India's future was now a contentious issue in the press and on the floor of the Commons, where a knot of right-wing Conservatives convinced themselves that the government was losing its nerve and allowing India to slip from Britain's grasp. On the left, there were protests that the reforms did not go far enough in the direction of democracy. These differences were voiced in the debate on the bill in June 1919, when opponents stressed the diversity of India's population and the fact that the peasant masses had no truck with political reforms, seeking nothing more than security of tenure and civil peace. The strongest denunciation came from Brigadier-General Henry Croft, the MP for Christchurch, who hinted at Montagu's origins and untrustworthiness by references to his 'Oriental fervour' in promoting a 'revolutionary measure', which had been hastily framed without seeking the opinions of the loyal martial classes.[45]

V

The India under Parliamentary scrutiny in 1919 was not the country it had been five years before. Like every other participant in the war, it had suffered severe internal strains which had bruised and shaken old social and economic structures. Soldiers serving in Europe had had their eyes opened to new worlds and opportunities. In October 1917, Khan Muhammad Khan of Jacob's Horse told his family that: 'The people of Europe live in ease and comfort simply through education . . . I wring my hands with regrets, that I did not set myself to acquire learning.' He promised himself that, if he returned home, his children 'will fashion their lives according to my new ideas'.[46] Others discovered new political insights. 'Only the ruling class that thinks so much of itself . . . stands in the way of any Indian reform,' a sepoy commented in November 1915. A Labour Corps coolie wrote home in January 1918 that the British government fully recognised the self-sacrifice of India and that Arthur Henderson, 'chief of the Labour Party', believed in Indian government and many other 'great sahibs' were of the same mind.[47]

Inside India, the war had quickened industrial growth. The expansion of the Jamshedpur works of Tata Iron and Steel Company was typical. Founded in 1907 with a workforce of 4,000, it was employing 30,000 in 1923 and production had risen a hundredfold. During the war its entire output had been consumed by the Middle East war effort.[48] Like their counterparts in the rest of India's fledgling industry, this company's managers had had to submit to centralised, official control. The Indian Munitions Board, set up in February 1917 in the wake of the Mesopotamian muddles, supervised the production of all raw materials and manufactured goods and acted as a central purchasing and distribution agency. By October 1918 it had spent £48.2 million.[49] As in Britain, wartime emergency conditions had forced the abandonment of traditional *laissez-faire* economic policies, and after the war the government planned to retain the board to oversee future investment and foster technical education, functions which were passed in 1919 to the new provincial assemblies.[50]

Wartime demands witnessed expansion in the production of such staples as cotton and jute and a rise of 6 per cent in overall exports over pre-war levels. Imports from Britain, hitherto India's main supplier of manufactured goods, fell, but the shortfall was made up by new trading partners, the United States and Japan, whose exports to India increased by 400 per cent. A dramatic indication of the new pattern of trade were the statistics for cotton imports: in 1913–14 India took £37.9 million from Britain and in 1918–19 £27.2 million, while Japan's share of the Indian market rose from £1 million to £9.6 million. Japan and the United States both accepted Indian raw materials, and in the final year of the war were taking over a quarter of India's exports, slightly less than Britain's share.[51] The war had fractured Anglo-Indian economic inter-dependency and started a trend that would become increasingly pronounced over the next twenty years.

The chief beneficiaries of this economic revolution were Indian businessmen who, after 1918, ploughed back their wartime profits into new and developing industries. These were still delicate plants and needed protection from the strong winds of foreign, mainly British, competition, which was why the Indian commercial community pleaded for an end to the free-trade policy which favoured Britain. Opposition to free trade helped swing businessmen and their funds behind Congress, whose economic policy of *swadesh* (economic self-sufficiency) was protectionism in all but name.[52] A step in this direction had been taken in 1917 when the Indian government agreed to take over £100 million of Britain's war debts in exchange for the right to tax Lancashire cottons.

The impact of the war on the countryside and the poorer classes was uneven and hard to quantify. The burden of tax rose steeply from an average of one and a half rupees (12p) a head to two and a half (20p). A detailed survey of the village of Pimpla Soudagar, near Poona, undertaken in 1916, revealed that the ryots continued to live a precarious existence. This predominantly Hindu community contained 556 inhabitants, of whom a quarter were children, and whose total income was 22,500 rupees (£3,150). It was calculated that a family of five received, on average, 218 rupees (£30.50) a year, of which 200 rupees (£28) went on food and clothing. Between them the villagers owed 13,300 rupees (£1,862) on which they paid 2,600 rupees (£364) in interest payments, which averaged 24 per cent, and the annual land revenue assessment was 1,160 rupees (£162). With necessities representing 91 per cent of its budget, the average family had to find the equivalent of an additional 16 per cent to satisfy moneylenders and the government. There was some temporary relief in that eighty-nine men and boys were employed in a munitions factory in nearby Khadki, but their wages were not enough to keep sixty-seven families out of the quagmire of cumulative debt which was passed to the next generation.[53]

Matters were made worse for those already on a tight margin by wartime inflation and price increases. Both rose steadily during the war years, despite ample harvests, and spiralled after the failure of the south-west monsoon in June–July 1918. Using official figures and taking 1913 price levels as a base of 100, it was calculated that at the close of 1918 the cost of food had risen to 143 and clothing to 167.[54] In Baluchistan and the Sind, grain and rice prices doubled and the United and Central Provinces were officially declared a famine zone in the autumn.

Food shortages coincided with the Spanish influenza pandemic. The virus came into India by way of a troopship which docked at Bombay at the end of May 1918, and was transmitted across the country by discharged soldiers, postal workers, railway passengers and the panic-stricken who fled from the countryside to the towns and cities. A second and more virulent strain arrived in the last week of August, and within three months had the whole of India in its grip. Within a year, influenza had, according to a conservative official estimate, killed 12–13 million, but the real figure was probably closer to 18 million.[55] Women between fifteen and fifty and children were especially vulnerable. One immediate consequence was what the Punjabi legal authorities described as 'the scarcity of women', which they believed was one of the factors for the sudden increase in murders during 1919.[56]

The amount of crime in the Punjab and Awadh had fallen during the war and rose rapidly during 1919 and 1920. Among other things, this upsurge was ascribed to the 'return of bad characters from abroad' or 'bad characters from the army'.[57] The ferocious qualities which the army prized in the 'martial classes' were obviously a nuisance in time of peace, but, as in Europe, it may have been that men who had grown hardened to slaughter and mayhem found it hard to shed their moral callouses.

The army had stayed true to its salt. Indian troops had played a vital part in campaigns which had added Iraq, Palestine and German East Africa to the British empire and Syria and the Levant to the French. They had also behaved gallantly on the Western Front, and the sum of their sacrifice is set in the roll call of the dead carved on the sides of the triumphal arch designed by Sir Edwin Lutyens and set, majestically, at the end of a sweeping avenue which leads to the government offices in New Delhi. More lives would be lost after November 1918. During 1919 and 1920 Indian units were deployed in wars on the North-West Frontier, against rebels in Kurdistan and Iraq and on ill-starred excursions against Russian Bolsheviks.

Indian soldiers who returned home from various fronts at the turn of 1918 found a country in a state of flux. It was entering the first phase of an industrial revolution and was distressed by food shortages, inflation, high prices and a devastating pandemic. Alongside the hunger and sickness there were their offspring: discontent and restlessness. In turn, these generated a feeling that great, perhaps catastrophic events were just round the corner. This unquiet mood of uncertainty was sensed by Lal Singh, a corporal returning from a prison camp in Germany in M. J. Anand's novel *The Sword and the Sickle*. As his train carried him from Bombay to his native Punjab:

> He felt himself in the presence of a new spirit, of something unusual, the echoes of some giant change, some great unrest, whose ominous waves spread out and hovered like a new doom, full of fearful expectations.

2

Strong Passion: Amritsar and After, 1919–22

I

Nineteen nineteen was a decisive year in Indian history. For those who ran and guarded the Raj, it was the year when another mutiny was averted by strong men and hard measures. Both saved the Raj; but they lost it untold numbers of friends and severely damaged its reputation for wisdom and humanity. Indians were alternately stunned and enraged by the terrible events in the Punjab. The old exclusive Congress was reborn as a dynamic mass movement which embraced the peasantry and the growing class of industrial workers. The midwife of this new, popular nationalism was Gandhi, who gave Congress its new mission and led it in directions which unnerved many of its older, more conservative members. They had no choice but to follow, for 1919 was the year in which Gandhi stamped his personality and principles on Congress. Another figure who had convinced himself that he knew what was best for India's future also occupied the centre stage that year: Brigadier-General Reginald ('Rex') Dyer. For Indians he was a devil incarnate, but for many, perhaps the majority of his countrymen and women, he was India's saviour. The year which marked a turning point in India's history also witnessed a parting of the ways between Britons and Indians.

It is hard to pass a historical judgement on Gandhi, let alone criticise a man who is still regarded in India and beyond as a saint. He towered over all those engaged in the struggle for Indian independence as a Mosaic figure, who led his people and fired them with a vision of themselves and their country, which most found impossible to fulfil. Gandhi's assassination in 1948 added to his sanctity, transforming him into a martyr for his country and his principles; to censure them and him is tantamount to blasphemy. The film of his life, made in 1982 by a British director, Richard Attenborough, is pure hagiography, the late-twentieth-century equivalent of a mediaeval encomium of a remarkable saint rendered in words and illuminated pictures. Gandhi was a miracle-worker. A tiny, frail man, he took on the Goliath of the British Raj and overcame it through his own interior moral strength: humility and rectitude proved more than a match for arrogance and armed might. As a twentieth-century parable, Gandhi's achievement was profoundly inspiring for the millions of individuals throughout the world who found themselves struggling against unyielding and all-powerful political systems.

And yet as an example of the triumph of the metaphysical over the physical, Gandhi's success was misleading. It rests on the shaky assumption that the Raj was monolithic and omniscient and that its masters were determined to keep their monopoly of power come what may. Furthermore, those in authority exercised their powers of coercion sparingly and often with considerable reluctance.

As Gandhi fully appreciated, his opponents were peculiarly susceptible to the moral force of his arguments and actions. Proposing a toast to the British empire at a dinner of the Madras Bar Association in March 1915, he reviewed his recent campaign for Indian rights in the Transvaal:

> As a passive resister I discovered that I could not have that free scope which I had under the British Empire. . . . I discovered the British Empire had certain ideas with which I have fallen in love ['Hear, hear'] and one of those ideals is that every subject of the British Empire has the freest scope for his energies and efforts and whatever he thinks he is, is due to his conscience.[1]

This is extraordinarily revealing. With their traditions of liberty and respect for the individual conscience, the British were bound to be more receptive to moral arguments than the Transvaal Boers, with their unthinking, master-race arrogance. Evidence of this had come from the backing Gandhi had received from the Indian government, in particular Lord Hardinge, for which he was grateful.

When Gandhi spoke to his fellow barristers, he was forty-six and still an unknown force in Indian political life. His efforts on behalf of Indian immigrants in the Transvaal had won him widespread respect and opened many doors within the Congress establishment. Nonetheless, he was and remained something of an oddity, with idiosyncratic views which were the product of his private religious convictions and meditations. For him, religion, in so far as it concerned man's knowledge of and relationship with God, was fundamental to the conduct of all human affairs. Gandhi's opinions on every public issue from the prevalence of spitting (which he deplored) to the future of India, had their roots in his own metaphysical preoccupations and personal quest for enlightenment. Whenever he pronounced on a subject, theology intruded and became inextricably entangled with his economic and political theories. For instance, in 1916 Gandhi condemned British civilisation as reproduced in India as 'decidedly anti-Christian' and claimed that 'England had sinned against India by forcing free trade upon her'.[2] If, in his cosmology, the Raj was a sort of Antichrist, Indian efforts to terminate it had to be rooted in faith. The masses were the 'living force of Indian life', who knew from experience how to deal with oppression. Once they recovered their spiritual energy they would do so again, Gandhi predicted.[3]

His appeal to godly Hinduism as a counter force to a godless Raj was not novel. It had been forcefully preached by Tilak and adopted with violent results by various underground movements in Bengal. On the eve of Montagu's visit in 1917, one Bengali cell called for a holy war:

> First and last spread terror. Make the unholy Government impossible. . . . We ask you once more in the name of God and Country and all, young and old, rich or poor, Hindus and Muhammadans, Buddhists and Christians to join this war of independence and pour forth your blood and treasure . . .[4]

Such appeals disturbed Gandhi who, despite Mrs Besant's efforts to silence him, forthrightly denounced the Bengali terrorist campaign during the 1916 Congress session. Murders and conspiracies soiled a noble cause, hindered rational debate and had so far accomplished nothing.

At this time Gandhi's attention was focused on the Indian peasantry, whom he was already regarding as allies in the national movement. Then and later he had viewed them and their world through rose-tinted Tolstoyan glasses, imagining them to be possessed of instinctive wisdom and goodness. Hitherto, the ryots had been largely ignored by a Congress dominated by rich men of Western education. The rural peasants 'recognise us not as much as they recognise the English officers', Gandhi wrote. 'Their hearts are an open book to neither.'[5] He was prepared to read their hearts, and between 1915 and 1918 travelled across the country making speeches and, most importantly, listening to what the peasants had to say. His holiness impressed them deeply, as did his willingness to use skills learned in the Inner Temple to defend them against high taxes and overbearing landlords. It was the beginning of a relationship with the poor which, in time, gave Gandhi enormous prestige among the masses. Courting the peasantry was a brilliant manoeuvre, for it struck at the roots of a Raj that had always justified itself as the spokesman and guardian of the silent masses of India. Gandhi intended to usurp both functions.

His excursions into what was an unknown world included a third-class return railway journey between Madras and Bombay to discover what was, so to speak, the darker, hidden side of the Raj. He paid thirteen rupees (91p) for what turned out to be a most unpleasant experience for a man from a middle-class background who would normally have paid 65 rupees for a first-class ticket. He squeezed into an over-crowded, dirty carriage, used a foul lavatory and, when the train halted for meal breaks, was served fly-blown food and unpotable tea – 'tannin water with filthy sugar and whitish looking liquid miscalled milk'. Railway officials hectored passengers and took their bribes.[6]

'I hold strong and probably peculiar views,' Gandhi confessed in August 1918, adding that they were not shared by the Congress leadership.[7] He was right. The championship of the rights of women and the assertion that the treatment of Untouchables was a 'blot on Hindu society' bewildered many from the higher castes and outraged others. It would have been difficult for educated, middle-class Indians to accept his quirky economic doctrines which demanded that, like everyone else, they learned how to spin cotton to promote national self-sufficiency and personal self-awareness. Nor would the urban businessman have applauded Gandhi's request to peasants to use their village baker rather than one from a nearby town.[8] This hostility to the large-scale producer, whether capitalist corporation or socialist co-operative, stemmed from a romantic attachment to the artisan and peasant, both of whom Gandhi saw as the backbone of India. He favoured man rather than machine power, distrusted all forms of modern technology and preferred Indians to be taught in Hindi rather than English. This was not a programme to attract the conventional liberal, progressive Congress member.

Had it not been for the government's decision at the end of 1918 to introduce stringent anti-terrorist laws, Gandhi might have stayed an eccentric philosopher on the fringes of the Congress, well-loved but with little influence. The legislation, known as the Rowlatt Acts, was the outcome of the deliberations of a committee which had been instructed to investigate sedition. Its findings were bleak: an under-manned police force which had scarcely contained terrorism was bound to be overwhelmed once wartime legislation lapsed, detainees were released and large numbers of ex-soldiers returned home. The answer was the abolition of normal legal processes for all political offences, which henceforward would be tried without juries in courts where the burden of proof would be weighted in favour of the prosecution. Gandhi was appalled and prepared for what he described as the 'greatest battle of my life' which, incidentally, he felt sure would restore his failing health.[9]

Gandhi's weapon would be the *satyagraha* he had perfected for his contest with the authorities in the Transvaal. It was often called 'passive resistance', a phrase he disliked because it missed the essence of what he had in mind. Satyagraha was a quality of the soul which enabled an individual to endure suffering for what he knew to be morally right. Injustice, as represented by the Rowlatt Acts, was profanity and would wither in the face of the superior moral stamina of those who had prepared themselves and taken the satyagraha pledge. The British were, he believed 'sound at heart' and so would bow to the 'supremacy of moral force'.[10] During February and March 1919, Gandhi outlined his philosophy and what would be expected from those who submitted to the vows of the satyagraha. What he had seen of India during the past four years had made him confident that even the peasantry would understand the nature of what he was demanding from them, and would behave with the necessary patience and restraint when confronting the police. And yet, remembering his Transvaal experiences, he noted that the warlike Pathan could not suppress his instincts sufficiently to accept the self-discipline needed not to lose his temper and lash out.[11]

II

Although the spirit of satyagraha was essentially Hindu, hundreds of thousands of Muslims agreed to participate in the protests planned for the end of March. They did so more out of sectarian sympathies than hostility to the Rowlatt Acts. Since the surrender of Turkey the previous October, Muslims had been disturbed by a persistent rumour that the Britain was bent on the abolition of the caliphate. The response was the Khalifat movement, which urged the British government to preserve the religious status of the Turkish sultan as head of Sunni Islam. As the agitation spread, Khalifat supporters became convinced that their faith was in some way imperilled. Ancient animosities against the infidels surfaced among India's Muslims and were expressed by the poet Akbar Ila Wahabi:

> *Our belly keeps us working with the clerks*
> *Our heart is with the Persians and the Turks.* [12]

Fissile, atavistic sentiments were being fomented by agitators based in Tashkent and Samarkand, where Russian agents were cultivating a Pan-Islamic–Bolshevik axis which would broadcast revolutionary propaganda in India, Persia and Iraq. During the winter of 1918–19 intelligence sources in Mashad reported that rumours were spreading to the effect that British troops had desecrated Muslim holy places and that the Afghans were poised to invade India. [13] The government took this superficially improbable alliance of Bolshevism and Islam seriously, and, in May 1919, Chelmsford was disturbed by the diatribes 'against the British who choke all native races' that were pouring from Tashkent. [14] More alarming were calls for revolution, like this one delivered by a Turkish agitator in Merv during the early summer:

> Oh working Muhammadans! The Soviet Government has been formed to free you all . . . Are you aware that your fellow labourers in other parts of the world are being cruelly and shamefully strangled in cold blood by the British – the greatest enemy of Islam? The British Government is the same which has enslaved 70 millions of Muslims in India, which rules Egypt with fire and sword, which had wiped out Tripoli and dismembered the Turkish Empire . . . You know that the Afghans have risen against them, and that the British are running like hares before the gallant Afghan troops. You can send your friends to the Indian sepoys . . . who are deceived by British pay to be against them in their right and win them to your side, turning them against their infidel employers. [15]

Appeals to mutiny always struck a chill note in India. There had been chronic unrest on the North-West Frontier since 1917 and it persisted until 1924, despite several punitive expeditions and the widespread use of aircraft. There were occasional signs of wobbling among Muslim troops, and, in January 1920, the commander in Waziristan thought it prudent to look out for signs of Pan-Islamic subversion among men being asked to fight their co-religionists.[16] Periods of uncertainty spawned rumours and they ran riot through India during 1919 and 1920, adding the authorities' headaches, for they could not be stifled and denials seldom convinced. Among the crop during the summer of 1920 were bizarre tales that the Russians had invaded Afghanistan, occupied Chitral and that Gandhi was on his way to Moscow.[17]

Even without Gandhi's satyagraha campaign, there was a prospect of serious unrest during the spring of 1919, although its form and extent were unclear to the government. It was simultaneously faced with Muslim apprehension about the future of the caliphate, distress in the wake of the recent influenza epidemic, prices outstripping wages, dearths and undercurrents of expectation stirred up by news of massive upheavals in Russia and the Middle East. As Chelmsford told the princes in November, they were living through unquiet, envious times. There was a 'new spirit abroad in the world . . . prone to look on order as tyranny, prosperity as profiteering, and expensiveness of living as the result of administration'.[18]

Riots marked the first satyagraha hartal in Delhi on 30 March. They had started, as they were bound to, when some food vendors refused to accept the closure of businesses and they ended with police and troops firing on mobs. The pattern was set for the next fortnight, when each hartal was marked by disorderly processions, looting, arson and attacks on police and Europeans. The trouble was worst in Delhi, Ahmadabad and the Punjab and worsened after 10 April when Gandhi was arrested and taken to Bombay. His crime, Chelmsford believed, was naïve irresponsibility. 'Dear me,' he wired Montagu on the 9th, 'what a damned nuisance these saintly fanatics are! Incapable of hurting a fly, honest, but he enters lightheartedly on a course of action which is the negation of all government and may lead to much hardship to people who are ignorant and easily led astray.'[19] As the anarchy and bloodshed spread, Gandhi gradually realised the ferocity of the passions he had unwittingly unleashed. On 5 April he blamed the Delhi disturbances on the police, but, on the 11th and 12th, he pleaded for restraint, asking his followers to stop mass demonstrations, stone throwing and railway sabotage. They ignored him and on 14 April he was forced to admit that he had 'over-calculated' his countrymen's capacity for self-discipline, but, and here the Hindu was speaking, wondered whether Muslim fervour had been the catalyst for the disorders.[20] The expressions of hatred towards the British, the murders and the savagery of Indians shocked Gandhi, who had ingenuously imagined them incapable of vindictiveness and violence.[21] Chelmsford believed his remorse was sincere, but thought him a 'tool' in the hands of 'revolutionists'.[22]

'Micky' O'Dwyer had no doubts as to the Indian capacity for mayhem and was ready for it in the Punjab, where he expected a repeat of the revolutionary conspiracy he had thwarted in 1915.[23] But the governor's preparations were insufficient to withstand the riots which convulsed Lahore, Kasur, Jalandhar, Multan and Amritsar on 10–12 April. They were, he informed Chelmsford, the pre-meditated work of 'an unholy alliance (chiefly Hindu) between a section of extremist Intelligentsia and the low class Muhammadans, workers, pimps and bravadoes'.[24] Their aim, O'Dwyer believed, was a full-scale uprising coupled with attempts to lure Indian soldiers into a mutiny and, as events unfolded, he found plenty of evidence which appeared to uphold his thesis. His reaction, therefore, was to treat the disturbances as the first stages of an insurrection intended to overthrow the Raj. Condign measures resolutely enforced alone would save the Punjab and with it British India.

O'Dwyer's views on the precariousness of the situation in the Punjab were shared by Brigadier-General Rex Dyer, a chain-smoking, 55-year-old career soldier who had been born in India. His *Times* obituary described him as a 'breezy, kind-hearted man' with a 'dauntless spirit' which had been proved when he commanded a detachment on the Indo-Persian border during the war.[25] He was the typical bluff, no-nonsense sahib, the epitome of a type which was happiest knocking a frontier into shape. Once he told a tribal chief that, 'No Englishman ever makes war against women and children.' On another occasion he warned a bandit: 'Halil Khan, if you play me false, or ever raise you hand against me, I will blow your head off.'[26] Dyer was not a natural subordinate and upset Chelmsford when, off his own bat, he began 'annexing large chunks of Persia' in 1918, and it was only his ill-health which saved him from being dismissed.[27] After he left the frontier, mothers invoked his name to still their fretful children. Outwardly tough, Dyer suffered considerable discomfort and pain from old injuries, which did nothing to improve an already brittle temper. At the beginning of April, he commanded the 45th Brigade based at Jalandhar.

In spirit and strength of will, Dyer was the natural partner of O'Dwyer at whose orders he was sent to Amritsar, where he arrived on the evening of 11 April. What he saw and heard had a powerful effect on his imagination: there were over 100 terrified European women and children crowded into the Gobindgarh fort, refugees from a city which had passed out of British control into that of the mob. During the past thirty-six hours it had stormed two banks, murdered three European members of their staff, burned their bodies and looted cash. The buildings had then been fired, as had two mission schools. Other Europeans had barely escaped alive and one, Miss Marcia Sherwood, a mission doctor, had been brutally beaten by Indian youths, an assault which outraged Dyer, for it seemed to symbolise the contempt in which his countrymen were now held.

Amritsar was a city of 150,000 which had exploded after the arrest of its two leading nationalists: Dr Saifuddin Kitchlew, a 31-year-old Cambridge barrister who was a strong supporter of the Khalifat movement and a fiery orator (he eventually became a Communist), and Dr Satya Pal, a medical practitioner. Both had organised the anti-Rowlatt hartals on 30 March and 6 April, which had been marked by enthusiastic displays of Hindu–Muslim unity, but no serious trouble. The riots on the 10th, ostensibly in support of the detained men, turned into a general attack on Europeans and their property. There had been some firing by police and troops which had been insufficient to coerce but enough to inflame the rioters. By the time of Dyer's arrival all attempts to restore order had been suspended; the Raj appeared paralysed.

Dyer had under his command over 1,100 troops, about a third of them British, and two armoured-cars equipped with machine-guns. On the morning of the 12th he led a detachment of over 400 and the cars through the streets and met a sullen, hostile reception. The following day he re-entered Amritsar and, at various places, a proclamation was read which imposed a curfew at 8.00 P.M. and banned all processions and meetings. Again, Dyer and his troops were ill-received: among the slogans shouted at them was 'The British Raj is at end.'[28] This appeared to be confirmed when Dyer heard garbled details of further commotions in Lahore and Kasur. Most disturbing of all were the reports which reached him of Amritsar agitators, who were alleging that if Indian troops were ordered to open fire on demonstrators, they would refuse.[29] Similar predictions were being broadcast elsewhere in the Punjab and heightened anxieties about a second mutiny.

By the evening of 13 April, if not before, Dyer had convinced himself that the recent disturbances in Amritsar were the prelude to a general uprising, that the city had to be recovered and some sort of deterrent punishment inflicted on its inhabitants which would convince them that the British will to rule was as strong as ever. Intelligence that, in defiance of the previous ban, a mass meeting had been planned that afternoon must have concentrated his mind on the possibility that the subversives wanted a trial of strength. His resolve and that of the Raj were about to be tested. The assembly, which attracted between fifteen and twenty thousand, was held in an enclosed area of wasteland, the Jallianwala Bagh. It is not known how many present had heard of Dyer's interdiction, although the appearance of an aeroplane overhead was a spur for some to leave. Earlier, there had been rumours that the city was to be bombarded in retaliation for the outrages.[30]

Dyer, accompanied by the two armoured cars and fifty Gurkha and Sikh infantrymen (O'Dwyer favoured the use of Indian troops to give the lie to rumours of imminent mutiny) and a further forty Gurkhas armed with kukris reached the bagh just after 5.00 P.M. The chosen entrance was too narrow for the cars, and so Dyer deployed his men facing the crowd and, without warning, ordered them to fire. They continued to do so, reloading twice, for the next ten minutes. Many years later, a Gurkha told a British officer: 'Sahib, while it lasted it was splendid: we fired every round we had.'[31] It was a methodical, directed fusillade with Dyer ordering volleys against parties of demonstrators who were scrambling over walls. When it was over 1,650 rounds had been fired, and 379 lay dead or dying and 1,500 wounded in an area about the same size as Trafalgar Square. Dyer and his party then departed, leaving the injured to fend for themselves, or wait for help from friends and kinsfolk who were willing to defy the curfew.

From then until his death eight years after, Dyer believed that at a stroke he had restored the authority and prestige of the Raj in the Punjab, and saved the lives of his countrymen and women in Amritsar and elsewhere. 'My duty and my military instincts told me to fire,' he would repeatedly claim.[32] At the time it was calculated that there had been about 200 casualties, the figure which reached Delhi and was relaid to London on 15 April. The cable ended: 'The effect of the firing was salutary.'[33]

In the meantime, O'Dwyer had been given permission to declare martial law and the process of pacification was under way across the Punjab which, Chelmsford assured Montagu, was now in 'open rebellion'.[34] At Gujranwala an aeroplane was used to strafe and bomb rioters attacking a railway station. In Amritsar, Dyer addressed the leading citizens in forthright terms. If they wanted war, the government was ready, if they did not then they were to open their shops. 'Your people talk against the Government,' he continued, 'and persons educated in Germany and Bengal talk sedition. I shall uproot all these.' Punishment had to be seen, felt and inflicted in ways which humiliated as well as hurt. In the street where Miss Sherwood had been attacked, all Indians were forced to crawl on their bellies, including perhaps those anonymous but brave folk who rescued the doctor and tended her wounds. British soldiers who enforced Dyer's orders found the business amusing and, in other parts, the British onlookers applauded floggings and some shouted out: 'Strike hard, strike more.'[35] Special care was taken to whip men from the higher castes in public places where their shame would be seen by all; in Kasur the punishment was carried out in the presence of local prostitutes.[36]

O'Dwyer's diagnosis and remedies for the Punjab's problems were accepted in Delhi, but not without qualms. 'If only people would realise that the day has passed when you can keep India by the sword,' an exasperated Chelmsford told Montagu on 28 April. Dyer, he thought, was beyond anyone's control, and he reminded O'Dwyer that, 'we have to live with Indians when this is all over'.[37] In private, the Viceroy had been appalled by the 'crawling order' which, he rightly believed, would raise 'racial animosity'. Nevertheless, Chelmsford praised 'Dyer's otherwise admirable conduct of a most critical situation'. If, as Montagu had demanded, he was recalled, his treatment would be most 'bitterly resented by all Englishmen in this country'.[38] The Secretary of State remained sceptical, and early in September Chelmsford had to remind him that the emergency in the Punjab would have had dire consequences had not O'Dwyer and Dyer acted so promptly and decisively. The unrest might easily have spilled over into the United Provinces and beyond, and 'at any moment the Army might have gone, and once they had gone we should have had a state of things which would have been infinitely more serious than the Mutiny of 1857'.[39] It was a view which was already generally accepted throughout the British community in India and would shortly gain wide currency in Britain.

Gandhi, dazed by the results of his satyagraha campaign, suspended it on 18 April. Not long afterwards, he spoke to Sir George Lloyd, the Governor of Bombay, who afterwards told Chelmsford that 'he feels that he has failed, but he is anxious to go down, if possible, with colours flying as a martyr'.[40] In June Gandhi wrote to Montagu, accepting a share of the blame for what had happened, shifted the bulk of it on to the authorities and pledged that he would renew the satyagraha campaigns at an unspecified date.[41]

III

A news blackout prevented exact details of what was happening in the Punjab from reaching newspapers in India and Britain until June, when martial law was lifted. At the beginning of May the war with Afghanistan became the centre of official and newspaper attention. It was a half-hearted affair in which Afghan units crossed the frontier from 4 May onwards, but were gradually pushed back during the next three weeks. The offensive was accompanied by some inflammatory pro-Islamic propaganda to the effect that Germany had restarted the war, there was a rebellion in Egypt (which was true) and Sikhs had turned their rifles on their British officers at Amritsar (which was not). Intelligence that the Afghan attack had been planned to coincide with uprisings in the Punjab gave substance to O'Dwyer's belief that he had been faced with a revolutionary conspiracy.

Dismal memories of previous incursions into Afghanistan and over-strained resources ruled out any bold counter-attack, and there was an additional problem in the form of the Wazirs, Mahsuds and Afridis who joined in the fray on the Afghan side. Some officers grumbled about not being allowed to take the offensive in the old frontier manner, but for Delhi and London the war was an embarrassing distraction which they hoped to end swiftly. Nonetheless, no risks were taken and 340,000 British and Indian troops were concentrated on the frontier, over two-thirds of India's garrison.[42]

Aggressive action was left to the Royal Air Force. Aircraft were widely employed, both against tribesmen and Afghans, and with encouraging results. Air Force officers boasted that the frontiersmen 'live in dread of aeroplanes', but they soon managed to overcome their fear. On 9 May three machines were brought down by ground fire, losses the RAF attributed to the 'intrepidity of the pilots' and 'the good marksmanship of the Afridi tribes'. An aircraft crashing on take-off at Miramshah inspired a local mullah to claim he could destroy them by spells, but subsequent raids against local villages undermined faith in his magic.[43] A series of heavy bombing raids was launched against strategic targets inside Afghanistan; six tons of bombs fell on Jalalabad in one attack and in another on Dacca machines flew in waves from morning to evening, inflicting an estimated 600 casualties, including two elephants. The climax of the air war came on 24 May (Empire Day) with a raid on Kabul by a four-engined Handley Page V 1500, named 'Old Carthusian', which had been specially flown from Britain.

Among the targets hit was the Amir Ammanullah's palace. He complained to Chelmsford, alleging that air raids against a people which did not possess aeroplanes had aroused bitter resentment.[44] This disadvantage was about to disappear; RAF intelligence had picked up rumours that the Afghans were getting four machines from Russia.[45] The British government was also considering raising the stakes to secure a speedy outcome to the war, and, on 14 May, offered Chelmsford supplies of poisoned gas. He replied that the military situation did not yet warrant its employment and 'until such is the case we consider it would be impolitic to initiate its use'.[46] The Indo-Afghan frontier was spared the horrors of the Western Front, as both sides agreed to a truce at the beginning of June. A peace was finally agreed in November 1921, which returned Anglo-Afghan relations to their pre-war status.

Tribal resistance continued to flare up for the next five years and was dealt with in the old way. Columns penetrated the valleys, extracted fines and pledges for good behaviour and, when neither were forthcoming, burned crops and villages. 'I am afraid that they will undergo most awful hardship this and next year, until they have got their crops going again,' Major-General Harold Lewis noted in his diary. But inaction would invite another 'show in the near future'. A further four months of campaigning against the Mahsuds left him wondering whether tenacity owed something to 'the Bolshevik menace'.[47] Russia too was suspected of having encouraged the Afghans in their cross-border venture, and, for some time to come, British and Indian intelligence collectors and analysts blamed Moscow for every challenge to the Raj.

Even the British soldier was succumbing to what his officers would have called 'Bolshevism'. Troops shipped from Iraq to meet the Afghan threat were sullen at having their demobilisation postponed and hooted at officers on the streets of Peshawar. There were murmurings among the British garrison in other areas. At Sialkot, men wanting to go home mutinied and were threatened by artillery in a episode reminiscent of the 1857 Mutiny.[48] A 'strike' among army account clerks in September 1919 at Poona spread to other units dissatisfied with the pace of demobilisation. 'It will be very bad if Indian troops get to know,' Chelmsford commented.[49] Demobilisation was accelerated and 48,000 men who had enlisted for the duration of the war were shipped home between October and December, over a year after the conflict in Europe had ended. The mood of those who stayed and the replacements remained cussed. In June 1920 there was a soldiers' strike over how their pay was rendered into rupees. 'The modern British soldier is thoroughly imbued with the idea of downing tools in the event of things not going his way,' Chelmsford informed London, 'and we have to face the fact that a very different spirit animates the modern British soldier from that which pervaded the pre-war British Army.'[50] More frightening was the mutiny by Irish nationalist sympathisers among the Connaught Rangers in July 1920, during which several men were killed. At one stage in this disturbance there had been a rumour that English detachments had machine-gunned a crowd of rebellious Irish soldiers at Jalandhar in what was, in effect, a second Amritsar.

III

After Amritsar, Dyer had proceeded to the frontier, where he distinguished himself as commmander of a force which relieved the fort of Thal during the Afghan war. Precise details of his actions in Amritsar and the nature of measures taken elsewhere in the Punjab were gradually coming to light in the summer of 1919. Much of the information was gathered from eye-witnesses by Congress supporters, many of them lawyers, who entered the province once martial law had been lifted.

This testimony was published the following March, shortly before the appearance of an official report compiled by a committee under Lord Hunter, a Scottish jurist. Its proceedings were public and conducted against a constant interruptions from indignant Indian spectators, whom Hunter did little to subdue. Two sharp-witted Indian lawyers acted, as it were, for their countrymen, and they found Dyer easy prey when he gave evidence during the third week of November. Unprepared, unrepentant and unrepresented, he admitted under cross-examination that he had first planned to use armoured-car machine-gun fire on the demonstrators and gave a distinct impression that, in the words of one of his inquisitors, he intended to 'strike terror' into the whole of the Punjab. Not long after, he spoke his mind again to some brother officers with whom he was sharing a sleeping car on the Amritsar to Delhi night train. Another passenger, Jawaharlal Nehru, then a young lawyer and Congress supporter, overheard him say that he had had Amritsar at his mercy and that he had been briefly inclined to reduce it to ashes.

Dyer's candour brought about his downfall and a major scandal which poisoned Anglo-Indian relations. Montagu was 'staggered' by the revelations and, quick to cover his flank, accused the Punjabi authorities of having been sparing with the truth in their accounts of what had occurred.[51] Chelmsford countered by saying that Dyer's frankness had made a 'favourable impression' on the committee, but, as the crisis deepened, he trimmed his sails and came down against the man he had once defended.[52] On 25 May 1920, two months after he had read Hunter's report, the Viceroy told King George V that, with 'the greatest reluctance', he had been forced to take an adverse view of Dyer's conduct. This change of heart was noticeable elsewhere, or so Gandhi imagined:

> I think the officials, too, are repenting. They may not do so in public, and General Dyer may say what he likes; they do feel ashamed, nonetheless. They dimly realise that they have made a mistake and, I am certain that, if we go about our task in a clean way, the time will come when they will repent openly.[53]

They did, but only up to a point. The majority of the Hunter committee severely censured Dyer but gently reprimanded O'Dwyer, while its three Indian members wholeheartedly condemned both. What followed was an official exercise in damage limitation, for the British and Indian press now knew everything there was to be known about the events in the Punjab. Dyer was the first casualty. A relieved Indian government had granted him six months' sick leave and he had left for England at the beginning of April 1920. He disembarked at Southampton on 3 May, and was greeted by a *Daily Mail* journalist to whom he admitted: 'I had to shoot. I had thirty seconds to make up my mind what action to take and I did it. Every Englishman I have met in India has approved my act, horrible as it was.' Twelve days later he was ordered to resign his command by Major-General Sir Charles Monro, the commander-in-chief in India, who told him that there was no longer any position open to him in India. If necessary, the general added: 'He should be made to retire.'[54]

This was also the opinion of Winston Churchill, the Secretary State for War, and it echoed the view of Montagu, who had long feared the worst about Dyer. Both found themselves under fierce attack in the press and the Commons from those who regarded Dyer as the man who, by his unwavering attachment to his duty, had saved India. His most forceful defender was the ultra-Conservative *Morning Post* which, on 28 May, proclaimed: 'For practical purposes, General Dyer was facing the core of the Punjab rebellion with fifty rifles.' He had rescued the Raj and now an ungrateful, cowardly government had 'decided to sacrifice General Dyer to the susceptibilities of native agitators'. A few days after, Sir Verney Lovett, a former member of the ICS and reader in Indian history at Oxford, reminded *Morning Post* readers that the disturbances in the Punjab in April 1919 had been the worst since the 1857 Mutiny. Another, anonymous correspondent ('Briton') quoted the Lahore *Pioneer* of 31 May 1919, which had described posters in Amritsar that invited Indians to rape white women 'in the blessed name of Mahatma Gandhi'.[55]

On 9 July the *Morning Post* opened a fund for Dyer as a recognition and reward for his 'prompt and stern measures' which had saved India. The response was astonishing. There was £1,100 from the 'Ladies of Calcutta', who were incensed by the posters inciting attacks on British women, and £100 from an American lady who had once visited India and wrote, 'I fear for the British women there now that Dyer has been dismissed.' Among the smaller donations were sums from Rudyard Kipling, 'An indignant Englishwoman', 'An Old Punjabi', 'A Mutiny veteran's daughter' and 'One who has been in the East and knows its perils'. Thirty-seven pounds was collected at an Alnwick livestock auction, including the proceeds from the sale of a sheep given by one well-wisher; Northumberland farmers and stockmen clearly understood the need for firmness in India. So did thousands of others: within three weeks subscriptions had reached £15,000, and when the fund was closed it totalled over £26,000. The figure was both a popular vindication of Dyer and a slap in the face for India.

The cash was a consolation for Dyer, whose dismissal had been upheld by the Commons. It was the subject of an acrimonious and rowdy debate during the afternoon and evening of 8 July which, in large part, was a motion of censure on Montagu. He began the proceedings with a plea for a liberal Raj which, he fervently believed, could only flourish so long as it enjoyed the goodwill of its subjects. This had been severely bruised by Dyer's acts and words; how could the British preach ideas about individual liberty on one hand and then, on the other, tell an educated Indian who took them at face value that he was an agitator? If Britain chose to rule India by the sword alone, it would, he predicted, 'be driven out by the united opinion of the civilised world'.[56] 'Bolshevism!' bellowed one furious Tory. Later another heckler of the same persuasion suggested send-ing Dyer to Ireland to deal with Sinn Féin. An Ulsterman, Sir Edward Carson, then spoke for Dyer, arguing that he had crushed an incipient rev-olution which was part of a global plot: 'It is all one conspriracy, it is engineered in the same way, it has the same object – to destroy our sea-power and drive us out of Asia.'

Variations on the theme of Dyer as India's saviour followed from his supporters, including the outspoken Sir William Joynson Hicks, who had the advantage of having recently toured India where he had found huge support for 'the inevitable and necessary blow' that had been struck at Amritsar. The government benches were rallied by Winston Churchill who, in characteristically trenchant manner, denounced the 'frightfulness' in the Punjab and expanded on Montagu's argument that the Raj rested not on force but on the co-operation of its subjects. In private, Churchill believed that Dyer had been right to 'shoot hard', to extricate his force before taking measures for the care of wounded and that the 'crawling order' was a 'minor issue'. What stuck in his craw and that of the army's high command was Dyer's repeated assertion that he would liked to have killed more.[57] Nonetheless, Churchill's castigation of the general helped swing the debate the government's way.

The Lords discussed Dyer eleven days later in a more sedate manner. The government's position was defended by an Indian peer, Lord Sinha, a barrister and Under-Secretary of State at the India Office. He reminded listeners of the 'strong passion' which had been aroused among his coun-trymen by the massacre and the racial humiliations subsequently inflicted on them.[58] Similar sentiments were expressed by R. G. Pradhan, the *New Statesman*'s Bombay correspondent:

> The notion that the loss of one English life demands the wanton sacrifice of hundreds of Indian lives is a mischievous and mistaken notion, and it ought not to influence at the least the policy of the British government.

The Raj, he concluded, depended for its survival on an appreciation by Indians of its sense of justice, fair play and 'Britain's freedom from racial-ism'.[59] All had been thrown into question by the events in the Punjab. The pro-Dyer *Spectator* blamed the whole sorry business on the pusillanimity of Montagu, whose 'inability to say "No" to traitors and conspirators' was the source of all the recent unrest. In the Commons debate he had sounded like an 'Asiatic agitator', and had lost the support of the British community in India and the confidence of the princes. As a Secretary of State he was no more than a 'Bolshevik Pasha dealing out revolutionary generalities with the insolence of a tyrant on the divan'.[60]

IV

This combination of two hateful stereotypes, like the language of others in the Dyer camp, reveal why the Amritsar incident generated so much passion, and sheds considerable light on why the general behaved as he did. Throughout 1919 and 1920 the pre-war order had come under a systematic and unrelenting assault. At home (as in India) there had been mutinies among soldiers impatient for their discharge, an upsurge in Trade Union militancy, and, most dangerous of all, the onset of Sinn Féin's terrorist war against what remained of British government in southern Ireland. Abroad, there were anti-British riots in Egypt, tumults in India and, at the end of May 1920, an Arab rebellion against the Anglo-Indian administration of Iraq. The British army of occupation in Constantinople, like the rest of the Allied forces engaged in the emasculation and partition of Asia Minor, found themselves on a collision course with the Turkish national movement led by Kamal Atatürk. The coincidence of these violent movements and their common anti-British objective nourished the growth of conspiracy theories. During the Commons Dyer debate, Carson had linked unrest in India with its mainfestations elsewhere and accepted that all were part of a world-wide plot against the empire. It went without saying in conservative circles that this intrigue was being masterminded in Moscow where, for the past eighteen months, Comintern had been preaching world revolution. Right-wing newspapers, politicians, generals and intelligence officers in Whitehall and Simla invariably detected the hand of Communism behind every expression of anti-British sentiment.

A further, sinister dimension had been given to this conspiracy by the circulation of the 'Protocols of the Elders of Zion', a fabrication of Czarist anti-Semites that had allegedly uncovered a Jewish plot for world domination which involved the overthrow of the British Empire. The *Morning Post* had given much space to this nonsense, and among the donors to the Dyer fund were 'a believer in the Jewish peril' and another in the 'Hun–Jew peril'. The fact that Montagu was a Jew would not have been lost on these two dupes. For them and others host to similar phantoms, the

Jewish international conspiracy and the Bolshevik were one and the same.

Paranoia about Russian intrigue was rife in India. Its agents had been busy on the Russian–Persian frontier since the middle of 1918, first sniffing out Turko-German subversion and, after November, keeping an eye on the Bolsheviks. Attention centred on the activities of the Tashkent Press Bureau, an offshoot of Comintern, which was run by Manabendra Nath Roy. In his teens he had been associated with Bengali terrorists and had travelled in the Far East and America, seeking to purchase arms. He joined the Mexican Communist party and made his way to Moscow, where he met Lenin. Afterwards he remarked: 'I have had the rare privilege of being treated as an equal by a great man.'[61] He ran the University of Toilers of the East in Moscow and then shifted to Tashkent to work with a small band of Indian Communist and Turkish Muslim propagandists, who had been generously provided with a Russian wireless transmitter. Its audience must have been tiny, given the number of receivers in India, but its messages were picked up by military intelligence. Among the broadcasts made during the first half of 1920 were claims that the British were poised to annex Afghanistan and Persia as a springboard for an invasion of Turkmenistan, and reports of strikes in India, British artillery fire smashing workers' barricades, and further massacres in the Punjab, where officials were said to have remarked that the only way to deal with crowds was to shoot them.[62] A 'revolutionary spirit is rampant in the East', proclaimed the Tashkent-produced *Communist* in July 1920; 'the British Empire in the East was and is in jeopardy'.[63] There was also, and this might have been ill-received in some quarters in India, a proto-feminist appeal which began:

> O Muslim ladies. You have, to this day, lived your lives without enjoying the rights of womanhood. You have been conceiving that you were created only to serve men. No, this is not the case . . .[64]

A government which was traditionally highly sensitive to the slightest hint of Russian meddling in Indian affairs was bound to be frightened by this sort of material. Moreover, it took little imagination to link present convulsions and the recent Afghan invasion with the secret machinations of a régime which was, incidentally, fighting a series of campaigns against British-backed anti-Communists in southern and northern Russia. During the winter of 1918–19 the former had been receiving direct assistance from India through Persia. In a situation which, in certain respects, resembled the Cold War, both sides were resorting to subversion. A thrilling and revealing account of India's brief participation in the anti-Communist movements in Central Asia was written by one of the agents involved, Reginald Teague-Jones, who died in 1988, having lived for over sixty years under an assumed name. He had been compelled to do so to escape the notoriety he had achieved in Soviet mythology for his supposed part in the execution of twenty-six commissars near Baku in September 1918.[65]

Fear of the partially known is as unnerving as fear of the unknown. In the months before and after the disorders in the Punjab, officials from the Viceroy downwards had been bracing themselves for possibly widespread, Russian-inspired subversion. Added to this preoccupation were older anxieties about the Raj being overturned by some bolt from the blue, of the sort which had appeared in 1857. And then there was the recent example of Russia, where a small but determined knot of revolutionaries had overthrown an outwardly powerful and monolithic state. This fearfulness had recently been increased by wartime conspiracies, which explains O'Dwyer's reactions and, to some extent, Dyer's. There appears to be no doubt that during the crucial second fortnight of April 1919, both men had diagnosed the symptoms of an insurrection whose ferocity might equal, possibly excel that of 1857. Each reacted in the customary manner: by a precipitate resort to the aggressive use of overwhelming force. In Dyer's case, loss of control over Amritsar and the psychological effect this might have had elsewhere in the Punjab might have justified limited firing on a demonstration whose purpose was deliberately to goad authority. But his use of firepower in what was tantamount to a test of the Raj's resolve was neither salutary nor surgical; it was, as he subsequently made plain, vindictive. Vengeance rather than pacification also underlay the subsequent measures taken in the Punjab.

In defence of his snap decision, Dyer stated many times that his mindset was that of a soldier. There seems no doubt that he subscribed to that persistent martial creed that the Raj had been created by the army and would always be sustained by force. In an emergency soldiers knew what had to be done and were not hamstrung by precedents and rules, unlike civilian administrators. Many soldiers believed that Dyer had done his duty and were bitter about his treatment by a pusillanimous government. 'They let those sweltering down in the plains do the dirty work and then censure them for doing it,' wrote Lieutenant-Colonel M. H. Morgan, who had been with Dyer at the Jallianwala Bagh.[66] Men of this stamp simply believed that condign remedies were the only ones understood by

Indians. After the 1919 disturbances there, the local commander at Delhi had described the rioters as 'the scum of Delhi'. He added: ' . . . if they got more firing so much the better. It would have done them a world of good . . . as force is the only thing that an Asiatic has any respect for.'[67]

Of course, there were officers in India who did not think in this way; the trouble was that one who did was sent to Amritsar. The result was described in a speech delivered by the Duke of Connaught in February 1921, when he opened the first session of new legislative council: 'I have felt around me bitterness and estrangement between those who have been and should be friends. The shadow of Amritsar has lengthened over the fair face of India.'[68]

V

There were very few Indian faces in the crowd when the Duke unveiled a statue of his elder brother, the King Emperor Edward VII, in Calcutta, where shops were closed throughout the city. Cold-shouldering a prince was part of a wider campaign of non-co-operation which had been under way since the Congress's annual meeting at Nagpur in December 1920. Gandhi had dominated the proceedings by the sheer force of his person-ality, his ability to bind together Hindus and Muslims, and the persuasive-ness of his arguments. He persuaded 1,855 present to vote for his programme, giving him a majority of just under a thousand over those who were uneasy about an alliance with the masses and the disruption of government. Having recovered from his dismay at the violent conse-quences of the 1919 satyagraha campaign, Gandhi won over Congress to his principles and their use in a new contest designed to make India ungovernable. If this was accomplished, Gandhi predicted that swaraj (self-government) would follow within twelve months.

His political strategy was called non-co-operation. Participants were instructed to hand back their titles and decorations, stay away from official levées and ceremonies, remove their children from government schools, boycott the courts, withhold taxes, shun imported goods and have noth-ing to do with the elections to the new legislative assemblies. In October 1921 Congress asked all government servants to leave their posts. This was an audacious initiative which, if successful, would detach from the Raj those Indian collaborators whose assistance was vital and, simultaneously, starve it of cash. As well as jamming the machinery of government, Gandhi was eroding its moral base by promoting Congress as the friend of and spokesman for the peasantry who, like Chesterton's people of England, had not yet found their voice. There were, of course, practical objections to this campaign. Many lawyers and businessmen were unwilling to bring about their own ruin, and middle-class parents refused to impede their children's education. Gandhi himself had to reprimand some over-zealous followers whose hartal included cutting off the water supplies of Barisal.[69]

Perhaps the most dynamic feature of the 1920–22 satyagraha campaign was Congress's recruitment of the ryots into the new *kisan* (peasant) organisations. One of those deeply involved was Jawaharlal Nehru, then in his early thirties, a Harrow- and Cambridge-educated lawyer and son of another Congress barrister, Motilal Nehru. In June 1920, the hot season, he passed through the remote rural backwaters of Awadh, holding meetings and discovering for the first time a wretched India, previously hidden from the sight of people of his background. Country people flocked to his impromptu meetings:

> They were in miserable rags, men and women, but their faces were full of excitement and their eyes glistened and seemed to expect strange happenings which would, as if by a miracle, put an end to their long misery.
>
> They showered their affection on us and looked on us with loving and hopeful eyes, as if we were the bearers of good tidings, the guides who were to lead them to the promised land. Looking at them and their misery and overflowing gratitude, I was filled with shame, shame at my own easy-going and comfortable life and our petty politics of the city which ignored this vast multitude of semi-naked sons and daughters of India, sorrow at the degradation and overwhelming poverty of India. A new picture of India seemed to rise before me, naked, starving, crushed and utterly miserable. And their faith in us, casual visitors from the distant city, embarrassed me and filled me with a new responsibility that frightened me.[70]

Nehru listened to long recitals of the misfortunes of the ryots: high rents and taxes, evictions and maltreatment by taluqdars, their agents and those eternal bugbears, the moneylenders. What struck him most forcibly was how the peasants imagined that his arrival might mark the beginning of a new era in which their burdens would somehow miraculously vanish.

This sense of being in the process of moving forward, even if there was no clear destination, permeated a contemporary peasants' demonstration in M. J. Anand's *The Sword and the Sickle*. The crowd marches along, shouting various slogans ('Relief to the Peasants! Down with Sarkar [government]!') in a sort of trance:

> Religion mixed with politics and the name Gandhi completed the curve in a natural flow, so that a completely new spirit of accumulated hatred and some concentration of purpose [appeared], for what the purpose was beyond being flogged no one seemed to have questioned, through obedience to a leader which was a remnant of their spineless acceptance.[71]

Anand, who at the age of fourteen had been flogged during the 1919 Punjabi disturbances, afterwards drifted towards Marxism, which made him believe that Gandhi was luring the peasantry away from the only goal which would end their suffering: social revolution.[72]

Paying off old scores, rather than an impulse to create a new order, drove some Awadh peasants to loot the property of a taluqdar, shouting pro-Gandhi slogans as they did so. Nehru investigated and discovered that they had been put up to the crime by another landowner, who had persuaded them that this was what Gandhi would have wished.[73] After explaining to them that satyagraha ruled out such behaviour, the culprits owned up and were arrested. Their misdeeds were used as the excuse for a systematic official campaign against the kisan movement in the area, and many of its members ended up in gaol. As in 1919, it was impossible to restrain crowds of protesters for whom the morality of satyagraha was incomprehensible. Violence erupted spontaneously in different regions at different times when those at the bottom of the pile snatched the opportunity to plunder or take revenge. The Bombay hartal which marked the arrival of the Prince of Wales at the end of November 1921 turned into a four-day riot in which shops were pillaged and Europeans attacked. In all, fifty-three demonstrators were killed and hundreds wounded when police and troops opened fire.

Zamindars and moneylenders were attacked in Rangpur, where social tension had increased in consequence of the meeting of the North Bengal Ryot conference, held there at the end of August 1920.[74] According to a plain-clothes detective, some of its sessions 'smelt high of Bolshevism', an understandable judgement given the tone of one speech: 'The aristocracy roll in luxury, but the ryots die in poverty; the wealthy man wears fine clothes, but the wives and daughters of the ryots wear rags and tatters.'[75] Elsewhere in Bengal liquor and ganja stores were broken into, and Santal tribesmen convinced themselves that wearing the distinctive Gandhi hat gave them immunity from police bullets, a nice merging of old magic and modern politics.[76] Outnumbered, and thinly spread, the local police were paralysed in many rural districts.

By the beginning of 1922 the civil disobedience movement was careering out of control. Confirmation of this came in February with the Chauri Chaura incident, in which a mob, waving swaraj banners, stormed a police station, beat to death twenty-two policemen and burned their bodies. Recognising that he could no longer restrain his followers, Gandhi called off the campaign, advising them to concentrate on spinning, educating the masses and forming local committees. His prestige now stood so high that his adherents acquiesced, although Nehru and many others were bitterly disappointed, believing the movement had been steadily gaining ground. It had, but slowly, and there had been no progress whatsoever in the princely states. It was less easy to work up a head of steam against administrations which were run by Indians than against a government in which white men dominated.

One outstanding feature of the 1920–22 agitation had been Congress's ability to exploit localised discontent and amalgamate it with the broader campaign for home rule. In the traditionally volatile and unruly Malabar region, Congress activists had won converts through taking on board the long-standing grievances of the Muslim Mapillas against the largely Hindu landlord class. The Khalifat movement was strong in this region and, during 1920, Congress membership rose from a handful to over 20,000. Gandhi was warmly welcomed during a brief visit in August, although he was uncertain whether the thousands of Muslims in their Khalifat green hats who turned out to cheer him would stick to non-violent forms of protest.[77] As was now happening so often throughout India, nationalist agitation was a catalyst for the release of long pent-up resentments and frustration whose mainsprings were regional, social and economic.

Mapilla rage was directed in more or less equal parts against an infidel government, its local representatives – mainly policemen – and Hindu landlords. It simmered during the first half of 1921 and boiled over in August, when a crowd armed with spears and swords expelled a party of policemen from Pukkotur. One act of defiance spawned others and, within a fortnight, the government's control over much of Malabar had snapped.

The rebels had few firearms, and encounters with the growing number of British and Indian troops summoned to the district were one-sided. At the very end of October, the Mapillas changed their tactics to guerrilla warfare, which prompted a staff officer to liken them to Sinn Féin in Ireland. The answer was to call in specialists in jungle warfare – Gurkhas and Chins and Kachins from the Indo-Burmese borderland.[78] It was less easy, however, to find local policemen to take charge of areas which the army had cleared of insurgents. There were, however, captured 'mops' who were willing to act as police spies, leading patrols to gangs.[79]

Among the rebels' aims was an independent Muslim kingdom in Malabar, and the process of bringing it about involved the forcible conversion, including circumcision, of nearly 700 Hindus; those who refused, or who happened to be landowners, were murdered.[80] At the end of a brief campaign, British losses were 43 dead and 126 wounded. Mapilla casualties were 2,339 dead, 1,652 wounded and just over 6,000 taken prisoner. A further 39,400 surrendered, among them 67 who were later suffocated to death in a closed railway carriage. It appeared that the ventilators had been inadvertently papered over. Inevitably in such a campaign there were charges and counter-charges of atrocity; in one report a police officer cynically noted that a local headman 'has made no complaints but he has probably been publicly buggered and his women raped'.[81] It was a strange irony that one of the detachments that took part in these operations was the Leinster regiment from Southern Ireland, a country which, in 1922 and after a three-year partisan campaign, had won a form of independence from Britain.

Gandhi and many other senior Congress figures were encouraged by what had happened in Ireland, as were nationalists in Egypt. Hopes that India might achieve what Ireland had were premature; in 1922 the Raj was still firmly in the saddle, although its officials had suffered some nerve-wracking moments during the past two years. The commander-in-chief, Lord ('Rawly') Rawlinson, had no difficulties on allocating troops to meet emergencies. Like many others at the top, he believed that Gandhi was 'manifestly incapable of leading the "frankenstein" which he has created'.[82] The view from below was different: Jawaharlal Nehru thought that its ancient mainstay, prestige, was withering in the face of the satyagraha protests. He and his father, Motilal, were arrested at the end of 1921 and given brief prison sentences, he by a court in a native state, Nabha. So far, the protest movement had made virtually no headway in the princely states, whose governments had taken a firm line with agitation. Their loyalty did not prevent some of their rulers, including the Raja of Nabha, from expressing disquiet over what had occurred at Amritsar and in the Punjab during 1919.[83] In the November of that year, Chelmsford took the precaution of giving an address to the princes in which he emphasised the need to smother sedition and reminded them that those behind the present agitation would not respect traditional authority.[84] It was a message that was taken to heart. In M. J. Anand's *Confessions of a Lover*, set in the early 1920s, the student hero is warned to steer clear of nationalist politics because his college is funded by the Maharaja of Patiala, who was pro-British.

The Raj's coercive machinery was able to cope with the restlessness without resort to the methods of O'Dwyer and Dyer, although the prison system was briefly shaken by the influx of thousands of protesters. There was also the bonus that flare-ups tended to be short-lived and, of course, sporadic. Moreover, it was common for non-violent protests to run out of steam, especially in the face of official determination. Bombay's protest movement collapsed after the riots and shootings at the end of November 1921, and many of its working-class supporters from the docks and mills turned to Trade Unionism.[85] It was also impossible to obtain solidarity among what might be termed the 'official and semi-official' nationalists, who refused to jeopardise their positions and salaries by withdrawing from government. For them to stick rigidly to the principles of non-co-operation was impossible: if they did so within government departments and legislatures they would harm the welfare and interests of their countrymen.

Working within the administration was already securing advantages. Under pressure from the Indian members of the Viceroy's legislative council, the Indian government refused to augment its military budget to satisfy London. In particular, the Indians objected to the deployment of sepoys in support of Britain's newly acquired pretensions in the Middle East. If Indian soldiers were to guard British oil wells in Persia, then Britain rather than India should foot the bill. The alternative was raise the military allowance to £60 million a year, two-fifths of India's revenues, something which in the present state of affairs was unthinkable. The ultra-imperialist Chief of Imperial General Staff, Sir Henry Wilson, grumbled that Montagu and Chelmsford were 'terrified of taxing India'. Maybe so, but they got their way.[86]

Dismayed by this response, Sir Henry Wilson gloomily wondered whether the Cabinet was already secretly thinking in terms of giving up India.[87] It was a thought which crossed the minds of Dyer's supporters, who detected a faltering of the will to rule in London and Delhi. What they had failed to recognise was that the India of 1922 was not that of 1919. The events of the intervening three years had revealed that the political opponents of British rule were now capable of mobilising considerable public support. India was not yet ungovernable, and there were still large areas barely affected by Congress agents, but the spread of unrest was a sharp reminder of that old truth: India could not be ruled without the co-operation of a substantial portion of its population.

This attempt to shift what was, in effect, the balance of political power within India had been undertaken by Gandhi. For those who dealt with him he was a perplexing phenomenon: the charismatic leader of a mass movement who, unlike his counterparts in Europe during the second quarter of the twentieth-century, abhorred violence. Furthermore, he had turned his back on those forces which were transforming the contemporary world: industrialisation, international trade and collectivism. In an age of secularism, he insisted that politics could not be separated from religion, and that metaphysical thought was the only guide to political action. On the face of it, he had nothing with which to appeal to the élite that had hitherto guided Congress and he never held any office within the movement. Nonetheless, he convinced the bulk of its members to swallow their prejudices and follow him along a path which seemed extremely hazardous. It was; but at the same time, it produced results. The combination of satyagraha, populism and non-co-operation seemed the only way by which the Raj could be made to yield. As Gandhi had repeatedly claimed, the British were susceptible to moral pressure, but they had not buckled. He had given the Raj a rough passage, but it had not given ground: the Rowlatt laws remained and swaraj had not been achieved by 1922.

For all his public humility, Gandhi was at heart a vain man who wanted Indian freedom on his own terms and through his own methods. When both had failed, he stepped down and turned his attention to spinning and Hindu education, giving the impression that he considered these equally important as the achievement of Indian nationhood. They were, for both were part of Gandhi's programme of national redemption, which was a vital part of the struggle for independence. So was he; his semi-monastic retirement in February 1922 was followed by six years in which Congressional energies were largely consumed by sterile internal debate. The Raj breathed again.

3

—◆—

This Wonderful Land: Anglo-Indian Perspectives

I

On 7 January 1922 readers of the *Sphere* were presented with two starkly contrasting images of India. The first showed a burning hut, the home of a 'loyal' Hindu who had been victimised for the help he had given the security forces in the bush war against the Mapillas. They were 'fanatical and malevolent' rebels and dacoits, preying on the Malabar Hindus, who were a 'gentle, peace-loving people, clean and courteous'. The photograph and its accompanying story were a vivid reminder that the Raj kept the peace and protected the weak. Its service to the progress of India was revealed by the second image, which showed the Prince of Wales conferring degrees on Indian graduates at the University of Lucknow. The same issue contained other, more glamorous scenes from the royal tour: the gorgeously robed Maharaja of Bikaner, his mailed lancers and exotically dressed sword dancers. The prince was lavishly received in every state he visited and the colourful ceremonies of greeting were ideally suited for what are now called 'photo-opportunities'. There were also plenty of excuses for journalistic hyperbole. After the Prince's reception at Udaipur, Reuter's correspondent wrote: 'Here indeed was the shining East – the mystic East – the East whose call conjures fancy with magical and fantastical spells.'[1]

The royal tour during the winter and spring of 1921–22 was designed to

· 491 ·

reassure the British people that the heart of the Indian empire remained sound and steadfast in spite of the past two years of protest and disorder. Glimpses of the prince shaking hands with grey-bearded and medalled veterans, riding on an elephant, posing beside one of the many tigers he had shot or with well-stuck pigs that had fallen to the royal spear indicated that he was a man fit to become King Emperor. A newspaperman noted that the future Edward VIII's sportsmanship won over even the Awadh nationalists. Congress hats disappeared from the urban crowds, and in the countryside, 'Natives completely won by a fleeting smile from the Prince would prostrate themselves to kiss the dust over which his car had passed.'[2] And then there was the glittering assembly of fifty princes at Delhi who, according to the *Graphic*, 'with manifest sincerity testified their fidelity to the Throne'.[3]

This was all very comforting and just what the the Prime Minister, Lloyd George, had in mind in 1919 when he had proposed a series of royal peregrinations around the empire. Young, handsome and with a breezy informal manner, the prince would win hearts and stiffen that attachment to the monarchy which was the principal bond that held together a scattered and disparate empire. This was emphasised by the prince at the political highlight of his tour, the dedication of the huge statue of his great-grandmother, Queen Victoria, in Calcutta. He recalled how the Queen Empress had had 'the peculiar power of being in touch with all classes on this continent' and that now her dreams were being fulfilled as India moved towards responsible government. Genuine affection for the Queen Empress had to be transferred to her successors. 'I want to know you and I want you to know me' the prince told British and Indian grandees as he stepped ashore at Bombay. But the human touch which worked so well in Canada and Australia was unsuited to India, or so the prince's father, George V, imagined. On his advice his son was hedged with protocol and guided by officials who equated regality with stiffness. For them, the Prince of Wales was in India to remind its people that they were the subjects of the King Emperor, which was why Gandhi and Congress had appealed for a boycott of all royal ceremonies. The British press claimed that this attempt to shun the prince was an abject failure, citing the crowds which turned up to see him as evidence. It was not; the urge to witness a splendid public spectacle did not mean that all who succumbed to it were simultaneously converted to supporters of the Raj. A Congressman could and did enjoy watching the prince play polo, which he did well, without shedding his political opinions. Among the sheaves of press photographs of Indian crowds is one in which an onlooker wears the distinctive Gandhi skullcap.[4] Prince Edward himself was astute enough to observe that Indians 'found it hard to resist the great public shows being organised in my honour'. As his father had reminded him before his departure, ritual and pageantry impressed 'the Oriental mind'.[5]

The British mind was also open to such forms of persuasion. Newsreels, press reports and pictures in the weekly illustrated journals regularly presented the public with the magnificent façade of the Indian empire. Princely India was always in the forefront of public consciousness, thanks to the appearance of princes as guests at coronations, royal jubilees, weddings and funerals. Ever since the Golden Jubilee of 1887 these had been essentially imperial celebrations contrived to proclaim the empire's unity and strength. Martial India was much in evidence. Indian ADCs and orderlies in striking uniforms and festooned with medals earned in their service attended Queen Victoria, Edward VII and George V, and Indian cavalrymen were regular performers in state pageantry of the new, imperial monarchy. The Queen Empress expressly asked that Indian horsemen escorted her carriage on its journey through London to St Paul's Cathedral for the Diamond Jubilee thanksgiving service on 22 June 1897. As the Bengal lancers trotted up Ludgate Hill, a voice in the crowd shouted, 'Three cheers for India,' and there was a hearty response. The spectators were watching more a display of imperial muscle, for among the contingents were Sikhs, once Britain's fiercest enemies and now some of the Queen's most loyal subjects and bravest soldiers. In India and elsewhere, Britain conquered and then embraced the defeated, winning their respect and friendship.

The enthusiast who had invited hurrahs for India may well have visited the spectacular Empire of India Exhibition, which had been staged between August and October 1895 and, in response to popular demand, between May and October 1896. It was the creation of Imrie Kiralfy, an impresario, and was a combination of pageant, staged at the 6,000-seat Empress's Theatre, Earls Court, and an instructive and entertaining exhibition nearby. The stage show was a sequence of scenes illustrating a thousand years of Indian history. There were grand spectacles, melodramatic incidents and a lively script in verse. The tableau which showed the Maratha hero Shivaji included some faqirs:

> *Cursing, crying, flesh chastising,*
> *See us Fakirs, martyrising;*
> *All the world despising.*

The climax came with 'The Glorification of Victoria, The Empress Queen' and was marked by an imperial ode:

> *Mother, crowned of East and West!*
> *Thou, for us, art proved the Best;*
> *India, nestling at thy Knee,*
> *Hath thy peace, and praiseth thee;*
> *In their Heaven our Gods recline,*
> *Well content that we are thine,*
> *Jai! Jai! Victoria! Be this seen:*
> *Eastern Empress! Western Queen!*

Before or after the show, the audience could stroll through an Indian wonderland which, in many ways, ressembled the great pleasure gardens of the eighteenth century. There were Indian streets, *chowks* (open town centres), mosques, a curry house, shops inhabited by native craftsmen, faqirs, snake charmers and jugglers, and Indian plants and shrubs grew in the gardens by the walkways. The site and theatre were on the newly-opened District Railway and proved an immense attraction for family excursions: about half a million saw the pageant and twelve million attended the exhibition.[6]

What they experienced both entertained and informed. The Victorian Raj represented the consummation of India's history: a golden age in which enlightenment was triumphant and for which all Indians were grateful. Within a few years the actual splendour of the Raj appeared on cinema screens, with newsreels of the 1903 and 1911 durbars. In the latter year there was another India Exhibition at Crystal Palace, complete with a raja's palace, a bazaar and a jungle in which animals wandered around. Like its predecessor, it was immensely popular with predominantly lower-middle and working-class day trippers.[7] For a substantial part of the British population, India was not a remote, unknown region, but a picturesque wonderland peopled by quaint but loyal people, glad to be ruled by Britain.

Spectacular imperial festivities, whether royal celebrations or exhibitions, were part of a process by which the public interest in the empire was aroused. On the whole governments approved, although the more serious-minded late-Victorian and Edwardian imperialists were uneasy about the empire becoming associated with nothing more than a cheery day out or a music-hall chorus. They could, however, take some comfort from the fact that there were other, more didactic but still palatable ways in which the imperial message could be transmitted to the masses. There were the lantern-slide lectures which were popular diversions before and for many years after the advent of the cinema and wireless. Among the many Indian subjects was George V's 1911 Delhi durbar, which offered a colourful evening's entertainment with pictures of the King Emperor riding into Delhi and receiving the homage of the princes. The notes, supplied with the slides, drew the audience's attention to the 'frank enthusiasm' of the Delhi crowds whose 'excitement rose to fever pitch' as the royal cavalcade approached. The King Emperor's meeting with the Mutiny veterans was singled out. 'One is glad to see the breasts of these noble old fellows covered with medals, which ensure them the highest respect in their villages and among their neighbours, as evidencing the fact that they are men whom the great British Raj delighteth to honour.'[8]

Through its public-service broadcasts, the BBC developed the traditions of the lantern-slide lecture. The continuing political turmoil and the fact that the British Parliament was having to decide the country's political future made India a favourite subject for short, educational talks by experts. During the first part of 1929, Professor H. G. Dalway Turnbull outlined the tenets of India's principal religions in a series of lectures which, while largely factual, included some personal comments. Hinduism, he observed, was a powerful social cement in times of upheaval, but its doctrines drained men of any 'spirit of adventure'. It was also, as it had been for nineteenth-century reformers and missionaries, an impediment to progress. Describing Hindu festivals and pilgrimages, the professor remarked that India was still 'a regular jungle of popular superstitions . . . much like those of the Dark Ages in Europe'.[9]

Modern, enlightened India was given its voice by Dhanvanth Rama Rau, who spoke on the women of India during the autumn of 1936. She described everyday chores undertaken by the Indian housewife and the increasing part women were playing in their country's public affairs. As well as being the pivots of their households, Indian women were becoming moral watchdogs, campaigning to raise the age of consent and reduce prostitution. The educated classes now universally condemned child marriages, but she defended arranged unions, which usually turned out happily, unlike so many entered on by free choice in Britain.[10] Older Indian marriage customs were described by Miss Mira Devi, who spoke about life inside the zenana in October 1937. She emphasised that women hidden from the eyes of men enjoyed an agreeable existence, in which considerable time and money were devoted to the purchase of clothes and 'on making themselves beautiful'. British women may well have been envious, but there were drawbacks, since the mother-in-law traditionally was mistress of the Indian household and the husband had to be obeyed unquestioningly as 'lord and master'.[11] Other, less contentious subjects covered by the BBC Home and Empire services during the 1920s and 1930s included peasant life in the Hunza district, Indian wildlife, and the language of Assam.

Recent political changes were occasionally explained. A former chairman of India's legislative council, Sir Frederick White, discussed the difficulties faced by the new elected ministries. The greatest of these was what he called 'the devil of feud' which prevented harmony between mutually resentful religious and racial groups.[12] A veteran Indian newspaperman, Sir Stanley Reed, used a talk on the opening of the new official buildings in New Delhi at the end of 1936 for an impassioned defence of the Raj. The great legislative and administrative complex was, he told listeners:

> . . . the symbol of our crowning work in India – a work which rescued this wonderful land and its generous peoples from anarchy, established the rule of law, implanted the seeds of human freedom, and now has passed the main responsibility of governance into the hands of a United India, retaining only certain essential powers until she reaches her destined status, a self-governing Dominion freely knit in the British Commonwealth.[13]

Like the Prince of Wales some years before, the speaker portrayed India's tentative steps towards self-government as a significant milestone on a journey towards national advancement, whose direction had been preordained by a wise and benevolent Raj. This was an optimistic gloss, for in India the recent reforms had been seen as too slow and timid, and in Britain a substantial lobby had denounced them as too fast and reckless. Whenever possible, the BBC always endeavoured to be positive and impartial.

II

By the standards of the time, the broadcasters' approach to India would have been regarded as too 'highbrow' and, therefore, unlikely to engage the masses. For them, India remained what it had always been in the popular imagination, a land of adventure, romance and mystery. In this form it continued to provide the scenarios and background for popular fiction, and, during the 1930s, movies. Although he died in 1902, G. A. Henty remained perhaps the greatest source of Indian lore for his countrymen. His was a narrow but attractive vision of a country filled with bold and resourceful young men serving the Raj with their wits and their swords. His tales of derring-do captured the imagination of the young, and their impact cannot be underestimated. Hugh Martin, the son of an Indian official who joined the ICS in 1938, recalled:

> From an early age I had been attracted by the idea of Empire, one of my favourite authors was G. A. Henty and I knew as much about the acquisition of the Indian Empire as I did about the Carthaginian War. I had enjoyed Kipling too, particularly when my mother read him aloud. Greek and Roman History seemed to lead in the same direction.[14]

The distinctive flavour of Henty's India lingered on in the North-West Frontier until the end of the Raj. It can be savoured in a lance corporal's memories of campaigning there during 1937: 'Razmak to me was as soldiering should be, a tough soul-stirring experience, something that I as an eager young NCO really enjoyed, each and every column a story unto itself.'[15] The same sense of excitement and love of adventure surface in the memoirs of officers like John Masters, who served on the frontier between the wars.

For all his often creaking plots and wooden characterisation, Henty offered an enthralling picture of the fighting man's India, with which he had a brief acquaintance as a correspondent covering the Prince of Wales's tour in 1874–75. His nine Indian novels were about various stages in the country's conquest, and their heroes are all athletic, often harum-scarum boys just out of school and ready to take on the world. Their exploits are intermingled with the deeds of actual heroes such as Clive and Sir Arthur Wellesley and, from time to time, Henty delivers a history lesson to explain the intricacies of high politics and strategy. Morality is clear-cut: the British stand for humanity and justice and their adversaries are either parasites or rogues, or both. This is a land where the strong get what they want and are admired for it, as Percy, the hero of *Through the Sikh Wars*, discovers when he enters the Company's service and is told: 'What do the natives care for our learning? It is our pluck and endurance and the downright love of adventure that have made us the masters of the great part of India, and ere long will make us the rulers of the whole of it.' Indians rarely intrude into this world, save as faithful servants or villains, and when not outwitting Marathas or dacoits, the heroes stay within the boundaries of the sahibs' India, usually shooting tigers and spitting pigs with a bravado that earns the admiration of their superiors.

It was intoxicating stuff, and widely read by boys from all backgrounds; at the turn of the century the annual print-run of Henty's yarns was between 150,000 and 200,000.[16] The Henty genre flourished well into the next century, when fresh generations of schoolboys were transported to an India where adventure and fame waited for the stout-hearted. In content and style, D. H. Parry's *Listed as a Lancer*, which appeared in *Chums* during 1913, may stand for many others. It recounts the picaresque career of Jack Robinson, who joins the cavalry after being expelled from school. On the North-West Frontier he wins the friendship of the regimental riding-master by saving his daughter from a fire, and the enmity of Lieutenant Foxwell Crawley, the son of a millionaire gin distiller who had 'none of the instincts of a gentleman'. Jack has, although a ranker; and he vainly attempts to save the life of an Indian barber who is being kicked to death by a British soldier. Aware of scandals caused by such brutality during Curzon's viceroyalty, the author comments: 'Now as everyone who has been to India knows, it is a most dangerous thing to hit a native in the stomach. It is very liable to rupture the liver.' The murdered man's brother turns out to be a Pathan spy who, bound by a debt of honour, assists Jack when he is taken prisoner by a fanatic mullah. During his captivity the hero meets some Russian officers, making mischief on the frontier, and, adding a modern touch, invokes the help of two Royal Flying Corps officers who bomb the mullah's headquarters – anticipating the type of warfare that would be introduced to India within the next three years. The climax comes when the Russians invade Afghanistan and the hero manages to capture their entire high command.

Less ambitious boys' stories exploited the 'mysterious' and invariably sinister aspects of India. *The Demons of the Pit*, serialised in *Chums* in 1920, concerns priests 'in remote districts . . . offering human sacrifices to their hideous gods', which was not as far-fetched as might have first appeared, for such practices were still occurring among tribes on the Burmese frontier. A tea plantation is the setting for *The Sacred Tiger*, in which the young hero becomes bored with his routine duties as manager: 'One soon tires of watching native pickers to see that they don't slack – as natives surely will if they are left to their own sweet inclinations.'[17]

Like other crude stereotypes, that of the idle native was part of the stock-in-trade of adult popular fiction with an Indian setting. And yet, many standard characters were rooted in reality, even if they were flatly rendered. The seventeen-year-old raja in Alice Perrin's *The Anglo-Indians* (1912) is bent on sybaritic self-indulgence despite the efforts of his tutor, Captain Somerton, to 'inculcate notions of manliness'. Later, he and his young wife are keen to travel to Europe, she mesmerised by London's shopping opportunities. Such creatures did exist and were a constant problem for the Raj. All this would have been understood by the authoress, who was the daughter of a Bengal cavalry general and the wife of an Indian official. Her theme is the aspirations of the three daughters of the Fleetwoods, one of those families with a long history of service in India. Their father is a district officer and their mother a memsahib of the old school who, like so many of her kind, was finding it very hard to come to terms with change of any sort. She regrets Indians adopting Western ways. 'To her it was "not suitable" that Orientals should dance with English girls considering their present attitude towards the Feminine, just as she would have deemed it unsuitable for an Englishwoman to sit on the floor and eat with her fingers.' Captain Somerton concurs: 'No Englishman would be happy if his wife became friendly with an Indian and vice-versa.' Just why is explained when Fay Fleetwood flirts with the raja, laying her hand on his as she tries to persuade him to govern justly, and mercifully unaware of 'the fierce flame of passion that surged through his being at her tender touch'.

As well as the lecherous prince there is another familiar figure, the sulking memsahib. Marion Fleetwood vents her discontent on her sister, Fay. India, she complains, is 'petty, and narrow, and second rate; people are too simple and commonplace out here. There's no life, only existence.' Like so many exiles who felt themselves circumscribed by the society and conventions of India, Marion yearns for England. Such women existed. In her memoirs, Phyllis Lawrence, the wife of a senior civil servant, recalled the young wife of a junior official 'eating her heart out for an English suburban villa with H and C laid on'. Lonely and distressed, she dies from dysentery while her husband is away on duty.[18]

Like Alice Perrin, Maud Diver was born in India, a soldier's daughter and the wife of an officer. In 1896 she returned to England and a busy literary career in which she wrote romances set against an Indian background; sixteen are listed in her entry in *Who's Who* for 1930. They included historical adventures set on the North-West Frontier and novels which dealt with the problems of contemporary India. Her *Far to Seek: A Romance of England and India* (1921) engages the awkward subject of the Anglo-Indian, but in a manner which would cause no unease or blushes. The hero, Roy Sinclair, is the son of an English baronet and a high-born Rajput lady, whose marriage has set her permanently apart from her kin. Her son learns of his ancient Indian inheritance from Rajput chivalric tales heard at his mother's knee, and encounters racial prejudice at his prep school, where he is befriended by Desmond, the son of an Indian army officer whose family record of service stretches back 100 years. So, two honourable traditions meet. Less fortunate is an Indian boy, Siri Chandranath, who suffers at the hands of 'Scab Major', the school bully.

Sinclair proceeds to Oxford where racial, caste and culinary taboos are suspended and he mixes freely with Indian men and women of his own age. He meets Dyan Singh, who voices the grievances of the educated Indian: 'We are all British subjects – oh yes – when convenient! But the door is opened only – so far. If we make bold to ask for the best, it is slammed in our faces.' Seeking his roots, Sinclair goes to India, now plunged into political turmoil. His maternal grandfather, a minister in a Rajasthan state, is a conservative who hopes that the princes can check sedition, but is also aware of the need for greater contacts between the races, particularly among their upper classes. Sinclair also attends a nationalist meeting in Delhi where he hears 'Swami', a thinly disguised Gandhi figure, preach the doctrines of 'yoga by action', randomly quoting Christian and Hindu scriptures to support his appeals to the youth of India. Another speaker is Siri Chandranath who, not surprisingly after his treatment at prep school, has became an anti-British firebrand, unlike Dyan Singh whose nationalism has not blinded him to the virtues of British government. Sinclair also confronts the ugly face of the Raj; sensing that a future baronet might be an ideal match for her daughter, a memsahib freezes with horror the moment she hears that he has an Indian mother.

The story concludes dramatically in Lahore at the height of the 1919 disturbances. Here, Mrs Diver is completely in sympathy with her countrymen and women embattled in the midst of the 'formidable depths of alien humanity hemming them in, outnumbering them by thousands to one'. 'Up against organised rebellion', the Europeans are terrified by rioters shouting, 'Kill the white pigs, brothers!' Order is restored and a good word is said for the 'strong action' taken at Amritsar, which was to be expected from an authoress who had contributed £7 to the General Dyer fund.[19] The moral is clear: for all its faults and those of its servants, the Raj is infinitely preferable to any alternative proposed by the nationalists, whose rhetoric leads to anarchy and bloodshed.

A fictional Dyer is the hero of 'The Bone of Contention' (1932), a short-story-cum-political-polemic by another prolific source of Indian fiction, Ethel Savi. Born in India, she spent some time during the 1880s in rural Bengal, an experience, she claimed, which earned her recognition as an expert on 'the inner life of the natives of India, their proclivities, castes and psychology'. Afterwards she mastered the equally arcane mysteries of life and manners in the European civil lines.[20] According to her *Who's Who* entry, these accomplishments qualified her to write over twenty novels on India. To judge from 'The Bone of Contention', her uncompromising views were frozen in a past inhabited by aggressive, no-nonsense sahibs and passive, deferential Indians.

In this story, Faisal Ali, a Muslim businessman, plans to clear away the ruins of a Hindu temple to make way for a road, and is opposed by Babu Nobin Biswas, a Bengali entrepreneur. He is also a Congress activist who encourages students to 'show signs of disloyalty to the flag and shout insults at Englishwomen'. Marius Brandon, a masterful young official, investigates the temple, overriding a Hindu who objects to his presence: 'Go to blazes! . . . Who the devil are you to dictate to a sahib what is to be done . . . son of a pig!' The upshot is that the Muslims demolish the temple and trigger a communal riot of the sort which were becoming commoner at this time. Brandon is more than up to the crisis and afterwards tells his superior: 'We gave them no quarter . . . None of that rot with blank cartridge. We let 'em have it straight and hot, and my word! it did the trick like magic.' Promotion beckons, 'if I am not sacked for having opened fire on the oppressed natives'. Mrs Savi approved, but in 1932 the Indian government would have been embarrassed by Brandon, to say the least. Nevertheless, there were plenty in Britain who respected men of his stamp. The popular illustrated weekly, *Picture Post*, wrote warmly of the former governor of Bengal, Sir John Anderson (of the Anderson Shelter), as one of those 'iron-fisted, steel-hearted men usually required, sooner or later, to serve the Empire in India'.[21]

Mrs Savi's short story also reflects a constant of Anglo-Indian life, the feeling that things were changing for the worst, and that there had once been a perfect age when everyone had known their place in the scheme of things and behaved accordingly. Of course, this is a theme which may be found in the literature of any generation, but in India it corresponded closely with reality. Civil servants' and officers' memoirs which appeared after 1914 lamented the deterioration and, the writers argued, the dilution of the Raj's prestige. Describing his final Indian posting in 1897, C. E. Goulding, a police officer, regretted that it was in a 'civilised' district which was administered by a 'Europeanised Babu'. 'I wished,' he wrote, 'to take away with me the recollection of what India had been.'[22] Similar sentiments run through the writings of Sir Michael O'Dwyer, William Horne and General Sir James Willcocks, all of whom regarded the political changes introduced after 1909 with trepidation. It was a reaction which transcended rank. Frank Richards, a private in the Royal Welch Fusiliers, recalled how, soon after his arrival in India in the early 1900s, he was rebuked by a veteran. 'Sonny, the soldiers of the old John Company drank rum and not shark's piss,' he observed, adding, 'the country is fast going to the dogs, by the way that some of the natives were strutting about.'[23]

Inter-war travel literature emphasised the immutability of India as its greatest appeal. 'Sudden glimpses of a world long lost' were promised to tourists in a 1938 advertisement for the Indian Railway Bureau. The accompanying drawing of fair-skinned nautch girls in long diaphanous dresses and princely, robed figures standing beside an elephant indicates that visitors would encounter sights already familiar from scenes in the illustrated weeklies and newsreels.[24] This was the timeless, picturesque country visited by an American travel writer, M. O. Williams, who exclaimed, 'If only the East would remain unchanged.' His piece appeared in the November 1921 issue of the *National Geographic Magazine*, which was largely devoted to India, no doubt in anticipation of the forthcoming royal visit. The 'magic' of the sub-continent was evoked by pictures of caparisoned elephants, mailed warriors and princely palaces, and there was praise for the work of the British. An article on Kashmir described the moral revolution accomplished at the Church Mission School at Srinagar by its muscular Christian headmaster, Edward Tyndale-Briscoe. He had invigorated the 'physically lazy' youth of Kashmir by a relentless programme of soccer, boxing and swimming. 'Here,' the author remarked, 'were people who, with all their age-old philosophy, did not know that physical courage, reserve and self-restraint, bred in muscle and bone, would do more than fanaticism to make them strong.'[25]

Indian incapacities were a persistent theme in books about India, whether factual or imaginary. 'Half of them don't believe in germs and the other half are too indolent to be enlightened,' laments a memsahib in Mrs Savi's *The Passionate Problem* (1935). Far better, thought Maud Diver, that Indians remained untaught. In her *Desmond V.C.* (1915), the hero presents a faithful Sikh NCO (a coloured portrait of the King Emperor is the sole decoration of his room) with a photograph of himself. 'To the unsophisticated native – and there are happily many left in India – a photograph remains an abiding miracle; a fact to be accepted and reverenced without explanation, like the inconsistencies of the gods.' In fact, Indians had been taking their own photographs for the past sixty years. Such an activity would have displeased Sir George Younghusband, for whom all educated Indians were an anathema, as he explained in his memoirs:

> The best Indians in the middle and lower-middle classes, and those who have the highest and best qualities, are the soldiers and servants who can perhaps neither read nor write, but who have lived all their lives within the honest atmosphere of Englishmen and Englishwomen. The worst are the so-called highly educated Indians, who get a smattering of algebra and John Stuart Mill.[26]

Real and fictional Indians found themselves snared in a moral trap. If they embraced Western learning they were despised, and, simultaneously, they were condemned for resisting improvement. Their supposed immunity to progress was censured in *Mother India*, a tendentious survey written by an American, Katherine Mayo, and published in 1927. At the beginning, she gives a nightmarish account of the sacrifice of a goat she had witnessed in Calcutta:

> The blood gushes forth on the pavement, the drums and gongs burst out wildly. 'Kali! Kali! Kali!' shout all the priests and the supplicants together, some flinging themselves down on the temple floor.[27]

This sets the tone for a book in which Indian backwardness is blamed upon Hinduism, which has 'devitalised' the Indian mind and filled it with meaningless abstractions which are summed up as 'nothingness'. Hinduism has also legitimised the degradation of women, about which Miss Mayo has much to say. For all its inability to push through profound reforms in this area, she still praises the Raj: 'Britain, by example and teaching, has been working for nearly three-quarters of a century to implant her own ideas of mercy on an alien soil.' She has sympathy too for the princes, one of whom tells her that: 'We made no treaty with the Government that included Bengali babus [i.e. Congressmen]. We shall never deal with this new lot of Jacks-in-office.' The pretensions of what he calls 'the babu' class disturb the fictional raja in *The Anglo-Indians*: 'Nowadays they tell me the tiger and the goat drink at the same stream.'[28]

The raja's forebodings are a reminder that Indian society, like that of the British in India, was hierarchical. During his voyage out in 1933, Pilot Officer David Lee was reprimanded for buying the wrong style of pith helmet. 'You will be taken for a bloody box wallah [non-official European],' he is warned, which would be unthinkable for an officer.[29] In *The Passionate Problem*, Edith Savi (herself the wife of a box wallah) describes guests from that class drinking too much at a ball and helping themselves to cigars. Their misconduct was 'holding British prestige up to contempt', and a shocked sahib and Indian banker swiftly bring proceedings to a halt to forestall further excesses.[30] Learning self-control and the correct forms of dress were part of a process of social and moral acclimatisation whose purpose was conformity and solidarity. Attitudes normal enough at home were unacceptable or even dangerous in India, where the prestige of the British race was still considered the mainstay of the Raj. 'You're superior to everyone in India except one or two of the ranis, and don't forget that,' Mrs Turton, the Collector's wife, tells Mrs Moore, the naïve newcomer at the beginning of E. M. Forster's *A Passage to India* (1924).

But the elevation of the ICS official was brief. 'At Chandrapore the Turtons were little gods; soon they would retire to some suburban villa, and die exiled from glory,' Forster observes with some pleasure, for on the whole he disliked the values of the Indian official class. He was unconsciously echoing a snobbery which could be found inside the Anglo-Indian hierarchy. In 1923, when a group of officers were discussing whether to open fire on rioters, one suggested consulting a civilian official. A furious brigade commander interrupted: 'Who do they think they are? Snivelling little intellectuals who, when they return from this God-forsaken country, try to pass themselves off as gentlemen. A lot of them settle in hideous little villas on the outskirts of my place in Surrey.'[31]

Indian society too is pyramidal and brutally exclusive. Its barriers and spitefulness are revealed in the picaresque tragedy of M. J. Anand's *Coolie*, which appeared in 1936 and gives a finely observed worm's-eye view of the Raj. The hero, Munoo, is a hill boy placed by his family in the service of an Indian bank clerk, whose status is announced by a blackboard set on his verandah: 'Babu Northoo Ram – Sub-Accountant of the Imperial Bank, Sham Nager.' Munoo is baffled by the ways of his new master and is soon in trouble after he excretes by the bungalow, infuriating his mistress. 'What will the sahibs think who pass by our doors every morning and afternoon! The Babuji had prestige to keep up with the sahibs.' So too has a neighbour, an Indian judge, whose wife is outraged when Munoo quarrels with one of her servants. 'These low babus are getting so uppish,' she exclaims. 'Let my husband come and we will show you what it is to insult your superiors.' Like Munoo, the greenhorn British official had to learn rules which were vital for his survival. Why was explained in *A Passage to India*, after his mother and prospective bride, Adela Quested, challenged Ronny Heaslop for behaving like a god. He replies:

> Here we are, and we're going to stop, and the country's got to put up with us, gods or no gods. 'Oh, look here,' he broke out, rather pathetically, 'what do you and Adela want me to do? Go against my class, against all the people I respect and admire out here? Lose such power as I have for doing good in this country, because my behaviour isn't pleasant? You neither of you understand what work is, or you'd never talk such eyewash. . . . I am out here to work, mind, to hold this wretched country by force. I'm not a missionary or a Labour Member or a vague sentimental sympathetic literary man. I'm just a servant of the Government; it's the profession you wanted me to choose myself, and that's that. We're not pleasant in India, and we don't intend to be pleasant. We've something more important to do.'

This is the cost of the Raj; its servants cannot fulfil their vocation without self-containment and setting a distance between themselves and those whom they govern. What the outsider, like Forster, interprets as haughtiness is essential for the perpetuation of a system which, its defenders believed, worked for the interests of India.

Forster was repeating what he must have heard many times during his time in India in 1912–13 and in the early 1920s as secretary to Tukoji Rao

II, the Maharaja of Dewas. An aesthete and intellectual who detested the athletic public-school spirit which pervaded the British community, and in particular its clubs, Forster was bound to recoil from much of what he saw and heard. It disturbed a man who believed with all his being in the value of human relationships that here was a world in which they were strictly regulated to the point where close contact between British and Indian was all but impossible. And yet, his India was, in its way, as subjective as Kipling's, and both were selective. Malcolm Darling, his Cambridge undergraduate friend and civil servant, was the antithesis to Mr Turton even though, in time, he came to share the general belief that the Westernised Indian did not represent the 'real' India.

There were certainly plenty of authentic Turtons in India, but the point was that they were there to govern fairly, not court the affection of those Indians who wanted to be their successors. They did not treat these people as equals simply because, as administrators, they had to appear dispassionate. The aloofness and emotional calluses which dismayed Forster were part and parcel of their job for many, but not all, British officials. They were in India to command respect and not cultivate intimate friendships, although the two were not always incompatible. There was a body of opinion, strong among the older generation of officials, that thought excessive familiarity might prove dangerous, even if it was desirable on a purely human level.[32] Sir Bampfylde Fuller, one of the old school, admitted that his countrymen's condescension upset Indian susceptibilities. Nonetheless, he wondered whether Indians who complained of British frostiness were employing a double standard. They forbade their wives and daughters to mix with Europeans and their womenfolk, and some high-caste Hindus refused to eat with Christians.[33] Not every Hindu was bound by taboos. Sir Henry Lawrence, commissioner of the Sind between 1916 and 1918, dined with Gokhale and other leading Hindu figures at their houses and invited them to his.[34]

Lawrence not only enjoyed warm relations with Indians, but favoured the land nationalisation and the state ownership of public utilities. The ICS was not solely the preserve of men of the same mental mould as Forster's sun-baked bureaucrats. Moreover, new generations of administrators discounted the shibboleths of the old hands. Penderel Moon, who joined the service in the early 1930s, caught the clash between old and new in an imaginary exchange between a new official and his older superior. The newcomer questioned whether India had been the net economic beneficiary of British rule, and the older replied testily:

Here are we who have spent our lives in India working for the peasants – devoting all our energies to their welfare in the heat of the day – and then you come out and tell us that they are worse off than when we began. I don't know where you get these notions.

He blamed them on the preparatory year spent studying at University, 'reading seditious literature and studying phonetics'.[35] There were other sceptical minds abroad. After a tour in a district near Benares in 1940, Hugh Martin was asked by the commissioner to list all that he had observed which could not have been seen 2,000 years ago. He truthfully answered kerosene, bicycles and Singer sewing machines.[36] This exchange would have unthinkable in Forster's Chandrapore at a time when the Raj, while under siege, still believed in its own durability. Nearly twenty years after, when it was clear that Indian self-government was inevitable and a new generation of officials were in place, attitudes had changed considerably.

Shared pleasure in sport demolished racial barriers. It was sadly ironic that the only satisfactory relationship Forster's Dr Aziz has with a European is playing an impromptu game of polo with a British subaltern – 'Aziz liked soldiers – they either accepted you or swore at you, which was preferable to the civilian's hauteur'. After a lively chukka, each goes their own way, each thinking: 'If only they were all like that.' Some time after, when Aziz is under arrest for the alleged assault on Miss Quested in one of the Marabar caves, and the white community coalesces around a shared sense of racial outrage, the officer appears and, somewhat tipsy, addresses his countrymen. 'The native is all right if you let him alone. . . . You remember the one I had a knock with on your maidan last month. Well, he was all right. Any native who plays polo is all right. What you've got to stamp on is these educated classes, and, mind, I know what I'm talking about this time.'

Here, *A Passage to India* conveys an authentic resonance of the Raj. B. N. Lahari, one of the first Indians to be admitted for training as a senior police officer in 1921, recalled that he was treated in a friendly manner by all his European colleagues. He was tolerated, he believed, because he did not chew betel or play Indian gramophone records and because of his willingness to engage in mess horseplay and fight back.[37] In the early 1940s Alan Flack got on splendidly with his superior, Muhammad Zillah Khan, who was 'a good tennis player, billiard player, shot and

in fact a fine chap of the old Mussulman school'. Yet despite their friendship, Slack never met his wife, who remained in purdah.[38]

IV

Contemporary law banned any explicit references in fiction to sexual contacts between British and Indians. Forster knew about them, probably in
some detail, through his shipboard meeting in 1912 with Lieutenant
Kenneth Seabright of the Queen's Own (Royal West Kent Regiment),
with whom he later stayed at Peshawar. Seabright was a homosexual with
an enthusiastic and insatiable appetite for teenage boys, and he seems intu-
itively to have recognised Forster's latent homosexuality, as did some young
Indians. The young subaltern, who struck Forster as a Byronic figure, was
already at work on an epic poem which recorded in lubricious detail his
encounters with various Indian partners, whose colour excited him.
Paradise for Seabright was the North-West Frontier, where his tastes were
abundantly catered for:

> *And now the scene shifted and I passed*
> *From sensuous Bengal to fierce Peshawar*
> *An Asiatic stronghold where each flower*
> *Of boyhood planted in its restless soil*
> *Is – ipso facto – ready to despoil*
> *(Or be despoiled by) someone else; they yarn*
> *Indeed so has it that the young Pathan*
> *Thinks it peculiar if you would pass*
> *Him by without some reference to his arse.*[39]

What is remarkable is that Seabright's activities appear either to have passed
undetected or have been ignored by his brother officers and superiors. If
revealed, his conduct would have rendered him liable for a court martial
and, at the very least, a dishonourable dismissal; an officer who merely
spoke to his men about sexual subjects was cashiered in 1916.[40] Seabright's
extraordinary career gives the lie to the predictable assertion of Baden-
Powell that polo and pig-sticking had purged the British subaltern of his
former vices.[41]

Evidence of their persistence, at least in matters of sex, comes from the
anonymous confession of a bisexual officer who was strongly attracted to

Asian women, particularly Japanese. His Indian experiences included affairs with British women (one married and another picked up at a ball), an orgy in a Bombay brothel which lasted three weeks, and a chance encounter with 'a fairly good-looking punkah woman', who opportunely turned up at his bungalow.[42] There is no reason to disbelieve this testimony, although corroboration is hard to find among the reminiscences of those who lived in a far more reticent age. Nonetheless, one survivor recalled an encounter in 1918 with the wife of senior civil servant, whose pastime it was to travel on trains heading northwards from Bombay and engage the more hand-some, newly-arrived subalterns as bedmate for the night.[43]

Imported Japanese prostitutes employed in Bombay brothels were highly rated by the unknown philandering officer. Several hundred Japanese girls, some as young as twelve, were hired by Rangoon whoremasters and, according to Private Frank Richards of the Royal Welch Fusiliers, they 'had the reputation of being the cleanest girls in town'. There was an inter-national flavour to Rangoon's Red Light district at the beginning of the century, with one street housing prostitutes from all countries. The patri-otic Richards remembered that 'I felt thankful when I was told there was not an English girl amongst them.' His memories of the Edwardian Raj were published in 1936 with the encouragement of Robert Graves, and were extremely frank for their time. Richards described the various broth-els reserved for British servicemen, which were flourishing, despite the exertions of various 'purity' lobbies over the past thirty years. The Agra prostitutes lived in a street in the Suddar bazaar, a short walk from the bar-racks, and had an exclusively military clientele. Regimental policemen patrolled the street and gave a savage caning to any Indian who had the temerity to speak to the girls. There were about forty of them, aged between twelve and forty, and each stood in front of her cabin proclaim-ing her skills in love's arts. Every prostitute was examined three times a week by army doctors, and any with venereal infections were removed for treatment in the native hospital. Some bold spirits ventured beyond the official pale of indulgence. 'If a man hired a gharri to go for a ride some-where, the driver would immediately say: "Sahib, you want nice bibi [concubine], me drive you to bungalow of nice half-caste, plenty clean, plenty cheap, only charge one rupee, Sahib." The result was often the pox, a spell in hospital and a punitive reduction in pay.'[44]

Indian lack of inhibitions about sex, which surprised many British sol-diers, horrified Katherine Mayo. She praised official efforts during the 1920s to crack down on newspaper advertisements for concoctions which revived virility and were vindicated by candid testimonials from satisfied customers.[45] Unlike them, the campaign flagged. The Delhi *Liberator* of 21 September 1947 contained a puff for 'Lifenjo', whose promoter, Mrs Swatty, a mother of ten, declared: 'The roses are still blooming on my face and my beauty is unmarred. My husband finds me good as a virgin of sixteen.' Those wishing to share her felicity were promised that 'our confidential letters shall guide you well in all matters relating to sexual science.'

British women too could learn some of the ploys of the zenana. During the autumn of 1919, advertisements for 'Wana Ranee' scent showed an Indian girl, one breast coyly uncovered, set against the outline of Oriental buildings. This 'Oriental fragrance' offered 'a mystic charm'. Women who suffered from unwanted facial and bodily hair were promised relief through an Indian remedy in an advertisement of 1922. The puff claimed that the formula for this depilatory had been disclosed to a British officer by a sepoy whose life he had saved. Hitherto it had been 'the closely guarded secret of the Hindu religion' which forbade women hair on any part of their bodies save the head. Now it was available through Mrs Hudson, who 'belongs to a family high in Society and is the widow of a prominent Army Officer, so you can write to her with every confidence'.

An oblique, literary admission of Indian sensuality was the country's frequent representation as a woman. In Sara Jeanette Duncan's novel about Indian nationalism, *Burnt Offering* (1909), Yavada, a pro-British guru, imagines his nation is Britain's bride. 'England is the husband of India,' he suggests, adding that in consequence, 'we are the children of England, also.' The authoress was borrowing a conceit from Kipling, who had used the metaphor of marriage to illuminate the relationship between the two countries. For him the bride was prone to wilfulness and, therefore, required a firm, wise groom.[46] India, a young woman clad in a sari, respectfully bows before her King Emperor in Bernard Partridge's *Punch* cartoon drawn to celebrate the durbar of 1911.[47] As a woman, India demanded respect and honour, a point made in Kipling's story 'The Man Who Would Be King'. In it, a pair of devil-may-care discharged soldiers make their way deep into the Himalayas to Luristan, where, with their modern weapons and tactics, they make themselves rulers. Revered as gods, they betray their subjects' trust by plundering their shrines and are ultimately destroyed. On one level, this is a parable of the ravishment of India that had been perpetrated by the greedy nabobs of Clive's era. They were, of course, as Kipling makes plain elsewhere, superseded by worthier suitors who chose to woo rather than rape.

V

It was Kipling's India of dashing men and their exploits rather than Forster's flawed Raj which filled the cinema screens during the inter-war years. His tales of the scapegrace but fundamentally decent British rankers were adopted by Hollywood for *Gunga Din* (1939). Like so many products of the American studios at this time, the film was a vehicle for its stars: Cary Grant, Douglas Fairbanks Jr. and Victor MacLagen. After a series of adventures, they, together with the humble bhisti, Gunga Din (Sam Jaffe), save the Raj from Hindu fanatics, one of whom in his simple dhoti bears more than a passing resemblance to Gandhi. He meets his death bravely, which prompts one of his antagonists to remark that he was, in his way, also serving his country. The climax of the film is a battle in a mountain pass in which the British forces (including kilted Highlanders who sing, with unintentional irony, the Jacobite ballad 'Will ye nae come back again') are saved from ambush by Gunga Din. There are Gatling guns, cannon mounted on elephants and a spectacular charge by Bengal lancers.

In *Gunga Din* and similar films, Hollywood producers saw India's North-West Frontier as an extension of America's Wild West, another region peopled by a race which had defiantly impeded the white man's progress. India's frontier was also the setting for *Lives of the Bengal Lancers* (1935), in which American actors play British cavalrymen under the stern eye and fierce moustache of C. Aubrey Smith, whose visage and bearing marked him out as the cinema's perfect sahib. From him the young men learn their duty and the meaning of service to a Raj which brings order and justice to the wayward tribesmen. The fanatic opponents of the King Emperor's peace are finally overcome after a fast-moving sequence of scenes in which pigs are stuck, anti-British conspiracies uncovered, and battles won in the nick of time. The films ends on a poignant note as the heroes receive medals for gallantry, one awarded posthumously and pinned to the saddlecloth of his horse. Self-sacrifice is the price of empire and, as the bugle sounds, one feels a wave of sympathy for the Raj and its gallant defenders.

Another blend of Henty and Hollywood appeared in 1935, with *The Charge of the Light Brigade*. In spite of a breathtaking historical contortion, in which the Cawnpore massacre precedes the Crimean war and is avenged by Errol Flynn and his horsemen, the film succeeds as pure romantic adventure. It was stirring stuff and audiences loved it. Another Indian release of the same year, *Clive of India*, was a British production. It starred

Ronald Colman as the hero and Loretta Young as his wife, and tended to concentrate on their private life, with tension created by her yearning to return to England. Nonetheless, and in spite of being shot in a studio, it contained what one critic called 'lively and picturesque moments' with elephants appearing at the battle of Plassey. There was also a political message, with Clive proclaiming his personal creed: 'India is a sacred trust. I must keep faith.' It was also, as British cinema-goers were aware, the lodestar of those responsible for the modern Raj.

How the present rulers of India kept faith with its people was shown in *The Drum*, produced by Alexander Korda in 1938 from a script by A. E. W. Mason, the author of *The Four Feathers*. The story revolves around anti-British subversion in the frontier state of Tokut, masterminded by the ruthless Ghul Khan (Raymond Massey), who embodies the two most potent sources of opposition to the Raj. He is Oxford-educated (Balliol, needless to say) and a fanatical Muslim, having fought alongside the Turks and against the British at Gallipoli and in Mesopotamia. Currently he is planning a jihadic uprising to unite the tribes, whom he will arm with modern weapons smuggled from another enemy of the Raj, Russia. Against him is the British resident, Carruthers (Roger Livesey) aided by Azim, the young, dispossessed Raja of Tokut (the fourteen-year-old boy star, Sabu), who is first won over to the sahibs by the bravery and kindness of Mrs Carruthers, played by Valerie Hobson. Ghul Khan decoys Carruthers, his wife and a small detachment of Highlanders to a party, in which they will be massacred. Carruthers suspects treachery, but attends alone, quietly telling his friends that individual self-sacrifice has always been necessary for the advancement of the empire and with it, peace and civilisation. He cites the example of Gordon at Khartoum. After his departure there is a moving vignette in which his wife plays the piano and is toasted, along with all the memsahibs in India, by the regimental adjutant and doctor, who praise them for their endurance and for making their menfolk's exile so agreeable.

Ghul Khan's plot is frustrated thanks to Carruthers's vigilance, the courage of Azim and the timely arrival of a relief column. The new raja finally enters Tokut with his British friends, from whom he had learned the values of a Raj which prizes integrity, fair play and humanity. Filmed in technicolor and including location footage shot in Chitral, *The Drum* is visually stunning and the battle scenes exciting and authentic, as they ought to have been, for Korda had hired regular British and Indian troops.

The film is a strong apologia for the Raj, and was welcomed by British audiences at a time when the North-West Frontier was making headlines. On 17 November 1936 the *Daily Sketch* led with the story 'British Column Ambushed' and a sensational account of how a force had been 'lured by treachery' into a Waziri valley, where it had suffered heavy losses – in fact seventeen dead. This skirmish was part of large-scale operations then in hand against Haji Mirza Ali Khan, the Faqir of Ipi, a charismatic holy man who had been rallying the Wazirs with the well-worn but still potent slogan of 'Islam in Danger'. Like Ghul Khan in *The Drum*, the Faqir was suspected of soliciting arms from Britain's enemies, and, on 16 April 1937, the *Daily Herald* claimed that he was being assisted by Mussolini through the Italian embassy in Kabul. This was strenuously denied by the British government. Nonetheless, there was a secret anxiety that, in the event of a European war, Italy might actively foster unrest on the North-West Frontier.[48] Italian and German propagandists used the frontier war as a device to blacken Britain's name and somehow exonerate their own governments' crimes. In November 1938 and in response to British press outrage at the horrors of the Krystallnacht, *Volkische Beobachter* alleged that Wazirs, fighting for their independence, had had their land invaded by tanks and aircraft and that thousands of women and children had been killed by bombs and shells.[49] Sensitivity to such criticism may explain why *The Drum* did not include aircraft and armoured vehicles in the Raj's armoury, even though the film was set in the present day.

What entertained British film-goers, enraged Indian. When *The Drum* was shown in Bombay and Madras, indignant audiences stormed out of the cinema and protested in the streets against what they considered to be British propaganda. The Indian government, which already had its hands full with communal and political unrest, ordered this fresh source of tension to be withdrawn from circulation. *The Drum*'s reception in India justified, after the event, a ban on the making of *The Relief of Lucknow* in 1938, which the Indian and British governments feared would exacerbate racial tension. Official censorship did not extend to the press, for, soon after, *Picture Post* did a feature on the Mutiny, illustrated by contemporary photographs. The text admitted that Indians were no longer 'wholly satisfied' with the Raj, but it still offered them 'vast benefits – medical, sanitary, educational and economic'.[50]

Nervousness over the presentation of the Indian Mutiny for a mass audience was a symptom of a wider anxiety about how the empire was treated by film-makers. Ever since its foundation in 1912, the British Board of Film Censors had proscribed a number of subjects, which included misconduct by British servicemen and, from 1928, any hint of sexual attraction between coloured men and white women. The celluloid sahib had no choice but to behave impeccably, since film-makers were forbidden to represent, 'White men in a state of degradation amidst Far Eastern and Native surroundings,' or suggest that British overseas possessions were 'lawless sinks of iniquity'.

Such interdicts were unneccessary, since Hollywood and British studios saw the empire through the eyes of Kipling and Henty as backcloths against which heroes could perform their exploits and keep audiences on the edges of their seats. The political message of 1930s films about India was favourable to a Raj which was always served by honourable, dedicated and gallant men.

VI

Cinema images and scripts confirmed popular perceptions of India which had their roots in the 1880s and 1890s. Images of India first projected by Kipling proved remarkably durable, even though their verisimilitude was sometimes questionable. 'Rudyard Kipling made the modern soldier' asserted Sir George Younghusband, who believed that rankers had deliberately modelled themselves on the characters in Kipling's ballads and short stories.

> My early recollections of the British soldier are of a bluff, rather surly person, never the least jocose or light-hearted, except perhaps when he had too much beer. He was brave always, but with a sullen, stubborn bravery. No Tipperary or kicking footballs about.

Afterwards, soldiers self-consciously adopted the demeanour and argot of Kipling's Cockneyfied, chipper soldiers; or so Younghusband and his brother officers believed.[51] Kipling's picture of India certainly had a strong and lasting appeal for soldiers. His lines on the terrors that awaited the British fighting man who had the misfortune to lie wounded on the 'Afghan plains' chilled the hearts of Private Swindlehurst and men from the Lancashire Fusiliers in 1920, as they prepared to embark for India and a posting on the North-West Frontier.[52]

Everyone who went to India travelled with preconceptions gathered from reading, hearsay, the advice of those who had gone before, and, from 1920 onwards, the cinema. After a visit to the small princely state of Khairpur in 1916, Lady Lawrence listed her impressions:

> Gorgeousness and squalor. Pageantry and over eating and making interminable state banquets. Intrigue, Red carpets. Rams fighting, fireworks, treachery and whispers of murder. Everything one is led to expect in a petty native state in fact.[53]

A trawl through other diaries and the contemporary reports of the Foreign Department would have revealed all these features, although randomly spread. Like everyone else who tried to portray India or make sense of it, Lady Lawrence fell back on generalisations or rough and ready syntheses.

Individual prejudice invariably dictated how India was interpreted. Between 1939 and 1947 the country came under closer scrutiny as thousands of British national servicemen were posted there. They brought with them assumptions about the country that had been picked up at home, and they did not always slip comfortably into traditional Anglo-Indian habits of mind. Captain Kingsford, a Marxist and an army education officer who arrived in 1944, was shaken by the degradation he witnessed and for which he was unprepared. He remembered his first impression of Bombay on a train bound for Peshawar:

> Cocooned in my first-class carriage, I felt the oppression of body and mind lift. I might still shudder at the sight of the poor, skinny, spindle-shanked, emaciated, filthy, diseased; they would be everywhere. But is specially horrible on the city pavements. The day I walked to the dhobi's [laundryman] quarters to get the washing as he had failed to deliver it, the wretched beings there, the old grey man, half-naked, emaciated asleep on the ground, and the small baby on a box, its thighs quite shrunken to a chicken's wing, flies crawling over its penis; outside Lloyd's Bank, a woman advanced in pregnancy lying prone on the pavement, her swollen belly fully exposed, her naked breast clutched by a baby spawling naked beside her. . . . Dirt prevailed everywhere, except in the expensive quarters. As you went along the street everyone seemed to be mixed up with the dust and refuse which the women scavenged for in the early morning, cool and golden before the heat came down.

When the monsoon came the poor cowered and clutched their soaked flimsy rags to their skinny bodies. Those who were slightly better off struggled for places on trams, buses and trains, forcing their way into an already solid mass of bodies. The overwhelming impression of chronic poverty had depressed us and induced apathy in most of us as well. I had become convinced of the essential hollowness and rottenness of our existence in India.[54]

Black, East African askaris, who served on the Burma front in 1944–45 and had only encountered prosperous Indian traders at home, were astonished by the poverty and begging they saw in Bengal.[55] United States servicemen (250,000 passed through India during the war) reacted in the same way, and soon transferred to Indians the same racial arrogance which they practised at home towards Negroes.[56] American journalists took a similar line; one wrote at the end of 1942: 'India is a miserably poor, hungry, retarded country. Most Indians are half-starved and three-fourths naked.'[57]

British troops too were stunned by what they saw of India, which seemed to be at odds with what they had been told about a benign, progressive Raj. Conscripts of the 1st Cameron Highlanders, their heads full of left-wing press reports of British misrule, found themselves being converted from thinking 'Why haven't we done more for these people?' to 'What can you do with these people?'[58] Les Blackie, a Tyneside national serviceman in the Tank Corps, concluded that the Indians were their own worst enemies. 'Religion,' he told his parents in 1946, 'retards the advance of civilisation . . . How can a country get on,' he asked, 'where boys are married at 14 and girls at ten and under?' The hucksters and beggars who hung around outside his barracks were 'black chunks of laziness' who, when not attempting to swindle British servicemen, did nothing but 'beg, pray and squabble'.[59]

Public defecation, an indifference to elementary sanitary precautions, and women carrying heavy burdens or undertaking heavy labour were regarded with a mixture of ridicule and disdain.[60] Such sights had aroused no adverse comments among soldiers a hundred, even fifty years before, because they would have been familiar to men raised in rural and urban slums. All that was different was the scale of deprivation. Britain had changed and was changing for the better, whereas India appeared to have stayed still, which was puzzling for a generation that had been brought up to believe that the peoples of the empire were making great leaps forward. In his last Empire Day broadcast before the outbreak of the war, George VI had spoken of an empire united by 'freedom, just laws and mutual confidence'. Symbolic sculptures of 'Science', 'Industry' and 'Health' had adorned the 1938 Empire Exhibition at Glasgow. It was the last of its kind and, unlike its predecessors, eschewed the picturesque, preferring through futuristic architecture to advertise a forward-looking empire which was striding onwards and upwards. Seen from the standpoint of the transient British serviceman, India appeared exempt from this process.

The war eroded barriers in Britain, but they stayed firm in India. 'The British civvies out here always classed the common soldier as scum!', Les Blackie told his parents. 'You see they have found that everyone does just as they order, due to the fact their servants etc are all "darkies".'[61] Other hierarchies remained frozen: in his autobiography, *Bugles and a Tiger*, John Masters recalled how in the 1930s Indian army officers sat, quite literally, well below the salt in British regimental messes. As a Gurkha officer, he was repelled by 'niggers', 'wogs', 'Hindoos', and 'black-bellied bastards': terms which still held their place in the vocabulary of racial abuse among some British other ranks and officers, and did so, sadly, until the final hours of the Raj.[62] 'To me already, from evenings I had spent in the messes of Indian regiments in Razmak and on column, they were Dogras, Bengalis, Afridis, Konkani Mahrattas,' he remembered.

As always with India, one impression is contradicted by another. Relations between Indians and men of the 9th Lancers stationed on the frontier in the late 1930s were friendly. James Squire, then regimental riding master, enjoyed polo chukkas with his opposite numbers from Indian cavalry regiments – 'They were splendid chaps among whom I made many friends.'[63] Touring the bazaars of Peshawar in the early 1920s, Private Swindlehurst of the Lancashire Fusiliers met an Indian with a shared interest in photography, which formed the basis for friendship. General Palit, one of the advance guard of Indian commissioned officers, thought that the social hurdles which separated him from some of his British colleagues were knocked away by the war, which brought with it an influx of young officers from Britain who were untainted by old prejudices.[64]

Understanding came through knowledge, and John Masters believed that where India was concerned his countrymen had little of either.[65] Very few ever met Indians; in 1931 the census revealed that 95,000 people in Britain had been born in India, and nearly all of them were of British parentage. Most Indians who lived in Britain were students, birds of passage confined to the university towns and cities and predominantly middle-class. A few, mostly physicians and former Bengali seamen, had settled in the country. The latter ran a handful of Indian restaurants, most of whose customers were Indians or Britons who had lived in India and developed a taste for its cooking. Eating a curry was an opportunity to relive old times; British customers liked to be called 'sahib' and referred to the waiters as 'bearers'.[66]

Ignorance of India was often collosal and inexcusable; Sir Zafrulla Khan, Minister of Commerce and a member of the viceregal council, once met a prominent British politician who believed that all Indians were Hindus. Newspaper reports of communal and political violence suggested that the entire country was convulsed with disorder, and literature, both fictional and factional, was often ill-balanced and misleading. He noted approvingly that in the wake of the outrage provoked by Miss Mayo's *Mother India*, an Indian had travelled to the United States and had returned to publish *Uncle Sham*, a catalogue of American excesses and vice.[67]

The truth was that India, like the rest of the empire, was taken for granted by the man and woman in the street. Its problems and future were relatively insignificant issues for a people facing economic stagnation, mass unemployment and, from 1933, Britain's relations with rising, virile, jealous and expansionist powers: Germany, Italy and Japan. In the latter context the empire did matter, for it made a Britain a world power and was an invaluable asset in an increasingly hostile world. 'The Empire true, we can depend on you' ran a line in 'There Will Always Be An England', a rousing patriotic song which appeared in October 1939. In many respects its sentiments belonged to that era of flag-waving jingoism which had been brutally terminated by the mass slaughter of 1914–18. Inter-war imperialism had been soberer, concentrating on the serious responsibilities of empire, although the public's taste for old-style imperial adventure stories remained as strong as ever. But those who read Kipling or thrilled to the derring-do of *Lives of the Bengal Lancers* or *The Drum* were also aware from the newspapers that Indians were becoming less and less satisified with the wise paternalism of the sahibs who, it had always been said, stood between them and anarchy.

4

A Great Trial of
Strength: Power
Struggles, 1922–42

I

After 1922 the Raj recovered its former composure, while its opponents fell temporarily into disarray. On his release from prison in
1924, Gandhi threw himself into preaching the gospel of cotton spinning
to the peasantry. Congress was in eclipse, with its members quarrelling
among themselves about aims and methods. Hindu–Muslim harmony
evaporated after Turkey's new president, Kamal Atatürk, abolished the
caliphate and with it the reason for the Khalifat movement. Communal
disorders increased in frequency and virulence.

Sectarian violence was one of the principal concerns of the new
Viceroy, Lord Irwin (later Lord Halifax), a pragmatic Conservative aristocrat of immense height and Anglo-Catholic inclinations. His appointment
in 1926 by Stanley Baldwin raised some eyebrows because Irwin knew
little of India beyond what he had gathered during a tour twenty-two years
ago, but, as the Prime Minister recognised, India needed a man whose
mind was flexible rather than over-burdened with local knowledge or
prejudices. Henceforward, British policy consisted in balancing the need to
keep overall control at the centre at the same time as making concessions
to Indians who were pressing for greater autonomy. The lines to be followed were those laid down by the Montagu–Chelmsford measures:
Britain retained responsibility for India's defence and foreign policies while

Indians took care of some financial and all social and welfare matters through their elected provincial and national legislatures. A great deal of good was accomplished by these bodies, not least the acceleration of the programme for innoculation against cholera.[1]

Co-operation with the Raj had much to offer Indians. Success and honours were the rewards of those who worked with the British. M. J. Anand's fictional Sir Todar Mal, Knight Commander of the Indian Empire, barrister, official prosecutor and a member of the Daulatpur municipal council, counted for something in his community. He wore a frock coat, carried a gold watch and chain and felt proud to ride through the bazaar with an Englishman in his carriage. Many envied his *izzat* (good fortune), some thought him a 'traitor', and 'everyone was afraid of him'.[2] There were plenty of Sir Todars at the disposal of the Raj, and they served their country well and also themselves, their kinsfolk and friends, or so the jealous believed.

The system under which they worked was due for official assessment in 1929, the year of a British general election. If the Labour Party won, then the review of Indian constitutional arrangements might be favourable to Congress, which had long had close links with the British Left. This was the fear of the Secretary of State for India, Lord Birkenhead (formerly F. E. Smith) and so he brought forward the date of the commission. It was headed by Sir John Simon, a virtuous but lifeless political packhorse, instructed to visit India, discover how the Montagu–Chelmsford arrangements were working and suggest possible adjustments. With the exception of the Labour MP, Major Clement Attlee, the committee members were all undistinguished British Parliamentarians. The message, as read by Congressmen, was clear and harsh: India's political future was to be shaped from above and without reference to its peoples' wishes.

Congress demonstrators with black flags and shouts of 'Simon go home' greeted the commissioners when they disembarked at Bombay in December 1928. Mournful processions and a boycott were not enough; Congress had to seize the political initiative. It did so at its annual conference in late December, when delegates backed two audacious motions. The first, framed with moderate backing by Motilal Nehru, called for instant Dominion status, and the second, proposed by his son Jawaharlal and another younger generation radical, Chandra Subhas Bose, demanded complete British withdrawal from its new dominion by 31 December 1929. The alternative was a renewed campaign of protest and disruption. This was blackmail, and only the most artless could have imagined that

Britain would give way. It was also an astute and well-calculated manoeuvre which shoved the Simon commission into the margins, and a timely reminder of Congress's historic claim that it alone spoke for the whole of India. The last few years had witnessed signs of the fragmentation of Indian political life, as local and religious factions proliferated. The Sikh Akali movement in the Punjab, although at first concerned with the administration of temples, contained the seeds of a separatist, national movement. Militant Hindus were attracted to the Mahasabha groups pledged to defend and purify their faith, industrial workers to the rapidly expanding Trade Unions, and peasants to their rural associations, concerned with rents, tenure and tax. The growth of such groups gathered momentum during the 1930s as it became clear that the Raj would shed more and more of its power. Those who were waiting in the wings to pick it up needed to be organised beforehand.

Most significant of all was the gulf that was opening between Hindus and Muslims within Congress. Given the bitterness and recrimination which surrounded – and still surrounds – the process by which this rift widened and led to the partition of India and communal massacres, it is extremely difficult to analyse dispassionately the events and personalities involved. The issues are further blurred by Indian assertions that Britain deliberately exacerbated tensions in fulfilment of a policy of divide and rule, in the hope that it might somehow perpetuate the Raj. And yet it is difficult to imagine how successive viceroys could have resisted demands for special representation from the spokesmen for nearly a quarter of India's population. To allege that the British could have disregarded or deflected this pressure assumes that the Raj was stronger than it was. A head-on collision with Muslim opinion would have invited calamity, since Muslims were disproportionately represented in the ranks of the police and army and the First World War had seen instances, admittedly on a small scale, in which soldiers had preferred their faith to their duty to the King Emperor. Moreover, fomenting religious antipathies ran counter to the purpose of a government which in large part justified its existence by its ability to restrain communal strife. For this reason, and against a background of a spiralling religious violence, Irwin supported efforts to foster tolerance. They failed, as did those of Jawaharlal Nehru and the Muslim Congressman, Dr Maulana Azad.

It was well-nigh impossible for two sophisticated members of the two communities to convince poor, credulous Hindus and Muslims that they had nothing to fear from each other. It required only one small incident or some snippet of hearsay to bring old suspicions to the surface, and they proved stronger than any calls for unity in the face of some external enemy. This is dramatically demonstrated in M. J. Anand's novel *Coolie*, in which a strike meeting of Bombay mill-hands is interrupted by a rumour that a Hindu child had been kidnapped by Muslims, presumably for conversion or forced marriage. As the tale goes round, the number of victims grows, and there are calls for revenge and counter cries of 'You black lentil-eaters! You Hindus!' Brawls spill into the street and within a few minutes the city is convulsed by murderous riots.[3] Fiction reflected reality. Music from Hindu processions which passed close to mosques, rows over cow slaughter and bazaar tales of forcible conversion were the commonest triggers for violence, but even something as trivial as a squabble between children could cause an explosion.[4]

At a high political level disagreements centred on the provision of seats for Muslims in elected assemblies. On this issue, the crunch came during the December 1928 session of Congress, when the prominent Muslim leader, Dr Muhammad Ali Jinnah, proposed not only the reservation of places for his co-religionists in national and provincial legislatures, but the creation of three designated Islamic states – Sind, Baluchistan, and the North-West Frontier Province – within a future Indian federation. Here and elsewhere, he was anxious that the Muslim minority should have its rights guaranteed under what democratic calculus dictated would be a Hindu central government. Jinnah lost the argument and afterwards Muslim support for Congress began to dwindle. With hindsight, it has been said that this setback marked the parting of the waves, which assumes that the 1919–24 Hindu–Muslim accord between them had been cemented by conviction rather than convenience. In fact, the situation remained fluid for some years after Jinnah's failure to secure his safeguards. Muslim militancy and demands for a separate state only emerged after 1937.

The strains created by the appearance of a host of smaller, political organisations made it imperative for Congress to re-emphasise its claim to speak for every Indian. If it did not, then the British would surely make deals with individual factions and play one off against another. It was, therefore, vital that Congress gathered as many as possible of the discontented under its wings, whatever their grievances. They had to be persuaded that their causes could only be advanced through Congress, which alone had the strength to stand up to the British. To prove this, it had to back up the bold challenge it had issued at the end of 1928 with a nationwide campaign of resistance the moment its deadline for British departure had passed. It would also have to maintain solidarity in the face of any counter-offer from the government, which was bound to fall short of the desired announcement of an evacuation on the last day of 1929.

Keeping the Congress ranks together proved hard, for in July 1929 a Labour government was elected in Britain. The new Prime Minister, Ramsay MacDonald, was sympathetic to Congress's aspirations, as was the new Secretary of State, William Wedgewood, who in the past had been a Parliamentary scourge of the Indian government. Both warmly welcomed Irwin's prosposal to announce Dominion status for India. There was support too from Stanley Baldwin, a bold step which distanced him from a substantial faction on the right of his party, which was determined to keep India, whatever the cost. Recent events indicated just what the cost might eventually might be: a strong, unswerving line in Ireland had led to a three-year partisan war against the Irish Republican Army, which had ended with a compromise in 1922. Likewise, prolonged resistance to British control over Egypt had ended with a bargain that took heed of Egyptian feelings. Whatever the diehards had said to the contrary, Ireland and Egypt could not be held by the sword alone, and nor could India.

Irwin's promise of Dominion status was delivered in October 1929, accompanied by an invitation of Indian representatives to a Round Table conference in London, where they were hammer out the arrangements for a new, federal constitution. Congress rejected an offer which was designed to trump its own proposals for India's future. Two months after, at its annual conference in Lahore, it prepared for a new round of non-violent resistance, scheduled to begin on 26 January 1930, which was declared 'Independence Day'.

An 'All-India' campaign was envisaged to reinforce Congress's self-image as the tribune of the entire nation. Gandhi's leadership was indispensable; quite simply he knew India and its masses knew him. His knowledge of the peasants was probably unique, and had been increased by his recent tours of the towns and countryside where he had explained how personal and national salvation could be achieved by spinning *khadi* (cotton cloth). To many of his listeners he was a messianic figure, a moral teacher whose image was already beginning to be carried alongside those of the Hindu gods in religious festivals. Those who did not know or care about Nehru or any other Congress leader had heard of Gandhi and his goodness.

Gandhi was also a consummate showman and a shrewd politician, with a knack of projecting himself in such a way as to attract the greatest possible attention in India and abroad. He gave press interviews in which he revealed a talent for self-dramatisation, which made striking headlines. On 22 January 1930 he told a *Daily Express* reporter that he was about to embark on a 'life-or-death struggle'. India would soon witness a 'great trial of strength' which could only be averted if the British government caved in and delivered a blueprint for complete independence. Not long after, he predicted a civil war in India if Irwin's Round Table conference proceeded.[5] Again in melodramatic vein, he answered the question whether anarchy would follow Britain's withdrawal by saying that he was unperturbed by the prospect of invasion or lawlessness. 'It won't be a new thing in the history of nations that have struggled for freedom.'[6] Whether his Indian audience understood the implications of this statement for themselves and their families is not known. Even Gandhi's now familiar loin cloth was a prop in a well-thought-out piece of political stagecraft. Wearing it, he appeared to the world as the living symbol of 'the semi-starved almost naked villagers' of India, for whom he spoke.[7] Or so he said when he set out for Britain in July 1931; and then and later he was taken at his word.

Behind the façade of the simple prophet-cum-saviour was an astute political brain. Like the rest of the Congress leadership, Gandhi knew that attendance at the London conference would be political suicide. Congressmen would be forced to follow an agenda set by the British and they were certain to return home with far less than they demanded. Moreover, and this galled, Congress would have to sit alongside other 'representatives' of India, most notably the princes. They were forthrightly denounced by Gandhi as 'pawns' created and used by the British. Their vices were those of their masters: 'As the Emperor so his vassals. Our Imperial Government is Satanic.' And yet even the most depraved prince would be spiritually reborn when India became independent. 'When the Imperial Government is replaced by a national government,' Gandhi prophesied, 'the rulers will become virtuous automatically.'[8] As ever, Gandhi was struggling against demonic forces unleashed on India by the West. Vaccination against smallpox was, like the princes, a British invention and, therefore, wholly evil. It was 'a filthy process . . . that is little short of eating beef', and the smallpox victim was advised to cure himself with enemas, fresh air, sleeping in a damp sheet and a new diet.[9] What became of those who took Gandhi's advice can only be guessed.

II

Gandhi's spiritual powers were invoked, like those of a god, by his followers when their satyagraha was tested. When Krishan Chander, the hero of
M. J. Anand's *Confessions of a Lover*, is set upon by lathi-wielding policemen, he implores the aid of Gandhi to give him inner fortitude:

'Mahatma [Great Soul], make my body non-violent!' I naively
  prayed.
And I pressed my body down to the earth.
'Give him a taste of the lathi.'
A blow fell on my back, which was very painful.
I said to myself I was not to feel pain, or be angry if I felt the pain.
A third blow fell on my feet.

Each satyagraha who passed the assay of beating, humiliation, arrest and
maltreatment in gaol became, as it were, Gandhi himself, and a spiritual
particle of his yet-to-be-born India. The satyagrahas were also an exercise
in political power which demonstrated that Congress, rather than the Raj
or those invited to London, was the true voice of India and it was clamouring for immediate independence.

Gandhi's own satyagraha was spectacular. He masterminded a mass defiance of the government salt tax, a survival of East India Company rule
which cost the average Indian no more than three annas (1.5p) a year. The
sum may have been a bagatelle, but what mattered for Gandhi was that the
monopoly over one of the essentials of life symbolised the power and
intrusiveness of the Raj. Followed by journalists and newsreel cameramen,
he set off from his house at Ahmadabad on 12 March 1930 for a 240-mile
march to Dandi on the Gujarat coast. Excitement increased as he walked
southwards and thousands joined him, including at his request, Untouchables, which displeased many Hindus and led to some resignations from
Congress. Muslims stood aloof. On 5 April, Gandhi reached the seashore,
bathed and then picked up a token piece of sea salt from the beach. The
government treated the episode with Olympian indifference and concentrated instead on mass arrests of national and local Congress leaders, including Jawaharlal Nehru. Cutting off the Hydra's heads would, it was assumed,
render the beast harmless, and its carcass could be disposed of by the
police and the army.

In what Gandhi rightly emphasised as a trial of strength, the two sides were evenly balanced. Congress had reluctantly accepted that the 'All-India' protests could not be extended to the princely states, where its local organisations had made very limited headway. In any case, Congress shied away from provoking the princes, which would certainly push them further behind the government. Where there were flickers of unrest, some rulers reacted vigorously. The Maharaja of Kashmir forbade all meetings and displays of the Congress flag and the Maharaja of Gwalior shut down the local Congress offices.[10] No coercive measures were needed in Mysore, a progressive state where Congress had yet to make any impact. Nor could Congress win ground in Travancore, a state run by educated Hindus where the literacy rate was 63 per cent, the highest in India.[11] Elsewhere protest movements which threatened withholding rent as well as tax naturally scared the landowning classes, who rallied to the Raj. The Maharaja of Hyderabad offered 200,000 rupees to the government to assist the suppression of the disturbances, and a Monghyr zamindar threatened to fine his tenants 150 rupees if they actively helped Congress. The Maharaja of Darbhanga, who was also the Bihar Landowners' Association representative at the London conference, founded and funded a pro-government newspaper.[12] This solidarity was a bonus for the government and was acknowledged in one official report which suggested that: 'The prestige and influence of the Chiefs can best be upheld by letting the peasantry see . . . there are two sets of Rulers, the British and the Native, but a single government.'[13]

Even where the local power-brokers were not hostile, popular participation in the protests was patchy and spasmodic, which was just as well since the police were thinly spread and their numbers were falling. There were approximately 215,000 policemen in India in 1930, over a third of them Muslims, which meant that on average there was one policeman to every 1,500 of the population. Police loyalty remained unshaken despite vicious intimidation of them and their families. But the force was aware of how the political pendulum was swinging and, in the wake of concessions made to the nationalists, there was apprehension about the future of the Raj. No one wanted to back a horse which was likely to lose.[14] Although considerable efforts were made to include as many races and religions within the the police as possible, the gathering and evaluation of political intelligence was only entrusted to Europeans and Eurasians, at least in Madras.[15] This was vital work, for, if forewarned of Congress's plans, the police could deploy more effectively and prepare counter-measures. Evidence of success in this murky area is hard to find, let alone assess; nonetheless, by 1939 Madras Special Branch had penetrated the local

Congress leadership to the point where it could secure copies of secret letters to Gandhi.[16]

The 1930 civil disobedience campaign followed the pattern of its predecessor. Congress adopted two complementary strategies. The first was an extension of the boycott of foreign textiles through the harassment and intimidation of anyone who bought or sold them. For instance, some sisters who had purchased imported silk for a wedding were pursued home by pickets who warned their mother that the marriage would be unlucky if the material was worn. Greatly distressed, she took the silk back to the dealer, who reimbursed her, no doubt fearing that he might be the next victim of the crowd.[17] Another form of social bullying was the mock funeral for and cremation of the effigy of a merchant who sold foreign cloth. Congress's second objective was the disruption of the machinery of government through withholding taxes, picketing liquor stores and mass infractions of the forest laws, during which peasants chopped down trees and grazed their stock at will.

Peaceful meetings and processions often became violent and each side blamed the other, although the question of who threw the first brickbat or delivered the first lathi charge was invariably pedantic. For every dedicated satyagraha there were hundreds, sometimes thousands, keen for a scrap with the police and a chance to use the breakdown in order to loot and settle old scores. The lukewarm attitude of the majority of Muslims towards the hartals, boycotts and mass marches added to the tension and led directly to communal riots, the worst in Bombay, Cawnpore and Benares. Official anatomies of the crowds singled out 'loafers and the unemployed' and '*badmashes*' (petty criminals) as the mainspring of all the trouble and accused Congress agents of training their followers in the use of lathis, swords and spears.[18] With equal predictability, Congress alleged that its peaceful supporters were provoked by police aggression.

The police just managed to keep the upper hand, save in Peshawar. Here political life was dominated by Abdul Ghaffar Khan, the leader of the Khudai Kidmatgar or 'Servants of God'. A tolerant Muslim who had been taught at a Christian mission, he believed, almost uniquely for a Pathan, in women's rights and education. Their emancipation was part of his dream of a Pathan renaissance in which his people would unite and build a new identity, free of such ancestral shackles as blood feuds. He was sometimes called 'the Frontier Gandhi' and his apostles wore red shirts, which alarmed the authorities who thought these young men might be covert Communists. Spurned by the Muslim League, no doubt unhappy with his heterodoxy, Abdul Ghaffar

Khan threw his weight behind Congress in 1930, and in April Peshawar was convulsed by a series of relatively peaceful demonstrations.

Violence exploded in the city after the arrest of its most prominent Congress activitists on 22 April. Trouble had been expected, and the civil authorities had troops on stand by, supported by a novelty in Indian crowd control, four armoured cars. (They were named after First World War battles, in the manner of warships, e.g. His Majesty's Armoured Car 'Bapaume'.) 'Bapaume', 'Bray', 'Bullicourt' and 'Bethune' trundled into the streets of Peshawar on the morning of 23 April, and were immediately beset by a mob which murdered a motorcycle despatch rider. Three cars collided, one was set on fire and only with difficulty was another able to lower its machine-gun to fire a couple of bursts, which drove off the rioters. The situation was saved by the arrival of several companies of the King's Own Yorkshire Light Infantry who fired over, and sometimes into, the crowds. It was a nerve-wracking experience for the troops, as one remembered long after. 'They came like a plague of locusts from nowhere', but 'we were soldiers paid to do these kinds of jobs' and 'under iron discipline'. When the volley had been fired, 'it was exciting seeing them running away for their lives'.[19] Thirty-three demonstrators died and thirty were injured before order was restored and it was safe to withdraw the soldiers.

The bloodshed in Peshawar had repercussions throughout the region. Abdul Ghaffar Khan's Red Shirts converged on the city from the countryside and Pathans, thinking that the Raj was on its last legs, snatched the opportunity for a fresh bout of mischief. The tribesmen had been puzzled by official tolerance of Congress and Red Shirt agitation and the steps already taken towards self-government. Pathans again wondered why the British would entertain ceding their power in India.[20] There was a further sign that the Raj might be entering its final days: two platoons of the Royal Garwhal Rifles refused to take part in operations at Peshawar. Thereafter, special care was taken to see that Indian troops were isolated from anti-government propaganda, but it proved unnecessary, for 'they were composed of the types of fighting men who thought and spoke in contempt of the townie "bunnia" [moneylender] caste and local pleader who went to make up the ranks of the Indian political bodies'.[21]

This was reassuring, since large numbers of Indian troops were needed during the second half of 1930 to quell what had quickly become a full-scale Mohmand and Afridi rebellion. It took over a year to suppress. As usual, there were plenty of collaborators on hand; 3,000 Kurram Valley 'militiamen', well-armed and under British officers, repelled an Afridi attack on their homeland and were afterwards rewarded with a year's remission of tax. Aircraft were extensively used during these and other operations, bombing concentrations of tribesmen and Red Shirts and defiant villages. Despite elaborate precautions, intelligence errors led to the wrong targets being chosen and the deaths of innocent non-combatants.[22]

The outbreak of war on the North-West Frontier added to the headaches of a government already distracted by large-scale civil disobedience. It was also contending with a sudden upsurge in terrorism, which had included an attempt to derail Irwin's train by a bomb at the end of 1929. He displayed commendable viceregal sang-froid, afterwards remarking that he was 'inured to that kind of thing by the Cona Coffee machine, which was always blowing up'.[23] Irwin was less collected at the beginning of August 1930, when he was seriously contemplating the imposition of martial law on the most disaffected regions as the only means of preserving order. Surrendering power to the army was both an admission of failure and, in the light of Amritsar, a hazardous resort. Irwin was spared the decision because Congress was also feeling the strain in what had turned into a war of attrition.

From the start, the quality of Congress's local organisations had been extremely variable and, as the campaign unfolded, it emerged that many were incapable of sustaining the effort needed. There was incapacity at the top as well, which had been revealed by the inability of the Congress high command to co-ordinate actions across the country. Furthermore, funding mass resistance was proving a problem, with cash needed to transport demonstrators by train and motor lorry and pay for the victuals of protesters in prison. These numbered 29,000 in November (revealingly, only 1,152 were Muslims), but for the moment there was no lack of volunteers, particularly schoolboys and university students. Women were also very much to the forefront in demonstrations and they were proving peculiarly effective when it came to the 'social' boycott of those, often of their own sex, who purchased forbidden, imported goods. But as the struggle dragged on into the winter with no end in sight, popular support began to dry up. Congress would face the new year with depleted ranks.

III

By the autumn of 1930 the Raj and Congress were in a stalemate, from which the only escape was a truce. It would require the consent of Gandhi who, since his arrest in May, had been a prisoner, enjoying a most comfortable régime by the standards of Indian detention. Conditions were such that he was able to devote himself entirely to his spiritual and dietary preoccupations. In the meantime, and in acknowledgement that the present campaign was foundering, the more extreme Congress leaders were considering new, openly aggressive tactics. After his release from gaol in October, Jawaharlal Nehru spoke of a new phase in the struggle, in which Indians would undertake 'the conquest of power', words which landed him back in prison. They disturbed Irwin, who feared that Congress might seek a way out of the present impasse by stepping up violence. Another course was a compromise with the government which would allow Gandhi to proceed to London and plead Congress's terms at the Round Table conference, which was opened by George V in November. Fully justifying his later nickname, the 'Holy Fox', Irwin had correctly identified two Gandhis. One was the saintly metaphysician prone to exaggerated rhetoric and postures, and the other a canny, hard-bargaining politician who fully understood reality. Irwin appealed to the latter and eventually got what he wanted, but it was not easy.

Conciliation took time and relied heavily on the goodwill and energies of moderate nationalists and businessmen, who were disturbed by the damage being inflicted on the Indian economy by the unrest. The first approaches to Gandhi were made in July, and it was only in February 1931 that he and Irwin met at Delhi to hammer out the terms of an armistice. The discussions were frank but courteous. In his reports of what passed, Gandhi referred to the Viceroy's belief in God and a universal moral order. 'He desires peace because he has been touched by the struggle.'[24] A common will for an accord existed, but it took many hours of tough horse-trading before it took shape. Irwin was in the slightly stronger position, for his intelligence services had alerted him to Congress's manpower and cash problems.[25] In the end he got what he was after: the suspension of Congress's civil disobedience and Gandhi's agreement to attend a second conference in London. In return, 19,000 Congressmen and women were set free, confiscated property was returned to its owners and there was a relaxation of some of the emergency coercive powers. The Raj had publicly acknowledged Gandhi's pre-eminence within Congress and India as a whole, and he had recognised that it would be better if it secured its independence relatively peacefully − with British co-operation rather than without it.

The Gandhi−Irwin pact provided everyone with a breathing space. The

1. On the look-out for Mapillas, Malabar, 1922.

2. Road-block: staff car halted by barricade, Malabar.

centre of political attention shifted from India to London, where the Round Table conference was adjourned in February. It represented every complexion of Indian political opinion save Congress, and had made considerable headway. It had been decided that India would acquire a form of Dominion status as a democratic federation that would embrace the princely states and the eleven British provinces. Indian participation in all levels of government would be accelerated. The second session, attended by Gandhi, opened in September 1931 and was soon in trouble. It was derailed by bickering over the balance of electoral power, involving the reservation of seats for racial and religious minorities which was considered essential for stability. This was already a well-chewed bone of contention which again led to divisions. Hindus and Muslims could not agree terms and Congress was apprehensive about the possible emergence of an axis between the Muslims and the princes.

The inability of this and a subsequent Round Table conference to produce a workable constitution placed the onus on the British Parliament. During the next two years the future governance of India was decided by Parliamentary committees, and the result was the India Bill which was introduced in November 1934 and passed the following August. Under its terms, the provinces of British India became self-governing and there was provision for an Indian federation. This would come into existence if and when a substantial number of the princes agreed to join, something they were presently disinclined to do, even though it was the expressed wish of their King Emperor. Like his ministers, George V hoped that the princes would join the federation to give it a ballast that would counterbalance Congress's headstrong professional politicians.[26] Until the princes complied, central authority in India, and with it control over defence and foreign policy, remained in British hands. The country was also finally relieved of the obligation to pay for its British garrison, whose costs were henceforward met by the Treasury.

At every stage of its evolution, the Government of India Act had been fought tooth and nail by a knot of determined Conservatives who joined forces with former generals and civil servants to form the India Defence League. Kipling, who seems to have forgotten his youthful notions of the Raj as the trustee for the people of India, was one of its vice-presidents, and Winston Churchill its most forceful spokesman. His view of India had been formed thirty-eight years before when he had been a subaltern there, and it remained substantially the same for the rest of his life. He could never bring himself to believe in complete equality between the races or the fitness of Indians to manage their own affairs honestly and efficiently. Hindu politicians and Gandhi in particular aroused his spleen:

> It is alarming and also nauseating to see Mr Gandhi, a seditious Middle Temple lawyer, now posing as a fakir of a type well-known in the East, striding half-naked up the steps of the Viceregal palace, while he is still organizing and conducting a defiant campaign of civil disobedience, to parley on equal terms with the representative of the King-Emperor.

Press support for the India Defence League came from Lord Rothermere, the proprietor of the *Daily Mail*, who dictated a series of explosive editorials under the general title 'If We Lose India —!' between March 1930 and April 1931. These polemics were published as a penny pamphlet which was illustrated by photographs of Gandhi, British troops on riot duty and corpses piled on a lorry after the recent communal riots in Lahore. At the beginning there was a compendium of 'facts', of which the first was: 'India never had unity, security, justice, communications, public health *until the British came*.'[27] The arguments that followed set out to prove that Gandhi and Congress were unrepresentative of India ('a numerically insignificant group of 400,000 semi-educated Babus who hanker after the spoils of minor office'), and had been pandered to for too long by a government that had lost the stomach to rule firmly. Indians understood the benefits of British rule and the British ought to understand the value of Indian trade at a time when their economy was in recession. If, as now seemed likely, the British withdrew from India, their departure would be the signal for 'carnage and chaos'.

More was at stake than the internal security of India. 'England, apart from her Empire in India, ceases for ever to be a Great Power,' claimed Churchill, echoing Curzon's words. Christian civilisation was in jeopardy, for, as Rothermere and many India Defence League members believed, Britain ruled India under a Divine dispensation. If Britain resigned this responsibility, then India would morally degenerate under Hindu government and might easily fall prey to Communism; the fear of a Russian invasion had never quite passed away.[28]

The India Defence League conducted a bad-tempered campaign from the backbenches, where Churchill now sat, and through public meetings and the editorial and correspondence columns of the press. It failed because of the moral courage of Baldwin, that most under-estimated of

British Prime Ministers, who stuck resolutely to the position he had taken in 1929 when he had approved the Irwin declaration. His strength lay in his quiet pragmatism, which enabled him to convince his traditionally imperialist party that the empire was an organism which would have to change in order to survive. Moreover, the measures of the India Act were, in a sense, a fulfilment of that nineteenth-century vision of the Raj as an agent for the elevation of the Indian people. As John Buchan, the novelist and Independent MP argued, India deserved Domininion status because it had fought alongside Britain and the other dominions during the war. 'The Dominions are equal and independent partners; so also must India be, but not necessarily *likewise*.' India would, he predicted, evolve its own forms of government in response to its peculiar needs, a task for which its own politicians were more than equal.[29] In essence this was the liberal imperialist philosophy as followed by Baldwin and, under his influence, the bulk of the Conservatives. No more than fifty ever followed Churchill into the lobbies.

Privately, Baldwin thought Churchill was 'quite mad'.[30] His unbending opposition to the India Act and his frequently lurid predictions of its consequences divorced him from his party and, some imagined, ruled out for ever his chances of continuing his ministerial career. The public showed little interest in the India issue; its mind was consumed with other matters of greater urgency and closer to home: recession, unemployment, rearmament and Britain's relations with Germany and Italy. Even if the British people had not been so distracted, there is no reason to believe that they would have endorsed a policy which would have transformed India into an occupied country, ruled by the sword and against the wishes of its population. This was, after all, the India Defence League's alternative to Dominion status.

IV

The force available to the Raj was sufficient to handle the disturbances which flickered on during 1933 and 1934. A formula for their containment had been devised which meant that the police never lost control on the streets or in the countryside for very long. Congress leaders and local organisers were arrested and imprisoned, and crowds broken up by lathi charges and sometimes, when matters looked like getting out of hand, by police volleys.

The energies of Congress were becoming increasingly consumed by finding ways in which to respond to political initiatives which were coming from London. In August 1932 Ramsay MacDonald issued the Communal Award, which designated the Sikhs, Indian Christians, Anglo-Indians and Untouchables as separate electorates with the same right to reserved seats as the Muslims. Gandhi interpreted the inclusion of the Untouchables or 'depressed castes' in this special category as a device to split the Hindus. Again in detention, he reacted with a dramatic gesture, a fast to death which, he announced, had been directly inspired by God.[31] He hoped both to draw attention to the iniquities of Untouchability, which he found deeply repugnant, and to blackmail the government into revoking the award. Neither Lord Willingdon, the new Viceroy, nor Congress wanted his death; for one he would be a martyr (which was why plans were in hand to release him from prison if he passed the point of recovery) and for the other an irreplaceable loss. In the end it was the Congress leadership which came up with a settlement that allowed the Untouchables to choose for themselves whether or not they remained attached to the Hindu electorate. Afterwards, Gandhi devoted himself to a nationwide personal campaign against Untouchability, which some Congressmen regarded as an irrelevancy in the struggle against the Raj and others as an assault on Hinduism.

Arrangements for voting were a prelude to the imposition of the federal constitution. Elections to the provincial assemblies were due at the end of 1936 and posed a dilemma for Congress. On one hand, the new arrangements fell far short of its demand for *purna swaraj* (complete independence), but on the other they offered an opportunity to secure it by working within the system. A total boycott would leave the field open to other parties and sever its links with the government. For these reasons it agreed at its Lucknow conference in April 1936 to participate in the elections, but with an important caveat which was explained by Jawaharlal Nehru:

> We go to the Legislatures not to co-operate with the apparatus
> of British imperialism, but to combat the Act and to seek to
> end it.[32]

Next to Gandhi, Nehru was now Congress's most widely known and popular leader and an invaluable asset in the election. What he called his 'hurricane tours', a hectic progress across India marked by rallies, speeches and processions, helped sway the electorate towards Congress. Alone of all the parties, it had a national organisation whose tentacles stretched everywhere and was enthusiastically served by an army of local activists, many of them students, who recruited members, collected funds and arranged meetings. Above all, Congress possessed Gandhi. His universal appeal was cunningly exploited to seduce peasant voters, who were told that each Congress candidate was personally endorsed by the Mahatma. Messages to Gandhi were found among the voting slips, written by voters who imagined that the ballot box was also a letter box through which they could contact him.[33]

The cult of Gandhi in part offset Congress's lack of a clear-cut programme. In terms of political tinctures, the party ranged from crimson to pale blue, embracing socialists, like Bose and Nehru, and moderates and conservatives who looked to Gandhi as a brake on the left. The manifesto which emerged reflected Nehru's preoccupation with the elimination of rural poverty and was designed to have the widest possible appeal. It did, but at the same time raised expectations which were beyond fulfilment. The ingenious beguiled the ingenuous: once a Congress worker collected a pile of grass, set fire to it and promised villagers that, 'As this grass burns, so will your debt disappear.'[34] Such stratagems were, perhaps, necessary to counter the intimidation of the regional landowners' parties: the National Agrarian Party of the United Provinces, the Unionists of the Punjab, and the Madras Justice Party. It was relatively easy for Congress officials, zamindars or their servants to threaten voters, since at many polling stations the parties were identified by different coloured boxes. In at least one polling station in Bihar, a Congress worker guided peasants towards his party's box, which was yellow.[35] All this was part of the Indian political tradition, as it had been of Britain's during the eighteenth and much of the nineteenth centuries. In 1931 electors in Lahore were impersonated, bribed and threatened by 'bosses' and a fifth of the votes cast were subsequently invalidated.[36]

The result of the 1936–37 elections was a sweeping victory for Congress. Fifteen and a half million Indians voted, just over half of those eligible, to give Congress overall control of the United and Central Provinces, Orissa, Bombay and Madras and make it the largest single party in Assam and the North-West Frontier Province. In practical terms, it had now become a partner in government, albeit without conviction. An analysis of the poll showed that Muslims had very little confidence in Congress, but scarcely more for the Muslim League, which had yet to present itself as a mass party.

The catalyst which transformed the League into a nationwide, popular party was the behaviour of Congress in power. A political spoils system operated, by which incoming Congress ministers distributed offices to party supporters, forcing Muslims out of jobs and diminishing their local influence and access to power. As Congress's capacity for patronage grew, so did its membership, which in 1939 stood at five million. In some states Congress's fiscal policies hurt Muslim landowners who were also being dis- countenanced by Nehru's attempts to draw poorer Muslims within his party's orbit. In Bihar the Congress-dominated legislature banned cow slaughter. And then there were the pinpricks: the hoisting of the Congress flag over public buildings and insistence on the singing of 'Bande Mataram' in schools. Many Muslim grievances were exaggerated, but this did not prevent the complainants from believing that they were witnessing the first stages in the creation of a Hindu Raj.[37] Now, as never before, Muslims would have to insist on the electoral safeguards that Jinnah and the League had long been demanding.

The only counterweight to Congress was a toned-up, vastly expanded Muslim League. At the head of this popular movement was Jinnah, who had been at the heart of the Congress movement for nearly thirty years. He was an imposing figure with aquiline features who chain-smoked, wore well-cut English suits and sometimes sported a monocle. His greatest strengths were his single-mindedness, tenacity and a rigorous legal mind. When he became president of the League in 1935, Jinnah still believed that a united, independent India was only possible if Muslim rights were prop- erly protected. On this he never wavered. He was not prepared to tack or compromise under pressure, which made him a formidable adversary. His resolution was often exasperating for the British government and Con- gress, but after 1939 neither could afford to ignore or bypass him, for he had made himself the voice of the Muslim community.

The cult of Jinnah, like that of Gandhi, was carefully orchestrated through personal appearances, mass rallies, processions and press inter- views. In October 1938 his supporters marched through Karachi accom- panied by Muslim 'National Guards' (in the manner of contemporary European mass movements, those of India were beginning to develop paramilitary units) and several brass bands. At Quetta in 1943 over 50,000 turned out to hear Jinnah, who now represented the embodiment of Muslim unity and dreams. Those who contrived the League's public spec- tacles deliberately harked back to the time of the state pageantry of the Mughal era. Former Muslim glories were resurrected; a 'Tipu Sultan Day' was celebrated in Mysore in 1946.[38] Jinnah made a point of cultivating the students of the Islamic university at Aligahr, long a powerhouse of Muslim thought and aspirations. His visit there in 1938 was recalled by a student, Ata Rabanni:

> Suddenly there was a lot of commotion and a burst of slogans from thousands of throats, and the whole crowd was on its feet. Amongst this uproar and shouts of *Allah-o-Akbar* [God is Great], a tall and elegant figure appeared from behind the dais and ascended the improvised steps from the rear of the raised platform. He was no other than Mr Jinnah, the Quaid-i-Azam [leader of the nation], my leader, our leader, everybody's leader. The public gave him a standing ovation, shouting slogans of welcome. I was overwhelmed and made my self hoarse shouting *Zindabad* [victory] slogans.[39]

Congress supporters had and were giving similar receptions to Nehru or Bose. But their prevailing atmosphere was always Hindu. In spite of all the endeavours of its leaders and, for that matter, Jinnah, Congress had never been able to persuade the Muslims that it was truly bipartisan. Their enthusiastic response to the League's mass rallies of the late 1930s and early 1940s were an indication of the extent to which Muslims had, rightly or wrongly, imagined themselves excluded from a national movement whose rhetoric and theatre was always distinctly Hindu. Whatever else he may have achieved, Jinnah had at last given the Muslims a sense of identity and purpose. The swiftness of his rise to power suggests that they had been seeking both for some time.

V

The success and stridency of the Muslim League was regarded with alarm in London and Delhi.[40] Its emergence was an unwelcome complication which added to the burdens of the Viceroy, the Marquess of Linlithgow, who was endeavouring to make the federation work. He was a Viceroy very much in the traditional patrician mould: he was six feet five inches in height, dropped the final 'g' from participles when he spoke, and, once during a tour of Kashmir, chased butterflies on horseback.[41] He prized wisdom above cleverness, had a high sense of personal honour and a taste for the knockabout comedy of Bud Flanagan and 'Monsewer' Eddie Gray. Since his arrival in April 1936, Linlithgow had listened to, charmed and cajoled Indian politicians, but to little avail. The attitude of the princes towards the new constitution gradually began to soften, and by the summer of 1939 a trickle of states agreed to join the federation. Fortified by his mass support, Jinnah insisted that the Muslims would never agree to any form of central government until the problem of their representation had been solved to their satisfaction. Congress was equally adamant in its demands for full independence and a democratically elected national assembly.

The outbreak of war on 3 September 1939 interrupted this protracted, three-cornered and, as it turned out, sterile debate. On that day and acting within the letter of his powers, Linlithgow declared war on Germany. Congress was initially indignant. The Viceroy had committed over 300 million Indians to a conflict without consulting a single one, and shown beyond question that Britain was ultimately still master of India. Once the shock of having been propelled unasked into a war had passed, Indian politicians began to seek ways in which they could gain advantage from the emergency. The League committed itself to support Britain for the duration of war as much out of hope for future favours as conviction. In broad principle, Congress was against Nazism and Fascism and, therefore, behind Britain. Gandhi was downcast at the thought of London being bombed and gave his sincere, wholehearted sympathy to the British people. 'We do not seek our independence out of Britain's ruin,' he declared shortly after the outbreak of war. 'That was not the way of non-violence.'[42]

The war did not change Indian political life. The haggling went on with Linlithgow inviting Congress and the League to participate in an executive that would direct the national war effort. Neither would agree, save on their own terms. Congress wanted an unconditional pledge that India was free to write its own constitution once the war was over, and Jinnah insisted that the League was recognised as speaking for every Muslim. In what was a fit of pique, the Congress leadership asked all its provincial ministries to resign on 22 December, which they did. Jinnah was jubilant and called upon Leaguers to celebrate their release from Hindu bondage on what he designated 'Deliverance Day'. It was also the day on which India's provinces reverted to a form of direct British government, something they had not known since 1919.

The Secretary of State, the Marquess of Zetland, suggested in February 1940 that the deadlock might be broken if Indian political leaders of all persuasions were brought together and asked to work out a constitution. This was wormwood to Churchill, now back in the Cabinet, where he made no bones about his pleasure at the fissure now opening up in India:

> . . . he did not share the anxiety to encourage and promote unity between the Hindu and Muslim communities. Such unity was, in fact, almost out of the realm of practical politics, while, if it were to be brought about, the immediate result would be that united communities would join in showing us the door. He regarded the Hindu–Muslim feud as the bulwark of British rule in India.[43]

Churchill became Prime Minister in May and made it abundantly clear, then and later, that he wished to extend the life of the Raj for as long as possible. Flirting with Congress would, he believed, undermine its authority and prestige and was to be avoided at all costs.

India's internal divisions widened even further when Jinnah, speaking in Lahore on 27 March 1940, explained why the divergence between the Muslim and Hindu communities was permanent. 'They are not religious in the strict sense of the word, but are in fact different and distinct social orders, and it is a dream that the Hindus and Muslims can ever evolve a common nationality.' Each had their own history and culture and refused to intermarry or eat together. His words were a call for a separate Muslim state, already spoken of as Pakistan, although he said nothing as to what might be its future relationship with India.

As he had intended, his language and the League's activities had cut Congress's scope for action. When its working committee met at Wardha in the third week of April, Rajendra Patel warned that to challenge the British government would invite a counter-attack from the Muslim League and the onset of a civil war. Others, including Gandhi, felt that the rank and file were unready for a further bout of civil disobedience.[44] Nehru was more vehement and keen for a showdown with the government. He denounced Pakistan as a 'mad scheme', and began touring the country to stiffen the nerve and sinews of Congress supporters. The young were highly receptive; they were already forming volunteer bands who wore uniforms, marched and drilled. Nehru reviewed one body holding an imitation field-marshal's baton. In October he was arrested and given another spell in gaol. Chandra Subhas Bose, whose fiery temperament Gandhi mistrusted, abandoned Congress completely and formed the

Forward Bloc, which aimed to direct India along the course which had been followed by Sinn Féin and the Russian revolutionaries in the last war.

External events during the early summer forced Congress's hand. The fall of France in May and Britain's isolation turned Indian minds to national defence, and a degree of co-operation with the government. This did not extend to acceptance of an offer of places on the Viceroy's council in return for yet another committee to discuss a constitution. Gandhi was drifting into a world of self-indulgent moral fantasy. At the end of June he suggested that if Europe had adopted his principles of non-violence in dealing with Hitler, 'it would have added several inches to its moral stature'. He advised Britain not to resist invasion and so 'confound Nazi wisdom and put all the Nazi armaments out of use'. Unconditional surrender would leave the British with their souls and minds intact, but he did not say what it might do for India.[45] Like so many of his contemporaries, he did not then fully understand the nature of Nazism and its unlimited capacity for cruelty and evil.

If its overriding purpose was holding on to power, the Raj at the close of 1941 seemed to be in a superficially strong position. After twenty years of wrangling and concessions, India, in the words of a group of Congress moderates, was still 'a dependency' which was 'ruled from Whitehall'.[46] At the insistence of Congress nearly all the provincial assemblies had dissolved themselves in 1939, leaving the way clear for the restoration of the old bureaucratic system they had superseded. There were significant differences, however, for the administrative machinery had quietly passed into Indian hands: less than a tenth of India's 2,500 judges were now British, and Indians outnumbered Britons in the ICS. In London and Delhi, the makers of policy were thinking in terms of a final handing-over of power to Indians. As yet no one knew for certain how the transfer might be achieved without chaos and bloodshed, or, and this was the knottiest of India's problems, who would receive power. The only two contenders, Congress and the Muslim League, refused to work in tandem and the British government refused to contemplate any arrangement that would involve the partition and, therefore, the weakening of India. Nevertheless, the majority of Indians imagined that once the war ended, their country would gain its freedom. This was the belief of nearly two-thirds of the Indian officers serving in Malaya in 1941.[47]

VI

India's mobilisation for war had proceeded remarkably well, considering the unrest of the past twenty years. By January 1941 the full strength of the Indian army was 418,000, of whom 37 per cent were Muslims and 55 per cent Hindus, mainly Rajputs, Jats and Dogras, whose warrior traditions remained strong. Congress did nothing actively to impede recruitment and no mass satyagraha materialised, largely because Gandhi feared that it would lead to violent collisions with Muslim Leaguers. Nevertheless, General Sir Robert Lockhart, who supervised recruitment to the Indian army, noted that only a trickle of volunteers was coming forward from Congress's strongholds: the United and Central Provinces, Bihar and Bombay.[48]

An Indian soldier of the old school, Lockhart suspected that the bulk of recruits were joining up only to make more money or learn a trade, such as driving, which would help them prosper after the war. 'The bulk of the Indian army are thus pure mercenaries, not actuated by love of country or devotion to a distant throne or hatred of the enemy,' he gloomily concluded in May 1943.[49] There was a distinct lack of fighting spirit in the impertinent request for a discharge delivered to his colonel by Lok Nath Pande of the 17th Dogras in the March of that year:

> I have paid fifty rupees for my membership of Congress. So I hope that you will kindly grant my application for discharge, or I will do some Congress work in your military. Then you will shoot me. But I do not care for it . . . I come here only to see the enjoyment of soldiership. But it is not good for myself. I cannot say it is bad. I will congratulate you with all my heart for my discharge.[50]

Pande was released from his obligations on the sensible grounds that the army was better off without grumblers whose discontent might prove infectious. To counter sedition, police recruitment was stepped up and an Emergency Powers Act was introduced in 1940 to crack down on any political activity which imperilled the war effort. Special care was taken to prevent interference with the armed forces. Here, the greatest danger lay not with the major political parties, but with the smaller extremist groups which had mushroomed over the past twenty years. The loyalty of the Indian soldier was a delicate matter, and the Indian army was extremely touchy about allegations that its men were even susceptible to subversive propaganda, let alone willing to give it the time of day. Even so, morale was diligently monitored, which was not always easy given the influx of new, inexperienced British officers.

Communist and Sikh ultra-nationalist agitation was responsible for two significant outbreaks of unrest in 1939–40. Both were blamed for a mutiny by over 300 men of the RIASC (Royal Indian Army Service Corps) in Cairo in January 1940, where they refused to load stores on to lorries. Among those arrested were several Sikh reservists who had pre-war connections with the Communist journal *Kirti Lehr*, and others from a village where Ghadrite sympathies were still strong. Army intelligence suspected that local German agents had had a hand in the mischief, but could find no direct evidence. A number of men from the RIASC were among the POWs who were reported to have defected to the Germans by the spring of 1942, but whether they were from the mutinous unit is not known.[51] Congress demands that Indian troops should be kept solely for Indian defence were among the complaints of just over a hundred men from Central Indian Horse, who mutinied on the quayside in Bombay in July 1940 in protest against being ordered to the Middle East. Investigation revealed that the ringleaders were Communist sympathisers who had manipulated the sepoys' grievances for political ends. India's Communists did as Comintern commanded and, after the German invasion of Russia in June 1941, they became fervent supporters of the war, as did their equally biddable British counterparts. At the end of the year, the Communist wing of Congress was clamouring for India to join the war against Fascism.[52]

Undercurrents of sectarian animosities broke surface during the mutiny of the Central India Horse. Some Punjabi Sikhs imagined that Muslims would raid their villages and rape their women if the regiment went on foreign service.[53] These sowars' anxieties were shared by many other Sikh soldiers, who feared that future shifts in power within India would leave them, their families and communities exposed to abuse by a 'hostile' Muslim government in the Punjab.[54]

Religious misunderstanding lay behind another serious outbreak of unrest in the army, the mutiny by Sikh artillerymen stationed in Hong Kong in December 1940. It was triggered by orders for the gunners to replace their turbans with regulation steel helmets. This and poor communications between officers and men was the army's explanation for the disturbance, but it was not the whole truth. There was evidence which pointed towards subversion by Indian agents employed by Japanese intelligence. At least one, who possessed three aliases, was a Ghadrite sympathiser. The presence of these shadowy figures on the fringes of the protest may have been why some of the mutineers expected Japanese assistance.[55] Britain was still at peace with Japan, but Military Intelligence felt certain that:

> There is undoubtedly a regular traffic of Indian professional subversive agitators up and down the Pacific coast, and there's definite proof that Sikh police in the Portuguese possession of Macao are affected. It is therefore reasonable to surmise that attempts to subvert the Sikh police in Shanghai, Malaya, Singapore and Burma are being made.[56]

This was substantially correct. A cell of the Indian Revolutionary Block had been established under Japanese patronage at Canton, and had attracted a trickle of Indian defectors during 1939 and 1940, including a sepoy who brought with him maps of Hong Kong's perimeter defences. These attempts to seduce sepoys were an indication that the Japanese government was already considering ways in which it might exploit Indian discontent and, once it had begun its offensive against British Asia, make an alliance with Indian nationalism. Three Ghadrite defectors, employed by Japanese Intelligence, appeared in Hong Kong immediately after its capture on Christmas Day 1941 to begin a campaign of anti-British propaganda.[57]

5

A Bad Knock: India at War, January–July 1942

Between February and May 1942 the Raj was stripped of what had long been considered its most precious asset, prestige. The process was painful and public. On 15 February Singapore surrendered and over 100,000 British, Indian and Australian troops laid down their arms after a 54-day struggle against a smaller Japanese army. Next, the Japanese thrust into Burma, capturing Rangoon in March and Mandalay six weeks later. India now faced an invasion by an adversary whose declared aim was to free Asians from European rule. Malays and Burmese took the Japanese at their word and welcomed them as liberators; so too did 40,000 Indian POWs who threw in their lot with the victors within a few weeks of the fall of Singapore. The balance of power in southern Asia was swinging decisively against Britain. During April a Japanese fleet cruised at will around the Indian Ocean, which had been a British waterway since 1800. Colombo was bombarded, and the threat to India's coastline and ports was only removed when the interlopers were defeated by the United States Navy in the battle of the Coral Sea at the beginning of May.

Nothing better illustrated the new dispensation of power in Asia or, for that matter, the rest of the world. Henceforward, India's seaborne security depended upon the United States rather than the Royal Navy. For a time, all that the Viceroy's advisers could come up with in the way of a defence strategy was a 'scorched earth' policy if Bengal was invaded. The Raj had lost one of its traditional justifications, the ability to protect India. Discredited by defeat and unable to defend itself, the Raj could no longer expect the co-operation of its subjects. Even before the disaster at Singapore, Linlithgow was aware that he and his government were facing harsh new realities. Their implication was chilling, as he explained in a cable to Leo Amery, the Secretary of State for India:

> The Cabinet will I think agree with me that India and Burma have no natural association with the Empire, from which they are alien by race, history and religion, and for which as such neither of them have any natural affection, and both are in the Empire because they are conquered countries which had been brought there by force, kept there by our controls, and which hitherto it has suited to remain under our protection. I suspect that the moment they think we may lose the war or take a bad knock, their leaders would be much more concerned to make terms with the victor at our expense than to fight for ideals to which so much lip-service is given . . .[1]

The Viceroy's mordant analysis was substantially correct. Similar conclusions were reached by the political and military experts who spent the next few months picking over the evidence which emerged from the débâcles in Malaya and Burma. High on the list of explanations was the racial hubris which clouded judgements at every level of command. 'Eastern races [are] less able to withstand [the] strain [of] modern war,' insisted General Harry Gordon Bennett at the start of his acerbic defence of his own and the Australian army's exertions in Malaya.[2] It was a barb aimed at the Indian army, which he blamed for the defeat, although his condescension embraced the victorious Japanese, an irony which Bennett lacked the wit to appreciate. Racial bigotry was endemic throughout European society in Malaya and, as elsewhere in the empire, was most virulent among the commercial and planter class whose members banned Indian officers from their swimming pools, tennis courts and clubs. This discourtesy was extended to men who, in India, had been treated in a warm spirit of comradeship within British army messes.[3] Not surprisingly, 'a good deal of bitterness' was aroused by the frostiness of Malaya's whites. One Indian officer spoke for many when he commented that he and his countrymen had travelled far to protect arrogant and pampered Europeans, 'and he was damned if he was going to lift a little finger to do it when the time came'.[4]

The crassness of the European community in Malaya was a bonus for Japan. It gave a convincing edge to propaganda which announced that a Japanese victory would overturn the old Asian racial pecking order. A new era was promised in one leaflet distributed as the Japanese advanced on Singapore:

> Malays, we are your friends, and intend to drive out the Europeans, who have enslaved you, also kill off the Chinese who have taken the wealth of your country. So that we can identify you at all times wear your hats. ASIA FOR THE ASIATICS.[5]

The slogan was repeated in Burma and its resonances were soon picked up in India. From September 1941, intelligence staff of the Japanese Army's Imperial General Headquarters (IGHQ) had been devising a propaganda offensive that emphasised Asian brotherhood and Japan's liberating mission. Delivering this message to Indians was the task of a former teacher with a special knowledge of Burma, Major Iwaichi Fujiwara, who had gathered around him a band of Sikh separatist and Indian nationalist exiles. Their objective was strategic rather than political: by undermining the morale of the Indian soldier, Fujiwara's agents would seriously damage Britain's capacity to defend Malaya and Hong Kong. The seditionists moved quickly. On 11 December 1941, two days after the landings at Ipoh, a Sikh civilian approached some Gurkha POWs and asked them to return to their lines and distribute leaflets which called on Indian troops to desert. Similar material was circulating among the Indian garrison in Hong Kong by 14 December.[6]

It is hard to assess the initial impact of either leaflets or Japanese broadcasts directed at Indians in Malaya. By 29 January 1942 at least 200 Indians had defected and, under the command of Captain Mohan Singh, who had turned his coat at the very beginning of the campaign, were serving as ammunition carriers in the Japanese army.[7] This trickle of deserters hardly supported Gordon Bennett's claim that sepoy morale had disintegrated. He drew a bleak picture of bored, homesick men, often placed in unfamiliar deep jungle for weeks on end, under an inexperienced and sclerotic command, which had succumbed to a 'retreat complex' at the beginning of operations.[8] His diatribe was vigorously rebutted and counter-charges were levelled against the Australians. 'General Gordon Bennett naturally does not mention the shortcomings of the Australians, of which there is much evidence from other sources,' one staff officer tartly minuted.[9] These 'other sources', some of them mere hearsay, revealed allegations of half-hearted resistance, malingering, theft, maltreatment of natives and mass desertion.[10] The last seems to have been true, but was perhaps excusable in the light of the Australian commander's example. Gordon Bennett cut and ran to get a ship out of Singapore the moment it appeared that surrender was imminent. Thereafter, Australian servicemen called their running shoes 'Gordon Bennetts'.[11]

General Sir Archibald Wavell, overall commander in Malaya and commander-in-chief in India, added his voice to the acrimonious post mortem. He avoided allocating guilt to individuals and armies, although candidly admitting that he and other officers had grossly underestimated the fighting capacity of the Japanese.[12] He stuck up for the Indians whose fighting spirit had been 'good' even during the 400-mile retirement through the jungle.

What he failed to understand was the cumulative effect of enemy propaganda, reverses and retreat. The Indian soldier was exposed to a sequence of severe psychological shocks which upset his view of the world and his place in it. Traditional respect and admiration for the white soldier were jolted by a series of disgraceful incidents of panic and cowardice. Unnerved by the flight of Royal Australian Air Force personnel from Khota Baharu airfield, a Hyderabad state battalion followed suit, murdering their colonel when he tried to turn them back. The helter-skelter rush of Australian airmen from Kuantan horrified a Sikh, who asked a British officer, 'How is this possible? They are all sahibs.' 'They are not sahibs, they are Australians,' was the reply.[13] Such incidents and the experience of seeing European soldiers running away from and then surrendering to Asians shook the Indian soldier's faith in his rulers and their power.[14]

Exhausted, separated from their officers, disorientated and with confidence in their rulers in shreds, many Indian fighting men easily succumbed to Japanese pressure. They were exhorted to align themselves with the new Asian order and help emancipate India at a mass rally on 17 February. Within days, recruits were flooding in to the Indian National Army (INA), a title chosen by Mohan Singh, its first commander.[15] The scale of the defection stunned the Indian military authorities, who at first imagined that every Indian and Burmese prisoner had become a Japanese soldier. Wild estimates put the total of renegades at 89,000 and, by September, details of their training and eventual purpose were trickling through to Simla. The volunteers were being assured that Japan had no plans to occupy India and were promised a part in the forthcoming Japanese offensive against eastern

Bengal. They would enter India as liberators.[16] This was how the Japanese had arrived in Burma and the Burmese had believed them, justifying Linlithgow's estimate of their loyalty to Britain. An American observer attributed Burmese perfidy to dissatisfaction with an unloved and distant administration. 'Unless the same decadent and unintelligent course in India is corrected,' he predicted, 'India may be expected to collapse under attack as Burma did.'[17] By midsummer the Japanese had installed a Quisling régime in Burma under a nationalist politician, Ba Maw. The new government was entirely Burmese and was soon persecuting the Karens, who were driven into the arms of the British.

The early history of the INA suggests that its Japanese godfathers were as astonished by its size as the British high command. No one had been prepared for such a rush of volunteers and, therefore, no plans had been made for their organisation, training and future employment. Nor, at the time of their initial offensives, had the Japanese contemplated the inclusion of India in their projected South-East Asia Co-Prosperity Sphere. Events in Malaya had created what neither Fujiwara nor his superiors had expected: an army of Indian deserters, some of whom believed they were patriots. What was to become of them, and what, if any, part would they play in Japanese strategy? Liaison was difficult; Fujiwara spoke little Hindustani or English, and his successor, Colonel Hideo Iwakuro, was similarly ill-equipped for everyday contact with his country's protégés. There was a shortage of translators to instruct the Burma Independence Army (BIA), who were forced to learn their drill by sign language.[18] To begin with, arms were in short supply, and what was delivered was either out of date or in poor condition.[19] As yet unaware of the INA's defects, the British feared that it would be deployed on the Arakan front in September in readiness for an invasion of Assam.[20] In fact, the INA and the BIA had not yet been assigned any definite military role. In April the Japanese Prime Minister, Admiral Hideki Tojo, had announced on the wireless that Japan would drive the British from India, but no date had been set for the invasion.

For the time being, Colonel Iwakuro was ordered to treat Indian and Burmese collaborators as a source of agents for behind-the-lines sabotage and espionage. During the summer of 1942 the Japanese opened two schools in Rangoon and Penang, where mainly young, civilian volunteers were taught how to operate wireless transmitters, blow up railway lines, spread sedition and collect military information. According to some agents who fell into British hands, their training had been inadequate, and at least one Indian instructor fell out with the Japanese after they had peremptorily removed twenty pupils from his class for a mission in India.[21] This clash was a reminder that the Japanese high command saw the INA as an instrument of imperial policy, whereas its more fervent members imagined themselves to be equal partners in an enterprise to liberate India. INA soldiers wore Congress colours on their uniforms and eventually would be mustered in brigades named after Gandhi and Nehru. And yet all their activities were strictly controlled by the Japanese, who did not hesitate to arrest anyone who showed the slightest signs of obstructiveness.

The INA's political wing was the Indian Independence League, a lustreless band of extremist exiles based in Bangkok and far removed from mainstream Indian politics. Its only big name was Rash Behari Bose, an ageing and tubercular Bengali terrorist who had organised the attempted assassination of Lord Hardinge in 1912 and afterwards fled to Japan. He offered little inspiration. Moderates initially seduced by the Japanese were soon disillusioned. Ten nationalists, including H. M. Parwani, a prominent Hong Kong Congressman who had recruited men for the INA, escaped from Burma to India in September 1942.[22] During the next twelve months INA deserters followed. They brought with them heartening stories of how a substantial number of its rank and file had joined not out of nationalist fervour, but out of terror or an understandable desire to secure decent treatment and better rations. There were also reports that many officers and other ranks had stayed true to their salt, even in the face of torture by Japanese and former Indian officers, who had quickly adopted their new masters' vicious habits.[23] Among the photographs discovered when Singapore was liberated in 1945 were pictures of Indian prisoners being shot and then bayoneted by Japanese soldiers. Such brutality and the mass murder of Chinese civilians and British and Australian prisoners in the days after Singapore had fallen drove many Indians to seek safety in the ranks of the INA.

II

Not yet fully aware of the INA's exact nature and the circumstances of its creation, the British regarded it as a potential source of enormous mischief inside India. There were two, closely connected dangers. The first was infiltration by expert saboteurs and seditionists, who would simultaneously disrupt communications, spread defeatism and foment unrest. And then there was the possibility that a Fifth Column already existed within India, waiting to assist the partisans and co-operate with a Japanese invasion. Intelligence analysts had concluded that a similar underground organisation had been in place before the Japanese attack on Malaya, and had done untold harm.[24]

There was anxiety too about German and Italian plans to launch diversionary, partisan operations on the North-West Frontier. The spectre of a fresh bout of trouble on the frontier gained substance during the summer of 1941, when the Wehrmacht thrust into southern Russia. Army Group A secured a foothold in the Caucasus by September and in July 1942 occupied Rostov. There was no way of knowing which way the developing struggle for Stalingrad would swing; if it went against the Russians, the Germans would be free to push eastwards into Central Asia. An advance in this direction would make it possible to airlift men and supplies to Afghanistan.

The Axis powers had been meddling in Afghan affairs since at least 1937. Their objective had been to unseat the British-inclining amir, Zahur Shah, and replace him by the deposed Ammanullah, who was a refugee in Rome, where he had acquired an Italian mistress and the attentions of Mussolini's foreign ministry.[25] His and his new friends' activities were closely watched, for the Foreign Office suspected that the Italian government intended to foment unrest among the border tribes as a device to distract British attention prior to a move against the Sudan or Egypt.[26] As in the heyday of the Great Game, Britain's international rivals recognised the value of the frontier as a means to divert troops. And with good reason; the 1936–37 campaign against Mirza Ali Khan, the Faqir of Ipi, had involved 54,000 men and RAF squadrons which were urgently required in the Middle and Far East.[27] A far greater effort would be needed if the faqir united all the tribes; there were just under half a million modern rifles distributed among them. During the next two years, Pietro Quanoni, the Italian minister in Kabul, made a number of clandestine approaches to the Faqir of Ipi, who was also being courted by agents of Ammanullah.[28] The faqir was a useful ally. His piety and supernatural powers made him widely revered among the Pathans – he had once promised to turn the RAF's bombs to paper, and when aircraft dropped the usual warning leaflets, his followers acclaimed a miracle! But the frontier messiah was also canny, cautious and not over-enthusiastic about an alliance with Fascism and Nazism, which he considered godless.

The German government was also meddling in Afghan affairs. In March

1938 it asked for landing facilities at Kabul for Lufthansa airliners, a request which was repeated in the spring of 1941.[29] By then, if not earlier, the *Abwehr* (Wehrmacht Intelligence) was concocting an audacious plan for a frontier campaign that would combine a mass tribal insurrection with cross-border sabotage. It was codenamed 'Operation Tiger' and was scheduled to commence in September. The groundwork was already in hand. Two agents, Lieutenant Dietrich Winckel (codenamed 'Pathan') and 'Rassmuss' were sent to Kabul, where they made contact with Indian members of the Forward Bloc and extended feelers towards the Faqir of Ipi. He set a high price on his co-operation: £25,000 a month for raising Waziristan and twice that amount if he could extend the uprising. In June, Enrico Anzoliti, a secretary at the Italian legation, disguised as a Pathan secretly visited the faqir, who asked him for a wireless set. A month later, two German agents, Professor Manfred Oberdorffer, an expert in tropical medicine, and Friedrich Brandt, a lepidopterist, attempted the perilous journey to the faqir, but were intercepted by Aghan troops. The physician was killed and his companion wounded.[30]

Meanwhile, the German and Italian armies were training specialist units for covert operations on the frontier. A German POW from the Brandenburg Leib Regiment revealed to British interrogators that during the summer of 1941 he had encountered NCOs from one of these groups who were undergoing instruction at the camp near Cassell. When they had completed their course, they were to be transported to Russia and then flown to the Afghan–Indian border, from where they were to 'make their own way to India as agents and saboteurs'.[31] Everything depended on a free passage across southern Russia. Another prisoner from the same regiment claimed that there had been nearly 300 men at Cassell in June 1942, a third of them Indians, who were receiving parachute training and were to be employed in the Khyber Pass.[32] This was the suspected destination of Indians who were being given parachute instruction by the Italians at training camps in Greece during the summer of 1942. At least sixty-two had taken the oath of allegiance to Italy, and a group had been spotted in Rome dressed in uniforms adorned with Fascist insignia and shoulder-straps in the Congress colours of green, white and orange.[33]

These Indians were all POWs, captured in North Africa and subsequently lured into the German and Italian armies. Their story and subsequent fate forms part of the background of Paul Scott's novel, *The Division of the Spoils*, in which they are depicted as tragic, misled creatures. No one was sure exactly how many changed sides: estimates made by

British Military Intelligence during 1943 have their total as between 2,000 and 2,500, which was probably not far from the truth.[34] All had been the subject of intensive propaganda by a handful of Indian renegades, including one who had worked for the Germans in the last war, and were promised preferential treatment. A few may have been threatened or roughly used. Many were sincere nationalists who believed that when they went into battle it would be for the liberation of their homeland. In November 1943, a party of 250, attached to the Italian army, was reported to have refused service against the British in North Africa and insisted that they would only fight in India.[35] As the tide of the war turned against their new masters, there was little that the Free Indian Legion could do to help their country. Most ended up in penny packets among the forces defending Hitler's Atlantic Wall in the summer of 1944.[36]

One name constantly cropped up in reports of the Free Indian Legion, Chandra Subhas Bose. Before the war he had been a prominent Congressman with a considerable popular following, which was strongest in his native Bengal. Military Intelligence in Simla rated him third to Gandhi and Nehru among India's political heroes, and it was not far wrong.[37] His nationalist credentials and record were impeccable. Born in 1897 to a prominent Bengali family, Bose passed from Calcutta university to Cambridge and from there to a place in the Bengal Legislative Council. In 1930 he was Mayor of Calcutta, but during the next decade he became increasingly disillusioned with Congress's political tactics. Imprisoned during the 1931 non-co-operation movement, he was disappointed with Gandhi's leadership, which he considered too hesitant. During the next five years Bose toured Europe, met Mussolini, and was impressed by the dynamism of the new politics of decisive action which were transforming Italy and Germany. Although a socialist, Bose warmed to the methods and sheer energy of the European radical right. In many ways, he closely resembled his contemporary, Sir Oswald Mosley, Britain's self-appointed man of destiny. Like him, Bose was a young man in a hurry and dismissive of his elders whose ideas and methods were manifestly failing to solve modern problems. How, wondered Bose, would the British government have reacted if it had been confronted by men of Mussolini's, Hitler's and Stalin's stamp, rather than Gandhi, who had left London with nothing more substantial than the goodwill of George Bernard Shaw and sundry Labour MPs?[38]

Hitler was strongly against any alliance between Germany and Indian nationalism. He was genuinely amazed by the lengths to which the Raj went to reach an accommodation with Congress. He once advised a dumbfounded Irwin (then Lord Halifax and Foreign Secretary) that Britain ought to shoot Gandhi and as many Congressmen as were needed to 'make it clear that you mean business'. The Führer admired the Raj and feared that its collapse would create a vacuum which either Russia or Japan might fill; a view he still held in April 1942, when he refused to give even verbal support for the Indian national movement.[39]

Despite this, and the contemptuous views of Indians set down in *Mein Kampf*, Bose imagined that he might reach some sort of arrangement with Germany. By 1940, he had discarded Gandhian orthodoxy in favour of an ideology based upon Communist and Fascist notions of direct, violent action. Gandhi distrusted his militancy and had exerted behind-the-scenes pressure to curb his influence within Congress. Nehru was distressed by Bose's plans to exploit Britain's wartime difficulties which, he believed, were tantamount to offering a helping hand to the Fascist powers. Bose's power base was now the radical, left-wing Forward Bloc and through it he appealed for a fresh campaign of civil disturbance. It was welcomed by the students and secondary-school pupils who had become his largest constituency. While Gandhi wavered, Bose preached popular revolution and seemed to be snatching the initiative and, incidentally, the limelight of the national movement. Freedom and independence on his terms demanded action inside India and help from outside. India's way ahead was along the path that had been taken by Sinn Féin (Bose had met De Valera) and Lenin in the last war. Early in 1941, disguised as a Pathan bricklayer, he travelled by road and mule from Rawalpindi to Kabul, where he arrived on 1 February. His guide, Bhagat Ram Talwar, and accomplices were Forward Bloc men and, unknown to Bose, Soviet agents.

Bose's first hope was Russia, but he was turned away from the Soviet legation. After a week of seeking an audience with the Russian minister, on Ram's advice he went to the German legation, where he was warmly welcomed and offered a passage to Berlin. The paperwork took time and so Bose availed himself of Italian help, and with the appropriate documents set out for Rome and a new career as India's Sir Roger Casement. All this and details of his and other Russian agents' dealings with Nazi intriguers in Afghanistan were revealed to the Indian CID by Ram after his arrest in November 1942. His offer of service as a double-agent was accompanied by a lengthy confession, which offered no hint as to why Bose had first sought Soviet patronage, or why it was refused at a time when Communists were doing all in their power to hinder the Indian war effort.[40]

In Italy and then in Germany, Bose was employed as the Free Indian Legion's recruiting sergeant. In one speech he assured POWs that 'Hitler is your friend, a friend of the Aryans, and you will march to India as your Motherland's liberators, maybe via the Caucasus and the Khyber Pass, maybe by some other route.'[41] Bose also broadcast to India on Azad Hind (Free India) Radio. It was transmitted on short-wave to an estimated 30,000 Indians who possessed the requisite receivers; a further 90,000 could have been reached if Berlin had possessed the technology for sending long-wave signals. Blending his own passionate nationalism with Dr Goebbels's 'perfidious Albion' line of propaganda, Bose declared on 9 March:

> Although British Imperialism is our particular enemy it is at the same time the greatest enemy of all mankind. By the needless exploitation of 500 million human beings and by a clever system of slavery, British Imperialism has prevented all true understanding between the various nations of the world and also a satisfactory solution of international problems.

Just over a month later, he promised Indians that his co-workers would soon be dropping from the skies and that patriots were to give these parachutists all the assistance they might need. On 22 May, Bose's colleague, William Joyce ('Lord Haw Haw' to his British listeners), announced that the parachutists had safely landed a fortnight before.[42] No trace of them was found but the news gave the jitters to the authorities, which was no doubt the Germans' intention. Fifth columnists were suspected as the cause of a brawl in the Grand Hotel, Lahore on 4 May, in which a crowd of Indians, many of them students, rescued a girl who had allegedly been dragged into the hotel compound by three British NCOs. She was whisked away in a tonga and the authorities wondered whether the incident had been deliberately manufactured by enemy agents, keen to stir up racial antipathy.[43]

III

Bose's broadcasts were heard in an India in which the Raj's position was becoming more and more precarious. Its prestige had disappeared, its army could no longer be relied upon, and it was doubtful whether it could defend its frontiers. Early in March, Linlithgow confessed that he lacked the forces to resist a Japanese landing on the Cuttack coast and could not prevent an advance into Orissa.[44] Japan and Germany were preparing for a partisan campaign which might draw upon help from an unknown number of Fifth Columnists. One of their potential allies, the Faqir of Ipi, acting off his own bat, re-opened hostilities in Waziristan in the spring, tying down three brigades which were desperately needed elsewhere.

Disaster could be averted if, by some means, Congress could be induced to become a partner in the war effort. The will was certainly there in some quarters. On 16 March, Nehru told a rally in Delhi:

> If today we were masters of our own destiny we would ask people to get ready and defend the country with all our might. Unfortunately obstinate worthless and incompetent Government still has its grip tight on us.[45]

The government which Nehru so despised was all too aware that its popularity would be immeasurably strengthened if, somehow, it could break the constitutional deadlock. Generous concessions to nationalist sentiment offered a remedy for the apathy and, in many instances, open hostility to Britain which infected millions of Indians. This was the view of President Roosevelt, who regarded the need to swing India behind the Allied war effort as a matter of great urgency. Like many Americans, he was also concerned about his country fighting a war in Asia and the Pacific which, on the surface, looked dangerously like a rescue operation for an embattled British empire.

American opinion and the pressure it could exert on Britain had become a factor in Indian politics. Even before the United States had entered the war, Roosevelt and Churchill had outlined their countries' war aims in the Atlantic Charter of August 1941. The promise of liberation for all oppressed peoples struck a chord in India; the *Bombay Chronicle* welcomed the declaration as the 'Magna Carta of the world'. This was not how Churchill interpreted the pledge; as he subsequently explained to the Commons it was inapplicable to India which, like Europe, was a patchwork of peoples and provinces. This casuistry angered Indians, and when it was discussed in the Viceroy's Legislative Council one Indian member, Jammadas Mehta, pertinently remarked that the Indians were dying to emancipate others while their countrymen remained enslaved.[46] Vinayak

Savarkar, president of the Hindu Mahasabha, appealed directly to Roosevelt and asked him whether America would guarantee India's post-war freedom.[47]

As Indians correctly sensed, Britain was now junior partner in the alliance and would find it hard not to bow to American pressure. This increased at the beginning of March and was augmented from within the War Cabinet by Attlee and Leo Amery, who had convinced himself that India's future safety demanded the swift creation of a genuinely national, that is popularly supported, government. Pushed into a corner, Churchill relented and the upshot was the despatch of the Lord Privy Seal, Labour MP Sir Stafford Cripps, to India. A socialist of the lofty-minded tendency, he was well known and liked within Congress circles, where his integrity was respected. Linlithgow and the Indian administration looked on him as a trespasser who came from London with a mandate to settle India's future over their heads. He was assisted by another interloper, Colonel Louis Johnson, a Virginian lawyer, who acted as President Roosevelt's personal representative. He was not an ideal choice; an American diplomat then stationed in India recalled him as lacking grace, tact and knowledge of local affairs.[48]

Cripps arrived in India on 23 March and left on 11 April without any agreement. As sincere in his desire to reach a settlement as Churchill was half-hearted, Cripps offered Indians a bargain. After the war India would become a dominion and its people would elect an assembly which would frame its constitution. If any province or princely state wished to dissociate themselves from the new state, they were free to go their own way, which was encouraging news for the Muslim League, for it brought nearer the prospect of Pakistan. In return, all Indian parties were invited to join an interim government of national unity under the Viceroy and his council. Congress rejected the first part of the bargain, but was willing to join the proposed government so long as it functioned as a genuine Cabinet with the Viceroy acting as a prime minister. Churchill and Linlithgow jibbed at this suggestion; neither was willing to countenance any dilution of viceregal power at a time of crisis. Furthermore, they refused Congress's demand that the defence ministry was given to an Indian. This question was highly sensitive, for there were fears that, given the perceived anti-British mood in India, there might be a move among Indian ministers to seek a separate peace with Japan.[49] British insistence on the preservation of the Viceroy's power and misgivings about Indian participation in the shaping of strategy proved insurmountable hurdles. Congress was affronted;

ultimately Britain would cling to power come what may, and was unready to accept Indians as equal partners.

Churchill had got what he wanted: continued control over the direction of India's war effort and a propaganda victory, for in the United States Congress was now seen as a dog in the manger. From Roosevelt downwards there was a temporary shift in opinion in Britain's favour.[50] Nonetheless, the Raj had to be prepared to face future American criticism and meddling while Congress welcomed a new potential ally. At the beginning of April, Nehru candidly admitted to Colonel Johnson that he was considering 'hitching India's wagon to America's Star and not Britain's'. He observed that Americans would back Britain to the hilt, and expected Congress to throw itself wholeheartedly into the war effort. If it did, then the United States would unreservedly support its post-war aspirations.[51]

IV

Uninvited but unavoidable United States meddling in Indian affairs was a disturbing prospect for the government. Secret measures were taken during the second half of 1942 to keep American journalists in the country under surveillance. Their private mail was regularly intercepted and read for evidence of anti-British sentiment. This was hardly necessary since it was plentiful in the American press. On 14 September, *Time* alleged that: 'The British clung to the contention that Mohandas K. Gandhi was a pacifist traitor, an irrational screwball and a menace to India's safety.' Less than a month after, *Life* published an open letter to the British people with the warning that, 'If your strategists are planning a war to hold the British Empire together they will sooner or later find themselves strategizing all alone.'

The correspondence of individual American reporters revealed a deep hostility to Britain and its administration in India. William Fischer of the New York *Nation* wrote several pieces on India which reflected badly on the Raj, leading British officials to conclude he was a Fifth Columnist.[52] Among the American journalists singled out as 'objectionable' by Military Intelligence was Mrs Soli Bilimoria, a sometime Seattle schoolmistress who ran the film section of the American Office of War Information. 'I certainly dislike the thought that American men are going to be killed to fight for the defense of India,' she wrote home. She was also irritated by the Anglo-Indian custom of dining at nine – 'they [the British] think all Americans barbarians because we don't like their damn eating hours'. On a graver note she likened Indian gaols to concentration camps.[53] The authorities asked for removal of this tiresome women, but were refused. There was no official love for her organisation, which was accused of producing advertisements and newsreels that exaggerated the United States's war effort and belittled Britain's.[54] The latter, presumably, were seen in Indian cinemas.

Opening American mail also uncovered hints of post-war plans for the penetration of Indian markets, for as a price for its war aid the United States had secured trade concessions throughout the empire. The Westinghouse Corporation asked its representatives in Delhi to procure useful business information from the Indian Department of Commerce and 'educators and missionaries'.[55] There were also enquiries about Indian air routes and future industrial investment. All this was clear evidence of America's aim of 'post-war world trade domination'.[56]

However vexatious it was, the Indian government had to take note of American anti-imperial prejudices. In June it took care to inform United States pressmen about punitive operations then under way against the Hurs of the Sind.[57] They were the followers of a Muslim holy man, the Pir Pagaro, and combined piety with preying on their neighbours. Since the outbreak of the war, the Pir and his adherents had been behaving as if the Raj was already extinct. They adopted uniforms of khaki shirts and shorts, drilled and became increasingly bold in their robberies. On 16 May a gang of sixty derailed the Lahore–Hyderabad mail train near Tando Adam and shot twenty-two passengers, including two British officers. In another raid a bus was ambushed and thirteen passengers murdered. Condign measures were needed to re-assert the government's authority and save the Sind from anarchy. Martial law was declared by Linlithgow and military columns, supported by aircraft, criss-crossed the Hurs' stamping grounds during June and rounded up 2,000 dacoits. Eighty-one were killed in action, seventy wounded and a further seventy-nine hanged for murder and sabotage. Stolen goods and cash worth over a third of a million rupees was recovered and the Hurs' families were confined in special settlement camps. The Pir Pagano had already been taken, and was tried and found guilty of rebellion and murder. He was duly executed which, Linlithgow claimed, was the only way for the Hur 'bubble to burst'. His corpse was buried secretly to forestall the growth of a cult.[58] Gandhi deplored the violence in the Sind and gave guarded backing for the government's efforts to overcome it, although he imagined that the Hurs could have been peacefully persuaded to change their ways.[59]

Internal enemies had to be eliminated if India was to face the danger to its frontiers. These were gravely imperilled during the late spring and early summer of 1942, when a war on two fronts seemed a possibility. Rommel's breakthrough in North Africa and continued advances into southern Russia forced India's high command to consider a Wehrmacht attack from the Middle East or through Afghanistan. Twenty new airfields were built in eastern Persia and Baluchistan (on the borders of the troubled Sind) in preparation for a land offensive which, if it materialised, was expected early in 1943.[60] And then there were the Japanese, whose offensive from the east had been momentarily halted by the monsoon and transport shortages, but was expected to be renewed in October. One danger had, however, been removed; in June the Japanese Navy had suffered a crushing defeat at the hands of the Americans at the battle of Midway, and what was left of its ships were engaged in the struggle for Guadalcanal during August. There were none to spare for those amphibious operations against India which had been a major source of anxiety to the Viceroy and his military staff.[61]

The external threat coincided with an internal one. Watching events from Berlin, Bose was confidently predicting an uprising in India in the wake of the collapse of the Cripps initiative. 'The unrest has been gathering in volume and intensity and will, before long, reach the boiling point,' he told a press conference on 12 June.[62]

The timing, extent and nature of the upheaval depended upon Congress and, above all, Gandhi. From April to July he was preparing for a campaign of civil disobedience which, he promised foreign newspapermen on 15 July, would be the biggest yet. His objective was the immediate departure of the British from India, an act, he sincerely believed, that would remove the threat of a Japanese invasion. So long as the British remained, the Japanese would be tempted to attack India. 'The very novelty of the British stroke will confound the Japanese,' he said with unintentional irony, and 'dissolve hatred against the British'.[63] If the Japanese belligerency did not evaporate in the face of this amazing gesture, and Gandhi was never sure that it would, Indians would have to oppose them non-violently. Just what this might entail, he revealed at the beginning of April:

> . . . the resisters may find that the Japanese are utterly heartless
> and that they do not care how many they kill. The non-violent

resisters will have won the day inasmuch as they will have preferred extermination to submission.[64]

Gandhi had become utterly careless with the lives of his countrymen. On
14 May he told a *News Chronicle* journalist that the British would have to
'leave India in God's hands, but in modern parlance to anarchy, and that
anarchy may lead to internecine warfare for a time or to unrestrained
dacoities'. 'From these,' he added, 'a true India will rise in the place of
the false one we see,' which no doubt would comfort the survivors.[65]
Alternately beset by Japanese, dacoits and British tax gatherers, Indians
might, he conceded, have to defend themselves. For this purpose, he recommended 'gymnastics, drill, lathi play and the like'.[66] All that mattered
for Gandhi was that the British left India; the future could take care of
itself.

This was the irresponsibility of a man for whom every other consideration was subordinate to a single aim: the emancipation of India on his
own terms. Nothing else mattered, least of all the reality of the war being
waged outside India. He must have known the human costs of a brief spell
of anarchy to the ordinary people of the Sind – his own journal, *Harijan*,
had described them in some detail.[67] It is also hard to believe that he was
unaware of the horrendous massacres of hundreds of thousands of unre-
sisting civilians by the Japanese army in China. Perhaps, and this is a
generous explanation, Gandhi could never comprehend the mindset of
those who were masterminding the Axis war effort. A less generous but
more plausible interpretation of his increasingly facile utterances was that
he and Congress had got themselves into what Linlithgow imagined to be
a 'desperate position'.[68] Gandhi was seventy-three and his personal vision
of Indian salvation and freedom was as far as ever from being fulfilled. He
was also aware that Bose (whom he promised to resist if he ever attempted
to set up a Quisling régime) and the Forward Bloc were also bidding for
popular support.[69] Congress's rank and file supporters were becoming
impatient and he had, therefore, to keep them in the fold through a fresh
effort of unprecedented intensity.

Speaking in secret to a meeting of Gujarat Congressmen, Gandhi
revealed that he was contemplating a new campaign of civil disobedience
in retaliation for Britain's refusal to heed his summons to withdraw. What
was said found its way on to the Viceroy's desk, thanks to the interception
of a letter from a Communist who was present. A massive and thorough
intelligence operation was soon in hand to discover the nature of and

timetable for the forthcoming campaign, so that counter-measures could be prepared. On 27 May, Linlithgow reported to London that 'secret sources' had revealed to him the overall political thrust of Gandhi's plans, and during the following weeks details of how they would be translated into action were gradually uncovered.[70] There was close CID surveillance of Congress officials, interception of correspondence, penetration of private meetings and seizure of documents.[71]

On 31 July, Madras CID carried out an intelligence coup by securing a vital secret paper, drawn up three days before, which described the organisation and phases of the resistance programme. This followed well-established lines in the first phases, with token infractions of minor laws, withdrawal of co-operation at all levels of government, boycotts and strikes. Stages five and six were novel and contrived to hamper the war effort: disruption of trains, cutting telegraph and telephone lines, withholding rents and taxes and picketing soldiers.[72] Participants were cautioned not to undertake any activity which might endanger life, but in the past such warnings had not been heeded. Linlithgow interpreted the document as an invitation to sabotage, and it was accepted as such when it was presented to the War Cabinet on 6 August. Its contents and tenor swayed Cripps and his Labour colleague Aneurin Bevan, both of whom had hitherto been very sympathetic to Congress.[73]

As it collected intelligence, the Indian government used some of it to influence opinion in America. It was considerably assisted by some of Gandhi's statements. What, for instance, could Americans make of his drawing attention to 'racial discrimination' and 'lynch law' in their country?[74] Or how would they react to his promise not to oppose the Japanese and repeated claims that he could discern no moral difference between the Allies and the Axis powers? Linlithgow saw his opportunity and instructed his official agent in Washington to brief American pressmen to the effect that Gandhi was either suffering senile decay, or had unthinkingly allowed himself to become a 'tool' of the Axis.[75] Likewise, Amery asked Lord Halifax, the Ambassador in Washington, to prepare Roosevelt and American opinion for the 'drastic measures' that the Indian government would be driven to take to frustrate Gandhi and protect the war effort.[76]

The burden of enforcing these 'drastic measures' would fall heaviest on the police. During the first two years of the war the total number of police had risen from 191,000 to just over 222,000, of whom a half were armed with rifles.[77] In the final week of July, Linlithgow approached each provincial governor for an assessment of police morale. The results were, on the whole, encouraging. In Bengal and the United Provinces, Madras policemen, like everyone else, were feeling the pinch as prices rose, and in the Central Provinces some constables were anxious about 'victimisation' in the event of post-war independence.[78] Only in Bihar was there any apprehension, since the province was a Congress stronghold and in rural districts scattered policemen were vulnerable to social pressure. Morale would stay high if officers were assured that the government was ready to act firmly.[79] It was; on 18 July a signal was sent to all British army and air force units, ordering them to be on stand-by to assist the civil power.[80]

On the last day of July, Linlithgow could feel satisfied that whatever action Congress decided to take, the government was prepared. Within a few weeks he would be facing what, with good reason, he described as the largest and most determined insurrection faced by the Raj since 1857. This time it knew what to expect and was ready, thanks to its intelligence services.

6

An Occupied and Hostile Country: India at War, August 1942– August 1945

After several months of debate and prevarication and not without severe misgivings among its members, the All-India Congress Committee took the plunge on 8 August. It invited the British to 'Quit India' and, correctly guessing what the response would be, called on its supporters to make the country ungovernable. Early the next day, Gandhi, Nehru and most of Congress's leadership were arrested and interned. Within the next fortnight thousands of local activitists were corralled, offices raided, files seized and party funds sequestered. The more important detainees were well-treated: Gandhi was held in the Aga Khan's palace at Poona and Babu Sri Krishna Sinha, the former prime minister of Bihar, was allowed a daily massage with coconut oil.[1] Others were not so fortunate.

The government had snatched the initiative and, caught off balance, Congress accused it of a pre-emptive strike. The old axiom that the Raj moved swiftly and decisively against its enemies had been revived and there was applause from some quarters. Major-General Sir John Kennedy, director of military operations at the War Office, welcomed Linlithgow's decision to use aircraft against railway saboteurs as 'an exhilarating departure from precedent'.[2] The left-wing weekly *Tribune* sensed that the Raj was returning to its old ways, claiming on 14 August that: 'The Imperial lion has roused itself, invoking the Spirit of Clive and of Hastings and Dyer, he roars again.' Such criticism was rare; on the whole the British press praised the Viceroy's action as well-timed and necessary. Japan was the only beneficiary of Gandhi's plans, argued the *Spectator*, which likened the Mahatma to another mischief-maker then in detention, Sir Oswald Mosley.[3] On the evening of the day of the arrests, Leo Amery broadcast on the BBC Empire service and to the United States. He reminded listeners of how Congress's proposed campaign would injure the Allied war effort: 'No worse stab in the back could be devised to all the gallant men, Indian or British, American or Chinese, now engaged on Indian soil in the task of defending India.' The government had had no choice but to 'cut the fuse leading from the arch-saboteurs to all the inflammable and explosive material which they hoped to set alight all over India'. Cabinet unity over Indian policy was reflected a week after when the Labour MP, Arthur Greenwood, told Americans that Gandhi's actions embarrassed the Allies and seriously damaged India's future chances of securing freedom.[4]

Tribune had been right in its depiction of the awakened imperial lion. Its roar was heard and its claws felt during the next three months wherever Indians defied the government. Just before his arrest Gandhi had called on his followers to 'go out to die not to live' and, aware that Congress's superstructure was about to swept away, urged every demonstrator to become his or her own leader.[5] From the start, he knew that it would be impossible for the movement to be directed or synchronised from above, although the resourceful Congress leaders in Delhi had procured loud-speaker equipment beforehand. They used it to broadcast the news of Gandhi's arrest in the streets on 9 August, in what turned out to be the prelude to over a week of riots, attacks on Europeans and damage to government and railway property. The pattern was much the same across the country. Hartals disrupted the distribution of food and caused shortages in the larger cities. Crowds gathered, clashed with the police and assaulted anybody or anything which represented authority. Revenue offices and police stations were the favourite targets for assaults and arson, and, most alarmingly in wartime, stations and signal boxes were burned. Railway tracks were torn up and telegraph and telephone lines torn down.

The threat to the transport of troops and war supplies was so great that on 14 August the RAF was ordered to fly sorties against crowds that threatened railway lines running across the eastern United Provinces and northern Bihar. Blenheim and Hudson bomber crews were instructed to fly low over the crowds, warn them that they meant business by firing Verey flares and then, if they had not scattered, spray them with machine-gun fire. Details of the measures and their application were to be kept secret. During the next fortnight a series of missions were flown and crowds of saboteurs were dispersed with fire, but there were no sightings of casualties. There were, however, signs of defiance: a mob looting trucks on the Katihar–Muzaffar line hurled stones at the aircraft, as did a small party caught damaging a bridge near Gilak.[6] One Blenheim crash-landed and two of its crew were murdered by a Bihari mob.[7] No one was certain how many were killed as a result of these aerial attacks, and Congress later claimed that there had been losses in Nilgiri (Tamil Nadhu) and Talcher, where it was alleged tear-gas bombs had been dropped.[8]

Strafing crowds was a signal of the government's determination to keep the upper hand come what may and by every possible means. The war had considerably increased its resources, with 35,000 British troops available to support the civil authorities and police. These reinforcements represented a substantial section of a strategic reserve that might well be needed to defend the frontier if, as was expected, the Japanese re-opened their offensive when the monsoon ended. This gave roughly six weeks in which to contain if not completely overcome the insurgents. Detachments of troops, often in penny packets, were dispersed across the disaffected areas, guarding lines of communications, public buildings and military stores. Others were rushed to areas where the police were hard pressed or had temporarily lost control. When fire had to be opened, shots were to be directed into the ground so that they would ricochet through the crowds.[9] Airmen were ordered to be ready to defend their bases with pepper bombs, lathis and fire hoses. 'In the case of women lying on the runways, rumour has it that by ordering airmen to lie down side by side with the woman this form of resistance is normally broken up.'[10] British troops undertook their duties with characteristic phlegm and good humour, although many were angered by atrocities, notably the burning alive of the wives and children of policemen. The Tommies' reputation for toughness was as strong as ever, and crowds prudently chose not to tangle with them.[11] Nonetheless, during the Delhi riots a few bold slogan shouters mockingly referred to the recent British defeat in Malaya. Indian soldiers were untouched by the agitation and the police were steadfast; there were only 216 desertions during the uprising.[12] Interestingly, some Congress supporters imagined that United States servicemen would be deployed against the demonstrators, although Roosevelt had ordered them to keep out of the troubles.

Loyalty below was matched by resolution at the top. Linlithgow never wavered from performing what he saw as his duty and this, above all, was to secure a tranquil India in which the war effort could proceed unhindered. 'I am engaged here in meeting by far the most serious rebellion since that of 1857,' he told Churchill on 31 August, 'the gravity and extent of which we have so far concealed from the world for reasons of military security . . . Mob violence remains rampant over large tracts of the countryside,' he continued, 'and I am by no means confident that we may not see in September a formidable effort to renew this widespread sabotage of our war effort.'[13] Churchill was at his most adamantine and could not conceal his pleasure in at last getting Congress 'on the run'.[14] He made clear his position on the uprising and India in general with a famous declaration: '. . . we mean to hold our own. I have not become the King's first minister in order to preside over the liquidation of the British Empire.' Tory backbenchers were solidly behind him, which explains their cheers when the question of bombing Indian rioters was raised in the Commons on 8 October.[15] This was regrettable but understandable. Britain was embattled and suffering regular air raids; its armed forces had still not gained mastery in the Atlantic or in North Africa; and the news from Russia was grim as the Germans pressed deeper into the Caucasus. Everywhere the Allied battle line was fragile, and India was imperilled by the Germans to the west and north-west and Japanese in the east. At the moment of crisis, the war effort was further jeopardised by a humbug who placed Congress's political ambitions before an Allied victory and simultaneously claimed he was a true friend of Britain. As well as dealing with the Indian crisis, the War Cabinet found itself having to fend off American criticism and the meddling of the warlord-turned-Chinese-Nationalist-leader, Chiang Kai-shek, who, for the past few months, had been offering gratuitous advice on Indian affairs.

Comparisons with the 1857 Mutiny were deceptive. In 1942 the Raj had been forewarned of the trouble and its machinery of coercion was already in place. Intelligence of Congress's intentions had been vital and, once the disturbances were under way, police raids on Congress offices yielded further details of its tactics in the provinces. By 19 August the local CID had obtained all the plans for disruption throughout the United Provinces. This and the interception of mail threw Congress activists on to their own devices and made co-ordination difficult, but not impossible. As events unfolded, they were often surprised by the extent to which under-cover CID men and informers had penetrated their organisation at every level.[16]

Being forewarned did not always mean that the authorities were fore-armed. On 14 August the police at Chimur heard that Congress agents were preparing for an attack on the police station two days later. The leaders were immediately arrested, but this did not prevent crowds from assembling on the arranged day. The local inspector warned them to disperse and was murdered by the mob, leaving his thirteen subordinates outnumbered and terrified into inactivity. Later, the rioters burned alive two Indian magistrates and set fire to official buildings, including a school. Order was restored on the 20th by police reinforcements and a detachment of the Green Howards. Afterwards, the police and soldiers were accused of various outrages, including rape, but here and elsewhere such politically-motivated charges were as easy to make as they were hard to prove or disprove.[17]

There were similar brief losses of control everywhere. At Ballia, where police were thin on the ground, the magistrate conceded defeat and burned banknotes worth 400,000 rupees in the local treasury to prevent them from falling into the rioters' hands. Local officials were nervous about their forthcoming pay, and soon after charred notes were picked up and returned to circulation, as it were, by their new owners.[18] At Sasaram, the strategically important railway line from Lucknow to Calcutta was attacked by a large body which included schoolchildren and students from Patna University, who were joined by local criminals.[19] The station and signal boxes were fired and some students raised the Congress flag over the local court house. Hindu policemen refused to interfere and their sergeant warned Hugh Martin, the District Officer, that they would be swamped by sheer weight of numbers if they opened fire. Martin and his men retired to make their stand in the treasury and the gaol, from where they were rescued by the timely arrival of twenty British soldiers. There were not enough of them to make an impact, but the appearance of a battalion of the Bedfordshire regiment tipped the balance and order was restored.

There was a distinct Mutiny feel to many of the small-scale actions fought during August 1942, as parties of British and loyal forces withdrew behind makeshift defences. When he arrived at Madhuban in the eastern United Provinces, the Anglo-Indian District Officer, R. H. Niblett, was disturbed by reports that large bodies of nationalists were converging on the local fortified *thana* (police station). A defence was improvised by a force of just over sixty Indian policemen and chowkidahs, who shared between them ten out-of-date police rifles, two sporting guns, a few revolvers, and some spears and lathis. Against them were ranged at least 4,000 villagers carrying lathis, spears, plough-shares, saws and spades, who claimed that swaraj had arrived and, in consequence, asked to hoist the Congress banner over the thana. They also wished to kill a local police superintendent who was British. After burning down the nearby houses of the postmaster and postman, the crowd opened its attack on the police station, supported by two elephants which were to be used to scale the perimeter walls.

A series of sallies followed. One was led by Ram Nachtar Tewari, who had a reputation as a local trouble-maker and possessed a touching faith in Gandhi. The Mahatma, he promised his followers, had miraculously rendered all bullets harmless. A few seconds after, he and eight or ten of those with him were shot dead. The contest lasted two hours and ended with the flight of the rebels. The defenders had fired 119 rounds, killed between forty and fifty and suffered no injuries beyond cuts and bruises from well-aimed brickbats.[20] Elsewhere the weight of numbers told and police stations were overrun or abandoned. In Bihar, where Congress was strong, the police undermanned and scattered, and the unrest most intense, there were weathercocks among Indian civil servants and landlords who hedged their bets by adopting a calculated neutrality. And with good reason, for they believed that at some as yet unspecified date the Raj would be replaced by Congress and it therefore made sense to keep on good terms with its local bigwigs.[21] Another form of insurance was a Congress flag hoisted over his house by an Orissa Congressman, who hoped it would provide immunity from Japanese air attacks.

II

As conceived by Gandhi, the Quit India campaign was a demonstration of Congress's continued hold over the masses, and proof that Indians wanted an end to the Raj and were willing to risk their lives to achieve it. The form of the protests owed much to the party's socialist wing, which had been advocating sabotage for some years. Communists within and outside Congress were divided; some threw themselves into the fray, while others stayed loyal to a government which, for all its faults, was still an ally of the Soviet Union. Among those who followed Moscow's line was a group which, with party backing, volunteered for behind-the-lines operations in Japanese-occupied territory.[22] The Muslim League would have no part in the Quit India campaign and, incidentally, Muslims were automatically exempted from the mass fines imposed by the government on the inhabitants of disturbed areas. On 31 July, Jinnah had asserted that, while Muslims were happy to see the dissolution of the Raj, he warned against any deal which appeased Congress at their expense. Two days before the Quit India campaign was launched he repeated his well-worn prediction that a precipitate British withdrawal would mean a Hindu Raj.[23] As the campaign spread, the League contrasted Muslim support for the war with Congress's disloyalty and demanded reward in the form of cast-iron guarantees for a post-war Pakistan. Sikhs also distanced themselves from the insurrections.

In geographical and demographic terms, the Quit India movement was an untidy affair. Support was confined almost entirely to Hindus, and the upheavals were most violent and persistent in Bombay, Delhi, Calcutta, northern Bihar, the eastern United Provinces, parts of the Central Provinces, West Bengal and Orissa. The princely states were no longer immune from large-scale unrest. Spontaneous street protests against Gandhi's detention led, as these things always did, to clashes with the police in Mysore. Popular anger in Travancore was directed against an administration which was seen as repressive and collaborationist.[24] And yet neighbouring Malabar remained quiet, even though it was notoriously fissile and had thrown itself behind Congress agitation ten years before. Another traditionally inflammable region, the North-West Frontier Province, was also quiet.

In many instances Congress provided a label for local dissidents whose immediate objectives had little to do with national self-determination. At the outset of the campaign, the leadership had hoped that overall direction would be in the hands of the educated élite, among whom Congress support was strongest. Professors, teachers, students, older schoolboys and girls were the yeast which would activate the peasants and labourers, who were, as it were, the movement's dough. During the second week of August, students from Benares and Patna Universities, egged on by their pedagogues, attacked railway property and fanned out across the countryside, raising the ryots. As more and more from the bottom of the pile were drawn into the protests, they began to elbow out their predominantly middle-class leaders. Peasants and labourers had been the hardest hit by wartime price rises and their first instinct was to fill their pockets and bellies. Attacks on and looting of district treasuries and granaries were common, particularly in Bihar. Longer-term economic aspirations broke surface in some regions. '*Raja Ku Manbu*' (Death to the Raja) and '*Chesi-Muha Sarkar Gadhibe*' (We will build a peasant-worker state) were slogans shouted by peasants and labourers in the tiny state of Talcher.[25] There were other, sporadic outbursts of class conflict, which Gandhi and the mainstream Congress leadership had wanted to discourage, not least because the movement depended upon support from the commercial community and landlords. Inevitably, a public emergency on this scale attracted the purely self-interested, and professional criminals soon joined in whenever there was a chance to loot.

But what did they, and the more nobly motivated, achieve? In March 1943, when the worst of the upheavals had been over for five months, General Lockhart chillingly concluded that henceforward India was 'an occupied and hostile country'. The bulk of its inhabitants were 'illiterate, superstitious [and] easily swayed by mischief mongers'.[26] If there was a recrudescence of the troubles at least 100,000 soldiers would be needed, and at the moment only two-thirds of that number were available. In Berlin, optimistic intelligence analysts imagined that the Quit India agitation had come within a stroke of toppling the Raj.[27] It was not a view held by Congress, which was disappointed by the results. An analysis of the campaign, which fell into the hands of Military Intelligence in March 1943, suggested that it had failed in its aim of paralysing the government, even in such highly militant districts as Bihar. The sole explanation was the loyalty of the army – 'You can break the police, but what of the military?'[28] There were other considerations. Where it existed, support had been passionate and individuals had shown an extraordinary courage and willingness to fight against the odds for the emancipation of India. Consider the 73-year-old Matagini Hazie, who advanced unflinchingly into police fire at Tamluk, holding Congress's flag in her hands, and was shot dead with several others.[29] But the pool of would-be martyrs was limited. By no stretch of the imagination had the campaign been universal in terms of geography, caste or religion. Nor, for that matter, had been its predecessors in 1919 and 1930. But each spasm of protest had severely shaken the Raj and added to the impression that it was losing the consent and goodwill of its subjects.

As in 1857, the Raj had been saved by the sword. But the circumstances had been exceptional, for the counter-insurgency operations of August and September 1942 had been undertaken against a background of war, under a virtual press black-out, and had the support of a home government headed by a Prime Minister who loathed Congress. If Delhi embarked upon a similar course in peacetime, public opinion in Britain and the rest of world might compel the Indian government to adopt less severe measures. Nonetheless, many who lived through the turmoil during August and September 1942 believed that the Raj had gained a victory which it could repeat if it still had sufficient willpower.[30]

The Indian government had lost none of its prediliction for statistics and, at the close of 1942, figures were produced that measured the scale of damage, human and material, caused by the uprising. Policemen and soldiers had opened fire 369 times, and had killed just under 1,000 and injured over 2,000. Congress challenged these figures and claimed that the death-toll had been between 4,000 and 10,000, which, of course, made a propaganda point. Nevertheless, many corpses must have been excluded from the official reckoning because they had been removed and cremated soon after the shootings. Ruins could not be moved and were duly counted: 1,318 government buildings and 208 police stations had been destroyed, and there were over 3,400 cases of damage to electrical installations, which included telegraph and telephone lines. The railway network had also been devastated, with 332 stations wrecked, 268 items of rolling stock damaged and lines torn up. All this had played havoc with the war effort. On 11 September, Wavell's staff calculated that British and Indian soldiers had lost between six and eight weeks' training, and railway sabotage had retarded troop movements by three weeks. The programme of airfield and base construction had been put back by three weeks thanks to shortages of coal, bricks and cement caused by strikes and transport delays. Deliveries of textiles had been held up for the same reasons, and the walk-out at the Tata steel works (the largest in the world outside the United States) had led to a shortfall of 10 per cent in steel production.[31]

Things could have been worse. No Japanese offensive materialised in the autumn, and at the end of the year the IGHQ decided to concentrate on the Arakan coastal strip, rather than the Imphal front, for its advance into India. It was strapped for men and transport and the big push was finally scheduled for the beginning of 1944. For the time being, the invasion threat was suspended. Churchill, in a speech on 10 September, had accused Gandhi and all involved in the Quit India movement of being no more than Fifth Columnists in the service of Japan. His charges distressed the moderate Congress leaders, Sir Tej Bahadur Shah Sapru and Chakvarti Rajagolachari, who were still at liberty and officially considered to be figures with whom the government might do business. Their indignation was justified, for, in spite of intensive investigation, no links were ever uncovered between Congress and the Japanese. Absence of proof did not deter conspiracy theorists, who convinced themselves that the Quit India movement had been secretly scheduled to coincide with a Japanese offensive on 15 September. It was noted that the areas where the convulsions had been greatest lay in the path of an imagined Japanese advance, but there was no explanation, beyond incompetence, as to why the uprising had been mistimed.

III

Dr Goebbels had instructed Azad Hind Radio to give every backing to the Quit India movement and Chandra Subhas Bose obliged, despite his feeling that Gandhi was prepared, as ever, to temporise with the British.[32] Any hope that Bose may have had of direct German assistance to the Indian national movement was dispelled by his meeting with Hitler in November. The Führer was still lukewarm towards Indian nationalism, fearing that if the Raj was overthrown Russia might occupy India. Bose had no further value in Berlin, and so it was agreed with the Japanese that he should be sent to the Far East to breathe fresh life into the flagging INA. On 3 February 1943 he boarded the U-180, which carried him to a rendezvous off the coast of Madagascar with the Japanese submarine, I-29. He reached Sabang on 1 May and was flown to Tokyo where, a fortnight later, he received Tojo's renewed pledges of assistance for the liberation of India. Henceforward, Bose was India's *Netaji* (Leader), a distinctly modern title which had the same resonance as 'Duce' or 'Führer'. He also dressed for the part of a modern, dynamic and purposeful leader, wearing a tight-necked khaki tunic and jackboots.

The Netaji had arrived too late. The tide of the war was swinging irreversibly against the Axis powers; in October 1942 the El-Alamein offensive began and the German 6th Army surrendered at Stalingrad in February 1943, by when Japan had lost command of the Pacific and was struggling against the odds to cling on to its conquests there. The INA had become an irrelevancy in Japanese strategy, save as a source of agents for behind-the-lines sabotage and spying in India. Twelve hundred men and women underwent training and small groups of graduates were regularly taken by submarine and put ashore on the Indian coastline. Nearly all were quickly

rounded up and willingly became British double agents; one party jettisoned their transmitter and arms and caught a train to get home. Only nine
refused to change sides and were executed.[33] Relations between the rump
of the INA and the Japanese became more and more vinegary. The latter
remained firmly in control; once when Indians grumbled about slights
they were brusquely told: 'You should be proud to be puppets of the
Japanese.' INA officers were not saluted by Japanese other ranks, while all
Indians had to salute Japanese officers.[34]

Bose reversed the decline in morale by the force of his personality,
rousing speeches and a slogan, borrowed from the 1857 mutineers: '*Chalo
Delhi*!' (Forward to Delhi). He fed his followers false hopes, with the
promise of a grand victory parade before the Red Fort in the summer of
1943. The truth was that the Japanese had no intention of invading India;
their plans were for a limited push against Imphal, which operational difficulties delayed until March 1944. While his followers kicked their heels
and waited on the Japanese, Bose regularly broadcast to India. He
denounced the rule of the new Viceroy, General Wavell, as a 'military dic-
tatorship' and reminded his audience of how 'the first Asiatic power to
resist foreign aggressions' had already granted independence to the
Burmese and Filipinos. Challenging British allegations of Japanese atrocities, Bose claimed that the Indian government had hanged thousands,
locked up leading nationalists and bombed 'innocent Hindus'.[35]

The INA was relegated to a minor role in the Imphal offensive, with
most of its men guarding supply dumps and lines of communication.[36] An
élite, known as *bahadurs* (fearless ones), was allocated to Japanese front-line
units with orders to penetrate behind Anglo-Indian positions and distribute propaganda leaflets. These were vividly drawn and called on Indian
soldiers to desert and turn their guns against the British. The image of
Churchill was prominent. Surrounded by servants who polish his boots
and bring him whisky, a uniformed Churchill-sahib leaps from an armchair, discomposed by the sight of Indians drubbing British soldiers outside
his bungalow. In another cartoon he resembles a pugnacious Mr Toad,
cigar clenched between his lips, a revolver in one hand and the other
pushing a reluctant Indian soldier towards the front. Behind him Indian
rebels wield lathis. Kites fly over starving Indians and corpses in a vignette
of India under British rule, set alongside another in which a contented
family enjoy a meal under a tree in 'Free India'.[37]

The broken-down figures might easily have been INA men at the front.
Of the 6,000 who eventually went into action with the Japanese in the

spring of 1944, over a tenth deserted to the British, 400 were killed in action, 800 surrendered, 1,500 died from malaria and dysentery, and 1,400 were invalided.[38] They had been under-equipped, irregularly supplied, lacked transport and wore uniforms of khaki, unlike the Japanese and Anglo-Indian army who wore jungle green.[39] A growing flood of desertions to the British marked the INA's end, and its last gasp came in April 1945, when the Anglo-Indian forces reoccupied Rangoon.

A leader without anyone to lead, Bose fled from Rangoon on 24 April, according to 'Agent 1189', a British spy who had penetrated the INA's high command and accompanied Bose on his final journey. This agent also revealed that Bose and his closest followers had intended to make their way to Yunnan and set up a provisional Indian government with Chinese Communist assistance. The party flew to Bangok, Saigon and Formosa. It then left for Tokyo in an aircaft which suffered engine trouble and crashed near Taihoku on 18 August, a few days after Japan's unconditional surrender. Several of the passengers were killed and others injured, including Bose, who had extensive burns to his head, thighs and legs and was semiconscious. He was taken to a nearby hospital, where he fell into a coma and died within four hours. His body was later cremated.[40] His last moments were witnessed by Captain Yoshida Taneyoshi and were revealed by him to British Intelligence officers in Stanley gaol, Hong Kong, in October 1946.

By this date, Bose was already a national hero in India. His name was a nationalist rallying cry and many Indians believed that he was still alive, which was why Military Intelligence went to such efforts to track down anyone who saw him die. In Indian mythology Bose had become a King Arthur figure who had gone into some secret retreat from which he might emerge to save his people. The folk myth of the lost saviour persisted until the 1980s, with tales of the Netaji seeking sanctuary in Russia, although no one knew exactly what he was doing there, or why the Soviet government and its successors have remained silent about his presence.[41] In death as in life, Bose disconcerted his enemies. He survived in political folklore as a lost leader, a patriot warrior who had scared the British. Thus transfigured he became a Congress hero, even though at the end of his life he had rejected much that the party had stood for.

The living Bose had made the British very nervous about the loyalty of the Indian soldier. That instinctive Cassandra, General Lockhart, drew up a secret report in May 1943 in which he expressed deep misgivings about the present moral stamina of the Indian soldier. Lockhart's prophecies of doom may have been unfair to the small minority whose motivation and loyalty remained steadfast, but on the whole his analysis was accurate. This unfortunate state of affairs was the result of the decline in influence of British district officers and the 'negative attitude' of a Raj which had refused to stand up to its traducers.[42] Isolated and petty outbreaks of unrest before 1942, evidence that Congress agitators were attempting to tamper with troops, and Bose's propaganda compelled Military Intelligence to monitor carefully the mood of the Indian army. Censors' reports were studied for signs of discontent so that grievances could be anticipated, and soldiers were encouraged to submit complaints anonymously. One, from May 1943, asked 'Why India is not set at liberty as the Government has done for Italy?' Another from the same time observed that: 'In the eyes of Mahatma Gandhi all are equal, but you pay the British soldier 75 Rupees [a month] and the Indian 18 Rupees.'[43] Discrepancies in pay between British and Indians were a common and justifiable source of bitterness.

There were also anxieties about India's future. During the winter and spring of 1944–45, home letters included fears about government by the 'bania' class and 'bad men' in the villages vexing the families of soldiers.[44] Mistrust of Indian officials was widespread and also justified. Soldiers were disturbed by letters from their families, which described the graft of the police and local officials in charge of food and cloth rationing. There were also allegations that soldiers' families were being victimised by Indian local government officers, who were often Congress placemen.[45] Close surveillance of Indian troops was part of a wider programme designed to stimulate their morale and prove that Britain and not Japan held the key to the happier future of their country.

A psychological warfare initiative was begun early in 1943 with the formation of a special unit whose task it was to prepare men to resist Japanese propaganda. The antidote to Bose's poison was called 'Josh', which may be translated as a 'positive spirit' or 'zeal'. All staff involved in the promotion of Josh were given special instructions, which included a breakdown of the personnel (Bose was mistakenly described as a Communist), methods and ideology of the INA. All defectors were known by the general title of Japanese Inspired Fifth Columnist (JIF), since the government was anxious that as few Indians as possible knew about the nature of the INA. Wherever possible British troops were kept in the dark about the INA, to avoid tension between them and Indians. Colonel J. A. Heard, a former air-conditioning engineer who had lived in India for thirteen years, was part of the Josh programme from its inception. He worked at training camps in Lahore, Firozpur and Sialkot, where he addressed Indian officers and NCOs and explained to them how a Japanese occupation would overturn traditional Indian values.

At the beginning of 1944, Heard took charge of a weekly news-sheet called *Josh* for circulation among all Indian units. It was written in English and Urdu, and he chose the image of the rat, which was both vermin and parasite for the Indian villager, as the symbol of Japan. As portrayed in the magazine, the rat had slit eyes, pebble glasses and buck teeth, wore a Japanese forage cap and carried a Japanese flag. The Japanese obligingly provided the Josh campaign with its most potent source of propaganda: random and hideous atrocities against civilians and POWs. On 8 February 1944 there was a report in *Josh* of how Japanese soldiers had raped Muslim women who had fled to a mosque in Hong Kong. A report of Muslim POWs forced to pray facing Japan rather than Mecca appeared on 15 November. Commonplace Japanese brutality towards civilians was rendered in a playlet that was performed for and by front-line units. It showed the Japanese occupation of a Burmese village, in which women are abducted and houses plundered. An India detachment arrives, expels the Japanese and fraternises with the grateful villagers. Discovery of a real outrage against a Burmese village made young Indian soldiers 'veterans in hate' according to *Josh* of 12 March 1945, and subsequent editions included details of the ways in which Indian POWs had been abused by their captors who had, among other things, forced Sikhs to shave off their beards. Great emphasis was laid on Anglo-Indian comradeship. The issue of 15 February 1944 described how recently Indian gunners had invited their British counterparts to dinner in their mess, where everyone had shared chapattis. And there were celebrations of the many acts of gallantry performed by Indian soldiers and details of the decorations they were awarded. *Josh* steered clear of political controversy and any possible postwar changes in India, and there was no mention of the atomic bombs dropped on Hiroshima and Nagasaki in August 1945.[46]

Josh lectures, weekly leaflets and cartoons all helped to boost the Indian soldier's fighting spirit and deflect Japanese-inspired propaganda. 'I get inspired by a sense of duty,' one sepoy wrote home, 'and get excited by the brutal atrocity of the uncivilised Japs. Please do not worry about me. I have taken part in a national war and if I die I shall have the consolation that I perform my duties.'[47] The warrior traditions of the Indian army were still as strong as ever. It must have been Josh which inspired the Indian soldier who, on hearing from a renegade in an opposite trench that the INA would be in Delhi within ten days, snapped back, 'Not on these ruddy railways, you won't.' Railway delays were a constant source of complaints from Indian soldiers on leave.

In the end the INA turned out to be a paper tiger, although its survivors have tended to exaggerate its importance on the battlefield and have sometimes been taken at their word.[48] From the start, the INA's fortunes were inextricably linked to those of Japan, which meant that from mid-1943, it was, in Von Ludendorff's famous phrase, 'shackled to a corpse'. The Japanese high command might equally have used the same expression to describe the INA, given its dismal operational record. Its detritus was sifted through by British and Indian intelligence officers, who split the survivors into three categories. There were 3,700 'whites', simple souls who had been misled and were always half-hearted; 5,000 'greys' who had some degree of political commitment; and 2,500 'blacks' who represented the hard-core followers of Bose. The latter were detained for further investigation and possible prosecution for treason and individual acts of murder and torture. A few INA men never reached the POW cages. When they surrendered, they were shot out of hand by Indian soldiers who had been incensed by Japanese outrages against the Burmese.[49]

IV

The Bengal famine of 1943–44 posed a greater threat to India's war effort than the INA. Its propagandists recognised this fact and graphic representations of starving men, women and children were among Bose's most potent anti-British images. They alarmed the military authorities, who feared the sepoy's will to fight might be eroded by anxieties about whether his wife and children had enough to eat. At the same time, food shortages would divert energies away from the war effort, cut industrial production and delay the counter-offensive against Japan.

The great Bengal famine of 1943–44 crept up on the administration slowly, taking it unawares and unprepared. In September 1942, official calculations predicted a shortfall in cereal production of 1.25 million tons for the following year and a further 1.47 million for 1943–44.[50] Matters were made worse by the loss of the 1.5 millions tons of rice which had been annually imported from Burma; a severe cyclone and tidal waves which hit Bengal in October 1942; and chronic wartime price inflation. Together these misfortunes added up to a crisis but not a disaster. Hitherto, domestic food production had kept narrowly ahead of the demand. Between 1936 and 1939 the average yield had been 53.5 million tons, and the total for 1942–43 was 54 million.[51] From this amount an extra 485,000 tons had to be found to satisfy additional Allied troops and personnel serving in India and the requirements of an enlarged Indian army.

The margin between subsistence and shortage had become dangerously tight by the first six months of 1943. There might have been just enough food available if there had been effective machinery in place for rationing, the control of distribution and, above all, a willingness to co-operate among peasant farmers and entrepreneurs. None existed. Furthermore, the war had played havoc with normal market forces. Crash industrial expansion had created a boom in cities like Calcutta, where wages rose and to an extent cushioned workers against higher food prices. Primary producers in the countryside were likewise protected because they could feed themselves and wherever possible offload their surplus on to a sellers' market.[52] Those with capital exploited the market, buying up stocks and holding on to them in the hope of further price rises. This left the poorest exposed: unable to afford food they flocked towards the cities and towns where they hoped for some form of relief, either employment or charitable food hand-outs. Calcutta in particular acted as a magnet for the most vulnerable: landless labourers, widows, deserted wives, children and the aged flocked to the city in desperate hope of finding relief. Many died within sight of well-stocked shops. Beggars swarmed into the city, travelling by train but without tickets, and making it impossible for the authorities to discriminate between opportunists and the genuinely needy.[53] Smallpox, cholera and malaria proliferated among the underfed, adding to a death toll which was officially put at 1.5 million between mid-1943 and mid-1944.[54] It is more likely that the total was nearer 3 million.

From the beginning of the crisis it was understood that localised dearths were the result of withholding or hoarding. In July 1943 Linlithgow unsuccessfully tried to discourage both by pledging to import grain which, he hoped, would drive peasants and dealers to disgorge their produce before prices fell.[55] At the same time, the provincial and now largely Indian-run governments were attempting to impose rationing and regulate food distribution. Their efforts came in for much criticism from British officials. Sir Thomas Rutherford, the Governor of Bihar, accused the authorities there of corruption and allowing surpluses to be sent for sale to the industrial workers of Calcutta, while people in the countryside starved. In October, when he was acting Governor of Bengal, Rutherford denounced local politicians, including the former premier of Bengal, Fazl-ul-Huq, for feathering their own nests by crooked schemes, including the forgery of permits to buy government grain stocks. Allegations of racketeering, maladministration and 'criminal incompetence' were also levelled by Congress against Bengal's government, and Britain was accused of partiality towards the Muslims by allowing it to remain in office.[56] Reports of hoarding, venality and inefficiency also surfaced in the British press.[57]

Provincial governments certainly dragged their heels. Of the 370,000 tons of rice promised to Bengal by the neighbouring governments of Bihar, Orissa and Assam in 1943, only 44,000 tons had been delivered by June. Bihar had sent only 1,000 tons of its 185,000-ton quota. According to Sir John Herbert, the Governor of Bengal, the chief obstacle was 'a deadweight of opposition' from the public, local politicians and district officials.[58] Further south, in Hyderabad, ryots resisted the compulsory purchase of their surpluses because they feared the food would go to the government rather than the starving. They sang:

> Do not give brother, levy to the sarkar.
> The famine cannot be wiped out by levy payment.[59]

Stockpiling by ryots and the middle classes, clandestine sales of food and graft among junior railway officials were blamed by the Governor of Madras for the shortfall in supplies in his province.[60] After a tour of Bengal in September, Linlithgow reported to Amery his dismay at 'the lack of public spirit' in Bengal, where the rich were only concerned with looking after themselves. His successor, Field Marshal Wavell, was similarly depressed by conditions in the province and the lassitude of its officials.[61] All this was undeniable; disheartening but unavoidable. Uncertainty was widespread and could not be dispelled by official propaganda. Regions which had an abundance were disinclined to deliver their excess produce to those where there was scarcity, for fear that they might suddenly face shortages. The imposition of an efficient nationwide system of rationing was beyond the capability of the administration and, even if the will and the machinery had existed, there remained the problem of convincing a largely illiterate rural peasantry to place national before personal interest. For food growers, dealers, anyone with cash to invest and many politicians and officials, a national emergency offered irresistible opportunities for gain.

In these circumstances, what was to some extent an artificial deficit had to made up by rice and grain imported from the Middle East and Australia. Linlithgow, Wavell and Amery had to persuade a far-from-sympathetic War Cabinet that India's needs were so great and so urgent that already scarce shipping had to be diverted from such vital wartime duties as the transport of men and ammunition. It was a hard and heart-breaking task, made worse by the interference of Churchill's courtier and adviser, Lord Cherwell, who held all non-white races in contempt and imagined himself an expert on Indian affairs. Wavell rated him 'a fraud and a menace', which was as good a judgement as any on Cherwell's talents and value.[62] But Cherwell's capacity for meddling and the War Cabinet's indifference were no match for Wavell's dogged persistence. At the beginning of 1944 he asked for a million tons of the grain, and at the end of the year he had got it, although it was delivered under pressure and grudgingly.[63] By early 1945 the worst of the famine was over.

V

Field Marshal Viscount ('Weevil') Wavell was probably India's most under-estimated Viceroy. Unlike his successor, Lord Louis Mountbatten, Wavell did not indulge in manic self-promotion, for he was by nature a thoughtful, taciturn man of cultured tastes. He compiled an anthology of his favourite verses (*Other Men's Flowers*) and, when briefly recalled to London for consultations in the spring of 1945, he took the opportunity to see John Gielgud in *Hamlet* and Laurence Olivier in *Richard III*, both of which he greatly enjoyed. Wavell was also the admirer and biographer of another soldier-turned-proconsul, Viscount Allenby, who, in the early 1920s, had defied the government by making concessions to Egyptian nationalists. His study of Allenby's career taught Wavell his pragmatism, a commendable impatience with bureaucratic procedures and an ability to recognise the forces of history. This virtue won him few friends among those old-guard Tories who shared Churchill's hope that somehow the Raj could be perpetuated. The Prime Minister spoke fulsomely of its glories at Wavell's farewell dinner on 6 October 1943. In a rambling oration he extolled the blessings British government had bestowed on the Indian masses, who would remember their benefactors warmly:

> . . . this episode in Indian history will surely become the Golden Age as time passes, when the British gave them peace

and order, and there was justice for the poor, and all men were shielded from outside dangers. The Golden Age. And I trust we may claim the work we have done, the great work we have done, standing alone for a whole year under this storm; and we ought to be proud of the work we have done in India, as we are of the contribution which we have made, the great contribution which we have made to the salvation and freedom of the whole world.

It must have come as a shock for Churchill to hear the new Viceroy speak 'of our goal of a self-governing India' and look forward to a time in the near future when India, at peace with itself, would be 'a partner in our great Commonwealth of nations'.[64] A year later, Wavell rebuked the Ministry of Information for setting so much store by what Britain had done for India. 'The approach must be to boost Indian achievements, with the implication that the British Commonwealth is very lucky to have so valuable a member.'[65] He warned Churchill that India could not be held by force, a policy which the British people would never tolerate and, in any case, British soldiers did not want to stay in the country once the war was over.[66] And yet for all his political realism, Wavell shared the paternalism of his predecessors, once likening India to an adolescent whose waywardness could be subdued by a latch key, sympathy and 'a good deal of freedom'. All of which he hoped he could provide at the same time as preserving India's integrity as a nation.[67]

In his dealings with India's leaders, Wavell projected himself as a plain-dealing, honest soldier. This was his way of saying that he had little truck with the deviousness and deliberate obfuscation which, he believed, were the hallmarks of professional politicians, a class he instinctively mistrusted. His feelings, however soundly based, were a handicap when it came to negotiations with Jinnah, Gandhi and Nehru, who were not only professional politicians but lawyers. Each was a product of the English Bar, where they had been trained in the techniques of combative debate in which compromise was always a poor second to outright victory. The adversarial dexterity of India's tribunes encouraged captiousness and a tendency to get bogged down in legal trivialities, which was how they appeared to Wavell, whose job was to solve rather than dissect problems. But constitutional quiddities were of supreme importance to Congress and the Muslim League. Each was seeking power and could only secure it through a constitutional framework that accommodated their interests;

the small print mattered because it could tip the future balance of political power within India.

Before the war that balance had been heavily weighted in favour of Congress. Like the Raj it had set out to remove, it was monolithic and extraordinarily resilient, having survived waves of mass arrests and the imprisonment of its leaders and thousands of its rank and file. In 1939 Congress was a well-organised, centralised movement with five million members and an army of dedicated local activists. It was generously funded by Indian businessmen and in Gandhi and Nehru it possessed two leaders who, for all the difference in their temperaments, enjoyed vast popular adulation. Congress could not overturn the Raj, but its record showed that it had the ability to paralyse India's day-to-day administration and show, in a spectacular manner, that Britain no longer ruled with the consent of all Indians. Two wartime blunders shook its position. The mass resignation of Congress ministries at the end of 1939 achieved nothing save to deprive its senior members of the chance to gain administrative experience. The next folly was Gandhi's Quit India campaign, which produced several weeks of murder and mayhem, did nothing to shorten the life of the Raj and left behind the impression that Congress was willing to jeopardise the war effort for short-term political gains.

The chief beneficiary of Congress's miscalculations was the Muslim League, which went from strength to strength during the war. It avoided any action which might have been seen as disloyal, and was free to drum up support among Muslims. Congress's monopoly of opposition was fractured and, as Jinnah never tired of proclaiming, the League had become the authentic voice of all India's 90 million Muslims. They were already in a formidable position, thanks to previous British concessions which had granted them a disproportionate share of electoral power in areas where they were a minority. During the war, Jinnah had grown more confident and clamorous, seeking nothing less than Pakistan, a Muslim state which would embrace the Sind, the North-West Frontier Province, Kashmir, the Punjab and Bengal. There were already clear indications that inclusion in the new state would be rejected in the Punjab, where Muslims made up 55 per cent of the population, and in Bengal, where they comprised 53 per cent.

So far as Nehru and Gandhi were concerned, India was indivisible and any form of partition a violation of their motherland. Congress suspected that the League had been secretly fostered by the British as a device to maintain its paramountcy – a crude form of 'divide and rule'. Even

London and Delhi regarded the prospect of Pakistan with apprehension. Emphasising the essential unity of all Indians, Gandhi reminded Muslims that their ancestors had once been Hindus. But neither he nor any other Congress leader could ever quite convince the Muslim masses that the movement was not at heart Hindu and that, given the chance, it would impose a Hindu Raj on India.

Muslim fears of future Hindu dominance were matched in intensity by those of the Punjabi Hindus and Sikhs whom religious demography would bring within Pakistan's sway. A time-bomb was beginning to tick away. In August 1944 the Governor of the Punjab predicted that the creation of Pakistan would provoke 'a civil war' in the province, with the entire Sikh and Hindu communities up in arms.[68] Elsewhere, communal tensions continued to simmer and sometimes boiled over. The murder of a Sikh by a Muslim led to religious riots and murders in Ahmadabad in April 1941. A provocative 'anti-Pakistan Day' held the same month in Bihar was followed by a spate of disorders which left thirty dead and over a hundred wounded. Another flashpoint was Dacca, where there were Hindu–Muslim clashes in July and October 1941. A nearby village was looted and several Muslims murdered by a party of Sikh signallers in May 1942, which may have led to a two-day communal riot in Dacca four weeks later. Here and in Bihar a sinister pattern was beginning to emerge, with an outrage in one district being quickly avenged in another.[69]

Cohesion at the top might reduce tension in the towns and countryside and prepare the way for a single Indian government. In London there was no enthusiasm for any fresh projects to re-order the Indian polity until after the war; Churchill saw to that. Wavell thought otherwise and, on the eve of the 1945 general election, secured Cabinet approval for an initiative designed to open the viceregal executive council to Indians from all parties. Internees, including Nehru and and an ailing Gandhi, were released, and the Viceroy even approached the ex-Communist M. N. Roy, now leader of the Radical Social Democrats. It said much for the changed nature of the Raj that Wavell was now contemplating a former terrorist firebrand as a minister. He liked Roy, whom he thought possessed more 'independence' and 'guts' than the run-of-the-mill Indian politician, but Wavell always had a taste for the quirky. As it was, Roy was enough of a politician to ask for extra seats for his colleagues and a subsidy, and so Wavell turned him down.[70]

Wavell's quest for an interim government of national unity ended in tears at Simla at the beginning of July. From start to finish, Jinnah had been

unbending in his insistence that all the fifteen Muslims on the new council should be nominees of the League. The Quaid's intransigence was part
of a calculated political manoeuvre designed to exclude from power the
League's rival, the Muslim Unionist Party, which presently controlled the
provincial government of the Punjab. The League desperately needed the
Punjab, for without it Pakistan would be a house of straw. This explains
why, when Wavell made his last appeal to Jinnah, he found the Quaid 'in
a high state of nervous tension'. 'I am at the end of my tether,' he told the
Viceroy, and appealed to him 'not to wreck the League'. Wavell did not
budge and again rejected Jinnah's demands; the League had wrecked the
chances of a ministry which offered some hope of national cohesion in
what would turn out to be a period of unprecedented trauma in India's
history.

At the end of July 1945 Labour won a landslide victory in Britain.
Wavell was cautiously optimistic: 'I think Labour is likely to take more
interest in and be more sympathetic towards India, but they will have
some weird ideas about it.'[71] In fact, the ideas of Clement Attlee were close
to Wavell's. Britain would disengage from India after having agreed a
political settlement which would transform the country into a friendly
partner within the Commonwealth. No timetable had yet been drawn up
for closing the Raj, although Indians were expecting the end to come
within two or three years. And yet, if the pace of negotiations since 1930
was anything to go by, finding an equitable solution would take considerable time. The undertaking was known by an official euphemism as the
'transfer of power', which suggested a smooth passage of authority from
donor to recipient. Nothing was further from the truth: the 1942 Quit
India movement and Jinnah's haggling at Simla were the opening rounds in
a scramble for power. Indians now sensed as never before that the days of
the Raj were numbered; as a Congress politician once remarked to Wavell:
'No one worships the setting sun.'

———— •◆• ————

7

What Are We Here For?:
September 1945–
February 1947

I

Winding up the Raj was rather like playing a convoluted and confusing board game, in which elements of chess were mixed up with those of snakes and ladders. Pure chance could wreck the most carefully-considered gambits and send a player sliding towards an abyss. Escape routes were rare and did not always lead to safety. To further complicate matters, each player followed a different set of rules and pursued different objectives, although partnerships of convenience were sometimes possible.

There were two teams of British players. The first was the Cabinet's India committee, headed by Attlee, which defined Britain's goal as a dignified transfer of power which would end with an undivided, independent India within the Commonwealth and a friendly partner in British foreign policy. This was to be accomplished in such a way that it would appear to the world as an act of consummate statesmanship, the natural and wholly admirable conclusion to a Raj which had always placed the welfare of India first. The committee also devised a strategy which was implemented by a subordinate team based in India. This comprised the Viceroy, the commander-in-chief, their staff, the administration, the police and the garrison of India, whose job it was to keep the peace.

The principal Indian players were the working committee of Congress, dominated by Nehru and another veteran *sardar* (chief), Vallabhbhai Patel, and the Muslim League, which meant Jinnah. There were also the princes, still rulers of two-fifths of India, but now all but edged out from the political process. Last, there was a miscellany of players who occupied the periphery, but had the power to upset the moves of the rest. These were former INA men, Indian servicemen, the Sikhs, smaller political parties, the urban and rural masses and sundry scoundrels who hoped to turn a public emergency to their own advantage. Congress's aim was to come to an accommodation with Britain that would preserve the integrity of India and install an elected central government for the whole country. The League demanded Pakistan, an independent Muslim state occupying north-western India and Bengal and embracing sizeable and largely unwilling Sikh and Hindu minorities. The princes were players to whom things happened, and when they did attempt positive moves it was to salvage something of their former powers and revenues. A few, like Osman Ali, the Nizam of Hyderabad, dreamed of setting up independent states, something that was frowned on by Congress, which was anti-monarchical, and the British, for whom a fragmented India was a vulnerable India.

A powerful moral impetus lay behind Labour's Indian policy. It had its roots in the party's libertarian philosophy and the late-Victorian and Edwardian idealism of the men who shaped it, the Etonian vegetarian, Lord Pethick Lawrence, the Wykehamist Cripps and the Haileyburian, Attlee. It was somehow appropriate that the Prime Minister had attended a public school which had been the nursery of so many Indian proconsuls and commanders, all of whom were imbued with a powerful sense of duty towards the country and its people. Attlee had seen India at first hand when he had been a member of the Simon commission and thereafter he, like his fellow committee members, had maintained a deep interest in Indian affairs. A concern for India's welfare and a wish to protect its people from what they considered to be the excesses of its rulers had been traditional in the Labour Party. Its founding fathers, Keir Hardie and Ramsay MacDonald, had toured the country as guests of Congress and declared their support for its aims. For conservative Indians the working-class origins of this pair were a source of bewilderment; how was it, some asked when MacDonald became Prime Minister, that the King Emperor had chosen a 'cooly' to run his government?

Congress had deliberately and successfully cultivated an alliance with Labour since the beginning of the century. Labour MPs had been its voice in Parliament and a number of close personal friendships had been formed between British and Indian socialists. The most important was that between Cripps and Nehru, each a high-minded, middle-class political theorist dedicated to remoulding his country. Shared objectives and a common political outlook created a Labour–Congress axis which made it easier for men of Cripps's cast of mind to deal with like-minded Indians and enjoy their confidence. Much was owed to the efforts of Khrisna Menon, a socialist based in London who glided through Labour's intellectual circles, acting as a lubricant between the party and Congress and, at the same time, advocating Nehru as India's future leader. This rapport between Labour and Congress made some problems easier to solve and others immeasurably more difficult. In its efforts to court the Labour Party, Congress had gone to considerable lengths to represent itself as a progressive, secular movement, whereas the Muslim League was portrayed as obscurantist and bent upon creating a theocratic state. Not surprisingly, the League suspected that, at heart, the Labour government was hostile, although it could count on some sympathy among Conservatives. As events unfolded, the Congress leadership convinced itself that there was a sprinkling of pro-League supporters among senior British administrators and the army's high command, who were covertly delivering information to Jinnah.

Domestic opposition to Indian independence was muted and confined to right-wing Conservatives, with Churchill uttering sibylline warnings about Britain's decline as a world power. The old arguments that Britain needed India no longer carried much weight. It was pointless to regard the Indian army as the bulwark for British power in Asia at a time when Indian politicians and some soldiers were vehemently protesting against the deployment of Indian forces in Indonesia and Indo-China, where they were upholding Dutch and French imperial pretensions. There were no British settlers in India, as there were in southern Africa, who could rally support in Parliament. Most important of all, India had ceased to be a commercial asset of any kind. The economic umbilical cord between the two countries had been effectively severed between the wars. During this period, India's tentative steps towards self-government had been accompanied by an economic revolution. British investment in India fell, with the shortfall being made up by Indian capitalists, often in partnership with their British counterparts. Imports from Britain declined steadily: in 1928–29 Indians spent £83 million on imported British goods, in 1935–36, £39 million. Adverse Indian duties and Japanese competition all but squeezed out Lancashire cotton from what had hitherto been a captive and highly profitable market. British manufacturers were also under pressure and conceding markets to Japanese, German and American rivals. Between 1929 and 1936 Indian imports of British cars, buses and lorries rose from 2,887 to 7,726, and American imports increased from 6,352 to over 12,000.

With the establishment in 1931 of the Reserve Bank of India, the country was free to set the value of its own currency without reference to sterling. At the same time, heavy burdens were being lifted from the Indian economy: in 1933 Britain provided an annual grant of £1.5 million towards the Indian army, and six years after agreed to underwrite its programme of modernisation. Most significant of all was Britain's acceptance of the bulk of the costs of India's war effort, which meant that by 1945 the Indian government had built up a sterling balance of £1,300 million. India had passed from being Britain's debtor to its creditor. By contrast, Britain was now £2,730 million in the red, mostly to the United States, and faced spiralling balance of payments deficits. 'You have been living in a land of milk and honey, now you are going to a land £170,000,000 in debt to the world, where everything is rationed except air,' national servicemen told sahibs and memsahibs as they carried their baggage for their final journey home in the summer of 1947.[1]

Britain's obligation to India was the result of an Indian mobilisation for the campaign against Japan, and the bills for Indian troops who served in North Africa and Italy. Thirteen million Indians had been employed in some form of war work and, as in the First World War, there had been a rapid upsurge in industrialisation. Two and a half million Indian men and women had joined the armed forces and pre-war training programmes for Indian officers were rapidly expanded. By August 1945 there were 15,740 Indian officers, many of them drawn from what had hitherto not been regarded as the warrior castes. The loyalty of the new officer class was to India rather than the King Emperor, as their commander-in-chief, Field Marshal Sir Claude Auchinleck ('the Auk'), appreciated. 'It is no use shutting one's eyes to the fact that any Indian soldier worth his salt is a Nationalist, though that does not mean . . . that he is anti-British.'[2] Indian officers asked, with good reason, how, 'If we had been a partner in war, could we revert to subjection in peace?'[3] Just as Indians were taking over their army, they were coming to dominate every level of the civil administration; there were 429 British and 510 Indians in a now undermanned ICS.

The machinery of power was now largely in the hands of Indians; all that remained was for them to take the levers with as little fuss as possible.

After consulations with Wavell at the beginning of September, the Cabinet's India committee decided to call elections at the end of the year for the provincial and central legislatures. The results would indicate Indian opinion and prepare the way for negotiations for a final political settlement. As yet there was no decision on Pakistan, and Cripps hoped that there would be no need for one. Faced with the choice between partition and all-India government, he believed Congress would evolve a constitution that would satisfy the Muslims. Wavell was not so sure, and was willing to concede a Pakistan which consisted of areas where the Muslims were in an overwhelming majority, but not the Punjab and West Bengal.

Pakistan (the land of the pure) was a prospect fraught with strategic danger, for it would place India's north-west frontier in the hands of a weak government, forever strapped for cash. The first chill of the Cold War against the Soviet Union was being felt during 1946, and once again strategists faced the old imponderables of Russian intervention in Afghanistan. As early as January 1945, British intelligence was keeping a watchful eye on Russian activity in Persia. Axis propaganda had promoted fears that the Soviet victory in Europe would be followed by a spread of Communism, and in September there were rumours of fresh Russian intrigue in Afghanistan.[4] As the uncertainty within India added to tribal unrest on the frontier, there were fears that Russia might seek to exploit it.[5] Whatever Russia's regional plans, it was vital that the Indian army remained intact which was why, however much they may have privately sympathised with the Muslim League, Auchinleck and the army's high command opposed the creation of Pakistan.

The election results of the winter of 1945–46 confirmed those of 1937. Congress retained control of Madras, Bombay, Orissa, the North-West Frontier (with stiff League opposition) and the United and Central Provinces. The League dominated the Muslim vote and secured Bengal and the Sind. It gained 79 out of 175 seats in the Punjab, but was excluded from power by a coalition of Sikhs, Hindus and the Muslim Unionist Alliance. The polls had been conducted against a background of collaps-ing public order, which perturbed Wavell. On 5 November he voiced his apprehensions in a letter to the government in which he predicted that Congress would attempt a violent coup the following spring. Its tactics would be those of 1942, with sabotage, rioting and the assassination of offi-cials. In evidence he cited the inflammatory rhetoric of Congressmen on the campaign trial and the growing cult of the INA, which Congress was encouraging. A nationalist insurrection, of the sort which was occurring in

French Indo-China and the Dutch East Indies, appeared imminent and the alternative to its suppression by British troops would be to surrender India to Congress.[6]

Viceregal pessimism was confirmed during the next three months. On 5 November the first of nine courts martial of INA leaders began in the Red Fort in Delhi (echoes of Bahadur Shah's trial and Bose's boast) against a background of nationwide rallies. 'Patriots not Traitors' read some of the placards brandished by demonstrators outside the Red Fort and, since some of the accused were Muslims, the League added its voice to the clamour. Street-level unity was brittle and to avoid brawls, protesters in Madras agreed not to shout '*Jai Hind*' (Long live India) and '*Pakistan Zindabad*' (Long live Pakistan), but instead called out for the release of the INA prisoners.[7] Prominent Congress lawyers, including Nehru, defended the first quartet of prisoners, at least one of whom (Dhillon Singh) was suspected by Military Intelligence of having tortured sepoys who had refused to join the INA. The four were found guilty and, on 1 January 1946, Auchinleck placed expediency before justice and quashed their prison sentences. As matters stood, the prosecution and punishment of the INA leadership would play into the hands of Congress and might lead to restlessness within the Indian army. Here, feeling against the INA was not as strong as might have been expected, although British officers were bitter about the Auk's decision.[8]

One of those released, Shah Nawaz, threw himself into politics. In January 1946 he addressed several meetings in Calcutta, where Bose's reputation was high. A non-League Muslim, he appealed to his co-religionists to join the Hindus and Sikhs and 'kick the British out of India'. On another occasion, he claimed that in Malaya swimming pools had notices which banned 'Indians and dogs'.[9] Nawaz soon fell foul of the Muslim League, whose members pelted his car in Jhansi, and his political career was suspended until after independence. Other INA men, now popular heroes, were in the forefront of agitation and Wavell feared that they might put their military training to use and become the 'spearhead' for a Congress uprising. In fact, by the spring of 1946 the Congress leadership was beginning to recognise that in exploiting the INA it had opened a Pandora's Box and released spirits which were hard to restrain.

Disturbances erupted against a background of post-war dislocation. At the beginning of 1946, between five and seven million Indians were in the process of demobilisation or being made redundant by war industries. The harvest forecast was bleak: in February there was a drought in southern

India and the government estimated that 4.27 million tons of imported grain would be required to avert famine. In preparation for an emergency, the daily grain ration was reduced from fourteen ounces to twelve.[10] Political and racial tension began to increase, and it was not significantly relaxed by the announcement on 19 February that a four-man ministerial mission would leave within a month to arrange the final transfer of power. In the meantime there were disquieting signs of frustration: 'bitter racial feeling' was reported from Calcutta, where British and Anglo-Indian women were assaulted in the streets and a mob of youths pelted an American military convoy. There were also the by now routine attacks on trams, a tram depot, police stations and post offices. A mood of panic infected service wives in Delhi, where the atmosphere was said to have been 'worse than the Mutiny'.[11] Allowing for the exaggeration which often crept into police and miliary intelligence reports, there was a strong sense that things might suddenly get out of hand, and it was not confined to the British. As India moved inexorably towards self-government, Congress had everything to gain by not unduly rocking the boat and everything to lose from a conflagration in which alternative sources of political power were bound to emerge.

II

The expected explosion erupted in the third week of February, and took the frightening and unlooked-for form of a mutiny by thousands of Indian sailors. The Royal Indian Navy (RIN) had an unenviable record for discipline, with nine minor mutinies between March 1942 and April 1945 and, as always in such cases, poor command was in large part to blame.[12] Service grievances were uppermost to begin with, but there were strong indications that the sailors had already been politically subverted, apparently by the better-educated, English-speaking signallers.[13] The slogans 'Jai Hind' and 'British Quit India' had been painted on the walls of the naval dockyard at Bombay (similar graffiti were appearing everywhere) and, on 31 January, two off-duty RAF officers had been attacked and robbed on a Bombay quayside by a gang which included two ratings in uniform.[14] On 18 February, Indian seamen were spotted among a crowd which tore down and burned the American flag from the United States Imigration Service office in Bombay, and in the evening several Congress flags were hoisted on warships in the harbour.[15]

Just after nine on the morning of the 19th, there was a commotion at the shore signals school, HMIS *Talwar*, which had once been a railway station. Angry sailors smashed a signals bicycle (surely the most bathetic start to any uprising) and within minutes they were arming themselves with hockey sticks and commandeering trucks. They were confronted by Rear-Admiral Arthur Rattray, the flag officer commanding Bombay, who listened to their grievances. The mutineers demanded the dismissal of *Talwar*'s commanding officer, Commander F. W. King, an acerbic officer who commonly called his men 'black buggers', 'coolie bastards' and 'jungli Indians'.[16] Such insults were a symptom of a style of leadership which extended to Indian as well as British officers; one engineer rating later complained of being called a 'bastard' by his Indian superior.[17] Other complaints concerned the abominable conditions on *Talwar*. The latrines were foul, cook houses filthy, water supplies contaminated and men were often forced to sleep on the floor for lack of mattresses. Pay and allowances were low (Indian sailors had compared these with British and Australian ratings) and there was no civilian clothing for demobilised men.[18] There were also allegations that British sailors had urinated on an area at the foot of a signal tower where Muslims regularly prayed. Rattray's response to the crisis was inept and fumbling. He did not investigate the extent of the discontent and refused to offer any redress beyond replacing King.[19] But he did take precautions to prevent the mutineers from securing firearms.

News of the disturbance spread quickly and other sailors joined in. Soon after midnight ratings from another shore station, HMIS *Hemla*, led by an officer, tried to break into a wireless communications centre. The naval authorities were reluctantly forced to admit that they could no longer control the situation unaided and so requested army assistance. By dawn on the 20th the 18th Maratha Light Infantry had been deployed in readiness for further trouble.

By the morning of the 20th, the mutiny was taking on a distinct political complexion. Leaflets began to appear. One announced that officers who called their men 'sons of coolies' had dismissed two merely for putting up 'Jai Hind' posters. 'We have been through all these years the helpless victims to the racial complexes of the British officers, maltreatment, harassment and insufferable persecutions,' the flysheet continued. It ended with an appeal to soldiers, workers and students to join them, united by the slogan: 'Long live the solidarity of workers, soldiers, students and peasants. *Inquilibad Zindabad* [Long live the revolution]!'[20] The plea to Indian soldiers was ignored by all save a detachment of the Royal Indian

Army Service Corps, stationed in Bombay, which unsuccessfully tried to join the mutiny.[21] When British troops began to appear on the streets, their sympathy was solicited 'in the name of the great tradition of Britain's working class!' 'Brothers in the British Army' and former comrades-in-arms in the defence of Britain and India were implored not to fire on the mutineers. 'To use bullets against a democratic movement is the way of imperialism, not of the people.'[22]

The phrases had a distinct Communist ring. The naval uprising was a godsend to Bombay's Communists and they moved swiftly to exploit it, mobilising the city's working classes. On the morning of 21 February there were strikes at all but four of Bombay's seventy-four cotton mills and crowds were gathering on the streets, where they began to set up barricades. Europeans were manhandled and hustled off buses and trams, and Indians in Western-style dress were forced to remove their hats and ties, presumably as a token of class and national solidarity. Robert Stimson, a BBC correspondent, was forced to dismount from his bicycle by a crowd of students armed with clubs. He said he was a newspaperman, and Gandhi always treated journalists with great courtesy, because he believed that two sides of any question should be freely aired. Mention of Gandhi's name had a magical effect on the students, who allowed Stimson to pass, having asked whether he had ever interviewed the Mahatma.[23] Such behaviour struck Stimson as out of character, for in his experience nationalist demonstrators were usually courteous towards the British. Nonetheless there was a mood of racial antipathy abroad in Bombay, as there had been in Calcutta a fortnight before: on 28 February a flybill found at the Victoria railway terminus had the slogan 'Kill the White Dogs' while another announced 'Bombay is Free'.[24] Over 7,000 sailors had joined the uprising and just before ten on the 21st the four-inch guns of the sloop *Jumma* were trained on the Castle Barracks. Other targets in the mutineers' sights were those twin bastions of the European community, the Bombay Yacht Club and the Taj Mahal hotel, but neither they nor the barracks were shelled. Ashore, mutineers and civilians were holding mass rallies under Congress, League and Communist banners. As ever, the meetings were a prelude to riots, and by the afternoon mobs were attacking, looting and setting fire to shops, banks and post offices and clashing with patrols of police and troops.

Counter-insurgency operations were placed in the hands of General Lockhart who, as he later admitted, was lucky in that he could deploy a substantial force of British troops, backed by Mosquito fighter-bombers based at Poona and the heavy cruiser, HMS *Glasgow*, which was heading for Bombay at full steam. Furthermore, he had the backing of Auchinleck, who was determined to put down the insurrection with whatever force proved necessary. Congress too was resolved to stifle an uprising which was not of its making and, therefore, an embarrassment. Furthermore, it had been discountenanced by the ease with which the Communists had been able to whip up and control what amounted to a mass insurrection. Vallabhbhai Patel was among the Congress leaders who successfully pleaded with the sailors for restraint, although, mindful of his nationalist credentials, he also asked Lockhart to show leniency to the mutineers, who were not to be victimised. His influence may have led to the cancellation of a stern broadcast by the General, scheduled for six in the afternoon of the 21st. Lockhart had intended to demand an immediate, unconditional surrender by the sailors and warn those who resisted that they would face courts martial and possibly execution.[25]

This robust admonition was not needed. The mutineers surrendered at six on the morning of the 23rd and were taken into custody. Within the next two days order was restored in Bombay by a mixed force of Marathas and men from the Royal Marines and the Queen's, Essex, Leicester and Gloucester regiments, supported by armoured cars. It was a bloody, one-sided affair in which 223 demonstrators were killed and over 1,000 injured, and the sailors suffered 9 dead and 51 wounded. British casualties were 1 dead and 12 wounded. As the figures suggest, British units were compelled to open fire frequently, and one eyewitness, a civilian, thought the men were 'trigger happy', having been hardened to killing by their wartime experiences.[26] Another onlooker, an officer with left-wing views, claimed to have seen an open lorry in which troops armed with rifles and a Bren gun fired at random into what he alleged was a harmless crowd, killing four and wounding twenty-five. This version of the incident was passed on to a Labour MP by an artilleryman, Sergeant A. B. Davies, in a letter which contained some grousing about the slowness of demobilisation. According to the sergeant an Indian bystander had commented: 'There is British socialism in action.' 'Many of us sympathise with the Indian cause,' Davies added. 'We Socialists in the Army, and there are many, are in a difficult position. Let not the people at home, therefore, blame us if "authority" finds that it has to deal with us, as well as with the Indian people.'[27] An official investigation revealed that the firing had been justified in so far as the crowd was engaged in arson and looting.

To judge by their propaganda, the RIN mutineers were aware that there were national servicemen of socialist inclinations whom, they mistakenly imagined, might desist from firing on Indian demonstrators. The sailors also knew about a spate of strikes which had broken out recently among RAF ground staff dissatisfied with the progress of demobilisation. Some were fearful that they might be transferred for duty in Indonesia – hence the slogan 'Ships for Blighty but not Java'.[28] The airmen's bad example was followed by 1,600 disgruntled men from the Royal Electrical and Mechanical Engineers (REME) at Madras on 23 February. Again grievances concerned the pace of demobilisation and were settled without undue disorder. Everyone involved believed that, since the war was over, they enjoyed civilian rights, including that to strike whenever faced with unpalatable duties, and that Labour was somehow on their side.[29] For this reason there was an upsurge in writing letters to MPs.

This cussedness provided an additional headache for the army authorities, not least because Indian servicemen might take it into their heads to imitate their British counterparts. British morale had certainly drooped during February, largely on account of hitches with demobilisation and resentment as to the fact that, for practical reasons, men serving in the East were unable to have the same home leave allowances as their comrades in Europe.[30] What seemed like an extended exile was a source of anxiety about jobs, broken marriages and errant girlfriends. But at no time was there any indication that British troops were unwilling to undertake policing duties in India, rather the contrary. There were some gung-ho young officers in one Bangalore mess who expressed a wish to lead 'black and tan units' against the 'wogs'.[31] It was with some pride that Private Blackie told his parents on Tyneside of how Trimulgary strikers took to their heels when British troops appeared: 'If there is one thing that makes an Indian's legs turn to water it is the sight of a bayonet.'[32] An official investigation into soldiers' attitudes undertaken after the Bombay communal riots in April revealed that they had little interest in the political background to the trouble. Indians were always 'most respectful' towards them and they vaguely imagined that the Hindus were now masters of India and the British were their protectors. There was also a groundswell of sympathy for the Muslim, 'with his sense of decency, clean fighting and even numbers'.[33]

Any romantic illusions the Tommy may have had of India did not last long. At the height of the Bengal famine, soldiers had told a visiting Tory MP: 'If this is what India is like and the Indians do not want us, what are we here for and why do we bother to fight?'[34]

On the march, men of the 1st Cameron Highlanders and perhaps other regiments chanted:

> *Land of shit and filth and wogs*
> *Gonorrhea, syphilis, clap and pox.*
> *Memsahibs' paradise, soldiers' hell.*
> *India fare thee fucking well.*

'Cheer, wogs, we are quitting India!' was chalked on railway carriages by men about to be shipped home.[35] Grumbling apart, the British garrison in India remained in good heart and ready to undertake the tricky duties that would be required of them if, as seemed likely, the unrest continued.

During the unquiet days of February and March 1946 the same was not true of the Indian services. The RIN mutiny had been a shock, and its repercussions added to fears that the government was about to face an epidemic of indiscipline. Sailors at other bases took their cue from the Bombay men. At Karachi on 21 February there was a two-hour duel between shore batteries and the guns of the sloop *Hindustan* before its crew surrendered. In his analysis of the troubles in Bombay, General Lockhart laid responsibility at the feet of the RIN's senior officers, Rattray and Admiral John Godfrey, its commander-in-chief. The latter was indecisive and lacked the 'human qualities necessary in a commander', which was why Lockhart concluded: 'I have not heard one good word spoken of him by naval or military officers nor by civilians.'[36] Both admirals were shunted on to the retired list. Godfrey blamed 'strong subversive political influences' with Congress connections for his men's disaffection, and believed they had never been adequately investigated.[37] Under Congress pressure, the mutineers were not punished and, in time, were discharged.

During the last week of February and the first of March there was a sequence of copycat mutinies among other Indian servicemen. The largest was of ground crew of the Royal Indian Air Force (RIAF) who, like British airmen, were protesting against slow demobilisation. The trouble affected bases at Madras, Karachi, Poona, Allahabad and Delhi, and was officially blamed on 'unreliable' Indian officers and the acute political awareness of the better-educated men who were employed in technical units.[38] Pro-Congress elements were believed to have had a hand in the mutiny by over 1,700 men from the Royal Indian Army Signals Corps (RIASC) at a training centre near Jabalpur on 28 February. Some of the signallers marched into the nearby town 'in ugly mood' and were eventually rounded up by detachments from the 27th Jats and the Somerset Light Infantry using rifle butts and bayonets.[39] There was simultaneous unrest among a detachment of Indian gunners at Madras, signallers at Allahabad, and Indian clerical staff at army headquarters in Delhi. Here, the source of the unrest was indignation at what was regarded as over-enthusiastic fraternisation between British other ranks and girls from the Indian Women's Army Corps. In one distasteful incident a girl who had been photographed with a British soldier was abused by 400 babus, who promised to beat up anyone else similarly compromised.[40] Curiously, the restless mood also infected Japanese POWs at camps near Deolali and Nasirabad, where there were riots on 25 February in which twenty-five were killed.[41]

III

The culminative effect of these mutinies was to generate a mood of despondency at the top. The weekly intelligence summary issued on 25 March bleakly admitted that the Indian army was wobbling and 'only day to day estimates of its steadiness' could now be made. All naval and air force units were no longer trustworthy.[42] It mattered little that 'fighting' units had been unaffected by the bouts of indiscipline, which had been largely confined to technicians and behind-the-lines staff. Transport, signals and other support units would have a vital part to play, if, as expected, there was large-scale civilian unrest. Moreover, the high command intended aircraft to play the same role in anti-insurgency operations as they had done in 1942. Mainstream politicians were also discomposed by incidents which indicated that their hold over the masses was by no means as assured as it had been, and might weaken further in the absence of an agreement with the British.

Settling India's political future was the task of the three-man Cabinet mission which arrived in Delhi on 19 March. As its leader, Cripps, later explained to the Commons, its overriding objective had been to create the machinery for making a new state which Indians would operate.[43] At the same time he had, or so he imagined, laid the foundations of an interim, all-party government which would superintend the transfer of power. It had been very hard work, an epic of physical and mental endurance which had told heavily on Cripps's two elderly colleagues, Pethick-Lawrence and A. V. Alexander. The former was a benign and gentle influence on the proceedings, while the latter, a Co-op MP and First Lord of the Admiralty, was a taciturn presence, although capable of making penetrating observations when needed. Of Jinnah, Alexander remarked: 'He is the only man I know who walks around with a built-in air cooler.'[44] Alexander's sharpness impressed Auchinleck's military secretary, Shahid Hamid: 'He is full of common sense as well as being shrewd and straightforward. He comes from peasant stock.'[45] The First Lord was also, like so many working-class Labour members, a bit of an imperialist at heart, which in part explains why he was soon exasperated by Gandhi and Congress.

Attlee had insisted that the Cabinet mission did all that it could to preserve India intact, so that it could become a self-supporting nation which would play a key role in Britain's future plans for security in Asia.[46] This ruled out the Pakistan of Jinnah's vision, but did not preclude the existence within India of a knot of semi-autonomous Muslim provinces, which the Quaid had hitherto contemptuously spurned as a 'moth-eaten' Pakistan. At the outset of the negotiations, Jinnah demanded a sovereign Pakistan made economically viable by the inclusion of regions with substantial Hindu minorities, including Calcutta. Congress, as ever, emphasised the need for an Indian state with a strong central government. One escape from this impasse was a plan presented on 16 May, when the commission had retired from the debilitating summer heat of Delhi to the cool of Simla. There would be an All-India Union which would be responsible for defence, foreign policy and internal communications and three clusters of provincial governments. The first (Group A) would embrace Madras, Bombay, Orissa, and the United and Central Provinces – in other words, Congress's Hindu heartland. The second (Group B) comprised Muslim and predominantly Muslim areas: Baluchistan, the North-West Frontier Province, the Sind and the Punjab. The third (Group C) contained Bengal and Assam, where the balance of religions was slightly weighted in favour of the Muslims. These provinces had no right of secession and were free to construct their own constitutions. Together with the princely states, the provinces would elect representatives to an assembly that would hammer out a national constitution. In the meantime, a stop-gap ministry would be nominated with six Congress ministers, six Leaguers and one each from the Sikh, Parsi and Christian communities.

The mission's proposals had been evolved against a background of bickering, horse-trading and mutual suspicion. Neither Nehru nor Gandhi could ever fully comprehend the depth of Muslim misgivings about a Hindu Raj, which meant that they could never understand the nature of

Jinnah's passion for Pakistan, or why it struck a chord with so many Muslims. At one stage, Gandhi nearly derailed the proceedings by insisting that a Muslim Congressman joined the interim government just to illustrate Congress's non-sectarian basis. He was overruled by the Congress Working Committee. In some Congress quarters it was hoped that by procrastinating, the party might splinter the League, whose strength ultimately depended on its ability to secure concessions.[47] After stonewalling, Jinnah finally accepted the mission's plan, as did Congress after some touch-and-go moments. Cripps and his team left India on 29 June, satisfied that they had achieved a breakthrough. On 18 July he reported to the Commons in a mood of guarded optimism; later the same day MPs debated bread-rationing, a reminder that the British people had other, more immediate problems than India.

Having climbed, as it were, a significant ladder in the Indian political game, the British government unexpectedly found itself sliding down a snake. It was hatched during a meeting of the All-Indian Congress Committee on 7 July, in which formal approval was given to the arrangements agreed with the Cabinet mission. Playing to a left-wing gallery, Nehru, just elected Congress president, promised that once his party had won control at the centre it would act as it pleased. Congress refused to be constrained by previous agreements which, in Nehru's opinion, were unworkable. At the press conference on 10 July, he predicted that the provincial groups would fall apart, with the North-West Frontier (where Congress was strong) and Assam disengaging. Only the Muslim League was in favour of the principle of binding together provinces, he continued, and it was unwelcome to large numbers in the Sind, the Punjab and the North-West Frontier.[48] If his analysis was right, and he was certain it was, then the foundations for Pakistan were blown away by the cold wind of political reality. Years afterwards, Nehru regretted his recklessness, which had thrown into jeopardy the admittedly brittle accord between Congress and the League. Moderate Congressmen vainly attempted to limit the damage caused by Nehru's tactlessness. He had, unwittingly perhaps, opened the way for communal strife on an unprecedented scale.

And yet what Nehru had said merely confirmed what the League had always suspected: Congress was perfidious and, whatever it said to the contrary, would use its ascendancy over central government to frustrate the creation of Pakistan. The League's reaction was predictably pugnacious: on 27 July it repudiated the agreement with the Cabinet mission and, two days after, Jinnah called upon all Muslims to take charge of their destiny.

'Today we have forged a pistol,' he declared, 'and are in a position to use it.' The first shot would be fired on 16 August, which the Quaid designated 'Direct Action Day'.

IV

No one in India could have had any doubt what the words 'Direct Action' would mean when translated on to the streets; if they did then they had only to recollect the Congress protest movements of the past twenty-five years. Even the League's adherents in London carried sandwich boards proclaiming 'Pakistan or Perish' or 'Muster call to Arms' as they marched from Blackfriars to Downing Street. These slogans were being taken at face value in India where, even before Jinnah's appeal, Hindu–Muslim conflict was spreading and becoming more intense. Violence was embedded in Indian political life and, with the Raj clearly coming to the end of its days, it was inevitable that those who regarded themselves as its heirs would fall to blows. Efforts by rival party machines to assert supremacy in areas where there was a balance between Hindus and Muslims were a major source of turmoil. In the Hindu state of Alwar (Rajasthan) there was a spate of commotions during the first half of 1946, when Muslim activists attempted to arouse their fellow believers, the Meos. Crowds armed with lathis and guns gathered, a district magistrate's camp was attacked and schools were disrupted as agents tried to inject sectarian fervour into their pupils.[49]

During May tension between Hindus and Muslims increased in the Punjab, where both sides were laying in arms and private political armies were drilling. In Jalandhar, knives and lathis were being hoarded and stones piled on roofs, together with bags filled with sand and red pepper.[50] Trouble was coming; of this everyone was certain, and the evidence could be read in the newspapers or heard on the wireless. Communal riots broke out in Bombay in April and Ahmadabad on 3 July, when 39 were killed and 260 wounded in four days of disturbances. A Hindu procession passing a mosque was the signal for a sectarian battle in Dacca on 2 July, in which mosques were burned and temples desecrated. Fear and rancour combined to create an atmosphere in which rumours of real and fictional outrages sparked off sudden explosions. The alleged rape of a Muslim girl by a Sikh in Abbottabad provoked the firing of a Sikh *gurdwana* (temple) and the retaliatory murder of several Muslims.[51] Indian troops stationed at

Jhansi became involved in heated rows after listening to wireless bulletins, and there were reports of communal friction among units serving in Burma.[52]

It had been hoped that the army might somehow remain immune from the sectarian contagion. At the end of March, Southern Command had undertaken a discreet enquiry into the temper of Indian officers of all religions. After hearing their views, it was concluded that soldiers' reactions to large-scale communal disorder would depend on their officers. Their loyalty was to the army, although some expressed a reluctance to command forces ordered to suppress communal riots.[53] Auchinleck took little comfort from this. He was convinced that Muslim and Hindu soldiers would refrain from firing into mobs of their co-religionists, and said as much when questioned on the matter by the chiefs of staff in London on 13 August. He rejected, however, a Joint Intelligence Staff assessment that India was plainly heading towards a civil war which the Indian army could no longer prevent.[54]

Wavell and his provincial governors were also facing up to the unthinkable: that the Raj no longer possessed the will and wherewithal to keep the peace. This was Wavell's conclusion after he had listened to the views of his provincial governors on 8 August. Sir Evan Jenkins, the recently appointed Governor of the Punjab, believed that its Indian ministry lacked the nerve to disband the province's growing private militia and that serious communal troubles would soon occur in the cities. Sir Frederick Burrows, the Governor of Bengal and a former president of the National Union of Railwaymen, did not expect serious mischief during Jinnah's day of action, which was just as well for the local police could no longer be depended upon. Wavell was gloomily realistic: Congress now controlled three-fourths of India and was unassailable. If there was a trial of strength with the Raj, then the knowledge that the British departure was now predetermined would sway police loyalty towards those who would inherit power and patronage.[55] Having weathered the tempests of February and March, the Indian government faced a fresh storm of even greater ferocity.

It broke on 16 August in Calcutta. Trouble had been expected, at least by Eastern Command's intelligence assessors, and four British, one Jat and one Gurkha battalion backed by the tanks of the 25th Dragoons were standing by in readiness for upheavals.[56] But, when the day of action began, they were still in their barracks on the city's outskirts. Huseyn Suhrawady, Bengal's Prime Minister and a future premier of Pakistan, had ordered a public holiday for the 16th which guaranteed a large Muslim turn-out.

During the morning there were scuffles whenever Hindu shopkeepers refused to close their businesses. At four in the afternoon, thousands of Muslims converged on the Ochterlony monument (a Muslim police intelligence officer estimated the crowd at 500,000, a Hindu colleague at 30,000) to hear a series of provocative speeches. Suhrawady proclaimed the beginning of the struggle for Muslim emancipation. There was nothing to fear, he assured his audience: 'I have made the necessary arrangements with the police not to interfere.'[57] These words must have made many hearts leap for joy – there were many *goondas* (gangsters) in the crowd who were to take a leading part in the slaughter, looting and arson which followed.

The rally was a signal for the killing to commence. Muslim gangs roamed the streets during the afternoon, evening and night murdering Hindus. The victims were beaten, stabbed and their corpses sometimes mutilated, usually in alleyways. Many were Biharis who worked as milkmen, rickshaw wallahs, carters and doormen. Following techniques developed over the past decade, the murder gangs would dissolve the moment they saw squads of policemen or soldiers, fleeing into sidestreets and alleys. Not that the assassins had much to fear from the police; during his tour of the city, Burrows was horrifed to find policemen standing by as a mob bludgeoned to death three individuals. One shot from a British sergeant sent the crowd scattering. Strangely, Burrows denied that the police had been 'fixed' by Suhrawady and his League cronies, and blamed their indifference on fear of being criticised in the press and by politicians if they opened fire.[58]

By the early hours of 17 August the police had lost control over much of the northern part of the city, where many buildings were on fire. By now Hindus were taking promiscuous revenge and casualties were mounting. Troops were deployed to patrol the streets, backed by tanks which had 'a considerable moral effect' on the crowds. It took six days to restore order, during which the army fired 2,000 rounds at the elusive bands of assassins, killing 115. The total casualties for the communal massacres were estimated to be at least 4,000 dead and 10,000 wounded. Among the survivors were a small party of Hindus and Muslims, including women and children, who attached themselves to a British businessman. He guided his flock through streets littered with overturned cars and burnt rickshaws until they found a place of safety.[59] Their faith in him and his courage were a metaphor for a Raj which was fast passing away. In its place was a government forced to make moral compromises: there were no recriminations when Wavell interviewed Suhrawady, the man who bore a considerable responsibility for the killings. The politician was merely told to do his duty in the future. But to whom did a party boss like Suhrawady owe his duty – certainly not to his King Emperor and the people of India.

The Calcutta massacres opened a new phase in the communal struggle. Refugees from the city fled to their native Bihar with horror stories which inflamed passions and triggered random, retaliatory murders of Muslims there. But the pattern of slaughter could be stopped by resolute men and tough measures. On 26 November, Hugh Martin was travelling by train through Bihar with a detachment of the 1st Madras regiment when he heard of an attack on the Muslim village of Nagarnausa. Taking a jeep and a lorry, he led a well-armed party of sixteen soldiers to confront a mob of 5,000 Hindus about to descend on the village. The outnumbered soldiers opened fire without orders and the crowd fled after twenty had been killed. It returned again at night and was dispersed again by shooting. In all, 1,600 lives had been saved and there was no further trouble in the district. Nonetheless, Martin had to face a clamour from militant Hindus who alleged that he was a second Dyer.[60]

Bombay's response to the events in Calcutta was a steep rise in communal violence. During September, 471 were killed and over 1,300 wounded in a series of small incidents in which bands of assassins sallied out of alleyways, stabbed their victims and melted away. The city's Muslims were also disturbed by tales that the Sikhs were now Congress's 'shock troops'.[61] At Agra ten died after Muslims ambushed Sikh and Hindu religious processions.[62] In what would turn out to be a sinister development in the tit-for-tat killings, a train bound from Cuttack to Madras was found to have the word 'Mussalmans' chalked on one of its carriages. This identification had been made, it was believed, to enable Hindu acid-throwers to find their targets.[63] Preparations for a trial of strength were well advanced in the North-West Frontier Province, where uniformed Muslim League National Guardsmen were parading openly and ex-INA men and released RIN mutineers were being secretly drilled as *Jambazes* (holy warriors).[64]

The worst trouble was in eastern Bengal, where there were sectarian killings in the city of Dacca and the Noakhali district. Here occurred a rural pogrom in which Muslim gangs burned Hindu villages, murdered men, kidnapped women and raped them. The death toll stood at 300 on 10 September in what was a carefully planned campaign of terror, contrived both to frighten Hindus generally and to expel them from a province which had been designated as part of a yet-to-be-defined Muslim state. After making allowances for the spontaneous element in the Calcutta massacres, it is possible to detect the same pattern of cause and effect there: the city's non-Muslim population had to be intimidated or driven out before it could become, as Jinnah wished, a part of Pakistan. Certainly the situation in the summer of 1946 demanded that the League flexed its muscles in a region where its pretensions were strongly challenged by Congress and the Communists, some of whom wanted a separate Bengali republic.

Spiralling Hindu–Muslim violence generated fear and loathing in equal parts. In November 1946, the Muslim Nawab of Bhopal felt certain that his fellow believers faced extermination.[65] At this time a black propaganda document was circulating among Hindus, which outlined details of how the Muslims were about to seize control over India. Pakistan would be their base, and their methods included the murder by a 'secret League Gestapo' of Congress leaders and Muslims who refused to join the League and the destruction of Hindu and Sikh temples. Systematic sabotage would paralyse urban life and Hindu women would be abducted, raped and converted.[66] Lurid images appeared on Hindu leaflets which showed prominent Leaguers washing their hands in blood and breasts being sliced off women. The League's newspaper, *Dawn*, printed photographs of Muslim bodies.[67] It was impossible for the authorities to suppress such material, and even if they had the means, nothing could have halted the diffusion of rumours or the eyewitness tales of refugees. Nor could the contagion be contained by the personal appeals of India's leaders who, often at great risk, visited the troubled areas and remonstrated with their inhabitants. Hugh Martin was moved by the dignity and courage shown by Nehru when he visited refugees in Bihar, including a Muslim wrestler whose family had been murdered.[68]

V

On 2 September Nehru had been sworn in as Prime Minister of an interim government, whispering the words 'Jai Hind' at the end of his oath to the King Emperor. There were no League nominees among his colleagues, for it continued to remain aloof from a ministry which it imagined to be an instrument of Congress. Wavell, whose powers of perserverance bordered on the miraculous, finally managed to coax Jinnah to join the government on 26 October. Not that this signified a breakthrough; far from it, for the five League ministers saw participation in the Cabinet as a means to pursue the goal of Pakistan. The Cabinet worked in uneasy harness against a background of arguments over procedures as the two factions struggled for future political leverage. There was deadlock too in the quest for a new constitution.

Like the Raj he served, Wavell was wilting. At the end of the year he wondered whether his constitution would continue to withstand the stress of an office which offered nothing but anxiety. 'The main trouble has been that I have been sleeping badly, waking up too early, to be assailed by doubts, fears and problems, official and private.' He added: 'It is a great strain on a small man to do a job which is too big for him, if he feels it too big . . . I am afraid that 1947 may be even more difficult and more of a strain.'[69] Nehru too was showing symptoms of mental and physical exhaustion, while Jinnah was suffering from the early stages of terminal cancer, a fact which was kept well hidden and may have stiffened his determination to secure Pakistan within a lifetime which had no more than two years to run.

Early in April, Wavell and his staff had begun contriving a plan that would bring the Raj to an end in March 1948. It finally emerged as Operation Ebb-Tide and, for all its flaws, it offered a means to side-step the political impasse. British administrators and soldiers would undertake a phased withdrawal from India, retiring from south to north. They would leave behind them Hindustan, a state where Hindus were in the majority, and Congress would rule through provincial assemblies. This would leave the British confined to India's northern and eastern periphery and bring about what was in effect a partition, for this was the area the League claimed as Pakistan. Wavell's scheme was coldly received by Attlee and the Cabinet. It smacked of defeatism and looked dangerously like an ignominious abdication of responsibility. Moreover, if implemented it would overturn the government's policy of remaking India as a Commonwealth partner and ally. As the Foreign Secretary, Ernest Bevin, pointed out, an evacuation of India in this manner might tempt the Soviet Union to intervene. Even if the Russians did not invade, Wavell's plan was bound to undermine Britain's political and strategic position in the Middle and Far East.[70] There was not only the psychological impact of Britain in retreat, but the fact that if the evacuation was accompanied by disorders, additional troops would have be drafted in from Germany, Greece, Palestine and Egypt. As in 1919, the imperial battle-line was stretched taut. Auchinleck was ill-disposed towards the scheme, which he believed would do enormous harm to the Indian army's morale.[71]

Operation Ebb-Tide was rejected by the Cabinet at the beginning of January 1947. So too was Wavell, whose outlook and actions had been under critical scrutiny for some time. In April 1946, Pethick-Lawrence, while praising the Viceroy's virtues, warned Attlee that the greatest forebearance might become exhausted.[72] Certainly Wavell's feelings towards Gandhi were hardening. Their often testy exchanges left the Viceroy convinced that behind the whimsical, saintly exterior lurked a malevolent Machiavelli. Shortly after the Calcutta massacres, Wavell had been genuinely appalled when Gandhi had remarked that if India wanted a blood bath, it could have it.[73] Jinnah also had the same relaxed attitude to other people's lives, once remarking that Pakistan was worth the sacrifice of ten million Muslims.

In the end it was Wavell's bluff, honest approach to delicate political negotiations which brought about his downfall. Attlee, Cripps and Pethick-Lawrence feared that this might be the case and were, therefore, susceptible to backstairs Congress pressure for the Viceroy's removal. During the second half of 1946, covert approaches were made to the three ministers by Congress's roving representative, Sudhir Ghosh, a young man who had been personal assistant to the managing director of the Tata steelworks. Ghosh probably exaggerated the effect of his intriguing, and Pethick-Lawrence, if not Cripps, found him a vexatious embarrassment.[74] Wavell, with characteristic forthrightness, called Ghosh 'that little rat' and suspected duplicity among his superiors in London.[75] Even without Congress wire-pulling in London, it was clear to Cripps and Attlee that a new man with fresh ideas was needed in Delhi, and on 18 December Attlee asked Mountbatten to become Viceroy. He agreed in the first week of January 1947.

Attlee wrote to Wavell on 31 January, giving him four weeks' notice to leave India and offering an earldom as a consolation. Wavell accepted his dismissal with a dignified letter, reminding the Prime Minister that it had always been customary for a Viceroy to be given six months' notice before he was recalled. Not that this counted for much any more; now all that mattered was expediency.

———◆———

8

Was It Too Quick?: Dividing and Departing, March–September 1947

I

Admiral Viscount Mountbatten of Burma ('Dickie') was forty-six years old when he was appointed India's last and most controversial Viceroy. He was English-born from German parents: Admiral Prince Louis of Battenberg and Princess Victoria, a daughter of Louis IV, Grand Duke of Hesse. Through her, Mountbatten was a grandson of Queen Victoria, a royal connection that he treasured and used whenever it suited him, which was often. Royal blood counted for something in his lifetime, which coincided with the heyday of that imperial monarchy which his grandmother had done so much to create. Proud of his common touch, Mountbatten also expected deference and, like all princelings, was susceptible to flattery. His father had been an able First Sea Lord, but had been forced to resign in 1914 on account of his German blood. A victim of xenophobia, he later Anglicised his surname and was created Marquess of Milford Haven.

Mountbatten's background, his father's treatment, his mildly leftish views, egotism and personal flamboyance placed a distance between him and the conservative, reticent British ruling class from which viceroys had traditionally been selected. As events would show, his outlook, values and priorities were far removed from those of the proconsuls who had ruled India for the past hundred years, which may explain why he got on so well with the men they instinctively disliked – Indian professional politicians. They appreciated a shrewd operator who understood the language of power politics and expediency, which was no doubt why those who had served the Raj and commanded its armies looked askance at him, then and later.

Of Mountbatten's boundless ambition there can be no doubt. Opinion is divided over his talents as a naval commander, strategic planner and as the Viceroy ordered to terminate the Raj. He believed that he had succeeded in all these undertakings in an exemplary manner and said so frequently, convincing himself and, he hoped, posterity that he was a truly great and heroic figure. In constructing his own legend, Mountbatten was aware that much of what he had done was open to reproof, and he went to considerable lengths to forestall his critics. In one highly revealing episode he asked Sir Evan Jenkins, the last Governor of the Punjab, not to have any dealings with Leonard Mosley, who was then engaged in a book on the last days of the Raj. Mountbatten's only motive could have been a fear that Jenkins might reveal details of a piece of illicit viceregal legerdemain during the drawing of the border between India and Pakistan. In the warning to Jenkins, Mountbatten hinted at arm-twisting elsewhere when he claimed that Longman had already assured him they would not publish Mosley's book on the grounds that it was hostile. On the other hand, Mountbatten was keen for Jenkins to see the historian John Terraine, who was then gathering material for a twelve-part television documentary on the Viceroy's career. He was 'a real man of honour and would not let you down', and, according to Mountbatten, proof of his integrity could be found in his studies of Field Marshal Lord Haig and British strategy on the Western Front.[1] Both were highly sympathetic to their subjects and evidence of their author's ability to defend a seemingly untenable position. The posthumous television vindication appeared after Mountbatten's assassination by the IRA in August 1979. As a case for the defence it was impaired by its protagonist's glib self-righteousness.

In the light of his extraordinary efforts to preserve and, wherever possible, add lustre to his reputation, Mountbatten deserves compassion rather than condemnation. Those who tamper with history are usually frightened by it, and, for all his colossal vanity, the Viceroy may have been conscious that on occasions his judgement had been mistaken and his achievements exaggerated, not least by himself. 'I am glad to tell you that I was right from the point of view of history,' he told *The Times* on 2 January 1969. He predicted that his grandchildren would say: 'Great grandpa wasn't such a bloody fool after all. He was right and all the others who criticised him were wrong.' There were many variations on this theme of rectitude; so many, in fact, as to leave listeners wondering whether they were uttered as an antidote to interior doubts rather than as affirmations of unshakeable self-confidence.

Speculation along these lines is hard to sustain, for Mountbatten was essentially a man of action rather than thought. In India he proceeded on the assumption that whenever faced with a crisis it was always better to *do* something rather than wait and see. Considered procrastination would have been a difficult alternative for a Viceroy whose masters had told him to stick to their timetable. To deviate from instructions would have been risky for an ambitious man, all too aware of what had happened when his predecessor had fallen out with the government. It was also important to be seen in action. Mountbatten was the first Viceroy to appoint a press attaché, Alan Campbell-Johnson, whose job it was to make sure that the Raj ended with a display of favourable publicity. Newsreel cameramen were shepherded to where they could obtain the best shots of the Viceroy and Vicereine, both of whom were always obliging in such matters. Campbell-Johnson was delighted when Gandhi met the couple and placed his hand on Lady Mountbatten's shoulder, providing a gesture of 'spontaneous friendship' for the press photographers.[2]

Such informality added to the carefully contrived impression of the new Viceroy as a gust of fresh air blowing through the fusty corridors of power. Not that Mountbatten shunned the theatre of viceregal power, for he had a Ruritanian taste for uniforms and never missed a chance to appear in them, adorned with the stars and ribbons of the various orders that came the way of minor royalty. Thus arrayed, he formally took over from Wavell in an unprecedented ceremony at the viceregal palace. Incoming and outgoing viceroys had hitherto never met, and by ignoring this custom Mountbatten compounded Attlee's humiliation of Wavell, or so many believed.

The new Viceroy took very seriously the Prime Minister's wish that the British should leave India in a spirit of goodwill. From the moment of his arrival in Delhi on 22 March, he went out of his way to win the hearts of India's leaders in what turned out to be a highly effective charm offensive. Beguiling politicians with whom he had to make some hard bargains made sense if one assumed, as Mountbatten clearly did, that in an atmosphere of affability old differences and intransigence might miraculously evaporate. The magic did not work for Jinnah, who was not a man to be won over by breezy ward-room good humour or soft words. Even if he had been, it is hard to imagine that Mountbatten could ever have persuaded him that he was an even-handed Viceroy.

The Mountbattens inclined to the left, and were seen by Muslims as pro-Congress. Lord Casey (Governor of Bengal, 1944–46) found Lady Mountbatten 'startlingly left-wing' when they met at a dinner party in February 1945.[3] Her husband was a close confidant of the Labour MP, Tom Driberg, whom he used both as a source of political inside information and a secret contact with the press and the Labour Left. Driberg surmised that his friend was a homosexual like himself, although it is unclear on what grounds.[4] The deviant MP was one of a wide circle of socialist luminaries, including Sir Stafford Cripps and Khrisna Menon, whom the Viceroy consulted before he left for India. Cripps was an admirer and offered his services on Mountbatten's staff.[5] Any doubts which Jinnah or his followers may have had as to where the Mountbattens' sympathies lay were soon dissipated: within a fortnight of their arrival, the pair had struck up cordial and close relations with Nehru, Gandhi and other leading Congressmen. By contrast, the Viceroy's first interview with Jinnah on 5 April was frosty, and set the tone for its successors. Mountbatten set great store by his magnetic personality, and the Quaid's rebuff peeved him. His response was to refer to Jinnah as an 'evil genius', a 'psychopathic case', a 'lunatic' and plain 'bastard'. This was folly at a time when security at the top levels of government had all but ceased to exist as Indian civil servants shed old loyalties and acquired new. As a result, there were plenty of eavesdroppers glad to divulge secret information to Indian politicians.[6]

The Viceroy's claims to political detachment were further compromised by the crass misconduct of his wife. Edwina Mountbatten was a jejune socialite with a record for infidelity which her husband appears to have overlooked. Whether in Singapore, where they first met in March 1946, or when they became re-acquainted in India, the Vicereine became infatuated with Nehru. This was a disastrous intrusion of private passion into public life, since their flirtations were observed and commented upon, unfavourably by Muslims. One, Auchinleck's military secretary, Shahid Hamid, remarked in his diary for 31 March: '. . . according to [V. P.] Menon, Nehru's relationship with Lady Mountbatten is sufficiently close to have raised many eyebrows'. They remained arched for the next few months, although to judge from what is known of the love letters that passed between them, her feelings for the older, wiser widower were those of schoolgirl with a crush. What was, in every sense, a trivial affair added to Muslim fears that her husband was in Congress's pocket.[7]

As far as the Muslim League was concerned, Mountbatten's well-intentioned policy of cultivating the friendship of the men with whom he had to bargain had failed. It did, however, result in him being the first Viceroy to enjoy warm relations with the Congress leadership. They were undoubtedly drawn towards him in the belief that the British government had granted him complete freedom of action as a power-broker. This was not so, although Mountbatten often gave the contrary impression. On 27 March, when they were dining together, he told Lieutenant-General Sir Reginald Savory, the Adjutant-General of the Indian army, that he had 'practically carte blanche' to settle all India's outstanding problems.[8] On other occasions the Viceroy claimed that he possessed 'plenipotentiary powers' and could do as he wished.[9]

The real master of events, Attlee, employed an analogy from his beloved cricket to describe the Viceroy's position. 'I put you in to bat on a very sticky wicket to pull the game out of the fire,' he told Mountbatten on 17 July, when it appeared that he was about to save the match.[10] The Prime Minister was the captain and the Viceroy his star batsman, under orders to rescue the innings before light failed. To prevent his player from stone-walling, Attlee had publicly announced on 20 February that the British would leave India by 30 June 1948, a deadline which was intended to concentrate the minds of Congress and the League and force them to agree terms. An accord between the two was still thought possible, in spite of past experience of Jinnah's interior resolve and the mentality of his followers. If, after independence, India chose to join what was still an all-white Commonwealth, so much the better, although there were official fears that it might prove an unco-operative, possibly disruptive member. In the case of the Congress and the League remaining at loggerheads, then the Prime Minister declared that Britain would deliver power to existing central and provincial governments, or 'in such other way as may seem most reasonable and in the best interests of the Indian people'. The alternative to conciliation was a solution imposed from above.

To help him carry out Attlee's mandate, Mountbatten was given a strong team of supporting players. The anchor man was General Lord ('Pug') Ismay, his chief of staff who, for the past six years, had been chief of staff at the Ministry of Defence, where he had been Churchill's right-hand man. He represented the British chiefs of staff, whose overriding concern was for India to be retained within the Commonwealth as a link in a strategic chain of allies and bases which stretched from Gibraltar through the Mediterranean to the Indian Ocean and the Far East. This had always been the traditional role of India; it had underpinned British pretensions in Asia and the Middle East and, indeed, Britain's claim to be a world power. Old shibboleths died lingering deaths and, even in 1947, when Britain was staying afloat on American loans, there were those who still thought in terms which would have been recognised by Victorian and Edwardian statesmen and strategists. The chiefs of staff, together with Ernest Bevin, bridged the gap between men of the Palmerstonian mould and the cold warriors of the second half of the twentieth century. They imagined that an armed confrontation with the Soviet Union was inevitable and likely to be prolonged. If this was so, then Indian co-operation was vital for the defence of Commonwealth communications and the oilfields of Iraq and Persia. Auchinleck concurred; in May 1946 he had suggested that if Pakistan became a reality it would need a British garrison to defend it against Afghan and maybe Russian encroachments.[11] At this time Attlee still had an open mind about the Russian threat and, despite objections from the chiefs of staff, was not prepared to press independent India too far on the matter of an alliance.[12]

II

Mountbatten's first four weeks in India were spent listening to the opinions of Indian ministers, politicians and his staff. What he heard and saw convinced him that partition was unavoidable and that it was best undertaken sooner rather later. This was not what Attlee had wanted and was, in a way, a betrayal of all that the Raj had achieved in creating a united India under a single government. The point was made by Mountbatten when he broadcast to the Indian people on the evening of 3 June, after the partition of India had been announced:

> For more than a hundred years 400 millions of you have lived together and this country has been administered as a single entity. This has resulted in unified communications, defence, postal services and currency; an absence of tariffs and customs barriers; and the basis for an integrated political economy. My greatest hope was that communal differences would not destroy all this.

Furthermore, surrendering to the forces which had sought to sunder India along the fault lines of religion was a concession to primitive ancestral prejudices of the kind the Raj had once hoped it could extinguish. It had, at least among India's educated élite, and for all its life the Raj had been a secular state which had done all that was humanly possible to govern dispassionately. This noble principle had been accepted by men like Gandhi, Nehru and the Muslim Congressman, Dr Azad, for whom a passionate attachment to the ideal of a nation was not a denial of personal faith. A pious Hindu and a devout Muslim could live together in harmony under a government that was blind to confessional differences; this had been one of the greatest triumphs of the Raj. The upper echelons of Congress, true to their Western education, hoped that they might perpetuate this system along with the unity that the Raj had given India. They failed because in this they did not truly reflect the feelings of the masses and, however hard they tried not to, most of them spoke with what seemed to be the voice of Hindu revivalism.

The decision to bisect India was the result of Mountbatten's hectic consultations with its political leaders. He and his staff worked with the dedication and demonic energy of men running a race against the clock. Everyone involved, British and Indian, exhausted themselves, and nerves and tempers often became frayed. The momentum had to be maintained, for, as Ismay reported to the Cabinet on 2 April, India was like a ship crammed full of combustible material. Fire had broken out and had to be extinguished quickly so that the vessel could proceed to a port, preferably British. In quenching the flames and steering the ship to safety, Ismay concluded that 'we must not allow the "best" to be the enemy of the "good". From now on, an improvised, workable but flawed plan was better than none at all.'[13] As early as 29 March, the Viceroy was examining the possibilities of a division, and his exchanges with Jinnah during the following week convinced him that some form of Pakistan was inevitable.[14]

The first blueprint for partition and the allocation of power was drawn up during April and May. In its first form, which appeared in mid-April, it was known as 'Plan Balkan' and, as its name suggested, it involved the fragmentation of India. This scheme evolved further after consultations with the Congress leadership and Jinnah, who continued to oppose any arrangement that might produce a shrunken and impoverished Pakistan. The issue of whether or not the successor states would enter the Commonwealth led to various scuffles up blind alleys, with Indian politicians anxious to avoid any settlement under which Dominion status allowed Britain to retain some executive powers. Nevertheless, and thanks to the manipulative skills of the hard-nosed Patel, Congress accepted the

principle of partition on 28 April. He and many others believed that
Pakistan would wither and, at some future date, be driven by economic
necessity to return to the greater India.

Inextricable from the questions of boundaries and constitutional for-
mulae was that of security. A divided India meant a divided Indian army,
whose two parts would be responsible for internal security and, in all likelihood, the policing of those areas in which partition was bound to lead to
upheavals. Auchinleck's emotional attachment to the Indian army was
deep, and he was saddened by the prospect of it being wrenched apart.
Given that Hindus and Muslims were mixed within nearly every unit, their
separation and the allocation of resources was a dauntless, as well as disheartening task for a soldier who was never happier than when sitting
cross-legged with his men and sharing their meals in an atmosphere of
comradeship. When asked by the Viceroy (whom he called 'Pretty Dickie')
how long it would take to split the army, Auchinleck replied two, three,
possibly five years. In the event he and his staff were given four weeks to
prepare a plan.[15] Among other things, it would involve the replacement of
all but 2,500 of the 13,500 British officers who were widely and rightly
seen in many quarters as the cement which was binding the Indian army
together.[16]

It would have been hard for the Indian army to have preserved any
cohesion if Plan Balkan was implemented. At its heart lay the idea that
Indian provinces and states would ultimately decide their own future, and
it was, therefore, an invitation to fragmentation and a violent free-for-all.
Just what this might involve was revealed by the Raja of Faridkot, who discussed the possibility of a war between his state and Nabha during a dinner
at which the Viceroy was present. Two days after, he informed Lieutenant-
General Savory of his intention to annex the Firozpur and Ludhiana
districts after independence. The general also heard that other princes
were considering retaining British officers to command their armies,
which struck him as a return to the days of the Raj's foundation, when
European officers like Dupleix and Boigne had commanded princely
forces and thereby made themselves kingmakers.[17] The princes may have
had fantasies about future power struggles, but real ones were already
underway in Rajasthan and the Punjab, where sectarian factions were
attempting to secure local dominance.

Plan Balkan was a recipe for anarchy. This point was trenchantly made
by Nehru to Mountbatten at a private meeting on the evening on 10 May
after the Viceroy had, quite improperly, allowed him a glimpse of the

secret plan. This breach of security and partiality was excused by
Mountbatten as a 'sudden hunch', but it turned out to be a lucky one.
Nehru objected to the scheme in forthright but essentially correct terms.
'The inevitable consequences of the proposals would be to invite the
Balkanisation of India; to provoke certain civil conflict and to add to violence and disorder; to cause a further breakdown of the central authority,
which alone could prevent the growing chaos, and to demoralise the army,
the police and the central services . . .' Congress would reject out of hand
a plan which would weaken it as much as India. In great haste, and greater
embarrassment, a new plan was concocted, largely by Bahadur Vapal
Pangunni Menon, an experienced civil servant and Reforms Commissioner. On 18 May it was carried to London by Mountbatten for Cabinet
approval.

III

There was a strong element of panic in Mountbatten's dash to fabricate a
second plan that would satisfy Congress. He had talked himself and the
Cabinet into believing that any delay might lead to them being overtaken,
and swamped by events which were beyond their control. Over the past
five years the Raj had successively lost its prestige and authority. The ICS,
once known as the 'steel frame' which held India together, had been
reduced to a few struts, and in many areas real power rested with Indian
administrations to whom their countrymen looked as sources of patronage
and advancement. A morally and physically diminished Raj was left with
what it had started with: the army. And this, while still loyal to its commanders, was about to become immobilised as detachments, command
structures, arsenals and stores were divided and parcelled out.

Worse still, large areas of north-western India were lurching towards
pandemonium, and the Viceroy, his staff, ministers and the provincial governments were unable to arrest this movement. They were constrained by
three factors. First, the religious truce established by the Raj had collapsed in ruins during the second half of 1946 and, despite appeals by
Jinnah and the Congress leadership, could not be rebuilt. Then there was
Attlee's declaration that the British would depart in June 1948, which had
signalled the start of a series of bloody contests for paramountcy in the
Punjab. These, in turn, intensified sectarian violence in Bihar, Bengal and
Rajasthan. In each area, the authorities' resources for upholding order

had been stretched to breaking point, and had snapped in Bihar. On the morning of 5 May, Auchinleck had warned the Cabinet's India committee that the situation in the country was now 'dangerous', and the same afternoon Ismay reported that communal antipathies were deepening and clashes proliferating.[18]

A week or so after, Attlee obtained grisly confirmation of the brass hats' prognosis when he received an eyewitness account of massacres near Rawalpindi in a private letter from a personal friend, Lieutenant-Colonel Reginald Schomberg. The colonel described how the police and administration had stood by helplessly during three days of anti-Sikh riots orchestrated by minions of the Muslim League. Sikhs and Hindus were fleeing in terror from northern and western Punjab. The fate of those who failed to escape was revealed by the colonel's photographs of bodies (most already stripped to skeletons by vultures, kites and pariah dogs) including those of Sikh women who had hurled themselves into a well rather than face rape by Muslim gangs. Schomberg, whose military and civilian career in India stretched back for nearly forty years, concluded that only the British and Indian armies were holding the country together. 'India is in a melancholy state. There is no evidence of any grasp of the fundamentals of administration; and the auguries for the future are not propitious . . . the general opinions is that the hand-over is too quick.'[19]

Schomberg's analysis was correct. On 14 June, Jenkins informed Mountbatten of the slump in morale among embattled British administrators in the Punjab. 'It seems doubtful if many of the British officials will wish to stay . . . The average British official does not in fact believe that the new Government will be fit to serve under – in his opinion they are likely to be communal and unfair, their administrative standards will be low, and their financial stability will at best be questionable. This goes apparently not only for the British members of the ICS and IP [Indian Police], but the majority of doctors and engineers.' Indian administrators were also uneasy about their futures. 'The Muslims are, I understand, already parcelling out the more lucrative Pakistan appointments among themselves. The non-Muslims do not think they would be safe in the Western Punjab, and hope to be accommodated in Hindustan.'[20] All this was to be expected and not confined to the Punjab. Over twelve months of high-level prevarication, political wrangles and uncertainty as to where their loyalty would ultimately lie placed an almost unbearable burden on the by now predominantly Indian civil service and police. Many became frightened men; at the end of March, as order dissolved in the Punjab, Muslim and Sikh clerks at army HQ in Lahore took to carrying knives and swords.[21] It was no longer easy for an Indian administrator or policeman to take condign measures whenever they were needed, for he could no longer rely on his judgement being upheld by sympathetic superiors. Impartial and firm enforcement of the law was not always politically expedient, and rigorous action was, therefore, best avoided.

After nearly six months of handling intermittent communal disorders, the Bihar police cracked up at the very end of March, in part, it was suspected, as a consequence of Communist subversion. The result was a police mutiny that was suppressed by the Bihar regiment and armoured cars of the 25th Dragoons.[22] The spirits of those responsible for keeping the peace must have sagged further after the government decided not to hold enquiries into what had occurred in Bengal and Bihar, for fear of causing further acrimony. Those with a direct or indirect hand in the disturbances must have been encouraged by this pusillanimous dereliction of duty.[23]

And yet everything was not quite lost; at least where determined men were willing to resort to tough measures. This was proved in Rajasthan during the recrudescence of conflict between Muslim Meos and Hindu Jats in mid-March. Attempts to uncover the source of the troubles produced the usual catalogue of petty incidents: a row over washing a bullock, a buffalo stolen by Muslims, a false rumour that Hindus had been stabbed in the small town of Rewari, a lewd remark by a Muslim boy to a Hindu girl at a bathing fair, and a Hindu–Muslim brawl at a railway station.[24] With religious tension acute, the slightest affront led to bands of armed men gathering and attacking and burning neighbouring villages. Police and troops were moved swiftly to the centres of the outbreaks which were often in remote, roadless areas. In the Mathura district Stuart tanks of the Poona Horse, each with a police officer sitting on the turret, criss-crossed disturbed areas.[25] All the troops conducted themselves well. 'The behaviour of the Indian soldier has been almost beyond praise,' ran the official report of the operations. 'He has shown to the whole district that the Indian soldier has no communal feeling in the execution of his duty.'[26] Among the units deployed was a local one, the Rajputana Rifles, whose steadfastness had been previously questioned.[27]

Order was restored and a fine of 90,000 rupees imposed, but, and this was a sign of official faint-heartedness, only 450 rupees had been collected by the beginning of August. Here, as elsewhere, there was a strong feeling that all penalties incurred under the British would be waived after independence.[28] Wrongdoers had only to wait and the slate would be wiped clean by a new régime whose minister had been covertly sympathetic to their cause; after all, political pressure applied by Congress had enabled INA ringleaders and RIN mutineers to escape punishment. The state governments of Alwar and Bharatpur connived at and assisted in what Liaquat Ali Khan, the secretary general of the Muslim League, described as a systematic attempt to wipe out the Meos of western Rajasthan.[29] It was an area which had been plagued by sporadic commotions for over a year, and both sides had been buying and manufacturing firearms, including home-made mortars, shells and sub-machine guns. There was a fresh wave of troubles in early May, accompanied by rumours that the Maharaja of Bharatpur intended to expel all Muslims and distribute their lands among the Hindus, to which end his regular troops joined Hindu mobs.[30] On 7 August, Alwar state forces and police armed with Bren guns and mortars combined with between 10,000 and 20,000 Hindus to besiege the Meo village of Silgaon. Two Meos, both former Indian army officers, attempted to negotiate, but they were shot as a prelude to a massacre. A fortnight or so later, and just after independence, a similar assault on a Meo village near Gurgaon was frustrated by a British officer commanding an Indian unit. He fired three and a half magazines from a Bren gun, killing about fifty of a 10,000-strong mob, which scattered.[31]

Delhi did not even admonish the rulers of Bharatpur and Alwar for misdemeanours which, a generation before, would have brought about their dethronement and exile. When he visited the disturbed region on 1 June, Sir Evan Jenkins found that less than 400 regular Indian troops had been deployed, a hopelessly inadequate force.[32] Mountbatten had accompanied Jenkins on his inspection of the stricken districts, seeing for himself the destruction and hearing how resolute officers in command of small units had been able to scatter the mobs with rifle fire. Two Congressmen, Patel, the Home Affairs Minister, and Sardar Baldev Singh, the Defence Minister, had also toured the area and once encountered Hindus setting fire to a village. The Viceroy hoped that such sights would inject them with a sense of urgency and make them amenable to his plan for partition.[33]

The recrudescence of the violence in Rajasthan during the early summer was in part a response to tales spread by Hindu and Sikh refugees from the Punjab, where there had been chronic disorder since the beginning of March. Communal violence had been expected for several years and police and military intelligence had monitored the stockpiling of weaponry, mostly bladed, and the mushrooming of political armies which were, in every respect, the counterpart of Hitler's Brown Shirts. Former soldiers (one in three of the Punjab's adult male population had served in the army) were prominent in these units, and, when the raids and massacres were under way, it was noticed that they had been planned with military precision.[34] There was no shortage of recruits or cash: police intelligence discovered that the League, Congress and the Sikh Akali party were secretly funding and encouraging groups responsible for the disturbances.[35] Many probably did not need money to kill their neighbours, for passions had been rising ever since November 1946, when Muslim refugees reached the Punjab with eyewitness accounts of how their fellow believers had been treated in Bihar.[36] Press photographs of corpses and charred pages from the Koran, together with clandestine wireless stations kept tempers close to boiling point.

But the miseries of the Punjab were not just the consequence of outraged individuals seeking revenge. They were, in great part, the result of a calculated use of terror by political parties whose objective, in the case of the League, was to secure complete dominance. At the end of February 1947, the League promoted a violent campaign of mass disobedience which was designed to destabilise a province which it coveted as part of Pakistan. Roughly 60 per cent of Punjabis were Muslims, but the League had never secured a monopoly in local political power, having been forced to share it with the Muslim Unionist party. This group, in tandem with the Sikhs and Hindus, formed the Punjabi government, which was the first target of League agitation. After vainly attempting to ban the private political armies, the coalition resigned on 2 March and no successor could be found. Control over the province passed into the hands of the governor, Sir Evan ('Jenks') Jenkins.

Jenkins was an upright, dedicated and thoroughly honourable proconsul who had joined the ICS in 1920, beginning his career in the Punjab. His experience and knowledge of the province were unequalled, and were reflected in his cogent and forthright analyses of its present problems. He refused to place expediency before principle and, in private, was contemptuous of the Muslim League leadership, admired the tenacity of the Sikhs, and found the hypocrisy of Congress leaders distasteful.[37] The League was well aware of his views and accused him of favouring its adversaries. If there were any heroes of the last days of the Raj, Jenkins would deserve a place among them: backed by a weary and often disheartened administration and police force, starved of soldiers and indifferently supported by Mountbatten, he did all that was humanly possible to prevent a catastrophe which cost hundreds of thousands of lives.

With the collapse of the elected government, the League unsuccessfully tried to cobble together a coalition. Simultaneously it launched a systematic campaign of intimidation, by which it hoped to assert its supremacy in the towns and countryside. Time was limited, for the British were scheduled to depart at the end of March 1948. As matters stood in March 1947, there was a distinct possibility that the Punjab might be bisected with the eastern segment attaching itself to India and the western to Pakistan. A truncated Punjab was wormwood to the League, adding to its economic disabilities, and was to be prevented at all costs. In any event, partition would be a complex business: 30 million Punjabis and Muslims, Sikhs and Hindu communities were everywhere intermingled.

The killing, rape and arson began on 4 March, and was at first concentrated in the cities and towns, with attacks on non-Muslims in Lahore, Amritsar, Multan, Rawalpindi, Jalandhar and Sialkot. Afterwards, the murder gangs spread out into the countryside. While the communal killings followed the pattern of the previous year, Jenkins was certain their motive was now political. In Rawalpindi and its hinterland: 'The underlying idea was to eliminate the non-Muslim fifth column; in Lahore the Muslims wanted to scare away the non-Muslim element in the population and so on.'[38] Inevitably, Hindus and Sikhs struck back and paid out their enemies in their own currency. Planning was methodical, with small bands of terrorists collecting at pre-arranged points before making their attacks. Their victims were stabbed or slashed to death, their property plundered and houses burned. Rape was a common instrument of coercion: it was a way of humiliating husbands, fathers and brothers which both demonstrated their powerlessness and, given local custom, violated their property. To avoid it, many women took their own lives, like the Sikhs in Rawalpindi, or were killed by their husbands.[39] In towns and cities, roving parties killed in what had now become the customary manner, stealing up on an isolated individual, stabbing him and then vanishing down alleyways. Bodies of assassins shifted quickly and melted away whenever troops or police approached, which made catching them hard. Nonetheless, the trouble was finally contained in the Rawalpindi district; patrols from the Norfolk regiment intercepted Muslim villagers armed with lathis as they approached the city and, together with police, opened fire on any mobs they encountered. By 25 March, army HQ at Rawalpindi reported that morale among British and Indian troops was high, with an absence of any communal feeling among the latter and a widespread revulsion against the communal violence. Why, soldiers asked, could people who had lived together for so long suddenly turn on each other?[40] Again, as in Rajasthan, Indian soldiers had remained true to the army.

The security forces had imposed what turned out to be a temporary armistice. After a period in which all sides re-grouped and re-armed, the massacres resumed on 10 May and worsened steadily for the next two months. Given enough troops, Jenkins believed that he could contain and eventually suppress the disturbances. On 21 May he saw Mountbatten at Simla and asked for at least 20,000 reinforcements, which would be needed if there was no co-operation from the party leaders.[41] Even if this was forthcoming, it was unlikely to have any impact in the Punjab. Jinnah, Nehru and Patel were already making appeals for calm and goodwill which were as sincere as they were ineffective. Only Gandhi, through personal appearances in which he used the full weight of his moral authority, had any success, and this was in Bihar and Calcutta. Jenkins suspected that when other politicians visited distressed areas they did so 'nominally as Members of the Central Government, but in fact as communal leaders'.[42]

The additional forces were refused by the Viceroy. His declaration on 2 June that the date of the transfer of power would be brought forward to 15 August, and the Punjab was to be divided between India and Pakistan, added immeasurably to the turmoil. On 24 June, Hindus and Sikhs appealed through Jenkins for a neutral frontier zone to be established immediately. This suggestion, which might have saved thousands of lives, was cursorily turned down on the grounds that Muslims would object.[43] They did not, for they were never asked. In the first week of August, when arrangements were in hand for the east–west division of the Punjab between India and Pakistan, 7,500 men (the Punjab Boundary Force) were allocated for the border area. Jenkins was appalled; he protested on 13 August that they were utterly inadequate to keep the peace in an area where 14 million people lived in nearly 18,000 villages.[44] Mountbatten knew exactly the nature and scope of the problem from the detailed and extensive reports collected by military and civil intelligence, and the assessors' accurate prognoses as to what would happen if preventive measures were not taken. These reports confirmed what he had seen at Gurgaon on 1 June and in other distressed areas on other, later occasions. When he recalled these experiences twenty-two years later, his strongest memory was of the warm welcome given to his wife by the refugees among whom she undertook charitable work.[45]

There were Cassandras among the Indian leadership. On 19 March, Patel had asked Wavell for martial law in the Punjab, but was refused since by this date the authorities were getting the upper hand. He repeated his request with the same result at the very end of May.[46] On 23 June, Jinnah pleaded with Mountbatten: 'I don't care whether you shoot Muslims or not, it has got to be stopped.' Nehru was of like mind, and internal security was the cause of hysterical exchanges during a Cabinet meeting two days later, during which Indian ministers slated the Viceroy for what they alleged was a British failure to maintain order. Mountbatten subsequently told London that

> the League started attacking me and saying that there would soon be no city left for them to inherit. Baldev [Singh] chimed in with a 'shoot everyone on sight' cry; upon which Patel pointed out that the only people shot by troops were the wretched householders who were forced into the streets during curfew hours when their houses were set on fire![47]

The session ended in a whimper, with a decision to form a local security commission in the Punjab with members drawn from all three communities. How this would stop the fighting, or save lives, was never made clear. What *was* clear, both then and as the Punjabi crisis became more acute, was that Mountbatten and the Indian leaders were primarily concerned with their public images. The search was for scapegoats rather than solutions.

The Punjab imbroglio was an irritating distraction for Mountbatten who, from the announcement of his final plan, was solely concerned with its implementation before his ten-week deadline. There was no room for flexibility of approach or interpretation, and momentum had to be sustained, come what may. Watching Mountbatten at work during this period, Shahid Hamid noted: 'He believes in giving no time to others to think, analyse or absorb.'[48] Such intellectual exercises did not come naturally to a man who believed that action was the essence of government. Internal security considerations were low on the viceregal list of priorities, which meant, ultimately, that the Punjabis would be free to kill, rape, steal and burn as they wished. In the meantime, two Indias had to be created, and the people, resources and treasures of the old divided equitably. Swift surgery was the only alternative to prolonged blood-letting – or so it seemed from the perspectives of Delhi and Simla.

IV

The first phases of the process of dividing and quitting passed remarkably smoothly. Attlee and the Cabinet rubber-stamped the viceregal plan and, when the time came for its implementation, the requisite legislation was rushed through Parliament in three days. India's political leaders and parties accepted the proposals, and measures were taken for the disputed regions – Bengal, the Punjab and the North-West Frontier Province – to decide their own destinies. By 17 July, and after a series of votes, the Bengal assembly agreed to split the province into two parts, with the western, including Calcutta, joining India and the eastern (from 1971 Bangladesh) joining Pakistan. The Punjabi assembly decided in like manner for an east–west partition, although there was a strong feeling among the Sikhs for their own, autonomous state. The future of the North-West Frontier Province was settled by a highly unsatisfactory referendum on 15–17 July, which was boycotted by Congress supporters, including Abdul Ghaffar Khan's Red Shirts. Only half the 573,000-strong electorate voted, with 289,000 opting for Pakistan and 2,900 for India.

There remained princely India, with its population of 100 million and over five hundred rulers whose ancestors had conceded British paramountcy in return for protection and co-operation. The states had been largely immune to pre-war nationalist agitation, although with the creation of the federation in 1935 many princes imagined that they were about to be thrown to the Congress wolves. During the war, the princes had been unsparing in their support of the war effort: the Maharaja of Travancore purchased a patrol boat for the RIN; the Nawab of Bhopal sold his American securities to pay for fighter aircraft; the Maharaja of Kashmir supplied eighteen field ambulances; and the Nizam of Hyderabad footed the bill for three squadrons of warplanes.[49] Three hundred thousand volunteers from the states had joined India's armed forces, and their rulers bought 180 million rupees' worth of war bonds. Yet the Raj which they had supported so generously seemed bent on seeking an accommodation with the politicians who had done all within their power to fracture the war effort. In November 1946, Hamidullah Khan, the Nawab of Bhopal, ruefully observed: 'The British seem to have abdicated power and what is worse have handed it over . . . to the enemies of all their friends.' He had in mind Congress, which was republican in spirit and determined to strip the princes of their sovereign powers. After consulting his court astrologer

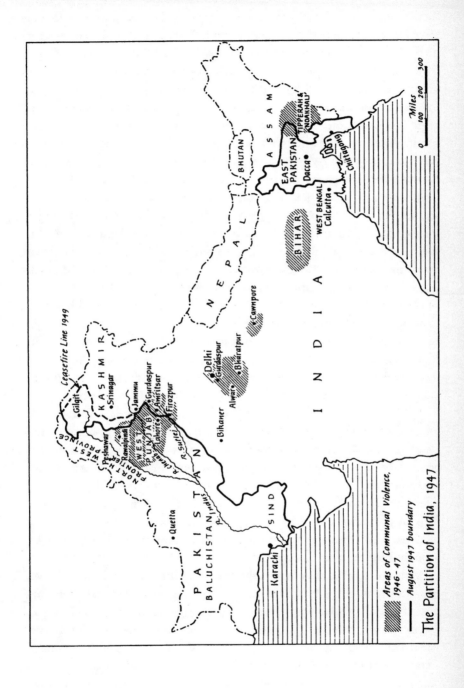

The Partition of India, 1947

Areas of Communal Violence, 1946–47

August 1947 boundary

in October 1946, Jeswant Rao Holkar, Maharaja of Indore, heard that: 'Guru has been the only protective planet in the Horoscope but he also becomes weak and evil from January 1947.' Between March and August malign influences hung over the maharaja.[50]

These foretokens proved remarkably accurate for Holkar and all his kind. Their ancestral loyalty to the Crown was now no more than a device to lever them from power. In March, George VI, the last King Emperor, asked his cousin, the last Viceroy, to persuade the princes to confront 'the inevitable' and inveigle them into whatever new state or states emerged. It was a task for which Mountbatten was ideally suited, since he had a taste for intrigue – many years later he was told by Field Marshal Lord Templar: 'You're so crooked, Dickie, if you swallowed a nail you'd shit a corkscrew.'[51] In private, the Viceroy was dismissive of the princes, whom he once characterised 'a bunch of nitwits' for not accepting democracy within their states and making terms with Congress.[52] In fact, for the past two years, the princes had been introducing reforms intended to transform their states into constitutional monarchies.[53]

The interests of the princes were upheld by an old-fashioned but fundamentally decent and honourable official, Sir Conrad Corfield, the head of the Political Department. He had little truck with India's professional politicians and sympathised with the princes' desire to keep them and their influence out of their domains. Aware of the drift of viceregal policy and unwilling to permit the states to be handed to Congress on a plate, Corfield discreetly approached the new Secretary of State, Lord Listowel. He secured a valuable concession: all the original agreements between the states and the Crown would lapse the day power was transferred to its successors. Neither India nor Pakistan would automatically inherit British paramountcy in so far as it affected the princes, who would become, in effect, independent rulers. Corfield also supervised the burning of four tons of documents held by his department which catalogued princely excesses and misdemeanours, to prevent them from being used by Congress for political blackmail.

Mountbatten had never taken the trouble to discover what precisely was meant by 'paramountcy' in the context of the princes. He had been outwitted by an official whom he consequently called 'a son-of-a-bitch'. Nehru was incensed to the point of apoplexy by Corfield's coup; it presaged a disunited India and was a reverse for Congress, which had intended to take over the states with the minimum of fuss. When the matter was discussed in Mountbatten's presence on 13 June, Nehru angrily accused

Corfield of dishonesty, and afterwards badgered the Viceroy to dismiss him as 'an enemy of India'.[54]

As usual, Mountbatten buckled under Nehru's pressure. Rather than legally unravel the problem of the princes' future status, the Viceroy resorted to machination. Effective control over the affairs of the states was removed from the Political Department and delivered into the self-interested hands of Congress and the League, who were permitted to form their own States Departments. The former were run by V. P. Menon and Sardar Patel, both of whom were prepared to employ underhand methods to prevent any princely declarations of independence. Stripped of British protection, the states, particularly the smaller ones, would be vulnerable to Congress subversion and, Menon imagined, it would be easy to engineer popular uprisings. Such devices might not be needed, for, as he rightly guessed, Mountbatten would offer himself as an accomplice in any political initiative designed to keep the states inside India or Pakistan.[55] Meanwhile, and with the encouragement of Corfield, the rulers of Travancore and Hyderabad (the largest, most populous and richest state) were entertaining daydreams of future independence. Far away to the north, and sensing the direction in which the wind was blowing, the Faqir of Ipi contemplated declaring himself amir of an autonomous Waziristan. He may have expected some assistance from Congress, to which he had contributed funds and support.[56]

Most of India's princes shared the apprehension of the Nawab of Bhopal. On 22 July he told Mountbatten:

> We wish to retain our relations with Great Britain, a monarchy, rather than to merge ourselves with an unfriendly political party which may tomorrow be ousted by Communist-dominated elements and which is almost certain to leave the British Commonwealth of Nations as soon as can be conveniently arranged. There is no guarantee of what the future Dominion of India will be. Are we to write out a blank cheque and leave it to the leaders of the Congress party to fill in the amount?

He concluded with a heartfelt appeal for an end to 'all this backhanded Balkan diplomacy' and the opening of 'negotiations on the level – fair and above board'. Mountbatten did not read the letter, but passed it to an experienced dabbler in 'backhanded Balkan diplomacy', V. P. Menon, for his advice.[57]

Menon drew up the form of accession, a document which asked each prince to attach his principality to either India or Pakistan before 15 August. Superficially open-ended, the paper was tantamount to a surrender of sovereignty, and acknowledgement that the new states had acquired paramountcy from the Raj. Despite the reservations of Listowel and the rest of the Cabinet, who believed the princes deserved more time, Mountbatten appealed to them on 25 July in terms which left no doubt that they had to sign immediately.[58] Like Chaucer's Pardoner, the Viceroy knew how to sell bogus wares through a mixture of flattery and threats. His most potent emotional weapon was his royal blood, and he used it skilfully, appearing before the princes adorned with all his decorations and warning them that if they refused his offer they would displease their King Emperor. Next came the menace: if the princes did not make terms with the politicians before the deadline, then would be deprived of the friendship of the Crown's representative in India and would be forbidden to buy modern weapons. There was time for clowning. When one diwan said he did not know his master's mind, Mountbatten picked up a glass paperweight, glanced at it and announced that it was a crystal ball which told him that the prince in question agreed to sign the accession document. The conjuror's patter worked; most present did sign, but with heavy hearts.

'For the Viceroy to use his influence, built upon the past exercise of paramountcy, in order to persuade trusting Rulers to accept such dubious propositions was, to say the least, unBritish,' observed Corfield some years later. During the next few days, the recalcitrant had to endure personal arm-twisting. After one session with Mountbatten, the Diwan of Gwalior told Corfield that he now understood how the Austrian chancellor, Dollfuss, must have felt after being harangued by Hitler. 'He had not expected to be spoken to like that by a British officer; after a moment's pause, he withdrew the word "British".'[59] By 15 August, and after some intensive persuasion by the Viceroy and V. P. Menon, only the rulers of Hyderabad, Kashmir and the tiny Kathiawari state of Junagadh had not caved in and attached themselves to either India or Pakistan. All kinds of sticks and carrots had been employed. At one stage in the negotiations with Hyderabad, Mountbatten was heartened to hear that the nizam might be swayed by his second son being accorded the title 'His Highness'.[60] More forceful measures were employed in Travancore, where an attempt was made to assassinate the diwan on 25 July against a background of threats of Congress-backed disturbances. On 1 August, a satisfied Viceroy reported to London that afterwards 'the States Peoples Organisation [i.e. V. P.

Menon and Sardar Patel] turned the heat full on and Travancore immediately gave in'. He added that Travancore's change of heart and the reasons for it have 'had a profound effect on all the other States and is sure to shake the Nizam [of Hyderabad]'.[61]

Milder but equally persuasive methods were employed by Mountbatten to tamper with the Boundary Commission. Its task was to draw a border between India and Pakistan which, as far as possible, would accommodate Hindus and Muslims. The Commission comprised two Muslim and two Hindu judges under the chairmanship of Sir Cyril Radcliffe, a jurist of the utmost integrity but with no Indian experience and a tendency to wilt under the heat. The five men were given five weeks in which to complete their task, a deadline which Radcliffe believed unrealistic.[61] Similarly unrealistic was the belief that the commissioners could undertake their evaluation in total secrecy. There were at least two of their staff who passed on secret information to Jinnah, Nehru and Menon, which enabled them to plead special causes to the theoretically impartial Mountbatten.

The most significant leak was made by Rao Bahadur Lala Adjudhia Khosla, the chairman of the Central Waterways, Irrigation and Navigation Committee, who delivered to Nehru details of the allocation of the districts of Firozpur, Zehra and Gurdaspur on the projected frontier between West (Pakistani) and East (Indian) Punjab. Called as a specialist witness, Khosla was concerned with the vital irrigation canal systems in these areas, and he revealed to Nehru that Radcliffe was contemplating handing Firozpur and Zehra to Pakistan and Gurdaspur to India. The former worried him: 'For the strategic and irrigation point of view it will be most dangerous to let Firozpur go to Pakistan.' The town was a natural defensive outpost, for it controlled the only bridge across the upper Sutlej, which was the natural barrier between India and Pakistan. Furthermore, the water supplies to Bikaner and East Punjab could be imperilled by whoever gained Firozpur. For these reasons, Khosla urged Nehru to approach Mountbatten, a suggestion which throws considerable light on the Viceroy's reputation for even-handedness.[63]

Another recipient of information about the future of Firozpur was the Maharaja of Bikaner, who wired Mountbatten on 10 August to protest against a threat to his state's life-line. He asked the Viceroy to give an interview to his diwan and Kanwan Sain, his chief engineer, who would, presumably, explain the technicalities. Years afterwards, Sain claimed that the meeting took place, but no record of it has survived among the official papers. All that remains are messages to Nehru and the maharaja in which

Mountbatten insisted he had no power to intervene.[64] He said the same to Liaquat Ali Khan who, on 11 August, had also got wind of the proposals for the disposal of East Punjab's water supplies.[65]

The truth was that for all his denials, Mountbatten was meddling in the Commission's business. On 9 August, one of his private secretaries, Walter Christie, noted in his diary that the Viceroy had to be restrained from interfering with the territorial award and was overstepping the limits of his authority.[66] Rumours to this effect also reached Shamid Hamid.[67] In the meantime, Jenkins had requested a draft of the Commission's map of the bisected Punjab so that he could deploy troops to forestall the commotions which were bound to occur on either side of the new border. One of the maps was flown to Lahore on 10 August, and it plainly showed the Firozpur and Zehra districts within Pakistan. The following day, Jenkins was instructed by telegram to 'eliminate the salient' and thereby place the region inside India.[68] Something hugger-mugger had been happening behind the scenes, but what?

This murky business was finally explained in 1992 by Christopher Beaumont, who had been secretary to the Commission. Nehru, it appears, was being kept well abreast of the commissioners' deliberations, not only by Khosla but also by V. P. Ayer, an Indian civil servant attached to the Commission. Forewarned, he was able to induce Mountbatten to exert pressure on Radcliffe, first indirectly through Menon and then in person. On the evening of 11 August, Menon tried to see Radcliffe secretly, but was quite correctly turned away by Beaumont. The following day, Radcliffe took luncheon with Ismay and Mountbatten, and the same evening a new map had been prepared for publication with the disputed districts as part of India.[69] It was a day after Jenkins had been instructed to disregard the old one, which indicates that Mountbatten felt absolutely confident in his ability to change Radcliffe's mind.

The snag was that the original chart had been circulated by Jenkins and, after it had been redrawn, Pakistani politicians were furious at what they considered to be a piece of flagrant gerrymandering by Mountbatten.[70] This was why, on 2 April 1948, Mountbatten wrote to Ismay to recall the meeting with Radcliffe and, to jog his memory, offered his recollections of what had passed. He also asked the general to burn the letter. According to the former Viceroy, Firozpur and the network of waterways had been briefly mentioned, but nothing was said which might have made Radcliffe reconsider his decision. 'My recollection of events is very different from yours' was Ismay's enigmatic answer.[71] From what has emerged since, it is clear that Mountbatten had demanded a radical alteration to Radcliffe's award in the interest of India and at the insistence of Nehru. His motives were those of expediency and a wish to appease the future rulers of India, who would be the losers if the Firozpur and Zehra districts joined Pakistan. Bikaner had threatened to transfer his state to Pakistan.[72] Most importantly, the area represented a bridgehead beyond the Sutlej, from which Pakistani forces could strike southwards towards Delhi in the event of war between the two successor states. Military considerations were believed to have been behind the delivery of the Gurdaspur region to India, for it provided overland access to Kashmir, whose Hindu maharaja had yet to decide whether to take his state and its predominantly Muslim population into India or Pakistan.[73] Not surprisingly, the leaders of the fledgling Pakistan believed that the Viceroy had worked tirelessly behind the scenes to pile up disadvantages for a nation which he had once likened to a Nissen hut, a temporary structure which would soon vanish. India, by comparison, he saw as a strong and durable building.

There was a paradox here. In his dealing with the princes, and backstairs intrigue over the splitting of the Punjab, Mountbatten had somehow reverted to that combination of dissembling and coercion which had prevailed in the time of Clive and Hastings. The moral tone which the Raj had acquired and so carefully preserved was one of the last of its trappings to be discarded.

V

Pomp remained to the end. The Viceroy was determined above all things that the Raj should end with a flourish, and he and Campbell-Johnson went to considerable efforts to stage-manage the independence day ceremonies. Whatever was happening elsewhere in India, a dignified façade would be maintained for the newsreel men, photographers and journalists who had flocked to Karachi and Delhi to witness the physical transfer of power. On 13 August the Mountbattens flew to Karachi where, in Campbell-Johnson's unintentionally revealing words, Government House was decorated 'just like a Hollywood film set'.[74] There were speeches at the official banquet that evening and Jinnah, now Governor-General of the dominion of Pakistan, proposed the King Emperor's health. His reign had seen, the Quaid observed, a voluntary surrender of imperial power 'unknown in the whole history of the world'. The next day saw that power formally terminated at a session of the new Pakistani parliament, during which Jinnah reminded his audience of the ancient Muslim tradition of religious tolerance. He then escorted the Mountbattens back to the aerodrome. As the viceregal aircraft flew over the Punjab, large fires could be seen below.[75]

Astrologers had chosen 15 August as a propitious day for India to begin its independent existence. Just before midnight, Nehru addressed the legislative assembly: 'Long years ago we made a tryst with destiny, and now the time comes when we shall redeem our pledge . . . At the stroke of the midnight hour, when the world sleeps, India will awake to life and freedom.' Indians in Delhi awoke to a day of colourful and cheerful festivities. First came the splendid ceremony in the Durbar Hall of Government House, where Mountbatten appeared in uniform and his wife in gold lamé for his installation as Governor-General. Next were the speeches in the legislative assembly and then the raising and lowering of flags. The crowds were immense, curious and good-natured. The Pathé newsreel described them as 'wild with joy' and showed pictures of the Mountbattens walking informally among Indians during the afternoon. The scene illustrated what the commentator called the new Governor-General's 'friendly, understanding manner' which had made Indian independence possible. In the evening there was a huge party in Government House which lasted until the early hours.

The cordiality which had marked independence day evaporated on the 16th, when the decisions of the Boundary Commission were announced. Mountbatten had expected angry reactions, and had postponed the declaration so that the two days of celebrations would not be marred. When the Indian Defence Committee met in Delhi on 16 August and heard accounts of escalating disturbances in the Punjab, the Governor-General wondered whether he had been wrong to defer publication of the awards.[76] Auchinleck thought so. After his visit to devastated Lahore on the 14th, the commander-in-chief reported: 'The delay in announcing the award of the Boundary Commission is having a most disturbing and harmful effect. It is realised of course that the announcement may add fresh fuel to the fire, but lacking an announcement, the wildest rumours are current, and are being spread by mischief-makers of whom there is no lack.'[77]

Auchinleck's bleak account of the situation in and around Lahore confirmed the urgent messages sent to Delhi by Jenkins and local commanders during the past three days. All described the spread of terror, hideous atrocities and the impending collapse of order throughout the region.[78] Military intelligence had also been recording the build-up of violence, although its files covering the vital period between 11 August and 11 September have somehow been mislaid.[79] The Auk was prepared to take immediate and overdue action. On 14 August he ordered two additional brigades – one Indian, the other Pakistani – to reinforce the woefully undermanned Punjab Boundary Force under Major-General Thomas Rees.[80]

The upsurge in communal violence in the Punjab was not a bolt from the blue. Mountbatten had expected it, although he admitted he was surprised by its scale.[81] This is difficult to understand, given the way in which the nature of communal disorders had changed during the past year. Spontaneous eruptions still occurred, triggered either by friction at a village or street level, or by an urge for vengeance. But the upheavals in Rajasthan and the Punjab in the early summer indicated that the killings, rapes and arson had been methodically planned and undertaken by groups which possessed a command structure, modern weaponry and an intelligence network. Just how sophisticated communal terrorism had become was revealed by Gerald Savage of the Punjab CID to the Viceroy, Jinnah, Liaquat Ali Khan and Patel on 5 August. Savage's investigations into the growing Sikh nationalist movement had led to the arrest on 4 June of Pritam Singh, an ex-INA man and Japanese-taught saboteur, who had been landed in southern India during the war. Under interrogation, Pritam Singh and other terrorists revealed the existence of an underground organisation which included trained bomb-makers, fire-raisers and railway saboteurs. Firearms and grenades were being purchased or covertly obtained from serving Sikh soldiers and stockpiled. Plans were in hand to derail trains and assassinate Jinnah in Karachi on 15 August. The Raja of Faridkot and Tara Singh, leader of the Sikh Akali party, were implicated in these conspiracies, and Mountbatten wisely instructed Jenkins to arrest all leading Sikh activists before independence day.[82] The governor's nerve failed him, and he decided to leave these men at liberty rather than risk further unrest, although it is hard to see how it could have got worse.[83]

Revenge against the Muslims was, Savage believed, the motive behind the Sikh plans, although the campaign in terrorism coincided with demands for an independent Sikh state. Adopting the well-tried methods of Congress and the League, Sikhs began a series of mass protests at the beginning of August which appeared to be the first stage of a coup. In the end, the only way in which militant Sikhs, Muslims and Hindus could be brought to heel was by the unwavering use of the iron fist. But who would apply it?

The Punjab crisis came at a time when neither the British nor the Indian army was in a position to take the kind of action that was needed. British troops and RAF squadrons had been scheduled to begin the evacuation of India on 15 August and to withdraw swiftly. Neither Mountbatten nor Nehru wished them to have any operational functions, including policing, between then and their final departure in February 1948.[84] Jinnah was against too much haste and would have liked to have kept some units for dealing with tribal unrest on the frontier. Arrangements were made for some detachments to stand by in readiness to protect British residents in Delhi, Karachi, Bombay and Calcutta, if the need arose.[85] It is impossible to know whether the presence of British forces would have prevented the communal massacres of August and September. Sir Khizr Hayat Khan, the former Muslim Unionist Prime Minister of the Punjab, believed that they could have done so. British soldiers, he claimed, 'didn't know a Muslim from a Hindu, they wouldn't shoot for fun and whatever they did, they would be trusted'.[86] Perhaps so; but the experience of Major J. L. Collard and a handful of unarmed men from the Green Howards suggested otherwise. They were on Delhi station on 8 September when they witnessed a gang of Sikhs killing some Muslims. The major approached one Sikh and asked him: 'Are you mad? And even if you had suffered in the Punjab, would you, if bitten by a mad dog, bite back?' Swearing profusely, the Sikh warned him to mind his own business or else he would 'get it as well'.[87] Of course, he might not have been so truculent had the British soldiers been carrying firearms.

As Mountbatten had intended, Indian and Pakistani troops would deal with what, from 15 August, was a problem for their governments. The operational implications of an essentially political decision were never carefully analysed. On 3 June, Listowel, taking his cue from Mountbatten, told the Cabinet's India committee that there was 'a considerable risk of further disturbances' during the process of petition. Six days after, he assured them: 'The Viceroy has, however, been authorised to take the strongest measures against any outbreak of communal warfare as a result of the recent announcement.'[88] In the same vein, Mountbatten promised Dr Maulana Azad that tanks and aircraft would be deployed against troublemakers.[89] In the event, willpower exceeded wherewithal; on 24 June the Viceroy confessed to Listowel that during the crucial period before and after partition the Indian army would be unable to render much assistance to the civil power. The majority of units would be in the middle of the complicated process of dividing.[90] Slavish adherence to Mountbatten's time-table meant that when the crisis broke in the Punjab, Auchinleck lacked the reserves to handle it.[91]

By 15 August, the disorientated and demoralised Punjabi police could no longer be relied upon to keep order; three-quarters were Muslims and, like everyone else trapped in the frontier zones, they were anxious to get themselves and their families across the boundaries into friendly territory. Only the army could maintain the peace. Contrary to some pessimistic analyses, Indian soldiers continued to act dispassionately whenever they had been called upon to disperse sectarian mobs or engage murder gangs. These rarely had any stomach for a fight. On 13 August, a Sikh Jatha (war band) armed with machine-guns was intercepted by tanks and scattered after sixty-one had been killed.[92] Elsewhere, disciplined and determined resistance, often by heavily outnumbered units, drove off marauding bands.

But the emotional strain on Indian troops was enormous. After four weeks of continuous action, Major-General Rees reported that his Punjabi soldiers had shown extraordinary moral resilience. As a result, 'only in those areas in which the P[unjab] F[rontier] F[orce] was present was there any semblance of security, law and order'.[93] Among the many horrific duties they had had to undertake was to rescue Muslim women who had been captured by Sikhs in Amritsar on 15 August, paraded naked, raped and then murdered. A few were saved and carried to sanctuary in the Golden Temple by Sikhs who had not abandoned their humanity.

The superhuman and courageous exertions of Rees and his men were not enough to prevent one of this century's most appalling human catastrophes. The statistics collected by the intelligence analysts reflected its scale: on 14 September, it was calculated that 1.25 million non-Muslims were on the move to East Punjab, while 898,000 Muslims were heading for West Punjab. The last figure rose to over a million within a week.[94] Refugees who travelled by foot in huge straggling convoys were preyed upon by gangs who tracked them like wolves, occasionally pouncing and then pulling back. Fugitives who travelled by train risked derailment followed by ambush. Assassins would sometimes hide among the passengers, concealing their knives and swords, and at a pre-arranged moment pull the communication cord. The halted carriages would then be attacked by their accomplices who had been waiting by the track.

In all, 5.5 million Hindus and Sikhs fled to India during the autumn and winter of 1947–48, and 5.8 million Muslims fled to Pakistan. It is impossible to calculate exactly how many died during this mass displacement. As with past Indian famines, the machinery did not exist to keep an exact tally of deaths, and in many cases the murder gangs buried their victims. The most credible estimates were obviously those made by the men on the spot: Sir Francis Mudie, the governor of West Punjab, estimated that 500,000 Muslims died trying to enter his province, while the British High Commissioner in Karachi put the full total at 800,000. This seems plausible given that, on 25 August, Indian intelligence sources in West Punjab calculated that at least 198,000 people had been killed in the provinces and a further 100,000 forcibly converted to Islam.[95] This makes a nonsense of the claim by Mountbatten and his partisans that only 200,000 were killed, but it does wholly substantiate his detractors' counter-claim that at least a million lost their lives.[96]

VI

Debates over digits cannot change the nature or the compass of the tragedy which occurred in the Punjab. They are, however, a reminder that Mountbatten's judgement over the partition of the province and the measures taken for local security were subsequently severely criticised. The hunt for scapegoats was quickly under way. On 10 September, the Pakistan Prime Minister, Liaquat Ali Khan, issued a communiqué to other Commonwealth governments in which he accused Mountbatten and Auchinleck of indifference towards the communal problem and what he described as an attempt to create a Sikh state on 9 August.[97] Tara Singh, the Sikh militant, charged the British with deliberately waging war on his people for their refusal to support the Muslim League.[98]

Tension had reached such a pitch that in mid-September the War Office commissioned a report on the possible course of a future Indo-Pakistani war. The border massacres apart, an obvious bone of contention was Kashmir, whose Hindu maharaja, Hari Singh, was still undecided about whether to plump for India or Pakistan. The latter engineered a *coup de main* on 22 October, in which Pathan 'volunteers' led by ex-INA men invaded Kashmir at the 'invitation' of some Muslim rebels. A fresh front was opened in the religious war, with killings of Hindus and mass kidnapping of women, often by tribesmen, Pakistani troops and police. Many of the victims were sold as additional brides to Muslim men; it was said that one member of the Karachi parliament had 500 women in captivity for this purpose.[99] As Muslim irregulars converged on Srinagar, Kashmir's capital, the maharaja hurriedly opted for India. Indian troops were rushed into the state, and after some heavy fighting gained the upper hand by the end of the year.

Jinnah had wanted to throw the Pakistani army into the conflict, but had been warned off by Auchinleck after some tense moments. The Auk's most compelling argument was that Pakistan was too weak to engage India; according to the partition award, 36 per cent of the Indian army (140,000 men) had gone to Pakistan and 270,000 to India. The balance of arms, equipment and supplies had gone heavily in India's favour and, most importantly, Pakistan had only received 17 per cent of India's sterling balances. The £147 million released to it was soon gobbled up in arms purchases for the country, which was forced to spend 70 per cent of its income on its armed forces and a further 18 per cent on administration.[100] Nonetheless, Pakistan pressed its claim to Kashmir, mounting a second invasion in the spring of 1948. The strategists' nightmare had come true; until its highly profitable alliance with the United States in 1954, Pakistan was a fragile, militarily and financially over-extended buffer state. India, by contrast, looked sturdier, although it too was forced to increase its armed forces and spend some of its sterling reserves on armaments and aircraft. The first political repercussion of partition was an arms race which has lasted to the present day.

VII

At a meeting of the Imperial General Staff on 3 October, Field Marshal Montgomery expressed his displeasure with how Mountbatten had wound up the Raj. 'He's made a mess of things. I'll write and tell him.'[101] As early as 10 August, Ismay had been disturbed by how events were turning out; he wrote to his wife that the British were departing from India 'with all our work destroyed and leaving behind anarchy and misery and measureless slaughter'. Two months afterwards, he had come to believe that Mountbatten had failed to show that quintessential viceregal quality – impartiality.[102] The Viceroy's relations with Auchinleck had been fraught since the end of July, when the former had sided with Nehru, who had accused the commander-in-chief of 'dabbling in politics'. Rather than confront the Auk with the charge, Mountbatten had asked his subordinate Savory to deliver the reproof.[103] An upright man, of formidable integrity,

Auchinleck was totally dedicated to India and its army. Devotion to the public service overruled private emotion, but for once the Field Marshal let his feelings get the better of him. When Mountbatten offered him an honour for his part in ending the Raj, the Auk told him he would take nothing for what had been 'the most painful and distasteful episode of my career'.[104] When it was all over, he came to Montgomery's conclusion that the Viceroy had made 'a mess of things'.[105]

Even Attlee briefly succumbed to the general mood of censure on the man he had sent in to save the game in India. 'Was it too quick?' he asked Lieutenant-General Savory when they discussed Indian affairs at Number 10 on 23 October.[106] The soldier did not record his answer. He had served gallantly with the Indian army since 1913, and his affection for the Raj was as strong as his faith in its virtues. On 15 August he had spoken sadly of the wretched state of India, cleft and sliding into anarchy. 'Is this to be the cul-mination of the British rule in India and the fulfilment of our great mission?' he asked colleagues at HQ.[107] Savory left India in December in the same sombre mood. He believed that nine-tenths of Indians secretly wished to have the British back, but the Raj had ceased to 'govern' in 1935 and thereafter it had been merely a matter of time before its bluff was called. As for the events of March to August, the British 'tried to make it appear to the Indians, the world and to *ourselves* that [we] were committing a Noble Deed'. Mountbatten had, he feared, 'forced the pace *too* much'.[108]

Savory, like the rest of Mountbatten's critics, was probably right to question his decision to end the Raj in seventy-three days and to stick unswervingly to a time-table which events revealed to be dangerously unrealistic. His treatment of the princes was shabby. Their new master proved tough and intolerant: the Maharaja of Jodhpur was ordered to cut down on whisky and women; the Raja of Faridkot was banned from going to Australia; various small states were annexed; and Hyderabad was occupied by the Indian army in September 1948. As for the slaughter in the Punjab, greater efforts should have been made to work out an adequate exigency plan in anticipation of a disaster which was plainly waiting to happen.

And yet to condemn Mountbatten for these oversights and underhand manoeuvres is to judge him by the vision and high moral standards of, say, Curzon or Irwin. They were architects and he was a demolition engineer, the nature of whose work demanded a very different outlook and meth-ods. In so far as it is a capacity to get things done, political power had all but passed into Indian hands by March 1947. Quite simply, the last Viceroy lacked the prestige, authority and resources of his predecessors and, therefore, placed himself in the hands of those who possessed all these assets – Nehru and the Congress high command. He found them congenial partners and performed his duties according to his lights; the trouble was that he had too much to say for himself and no humility.

Epilogue

What had ended at midnight on 15 August 1947? Certainly not the Raj which Sir Winston Churchill had known fifty years before and had subsequently defended with all his emotional energy. This had withered away after 1919 and been replaced by a system of government shaped by Westminster politicians, run by Indians and supervised by a dwindling band of British officials. Whatever its final form, Churchill had nothing but praise for the Raj; it had been 'a monument worthy of the respect of nations' and the 'finest achievement' of his countrymen.

All this was true, up to a point. But the Raj also represented a bargain. For over a hundred years India had underpinned Britain's status as a global power and provided it with markets, prestige and muscle. Ever since sepoys had been sent to Egypt in 1800 to evict the detritus of Napoleon's army, Indian manpower had upheld British pretensions in the Middle East, East Africa and the Far East. Millions of Indians had volunteered to serve Britain in both world wars. Veterans of the Second, many of whom served in Italy and afterwards settled in Britain, are justly proud of their exertions in the cause of freedom. Their feelings were voiced by Sergeant-Major Rajinder Singh in November 1993, when he and his comrades were lamenting the election of a British National Party candidate in an East End council election. 'I am a proud and loyal man,' the veteran remarked. 'We had much faith in this country. In the war, I thought it was time to help Britain to save democracy and fight fascism.'[1] Like many other Indian ex-servicemen, he was sad that his and his comrades' efforts have been largely forgotten in Britain.

India's own liberation signalled the end of Britain as a world power. Its international standing had already declined beyond the point of recovery. The recent, Herculean war effort had only been possible thanks to American credit, and the loss of Singapore had shown in the most dramatic way that Britain could no longer uphold its claims to be a major Asian power. India had always been the keystone of the British Empire, and once it had been removed the structure swiftly fell apart, as Victorian statesmen and Churchill (who was one of them in spirit) had foretold. And yet in the quarter-century after Indian independence, British politicians, diplomats and strategists talked themselves into believing that their country was still a world power and behaved accordingly. In fact, it was downhill all the way with some awkward bumps: the British were successively evicted from Persia and Egypt and an attempt to reverse fate ended disastrously with the Suez débâcle in 1956. Within the next decade, Britain's Far-Eastern and African empire had been dismantled with little heartache. Revealingly, the African National Congress had been modelled on its Indian counterpart, and many African nationalist leaders looked to India for example and encouragement.

The end of the Raj also marked the final settlement of a bargain. In return for its moment of greatness on the world stage, the Raj had offered India regeneration on British terms. It had been the most perfect expression of what Britain took to be its duty to humanity as a whole. Its guiding ideals had sprung from the late-eighteenth and early-nineteenth-century Evangelical Enlightenment which had dreamed of a world transformed for the better by Christianity and reason. The former made little headway in India, but the latter, in the form of Western education and the application of science, did. No one could guess how the long the task of India's moral and physical regeneration might take, nor were there any illusions as to the obstacles in the way, not least of which was the reluctance of many Indians to have their world remoulded. For all their faults, and the worst were spasms of impatience and high-handedness, those who set about the remaking of India showed remarkable dedication to their ideals and the welfare of its peoples. Figures such as Metcalfe, Elphinstone, Sir Henry and Sir John Lawrence, Curzon and Irwin represent the highest ideals of public service, and they and many others deserve respect and admiration. In the course of the everyday administration of a country which many of its rulers found hard to comprehend, misunderstandings frequently arose, sensibilities were bruised and Indians were too often made to feel inadequate or patronised. Nanny may well have known best, but this did not make her monopoly of rectitude welcome or bearable. Moreover, by the beginning of this century, a small but significant body of Indians believed that they and the rest of their countrymen no longer needed her ministrations.

Today, the principles which underlay the Raj are unfashionable. We dislike the notion of one people assuming superiority over another and re-ordering their lives. Imperialism, however well-meaning it may have been (and it was not always), is a discredited creed and the benefits it brought are either overlooked or devalued. By contrast, and often in the teeth of much recent experience, national self-determination is considered to be a source of human happiness. The right of peoples to decide their own future is inviolate, irrespective of whether they choose wisely or whether the government which emerges is just, honest and humane. Late-twentieth-century political correctness has been added to post-colonial guilt syndromes and the residual Marxism which still lurks on many university campuses, with the result that hardly any British, Indian or American historians have a good word to say about the Raj, or, for that matter, any other type of colonial government. At their poor best, colonial régimes are portrayed as expressions of incompetent paternalism, and at their worst as oppressive, racialist, exploitative and the source of the Third World's present woes. The balance is slowly being adjusted, not least because the recent history of so many of Europe's colonies has been a saga of a decline into tyranny, chaos and internecine war from which they seem unable to rescue themselves.

A past shaped by foreigners, however well-intentioned, can be an incubus for the descendants of those who were once imperial subjects. It does not foster national pride and self-confidence because it is a reminder of submission and collaboration. This explains why, within days and sometimes hours of independence, Indians and Pakistanis emancipated themselves from their recent history by a systematic assault on the statues of British monarchs, generals and proconsuls which overlooked public places. Like the Romans, the British were addicted to setting the seal on their conquests with sculpture. The offending figures were hauled down and exiled to obscure places where they now crumble away. Fifty years on, the exorcism continues. In 1995, the Gandhi dynasty surplanted the House of Windsor in Delhi, where Connaught Place (named after the Duke of Connaught, one of Queen Victoria's younger sons, also of London grill fame) became Indira and Rajiv Chowk (square). For some Indians the change of name was ridiculous. 'What are we going to tell our children?' one protester asked. 'That the British never ruled here? Then how did the

English language come here – from the Russians?'[2]

British monuments which owed their existence to the Raj have survived undisturbed, although fewer and fewer people now understand why they were erected. Havelock, the hero of Lucknow, still stands on his plinth in a corner of Trafalgar Square and Roberts, the hero of Afghanistan, sits astride his stone charger in Kelvingrove Park, Glasgow, although their deeds have been forgotten. Church memorials are a reminder of the human cost of the Raj. None more so than that in St Giles Cathedral, Edinburgh, which records how 488 soldiers, 47 wives and 124 children of the 78th Highlanders died from cholera on the 'banks of the Indus' between September 1844 and March 1845. And then of course there are the Indian words which have become embedded in the English language: words like bungalow, jodhpurs, verandah, gymkhana and pyjamas reflected the everyday world of the sahibs, while from that of the British soldier came 'blighty' and 'dillaly'. The former was a corruption of the Hindi *bilati*, meaning country; the latter derived from Deolali, where there was a hospital for the deranged victims of sunstroke.

Modern British perceptions of the Raj depend more on literature and cinema than history. Kipling, Forster, John Masters and Paul Scott command audiences made larger through the adaptation of their works for the cinema and television. The latter have generated a popular nostalgia, at least for the external trappings the Raj. This is not surprising, for the screen Raj is striking in its authenticity, bringing to life, as it were, those photographs of sahibs and memsahibs taking tea on well-groomed lawns with servants hovering in the background. Equally vivid are two post-imperial adventure films: an exciting version of Kipling's short story, *The Man Who Would Be King* (1975) and Ismail Merchant's visually stunning production of John Masters's *The Deceivers* (1988). Perhaps the best, and certainly the most thoughtful, cinematic evocation of the Raj is Satyajit Ray's *The Chess Players* (1977), which chronicles the political legerdemain which preceded the deposition of the last king of Awadh in 1853. While the Company's officials plot, two zamindars indulge their insatiable passion for chess to the point of forsaking their wives. They withdraw with their board and pieces to a village, squabble, and are suddenly made aware of how they and their fellow countrymen have been checkmated by an infinitely cunning and ruthless adversary. As the film ends, they watch, stunned and powerless, as the Company's army advances into Awadh. The parable is simple but still potent: Indian divisions, particularly those of the ruling class, had facilitated British conquest.

Curiosity and a taste for the exotic draw more and more British visitors to India, but not to bask in the afterglow of the Raj or marvel at its works. The tourist is directed towards the architecture and artefacts which are the products of a purely Indian genius, created before the dominance of the British. Naturally Indians wish to draw attention to the achievements of their own rather than someone else's civilisation. Nevertheless, the mark of the Raj can still be detected. The cast-iron railway bridge across the Jumma at Agra may not evince the same gasps of admiration as the nearby Taj Mahal, but it is a monument worthy of respect. More so, perhaps, because the mausoleum was a token of the self-indulgence of a Mughal emperor who was able to harness the resources and energies of his people to satisfy a whim. By contrast, the severely utilitarian bridge reminds us that the British set considerable store by using public funds for the public good, and acted accordingly.

The Raj did bring benefits to the Indian people, and its importance to the successor states of India, Pakistan and Bangladesh (former East Pakistan, which became independent in 1971) cannot be overstated. Whether they like the fact or not, these countries are what they are now because they were once governed by Britain and brought directly into contact with British ideas, values, learning and technology. The process of exposure and absorption was slow and uneven; old faiths, customs and habits of mind proved remarkably durable, and outlasted a Raj which lacked either the capacity or will to uproot them. There were enduring features of British rule, too. Attachment to the democratic idea remains strong in India, Pakistan and Bangladesh. Although this is not the place to chart the political and economic fortunes of the states which followed the Raj, it is worth saying that democracy has proved exceptionally popular and resilient. In Pakistan it has survived a series of military autocracies, and in India, eighteen months of Indira Gandhi's personal rule, during which she earned the mocking title 'the last viceroy'. None of these excursions into authoritarianism proved successful: Indians, Pakistanis and Bangladeshis remain convinced that their country's social and economic problems can only be solved by elected governments. At the same time, there is a consciousness of what constitutes good and honest administration, and the periodic outbursts against corruption in all three countries are a reflection that their people judge their officials by standards laid down during British rule.

Any balance sheet of the Raj would not be complete without a reference to its public utilities. When it ended, the sub-continent possessed what today would be called a communications 'infrastructure' which included over 40,000 miles of railways. The last all-India census, undertaken in 1941, revealed that just under 8 per cent of the population was literate. By 1961 this figure had risen to 21 per cent in India, and in 1991 it stood at 52 per cent in India and 34 per cent in Pakistan. Enormous headway has been made in education by the successor states, but it could not have been achieved without foundations laid down during the Raj, and the same holds true in public health. Likewise, the criminal and civil law codes of the entire sub-continent are a legacy of the Raj. When the British measured what they considered to be the physical and moral progress of India, they also revealed how much remained to be accomplished. During the war, British servicemen, among others, were dismayed by how little seemed to have been achieved: chronic poverty was endemic and famine always just round the corner.

The Raj's critics expected too much. It was never a totalitarian state which could do what it liked when it chose. Throughout its history the Raj operated under powerful constraints. These were the costs of its armed forces and administration, the amount of revenue it could raise and the need to conciliate Indian opinion. Behind the Raj's impressive façade lay a mass of compromises and accommodations made by a government which was always well aware that it lacked the manpower and resources to ride roughshod over its subjects' wishes. The 1857 Mutiny proved this, and Gandhi's non-co-operation campaigns confirmed the point. Nearly a third of Indians were subjects of the Raj only by association, being governed by their own princes who had chosen to become partners in government. The Raj could not have lasted as long as it did without the co-operation of millions of lesser Indians who filled the ranks of its army, undertook its bureaucratic drudgery and served in its perpetually undermanned police force. In the countryside where most Indians lived, often without ever seeing a European, village headmen, chowkidahs and a legion of fiscal and transport functionaries kept the machinery of government ticking over. In return they received local power and status. Such figures are easily overlooked, but they were the bedrock on which the Raj rested.

The existence of a substantial body of Indians who actively co-operated with alien rulers is a source of unease for modern Indian, Pakistani and Bangladeshi historians. How does one promote a sense of national identity in the knowledge that, during the recent past, the great majority of one's countrymen either submitted to or were the accomplices of foreign rulers? One answer is to elevate those who, often for private rather than 'national'

reasons, opposed the Raj. Thus the Rani of Jhansi has a splendid eques-
trian statue on the site of her cremation in Gwalior. Tikendrajit Singh, the
ambitious dynast who violently ejected the British resident from Manipur
in 1891, becomes a 'freedom fighter' in the Indian *Dictionary of National
Biography*, where it is claimed that his state needed a very strong, rather
ruthless ruler to withstand the Raj. Home-grown tyranny, it seems, is
better than the imported government, and it is hard to see how an aristocrat fighting for his privileges was a proto-nationalist. Nevertheless, it is
reassuring for Indians to know that there were men and women who
resisted the Raj, and they honour their spirit in the same way as Boadicea's
has been in England.

Twentieth-century nationalist leaders qualify more easily for the national
Pantheon. Moreover, although their arguments were grounded in British
political and legal philosophy, men like Gandhi and Nehru possessed distinctly Indian qualities. Here lay their immense strength: they could reason
with their rulers in terms the latter understood and simultaneously appeal
to the Indian masses. And yet, and this is perhaps the greatest irony of the
Raj, both men argued passionately for the preservation of India's integrity,
something which was a direct result of British rule. It is of course right and
proper that Gandhi, Nehru and Jinnah should be revered as national heroes,
but it should not be forgotten that each in his way was a product of political and intellectual traditions which had been imparted into their country
by the British.

Quite simply the Raj cannot be disinvented. It happened, and its consequences, from a passion for cricket to a faith in democracy, remain
deeply rooted in Indian soil. No one can ever know what course Indian
history would have followed if the British had not intervened so decisively in its eighteenth-century power struggles. Would a dominant,
centralising power have emerged from among the greater Indian states?
Would it have been Hindu or Muslim? Most importantly, how long
would it have lasted, and could it have resisted its neighbours? The history of independent states in Asia during the nineteenth century suggests
strongly that India might have endured some form of European domination, as Persia and China did, or direct occupation like Indo-China.
Would a non-British India, united or fragmented, have attracted the
investment which financed its railways, or would a native entrepreneur-
ial class have emerged with the capital which was ploughed into
industrialisation during the two world wars? And would hundreds of
thousands of Indians, Pakistanis and Bangledeshis have settled in Britain

to enrich it with their talents and, among things, make curry its most popular dish?

Subjunctive history is more than a diverting pastime, for it reminds us how much the present pivots on the past. For better or worse (and on the whole I think it was for the better), the British Raj shaped the sub-continent that is now shared by India, Pakistan and Bangladesh. The period of foreign rule has been likened to a love affair between a couple whom unexpected circumstances had thrown together. Initial fascination was followed by exploration and rough wooing, then came harmony, and fast behind rows, estrangement and separation. After fifty years the partners have calmed down and come to appreciate the value of what bound them together and the experiences they shared. The result is a restored goodwill, affection and a new partnership of interest with steadily rising Anglo-Indian trade and British investment in one of the world's most dynamic and expanding economies. I hope that this survey of the Raj will strengthen the bonds between Britons and Indians, and make them look again at their common past without shame or recrimination.

Bibliography

Abbreviations

BL	British Library
BLO	Bodleian Library, Oxford
EHR	*English Historical Review*
EcHR	*Economic History Review*
HJ	*Historical Journal*
IESHR	*Indian Economic and Social History Review*
IJMES	*International Journal of Middle East Studies*
ILN	*Illustrated London News*
IOL	India Office Library
IWM	Imperial War Museum
JAS	*Journal of Asian Studies*
JICH	*Journal of Imperial and Commonwealth History*
JIH	*Journal of Indian History*
JRAS	*Journal of the Royal Asian Society*
JSAHR	*Journal of the Society for Army Historical Research*
LHC	Liddell Hart Centre
MAS	*Modern Asian Studies*
NAM	National Army Museum
NLS	National Library of Scotland
NRO	Norfolk Record Office
PP	*Past and Present*
PRO	Public Record Office
RID	*Records of the Intelligence Department*
SRA	Strathclyde Regional Archives
SRO	Scottish Record Office
TP	*Transfer of Power*
TRHS	*Transactions of the Royal Historical Society*
VS	*Victorian Studies*

Sources

Unpublished

Bodleian Library, Oxford
Attlee Papers

British Library, London
Add Mss 37,689–718: Indian papers of the 1st Earl of Auckland; Add Mss
39,390–45,406: Diaries of Robert Cust; Add Mss 38,911–12: Journal of Lieutenant
Thomas Blackwell, 13th Regiment; Add Mss 40,172–228: Papers of Major Henry
Broadfoot; Add Mss 41,300: Papers of Captain J. Paton, Assistant Resident,
Lucknow; Add Mss 42,105–6: Journal of Captain J. Hyde, 13th Regiment; Add
Mss 42,500: Letters of Colonel Thomas Pierce (1857); Add Mss 42,807: Letters and
papers of General Sir Hugh Rose (Lord Strathnairn); Add Mss 43,574–87: Official
correspondence of 1st Marquess of Ripon; Add Mss 43,996–9: Correspondence of
Lieutenant-Colonel Herbert Bruce; Add Mss 44,218C: Letters of Mrs Francis
Duberly (1857–58); Add Mss 50,832–3: Letters of Sir George Clarke (Lord
Sydenham); Add Mss 49,876: Letters of Sergeant John Ramsbottom

Imperial War Museum, London
Letters, papers and correspondence of: Corporal Leslie Blackie, Royal Tank Regiment;
Admiral John Godfrey ('The Naval Memories of Admiral J. H. Godfrey',
Volume 6); Lieutenant I. J. N. Jukes RN; Dr P. W. Kingsford; L. Marsland Gander;
Major-General Harold Lewis; Colonel M. H. L. Morgan, 124th Balachis ('The
Truth About Amritsar')

India Office Library and Records, London
Official files: H (Home Miscellaneous series); L.Mil (Military Department); LPJ
(Public and Judicial); LPS (Letters Political and Secret); LWS (Letters, War Staff);
R (Records of Agents and Residents in Princely States); Mss Eur F 84 (Official
correspondence of the 9th Earl of Elgin); Mss Eur E 264 (Official correspondence of
the 1st Viscount Chelmsford); Mss Eur D 523 (Official correspondence of Edwin
Montagu)
Private papers, Mss Eur series: Anonymous Journal of the Karnatic campaign,
1780–81; Christopher Beaumont; Carnac Collection; Lord Casey (Sir Richard
Casey, Governor of Bengal, 1944–46); Lady Francis Chambers; Walter Christie;
Edward Colebrook; Alan Flack; Philip Francis; Charles Horne; Lieutenant Charles
Horwood, 12th Bengal Infantry; Brigadier John Jacob (Letters of Sir James
Outram); Lushington Collection; Lieutenant-Colonel Chardin Johnson, 9th
Lancers; Captain Robert Knolles; Hugh Martin; Lieutenant Godfrey Pearce, Bengal
Artillery; Lieutenant Thomas Pierce, 48th Bengal Infantry; Sidney Muspratt;
Lieutenant-Colonel Sir Jasper Nicholls; Samuel Roakes; John Shore; Strachey
Collection; M. M. Stuart; Sir Evan Thomas; Sir Charles Wood; Yule family
Recordings: C. P. Bramble; Major-General Palit; Govind Narain

Liddell Hart Centre for Military Studies, London
Letters, papers and correspondence of: Colonel J. A. Heard; Major A. C. Moore;
Captain S. J. Thompson RN

National Army Museum, London
Letters, papers and correspondence of: Brigadier William Alston, Bombay Pioneers;
Colonel B. J. Amies; Anonymous officer of Bengal Infantry (? Lieutenant-Colonel

Joseph Leggatt, 3rd NI); General Sir Arthur Becher; General Sir Roy Bucher; Private Jonathan Cottrill, 39th Regiment; Lieutenant John Daniel, RA; Colonel George Kellie, Indian Medical Service; General Sir Robert Lockhart; General W. L. Maxwell; Lieutenant Hooke Pearson, 11th Light Dragoons; Private H. Plumb, 24th Regiment; Private Potiphar, 9th Lancers; Ensign Alexander Rose, 54th Bengal Infantry; General Sir Reginald Savory; Private George Tookey, 3rd Light Dragoons; Lieutenant C. F. Trower, Bengal Light Infantry; Charles Waddington (Narrative of the Battle of Miani); Notes for General Officer Commanding, HQ Eastern Command, 24 August 1947

National Library of Scotland, Edinburgh
Official files and Indian correspondence of: the first and fourth Earls of Minto
Letters, papers and correspondence of: General Sir George Brown; Alexander Grant; Edward Grey, Veterinary Officer, 8th Hussars; Colonel James Halket; B. N. Lahari ('Leaves from a Policeman's Diary'); Assistant-Surgeon M. R. Oswald; Marquess of Tweeddale; Brigadier Alexander Walker

Norfolk Record Office, Norwich
Letters, papers and correspondence of: Captain Frank Cubitt; Andrew Leslie; Colonel Charles Windham

Public Record Office, London
Air (Air Ministry) 8, 23; DO (Dominions Office) 142; FO (Foreign Office) 65, 248, 402, 406, 539; HD (Home Department) 2, 3, 4; WO (War Office) 33, 71, 88, 92, 105, 106, 110, 157, 164, 203, 208; Papers of the 5th Marquess of Lansdowne (FO 800); Papers of Field Marshal Lord Roberts of Kandahar (PRO 30/57)

Scottish Record Office, Edinburgh
Letters, papers and correspondence of: Lieutenant-Colonel James Brunton, Madras Army; Alexander Campbell; Sir Montstuart Elphinstone (Seaforth Papers); Sir Archibald Grant; Captain William Hume, Bengal Army (Home of Wedderburn Papers); Lieutenant Alexander Lindsay, Bengal Horse Artillery; William Read (Cochrane Papers); Lieutenant James Whitton, Royal Scots Fusiliers

Strathclyde Regional Archives, Glasgow
Campbell of Succoth Papers

Published

Save where stated, all published in London.

Abbott, J., *Narrative of a Journey from Heraut to Khiva, Moscow and St Petersburg* (2 vols, 1867)
Adams, C., 'Across Seven Seas and Thirteen Rivers', *Oral History*, 19 (1991)
Adams, J., *The Western Rajputana States* (1899)
Addy, P., *Tibet on the Imperial Chessboard* (Calcutta, 1984)
Administrative Report of the Rajputana State Railway for the Years 1878–79 (Agra, 1879)
Aitken, B., 'The Coming Famine in India', *Contemporary Review*, XCIII (1908)
Aiyar, S., 'August Anarchy: The Pakistan Massacres in Punjab, 1947', *South Asia*, 18 (1995)
Alder, G. J., 'India and the Crimean War', *JICH*, 11 (1971)
Allworth, C. E. (ed.), *Central Asia: A Century of Russian Rule* (New York, 1967)
Amery, L., *My Political Life, III: The Unforgiving Years, 1929–1940* (1955)

——, *The Empire at Bay: The Leo Amery Diaries, 1929–1945*, ed. J. Barnes and D. Nicholson (1988)

Anand, M. J., *Coolie* (1972 edn)

——, *The Sword and the Sickle* (Liverpool, 1986 edn)

——, *Confessions of a Lover* (Liverpool, 1988 edn)

Andrew, W. P. ('An Old Indian Postmaster'), *Indian Railways as Connected With the Power and the Stability of the British Empire in the East* (1846)

Annals of the Indian Administration, ed. M. Townsend, I–IX (1856–58)

Annual Medical and Sanitary Report: Report on Civil Dispensaries and Special Hospitals in Mysore for the Year 1877 (Bangalore, 1878)

Annual Medical and Sanitary Report: Report on Civil Dispensaries and Special Hospitals in Mysore for the Year 1879 (Bangalore, 1879)

Annual Medical and Sanitary Report: Report on Civil Dispensaries and Special Hospitals in Mysore for the Year 1880 (Bangalore, 1880)

Annual Medical and Sanitary Report: Report on Civil Dispensaries in Coorg for the Year 1877 (Bangalore, 1878)

Anon, *The Morning Walk or the City Encompass'd* (1751)

Anon ('An Officer Who Serv'd in Those Squadrons'), *A Narrative of the Transactions in the East Indies During the Late War* (1751)

Anon, *The Dangers of British India from French Invasion and Missionary Establishments* (1808)

Anon, *The Opinions of Lords Wellesley and Grenville on the Government of India* (1832)

Anon ('A Lady'), *The East India Sketch Book* (2 vols, 1833)

Anon ('A Light Dragoon'), 'Reminiscences of a Light Dragoon', *Colburn's United Services Magazine*, 1833, Part III

Anon, 'The Douranee Empire', *Blackwoods Magazine*, XLIX (1841)

Anon, 'The Evacuation of Kabul', *Blackwoods Magazine*, LIII (1843)

Anon, 'Duelling in the British Army', *Colburn's United Services Magazine*, 1844, Part III

Anon, 'The Battle of Chillianwallah', *Colburn's United Services Magazine*, 1850, Part III

Anon, 'The Battle of Goojerat and Subsequent Events', *Ibid*

Anon, 'The Action at Ramnugger', *Ibid*

Anon, *By Authority! A Full Exposure of all the Horrible Tortures inflicted on the Natives of India by the Officers of the East India Company* (1855)

Anon, *A Psalm of Lamentation and Supplication to Almighty God concerning India* (*c.* 1857–58)

Anon, *Hymn for thew General Thanksgiving of the Suppression of the Indian Rebellion* (1858)

Anon, *The Indian Cookery Book: A Practical Handbook to the Kitchen in India* (Calcutta, *c.* 1860)

Anon, 'The Pursuit of Tanti Topi', *Blackwoods Magazine*, LXXXVI (1860)

Anon ('An Indian Gentleman'), *A Bird's Eye View of Indian Society* (1873)

Anon, 'The Romance of India', *Quarterly Review*, 196 (1902)

Anon, 'The Unrest in India', *Quarterly Review*, 209 (1908)

Anon, 'A Lady's Experience of the Singapore Mutiny', *Blackwoods Magazine*, CXCIII (1915)

Anon, 'History as she is wrote', *JSAHR*, 16 (1937)

Arasaratnam, S., 'Weavers, Merchants and the Company: The Handloom Industry in Southern India, 1750–1790', *IESHR*, 17 (1980)

Archer, M., *India and British Portraiture* (1979)

Arneil, B., 'Trade, Plantations and Poverty: John Locke and the Economic Defense of Colonialism', *Journal of the History of Ideas*, 55 (1994)

Argov, D., *Moderates and Exiles in the Indian National Movement* (1967)

Arnold, D., 'Industrial Violence in Colonial India', *Comparative Studies in Society and History*, 22 (1980)

———, 'Colonisation and Labour in Nineteenth Century India', *JICH*, II (1983)

———, 'Bureaucratic Recruitment and Subordination in Colonial India: The Madras Constabulary', *Subaltern Studies*, IV (1985)

———, 'Cholera and Colonialism in British India', *PP*, No. 113 (1986)

———, 'The "Discovery" of Malnutrition and Diet in Colonial India', *IESHR*, 31 (1994)

Ashburner, L. R., 'Gujerat Disturbances, 1857–1859', *Bombay Gazetteer*, I (Bombay, 1896)

Baden-Powell, R., *Indian Memories* (1915)

Bagot, D., *Psalm XLVI (Suited to the Indian Crisis)* (Dublin, 1857)

Baines, J. E., 'Maratha History of Gujarat, 1750–1819', *Bombay Gazetteer*, I (Bombay, 1896)

Bald, S. J., 'The Politics of a Revolutionary Elite: A Study of Mulk Raj Anand's Novels', *MAS*, 8 (1974)

Ballhatchet, K., *Race, Sex and Class Under the Raj* (1980)

Banerjea, S. N., *An Address to the Study of Indian History* (Calcutta, 1876)

Banerjee, A. C., *The Khalsa Raj* (Delhi, 1985)

Banerjee, S., *Studies in the Administrative History of Bengal, 1880–1898* (New Delhi, 1978)

Barrier, N. G., 'The Punjab Disturbances of 1907: The Response of the British Government in India to Rural Unrest', in D. Hardiman (ed.), *Peasant Resistance in India 1858–1914* (Oxford, 1993)

Barton, R. G., *Sport and Wild Life in the Deccan* (1928)

Bayley, C. A., *Imperial Meridian: The British Empire and the World, 1780–1830* (1989)

———, *Indian Society and the Making of the British Empire* (The New Cambridge History of India, II, i) (Cambridge, 1988)

———, 'The British Military-Fiscal State and Indigenous Resistance, India 1750–1820', in L. Stone (ed.), *The Imperial State at War: Britain from 1689 to 1815* (1994)

Beace, G. D., *British Attitudes towards India* (Oxford, 1961)

Beavan, H., *Thirty Years in India* (2 vols, 1839)

Bence-Jones, M., *Clive of India* (1974)

Bhadra, G., 'Four Rebels of Eighteen Fifty-Seven', *Subaltern Studies*, IV (1985)

Birom, Major, *A Narrative of the Campaign in India Which Terminated the War With Tipoo Sultan in 1792* (1793)

Blacker, V., *Memoires of the British Army in India During the Mahratta War of 1817, 1818 and 1819* (1821)

Bloch, I., *Sexual Life in England Past and Present*, trans. W. Forstern (1938)

Blood, B., *Forty Score Years and Ten: Sir Bindon Blood's Reminiscences* (1933)

Boal, B. M., *The Konds* (Warminster, Wilts, 1982)

Bose, S., *Peasant Labour and Colonial Capital: Rural Bengal since 1770* (The New Cambridge History of India, III, ii) (Cambridge, 1993)

Bosworth Smith, R., *Life of Lord Lawrence* (3 vols, 1883)

Bourchier, G., *Eight Months Campaign against the Bengal Sepoy During the Mutiny of 1857* (1858)

Bowen, H. V., 'Investment and Empire in India in the Late Eighteenth Century: East India Stockholding, 1756–1791', *EcHR*, 2nd Series, XLII (1989)

Bowrey, T., *A Geographical Account of the Countries Round the Bay of Bengal 1669 to 1679*, ed. Sir Richard Temple, Hakluyt Society, 2nd Series, XII (1895)

Bradley-Birt, F. D., *The Story of an Indian Upland* (1905)

Brass, P. R., *Language, Religion and Politics in North India* (Cambridge, 1974)

Bright, J., *The Diaries of John Bright* (1930)

British Parliamentary Papers: Colonies, East Indies, 1804–1874 (22 vols, Shannon, 1970)

Brodkin, E. I., 'The Struggle for Succession: Rebels and Loyalists in the Indian Mutiny of 1857', *JRAS*, 6 (1972)

Broughton, T. B., *Letters from a Mahratta Camp*, ed. M. E. Duff (1893)

Brown, J., 'Notes on Surgery of the Indian Campaign of 1857–58', *Monthly Journal of Medical Sciences*, VI (1861)

Browning, O., *Impressions of Indian Travel* (1903)

Bryant, G. J., 'The East India Company and the British Army: The Crisis at Madras in 1789', *JSAHR*, LXII (1984)

——, 'Scots in India in the Eighteenth Century', *Scottish Historical Review*, LXIV (1985)

——, 'Pacification in the Early British Raj, 1755–1785', *JICH*, 14 (1985)

Buck, E. J., *Simla Past and Present* (Bombay, 1925)

Buckle, G. E., and Moneypenny, W. F., *The Life of Benjamin Disraeli, Earl of Beaconsfield*

Buckley, R. B., *Irrigation Works in India* (1898)

Burnes, A., *Travels in Bokhara* (3 vols, 1834)

Butler, I., *The Eldest Brother: The Marquess of Wellesley, the Duke of Wellington's Eldest Brother* (1973)

Cadell, J., 'The Outbreak of the Indian Mutiny', *JSAHR*, XXXIII (1955)

The Cadet's Guide to India, Containing Information and Advice to Young Men about to enter the Army of the Honourable East India Company (1826)

Calcutta University Calendar 1866–67 (Calcutta, 1868)

Campbell, J., *Narrative of Major-General John Campbell of his Operations in the Hill Tracts of Orissa* (1861)

Campbell-Johnson, A., *Mission with Mountbatten* (Bombay, 1951 edn)

Candler, E., *The Unveiling of Lhasa* (1905)

——, *The Long Road to Baghdad* (2 vols, 1919)

——, *The Sepoy* (1919)

Carver, Lord, *Wellington and his Brothers* (Southampton, 1989)

Carrington, C. E., *The Life of Rudyard Kipling* (1956)

Casserly, G., *Life in an Indian Outpost* (n.d. *c.* 1915)

Cave-Brown, J., *The Punjab and Delhi in 1857* (2 vols, 1861)

Chand, T., *A History of the Freedom Movement in India* (2 vols, Delhi, 1961)

Charlesworth, N., 'The Myth of the Deccan Riots of 1875', *JMAS*, 6 (1972)

Chatterji, B., 'The Darogah and the Countryside: The Imposition of Police Control in Bengal and Its Impact (1793–1837)', *IESHR*, 18 (1981)

Chaudhuri, N. C., *Clive of India* (1975)

Chaudhuri, S. C., *English Historical Writings on the Indian Mutiny 1857–1859* (Calcutta, 1979)

Chaudhuri-Soas, K. N., 'The Structure of the Indian Textile Industry in the
    Seventeenth and Eighteenth Centuries', *IESHR*, 11 (1974)
Chevers, N., *A Manual of Medical Jurisprudence in India* (Calcutta, 1870)
Chopra, P. N., '"Quit India" Movement of 1942', *JIH*, 49 (1971)
——, *Quit India: British Secret Documents* (New Delhi, 1986)
Chunder, B., *Travels of a Hindoo to various parts of Bengal and Upper India* (2 vols, 1869)
Churcher, E. J., *Some Reminiscences of a Century in India* (1904)
Churchill, R., *Winston S. Churchill*, I (1966)
Churchill, W. S., *My Early Life* (1941 edn)
——, *Frontiers and Wars* (1962 edn)
Cobbold, R. P., *Innermost Asia: Travel and Sport in the Pamirs* (1900)
Cohen, S., 'Mesopotamia in British Strategy, 1903–1914', *IJMES*, 9 (1978)
Cohn, B. S., 'Structural Changes in Indian Rural Society', in R. E. Frykenberg
    (ed.), *Land, Control and Social Structure in Indian History* (Manohar, WI, 1979)
——, 'The Command of Language and the Language of Command', *Subaltern
    Studies*, IV (1985)
College of Fort William in Bengal, The (1805)
Colvin, I., *The Life of General Dyer* (1929)
Connolly, A., *Journey to the North of India* (2 vols, 1834)
Coopland, Mrs R. M., *A Lady's Escape from Gwalior and Life in the Fort of Agra
    During the Mutinies of 1857* (1859)
Coorg Medical Report of 1873 (Bangalore, 1875)
Copland, I., *The British Raj and the Indian Princes: Paramountcy in Western India,
    1857–1930* (New Delhi, 1982)
——, *The Princes in India in the End Game of Empire, 1917–47* (1997)
*Criminal Statistics of the High Court of Judicature at Lahore and the Courts in the Punjab
    . . . for the Calendar Year ending the 31st of December 1919* (Lahore, 1920)
Cruikshank, C., *SOE in the Far East* (Oxford, 1986)
Currie, K., 'Famines in 19th Century Indian History: A Materialist Alternative to
    Ecological Reductionism', *Journal of Contemporary Asia*, 16 (1986)
Cust, R. N., *Sorrows of Anglo-Indian Life, by a Sufferer* (1889)
——, *Memoirs of Past Years as a Septuagenarian* (1899)

Daily Mail Blue Book on the India Crisis (1931)
Das, B. S., *Civil Rebellion on the Frontier Bengal, 1760–1805* (Calcutta, 1975)
Das, M. N., *India under Morley and Minto* (1964)
Das, S., *Myths and Realities of French Imperialism in India, 1763–1783* (New York,
    1992)
Datta, P., 'Strikes in the Greater Calcutta region, 1918–1924', *IESHR*, 30 (1992)
Davies, C. C., 'Warren Hastings and the Younger Pitt', *EHR*, LXX (1955)
Defoe, D., *A Plan of English Commerce* (Oxford, 1927 edn)
de Lacy Evans, G., *On the Practicability of an Invasion of British India* (1829)
Desai, A. R., *Social Background to Indian Nationalism* (1966 edn)
'Devereux, C.', *Venus in India or, Love Adventures in Hindustan* (reprint, 1973)
Devi G., and Rav, S. R., *A Princess Remembers: The Memoirs of the Maharani of Jaipur*
    (New Delhi, 1976)
Dewey, C., *Anglo-Indian Attitudes: The Mind of the Indian Civil Servant* (1993)
Dey, R. S., *A Brief Account of the Punjab Frontier Force* (Calcutta, 1905)
Dickens, C., *Letters of Charles Dickens*, VII, ed. G. Strong and K. Tillotson (Oxford,
    1995)

Dictionary of National Biography, ed. S. P. Sen (4 vols, Calcutta, 1972–74)

Dilke, C. W., *Greater Britain: A Review of Travel in English-Speaking Countries During 1866 and 1867* (2 vols, 1869)

Directions for Settlement Officers (Agra, 1844)

Diver, M., *Far to Seek: A Romance* (1921)

Dodwell, H., 'Warren Hastings and the Assignment of the Carnatic', *EHR*, XL (1925)

Downs, T., 'Fear and Loathing in Bhadoli: The Revolt of the Minas Rajputs', *IESHR*, 27 (1990)

Douds, G., 'Matters of Honour: Indian Troops in the North African and Italian Theatres', in P. Addison and A. Calder (eds), *Time to Kill* (1997)

D'Oyly, C., *A Civilian and an Office: Tom Raw, the Griffin* (1828)

Draper, A., *The Amritsar Massacre: Twilight of the Raj* (1985 edn)

Dunlop, R. H. W., *Service and Adventure with the Khakee Ressalahar, Meerut Volunteer Horse During the Mutinies of 1857–58* (1858)

Dunsterville, L. C., *Stalky's Reminiscences* (1928)

Dutton, D., *Austen Chamberlain: Gentleman in Politics* (1986)

Durand, A., *The Making of a Frontier* (1899)

——, *The Life of Field-Marshal Sir George White* (2 vols, 1915)

Dyer, R. E. H., *The Raiders of Sarhad* (1921)

Dyson, C. C., *From a Punjab Pomegranate Grove* (1913)

The Early Annals of the the English in Bengal, II, ii, ed. C. R. Wilson (Calcutta, 1911)

The East India Examiner: Reprinted from the Original Papers in that Periodical Publication (1766)

The East India Military Calendar, Containing the Services of General and Field Officers of the Indian Army (1823)

The East India Register and Directory for 1803

The East India Register and Directory for 1809

The East India Register and Directory for 1813

[East India Merchant], *A Letter to the Right Honourable Lord John Russell, M.P. on the Subject of Indian Railways* (1848)

Edwards, H. B., *A Year on the Punjab Frontier in 1848–49* (2 vols, 1851)

Edwards, M., *Red Year: The Indian Rebellion of 1857* (1977 edn)

Egan, P., *Boxiana or Sketches of Ancient and Modern Pugilism, II* (1818)

Ellenborough, Lord, *Political Diaries, 1828–1830*, ed. Lord Colchester (2 vols, 1881)

Elphick, P., *Singapore: The Pregnable Fortress* (1995)

Elphinstone, M., *The History of India* (2 vols, 1841)

Elsmie, G. R., *Thirty-five Years in the Punjab* (Edinburgh, 1908)

Embree, A. T., 'Landholding in India and British Institutions', in R. E. Frykenberg (ed.), *Land, Control and Social Structure in Indian History* (Manohar, WI, 1979)

Empire Exhibition Glasgow: A Souvenir (Glasgow, 1938)

English, B., 'The Kanpur Massacre in India in the Revolt of 1857', *PP*, No. 142 (1994)

Eyre, V., *The Military Operations in Cabul Which Ended in the Retreat and Destruction of the British Army, January 1842, With a Journal of Imprisonment in Affghanistan* (5th edn, 1843)

Falconer, J., 'Ethnographical Photography in India, 1850–1900', *The Photographic Collector*, 5 (1984–6)

Fane, H., *Five Years in India* (2 vols, 1842)

Fass, V., *The Forts of India* (1986)

The Fast Day Sermons: 'The Indian Mutiny': Twelve Sermons Delivered on Wedenesday October 7, 1857 (1857)

Fay, W., *The Forgotten Army: India's Armed Struggle for Independence, 1942–1945* (New Delhi, 1994)

Feiling, K., *Warren Hastings* (1954)

Fincastle, Viscount, and Elliot-Lockhart, P. C., *A Frontier Campaign* (reprint, 1990)

Foote, S., *The Nabob: A Comedy in Three Acts* (1778)

Forbes, G., *Women in Modern India* (The New Cambridge History of India, IV, ii) (Cambridge, 1996)

Forbes, J., *Oriental Memoirs: A Narrative of Seventeen Years Residence in India* (3 vols, 1834)

Forbes-Mitchell, W., *Reminiscences of the Great Mutiny, 1857–1859* (1893)

Forrest, Lieutenant-Colonel, *A Picturesque Tour Along the River Ganges and Jumma in India* (1824)

Forrest, G., *The Life of Lord Clive* (2 vols, Delhi, 1976 edn)

Forster, E. M., *A Passage to India* (1979 edn)

——, *Selected Letters of E. M. Forster*, I (1879–1920), ed. M. Lago and P. Furbank (Cambridge, 1983)

Fort William–India House Correspondence and Other Contemporary Papers Relating Thereto, II (1757–59), ed. N. H. Sinha (India Records Society, Delhi, 1957)

Fortescue, J. W., *A History of the British Army* (13 vols, 1899–1930)

Fraser, A., 'The Situation in India', *Contemporary Review*, XCVI (1909)

Fraxi, P., *Indix Librorum Prohibitoru, being notes, Bio-, Bioblio-, Iconographical and Critical on Uncommon Books* (1877)

French, P., *Younghusband: The Last Great Imperial Adventurer* (1994)

Friedberg, A. L., *Change, Assessment and Adaptation: Britain and its Experience of Relative Decline, 1895–1905* (Ann Arbor, 1987)

Fuller, B., *Studies of Indian Life and Settlement* (1910)

——, *The Empire of India* (1914)

Fuller, W., *Strategy and Power in Russia, 1600–1914* (New York, 1992)

Furber, H., *Rival Empires of Trade in the Orient, 1600–1800* (Minneapolis, 1976)

Gallagher, J., Johnson G., and Seal, A., *Locality, Province and Nation: Essays on Indian Politics, 1870 to 1940* (Cambridge, 1973)

Galwan, R., *Servants of the Sahibs* (Cambridge, 1923)

Gandhi, M., *The Collected Works of Mahatma Gandhi* (82 vols, Delhi, 1958–80)

Gazetteer of the Bombay Presidency, VII (Baroda), XV, ii (Kanara) (Bombay, 1883)

Ghose, M., *The Open Competition for the Civil Service in India* (Calcutta, 1866)

Gibney, Captain ('A Wounded Officer'), *My Escape from the Mutineers of the Oudh* (2 vols, 1858)

Gilchrist, J., *The Anti-Jargonist, or: A Short Introduction to the Hindoostani Tongue* (Calcutta, 1800)

Gilmour, D., *Curzon* (1994)

Gilmour, J., *The Idea of the Gentleman in the Victorian Novel* (1981)

Gleig, G. R., *The Life of Major-General Sir Thomas Munro* (3 vols, 1840)

Glendevon, J., *Viceroy at Bay* (1971)

'The Letters of Lieutenant Edmund Goodbehere, 18th Madras NI, 1803–1809', ed. S. G. P. Ward, *JSAHR*, LVII (1979)

Gopal, S., *British Policy in India, 1858–1905* (Cambridge, 1965)

Gordon, L. A., *Bengal: The Nationalist Movement, 1876–1940* (1974)

Gordon, S., *The Marathas, 1600–1818* (The New Cambridge History of India, II, iv) (Cambridge, 1993)

Gordon, T. E., *A Varied Life* (1906)

Gouldsbury, C. E., *Tigerland: Reminiscences of Fifty Years Sport and Adventures in Bengal* (1915)

Graham, M. [Lady Callcott], *The Journal of a Residence in India* (Edinburgh, 1812)

Grant, G., *First and Last Love: A Tale of the Indian Mutiny* (3 vols, 1868)

Grant Duff, J., 'India, Political and Social', *Contemporary Review*, XXVI (1875)

——, *A History of the Mahrattas* (3 vols, Calcutta, 1918)

Great Delhi Durbar of 1911 (1912)

Greaves, R. L., *Persia and the Defence of India, 1884–1892* (1959)

Gregory, B., 'Staging British India', in J. S. Bratton, R. A. Cave, H. J. Holden, B. Gregory and M. Pickering, *Acts of Supremacy: The British Stage and the Empire, 1790–1930* (Manchester, 1991)

Griffiths, P., *To Guard My People: The History of the Indian Police* (1971)

St Clair Grimwood, E., *My Three Years in Manipur and Escape from the Recent Mutiny* (1891)

Gubbins, M., *An Account of the Mutinies in the Oudh and the Siege of the Lucknow Residency* (1858)

Guha, S., 'Mortality Decline in Early-Twentieth-century India: A Preliminary Enquiry', *IESHR*, 28 (1991)

Gupta, A., *The Police in British India, 1861–1947* (Delhi, 1979)

Gupta, M., 'The Vellore Mutiny of 1809', *JIH*, 49 (1971)

Gupta, P. C., *Nana Sahib and the Rising at Cawnpore* (Oxford, 1963)

Haight, G. S., 'Male Chastity in the Nineteenth Century', *Contemporary Review*, CCIX (1971)

Hamid, N., 'Dispossession and Differentiation of the Peasantry During the period of Colonial Rule', *Journal of Peasant Studies*, 10 (1982–83)

Hamid, S., *Disastrous Twilight: A Personal Record of the Partition of India* (1986)

Hamilton, A., *A New Account of the East Indies* (2 vols, Edinburgh, 1727)

Hardiman, D. (ed.), *Peasant Resistance in India, 1858–1914* (Delhi, 1993)

——, 'Community, Patriarchy, Honour; Raghu Bhanegre's Revolt', *Journal of Peasant Studies*, 23 (1995–96)

The Letters of the First Viscount Hardinge of Lahore to Lady Hardinge and Sir Walter and Lady James, ed. B. S. Singh (Camden Society, 4th series, 32 [1986])

Harrington, P., *British Artists and War: The Face of Battle in Paintings and Prints, 1700–1914* (1993)

Harrison, M., 'Quarantine, Pilgrimage and Colonial Trade: India 1866–1900', *IESHR*, 29 (1992)

Harvey, A. D., 'Prosecutions for Sodomy in England at the Beginning of the Nineteeth Century', *HJ*, 21 (1978)

The Private Journal of the Marquess of Hastings K.G., Governor-General and Commander-in-Chief in India, ed. Marchioness of Bute (2 vols, 1858)

Hauner, M., *India in Axis Strategy* (Stuttgart, 1981)

——, 'One Man Against the Empire: The Faqir of Ipi and the British in Central Asia on the Eve of and During the Second World War', *Journal of Contemporary History*, 16 (1981)

Memoirs of Major-General Sir Henry Havelock, ed. J. C. Marshman (2 vols, 1860)

[Henderson, H. B.], *The Bengalee, or: Sketches of Society and Manners in the East* (1829)

Henningham, S., 'Quit India in Bihar and the Eastern United Provinces: the Dual Revolt', *Subaltern Studies*, II (1983)

Henty, G. A., *Through Three Campaigns* (1898)

——, *A Soldier's Daughter* (1906 edn)

Hibbert, C., *The Great Mutiny* (1978)

HMC, *Reports of the Manuscripts of Earl Bathurst preserved at Cirencester Park* (1923)

HMC, *The Prime Minister's Papers: Wellington's Political Correspondence*, I, ed. J. Olney and J. Malvin (1976); II, ed. J. Brooke and J. Gaudy (1986)

Hodson, V., 'The Baraset Cadet College, East Indies', *JSAHR*, II (1922)

Hoghton, F. A., *Operations of the Mohmand Field Force in 1897* (Simla, 1899)

Holdich, T. H., *The Indian Borderland* (1901)

Hoole, E., *Personal Narrative of a Mission to the South of India* (1829)

——, *Madras, Mysore and the South of India; or: A personal Narrative of a Mission to those Countries* (1844)

Hopkirk, P., *The Great Game* (1989)

——, *On Secret Service East of Constantinople* (1994)

Horne, W. O., *Work and Sport in the Old ICS* (1928)

House of Commons Sessional Papers 54–59: (George III: Reports and Papers relative to Hastings's Impeachment), ed. S. Lambert (Wilmington, DE, 1975)

Hubel, T., *Whose India? The Independence Struggle in British and Indian Fiction and History* (Leicester, 1996)

Hunter, W. W., 'Popular Movements in India', *Contemporary Review*, LIX (1891)

Husain, I., *The Ruhela Chieftaincies: The Rise and Fall of Ruhela Power in the Eighteenth Century* (Delhi, 1994)

Hyam, R., *Elgin and Churchill at the Colonial Office, 1905–1908* (1968)

——, *Empire and Sexuality: The British Experience* (Manchester, 1990)

Imlah, A. H., *Lord Ellenborough: A Biography of Edward Law, Earl of Ellenborough* (Cambridge, MA, 1939)

Indian Munitions Board: Industrial Handbook (Calcutta, 1919)

Indus Valley State Railway: Administration Report (Rorkee, 1879)

Irvine, A. A., *Land of No Regrets* (1938)

Ives, E., *A Voyage from England to India in the Year MDCCLVI and a Historical Narrative of Operations of the Squadron and Army in India* (1773)

Jalal, A., 'India's Partition and the Perspective of Pakistan: An Historical Perspective', *JICH*, 15 (1986–87)

James, L., *The Iron Duke: A Military Biography of the Duke of Wellington* (1992)

——, *The Rise and Fall of the British Empire* (1994)

Jeffrey, K., *The British Army and the Crisis of Empire* (Manchester, 1984)

Jeffrey, R., 'A Sanctified Label – "Congress" – in Travancore Politics, 1938–1948', in D. A. Low (ed.), *Congress and the Raj: Facets of the Indian Struggle* (1977)

Jefferson, M., 'Lord Salisbury's Conversations With the Tsar at Balmoral, 27–29 September 1897', *The Slavonic and Eastern European Review*, XXXIX (1960–61)

Johnson, G., 'Partition, Agitation and Congress: Bengal 1904 to 1908', *MAS*, 7 (1973)

*Journals and Diaries of the Assistants to the Agent and Governor-General North-West
   Frontier and Resident in Lahore, 1846–1849* (Allahabad, 1911)

Kay, R. D. ('A Bengal Officer'), *Recollections of the First Campaign West of the Indus
   and the Subsequent Operations of the Candahar Force* (1845)
Kaye, J. W., *The Life and Correspondence of Charles, Lord Metcalfe* (2 vols, 1854)
———, *History of the Sepoy War in India, 1857–1858* (3 vols, 1876)
———, *History of the War in Afghanistan* (3 vols, 1878)
Kennedy, J. P., *A Railway Caution!* (1849)
Kiernan, V., *A History of European Empires from Conquest to Collapse, 1815–1960*
   (1982)
———, *The Duel in European History* (1988)
Kipling, R., *Departmental Ditties* (1897)
———, *Plain Tales from the Hills* (1899 edn)
———, *The Day's Work* (1914 edn)
———, *The Letters of Rudyard Kipling*, ed. T. Pinney, I (1990)
Khan Kirmani, M. H. Ali, *The History of Hydur Naik*, trans. W. Miles (1842)
Khrisnan, Y., 'Mountbatten and the Partition of India', *History*, 67 (1983)
Klein, I., 'When the Rains Failed: Famine Relief and Mortality in British India',
   IESHR, 21 (1984)
———, 'Imperialism, Ecology and Disease: Cholera and India', *IESHR*, 31 (1994)
Knight, C. A., 'The Images of Nations in Eighteenth-century Satire', *Eighteenth
   Century Studies*, 22 (1989)
Knight, E. F., *Where Three Empires Meet* (1896)
Koss, S. E., *John Morley at the India Office, 1905–1910* (New Haven, 1969)
Krishnamurty, J. (ed.), *Women in Colonial India* (Delhi, 1989)
Kubicek, R. V., 'The Role of the Shallow-Draught Steamboat in the Expansion of
   the British Empire, 1820–1914', *International Journal of Maritime History*, 6
   (1994)
Kumar D., and Desai, M. (eds), *The Cambridge Economic History of India*, II,
   c. 1757–*c.* 1970 (Cambridge, 1983)
Kumar, R., 'From Swaraj to Purna Raj: Nationalist Politics in the City of Bombay',
   in Low (ed.), *Congress and the Raj: Facets of the Indian Struggle, 1917–1947*
   (1977)
———, 'The Deccan Riots of 1875', in D. Hardiman (ed.), *Peasant Resistance in
   India, 1858–1914* (Oxford, 1993)

Lambrick, H. T., *Sir Charles Napier and the Sind* (Oxford, 1952)
———, *Sind: A General Introduction* (Hyderabad, 1964)
Landa, L. A., *Essays in Eighteenth-century Literature* (Princeton, 1980)
Lanereux, E., *A Treatise on Syphilis*, trans G.Whitly, The New Sydenham Society
   (1869)
Lang, A. M., *Lahore to Lucknow: The Indian Mutiny Journal of Arthur Moffat Lang*, ed.
   D. Blomfield (1992)
Lawrence, H. M., *Essays, Political and Military Written in India* (1859)
Lawrence, Lady (Phyllis Lawrence), *Indian Embers* (n.d.)
Lawrence, W. R., *The India We Served* (1928)
———, 'The Indian Village', *Geographical Magazine*, 6 (1937–38)
Lee, D., *Never Stop the Engine When it's Hot* (1983)
Lee Warner, W., *The Native States of India* (1911)

le Mesurier, A., *From London to Bokhara and a Ride through Persia* (1889)

Lenman, B., 'The Weapons of War in 18th-Century India', *JSAHR*, XLVI (1968)

Leopold, J., 'British Applications of the Aryan Theory of Race to India, 1850–1870', *EHR*, LXXXIV (1974)

Lindholm, C., *Generosity and Jealousy: The Swat Pukhtun of Northern Pakistan* (Columbia, NY, 1982)

Lindsay, A. B., 'Letters from the Abor Expedition, 1911–12', *JSAHR*, LIV (1976)

Low, D. A. (ed.), *Soundings in South Asian History* (Berkeley, CA, 1968)

——, *Eclipse of Empire* (Cambridge, 1993 edn)

Lyall, A., *The Life of the Marquis of Dufferin and Ava* (2 vols, 1905)

Lytton, R., *Personal and Literary Letters of Robert, first Earl of Lytton*, ed. Lady Betty Balfour (2 vols, 1906)

Life and Works of Lord Macaulay (10 vols, 1897)

MacKenzie, C., *Life in the Mission, the Camp and the Zenana, or: Six Years in India* (2 vols, 1854)

Mackenzie, D., 'The Conquest and Administration of Turkestan, 1860–85', in M. R. Rwykin (ed.), *Russian Colonial Expansion to 1917* (1988)

Mackenzie, J. M., *Propaganda and Empire* (Manchester, 1984)

—— (ed.), *Popular Imperialism and the Military* (Manchester, 1995)

Mackinnon, D. H., *Military Service and Adventures in the Far East* (2 vols, 1849)

Maclean, D., *Britain and her Buffer State: the Collapse of the Persian Empire, 1890–1914* (1979)

Maconochie, E., *Life in the Indian Civil Service* (1926)

Macpherson, J. W., 'Investment in Indian Railways', *EcHR*, 2nd Series, 8 (1955)

Macpherson, W. G., and Mitchell, T. J., *Medical Services: A General History* (4 vols, 1924, History of the Great War Based on Official Documents)

Macpherson, W. G., Horrocks, W. H., and Beveridge, W. W. O., *Medical Services of the Great War* (2 vols, 1923, History of the Great War Based on Official Documents)

Macrory, P., *Kabul Catastrophe: The Retreat of 1842* (Oxford, 1986 edn)

[Madras Officer], *A Sketch and Review of Military Service in India* (Edinburgh, 1833)

Mahatra, A., 'The Demography of the Bengal Famine of 1943–1944', *IESHR*, 30 (1994)

Maitra, K., 'Lenin and Roy on National and Colonial Questions at the Second Congress of the Third International', *India History Congress, 37th Session* (Calicut, 1976)

Majendie, V. D., *Up Among the Pandies, or: A Year's Service in India* (1859)

Major, A. J., 'The Chief Sufferers: Abduction and Women During the Partition of the Punjab', *South Asia*, 18 (1995)

Malhotra, P. L., *The Administration of Lord Elgin in India* (New Delhi, 1979)

Malleson, G. B., *The Indian Mutiny of 1857* (reprint, 1993)

Mangan, J. A., *The Games Ethic and Imperialism: Aspects of the Diffusion of an Ideal* (1986)

Mann, H. H., *Land, Labour and a Deccan Village* (University of Bombay Economic Series, I) (Oxford, 1917)

Marshall, P. J., *The Impeachment of Warren Hastings* (Oxford, 1965)

——, 'The Personal Fortune of Warren Hastings', *EcHR*, 2nd series, XVII (1964–65)

———, *East India Fortunes: The British in Bengal in the Eighteenth Century* (Oxford, 1976)

———, *Bengal: the British Bridgehead* (New Cambridge History of India, II, ii) (Cambridge, 1987)

Martin, E. J., 'An Engineer in the Mysore War of 1791–1792', *JSAHR*, (1943–44)

Martin, G., 'The Influence of Racial Attitides in British Policy towards India during the First World War', *JICH*, 14 (1985–86)

Mason, A. H., *Expedition Against the Hasanzai and Arazai Tribes of the Black Mountains* (Simla, 1894)

———, *Report on the Hindustani Fanatics* (Simla, 1895)

Mason, P., *A Matter of Honour* (1976 edn)

Masters, J., *Bugles and a Tiger* (1957 edn)

Mathur, R. M., *Rajput States and the East India Company* (Delhi, 1979)

Matthew, J. C., *The Story of St Andrew's Church, Bombay* (Bombay, 1913)

Mavor, W., *Voyages, Travels, Discourses from the Time of Columbus to the Present Period*, V ('Voyage of Mr Grose to the East Indies') (1796)

Mayo, K., *Mother India* (1927)

McCalman, I., 'Unrespectable Radicalism: Infidels and Pornography in Early Nineteenth-century London', *PP*, 104 (1984)

McGuffie, T. H., 'Lake's Mahratta Campaigns: Report on the Call Journals, 1803 to 1805, now in the R.U.S.I.', *JSAHR*, 29 (1951)

Mehta, M. J., 'Indian Relations With the Native State of Cambay', *JIH*, 22 (1982)

Mehta, M. S., *Lord Hastings and the Indian States* (Delhi, 1986)

Memorial of the Hindoo Inhabitants of Bengal (Calcutta, 1850)

Menenzes, S. L., *Fidelity and Honour: The Indian Army from the Seventeenth to the Twenty-first Century* (1993)

Metcalfe, T. C., 'From Raja to Landlord: The Oude Talukdar, 1850–1870', in R. E. Frykenberg (ed.), *Land, Control and Social Structure in Indian History* (Manohar, WI, 1979)

Metcalfe, T. R., *Ideologies of the Raj* (The New Cambridge Modern History of India, III, iv) (Cambridge, 1994)

Middlemas, K., and Barnes, J., *Baldwin* (1969)

Mill, J., *The History of British India* (4th edn, 8 vols, 1840)

Mills, I. D., 'The 1918–19 Influenza Pandemic: The Indian Experience', *IESHR*, (1986)

Minto, Mary Countess of, *India, Minto and Morley, 1905–1910* (1934)

Mollo, B., *The Indian Army* (Poole, Dorset, 1981)

Moon, P., *Strangers in India* (1942)

Moore, G., '*Just as Good as the Rest*' (Buckden, Hants, n.d.)

Moore, R. J., *Churchill, Cripps and India* (Oxford, 1979)

———, *Escape from Empire* (Oxford, 1983)

Morehead, C., *Clinical Researches on Disease in India* (2 vols, 1856)

Moreman, T. R., 'The British and Indian Armies on the North-West Frontier, 1849–1914', *JICH*, 20 (1992)

———, 'The Arms Trade and the North-West Frontier Pathan Tribes, 1890–1914', *JICH*, 22 (1994)

Morier-Williams, M., 'Facts on Indian Progress', *Contemporary Review*, XXXII (1878)

Morley, J., *Recollections* (2 vols, 1917)

Morris, I. P., 'British Secret Service Missions in Turkestan, 1918–19', *Journal of Contemporary History*, 12 (1977)

———, 'British Secret Service Activity in Khorassan', *HJ*, 27 (1984)

———, 'Intelligence and its Interpretation, Mesopotamia 1914–18', in C. Andrew and J. Noakes (eds), *Intelligence and International Relations, 1900–1945* (Exeter, 1987)

Morris, J., *Hired to Kill* (1960)

Mortimer, J. S., 'Annie Besant, India 1913–1917', *Journal of Contemporary History*, 18 (1983)

Mosley, N., *The Last Days of the British Raj* (1961)

Mukhergee, N., *The Ryotwari System in Madras* (Calcutta, 1962)

Murkerjee, R., 'Satan let loose upon Earth: The Kanpur Massacres in India in the Revolt of 1857', *PP*, 128 (1990)

Murray, J., 'Field Surgeon at the Battle of Aliwal: The Letters of Dr John Murray During the First Sikh War', ed. J. Fraser, *JSAHR*, 72 (1994)

Mutiny Correspondence (2 vols, Lahore, 1911)

Mutiny Reports (2 vols, Lahore, 1911)

Naidis, M., 'G. A. Henty's Idea of India', *VS*, 8 (1964–65)

Namier, L., and Brooke, J., *The History of Parliament: The House of Commons, 1754–1790* (3 vols, 1964)

Narain, P., *Press and Politics in India, 1885–1905* (Delhi, 1970)

———, 'Interaction of Nationalism and Imperialism in India in the 1880s: A Survey of the Vernacular Press', *JIH*, 57 (1979)

The National Mirror, Being a Series of Essays on the Most Important Concerns; but particularly those of the East-India Company (1771)

The Naval Brigade in the Indian Mutiny, 1857–1858, ed. W. B. Rowbotham (Naval Records Society, 1947)

Nayeem, M. A., *Mughal Administration of Deccan under the Nizam Ul Mulk Asaf Jau, 1720–48* (Bombay, 1985)

Neale, W. C., 'Land is to Rule', in R. E. Frykenberg (ed.), *Land, Control and Social Structure in Indian History* (Manohar, WI, 1979)

Neill, S., *A History of Christianity in India* (Cambridge, 1985)

Newton, Lord, *Lord Lansdowne: A Biography* (1929)

Nicolson, H., *King George the Fifth: His Life and Reign* (1952)

Nigam, S., 'Disciplining and policing the "Criminals by birth",' *IESHR*, 27 (1990)

Norris, J. A., *The First Afghan War* (Cambridge, 1967)

Notes on the Administration of Criminal Justice in the Province of Oudh During the Calendar Year Ending 31st December 1918 (Allahabad, 1919)

Notes on the Administration of Criminal Justice in the Province of Oudh During the Calendar Year Ending 31st December 1919 (Allahabad, 1920)

Notes on the Administration of Criminal Justice in the Province of Oudh During the Calendar Year Ending 31st December 1920 (Allahabad, 1921)

Notes on the Criminal Statistics of 1871, North-Western Provinces (Allahabad, 1872)

Notes on the Maps of Central Asia, Turkestan &c. (Dehra Dun, 1873)

Nott, W., *Memoirs and Correspondence of Major-General Sir William Knott*, ed. J. H. Stocqueler (2 vols, 1854)

O'Donovan, E., *The Merv Oasis: Travels and Adventures East of the Caspian During the Years 1879–80–81* (2 vols, 1882)

O'Dwyer, M., *India as I knew it, 1885–1925* (1926 edn)
Officers of the Bengal Army, ed. V. C. P. Hudson (4 vols, 1927–47)
Omissi, D., *The Sepoy and the Raj* (1994)
The Oriental Baptist (vols 1–4, Calcutta, 1847–50)
Orme, R., *A History of the Military Transactions of the British National in Indostand from the Year MDCCXLV* (2 vols, 1763)

Palmer, J. A. B., *The Mutiny Outbreak at Meerut* (Cambridge, 1966)
Pandey, B. N., *The Break-up of British India* (1969)
Pannikar, N. N., *Against Lord and State: Religion and Peasant Uprisings in Malabar, 1836–1921* (Oxford, 1989)
The Parliamentary History of England from the Earliest Period to the Year 1803 (36 vols, 1803–20)
Parry, D. H., *Britain's Roll of Glory, or The Victoria Cross, Its Heroes and Their Valour* (1906 edn)
Sardar Patel's Correspondence, ed. D. Das (10 vols, Ahmadabad, 1972)
Pati, B., 'The Climax of Popular Protest: The Quit India Movement in Orissa', *IESHR*, 29 (1992)
Paul, S. N., *Public Opinion and British Rule* (New Delhi, 1979)
Paxton, N. L., 'Mobilising Chivalry: Rape in British Novels about the Indian Uprising of 1857', *VS*, 36 (1992–93)
Pearce, C., *Indian Copper* (Lewes, 1990)
Pearson, H., *The Hero of Delhi* (Harmondsworth, 1948)
Peers, D. M., 'Sepoys, Soldiers and the Lash: Race, Caste and Army Discipline in India, 1820–50', *JICH*, 23 (1995)
Pemble, J., 'Resources and Techniques in the Second Maratha War', *HJ*, 10 (1976)
Penzer, N. M., *Poison Damsels* (New York, 1980)
Perrin, A., *The Anglo-Indians* (Leipsig, 1912)
Perry, P. W., *The Commonwealth Armies* (Manchester, 1988)
Phillips, C. H., 'The East India Company "Interest" and the English Government', *TRHS*, 4th Series, XX (1937)
The Private Diary of Ananda Ranga Pillai from 1736 to 1751 (12 vols, Madras, 1904–28)
Poddar, A., *Renaissance in Bengal: Quests and Confrontations, 1800–1860* (Simla, 1970)
Political Diaries of H. B. Edwardes, Assistant to the Resident at Lahore, 1847–49 (Allahabad, 1912)
Popplewell, R. J., 'British Intelligence in Mesopotamia, 1914–1916', in M. I. Handel (ed.), *Intelligence and Military Operations* (1990)
———, *Intelligence and Imperial Defence: British Intelligence and the Defence of the Indian Empire, 1904–1924* (1995)
Powell, A. A., 'Maulana Rahmet Allah Kairanawi and Muslim–Christian Controversy in India in the Mid-Nineteenth Century', *JRAS* (1976)
Speech of John Poynder Esquire at East India House on 20th March 1839 on the Subject of the Directors' Last Despatch (1839)
Press Lists of the Punjab Civil Secretariat (XVII): *From 1859 to 1868, Judicial Department* (Lahore, 1925)
Press Lists of the Punjab Civil Secretariat (XX): *From 1859 to 1868, Political Department* (Lahore, 1928)

Rabbani, M. A., *I Was the Quaid's Aide-de-Camp* (Oxford, 1996)

Rahim, M. A., *Lord Dalhousie's Administration of the Conquered and Annexed States* (Delhi, 1963)

Railways in India (1845)

Raj, J., *Economic Conflict in North India* (Delhi, 1978)

Rajasekhar, D., 'Famines and Peasant Mobility: Changing Agrarian Structure in Kurnool District, 1870–1900', *IESHR*, 28 (1991)

Rajendram, N., *Establishment of Power in Malabar, 1664–1799* (Allahabad, 1979)

Ram, S., *From Sepoy to Subedar*, ed. J. Lunt (1970)

Rana, R. P., 'Agrarian Revolts in Northern India during the 17th and Early 18th Centuries', in R. E. Frykenberg (ed.), *Land, Control and Social Structure in Indian History*, (Manohar, WI, 1979)

Rao, S., 'My Ways and Days in Europe and India', *Nineteenth Century*, XLIX (1901)

Ray, A., *Some Aspects of Mughal Administration* (Ludhiana, 1984)

Ray, R., *Urban Roots of Indian Nationalism* (New Delhi, 1979)

Ray, R. K., 'Masses in Politics: The Non-Cooperation Movement in Bengal, 1920–1922', *IESHR*, 11 (1974)

Raychaudhuri, T., 'Permanent Settlement in Operation: Bekargani District, East Bengal', in R. E. Frykenberg (ed.), *Land, Control and Social Structure in Indian History* (Manohar, WI, 1979)

Raza, S. H. (ed.), *Mountbatten and Pakistan* (Karachi, 1982)

Records of the Delhi Residency and Agency (Lahore, 1911)

Records of the Intelligence Department of the Government of the North-West Provinces of India during the Mutiny of 1857, ed. W. Coldstream (2 vols, Edinburgh, 1902)

Records of the Ludhiana Agency (2 vols, Lahore, 1911)

Rees, J. D., *The Real India* (1908)

Reid, R., *History of the Frontier Areas Bordering on Assam from 1883 to 1941* (Assam, 1942)

Renford, R. K., *The Non-Official British in India to 1920* (Delhi, 1987)

Rennie, Y., *The Search for Criminal Man: A Conceptual History of the Dangerous Offender* (Lexington, MA, 1978)

Report of the Commissioners Appointed by the Punjab Sub-Committee of the Indian National Congress (2 vols, n.p., 1920)

Report on the Administration of Criminal Justice in the Lower Province of Bengal (Calcutta, 1879)

Report on the Progress and Administration of the Holkar and Sindia Neemuch State Railway for the Year 1878–79 (Bombay, 1879)

Report on the Working of Dispensaries, Jail Hospitals and the Registration of Vital Statistics for the Central India Agency for 1909 (Calcutta, 1910)

Report on the Working of Dispensaries, Jail Hospitals and the Registration of Vital Statistics in the Central India Agency for 1912 (Calcutta, 1913)

Reports on the Calcutta University Commission, 1917–1919 (13 vols, Calcutta, 1919)

Richards, F., *Old Soldier Sahib* (1965 edn)

Richards, J. F., 'The Hyderbad Karnatic, 1687–1707', *MAS*, 9 (1975)

—— , 'The Imperial Crisis in the Deccan', *Journal of Asia Studies*, 35 (1976)

Richards, J. F., and Rao, V. N., 'Banditry in Mughal India: Historical and Folk Perceptions', *IESHR*, 17 (1980)

Ricketts, L., 'English Society in India', *Contemporary Review*, CI (1912)

Rizvi, G., *Linlithgow and India: A Study in British Policy and the Political Impasse in India, 1936–43* (1978)

Robb, P., 'The Ordering of Rural India: the Policing of Nineteenth-century Bengal', in D. M. Anderson and D. Killingray (eds), *Policing the Empire: Government, Authority and Control, 1830–1940* (Manchester, 1991)

Roberts, A., *The Holy Fox: A Biography of Lord Halifax* (1991)

———, *Eminent Churchillians* (1994)

Roberts, F., *Forty-one Years in India* (1 vol, 1898 edn)

Roberts in India: The Military Papers of Field-Marshal Lord Roberts, 1876–1893, ed. B. Robson (Army Records Society, 1993)

Robertson, G., *Chitral: The Story of a Minor Siege* (1898)

Robson, B., 'Maiwand, 27 July 1880', *JSAHR*, LI (1972)

———, 'The Kandahar Letters of Alfred Cave', *JSAHR*, LXXIX (1991)

Roche, P. A., 'Caste and the British Merchant Government in Madras, 1629–1749', *IESHR*, 12 (1975)

The Embassy of Sir Thomas Roe to the Court of the Great Mogul, 1615–1619, ed. W. Forster (Hakluyt Society, 2nd series, 2 vols, 1889)

Role, M., 'La Stratégie Japonaise dans l'Océan Indien', *Guerres Mondiales et Conflits Contemporains*, 159 (July 1990)

Rousseau, G., and Porter, R. (eds), *Exoticism in the Enlightenment* (Manchester, 1990)

Royle, T., *The Last Days of the Raj* (1997 edn)

Russell, H., *With the Prince in the East* (1922)

Russell, R., and Islam, K., 'The Satirical Verse of Akbar Ilahabad (1846–1921)', *MAS*, 8 (1974)

Russell, W. H., *My Diary in India in the Year 1858–9* (2 vols, 1860)

———, *The Prince of Wales's Tour: A Diary of India* (1879)

Ryder, M., *Four Years Service in India* (Leicester, 1853)

Rywkin, M. (ed.), *Russian Colonial Expansion to 1917* (1988)

Sala, G. A., *A Journey Due North, being Notes on a Residence in Russia during the Summer of 1856* (1858)

Sale, F., *A Journal of the Disasters in Afghanistan, 1841–42* (1843)

Savi, E. W., *The Passionate Problem* (1935)

Savi, E. W., and Barry, C., *Mixed Cargo: Stories of Indian and English Romance and Adventure* (1932)

Schendel, S. van, '"Madmen of Mymemsingh": Peasant Resistance and the Colonial Process in Eastern India, 1824 to 1833', *IESHR*, 22 (1985)

Scott, W., *The Surgeon's Daughter* (Waverley Novels, XLVII, ii, Edinburgh, 1903)

Sedition Committee Report, 1918 (Calcutta, 1918)

Sellon, E., *Herbert Breakspeare: A Legend of the Mahratta War* (1848)

Sen, A., 'The Food Problem: Theory and Practice', *Third World Quarterly* (1982)

Senelik, L., 'Politics and Entertainment: Victorian Music Hall Songs', *VS*, 19 (1975–76)

Sharma, B. B., 'Darogha Ubbas Ali, An Unknown Indian Photographer', *History of Photography*, 7 (1983)

Siddiqi, A., 'Money and Prices in the Earlier Stages of Empire: India and Britain, 1760–1840', *IESHR*, 17 (1981)

Simeon, D., 'The Great TISCO Strike and Lockout of 1928', *IESHR*, 30 (1993)

Sindia State Railway: Administration Report on the Construction of the Railway from April 1874 (Rorkee, 1877)

Singh, H. L., *Problems and Policies of the British in India* (1963)

Sleeman, W., *Rambles and Recollections of an Indian Official* (2 vols, 1893 edn)

Smalley, A., 'The Colonial State and Agrarian Structure in Bengal', *Journal of Contemporary Asia Studies*, 13 (1988)

Smith, H., *The Autobiography of Lieutenant-General Sir Harry Smith*, ed. G. C. Moore Smith (1903)

Smith, M., 'Sketch of Major-General Pollock's Campaign in Afghanistan in 1842', *Colburn's United Services Magazine*, 1844, Part III

Sprague Allen, B., *Tides in English Taste* (1619–1800) (2 vols, New York, 1958)

Statement Exhibiting the Moral and Material Progress and Condition of India During the Years 1889–1890 (1891)

Statistical Abstract for the British Empire for Each of the Ten Years 1926 to 1935 (1936)

Steadman, J. M., 'The Asiatick Society of Bengal', *Eighteenth Century Studies*, 10 (1977)

Steinbuck, Lieutenant-Colonel, *The Punjaub: Being a Brief Account of the Country of the Sikhs* (1848)

Sterling, A. C., *Russia under Nicholas the First* (1840)

Stewart, L., 'A Surgeon in the Second Sikh War: Ludovick Stewart's Account of the Battle of Chillianwala', ed. M. Nicholls, *JSAHR*, LXXI (1993)

Stewart, N., *My Service Days: India, Afghanistan, Suakim '85 and China* (1908)

Stocqueler, J. H., *India: Its History, Climate and Field Sports* (1853)

Stoddart Kennedy, G., 'The Christian Imperialism of the Die-Hard Defenders of the Raj, 1926–1935', *JICH*, 18 (1990)

Stokes, E., 'Rural Revolt in the Great Rebellion of 1857 in India: A Study of Saharanpur and Muzaffanum Districts', *HJ*, 12 (1970)

——, 'Traditional Resistance Movements in Afro-Asian Nationalism: The Context of the 1857 Mutiny Rebellion in India', *PP*, No. 48 (1970)

——, *The Peasant and the Raj: Studies in Agrarian Society and Peasant Rebellion on Colonial India* (Cambridge, 1978)

——, *The Peasant Armed: The Indian Revolt of 1857* (Cambridge, 1986)

Strachan, J. M., *The Connexion of the East India Company with Superstitious and Idolatrous Customs and Rites of the Natives of India* (1840)

Stuart, W. K., *Reminiscences of a Soldier* (2 vols, 1874)

Subramaman, L., 'Bombay and the West Coast in the late 1740s', *IESHR*, 17 (1981)

Sudhur, P., 'The Indian States and the Civil Disobedience Movement of 1930–31', *Indian History Congress* (Calicut, 1976)

Sundaram, C. S., 'A Paper Tiger: The Indian National Army in Battle, 1944–45', *War and Society*, 13 (1995)

Talbot, I., 'Mountbatten and the Partition of India: A Rejoinder', *History*, 69 (1984)

——, 'The Role of the Crowd in the Muslim League Struggle for Pakistan', *JICH*, 21 (1993)

Taylor, M., *A Student's Manual of Indian History* (1870)

Thackeray, W. M., "A History of India" by the Hon. Montstuart Elphinstone', *Quarterly Review*, LXXVII (1841)

Thirumati, I., 'Peasant Class Assertions in Nalgona and Warangal Districts of Telangana, 1936–1946', *IESHR*, 31 (1994)

Thorne, C., *Allies of a Kind: The United States, Britain and War Against Japan, 1941–1945* (Oxford, 1979)

Thornhill, M., *The Personal Adventures and Experiences of a Magistrate during the Rise, Progress and Suppression of the Indian Mutiny* (1884)

Tinker, H., 'India in the First World War and After', *Journal of Contemporary History* 3 (1968)

Tod, J., *Annals and Antiquities of Rajasthan* (3 vols, ed. W. Crooke, reprint Delhi, 1993)

Tomlinson, B. R., *The Indian National Congress and the Raj* (1976)

——, *The Political Economy of the Raj* (1979)

Tribe, D., *President Charles Bradlaugh M.P.* (1971)

The Transfer of Power: 1942–47, ed. N. M. Mansergh, E. W. R. Lumby and P. Moon (12 vols, 1970–87)

Tripathi, A., *The Extremist Challenge: India Between 1898 and 1910* (Bombay, 1967)

Tuker, F., *The Yellow Scarf* (1961)

Tupp, A. C., *The Indian Civil Service and the Competitive System* (1875)

Vansittart, H., *A Narrative of the Transactions in Bengal from the Year 1760 to the Year 1764* (3 vols, 1766)

Veitch, *Songs of an Exile* (Edinburgh, 1820)

Vernon, N. P., 'Soviet Historians on the Russian Menace to India in the Second Half of the 19th Century', *Indian History Congress* (Calcutta, 1976)

A Voice from the Men of Manchester (1858)

Vigié, H., *Dupleix* (Paris, 1993)

von Albertini, R., *European Colonial Rule, 1880–1940: The Impact of the West on India, Southeast Asia and Africa*, trans. J. G. Williamson (1982)

Walpole, H., *Horace Walpole's Correspondence*, ed. W. S. Lewis (48 vols, Oxford, 1937–48)

Walters, H. K., *The Operations of the Malakand Field Force and the Buner Field Force 1897–1898* (Simla, 1900)

Warburton, R., *Eighteen Years in the Khyber, 1879–1898* (1900)

Warner, P., *Auchinleck: The Lonely Soldier* (1982 edn)

Washbrook, D., 'Economic Depression and the Making of Traditional Society in Colonial India, 1820–1855', *TRHS*, 6th Series, 3 (1993)

Wavell, Lord, *The Viceroy's Journal*, ed. P. Moon (1973)

Webber, T. W., *The Forests of Upper India* (1902)

Webster, M., 'Zoffany in India: 1, The Mystery of the Lucknow Cockfight' and '2, Hunting the Royal Tiger', *Country Life* (8 and 15 March 1973)

Weeks, J., *Coming Out: Homosexual Politics in Britain from the Nineteenth Century to the Present* (1983 edn)

The Despatches, Minutes and Correspondence of the Marquess of Wellesley, K.G., During his Administration in India, ed. M. Martin (5 vols, 1836–37)

Welsh, J., *Military Reminiscences from a Journal of nearly Forty Years Active Service in the East Indies* (2 vols, 1830)

Wheen, F., *Tom Driberg: His Life and Indiscretions* (1990)

Willcocks, J., *The Romance of Soldiering and Sport* (1925)

Williams, Captain, *An Historical Account of the Rise and Progress of the Bengal Native Infantry from its First Formation in 1757 to 1796* (1817)

Williamson, T., *The East-India Vade-Mecum* (2 vols, 1810)

Wilson, A., *Sport and Service in Assam and Elsewhere* (1924)

The Military Correspondence of Field-Marshal Sir Henry Wilson, 1918–1922, ed.
    K. Jeffrey (Army Records Society, 1985)
Wilson, J., 'The History of an Indian District: An Example of the Benefits of British
    Rule in India', *National Review*, VI (1885–86)
——, *The Indian Civil Service as a Career for Scotsmen* (Edinburgh, 1885)
Duke of Windsor, *A King's Story* (1951)
Wink, A., *Land and Sovereignty in India* (Cambridge, 1986)
Wood, C., 'Peasant Revolt', in D. Hardiman (ed.), *Peasant Resistance in India,
    1858–1914* (Oxford, 1993)
Wood, J., *A Personal Narrative of a Journey to the Source of the River Oxus* (1841)
Wolf, L., *The Life of the First Marquess of Ripon* (2 vols, 1921)
Woolf, L., *Growing: An Autobiography of the Years 1904 to 1911* (1961)
Wolpert, S. A., *Morley and India, 1906–1910* (Berkeley, CA, 1967)
——, *Nehru: A Tryst With Destiny* (Oxford, 1996)
Wrong, G. M., *The Earl of Elgin* (1905)

Xeres [W. Lowry-Cole], 'On Tour With an Indian Proconsul', *Blackwoods
    Magazine*, CCII (1917)

Young, J., 'The Siege of the Fort of Deeg, 9 December to 26 December, 1804', ed.
    D. O. Khanse and T. R. Tandon, *JSAHR*, LXXIII (1985)
Young, K., *Delhi – 1857*, ed. H. W. Norman and Mrs K. Young (1902)
Younghusband, G., *Indian Frontier Warfare* (1898)
——, *A Soldier's Memories of Peace and War* (1917)
——, *Forty Years a Soldier* (1923)
Younghusband, G. J. and F. E., *The Relief of Chitral* (1895)

Zastoupil, L., 'Mill and India', *VS*, 32 (1988)
Ziegler, P., *Mountbatten* (1985)

The following journals and newspapers have also been used: *Asiatic Journal, British and
Foreign Medical Review, Chambers Information for the People, Chums, Daily Express, Daily
Graphic, Daily Mail, Daily Telegraph, Dublin Review, Edinburgh Review, The Graphic,
Lancet, Macphail's Edinburgh Ecclesiastical Journal, Medical Review, Medical Times and
Gazette, National Geographic Magazine, Naval and Military Magazine, New Statesman,
Picture Post, Punch, Quarterly Review, Saturday Review, Spectator, The Times.*

Notes

Part One: The Company Ascendant

1: Prologue

1 Roe, II, 225, 537.
2 Wink, 39.
3 J. F. Richards, 'The Imperial Crisis &c.', *JAS* 35, 239.
4 J. F. Richards, 'The Hyderabad Karnatik &c.', *MAS* 9, 247–8.
5 J. F. Richards and V. N. Rao, 'Banditry in Mughal India &c.', *IESHR* 18, 99–102.
6 Husain, 38ff.
7 *Ibid.*, 214.
8 Baines, 'Maratha History of Gujarat', *Gazetteer of the Bombay Presidency*, I, i, 399, 401.
9 Chand, 163–4.
10 *Fort William–India House Correspondence*, I, 470.
11 *Early Annals of the English &c.*, II, ii, 12, 15.
12 Hamilton, II, 13.
13 Orme, I, 38, 41.
14 SRO, Campbell, GD 87/1/34.

2: A Glorious Prospect

1 IOL, Mss Eur, Yule, E 357/1, I.
2 SRO, Grant, GD 345/1179, 2–3.
3 Landa, 296.
4 Defoe, *A Plan of English Commerce*, xiv–xv, 273.
5 Chaudhuri-Soas, 'The Structure of the Indian Textile Industry &c.', *IESHR* 11, 127–8.
6 Sprague Allen, 242.
7 Bowan, 'Investment and Empire &c.', *EcHR* (2nd series), XLII, *passim*.
8 Das, *Myths and Realities &c.*, 14, 22, 23, 33.
9 Vigié, 241.

10 *Fort William–India House Correspondence*, I, 349, 356.
11 Pillai, I, 140, 150.
12 Vigié, 241.
13 *Ibid.*, 453.
14 Orme, I, 165–6, 254, 378.
15 *Ibid.*, 78.
16 Ives, 23.
17 SRO, Campbell, GD 87/1/34.
18 Orme, I, 106.
19 Vigié, 263; Orme, I, 125–6.
20 *Fort William–India House Correspondence*, II, x–xi.
21 Arasaratnam, 'Weavers, Merchants &c.', *IESHR* 17, 271–3.
22 Vigié, 384.
23 *Ibid.*, 323–6.
24 Das, *Myths and Realities*, 7.
25 Forrest, I, 143.
26 Bence-Jones, 48–9.

3: New Strength from Conquest

1 *Parliamentary History of England*, 17, 355; *East India Gazetteer* (1828), I, 190–1.
2 Williamson, I, 188–9.
3 Bence-Jones, 123.
4 *Fort William–India House Correspondence*, I, 1011–12.
5 *Ibid.*, xvii–xviii, 563, 1009–10.
6 *Ibid.*, 1009, 1015–16, 1020.
7 Chaudhuri, *Clive of India*, 163–4.
8 Orme, I, 167; Marshall, *East India Fortunes*, 167.
9 Ives, 152–3; Orme, II, 173.
10 *Fort William–India House Correspondence*, II, 231.
11 *Ibid.*; IOL, Mss Eur, Strachey, F 128/141, 175d.
12 *Annual Register* (1758), 398.
13 *Fort William–India House Correspondence*, II, 250.
14 *The East India Military Calendar* (1823), 44.
15 Taylor, 134.
16 Kaye, *A History of the Sepoy War*, I, 484–5.
17 Hunter, *Imperial Gazeteer &c.*, IX, 193–4.
18 Kaye, *A History of the Sepoy War*, I, 485–6.
19 NLS, Minto, Ms 12,756, 493; Barrier, in *Peasant Resistance &c.*, 245.
20 Gilmour, 370–1.
21 NLS, Minto, Ms 12,757, 310.
22 IOL, Mss Eur, Strachey, F 128/141, 4.
23 Marshall, *East India Fortunes*, 117–18, 128.
24 Vansittart, II, 412–13.
25 Arasaratnam, 'Weavers, Merchants &c.', *IESHR*, 17, 275.
26 Bence-Jones, 173–4.
27 Vansittart, I, 151.
28 SRO, Grant, GD 345/916, B.
29 *House of Commons Sessional Papers &c.*, 54, 168–71; Marshall, *East India Fortunes*, 168–9.

30 IOL, Mss Eur, Strachey, F 128/45, 75–8, 80, 81.
31 *Ibid.*, 82d.
32 IOL, Mss Eur, Strachey, F 128/6, 9d.
33 *Ibid.*, 8–9.
34 *Ibid.*, 16d, 33.
35 *Ibid.*, 15.
36 Fortescue, III, 100.
37 IOL, Mss Eur, Strachey, F 128/141, 61.
38 Das, *Myths and Realities*, 71.
39 Vansittart, I, 39.
40 IOL, Mss Eur, Strachey, F 128/141, 14–15.

4: An Empire Within an Empire

1 Foote, 58–9.
2 *Ibid.*, 37–8.
3 Marshall, 'The Personal Fortunes &c,'. *EcHR* (2nd series), XVII, 295.
4 Walpole, XXIII, 400, 499, 524.
5 Namier and Brooke, II, 152; NRO, BEA, Grey, 419/439.
6 Phillips, 'The East India Company &c.', *TRHS* (4th series), XX, 95.
7 *The National Mirror* &c., 29, 78–9.
8 *Parliamentary History of England*, 17, 474.
9 *Ibid.*, 354.
10 Marshall, 'The Personal Fortunes &c.', *EcHR* (2nd series), XVII, 288, 291.
11 C. C. Davies, 'Warren Hastings &c.', *EHR*, 70, 616.
12 *House of Commons Sessional Papers &c.*, 58, 46.
13 Phillips, 'The East India Company &c.', *TRHS* (4th series), XX, 88.
14 *Ibid.*, 97–8.
15 Wellesley, III, 76, 96; *Asiatic Journal*, I, 149.
16 *House of Commons Sessional Papers &c.*, 58, 21–2.
17 Forbes, I, 242–3.
18 *Ibid.*, II, 378–9; IOL, L.Mil 5/482, *passim*.
19 Anon (Madras Officer), *A Sketch and a Review*, 68.
20 Bowrey, 24.
21 Mill, II, 4–5.
22 Hastings, I, 340.
23 Mill, II, 10.
24 Fraxi, 3–4.
25 Hamilton, I, 152.
26 Bowrey, 23.
27 Anon, *A Narrative and Transactions &c.*, 27.
28 Knight, 'Images of Nations &c.', *Eighteenth Century Studies*, 22, *passim*.
29 IOL, LPS 5/363, Memo of Colonel Alexander Walker, 28 January 1810.
30 *House of Commons Sessional Papers &c.*, 58, 12.

Part Two: The Conquest of India

1: *No Retreat*

1 Kaye, *Life &c. . . . of John Malcolm*, I, 320–1.
2 PRO, WO 1/357, 381–2.
3 *British Parliamentary Papers: East India Company Affairs*, 11, 824–5.
4 Gleig, I, 24.
5 Wellesley, II, 131.
6 Mathur, 11–12.
7 HMC, *Bathurst*, 363,
8 NLS, Walker, Ms 13,665, 10.
9 *Asiatic Journal*, 3rd series, I, 601.
10 James, *Iron Duke &c.*, 77.
11 Hardinge, 36.
12 Wellesley, IV, 226–7.
13 Lenman, 'The Weapons of War &c.', *JSAHR*, LVI, *passim*.
14 PRO, Adm 2/5119.
15 PRO, WO 1/854, 519.
16 Hastings, I, 35; II, 101–2.
17 *British Parliamentary Papers: East India Company Affairs*, 11, 234.
18 Hastings, I, 36.
19 Blacker, 375.
20 *Records of the Delhi Residency and Agency*, 242–43.
21 *Hansard's Parliamentary Debates*, new series, XVII, 669.
22 Butler, 192, 194.
23 Hastings, I, vi.
24 *Asiatic Journal*, 3rd series, I, 69–70.
25 PRO, WO 104/440.
26 NLS, Walker, Ms 13,667, 12–12d; 13,707, 8–14.
27 SRO, Elphinstone, GD 46/17/42, 24 June 1813.
28 Kaye, *Life &c. . . . of John Malcolm*, I, 51n, 208, 259; II, 416.
29 Wellesley, V, 161.
30 *Cobbett's Parliamentary Debates*, II, 22–3, 105, 372–3, 976, 1078.
31 Norris, 6.
32 Butler, 193.
33 *Blackwood's Magazine*, 52, 608.
34 Gleig, I, 464.
35 Ellenborough, II, 61–2.

2: *The Cossack and the Sepoy*

1 Abbott, I, 82, 96, 97, 98.
2 Burnes, I, 296.
3 PRO, FO 65/276, 9 March 1841.
4 PRO, FO 65/286, 31 January 1842.
5 Connolly, I, 155.
6 *Ibid.*, 327, 329, 382–3.
7 Burnes, II, 136.
8 Hopkirk, *Great Game*, 152.
9 Kaye, *War in Afghanistan*, II, 37.

10 Burnes, II, 217.
11 Wood, 371–2.
12 Mackinnon, I, 88.
13 NLS, Minto, Ms 11,322, 1–2, 9–10, 13d.
14 IOL, LPS, 5/363, 27 March 1810.
15 De Lacy Evans, 50–3.
16 *Asiatic Journal*, I, 216–17.
17 Hastings, II, 17, 35.
18 De Lacy Evans, 50–3.
19 SRO, Brunton, GD 214/677, 1.
20 NLS, Minto, Ms 11,322, 104d.
21 BL, Auckland, Add Mss 37,689, 11.
22 HMC, *Wellington*, 2, 457.
23 Nott, I, 47.
24 Norris, 83.
25 Fuller, 226.
26 Norris, 180.
27 Kaye, *War in Afghanistan*, I, 296–97.
28 Sterling, vi–vii, viii–ix.
29 Sala, 88.
30 Anon, *Great Britain and Russia*, 48.
31 Napier, 52.
32 Nott, I, 69.
33 *Asiatic Journal*, 3rd series, IV, 485–7, 491, 497–8.
34 Norris, 216, 218–19.
35 Nott, I, 100.
36 Burnes, II, 312.
37 Fane, II, 58.
38 NAM, Anon, 3rd NI, 85.
39 Kaye, *War in Afghanistan*, III, 32–3.
40 Mackinnon, I, 170–1.
41 BL, Broadfoot, Add Mss 40,182, 298.
42 PRO, FO 248/100, 20 June 1840.
43 Anon, 'The Evacuation of Kabul', *Blackwoods*, LIII, 276; Macrory, 114–15.
44 NAM, Daniel, 9 December 1838.
45 NAM, Anon, 3rd NI, 15; Kaye, 5.
46 Mackinnon, I, 79.
47 Ram, 88.
48 NAM, Anon, 3rd NI, 55.
49 Kaye, 42.
50 Fane, II, 172.
51 PRO, WO 164/441.
52 PRO, FO 248/100, n.d., 7 May 1840; Macrory, 107–8.
53 Norris, 353.
54 PRO, FO 248/100, 1 January 1842.
55 Sale, 47.
56 BL, Broadfoot, Add Mss 40,182, 136d; Eyre, 95; Norris, 446–50.
57 Havelock, I, 100–1.
58 Napier, 150.
59 Norris, 433.

3: The cast of a Die

1 *Hansard*, 3rd series, LXII, 382, 390.
2 *Punch*, 6 (1844), 118, 202.
3 Smith, *Autobiography*, 491.
4 Lambrick, *Sir Charles Napier &c.*, 14, 22, 23, 25.
5 *Ibid.*, 61.
6 Napier, 179.
7 *Ibid.*, 167.
8 Hansard, 3rd series, LXII, 382.
9 NAM, Waddington, n.p.
10 Lambrick, *Sir Charles Napier &c.*, 174–5.
11 Napier, 516.
12 IOL, Mss Eur, Jacob, F 75/1, 113–15.
13 *Ibid.*, 113, 119.
14 *Hansard*, 3rd series, LXII, 443–4.
15 Lambrick, *Sir Charles Napier &c.*, 243.
16 Hardinge, 3–4, 9.
17 *Ibid.*, 63, 121–2.
18 *Ibid.*, 49, 64.
19 *Ibid.*, 116.
20 BL, Broadfoot, Add Mss 40,127, 391–391d; Lawrence, *Essays &c.*, 270.
21 SRO, RH 2/8/69, 26.
22 Mackinnon, II, 82, 119.
23 IOL, L.Mil 3/56, 45.
24 Hardinge, 119, 136–7.
25 NLS, Brown, Ms 2845, 16–16d, 18.
26 NAM, Tookey, 24.
27 NLS, Brown, Ms 2845, n.p.
28 Smith, *Autobiography*, 545.
29 Banerjee, *Khalsa Raj*, 202–3, 214.
30 IOL, Mss Eur, Pierce, A 106, 5.
31 Ram, *From Sepoy to Subedar*, 137.
32 *Ibid.*, 138–9.
33 Mackinnon, II, 105, 114.
34 Smith, *Autobiography*, 552.
35 *Ibid.*
36 Mackinnon, II, 233.
37 NLS, Brown, Ms 2845, 66d.
38 Lawrence, *Essays &c.*, 312.
39 Edwardes, *A Year &c.*, I, 28.
40 *Political Diaries of Lieutenant H. B. Edwardes*, 5, 7.
41 BL, Cust, Add Mss 45,392, 64.
42 Edwardes, *A Year &c.*, I, 19; *Journals and Diaries of the Assistants to the Governor General &c.*, 59.
43 Edwardes, *A Year &c.*, I, 306.
44 Stewart, 'A Surgeon in the Second Sikh War &c.', *JSAHR*, LXXI, 218.
45 Edwardes, *A Year &c.*, I, 285.
46 *Journals and Diaries of the Assistants to the Governor General &c.*, IV, 165–6.
47 Ryder, 38, 44.

48 Edwardes, *A Year &c.*, II, 623–7.
49 IOL, Mss Eur, Pearse, B 115, 85d; Ryder, 46–7.
50 *Ibid.*, 126.
51 *Ibid.*, 132–3.
52 NLS, Grant, Ms 17,901, 135d.
53 NLS, Baird Smith, Ms 10,983, 14.
54 IOL, Mss Eur, Pearse, B 115, 21d; Ryder, 46–7.
55 *Hansard*, 3rd series, CIV, 755; *Dublin University Magazine*, XXXV (1850), 205.
56 NLS, Baird Smith, Ms 10,983, 25.
57 Stewart, 'A Surgeon in the Second Sikh War &c.', *JSAHR*, LXXI, 220.
58 *Dublin University Magazine*, XXXV (1850), 207.
59 *Ibid.*

4: Robust Bodies and Obstinate Minds

1 Hardinge, 221.
2 (Henderson), *The Bengalee &c.*, 31.
3 *British Parliamentary Papers: Indian Territories &c.*, 13, 116.
4 Blacker, 25–6; *Asiatic Journal*, I, 132–3.
5 IOL, LPS, 5/363, 23 March and 10 April 1812.
6 Blacker, 185n.
7 Murray, 'Field Surgeon &c.', *JSAHR*, LXXII, 40.
8 Wellesley, IV, 396, 446, 449.
9 SRO, Brunton, GD 214/677, 1.
10 Blacker, 63, 67–70.
11 IOL, LPS, 5/363, Elphinstone to Nepean, 17 November 1817.
12 Forbes, I, 339–40, 341–2; Beaven, I, 123; Elphinstone, I, 553–4.
13 *British Parliamentary Papers: Indian Territories &c.*, 13, 25.
14 IOL, Mss Eur, Pearse, B 115, 84.
15 Anon, 'The Battle of Chillianwallah', *Colburn's United Service Magazine*, 1850, Pt III, 10.
16 Anon, 'History as she is wrote', *JSAHR*, XVI, *passim*.
17 *Naval and Military Magazine*, 1831, Pt I, 151.
18 Stewart, 'A Surgeon in the Second Sikh War &c.', *JSAHR*, LXXI, 220.
19 Welsh, I, 181–2, 194–5.
20 Fortescue, XII, 368.
21 Young, 'The Siege of the Fort of Deeg', *JSAHR*, LXIII, 37, 43.
22 Fortescue, XII, 332–3.
23 Birom, 71–2, 80.
24 Stewart, 'A Surgeon in the Second Sikh War &c.', *JSAHR*, LXXI, 221.
25 Anon (A Light Dragoon), 'Reminiscences &c.', *Colburn's United Service Magazine*, 1843, Pt III, 586.
26 Anon, 'The Action at Ramnuggar', *Colburn's United Service Magazine*, 1850, Pt III, 566.
27 Blacker, 19–20.
28 *Ibid.*, 27; Hastings, I, 35.
29 SRO, Brunton, GD 214/682, 4.
30 Macrory, 94.
31 Young, 'The Siege of the Fort of Deeg', *JSAHR*, LXIII, 44.
32 *Ibid.*, 52.

33 NAM, Pearson, 1, 4.
34 PRO, WO 64/ 438.
35 IOL, L.Mil 5/150.
36 Anon (Lieutenant of the Bengal Establishment), *The Cadet's Guide &c.*, 33.
37 SRO, Home, GD 1/384, 20 February 1806.
38 *Ibid.*, 5 September 1807.
39 *Officers of the Bengal Army*, II, 473.
40 Bryant, 'Scots in India &c.', *Scottish Historical Review*, LXIV, 22.
41 SRA, Campbell, TD 219/110/70, 36, 37.
42 Goodbehere, 'The Letters &c.', *JSAHR*, LVII, 18–19.
43 SRA, Campbell, TD 219/110/70, 40, 107i, 121i, 131, 134, 137, 137i.
44 Hodson, 'The Baraset Cadet Camp &c.', *JSAHR*, II, *passim* ; NLS, Minto, Ms 11,306, 26, 38d.
45 Anon (Lieutenant of the Bengal Establishment), *The Cadet's Guide &c.*, 13–14, 41.
46 Anon (Madras Officer), *A Sketch and a Review*, 4.
47 Blacker, vi.
48 Anon (Madras Officer), *A Sketch and a Review*, 4, 7.
49 IOL, Mss Eur, Horwood, C 570, 26, 28.
50 *Ibid.*, 80.
51 Peers, 'Sepoys, Soldiers &c.', *JICH*, 23, 214.
52 NLS, Walker, Ms 13,707, 38–39.
53 IOL, L.Mil 5/255.
54 IOL, Mss Eur, Anon, D 1146/6, 80.
55 Ram, 14–15.
56 Williams, *An Historical Account &c.*, 373–4.
57 *Ibid.*, 375.
58 NLS, Walker, Ms 13,307, 38–9; *Asiatic Journal*, 11, 274; *Ibid.*, 13, 480.
59 NLS, Minto, Ms 11,322, 95.
60 Gupta, 'The Vellore Mutiny &c.', *JIH*, 49, 97.
61 SRO, Brunton, GD 214/677, 11ff; Goodbehere, 'The Letters &c.', *JSAHR*, LVII, 13.
62 NLS, Minto, Ms 11,322, 105d–106.
63 Blacker, 252n, Beaven, I, 98.
64 BL, Blackwell, Add Mss 39,811, 78.
65 NLS, Tweeddale, Ms 14,559, 83.
66 *Ibid.*, 96.
67 Beaven, I, 85.
68 NLS, Minto, 11,322, 3.
69 *British Parliamentary Papers: Indian Territories &c.*, 35.
70 IOL, L.Mil 10/134, 3ff.
71 Fane, I, 256–7.
72 BL, Blackwell, Add Mss 39,812, 7–7d.
73 Ryder, 3.
74 NAM, Cottrill, 1, 3.
75 NAM, Tookey, 3d.
76 IOL, L.Mil 5/3/289.
77 Morehead, II, 562–3.
78 NLS, Tweeddale, Ms 14,559, 1, 29.
79 IOL, L.Mil 5/407, 171, 175.

80 IOL, L.Mil 5/376, 120, 132–3, 232–3.
81 *Ibid.*, 133.
82 Morehead, I, 20.
83 Stuart, II, 214.
84 IOL, L.Mil 3/289.
85 Morehead, I, 365–7.
86 IOL, L.Mil 3/289; Morehead, I, 369, 379.
87 Anon (A Light Dragoon), 'Reminiscences &c.', *Colburn's United Service Magazazine*, 1843, Pt III, 389.
88 McGuffie, 'Lake's Mahratta Campaign &c.', *JSAHR*, XXIX, 57.
89 NAM, Plumb, 2.
90 Young, 'The Siege of the Fort of Deeg &c.', *JSAHR*, LXIII, 42.
91 Hastings, II, 249.
92 Ryder, 105.
93 Birom, 72.
94 IOL, L.Mil 5/318. The letters in this file are unnumbered; Private Tolney lived in Sandwich, Kent, and approached the Company for prize money in March 1816 and August 1817.
95 PRO, WO 64/438 and 441.
96 PRO, WO 64/440.
97 IOL, Mss Eur, Nicholls, F 175/33, 17.
98 Birom, 24.
99 IOL, LPS, 5/364, 'Copies of Letters from an Officer on the Staff, the Poona Brigade'.
100 IOL, L.Mil 3/56, 329.
101 IOL, L.Mil 13/1196, 597 (for issue of revolvers).
102 Blacker, 212–13.
103 Birom, 87–8.
104 *Ibid.*, 86–7.
105 Mackenzie, *A Sketch of the War &c.*, II, 25.
106 Goodbehere, 'The Letters &c.', *JSAHR*, LVII, 9.
107 IOL, L.Mil 3/56, 171; *British Parlimentary Papers: The Indian Territories &c.*, 59.
108 IOL, L.Mil 3/56, 598d.
109 IOL, L.Mil 5/364, Elphinstone to Hastings, 23 March 1817.
110 IOL, L.Mil 5/363, Carnac to Governor of Bombay, 23 March and 10 April 1812.
111 Blacker, 110.
112 NLS, Walker, Ms 13,665, 2–48.
113 Young, 'The Siege of the Fort of Deeg', *JSAHR*, LXIII, 43.
114 BL, Broadfoot, Add Mss 40,127, 38.
115 PRO, FO 248/100, 1 January 1842.
116 *Records of the Delhi Residency and Agency*, 45.
117 Blacker, 280.

Part Three: The Raj Consolidated

1: European Gentlemen

1 Harrington, 56–8.
2 In private hands.
3 Anon (A Light Dragoon), 'Reminiscences &c.', *Colburn's United Service Magazine*, 1843, Pt III, 586.
4 Anon, *The College of Fort William &c.*, 1–2.
5 Kaye, *Life &c.* . . . *Charles, Lord Metcalfe*, I, 106.
6 Wellesley, I, 54.
7 Gleig, I, 155.
8 SRO, Read, GD 1/594, 4 September 1800.
9 NLS, Minto, Ms 11,600, 41, 81–3.
10 Lahore Political Diaries, IV, 6.
11 Anon, *The College of Fort William &c.*, 5–6, 9; Wellesley, II, 131–2, 346.
12 NRO, De Grey, WLS 11/8, 1 September 1798.
13 Colley, 168–9.
14 Wellesley, II, 323–4.
15 *Ibid.*, III, 64.
16 Egan, 4.
17 *Naval and Military Miscellany*, I (1827), 147.
18 Kaye, *Life &c.* . . . *Charles, Lord Metcalfe*, I, 2, 13.
19 *Records of the Delhi Residency*, 2.
20 Edwardes, *A Year &c.*, I, 113 and note.
21 Anon (Henderson), 117–18.
22 *Ibid.*, 189.
23 NLS, Walker, Ms 13,739, 6d ff.
24 Wellesley, V, 174.
25 Broughton, 3.
26 Ryder, 66–7, 95.
27 Leopold, 'British Applications &c.', *EHR*, LXXXIV, 584 and note.
28 Welsh, I, 2.
29 Hastings, I, 31–2.
30 Gilchrist, ix.
31 *Ibid.*, 232ff.
32 Beaven, I, 19.
33 *Asiatic Journal*, I, 7.
34 NLS, Halket, Ms 14,207, 116.
35 IOL, Mss Eur, Knolles, C 598, 8 May 1819.
36 BL, Blackwell, Add Mss 39,811, 12.
37 Forrest, 125.
38 NAM, Becher, n.d.
39 SRO, Read, GD 1 594/2, 21 December 1797.
40 Cohn, 'The Command of Language &c.', *Subaltern Studies*, IV, 310.
41 IOL, L.Mil 5/383, 6–8, 17d.
42 Webber, 72.
43 *Asiatic Journal*, 3rd series, I, 145.
44 Forrest, 168–70.
45 BL, Cust, Add Mss 45,390, 266.

46 NLS, Halket, Ms 14,207, 17.
47 Beaven, I, 84–5.
48 Hastings, I, 109–110.
49 SRO, Elphinstone, GD 46/17/42, 10 April 1814.
50 Tod, II, 900–1.
51 Forrest, 163.
52 NLS, Walker, Ms 13,840, 96.
53 Hastings, I, 12.
54 Fane, I, 263–65, 268.
55 BL, Hyde, Add Mss 42,105, 5.
56 Beaven, I, 18–19.
57 Buck, 27.
58 Anon (Henderson), 73.
59 Anon, 'Duelling &c.', *Colburn's United Service Magazine*, 1844, Pt III, 237.
60 *Ibid.*, 238–39.
61 Kiernan, *The Duel &c.*, 297.
62 BL, Broadfoot, Add Mss 40,127, 30d.
63 Cust, *Memories*, 87.
64 Sleeman, *Rambles &c.*, II, 255–6.
65 BL, Blackwell, Add Mss 38,911, 17.
66 Welsh, I, 4.
67 SRO, Read, GD 594/2, 1 October 1798.
68 NLS, Oswald, Ms 9008, 8.
69 Buck, 9.
70 Williamson, II, 116–19.
71 *Ibid.*, I, 220–5.
72 SRO, Home, GD 1/384, 15 May 1811; BL, Blackwell, Add Mss 39,811, 17;
    BL, Cust, Add Mss 45,390, 58; NLS, Oswald, 9006, 2d.
73 Fane, II, 193–4.
74 NAM, Pearson, I, 58–9.
75 IOL, Mss Eur, Chambers, A 172, *passim.*
76 Williamson, I, 213.
77 *Ibid.*, 162,
78 PRO, WO 71/217.
79 Anon (Madras Officer), *A Sketch &c.*, 17.
80 IOL, Mss Eur, Pearse, B 115, 86.
81 NLS, Minto, Ms 12,756, 338.

2: Utility and Beneficence

1 Forbes, II, 74–6.
2 *The Oriental Baptist*, IV, 286.
3 Kublicek, 'The Role of the Shallow-Draught Steamer &c.', *International Journal of Maritime History*, 6, 87.
4 Chunder, I, 140–1.
5 *British Parliamentary Papers: East Indies*, 15, 205.
6 Andrew, *Indian Railways &c.*, 86–7.
7 BL, Auckland, Add Mss 13,709, 94d.
8 Kaye, *Life &c. . . . Charles, Lord Metcalfe*, I, 55.
9 Tod, II, 900–1.

10 IOL, LPS, 20, F 52, 55–6.
11 IOL, LPS, 5/363, Memo, 20 January 1810.
12 NLS, Walker, Ms 13,840, 45–46.
13 NLS, Walker, Ms 13,712, 9; *East India Military Calendar* (1823), 151–2.
14 NLS, Walker, Ms 17,739, 33.
15 Chevers, 3n.
16 NLS, Minto, Ms 11,722, 6.
17 Mill, II, 213, 517–18.
18 *British Parliamentary Papers: East Indies*, 6, 48.
19 Macaulay, VII, 389.
20 NLS, Walker, Ms 13,840, 45–6, 48.
21 Mehta, *Lord Hastings &c.*, 208–10.
22 IOL, LPS, 5/363, Memo 28 January 1810.
23 Hardinge, 206.
24 *Memorial of the Hindu Inhabitants &c.*, 8.
25 BL, Auckland, Add Mss 37,689, 34–6.
26 Methur, 98–9, 112–13.
27 BL, Auckland, Add Mss 37,692, 10.
28 IOL, BH 3/106 (R/2 475/3) *passim.*
29 *British Parliamentary Papers &c.*, 15, 680, 682.
30 Anon, *Railways in India*, 33.
31 Andrew, *Indian Railways &c.*, 27–8.
32 Hardinge, 63.
33 Macpherson, 'Investment in Indian Railways &c.', *EcHR* (2nd series), 8, 181.
34 Kennedy, *A Railway Caution!*, 13.
35 Anon, *Railways in India*, 3.
36 *Annals of the Indian Administration*, I, 125.
37 *Ibid.*, IX, 366.

3: *Gradual and Mild Correction*

1 *Records of the Delhi Residency*, 70ff.
2 *Directions for Settlement &c.*, 53–4.
3 SRO, GD 1/594, 4 September 1800; Gleig, I, 155.
4 *Directions for Settlement &c.*, 19.
5 Panikar, 3–5, 7, 8.
6 Neale, 'Land is Rule &c.', in Frykenberg (ed.), *Land, Control &c.*, 19.
7 Raychaudhuri, 'Permanent Settlement &c.', in *Ibid.*, 163, 167.
8 *Annals of the Administration*, I, 2, 18.
9 Poddar, 49–68.
10 Cohn, 'Structure and Change &c.', in Frykenberg (ed.), *Land, Control &c.*, 78.
11 Van Schendel, '"Madmen of Mymensigh" &c.', *IESHR*, 22, 143.
12 *By Authority! A Full Exposure &c.*, 14–15.
13 IOL, BH 106 (R/2 475/3) *passim.*
14 Rana, 'Agrarian revolts &c.', *IESHR*, 18, 294, 296, 299; Ray, *Some Aspects &c.*, 167.
15 *Land Revenue Policy*, 150.
16 Panikar, 1.
17 *Annals of the Administration*, III, 326–33.
18 Hamid, 'Dispossessions &c.', *Journal of Peasant Studies*, 10, 57.

19 *Gazetteer of the Bombay Presidency*, VII, 110–11, 113, 119, 126.

20 Ray, *Economic Conflict &c.*, 4–5, 7.

21 Hamid, 'Dispossessions &c.', *Journal of Peasant Studies*, 10, 59.

22 Mukherjee, 284, 290.

23 Wood, 'Peasant Revolt &c.', in Hardiman (ed.), *Peasant Resistance &c.*, 137–43.

24 Bradley-Birt, 198.

25 Van Schendel, '"Madman of Mymensigh" &c.', *IESHR*, 22, 165.

26 NLS, Tweeddale, Ms 14,558, 30.

27 IOL, Wood, Ms Eur, F 78, 27–36d.

28 Mukherjee, 315.

29 Nigam, 'Disciplining and Policing &c.', *IESHR*, 27,151.

30 BL, Auckland, Add Mss 37,692, 40.

31 Chevers, 654–55.

32 *Ibid.*, 6.

33 BL, Paton, Add Mss 41,300, 101–29.

34 *Ibid.*, 1–2, 12.

35 *Ibid.*, 339, 341.

36 *British Parliamentary Papers: East Indies*, 10, 217; *Ibid.*, 13, 352.

37 BL, Paton, Add Mss 42,300, 409.

38 *Ibid.*, 407–8.

39 NLS, Minto, Ms 11,600, 8–10.

40 Chevers, 535.

41 Hardiman, 'Community, Patriarchy &c.', *Journal of Peasant Studies*, 23, 90.

42 *Gazetteer of the Bombay Presidency*, VII, 439.

43 Nigam, 'Disciplining and Policing &c.', *IESHR*, 27, 136–7.

44 BL, Ripon, Add Mss 43,614, 137, 142–142d.

45 Mathur, 97–9.

46 *Ibid.*, 148–9.

47 BL, Paton, Add Mss 41,300, 358.

48 Campbell, *Narrative &c.*, 33.

49 Hardinge, 83–4.

50 Campbell, *Narrative &c.*, 43; Boal, 74.

51 *Ibid.*, 77–8.

52 Pennier, 61.

53 *Ibid.*, 69–70.

54 Chevers, 165n.

55 *Ibid.*, 152–3.

56 IOL, LPS, 20/F 52, 51–6.

57 Chatterjii, 'The Daroga &c.', *IESHR*, 18, 37.

58 Chevers, 569, 573.

59 *Reports . . . on the Administration of Criminal Justice under the Madras Presidency for the Year 1849*, 13, 22, 28; *Ibid. . . . . for 1853*, 3.

60 *Ibid. . . . . for 1849*, 7–12.

61 Chevers, 343, 447, 544–6, 554.

62 *Ibid.*, 435.

63 *Reports . . . on the Administration of Criminal Justice under the Madras Presidency for the Year 1849*, 5.

64 Chevers, 755–9.

4: A Hearty Desire

1 Fraxi, 380.
2 NAM, Daniel, 7 June 1836.
3 Bloch, 133–4.
4 Carver, 14.
5 Hyam, 117; Kaye, *Life &c. . . . Charles, Lord Metcalfe*, I, 82, 111–12.
6 Hyam, 115.
7 Haight, 'Male Chastity &c.', *Contemporary Review*, 219, 252–53.
8 *Westminster and Foreign Quarterly*, LIII, July 1850, 475.
9 Weeks, 37.
10 McCalman, 'Unrespectable Radicalism &c.', *PP*, 104, 101.
11 Fraxi, 133–7.
12 *Westminster and Foreign Quarterly*, LIII, July 1850, 457.
13 Fraxi, 380–1.
14 *Ibid.*, xliv-xlvi.
15 Hamilton, II, 19.
16 Penzer, 139, 171.
17 NLS, Halket, Ms 14,207, 17d–18.
18 Fraxi, 380.
19 *Westminster and Foreign Quarterly*, LIII, July 1850, 488.
20 Harvey, 'Prosecutions &c.', *HJ*, 21, 943.
21 Bloch, 425.
22 Harvey, 'Prosecutions &c.', *HJ*, 21, 939–40.
23 Chevers, 707.
24 Williamson, II, 428–9.
25 Brodie, 76–7.
26 IOL, L.Mil 5/408, *passim.*
27 Mukherjee, 'Satan let loose &c.', *PP*, 93, 128.
28 Ryder, 129.
29 IOL, LPS, 5/364, Elphinstone to Nepean, 17 November 1817.
30 Krishnamurty, 81, 83.
31 *Ibid.*, 40–1, 45, 50–1.
32 NLS, Minto, Ms 11,322, 105d-106.
33 Beaven, I, 18–19; Williamson, I, 450–1.
34 Brodie, 58–9.
35 *Ibid.*
36 SRO, Elphinstone, GD 46/17/42, 20 March 1813.
37 Henderson, 298.
38 Fraxi, 74–5.
39 NLS, Halket, Ms 14,207, 17d-18.
40 Mackenzie, *Life in the Mission &c.*, I, 278, 287.
41 *British and Foreign Medical Review*, 15, January 1845, 73.
42 *Lancet*, 31 January 1829.
43 Lancereux, 295–6.
44 *Lancet*, 31 January 1852.
45 IOL, L.Mil 5/376, 120.
46 *Ibid.*, 132–3, 282–3.
47 Hyam, 117.
48 Warburton, 3–10.
49 Anon (Lieutenant of the Bengal Establishment), *The Cadet's Guide &c.*, 43.

50 Goodbehere, 'The Letters &c.', *JSAHR*, LVII.
51 Anon (A Lady), *East India Sketchbook*, 29.
52 Mackenzie, *Life in Mission &c.*, I, 270.
53 Lehmann, 80.
54 *Medical Times and Gazette*, new series, 5 (1852), 477.
55 *Lancet*, 12 and 19 September 1829.
56 Cust, *Sorrows of an Anglo-Indian &c.*, 14.
57 Buck, 29.
58 Veitch, 38.
59 Anon (A Lady), *East India Sketchbook*, 126.
60 IOL, Mss Eur, Horwood, C 570, 18.
61 BL, Ramsbottom, Add Mss 59,876, 1d, 10.
62 Anon, 'Duelling &c.', *Colburn's United Service Magazine*, 1844, Pt III, 240.
63 E.g., *The Indian Cookery Book: A Practical Handbook to the Kitchen in India* (Calcutta, *c.* 1860).
64 Neill, 151.
65 Ives, 73.
66 Beare, 82.
67 *Macphail's Edinburgh Ecclesiastical Journal*, I, February 1846, 60.
68 Matthew, *The Story of St Andrew's Church, Bombay*, 2–10.
69 NRO, Leslie, MC 64/2/4; Hoole, *Personal Narrative &c.*, 81.
70 *AJ*, I, 145.
71 *Macphail's Edinburgh Ecclesiastical Journal*, II, March 1846, 140.
72 Beare, 85–8.
73 Hoole, *Personal Narrative &c.*, 131–2, 138–9.
74 *The Oriental Baptist*, I, February 1847, 58–9; *Ibid.*, IV, April 1850, 283.
75 NLS, Tweeddale, Ms 14,558, 1–26.
76 Strachan, 10.
77 *Gazetteer of the Bombay Presidency*, VII, 249.
78 *The Oriental Baptist*, II, March 1848, 90.
79 *Memorial of the Hindu Inhabitants*, 8.
80 Powell, 'Maulana Rahmet &c.', *JRAS*.
81 Mackenzie, *Life in Mission &c.*, I, 29.
82 Hoole, *Madras, Mysore &c.*, xl–xliii.
83 Hoole, *Personal Narrative &c.*, 124.
84 *Macphail's Edinburgh Ecclesiastical Journal*, V, July 1846, 438.

Part Four: The Mutiny

1: *The Sahib Paid No Attention*

1 *RID*, I, 3.
2 BL, Holmes, Add Mss 41,489, 30d.
3 SRO, Lindsay, GD 254/713, 17, 28.
4 Raj, *Economic Conflict &c.*, 58–9.
5 BL, Holmes, Add Mss 41,488, 54.
6 Hibbert, 59–60.
7 Ashburner, 'Gujarat Disturbances &c.', *Bombay Gazetteer*, I, i, 434–5.

8   BL, Holmes, Add Mss 41,489, 35.

9   *Ibid.*, 3–4d; Hibbert, 51.

10 BL, Holmes, Add Mss 41,489, 11d, 13–13d.

11 *Mutiny Correspondence*, I, 3.

12 BL, Holmes, Add Mss 41,489, 147.

13 Kaye, *Sepoy War &c.*, II, 426–27.

14 Ashburner, 'Gujarat Disturbances &c.', *Bombay Gazetteer*, I, i, 433.

15 Gubbins, 95–6.

16 BL, Holmes, Add Mss 41,489, 36.

17 Gubbins, 13.

18 Cadell, 'The Outbreak of the Indian Mutiny &c.', *JSAHR*, LV, 121.

19 IOL, H 725, 149.

20 *RID*, I, 454.

21 *Ibid.*, 105.

22 Kaye, *Sepoy War*, II, 244–5.

23 *Ibid.*, 246–7.

24 *Mutiny Correspondence*, I, 20–1, 23.

25 BL, Pierce, Add Mss 42,500, 2–2d, 83.

26 BL, Rose, Add Mss 42,807, 71–2.

27 Kaye, *Sepoy War*, II, 423–4.

28 Cave-Brown, I, 98–9.

29 IOL, Mss Eur, Horne, D 533, i, 7–8, 10, 12, 14.

30 Mathur, 187–9.

31 Young, *Delhi – 1857*, 63, 207.

32 Coopland, 83, 85, 87.

33 BL, Pierce, Add Mss 42,500, 40.

34 *RID*, I, 275; Stokes, *Peasant Armed*, 7–8.

35 BL, Pierce, Add Mss 42,500, 9.

36 IOL, H 725, 390–1.

37 Thornhill, 10, 20, 68, 71.

38 IOL, H 725, 151.

39 *Mutiny Correspondence*, I, 47.

40 Forbes-Mitchell, 5.

41 NLS, Grey, Ms 15,394, 2–8d.

42 *Mutiny Correspondence*, I, 121.

43 Gupta, *Nana Sahib &c.*, 38; IOL, H 725, 615–16.

44 Gupta, *Nana Sahib &c.*, 53, 64, 70.

45 Gubbins, 102–3.

46 *Ibid.*, 118; BL, Bruce, Add Mss 44,003, 113.

47 Kaye, *Sepoy War*, II, 268–9 and notes.

48 *Ibid.*, II, 284n.; Hibbert, 202.

49 Kaye, *Sepoy War*, II, 270–1; also Mukherjee, 'Satan let loose &c.', *PP*, 128, *passim*; and English, 'The Kanpur Massacre &c.', *Ibid.*, 42, *passim* for an academic debate of the possible social and political significance of the terror and counter-terror in June–July 1857.

50 Dunlop, 47–8.

51 NAM, Potiphar, 9.

52 Mukherjee, 'Satan let loose &c.', *PP*, 129, 110.

53 *Mutiny Correspondence*, I, 193.

54 Forbes-Mitchell, 16–19; Lang, *Lahore to Lucknow*, 121.

2: Very Harrowing Work

1 *Medical News*, 19 July 1858.
2 *Ibid.*; Kiernan, *European Empires &c.*, 48.
3 J. Brown, 'Notes of the Surgery of the Indian Campaign &c.', *Monthly Journal of Medical Sciences*, VI, 328 and *passim*; *Lancet*, 3 July 1858.
4 *The Naval Brigade &c.*, 139; IOL, L.Mil 3/667, 26 February 1858 for example of prisoners taken during an engagement.
5 Anon, 'The Pursuit of Tanti Topi', *Blackwoods Magazine*, LXXXVII, 175.
6 *Medical News*, 7 August 1858.
7 Majendie, 264.
8 NRO, MC 6/Cubitt 1, 5–6 November 1857.
9 Coopland, 107; Cave-Brown, 1, 194n; SRO, Lindsay GD 254/713, 31.
10 NAM, Potiphar, 38; Lang, 59.
11 NRO, MC 6/Cubitt 1, 1 January 1858.
12 Thornhill, 306, 313.
13 Majendie, 186–7.
14 IOL, Mss Eur, Chardin Johnson, A 161/b, 30; NAM, Potiphar, 7; SRO, Lindsay, GD 254/17, 31; Young, *Delhi – 1857*, 26.
15 Pearson, 233.
16 NAM, Potiphar, 53; *RID*, I, 479.
17 Stokes, *Peasant Armed*, 88.
18 *Ibid.*, 92.
19 *Mutiny Correspondence*, II, 56.
20 *Press Lists &c. . . . Political Department from 1859 to 1863*, 125, 132, 140.
21 Lang, 100.
22 NAM, Potiphar, 53.
23 Hibbert, 321.
24 NLS, Grey, Ms 13,396, 30–1.
25 Russell, I, 290–1.
26 Majendie, 178–9; Bourchier, 95.
27 NLS, Grey, Ms 13,396, 32–33d.
28 *RID*, I, 531.
29 *Press Lists &c. . . . Political Department from 1859 to 1863*, 122.
30 *Ibid.*, 103, 110.
31 BL, Bruce, Add Mss 43,996, 116–116d; 44,003, 29d–30.
32 *Mutiny Reports*, I, 189, 190–2; Russell, I, 170–1.
33 BL, Pierce, Add Mss 42,500, 46, 48, 67.
34 BL, Holmes, Add Mss 41,489, 120; *RID*, I, 206, 397ff; *Ibid.*, II, 2, 9, 10, 11, 16, 25, 30, 117.
35 IOL, Mss Eur, Horne, D 533, 82; Thornhill, 38–9.
36 *RID*, II, 39.
37 BL, Bruce, Add Mss 44,003, 8, 29d.
38 BL, Bruce, Add Mss 44,002; IOL, Mss Eur, Horne, D 533, 44; Gubbins, 169; Cave-Brown, I, 175–6; *Press Lists &c. . . . Political Department from 1859 to 1863*, 13, 15, 18, 20, 21, 38, 48, 77.
39 BL, Bruce, Add Mss 43,996, 128d; *Mutiny Correspondence*, I, 290, 303, 357; *Ibid.*, II, 2; *Press Lists &c. . . . Judicial Department*, 95.
40 *RID*, II, 39, 92.
41 *Ibid.*, I, 304–5, 444; II, 135, 316.

42 *Ibid.*, I, 39, 92.
43 *Ibid.*, I, 341; II, 130, 138.
44 *Mutiny Reports*, I, 148, 229.
45 *Ibid.*, II, 245.
46 *Ibid.*, I, 142; II, 275, 288.
47 Forbes-Mitchell, 47.
48 IOL, Mss Eur, Chardin Johnson, A 161/b, 5.
49 *RID*, I, 92, 202.
50 IOL, L.Mil 5/290.
51 IOL, L.Mil 5/295.
52 BL, Rose, Add Mss 22,807, 1–17.
53 Stokes, *Peasant Armed*, 54n.
54 BL, Bruce, Add Mss 44,002, 5.
55 Stokes, *Peasant Armed*, 53–4.
56 BL, Holmes, Add Mss 41,488, 47–51d.
57 *Mutiny Records*, II, 283.
58 IOL, H 725, 615–626d.
59 Bhadra, 'Four Rebels &c.,', *Subaltern Studies*, IV, 263–73.
60 Powell, 'Maulana Rahan Allah &c.', *JRAS*.
61 BL, Bruce, Add Mss 44,003, 80–80d; 44,004, 1, 64.
62 Thornhill, 114.
63 Bhadra, 'Four Rebels &c.', *Subaltern Studies*, IV, 243–5; Thornhill, 102–3.
64 Majendie, 187.
65 Bhadra, 'Four Rebels &c.', *Subaltern Studies*, IV, 242.
66 BL, Pierce, Add Mss 42,500, 24–24d; Dunlop, 3.
67 Kaye, *Sepoy War*, II, 257n.
68 IOL, H 725, 393.
69 Forbes-Mitchell, 182–6.
70 IOL, L.Mil 3/1196, 427, 567.
71 IOL, R/2/240, 12 November 1858.
72 Ashburner, 'Gujarat Disturbance', *Bombay Gazetteer*, I, i,444–8.
73 Forbes-Mitchell, 76–7.
74 Bhadra, 'Four Rebels &c.', *Subaltern Studies*, IV, 235.
75 Stokes, *Peasant and the Raj*, 143–51.
76 Downs, 'Fear and Loathing &c.', *IESHR*, XXVII, *passim*.
77 Stokes, *Peasant and the Raj*, 127.
78 *Ibid.*, 149.
79 Churcher, 60–6.
80 IOL, L.Mil 17/2/503, 41.
81 Dunlop, 94.
82 *Press Records &c. . . . Judicial from 1859 to 1863*, 74.
83 *RID*, I, 209.
84 IOL, L.Mil 3/667, 77.
85 NLS, Grey, Ms 13,396, 9, 9d, 10d.

3: *Like Elephants on Heat*

1 *Saturday Review*, 4 July 1857.
2 Thackeray, 'A History of India &c.', *Quarterly Review*, LXVIII, 377.
3 Leopold, 'British Applications &c.', EHR, LXXXIX, 581.

4 Thackeray, 'A History of India &c.', *Quarterly Review*, LXVII, 402.
5 *Chamber's Information for the People*, I, 188, 370.
6 *Illustrated London News*, 10 March 1849.
7 *Ibid.*, 28 February 1846.
8 Dickens, II, 459; 473.
9 Bosworth-Smith, II, 275, 279, 289, 295.
10 *Punch*, 12 September 1857.
11 *Manchester Guardian*, 7 October 1857.
12 *Edinburgh Evening Courant*, 29 September 1857.
13 Crooke, 'Songs of the Mutiny', *Indian Antiquary*, XL, 123, 168; Edwardes, *Red Year*, 180–2.
14 Harrington, 165–7.
15 *Fast Day Sermons*, 27, 66.
16 Dickens, VII, 459, 472–3.
17 *Hansard*, 3rd series, CXLVIII, 148, 703.
18 *Invergordon Times and General Advertiser*, 19 January 1858.
19 Paxton, 'Mobilising Chivalry &c.', *Victorian Studies*, 36, 8.
20 BL, Duberly, Add Mss 47,218C, 34.
21 Grant, *First Love, Last Love*, II, 76.
22 *Atheneum*, 18 September 1858.
23 Gibney, II, 176.
24 *Punch*, 18 October 1857.
25 *The Times*, 3 November 1857.
26 *Hansard*, 3rd series, CXLVI, 146, 1323–4, 1456–61.
27 *Ibid.*, 147, 446.
28 *Saturday Review*, 25 July 1857.
29 *Fast Day Sermons*, 75, 147–8.
30 *Hymn for the General Thanksgiving of the Suppression of the Indian Mutiny.*
31 *Edinburgh Review*, CVII, 2.
32 *The Times*, 3 November 1857; the same point was made in the *Manchester Guardian*, 7 October 1857.
33 *Saturday Review*, 4 July 1857.
34 *National Review*, VI, 3.
35 BL, Cust, Add Mss 43,395, 355.
36 *Fourth Report on Colonisation and Settlement*, 149, 202.
37 IOL, Mss Eur, Montagu, D 528/9, 215.
38 IOL, Mss Eur, Chelmsford, E 264/1, ii, 44.
39 I am indebted for this point to the late General Sir Ouvry Roberts.
40 Malleson, 88n.
41 IOL, L.Mil 17/2, 5, 503.
42 Mason, *Report on the Hindustani Fanatics*, 3–4.
43 Chaudhuri, 19.
44 IOL, L.Mil 3/1196, 323.
45 NLS, Minto, Ms 12,758, 688d, 692.
46 *National Review*, VI, 15.
47 *Ibid.*, 7.
48 *Spectator*, 9 May 1868.

Part Five: Triumphs and Tremors

1: *Low and Steady Pressure*

1 *Indus Valley State Railway, Administrative Report*, Appendix i.
2 Kipling, *Letters*, I, 100–1.
3 Gilmour, 168.
4 Arnold, 'The "Discovery" of Malnutrition &c.', *IESHR*, 31, 6–7; Klein, 'When the rains failed &c.', *Ibid.*, 21, 195; Rajaskhar, 'Famine and peasant mobility &c.', *Ibid.*, 34, 121, 124.
5 *Annual Medical and Sanitary Report . . . Mysore 1877*, 11.
6 Buckley, 277–8.
7 Mulhotra, 134.
8 IOL, Mss Eur, Elgin, F 84/1, 19, 25; Malhotra, 116–17.
9 IOL, L.Mil 17/11/94, 106, 113–14, 180, 269, 273; Malhotra, 133.
10 Gilmour, 173.
11 Wilson, 'The History of an Indian District &c.', *National Review*, VI, 325.
12 Barrier, 'The Punjab Disturbances &c.', in Hardiman (ed.), *Peasant Resistance*, 230–7.
13 Buckley, 324.
14 Aitken, 'The Coming Famine in India', *Contemporary Review*, XCIII, 15.
15 Horne, 3, 23, 99–100.
16 O'Dwyer, 25.
17 Grant-Duff, 'India: Political and Social &c.', *Contemporary Review*, XXVI, 866.
18 Wilson, *Indian Civil Service &c.*, 22.
19 Tupp, 42.
20 Bosworth-Smith, I, 291–2.
21 Horne, 121.
22 Lawrence, *The India We Served*, 275.
23 Dewey, 157.
24 Kipling, *Departmental Ditties*, 'One Viceroy Resigns'.
25 Ricketts, 'English Society and India', *Contemporary Review*, CI, 688.
26 Anon, 'The Romance of India', *Quarterly Review*, XCCVI, 51.
27 Lytton, II, 4–5.
28 Wilson, *Sport and Service*, 36–7.
29 Kipling, *Departmental Ditties*, 'One Viceroy Resigns'.
30 Forster, *Letters*, I, 186.
31 Lansdowne, 78–9, 92–3, 122–3.
32 Lyall, II, 68–9.
33 Gilmour, 151–3.
34 Lytton, II, 48–9.
35 Russell, *The Prince of Wales's Tour*, 447.
36 Warburton, 213.
37 Lawrence, *The India We Served*, 239–41.
38 Curzon, in *Nineteenth Century and After*, XLIX, 949.
39 IOL, Mss Eur, Elgin, F 84/1, 5–6, 13.
40 IOL, L.Mil 5/825, i, 1440.
41 NLS, Minto, Ms 12,756, 528.
42 IOL, LPS, 10/2, P 3763.
43 *The Times*, 2 January 1912.
44 IOL, LPS, 10/264, i, n.n.

2: *Not as Relics but as Rulers*

1 Casserly, 223.
2 Devi and Ran, 36.
3 Adams, *Western Rajputana*, 58.
4 NLS, Minto, Ms 12,589, Pt III, 1–3; Gilmour 190.
5 *Ibid.*, 191.
6 NLS, Minto, Ms 12,589, Pt I, 51.
7 BL, Ripon, Add Mss 43,511, 11d, 91.
8 Horne, 133–4.
9 Dyson, 114.
10 Copland, *The British Raj &c.*, 61.
11 Lee-Warner, 305–6.
12 Reid, 53.
13 BL, Ripon, Add Mss 43,614, 52.
14 IOL, LPS, 10, 40, 98.
15 NLS, Minto, Ms 12,589, 25.
16 IOL, Mss Eur, Elgin, 84a, i, 89.
17 NLS, Minto, Ms 12,756, 235–36.
18 Lawrence, *The India We Served*, 187.
19 Copland, *The British Raj &c.*, 63.
20 BL, Ripon, Add Mss 43,613, 165d.
21 Grimwood, 149–50.
22 Reid, 54–6.
23 *Ibid.*, 58; *The Times*, 4 May 1891.
24 Willcocks, 75.
25 IOL, LPS, 10, 1 and 2.
26 NLS, Minto, Ms 12,589, Pt I, 1.
27 IOL, L.Mil 17/11/196, 22.
28 Raj, *Economic Conflict*, x.
29 NLS, Minto, Ms 12,758, 688d.
30 Copland, *The British Raj &c.*, 134.
31 Mangan, 134.
32 *Ibid.*, 133–4.
33 NLS, Minto, Ms 12,757, 203–4.
34 IOL, BH 3/106 (R/2 475/3) *passim*.
35 BL, Ripon, Add Mss 43,615, 103d.
36 Sayagi Rao, 'My Ways and Days', *Nineteenth Century and After*, XLIX, 223.
37 Gilmour, 189.
38 Singh, *Problems and Policies*, 244.
39 IOL, LPS, 264, I, *passim*.
40 Copland, *The British Raj &c.*, 235.
41 IOL, LPS, 264, I, P 2255; II, P 173.
42 Browning, 193–4.
43 Copland, *The British Raj &c.*, 235; Mehta, 'Relations &c.', *JIH*, 50, *passim*.
44 Adams, *Western Rajputana*, 19–20, 115–16.

3: We are British Subjects

1 SRO, Whitton, GD 1/927, I, 107–8.
2 *Spectator*, 5 June 1875.
3 Ghose, *Open Competition*, 21n.
4 Lytton, II, 22.
5 O'Dwyer, 25.
6 Gupta, 'The Agrarian League &c.', in Hardiman (ed.), *Peasant Resistance*, 117.
7 Lytton, II, 21–2.
8 Singh, *Problems and Policies*, 28, 105–6.
9 Lansdowne, 74.
10 *Ibid.*, 61.
11 *Hansard*, 4th series, XCIII, 75–6, 476, 1310–11.
12 *Report of the Calcutta University Commission*, XII, 41.
13 *The Economist*, 22 November 1877.
14 Morier Williams, 'Facts on India', *Contemporary Review*, XXXII, 419.
15 *Calcutta University Calendar, 1866–67*; *Ibid., . . . 1867–68*, appendices.
16 *Report of the Calcutta University Commission*, XI, 17.
17 *Ibid.*, X, 122.
18 *Ibid.*, I, 49; Gosh, 'Social Reform in India', *National Review*, VIII, 367.
19 *Report on the Working of the Dispensaries . . . in the Central Indian Agency for 1912*, 2–3.
20 Von Albertini, 69.
21 Poddar, 62.
22 Quoted in *Edinburgh Review*, January 1858, 46.
23 Dyson, 36.
24 Ghose, *The Open Competition*, 5.
25 Chunder, I, 115.
26 *Ibid*, II, 386, 408–9.
27 Renfold, 205–6.
28 *Ibid*.
29 Kipling, *Letters*, I, 35.
30 Wolf, II, 131.
31 IOL, LPJ, 5/410 *passim*.
32 Renfold, 35.
33 Dilke, II, 194.
34 Argov, 14.
35 *Ibid.*, 81.
36 Narain, 'Interaction &c.', *JIH*, 57, 404.
37 Narain, *Press and Politics*, 275–6.
38 Kipling, *Letters*, I, 99.
39 Narain, *Press and Politics*, 67–8.
40 Forbes, 83.
41 Argov, 31.
42 *The Times*, 6 August 1892.
43 Campston, 'Some Early Indian Nationalists &c.', *EHR*, 76, 296.
44 Tribe, 275, 280.
45 Narain, 'Interaction &c.', *JIH*, 57, 406, 412.
46 *Ibid.*, 407.
47 *Ibid.*, 413.

48 Narain, *Press and Politics*, 32.
49 *Lancet*, 8 January 1898.
50 Malhotra, 148.
51 Paul, 15–18; Popplewell, *Intelligence &c.*, 32.
52 Argov, 74.
53 *Lancet*, 28 February 1898; Paul, 60.
54 Gilmour, 137.
55 *Ibid.*, 170.
56 *Ibid.*, 245.
57 PRO, WO 88/1, 293–4.
58 Narain, *Press and Politics*, 172.
59 Wilson, *Sport and Service*, 264.
60 Webber, 71–2.
61 Renfold, 296.
62 Argov, 105
63 NLS, Minto, Ms 12,756, 202.

4: Not Worth the Candle

1 Hopkirk, *Great Game*, 363.
2 Lytton, II, 65.
3 *Ibid.*, 133–4.
4 PRO, FO 65/1213, 299–300.
5 Cobbold, 200.
6 Friedberg, 389–90.
7 IOL, L.Mil 17/5/1739, 17.
8 PRO, WO 105/42, 'Memo . . . Military Requirements for the Defence of India', 4.
9 Durand, *The Making of a Frontier*, 41.
10 Allworth, 7.
11 Rwykin (ed.), *Russian Colonial Expansion*, 215–16.
12 Vernon, 'Soviet Historians &c.', *Indian History Congress*, 484.
13 Memo from Lawrence in, NLS (Printed Books) IP/AA/31/1.
14 *Notes on the Maps of Central Asia and Turkestan, passim.*
15 Mackenzie, 'The Conquest &c.', in Rwykin (ed.), *Russian Colonial Expansion*, 19n.
16 O'Donovan, II, 58.
17 Allworth, 159, 217–18.
18 PRO, WO 110/9, 5.
19 Vernon, 'Soviet Historians &c.', *Indian History Congress*, 487.
20 Lytton, II, 103–04.
21 Mackenzie, 'The Conquest &c.', in Rwykin (ed.), *Russian Colonial Expansion*, 225.
22 *Ibid.*
23 Lytton, 133.
24 NLS, Minto, Ms 12,536, 13.
25 Roberts, *Forty Years &c.*, 406n.
26 *Ibid.*, 457.
27 *Roberts in India*, 64.
28 NLS, Minto, Ms 12,537, 21–2.

29 *Roberts in India*, 120.
30 *Ibid.*, 164.
31 *Illustrated London News*, 24 January and 24 April 1880.
32 Robson, 'Kandahar Letters &c.', *JSAHR*, 69, 149.
33 Robson, 'Maiwand, 27 July 1880'; *Ibid.*, 51, *passim*.
34 *Roberts in India*, 293; Omissi, 12.
35 PRO, FO 65/1236, 134–6.
36 Holdich, 3, 10.
37 Gordon, *A Varied Life*, 171–3.
38 Morris, 'British Secret Service &c.', *HJ*, 27,661.
39 Hopkirk, *Great Game*, 416–17.
40 PRO, FO 65/1213, 10–11; FO 65/1235, 86.
41 PRO, FO 65/1235, 85, 136.
42 PRO, FO 65/1236, 22.
43 PRO, FO 65/1236, 48.
44 PRO, FO 65/1236, 39, 268, 327.
45 PRO, FO 65/1236, 5; Holdich, 126.
46 Fuller, 337–8; Rwykin (ed.), *Russian Colonial Expansion*, 229.
47 PRO, WO 110/9/8.
48 Holdich, 156.
49 French, 75–80.
50 Morris, 'British Secret Service &c.', *HJ*, 27, 666.
51 PRO, HD 2/1, 8, 9, 12, 16.
52 PRO, HD 2/1, 9, 10.
53 PRO, HD 2/1, 5.
54 PRO, HD 2/1, 104, 105, 109.
55 PRO, FO 65/1347, 1–2, 40–6, 47–8, 54–7, 163.
56 Le Mesurier, 19.
57 PRO, WO 33/49, 'Memo on the Strategic Situation in Central Asia', 2.
58 Lansdowne, 78–9.
59 Jefferson, 'Lord Salisbury's Conversation &c.', *Slavonic and Eastern European Review*, XXXiX, 217–18.
60 PRO, FO 539/51, 2–3.
61 PRO, WO 106/48, *passim*.
62 Cobbold, 231.
63 PRO, WO 65/1574, 179d.
64 Cobbold, 200.
65 Rwykin (ed.), *Russian Colonial Expansion*, 65.
66 PRO, HD 3/117 and 118.
67 PRO, WO 105/42; IOL, L.Mil 17/5/1739.
68 PRO, HD 3/118B.
69 Narain, *Press and Politics*, 254–5.
70 *Daily Graphic*, 28 August 1898.
71 PRO, FO 800/140, 56.
72 Addy, 69.
73 PRO, FO 800/140, 145.
74 E.g. Fleming, *Bayonets to Lhasa* (1961) and French, *Younghusband*, 154–252.
75 PRO, HD 3/125, I, Hardinge to Stevenson, 17 June 1904.
76 PRO, HD 3/125, II, *passim*.
77 NLS, Minto, Ms 12,695, 2, 55, 87, 97.

78 Cobbold, 311.
79 Morris, 'Intelligence and its interpretation &c.', in Andrew and Noakes (eds), *Intelligence and International Relations*, 81.
80 IOL, LPS 10/270, *passim*.
81 Robertson, *Chitral &c.*, 50–51.

5: Never at Peace

1 Younghusband, *Indian Frontier Warfare*, 141.
2 Hopkirk, *Great Game*.
3 *Chums*, 4 May 1898.
4 *Chums*, 24 August and 30 November 1898.
5 Henty, *Through Three Campaigns*.
6 Henty, *The Soldier's Daughter*.
7 *Daily Graphic*, 31 August, 10 and 15 September 1897.
8 *The Times*, 4 October 1897.
9 *Daily Graphic*, 10 August and 18 December 1897.
10 *Illustrated London News*, 28 August and 30 October 1897.
11 *Illustrated London News*, 4 December 1897.
12 *Daily Graphic*, 15 November 1897.
13 *Chums*, 21 September 1898.
14 Mackenzie (ed.), *Popular Imperialism and the Military*, 65, 77.
15 *Ibid.*, 149.
16 Parry, 308–9, 310.
17 Younghusband, *Forty Years &c.*, 135–6.
18 R. Churchill, 359–60.
19 Parry, 297.
20 W. Churchill, *Frontiers and Wars*, 17.
21 Fincastle and Elliot-Lockhart, 229.
22 Moreman, 'The British and Indian Armies &c.', *JICH*, XX, 36.
23 W. Churchill, *My Early Life*, 149.
24 Moreman, 'The Arms Trade &c.', *JICH*, 23, 194–5.
25 Dunsterville, 130–1.
26 Moreman, 'The Arms Trade &c.', *JICH*, 23, 205.
27 Younghusband, *Forty Years*, 247.
28 Lindholm, 163.
29 Blood, 313.
30 Mason, *Report on the Hindustani Fanatics*, 14.
31 Walters, 35.
32 Hoghton, 19.
33 PRO, WO 106/108.
34 Fincastle and Elliot-Lockhart, 22.
35 Russell and Khan, 'The Satirical Verses &c.', *MAS*, 8, 11.
36 Younghusband and Younghusband, 85; Churchill, *My Early Life*, 145.
37 Warburton, 343.
38 Robertson, *Chitral &c.*, 7, 30.
39 IOL, L.Mil 5/825, I, 312.
40 PRO, WO 106/290, 2, 13.
41 NAM, Alston, 8005-151-2, n.n.
42 NLS, Minto, Ms 12,537, 12.

43 SRO, Lindsay, RH 2/8/69, 36, 30–5.
44 James, *Rise and Fall &c.*
45 *Hansard*, 4th series, LIV, 283–4, 403.
46 *Ibid.*, 3rd series, CCCII, 188–9; 314–18, 1038–9.
47 Durand, *Life of Field Marshal Sir George White*, I, 353.
48 *Ibid.*, 348, 353.
49 *Roberts in India*, 359, 365.
50 Younghusband, *Frontier Warfare*, 52.
51 Lindsay, 'Letters &c.', *JSAHR*, LIV, 152, 154, 157, 160.
52 LHC, Moore 2 (H. E. Mitchell, 'Reports on the Naga Hills &c.', 8, 9, 16).
53 *Ibid.*, 11.
54 NAM, Alston, 8005-151-2, n.n.
55 *Hansard*, 4th series, LIII, 2.
56 Moreman, 'The Arms Trade &c.', *JICH*, XXII, 194.
57 Minto, 35.
58 Willcocks, 225–6.

6: *Conciliatory Sugar Plums*

 1 Wolpert, *Morley &c.*, 236.
 2 *Ibid.*, 151.
 3 Koss, 136–7, 142.
 4 Das, *India under Morley*, 147–8; NLS, Minto, Ms 12,756, 196–7, 520.
 5 Pandey, 'Rallying round the Cow &c.', *Subaltern Studies*, II, 110.
 6 Low (ed.), 133.
 7 Wolpert, *Morley &c.*, 39.
 8 *Sedition Committee Report*, 76.
 9 Letter in *The Times*, 6 June 1908.
10 Koss, 103.
11 *Ibid.*, 100.
12 *The Times*, 14 and 26 November 1906.
13 Hansard, 4th series, CLXV, 971; CLVIII, 1129; CLXII, 414.
14 NLS, Minto Ms 12,756, 204.
15 *Ibid.*, 109–13, 494–5, 496, 528.
16 Barrier, 'The Punjab Disturbances &c.', in Hardiman (ed.), *Peasant Resistance*, 291–2.
17 *Ibid.*, 493.
18 Wolpert, *Morley &c.*, 107.
19 NLS, Minto, Ms 12,757, 188.
20 *Ibid.*, 12,756, 520.
21 *Ibid.*, 511.
22 *Ibid.*, 203.
23 *Ibid.*, 328.
24 Barrier, 'The Punjab Disturbances &c.', in Hardiman (ed.), *Peasant Resistance*, 251–2.
25 BL, Spender, Add Mss 46,391, 256.
26 Tripathi, 115, 132–3.
27 BL, Sydenham, Add Mss 50,832, 206–7.
28 *The Times*, 24 July 1909.
29 *Ibid.*, 1 and 10 August 1908.

30 Popplewell, 143.
31 BL, Sydenham, Add Mss 50,833, 108.
32 Popplewell, *Intelligence &c.* 127–8.
33 Omissi, 20.
34 *Sedition Committee Report*, 58.
35 IOL, Mss Eur, Muspratt, F 223/92, 50.
36 Wolpert, *Morley &c.*, 164.
37 Letter to *The Times*, 6 June 1908.
38 Arnold, 'Industrial Violence in Colonial India &c.', *Comparative Studies in Society and History*, 22, 241.
39 Casserly, 311.
40 'Xeres', 'On Tour with an Indian Proconsul', *Blackwoods*, 201, *passim*.
41 Baden-Powell, 17.
42 Fuller, *Empire of India*, 375–76.
43 Dewey, 204.
44 Anon, 'Unrest in India', *Quarterly Review*, 209, 248; Fuller, *Studies in Indian Life*, 343–4.
45 *Ibid.*, 222.

Part Six: Disturbances and Departures

1: *True to Our Salt*

1 *The Times*, 17 August 1914.
2 Menezes, 266.
3 IOL, L.Mil 5/825, I, 545–6, 838, 1010–11, 1440.
4 IOL, L.Mil 5/825, 6.
5 NAM, Maxwell, 7402-28-109, 18 September 1884.
6 Durand, *The Making &c.*, 21.
7 Younghusband, *A Soldier's Memories*, 301–3, 311–12.
8 Browning, 31.
9 Cohen, 'Mesopotamia in British Strategy &c.', *IJMES*, 9, 172–3.
10 Moberley, I, 86–7.
11 IOL, L.Mil 17/5/3223, 6, 8, 13, 20.
12 IOL, L.Mil 17/3224, 22, 31, 39.
13 Moberley, I, 172–3.
14 Popplewell, 'British Intelligence in Mesopotamia', in Handel (ed.), *Intelligence and Military Operations*, 139.
15 Moberley, I, 343.
16 PRO, WO 33/768, 3749, 3852.
17 PRO, WO 32/5198, nos 99 and 102.
18 IOL, L.Mil 17/5/3250, 43.
19 PRO, WO 158/668, 149.
20 IOL, L.Mil 17/3250, 28–9, 60, 90, 111.
21 Macpherson and Mitchell, IV, 211, 215–16.
22 Macpherson, Horrocks and Beveridge, I, 152–3.
23 IOL, L.Mil 5/825, I, 19, 54; also 70, 204, 458.
24 PRO, WO 95/ 575, App. 116.

25 IOL, L.Mil 5/825, I, 23.

26 IOL, L.Mil 5/825, I, 826, 1292.

27 Martin, 'The Influence of Racial Attitude &c.', *JICH*, 14, 93, 94, 96.

28 IOL, L.Mil 5/827, 544.

29 IOL, L.Mil 5/825, 120, 121, 138, 189, 258, 649–50.

30 Anon, 'A Lady Experiences &c.', *Blackwoods*, 193, 783.

31 PRO, WO 32/8560.

32 IOL, L.Mil 5/827, 676–7.

33 Popplewell, *Intelligence &c.*, 174–5.

34 PRO, WO 106/1413, GOC Singapore to WO, 3 September 1915.

35 *Ibid.*

36 Hopkirk, *On Secret Service &c.*, 189–91.

37 Menezes, 281.

38 Gandhi, XIV, 484.

39 For an entertaining account of the activities of Mrs Besant and her fellow Theosophists, see P. Washington, *Madame Blavatsky's Baboon* (New York, 1993).

40 Mortimer, 'Annie Besant &c.', *Journal of Contemporary History*, 18, 63–4.

41 Montagu, 16, 17, 59, 60.

42 *Hansard*, 5th series, 116, 2320, 2347.

43 *Spectator*, 20 July 1918.

44 *Saturday Review*, 13 July 1918.

45 *Hansard*, 5th series, 116, 2324, 2338, 2392–5.

46 IOL, L.Mil 5/827, 650.

47 IOL, L.Mil 5/825, 1216; 827, 840.

48 Simeon, 'The Great TISCO Strike &c.', *IESHR*, 30, 135–6.

49 *Indian Munitions Board*, 11.

50 Tomlinson, *The Political Economy of the Raj*, 58–9.

51 *The Economist*, 5 April and 1 November 1919.

52 Ray, *Urban Roots &c.*, 82.

53 Mann, 43, 126–39.

54 *The Economist*, 8 March and 27 September 1919.

55 Mills, 'The 1918–1919 Influenza Pandemic &c.', *IESHR*, 23, 2, 7, 36.

56 *Criminal Statistics of the High Court of Judicature . . . and the Courts of the Punjab for the Calendar Year ending the 31st of December 1920*, 9.

57 *Ibid.*; . . . *for the Year ending the 31st of December 1919*, 7; *Note on the Administration of Criminal Justice in the Province of Oudh . . . during the Calendar Year ending 31st December 1919*, 2.

2: *Strong Passion*

1 Gandhi, XIII, 59.

2 *Ibid.*, 223, 440.

3 *Ibid.*, 222.

4 *Sedition Committee Report*, 73–4.

5 Gandhi, XIII, 223.

6 *Ibid.*, 548–51.

7 *Ibid.*, XV, 15.

8 *Ibid.*, XIII, 231.

9 *Ibid.*, XV, 107.

10 *Ibid.*, 142.
11 *Ibid.*, 132.
12 Russell and Islam, 'The Satirical Works of Akbar Illahabad', *MAS*, 8, 55.
13 PRO, WO 157/1260, Summary 1.
14 IOL, Mss Eur, Chelmsford, E 264/10, 409.
15 PRO, WO 157/1260, Summary 33.
16 IOL, Mss Eur, Montagu, D 523/10, App. C, Enclosure B.
17 PRO, FO 371/5832, N 1253, 8; N 2965, 6–7.
18 IOL, Mss Eur, Montagu, D 528/9, 303.
19 IOL, Mss Eur, Chelmsford, E 264/8, 103.
20 Gandhi, XV, 179, 212, 213, 220, 230.
21 *Ibid.*, 273, 280.
22 IOL, Mss Eur, Chelmsford, E 264/10, ii, 230.
23 O'Dwyer, 272, 280.
24 IOL, Mss Eur, Chelmsford, 264/8, Enclosure B, 2.
25 *The Times*, 25 July 1927.
26 Dyer, 141, 217–18.
27 IOL, Mss Eur, Chelmsford, E 264/1, ii, 43–4.
28 Draper, 82.
29 IWM, Morgan, 72/12/1.
30 Draper, 75–6, 86.
31 *Ibid.*, 91.
32 Colvin, 246.
33 IOL, Mss Eur, Chelmsford, E 264/10, 217.
34 *Ibid.*, 216.
35 *Report of the Commissioners . . . Punjab Sub-Committee of the India National Congress*, 169, 274, 326, 340.
36 *Ibid.*, 292, 372–3.
37 IOL, Mss Eur, Chelmsford, E 264/8, 118.
38 *Ibid.*, 10, ii, 436.
39 IOL, Mss Eur, Montagu, D 528/9, 215.
40 *Ibid.*, 171.
41 Gandhi, XV, 367–8.
42 Jeffrey, 101.
43 PRO, Air 2/125/ B 11395.
44 IOL, Mss Eur, Chelmsford, E 264/10, 403.
45 PRO, Air 2/125/B 11395.
46 IOL, Mss Eur, Chelmsford, E 264/10, 363.
47 IWM, Lewis, 74/48/1, 29 February and 22 May 1920.
48 Information from the late General Sir Ouvry Roberts.
49 IOL, Mss Eur, Chelmsford, E 264/1, 146, 298–9.
50 *Ibid.*, 11, 302–3.
51 IOL, Mss Eur, Montagu, D 523/10, 99.
52 IOL, Mss Eur, Chelmsford, E 264/11, 10, ii, 264.
53 Gandhi, XVI, 330.
54 PRO, WO 33/990, 13701.
55 *Morning Post*, 1 June and 6 July 1920.
56 *Hansard*, 5th series, 131, 1710.
57 Wilson, *Military Correspondence*, 187.
58 *Hansard*, 5th series, Lords, 41, 248.

59 *New Statesman*, 1 May 1920.
60 *Spectator*, 17 July 1920.
61 Matra, 'Lenin and Roy &c.', *Indian History Congress*, 500.
62 PRO, WO 157/1261, 6 and 7 March and 17 July 1920.
63 PRO, FO 371/5832, N 230.
64 PRO, WO 157/1261, 27 March 1920.
65 Teague-Jones (R. Sinclair), *The Spy who Disappeared* (1992).
66 IWM, Morgan, 72/22/1.
67 *Hansard*, 5th series, 131, 1739.
68 Quoted in Dyer's obituary, *The Times*, 25 July 1927.
69 Ray, 'Masses in Politics &c.', *IESHR*, 11, 380.
70 Nehru, *Autobiography*, 52.
71 Anand, *Sword and Sickle*, 54.
72 Bald, 'Politics of a Revolutionary Elite &c.', *MAS*, 8, *passim*.
73 Nehru, *Autobiography*, 61.
74 Ray, 'Masses in Politics &c.', *IESHR*, 11, 389–90, 408.
75 PRO, FO 371/5382, N 1253, 7.
76 Ray, 'Masses in Politics &c.', *IESHR*, 11, 398.
77 Pannikar, 128.
78 PRO, WO 106/157; *Intelligence Review*, 28 October 1921, 2–3; IOL, Mss Eur, Colebrook, D 789/2, L, 124, 248.
79 PRO, WO 106/156, 4.
80 *Ibid.*, 156, 1.
81 *Ibid.*, 156, 10; IOL, Mss Eur, Colebrook, D 789/2, L 125, 7.
82 IOL, Mss Eur, Montagu, D 528/9, 301, 303.
83 Wilson, *Military Correspondence*, 307.
84 IOL, Mss Eur, Montagu, D 528/9, 319, 2.
85 Kumar, 'From Swaraj &c.', in Low (ed.), *Congress and the Raj*, 93.
86 Wilson, *Military Correspondence*, 211; Tomlinson, *The Indian National Congress*, 12.
87 Wilson, *Military Correspondence*, 289.

3: This Wonderful Land

 1 Russell, *With the Prince &c.*, 41.
 2 *Ibid.*, 26, 63–4.
 3 *Daily Graphic*, 18 March, 1922.
 4 *Daily Sphere*, 14 January 1922.
 5 Duke of Windsor, 163, 169.
 6 Gregory, 'Staging British India', in Britton, Cave, Holden, Gregory and Pickering, 53.
 7 Mackenzie, *Propaganda and Empire*, 106.
 8 *The Great Delhi Durbar*, 18–19, 20–21.
 9 *Listener*, 20 and 27 February 1929.
10 *Ibid.*, 30 September 1936.
11 *Ibid.*, 30 October 1937.
12 *Ibid.*, 27 August 1932.
13 *Ibid.*, 23 December 1936.
14 IOL, Mss Eur, Martin, F 180/21, 3.
15 Moore, *Just as Good as the Rest*, 31.

16 Naidis, 'G. A. Henty &c.', *VS*, 8, 51.
17 *Chums*, 22 May and 7 June 1920.
18 Lady Lawrence, 63.
19 *Morning Post*, 13 July 1920.
20 *Who's Who, 1930*, 2760.
21 *Picture Post*, 3 June 1939.
22 Gouldsbury, 255.
23 Richards, *Old Soldier Sahib*, 86–7.
24 *ILN*, 18 June 1938.
25 *National Geographic*, LVI, 445, 502.
26 Younghusband, *A Soldier's Memories*, 273.
27 Mayo, 15.
28 Perrin, 125–6.
29 Lee, *Never Stop the Engine*, 8.
30 Savi, *The Passionate Problem*, 44.
31 Morris, *Hired to Kill*, 207.
32 Anon, 'Unrest in India', *Quarterly Review*, 209, 248.
33 Fuller, *The Empire of India*, 375–6; *Studies in India Life &c.*, 343.
34 Lady Lawrence, 42.
35 Moon, *Strangers &c.*, 20.
36 IOL, Mss Eur, Flack, F 180/21, 21–2.
37 NLS, Lahari, Acc 8122, 7–8.
38 IOL, Mss Eur, Flack, F 180/17, 8.
39 Hyam, *Empire and Sexuality*, 130–1.
40 PRO, WO 92/3, 6d.
41 Baden-Powell, 31.
42 Hyam, *Empire and Sexuality*, 132–3.
43 Private information.
44 Richards, *Old Soldier Sahib*, 197–9, 303–4.
45 Mayo, 35–6.
46 Huben, 46–8.
47 *Punch*, 13 December 1911.
48 PRO, FO 371/21065, 87, 114, 256.
49 PRO, WO 106/1594C.
50 *Picture Post*, 3 June 1939.
51 Younghusband, *A Soldier's Memories*, 187–8.
52 IWM, Swindlehurst, n.n.
53 Lady Lawrence, 213.
54 IWM, Kingsford, 84/29/1, 18.
55 PRO, WO 203/2356, Summary of 22 February 1946, 15.
56 Thorne, 239.
57 PRO, WO 208/816, 14–15.
58 I am indebted to Lieutenant-Colonel David Murray for this point (letter, 3 October 1996).
59 IWM, Blackie, 27 August and 7 September 1946.
60 I am indebted to Lieutenant-Colonel David Murray for this point (letter, 6 October 1996).
61 IWM, Blackie, 4 September 1947.
62 Masters, 63; see also IOL, Mss Eur, Palit, R 142 and IWM, Blackie, 19 August, 1946.

63 I am indebted to Captain James Squire for this point (letter, 20 September 1996).
64 IOL, Mss Eur, Palit, R 142.
65 Masters, 83.
66 Adams, 'Across Seven Seas &c.', *Oral History*, 9, 34.
67 *Listener*, 6 October 1937.

4: *A Great Trial of Strength*

1 Arnold, 'Cholera and Colonialism &c.', *PP,* No. 133, 149.
2 Anand, *Coolie*, 99–100.
3 *Ibid.*, 267–78.
4 Griffiths, 302–3.
5 Gandhi, XLII, 419–22; XLIII, 39.
6 *Ibid.*, XLII, 425.
7 *Ibid.*, XLVII, 119–20.
8 *Ibid.*, XLII, 223, 433.
9 *Ibid.*, XLII, 470–1; XLIII, 224.
10 Sudhur, 'The Indian States &c.', *Indian History Conference*, 365–66.
11 Jeffrey, 'A Sanctified Congress &c.', in Low (ed.), *Congress and the Raj*, 435.
12 Mukherjee, 'Radicalism in Bihar &c.', *Indian History Conference*, 370.
13 *Ibid.*, 369.
14 IOL, *LPJ,* 8/609, 403, 407; Gupta, *The Police of British India*, 374, 469.
15 IOL, Mss Eur, Colebrook, D 789/2, 77–80.
16 *Ibid.*, 82.
17 Brown, 127.
18 Mukherjee, 'Radicalism in Bihar &c.', *Indian History Conference*, 371.
19 I am indebted for this observation by W. A. Simms, who was then a corporal in the King's Own Yorkshire Light Infantry.
20 NAM, Alston, 8005-15-2, n.n.
21 *Ibid.*
22 PRO, Air 8/121, Memo, 20 July 1930, DI (Ap) 5.
23 Roberts, *The Holy Fox*, 31.
24 Gandhi, LXIV, 188.
25 Roberts, *The Holy Fox*, 39.
26 Nicolson, 509.
27 *Daily Mail Blue Book &c.*, 9.
28 Stoddart-Kennedy, 'The Christian Imperialism &c.', *JICH*, 18, 348, 350, 352–3.
29 *Spectator*, 26 July 1930.
30 Middlemas and Barnes, 583.
31 Gandhi, LI, 140.
32 Rizvi, 18.
33 *Ibid.*, 28.
34 *Ibid.*
35 IOL, Mss Eur, Flack, F 180/7, 34.
36 Dewey, 352–63.
37 Moore, *Churchill &c.*, 2–3, 13, 98–100; Glendevon, 87.
38 Talbot, 'The Role of the Crowd &c.', *JICH*, 313, 314.
39 Rattani, 11.

40 Moore, *Churchill &c.*, 23; Rizvi, 118–19.
41 IWM, Marsland Gander, 78/62/1m, 14 May 1943; Glendevon, 48.
42 Gandhi, LXXI, 804.
43 Moore, *Churchill &c.*, 28.
44 Gandhi, LXXII, 6; Moore, *Churchill &c.*, 38–9.
45 Gandhi, LXXII, 188, 214–15.
46 *TP*, I, 4.
47 PRO, WO 208/804A n.n.; WO 208/819A, App. D, 35C.
48 *TP*, I, 238.
49 NAM, Lockhart, 8310-154, 33, 5–6.
50 PRO, WO 208/819B, App. A, 8.
51 PRO, WO 208/763, 1A, 7B; WO 208/802, 70B.
52 *TP*, I, 36–7.
53 *PRO*, WO 208/763, 14A, App. C; LHC, Heard, 27.
54 NAM, Lockhart, 8310-154, 5.
55 PRO, WO 208/763, 4; WO 71/1057 for the court martial.
56 PRO, WO 208/807, 5–6.
57 PRO, WO 208/763, *passim*.

5: *A Bad Knock*

1 *TP*, I, 48–9.
2 PRO, WO 106/2569, 1.
3 Fay, 29.
4 PRO, WO 208/819A, n.n.
5 PRO, WO 106/2744A, 6.
6 PRO, WO 203/516, 38; WO 208/807, 1.
7 PRO, WO 203/516, 38–9.
8 PRO, WO 106/2569, 4, 10, 26, 32–3, 45–6.
9 *Ibid.*, 'Comments on General Gordon Bennett's Report', 5.
10 PRO, WO 106/2591, 4A, 4B, 5A.
11 Elphick, 177.
12 PRO, WO 106/2574A, 1B, 1.
13 Elphick, 221, 230.
14 NAM, Lockhart, 8310-154, 33, 5–6.
15 Sundaram, 'A Paper Tiger &c.', *War and Society*, 13, 36.
16 PRO, WO 208/219A, 10A.
17 Thorne, *Allies &c.*, 208.
18 PRO, WO 106/3723A, 125.
19 Fay, 143.
20 PRO, WO 208/819, 10A.
21 PRO, WO 208/803, 60B, 72B; Fay, 146.
22 PRO, WO 208/807, 4.
23 PRO, WO 208/804A, n.n.
24 PRO, WO 106/2574m, 3–5.
25 PRO, FO 406/81, Pt 55, 10.
26 PRO, FO 370/21065, 256.
27 PRO, Air 8/529, Air Staff Memo (July 1937), 1–2.
28 PRO, FO 371/21065, 3; FO 371/23620, 70, 76–7; FO 402/22, 100.
29 PRO, FO 371/2360, 32; WO 208/773, Report of 2 April 1941.

30 Hauner, 'One Man Against the Empire &c.' *Journal of Contemporary History*, 16, 199, 200–1, 211.
31 PRO, WO 208/802, 8B.
32 *Ibid.*, 134B.
33 *Ibid.*, 22B.
34 *Ibid.*, 98A.
35 *Ibid.*, 158A.
36 *Ibid.*, 176 and n.n (September 1944).
37 PRO, WO 208/819A, 24A.
38 Fay, 190.
39 Hauner, *India in Axis Strategy*, 28, 29, 479.
40 Bhagat Ram Talwar's confession is in WO 208/773.
41 Menenzes, 376.
42 PRO, WO 208/812, 2A.
43 IOL, LPJ, 8/572A, 24–5.
44 *TP*, I, 298–9.
45 *Ibid.*, I, 432.
46 IOL, LPJ, 8/558, 122.
47 *Ibid.*, 70.
48 Thorne, *Allies &c.*, 242.
49 Pandey, 162–63.
50 Thorne, *Allies &c.*, 245–7.
51 *TP*, II, 665–6.
52 PRO, WO 208/816, 14–15.
53 *Ibid.*, 35, 36, 49, 51, 55–6, 60, 73.
54 *Ibid.*, 38.
55 *Ibid.*, 21–22.
56 *Ibid.*, IF.
57 WO 208/795, Linlithgow to Secretary of State, 3 June 1942.
58 *Ibid.*, *passim.*
59 Gandhi, LXXVI, 126–7.
60 Hauner, *India and Axis Strategy*, 500–1.
61 Role, 'La Stratégie Japonaise &c.', *Guerres Mondiales et Conflits Contemporains*, 159, 68–70.
62 Hauner, *India and Axis Strategy*, 487.
63 Gandhi, LXXVI, 67–8.
64 *Ibid.*, 5.
65 *Ibid.*, 105.
66 *Ibid.*, 133.
67 *Ibid.*, 122–7.
68 *TP*, II, 122, 134.
69 Gandhi, LXXVI, 109–10.
70 *TP*, II, 134.
71 Chopra, *Quit India &c.*, 1, 6–7.
72 *TP*, II, 557–8.
73 Amery, *Empire at Bay*, 823–4.
74 Gandhi, LXXVI, 212.
75 IOL, LPJ, 8/597, 234.
76 *TP*, II, 223.
77 Gupta, *The Police &c.*, 526–7.

78 IOL, LPJ, 8/609, 398, 400, 407.
79 *Ibid.*, 403.
80 PRO, Air 23/2052, GHQ to HQ RAF, Bengal, 28 July 1942.

6: An Occupied and Hostile Country

1 IOL, Mss Eur, Flack, F 180/17, 19–20.
2 PRO, WO 106/3721A, 1.
3 *Spectator*, 4 and 14 August 1942.
4 *The Times*, 17 August 1942.
5 Gandhi, LXXXVI, 403.
6 PRO, Air 23/2052, *passim*.
7 *Hansard*, 5th series, 383, 948–9.
8 Chopra, 'Quit India &c.', *JIH*, 49, 39–40.
9 PRO, Air 23/2053, 5, 13.
10 *Ibid.*
11 I am indebted to Lieutenant-Colonel Murray for this point.
12 PRO, WO 208/819, 1A; Gupta, *The Police &c.*, 542.
13 *TP*, II, 853–4.
14 Amery, *Empire at Bay*, 830.
15 *Hansard*, 5th series, 383, 1342.
16 Chopra, *Quit India &c.*, 20–1, 59–63, 218–19.
17 IOL, LPJ, 8/609, 361–2, 323–7, 375.
18 NLS, Lahari, Acc 8122, 179–81.
19 IOL, Mss Eur, Martin, F 180/21, 34–6.
20 Henningham, 'Quit India &c.', *Subaltern Studies*, II, 131–5.
21 IOL, Mss Eur, Martin, F 180/21, 33.
22 Cruikshank, 85–6.
23 *The Times*, 1 and 7 August 1942.
24 Manor, 'Gandhian Politics &c.', in Low (ed.), *Congress and the Raj*, 419–21; Jeffrey, 'A Sanctified Label &c.', in *Ibid.*, 452–3.
25 Pati, 'The Climax of Popular Protest &c.', *IESHR*, 29, 26–7.
26 PRO, WO 106/3757, 1B.
27 Hauner, *India and Axis Strategy*, 551.
28 PRO, WO 208/819A, 25C.
29 Chopra, 'Quit India &c.', *JIH*, 49, 32.
30 IOL, Mss Eur, Jenkins, D 807, 1.
31 *TP*, II, 933.
32 Hauner, *India and Axis Strategy*, 544, 546.
33 Menenzes, 399.
34 Hauner, *India and Axis Strategy*, 597–9; Fay, 286.
35 PRO, WO 208/819A, 25C, App. C; WO 208/3812, 2A.
36 Hauner, *India and Axis Strategy*, 605; Sundaram, 'A Paper Tiger &c.', *War and Society*, 13, *passim*.
37 In the National Army Museum (7903–46).
38 Hauner, *India and Axis Strategy*, 608.
39 Fay, 297, 300; Menenzes, 395.
40 PRO, WO 208/3812, *passim*.
41 Hauner, *India in Axis Strategy*, 607.
42 NAM, Lockhart, 8310-54, 33, 4–6.

43 PRO, WO 208/819B, App. A, 8.
44 PRO, WO 208/2268, 1L.
45 PRO, WO 203/2045, 10P, 14Q.
46 From copies of *Josh* in LHC, Heard 1.
47 PRO, WO 208/2268, Report of January 1945, 14–15; PRO, WO 203/2268.
48 Fay, *passim*; but for a more balanced verdict see Sundaram, 'A Paper Tiger &c.', *War and Society*, 13, *passim*.
49 PRO, WO 203/2045, 10E.
50 *TP*, IV, 278, 683.
51 *Ibid.*, 682–3.
52 Sen, 'The Food Problem &c.', *Third World Quarterly*, 31, 172–73.
53 *TP*, IV, 112.
54 Maharatna, 'The Demography of the Bengal Famine &c.', *IESHR*, 31, 172–3.
55 *TP*, IV, 79.
56 *Ibid.*, 358–9; Patel, III, 179.
57 *The Economist*, 28 August and 4 September 1943.
58 *TP*, IV, 43.
59 *Thirumati*, 'Peasant Classes &c.', *IESHR*, 31, 232.
60 *TP*, IV, 82.
61 *Ibid.*, 297, 413.
62 Wavell, 81; Thorne, 6, 357.
63 Wavell, 46, 61, 92, 95, 107.
64 *TP*, IV, 376, 378.
65 Wavell, 101.
66 *Ibid.*, 97.
67 *Ibid.*, 108.
68 *TP*, IV, 1224.
69 IOL, LPJ, 8/572A, 23, 27, 175–7.
70 Wavell, 50, 51, 55.
71 *Ibid.*, 159.

7: *What Are We Here For?*

 1 IWM, Blackie, 6 September 1947.
 2 Warner, 249–50.
 3 LHC, Heard, 1, 52.
 4 PRO, WO 208/828, Report, 3 January, 1945, 2, 4–5; Report, 7 February, 1; 4 September, 1.
 5 IOL, LWS, 1/1/1029, 7.
 6 Wavell, 181–4.
 7 Fay, 499–500.
 8 For the reactions of Indian other ranks I am grateful to Philip Mason; for British officers, see IOL, LWS, 1/1/1029, 69, 74.
 9 PRO, WO 208/3817, 44, 298.
10 *The Times*, 8, 11 and 14 February 1946.
11 PRO, WO 208/3817, 268, 276.
12 IWM, Godfrey, 6, 97.
13 NAM, Lockhart, 8310-154, 1–2.
14 IWM, Godfrey, 6, 99d–100; PRO, WO 208/3817, 281.
15 *Ibid.*, 264, 266.

16 I am indebted to John Hailwood for this and other details of the mutiny.
17 LHC, Thompson (Findings of the Board of Enquiry . . . into the Mutiny at the Castle Barracks, 11).
18 *Ibid.*; NAM, Lockhart, 8310-154, 54, 68, 72; App. 8, 2.
19 *Ibid.*
20 PRO, WO 208/3817, 252.
21 PRO, WO 208/3816, 2B.
22 *Ibid.*, 245.
23 *The Times*, 23 February 1946; *Listener*, 24 March 1949.
24 PRO, WO 208/3817, 222.
25 NAM, Lockhart, 8310-154, 67.
26 IOL, Mss Eur, Bramble, R 143/2.
27 IOL, LPJ, 8/574, 120–1.
28 BLO, Attlee, 31, 169.
29 PRO, WO 208/761A, Intelligence Report, 14 September 1945, 3–4.
30 PRO, WO 203/2356, Report, 22 February 1946.
31 IWM, Kingsford, 107.
32 IWM, Blackie, 28 August 1946.
33 PRO, WO 208/3818, 194.
34 Thorne, 237.
35 I am indebted to Lieutenant-Colonel Murray for these quotations.
36 NAM, Lockhart, 8310-154, 74.
37 IWM, Godfrey, 6, 98d, 100, 101.
38 IOL, LWS, 1/1/1029, 71.
39 *Ibid.*, 71–3; PRO, WO 208/3817, 220, 242.
40 *Ibid.*, 234.
41 *Ibid.*, 248.
42 PRO, WO 208/761A, n.n.
43 *Hansard*, 5th series, 425, 1414–15.
44 Mosley, 22.
45 Hamid, 77.
46 Moore, *Escape &c.*, 63, 67.
47 Patel, 3, 105.
48 *TP*, VIII, 25–7.
49 IOL, R2/139/65, 4–5, 16, 37.
50 PRO, WO 208/3817, 80, 87, 98, 107, 121.
51 *TP*, VIII, 207n.
52 PRO, WO 208/3817, 38, 46, 52, 65.
53 *Ibid.*, 137–38.
54 *TP*, VIII, 225–7.
55 *Ibid.*, 205, 209.
56 NAM, Bucher, 7901–87, 2 (Report of Disturbances in Calcutta &c., 1); PRO, WO 208/3818, 290; *TP*, VIII, 313.
57 NAM, Bucher, 7901–87, 2 (Report of Disturbances in Caclutta &c., 2); *TP*, VIII, 297 (slightly doctored text from Burrows's report).
58 *Ibid.*, 297–8.
59 *The Times*, 28 August 1946.
60 IOL, Mss Eur, Martin, F 180/21, 50–53.
61 PRO, WO 208/3818, 236, 240; *TP*, VIII, 532–3.
62 PRO, WO 208/3818, 211.

63 *Ibid.*, 147.
64 *Ibid.*, 181, 185, 220.
65 Copland, *The Princes in India &c.*, 236.
66 Patel, 3, 87–8.
67 *TP*, VIII, 372, 472.
68 IOL, Mss Eur, Martin, F 180/21, 54.
69 Wavell, 403.
70 Moore, *Escape &c.*, 187–8, 190–1, 208.
71 Hamid, 118.
72 BLO, Attlee, 36, 22.
73 Wavell, 341n.
74 *TP*, VIII, 575, 747–78; Moore, *Escape &c.*, 202–3.
75 Wavell, 367.

8: *Was It Too Quick?*

1 IOL, Mss Eur, Jenkins, D 807, 166–7.
2 Campbell-Johnson, 40, 43, 55–6.
3 IOL, Casey, Ms Photo Eur 48/3, 267.
4 Wheen, 211.
5 Moore, *Escape &c.*, 218–19.
6 I am indebted for this point to Trevor Royle; see also *Spectator*, 12 December 1947 and Talbot, 'Mountbatten and the Partition &c.', *History*, 68, 32.
7 Hamid, 153, 172–3, 186; Roberts, *Eminent Churchillians*, 107–8; Rabbani, 101.
8 NAM, Savory, 7603-93-87, 27 March 1947.
9 Royle, 146, 148.
10 *TP*, XII, 215.
11 *Ibid.*, 801–6.
12 I am indebted to Francis Beckett, Attlee's most recent biographer, for this point.
13 Moore, *Escape from Empire &c.*, 238.
14 NAM, Savory, 7603-93-87, 29 March 1947.
15 *TP*, XII, 75.
16 NAM, Savory, 7603-93-87, 18 April 1947.
17 *Ibid.*, 19 April 1947.
18 *TP*, X, 625–6.
19 BLO, Attlee 53, 268, 285, 288.
20 Patel, 4, 142.
21 PRO, WO 208/3818, 242.
22 PRO, DO 142/415, 20–21.
23 *TP*, X, 75.
24 IOL, R 2/139/65, 65; NAM (Notes for GOC HQ Eastern Command, 24 August 1947), 7707-35, 1; Pearce, 127.
25 *Ibid.*, 128.
26 NAM (Notes for GOC HQ Eastern Command, 24 August 1947), 7707-35, 2.
27 PRO, WO 208/3819, 315.
28 IOL, Mss Eur, Jenkins, D 807, 25.
29 *TP*, XI, 20–2.
30 NAM (Notes for GOC HQ Eastern Command, 24 August 1947), Appendix A, ii; Pearce, 133–5.

31 *Ibid.*, 137.
32 *TP*, XI, 31n.
33 *Ibid.*, 158–9.
34 Aiyar, 'August Anarchy &c.', *South Asia*, 18, 28–31.
35 PRO, WO 208/3818, 94, 95.
36 *TP*, XII, 512.
37 IOL, Mss Eur, Christie, D 713, 3a, 68.
38 *TP*, XII, 512.
39 Major, 'The Chief Sufferers &c.', *South Asia*, 18, 60.
40 PRO, WO 208/3819, 212, 297, 319.
41 IOL, Mss Eur, Jenkins, D 807, 13 (Marginal note by Jenkins, dated 3 March 1950); NAM, Savory, 7603-98-87, 21 May 1947, confirms Jenkins's request.
42 *TP*, XII, 512.
43 *Ibid.*, XI, 587–8.
44 *Ibid.*, XII, 702.
45 *The Times*, 2 January 1969.
46 Patel, 4, 11–13, 20–4.
47 *TP*, XI, 680.
48 Hamid, 198.
49 Copland, *The Princes &c.*, 185.
50 *Ibid.*, 229, 236.
51 Roberts, *Eminent Churchillians*, 133.
52 Mosley, 158.
53 Copland, *The Princes &c.*, 212–13.
54 Mosley, 164–5; Hamid, 196.
55 Mosley, 169–70.
56 *TP*, XII, 295, 297.
57 NAM, Lockhart, 8310-154, 257–8.
58 Moore, *Escape &c.*, 312–13.
59 Mosley, 173–4; Copland, *The Princes &c.*, 257–8.
60 *TP*, XII, 345–6.
61 *Ibid.*, 453.
62 Hamid, 222.
63 *TP*, XII, 618–20.
64 *Ibid.*, 638–9, 662.
65 *Ibid.*, 633.
66 IOL, Mss Eur, Christie, D 718, 3b, 255.
67 Hamid, 222.
68 IOL, Mss Eur, Jenkins, B 807, 178–178d, 205; Mss Eur C 645, 3.
69 IOL, Beaumont, 358, 1–4; Roberts, *Eminent Churchillians*, 99–100; *Daily Telegraph*, 24 February 1992.
70 Hashim Raza, 92.
71 Roberts, *Eminent Churchillians*, 100.
72 Copland, *The Princes &c.*, 260.
73 Hashim Raza, 93–4.
74 Campbell-Johnson, 179.
75 *Ibid.*, 183.
76 Hamid, 234.
77 *TP*, XII, 736.
78 *Ibid.*, XII, 700–4, 704–5.

79 PRO, WO 208/3520, 135.
80 *TP*, XII, 736–7.
81 Hamid, 234.
82 *TP*, XII, 537–8, 589.
83 *Ibid.*, XII, 636.
84 *TP*, XI, 469, 572, 614, 668; XII, 75, 181–2.
85 *Ibid.*, XI, 530.
86 PRO, DO 142/416, 166.
87 NAM (Notes for GOC HQ Eastern Command, 24 August 1947), 7707-35, Appendix A, ii.
88 PRO, DO 142/425, n.n.
89 Roberts, *Eminent Churchillians*, 117.
90 *TP*, XI, 613–14.
91 *Ibid.*, XII, 736–7.
92 *Ibid.*, XII, 709.
93 IOL, Mss Eur, Jenkins, D 807, 38.
94 PRO, WO 208/3820, 51, 65.
95 Patel, 4, 278–9.
96 Roberts, *Eminent Churchillians*, 129–32.
97 PRO, DO 142/416, 172.
98 PRO, WO 208/3811, n.n.
99 Major, 'The Chief Sufferers &c.', *South Asia*, 18, 62–3.
100 Jalal, 'India's Partitition &c.', *JICH*, 15, 298, 305–6.
101 Roberts, *Eminent Churchillians*, 109–10.
102 NAM, Savory, 7603-93-87, 7 October 1947.
103 *Ibid.*, 26 and 28 July 1947.
104 Roberts, *Eminent Churchillians*, 130.
105 NAM, Savory, 7603-93-87, 20 November 1947.
106 *Ibid.*, 23 October 1947.
107 Hamid, 231.
108 NAM, Savory, 7603-93-87, 12 December 1947.

Epilogue

1 Douds, 'A Matter of Honour &c.', in Addison and Calder (eds), *A Time to Kill*, 128.
2 *Independent*, 23 January 1996.

Index